Cyberpsychology: An Introduction to Human–Computer Interaction

Kent L. Norman

University of Maryland

CAMBRIDGE UNIVERSITY PRESS

CAMBRIDGE UNIVERSITY PRESS
Cambridge, New York, Melbourne, Madrid, Cape Town, Singapore, São Paulo, Delhi

Cambridge University Press
32 Avenue of the Americas, New York, NY 10013-2473, USA

www.cambridge.org
Information on this title: www.cambridge.org/9780521687027

First published 2008

Printed in the United States of America

A catalog record for this publication is available from the British Library.

Library of Congress Cataloging in Publication Data

Norman, Kent L.
Cyberpsychology : An introduction to human–computer interaction / Kent L. Norman.
p. cm.
Includes bibliographical references and index.
ISBN 978-0-521-86738-2 (hardback) – ISBN 978-0-521-68702-7 (pbk.)
1. Human–computer interaction. I. Title.
QA76.9.H85.N668 2008
004.01′9–dc22 2008008536

ISBN 978-0-521-86738-2 hardback
ISBN 978-0-521-68702-7 paperback

This book is dedicated to past, present, and future generations who have and will have to suffer through the psychological ravages of the computer revolution. To the survivors! To us!

Contents

Preface

This book has been more than 20 years in the making. In 1984, I taught my first college course titled "Psychology in the Age of Computers." Over the years, I have collected material and references, added to my notes for the course, conducted empirical research, and thought a lot about the topics and issues. Since the introduction of the first personal computer in the 1970s, computer technology has developed into such a rich and pervasive presence that it affects nearly everyone in the world. "Cyberpsychology" has become the portmanteau that now encompasses where we are in psychology and technology. Consequently, the time has come for a general textbook on cyberpsychology.

This book is meant to be an "introduction." First, it encourages the reader to come to the topic with a fresh and ready mind. There are no prerequisites. Second, as an introduction, it emphasizes breadth rather than depth. It attempts to cover a variety of topics in the psychology of human–computer interaction rather than exhaustively delve into one topic. Finally, as an introductory textbook, it attempts to be engaging, to provide a good first impression of cyberpsychology, and to prompt the reader to follow up on the invitation to spend more time with the topics and ideas presented therein.

The title includes the word "psychology." This is done to emphasize the fact that this book is more about people than about machines. The organization and the perspective of the book come from psychology, not from computer science. Although the book is expected to be used in disciplines other than psychology, the point is that it is centered around human issues first and issues in technology second.

Finally, "human–computer interaction" is a rich term that has developed meaning over several decades. It is important to note that in using this term, although the terms "human" and "computer" appear side by side, the human takes precedence over the computer rather than being on the same plane. This perspective is emphasized throughout the book.

Readers will have to relax their psychological need for closure in this book. Technology is changing too fast and, with it, our theories and research change. Writing this book has been like painting a vertical stripe on a moving train. Each topic is a point of departure or a list of search terms for readers who want to know more, and the Web has become the vehicle for this search.

There are many people to thank and acknowledge for this book. First and foremost, I have to acknowledge the scholars, leaders, and entrepreneurs in technology who created the computer revolution and led to my involvement in the Human–Computer Interaction Laboratory at the University of Maryland, especially my good friends Ben Shneiderman in computer science and Nancy Anderson in psychology.

I want to thank the students, both undergraduate and graduate, who participated in my classes on cyberpsychology over the years for their suggestions and contributions, especially my current graduate students Susan Campbell, Walky Rivadeneira, and Ben Smith.

I express great appreciation to Karen Norman, my wife, for the drawings of the "dead psychologists" and a few computer scientists; to Katryn Norman, my eldest daughter, for her help with the figures; and to my other children, Kirk, Karitsa, and Kaleb, for their helpful comments, observations, and encouragement. Above all, honor and glory and praise to our God, the creator of all.

PART I

Fundamentals

One

Introduction

Importance, Implications, and Historical Perspectives

Scenario 1

Mary heard the familiar sound of a buddy coming online in iChat. She looked to the upper left of her screen and saw it was her friend Molly. She clicked on Molly; a pop-up window opened; and she typed, "Hey, what's up?" A few seconds later she read, "Have an intro psyc test tomorrow . . . studying the notes online. How about you?" Mary typed, "Not much, trying to write a paper and looking for refs. Doing a little shopping on the side." She glanced at her "shopping cart," which held a t-shirt and coffee mug she was getting for her brother's birthday. Just then, both of them noticed that their friend Martha came online, so they opened a multichat window. Each girl had her own icon. Mary had a picture of a female vocalist, Molly was a kitten, and Martha had a miniature picture of herself with a big grin. As it turned out, Martha was checking the movie listings and hoping to get the other two girls to go with her to a movie. Martha enticed them with a movie they had all been talking about seeing together. Mary typed, "OK, I'm done with shopping and my paper isn't due until next Monday. I'm ready." Mary keyed in, "Hey, it's a psyc test, I can wing it. I'm in. Let's go." Mary, Martha, and Molly got up and left the dorm room where they had been sitting together for the past hour, each at her own computer.

Scenario 2

Dr. Mike J.: *Mark can you move that scope just a little to the left? OK, I see it. Yes, there it is. Apply the clamp just to the left on the artery. Perfect. OK, let's get a biopsy on that tissue.*

Dr. Mark M.: *OK, Mike, I've got the biopsy. Let me just scan it in. Melvin, what's your read on it?*
Dr. Melvin N.: *Just a second, I am running a full DNA sequence on it. So, how was the fishing trip, Mark? Catch any trout?*
Dr. Mark M.: *Great. Would have got my limit if it hadn't been for this emergency. How was your golf game, Mike?*
Dr. Mike J.: *Terrible, I was glad to get out of the game.*
Dr. Melvin N.: *The analysis just finished. Take a look. Everything is OK.*
Dr. Mike J.: *Wonderful! Mark, you want to close him up and give his wife the good news. Wish I could join you fishing out there in Wyoming. Got to go to a faculty meeting here at Johns Hopkins. Melvin, thanks for quick analysis from DNAtronics, UK!*

Overview

Since the beginning of the computer revolution, a number of us have been trying to convince our colleagues in psychology about the importance of human–computer interaction (HCI). Some got it, but many didn't, and some still don't. Many psychologists view computer technology as a powerful research tool, but stick to "basic psychology" for their research. The study of human–computer interaction is "too applied" to be of central importance in psychology. Yet, many of our colleagues study the psychology of sports, the psychology of women, and the psychology of sex. Although not downplaying the importance of these, it can be asserted that we spend more time watching our computer screens than watching or playing sports; although men may be from Mars and women are from Venus,[1] computers are taking over the Earth; and although not as stimulating or reproductive, we have more interaction with our computers than with our partners (hence, the term "computer widows").

Meanwhile, we have quickly transitioned from a generation of computer illiterate students to a generation of computer savvy professionals. Thirty years ago, most computers were locked away behind heavy security doors, and only computer technicians had access to them. Today, personal computers are a common retail item. Access to the Internet is an essential service. We spend so much time interacting with computers, e-mail, and instant messaging that we may forget that we are communicating with people in the same room, as in Scenario 1. Nearly every job entails the use of computers on a constant basis. Every cash register, filling station pump, and auto parts lookup station is a computer. Every bank, hospital, airline, and social agency runs off networked computers and databases. Scenario 2 illustrates their use

[1] A reference to the book by Gray (1993).

in telemedicine. Computers are ubiquitous and pervasive. They are hidden behind the dashboards of our cars; they are at the other end of telephone calls to credit card companies; and they are the brains of automated teller machines (ATMs), cell phones, personal digital assistants (PDAs), digital cameras, DVD players, and digital cable boxes. There are no computer-free days. There is no escaping daily time with computers. Consequently, we have to come to grips with their presence in our psychological reality.

Living in a computerized, automated, digital world is different than living in the manual, analog world of the past. What we see and hear today is mediated by computer displays. How we take actions to do things is channeled through computer input devices. Where and how we store and organize things is determined by computer storage media and data structures. How we think and solve problems is either limited or augmented by computer functionality. Who we are, our goals and aspirations, and even our sense of self are altered by the electronic environment with digital communications, digital images, artificial intelligence (AI), icons, screen names, and passwords.

Psychology as a science and a discipline must do more than merely acknowledge that we live in a digital environment with computers and automation. It must do more than add a footnote, chapter, or illustration to current texts while perpetuating theories developed in the pre-digital world. Instead, it must rethink its basic theories in every area – from sensory and perception to social and clinical.[2] Fortunately, this is occurring in some areas. Cognitive science and neuroscience were founded in the digital age, and human factors psychology has embraced the interaction with computers, but a number of areas have fallen behind. Rather than make too much of this now, we instead develop and push these areas forward as we go through the successive chapters of this book. Finally, we try to cover the full range of psychology. To do this, we use as our guide the list of topics and chapters in a typical Introduction to Psychology course.

Psychology or Computer Science: Two Paths, One Journey

In high school, I was interested in science and electronics. So, naturally, I should have majored in science or engineering in college; yet, when I entered Southern Methodist University as a freshman, I decided to major in psychology. My reasoning was that what the world needed was not a better transistor radio or a new formula for plastics, but solutions to the deeper problems of the human mind. I did, however, take one introductory course in computer science, Computers and Society, in which the instructor taught us how to program in a language called PL/1 and covered a wide range of social issues. Many of these issues are still central today, such as computer fraud, AI,

[2] I am not as extreme as to say that basic theories need to be discarded or reinvented. I am only saying that we need to think about them in light of the computer revolution.

privacy, and secrecy. Although tempted to change majors, I stayed in experimental psychology with a parallel interest in computers and mathematics. Through my graduate studies at the University of Iowa and postgraduate work at the University of California at San Diego, I looked for avenues that connected psychology and computer science. I focused on mathematical psychology and computer simulations of human judgment and decision making. We were looking for ways of modeling human behavior using equations and computer programs. Along with many others in experimental psychology, I used computers to plan, control, and analyze experiments on learning, memory, judgment, and decision making, using minicomputers such as the PDP-12 and mainframe computers such as the IBM 360.

As it turned out, over the years there were many avenues between psychology and computer science. Psychology used computers as research tools and to model human behavior. The Society for Computers in Psychology (SCiP) was and remains a lively forum for psychologists to share ideas and software.

Computer scientists also had several reasons for being interested in psychology. First, those who were developing ideas in AI were interested in studying human problem solving as a starting point for heuristics and strategies, for common sense and expert knowledge about the world, and sometimes as a last resort after they had tried everything else they could think of. Second, as computers started to be used by the masses, those who were programming the computer interface needed to know how people interacted with the computer and why so many "human" errors were occurring. This group continues to study the human–computer interface in order to make it more intuitive, easy to use, error free, and require little or no training.

Moreover, there has been a realization in psychology that the world has changed and that there are significant forces on psychological and sociological processes from the digital environment. This has given birth to what is now called "cyberpsychology." Some of this is "pop" psychology, but much of it is a serious study of the consequences for humans using computers and the Internet.

This book attempts to cover the following four areas of overlap: 1) the use of computers as a research tool for studying psychological processes, 2) human–computer interaction, 3) AI, and 4) cyberpsychology.

Finally, we find two groups of people on the path between psychology and computer science: those interested in psychology but looking in the direction of computers for answers, and those interested in computers but looking in the direction of psychology for answers.

What Is the Psychology of Human–Computer Interaction?

As psychologists, we are interested in studying human behavior. Why do people act the way that they do? How can we explain and predict behavior?

How do people learn, modify, and correct behavior? We are also interested in subjective feelings, perceptions, moods, and emotions. We want to understand how people think, solve problems, and make decisions. All of this has to do with people in the environment interacting with physical stimuli and with one another. As computers become a greater part of that environment, psychologists will have to come to grips with their impact.

Computer scientists are interested in the theory of computing, the design and construction of computers, the development of computer programs and operating systems (OSs), and their application to real-world systems such as personal computers, the Internet, and a variety of software applications in business, government, education, and personal use. Ultimately, computer scientists have to deal with the "user" (i.e., the person interacting with the system) at some point. To know what to display on the screen and how to interpret user input, they have to ask, "What is this person thinking?" Computer scientists working with the human–computer interface, like psychologists, want to explain and predict user behavior. They want to know how people learn to use computers, how they modify their input, and how they identify and correct their mistakes. They are also interested in subjective impressions. What is the attitude of the user? Is the user frustrated, satisfied, or anxious about the interaction? Finally, how do users solve problems, search for information, and make decisions? Today, it seems that most computer scientists working with the human–computer interface and most designers of interactive technologies are doing the work of psychologists.

Thus, the psychology of the human–computer interface is the study of thinking, behavior, and attitudes of the person or groups of people using the computer or computer system. In Chapter 3, we develop this in greater detail by discussing a number of theories and models of the human–computer interface.

What Is Cyberpsychology?

Is "cyberpsychology" just another techie buzzword, or is there really something behind it? The prefix "cyber" comes from the word "cybernetics," the study of the operation of control and communication systems, and comes from the Greek word for steersman. Cybernetics was popularized by Norbert Wiener (1948/1961) in his book by the same name, *Cybernetics*. In it, Wiener discusses the primary ideas of feedback loops, homeostasis, and the hierarchical structure of machines.

The second part of cyberpsychology, "psychology," refers to the study of human behavior and cognitive processes. When we put the two parts together to create the term cyberpsychology, we engender a unique synergistic combination. Why? Because we, as humans, are inherently involved in control and communication. When these are mediated by machines, new factors and forces enter in that enhance and extend the purposes and intentions of the individual human mind and the collective purposes of communities of minds.

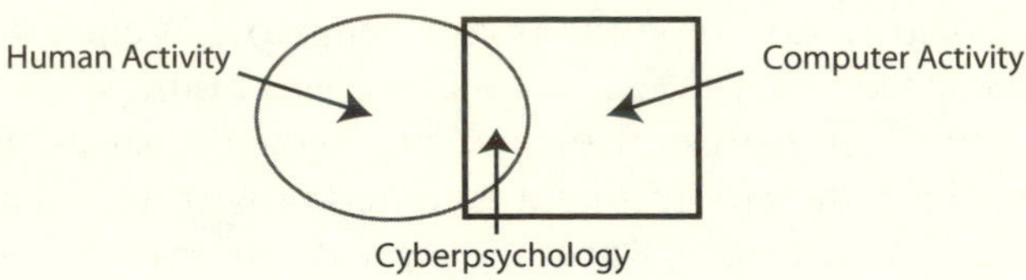

Figure 1.1. Cyberpsychology as the intersection of human and computer activity.

The study of cyberpsychology involves all aspects of human behavior and thought. One could easily pick up an introduction to psychology textbook and use the table of contents as the collection and the organization of topics. In fact, that is my plan for this book. We may talk about everything from the biological bases of behavior, sensation and perception, learning and motivation, thinking and problem solving, social processes, and developmental stages, to clinical and counseling psychology and psychotherapy! The difference is that in approaching each topic, we explore the avenues of contact between psychology and the emerging world of computers.

On the computer side, we talk about hardware and software, personal computers and central servers, OSs and human–computer interfaces, local area networks (LANs) and the World Wide Web (WWW), programming and debugging, multimedia and hypermedia, AI and software agents, and so on.

Cyberpsychology is not a course on how to use computers. In a sense, it transcends the "how-to" level to a metalevel in which we are interested in the "how-about" humans using computers. Most of the discussion is about others using computers rather than us. This is not to downplay experiential learning, but only to put it in its proper place. Computers, computer science, and technology are important. However, they do not supply the main content or the necessary organization of cyberpsychology. Instead, they provide the context in which we focus on psychological processes.

Cyberpsychology as a study is daunting. On one side, we have psychology where despite more than 100 years of study and research, we still know so little about the human mind. On the other side, we have computers, where technology is complex and changing rapidly. How can we cope intellectually between two such unknowns with one foot in psychology and the other in computer science? The good news is that instead of there being a void of confusion between the two, there are a number of commonalities, links, and analogues that turn it into an intellectual playground for ideas and theories and a powerful laboratory for exploring and testing these ideas.

In sum, cyberpsychology is the study of the impact of computers, technology, and virtual environments on the psychology of individuals and groups.

Although human–computer interaction refers more to an interface, cyberpsychology includes more of an overlap of space. It is the study of things that pertain to both the lives of humans and the activities of computers. As we go through the topics of this book, we explore what is in the overlap.

Figure 1.1 shows a diagram of the areas covered by human activity and computer activity. Over time, the area covered by computer activity has

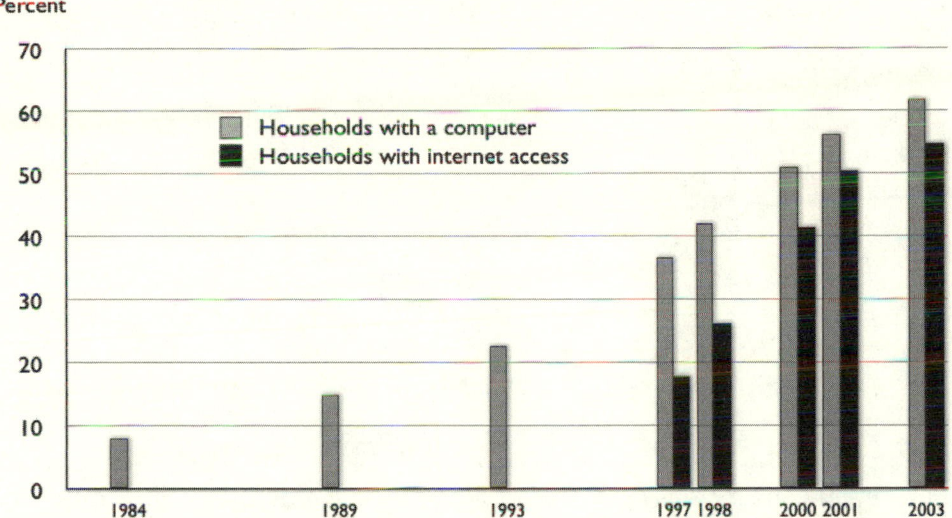

Figure 1.2. Households with a computer and Internet access from 1984 to 2003. (From Day, Janus, & Davis, 2005.)

dramatically increased, whereas the size of the area covered by human behavior has remained relatively the same. But as the area covered by computer activity has increased, the overlap has increased with it.

Impact and Importance of Cyberpsychology and the Human–Computer Interface

The break point in penetration of computers, the Internet, and related technologies is the beginning of the twenty-first century. It was roughly around the turn of the millennium that we in the United States broke the 50 percent mark in Internet use (Figure 1.2), personal computer use, and cell phone use. Some countries were ahead, and many have followed, but overall more than 50 percent of the populations of most industrialized countries now spend significant amounts of time interacting with computers and the Internet. Our perception goes beyond the objects and images in our natural environment, and now includes the graphics and images on the computer screen. When students look for information, more than 50 percent of them will go to the Internet rather than to books and library reference materials. The sphere of activities of computers has grown drastically over the past decades and engulfed larger amounts of human activity, as graphed in Figure 1.3. What is it that fills these areas of overlap between humans and computers? In the early years, it was primarily computer programming, database management, and mathematical and statistical computing. The overlap was limited to a select few computer programmers and analysts, and it was not much of an interface with teletypewriters and line printers. When the personal computer was introduced in the early 1980s, many more people

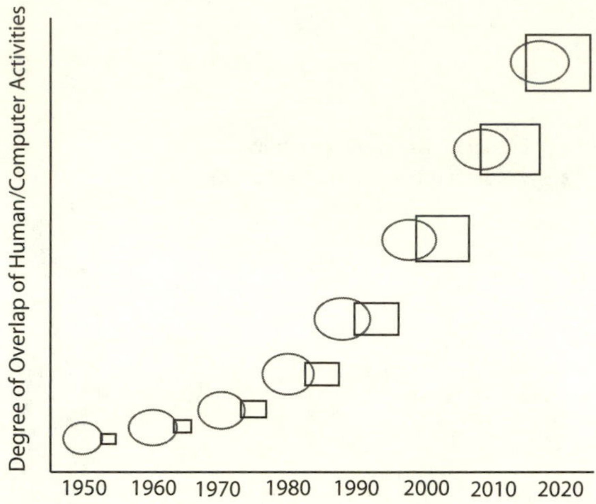

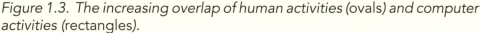

*Figure 1.3. The increasing overlap of human activities (*ovals*) and computer activities (*rectangles*).*

and activities were drawn into the overlap. With the introduction of word processors, more people composed and edited online rather than using paper and pencil or typewriters. Increasingly more of our conscious moments are spent in front of the computer, interacting with the mouse and keyboard. With personal management applications, people started to use electronic calendars, address books, notebooks, and planners. Our cell phones and PDAs are ever with us. Our entertainment centers, kitchens, and cars are filled with computer interfaces of one type or another. At the workplace, we have seen a mass conversion to digital devices and databases for secretaries, accountants, lawyers, librarians, and so on. Nearly every profession has been computerized.

In fact, the overlap has been so encompassing, pervasive, and ubiquitous that in just a few years we have taken it for granted. Now that we live in the age of computers, we must consider ourselves in light of the new environment with all of its enabling powers, all of its stresses, and all of its limitations. We must explore the overlap between human activity and computer activity. To do this, we need to understand things from both the perspective of psychology and the development of computers.

A Brief History of Psychology

Modern beginnings of psychology are credited to a number of influential scientists who pioneered theory and experimental research on behavior and the mind. Among them are Wilhelm Wundt, John Watson, Max Wertheimer, William James, and Sigmund Freud. Extensive histories can be found in other texts (Schultz & Schultz, 2004), but a brief history and a listing of a few names is given here as a review to set the perspective of what modern psychology

Figure 1.4. Wilhelm Wundt (1832–1920).

is founded on and to relate historical forces to current and future directions.

The origins of psychology come from different countries, laboratories, and perspectives. Its origins are so diverse that it is amazing that it coalesced into one discipline.

Wilhelm Wundt

Wilhelm Wundt (1832–1920) (Figure 1.4) is credited as being the "world's first psychologist." In 1874, he wrote the first textbook having to do with the field of psychology and conscious experience. In 1879, he established the first institute for experimental psychology at the University of Leipzig in Leipzig, Germany. Wundt used the method of introspection to study conscious processes. Observers were trained on how to report the contents of their own immediate states of consciousness (Humphrey, 1963). The purpose of the research was to determine the components of the conscious mind. He emphasized the elements of sensory, perceptual, and response processes.

Wundt used the person as the observer of his or her own impressions, thoughts, and behavior, an important concept in current psychology and in research on human–computer interaction. He conceived of the idea that elemental components of consciousness combine to form experiences that are more complex. Consequently, the first thing that researchers needed to do was to identify these components. This idea was later termed "structuralism" by Edward Titchner (1867–1927), one of Wundt's students who popularized the idea in America. Structuralism is an important concept for understanding how models of human–computer interaction are constructed today.

Wundt could also be called the "father of psychology" because between 1876 and 1919 he had more than 100 students who obtained doctoral degrees under his supervision (Fernberger, 1933; Tinker, 1932). A number of these

Figure 1.5. William James (1842–1910).

students went on to become famous in their own right. For example, G. Stanley Hall (1844–1924) founded the American Psychological Association in 1892, and James McKeen Cattell (1860–1944) developed the area and methodology for the study of individual differences, an extremely important concept in human–computer interaction.

William James

Although William James (1842–1910) (Figure 1.5) from America visited Wundt's laboratory in Liepzig, he agreed with neither his structuralist approach to consciousness nor with his laboratory studies. Instead, James was interested in how the mind functions to determine what people do and how they behave. He was especially interested in how the mind helps people adapt to their environment. Survival depended on adaptation. The central function of human thought was to adapt human behavior to the environment. With the addition of technology to the environment today, the mind is particularly challenged to constantly adapt to new ways of doing things.

In psychology, James' approach became known as "functionalism." Today, we go even further by transferring this idea to the computer and talking about its functionality. A word processor, for example, must have the functionality to input, format, and store text, but it would be helpful to have the functionality of a spell checker as well. The human mind in contrast to the computer has amazing functionality, which increases with learning and experience.

William James attempted to survey the whole range of human behavior and thought. In his two-volume book, *Principles of Psychology*, James (1918) covered the whole gamut of human experience, thought, and behavior, helping promote and unify psychology as a scientific discipline. It was in this

Figure 1.6. John Watson (1878–1958).

work that he gave us such ideas as "the stream of thought" and the baby's impression of the world "as one great blooming, buzzing confusion" (p. 462).

In his later years, however, James turned entirely to philosophy and established the idea of pragmatism in America. In his book, *Pragmatism*, James (1907) wrote about five things: a philosophical temperament, a theory of truth, a theory of meaning, a holistic account of knowledge, and a method of resolving philosophical disputes. To James, truth was "a species of the good," like health (p. 75). He explains that truths are goods because we can "ride" on them into the future and avoid being unpleasantly surprised. They "lead us into useful verbal and conceptual quarters as well as directly up to useful sensible termini. They lead to consistency, stability, and flowing human intercourse. They lead away from eccentricity and isolation, from foiled and barren thinking" (p. 103). James holds that truths are "made" (p. 104) in the course of human experience.

The philosophy of pragmatism fits into psychology in terms of the functionality of experience and belief. Interestingly, pragmatism later found itself useful in the development of theories of computing. Computer scientists, particularly those working on AI, needed to resolve issues about truth, meaning, and belief. Pragmatism and its emphasis on experiential learning and truth helped resolve a number of inherent logical conflicts in AI (Susskind, 1989).

John Watson

Up to this point, the study of psychology was driven by an interest in conscious experience and the use of introspection. When John Watson (1878–1958) (Figure 1.6) was awarded the first Ph.D. degree in the department of psychology at the University of Chicago in 1903, all of this was about to change. Watson did his research with rats, dogs, and other animals, and observed their behavior. He could not rely on introspection. Instead, he emphasized the study of observable behavior, and later, he altogether banned the use of introspection and subjective experience in psychological research. He focused on stimulus and response. The mind was a black box. With the new idea of behaviorism, researchers sought to describe, explain, predict, and control behavior. The opening paragraph of Watson's 1913 article, titled "Psychology as the Behaviorist Views It," laid out the direction of research in psychology for decades to come:

> Psychology as the behaviorist sees it is a purely objective, experimental branch of natural science. Its theoretical goal is the prediction and control of behavior. Introspection forms no essential parts of its methods, nor is the scientific value of its data dependent upon the readiness with which they lend themselves to interpretation in terms of consciousness. The behaviorist, in his efforts to get a unitary scheme of animal response, recognizes no dividing line between man and brute. The behavior of man, with all its refinement and complexity, form only a part of the behaviorist's total scheme of investigation. (p. 158)

Behaviorism was quickly adopted by many leading psychologists, particularly in learning and motivation, such as Edward Thorndike, B. F. Skinner, and Kenneth Spence. Behaviorism, while closing the door to conscious processes and introspection, opened a vast array of environmental variables, empirical research methods, and scientific rigor that helped psychology become an empirical science.

Philosophically, behaviorism attempted to remove the line between humans and animals. Later, behaviorism's influence would do the same for the distinction between humans and machines. Moreover, with the term "consciousness" stricken from the vocabulary, one did not need to speculate about machine consciousness. Ultimately, this became a stumbling block for behaviorism. Computer scientists found it necessary to speculate about internal cognitive processes and could not resist the idea of consciousness as a fundamental aspect of AI.

Ivan Pavlov

Ivan Pavlov (1849–1936) (Figure 1.7) was a physiologist, not a psychologist, but his work on the conditioned reflex of salivation in dogs, which won him the Nobel Prize in 1904, also brought an important and influential direction to psychology. Our nervous systems are conditioned by predictable events in our environment, and the mechanism for this learning is grounded in physiology. Taken to the extreme, we are machines programmed by events around us. All behavior, thought, and emotions are biologically based. In the rational mind of a reductionist, all of psychology can be reduced to the firing of neurons in the nervous system in response to stimuli in the environment.

Figure 1.7. Ivan Pavlov (1849–1936).

Prior to Pavlov's work, the response of salivation to the sight of food at a distance was believed to be due to "psychic" activity. A series of experiments caused Pavlov to reject the subjective interpretation of the "psychic" salivary secretion and to conclude that a conditioned reflex was involved. The discovery of conditioned reflexes made it possible to study all psychic activity objectively, without resorting to subjectivity. It was now possible to investigate by experimental means the most complex interrelations between an organism and its external environment.

Experiments carried out by Pavlov and his pupils showed that conditioned reflexes originated in the cerebral cortex, which acted as the "prime distributor and organizer of all activity of the organism." It was established that any external agent could, by coinciding in time with an ordinary reflex, become the conditioned signal for the formation of a new conditioned reflex. Following the discovery of this general postulate, Pavlov proceeded to investigate "artificial conditioned reflexes." Research in Pavlov's laboratories over a number of years revealed for the first time the basic laws governing the functioning of the cortex of the great hemispheres. Many scientists were drawn to the problem of developing Pavlov's basic laws governing the activity of the cerebrum. Because of this research, there emerged an integrated Pavlovian theory on higher nervous activity.

The biological basis of behavior is firmly rooted in modern psychology. Many psychologists have believed that by studying and mapping out the nervous system, we would develop a comprehensive theory of behavior. This was the pursuit of Karl S. Lashley (1890–1958) and many others, who believed that in their lifetimes we would bridge the gap between neural firing and higher thought processes. Unfortunately, the distance seems to grow the more we know about the complexities of the brain. Nevertheless, there is

Figure 1.8. Max Wertheimer (1880–1943).

much to learn about behavior from the nervous system, in the same way that one may learn about a computer from its circuit diagram.

Max Wertheimer

One of the main problems faced by theories in psychology has been the leap from the basic elements of the theory, whether units of experience, specific behaviors, or neural firings, to an overall effect. An important movement in German psychology sought to address this problem. It was Gestalt psychology founded by Max Wertheimer (1880–1943) (Figure 1.8). Wertheimer argued that you cannot build up knowledge merely from the parts. Consciousness cannot be understood by identifying and analyzing its components and then merely adding or linking them together as the structuralists assumed. Instead, "the whole is different from the sum of its parts." Our perceptions and understanding of things come about not by a passive combination of the parts, but by an active organization of the stimuli into a coherent whole. Much of the early work of Gestalt psychology used demonstrations in perception. Most of these are still cogent today. Later work in Gestalt psychology studied problem solving, the "Ah ha!" phenomenon, and insight as a reorganization of problem parts into a unique solution to the problem.

Gestalt psychology has had a significant impact on human–computer interaction. Many of the principles of Gestalt psychology are used in screen design. The idea of a perceptual foreground and background has been important in organizing screens into active and nonactive windows. We explore this in detail in Chapter 5.

Gestalt psychology would probably have had a greater and earlier impact in psychology had it not been for political developments in Germany. The Nazis

Figure 1.9. Sigmund Freud (1856–1939).

totally squelched Gestalt psychology. The four leading Gestalt psychologists (Max Wertheimer, Kurt Lewin [1890–1947], Wolfgang Kohler [1887–1967), and Kurt Koffka [1886–1941)] were all expelled from Germany and relocated in the United States. Unfortunately, behaviorism had taken foothold in American psychology, so Gestalt psychology had only a limited influence until the rise of cognitive psychology in the 1960s and 1970s.

Sigmund Freud

One cannot conclude a brief history of psychology without mentioning Sigmund Freud (1856–1939) (Figure 1.9), one of the most influential psychologists of all time. Like Pavlov, Freud was not a psychologist. He was a physician trained as a neurologist. But unlike Pavlov and many others in psychology, he did his research in the office and not in the lab. He based his theories on case observations from his clinical practice. Moreover, rather than basing his theories on conscious experience as did Wundt, Freud based them on unconscious processes. Freud believed that most of the mind, the factors that determine one's personality, and the forces of motivation are unconscious and hidden from conscious awareness. Consequently, Freud attempted to develop therapeutic techniques that probed the unconscious using a variety of methods such as psychoanalysis, hypnotism, personality tests, and dream interpretation.

Freud also emphasized the tripartite "self" composed of the ego, id, and superego. The ego is the rational self that plans, manages, and evaluates our motives and activities. It is the one part that is most conscious of its activities. The id is the part of the self that is entirely unconscious. It operates on the pleasure principle and is primitive, irrational, and illogical. The superego, in contrast, is the repository of moral teaching. It is the conscience that tries to do good. Although Freudian theory itself is no longer held in modern psychology, the concepts play an important part in cyberpsychology in terms of how we relate to others, the computer, and ourselves.

Current Trends in Psychology

The past two decades of psychology have seen many new developments. Radical behaviorism has been replaced by more balanced approaches in cognitive psychology. Psychology has become very interdisciplinary by attempting to connect with the brain sciences, linguistics, and AI under the term "cognitive science."

What we have not seen is the emergence of any new unifying of theories of psychology. Instead, we find many "microtheories" that deal with very specific areas such as attitude formation, focus of attention, organization of memory, language, self-image, and so on. Psychology has continued to use rigorous experimental methods and laboratory research, adding to our knowledge in every area of psychology.

Finally, psychology has become more applied, eclectic, relativistic, and data driven. Real problems need practical solutions. If it works, it must be right. It almost seems that we have returned to the pragmatism of William James. Clinical psychology has moved away from Freudian psychodynamic models to diagnostic techniques, practical methods of intervention, and drug therapy. The major "schools" of psychology seem to have dispersed. Psychology departments have lost faculty to other departments (e.g., biosciences, informatics, education, linguistics), and the research problems that have in the past been in the domain of psychology are now studied in new homes. Lacking a vision for psychology as a unified discipline, some have wondered if the grand day of psychology is waning.

It is unlikely that psychology will in itself develop a new unifying approach in the near future. However, in light of the new age of technology, it is possible that the unifying theory will come from the dynamic properties of the human–computer interface. The human–computer interface could itself provide the needed unifying perspective that will reinvent psychology. In Chapter 3, we investigate this possibility.

A Brief History of Computers

Although the history of psychology is based on a number of influential individuals, the history of computing seems to focus more on a series of milestones in the development of computing hardware. Of course, significant individuals were involved, but greater attention is paid to the technology developed than the personalities involved. A strange similarity, however, exists between the history of psychology and the history of computing. At the beginning of the twentieth century, Hermann Ebbinghaus (1850–1909)

Figure 1.10. Colossus (1943).

wrote "Psychology has a long past, but only a short history" (1908, p. 3). In the same way, computing has a long past, but a short history. Here, we begin with the modern history of computing starting in the 1940s. We break the history into three parts: hardware, software, and networks.

History of Hardware

First Generation

The first machines that could be called modern "computers" were based on wired circuits, electromagnetic relays, and vacuum tubes. They were very large, very unreliable, and used a lot of electricity. Typically, they used punched cards or tape for the nonvolatile storage media. Among the first of these were the Harvard Mk I and Colossus (both of 1943). The Colossus (Figure 1.10) was built in Britain at the end of 1943 during World War II to help crack the German coding system, the Lorenz cipher. The Harvard Mk I was built at Harvard University with backing from IBM. It was electromechanical and was meant to be a more general-purpose programmable computer.

The ENIAC (Electronic Numerical Integrator And Computer) (Figure 1.11) was completed in 1946 by the Army Ordnance Ballistic Research Laboratories, Aberdeen Proving Ground, Aberdeen, Maryland, to compute ballistic firing tables during World War II. It was also a general-purpose machine and was typical of the first-generation computers. It weighed

Figure 1.11. ENIAC (Electronic Numerical Integrator And Computer) (1946).

30 tons, contained 19,000 electronic valves, and consumed almost 200 kilowatts of electrical power. However, it was fast, capable of an amazing 100,000 calculations a second. Although the first generation of computers embodied the basic concepts and theory of computing with programming, instructions, data, storage, and so on, they were limited by their size, power consumption, and speed.

Second Generation

The next generation of computers came about with the invention of the transistor in 1947. The transistor replaced the relays and vacuum tubes of the first-generation computers. Printed circuit boards helped reduce the size of the computers during the 1950s and 1960s. Computers were still very experimental and limited to university research centers and government/military centers. But during this time, computer science and theories of programming developed.

Third Generation

The next significant breakthrough was the invention of the integrated circuit in 1958. The computer "chip" incorporated many transistor gates on one microchip. This began the era of the large "mainframe" computers of the 1960s and 1970s, such as the IBM 360 and the UNIVAC 1100 Series. The integrated circuits increased storage and processing capacities and brought computing to big business and government agencies. During this time, integrated circuits allowed the development of minicomputers such as the DEC-PDP computers, bringing computer power to smaller businesses and research labs. Computers really took off during this time and clearly demonstrated their potential in business, management, banking, information systems, and research. Everyone was considering computerization, but computers were still very expensive, far from their potential, and far from the hands of individual computer enthusiasts.

Fourth Generation

The most significant breakthrough for modern computing came in 1971, when Intel released the first commercial microprocessor, the 4004. The microprocessor put all of the computer's processing into one LSI (large-scale integration) chip or one VLSI (very large-scale integration) microchip. Around the same time, Intel produced the first RAM (random access memory) chip, putting large amounts of memory on one chip. The microprocessor opened the door to further advances in speed and power of the computers and made possible supercomputers such as the Cray-I. It also opened the door to personal computing. In 1974, MITS released the first personal computer, the Altair 8800, that anyone could buy, but only a few could figure out how to use it. This was followed by the first wave of personal computers that anyone could use–the Apple I and II, the Commodore PET, and, eventually, the original IBM PC in 1981.

Although the power of computer hardware has increased by orders of magnitude since the introduction of the microprocessor, the underlying technology has remained virtually the same. Most authorities agree that computers today are still in the fourth generation.

History of Software

The history of software is more difficult to trace. The hardware of computers is easy to identify, but software is not so apparent. It is the method of programming the hardware, the computer languages used for programming, and theoretical concepts involved in programming.

Programming

The idea of programming predated modern electronic or even electromagnetic computers. The first programming was for the loom. In 1804, Jacquard designed a loom in France that performed predefined tasks by feeding punched cards into a reading mechanism that automatically switched

Figure 1.12. Herman Hollerith (1860–1929).

weaving rods. The idea of using punched cards for programming and for storing data lasted for an amazing 150 years! It was used by Herman Hollerith (1860–1929) (Figure 1.12) for the U.S. Census in 1890 and continued to be used for program and data entry into the 1970s.

Here, several personalities were involved in the early concepts of programming. Ada Lovelace pushed the idea of programming machines with a rudimentary program in 1843 for the Analytical Machine, designed by Charles Babbage in 1827. The machine never came into operation, but the idea of programming was established.

Binary Code and Logic

One of the fundamental principles of modern computers and programming is binary coding and binary logic. George Boole (1815–1864) (Figure 1.13), a British mathematician, proved the relation between mathematics and logic with his algebra of logic (BOOLEAN algebra or binary logic) in 1847. His work in logic and mathematics laid the foundation of modern computing, but it would be 100 years before the idea would take root as the basic logic of computers.

Finally, in 1948, Claude Shannon (1916–2001) (Figure 1.14) wrote a paper, "A Mathematical Theory of Communication," published in the *Bell System Technical Journal*, on how binary logic could be used in computing. This theory was based on his 1937 master's thesis and earned him the Alfred Noble American Institute of American Engineers Award in 1940. The significance of this theory cannot be understated. Ultimately, it resulted in the development of binary code and computing and is the foundation of all

Figure 1.13. George Boole (1815–1864).

modern digital technology from computers to the Internet and from digital cameras to digital music. But binary code meant programming the computer using 1s and 0s. A programmer had to enter long strings of 1s and 0s to tell the computer what to do or what data to store. Various media such as punched cards and tape could store the programs, but programming was very tedious and error prone.

Languages

The solution was to have the computer do part of the work by converting shorthand code called "opcode" into groups of binary instructions. This

Figure 1.14. Claude Shannon (1916–2001).

was the introduction of assembly language. For each opcode, there was one instruction. Consequently, programs were very long and complicated.

When programs were written, some code was copied repeatedly or the instructions looped in what was called "spaghetti code." To unravel this code, Maurice Wilkes invented the idea of subroutines. Subroutines reused modules of code and made programming easier. Maurice Wilkes, David Wheeler, and Stanley Gill (1951) wrote the first textbook on programming, *The Preparation of Programs for an Electronic Digital Computer.*

The idea of a programming language really began with FORTRAN, shortened for FORmula TRANslator, in 1952. It was written by a team at IBM led by John Backus.

When COBOL (COmmon Business-Oriented Language) was published in 1960 by the CODASYL (Conference on Data Systems Languages) committee, of which Grace Hopper was a member, the idea of a programming or computer language was an established concept. The term "programming language" was used because like any language, it had a vocabulary or list of words and a grammar or syntax, and it had to produce unique code.

Like all programming languages at the time, FORTRAN and COBOL were machine specific. A different "compiler" was required to convert the program code into machine code for each type of machine. The idea of portability and machine independence came into being when "C" was developed by Dennis Ritchie and Brian Kernighan from 1969 to 1973, while they were working for Bell Laboratories. The power of "C" was that it had a small language base (vocabulary) but relied heavily on what they called "libraries." Libraries contained machine-specific instructions to perform tasks. The libraries were the only parts that had to be rewritten for different machines.

Since then, a number of new concepts have been developed such as object-oriented programming (OOP), visual languages, and Java. Each idea pushes to increase the ease of programming and portability of code from one platform to another (e.g., from Windows to Macintosh and back).

Operating Systems

Parallel with the development of computer languages, OSs were being developed. OSs were written to handle a lot of the common functions that most programs needed rather than writing machine-specific code over and over again. The principle of the OS was to take over almost all input and output tasks, such as writing data to and from memory, saving data on external storage devices, writing data to screens and printers, and scheduling tasks. Every computer had to have its own OS – from the big "mainframe" computers to new "microcomputers." The first real OS for a microcomputer was CP/M (control program/monitor), written by Gary Kildall (1942–1994) for the Intel 8080 chip. QDOS (quick and dirty operating system) was a clone of CP/M, purchased by Microsoft for $50,000 and developed into MS-DOS for the IBM-86 microcomputer.

In addition to "C," Richey and Kerningham at Bell Labs also developed UNIX, a generic OS. This, like "C," could be run on different machines by rewriting the libraries. The ideas behind UNIX continue in a number of OSs today (Linux, Mac OS X) in competition with Microsoft Windows OSs.

History of the Internet

Today, we know that it is not just the computer that matters, but it is the network that it is connected to that makes the difference. Like the computer, the Internet had significant input and funding from the military. ARPAnet (Advanced Research Projects Agency Network) was founded by the U.S. Department of Defense in 1969 for research on networking computers to share information and processing capacity. In the 1970s, ARPAnet was opened to nonmilitary users such as universities and research institutes.

Early users shared data and code between computers, but it was not until the mid-1980s that a number of services were standardized that allowed a wider community of users to take advantage of the Internet. First, the concept of "domain names" (e.g., www.apple.com) and domain name servers was introduced around 1984, so that people did not need to use numeric Internet protocol (IP) addresses. Second, protocols for e-mail and other services like file transfer protocol (FTP) were standardized.

But the major breakthrough for the Internet was the invention of the WWW by Tim Berners-Lee in 1989. He was a physicist working at CERN, the European Particle Physics Laboratory, and looking for a way for physicists to share information about their research. His idea was to think of files on servers distributed throughout the network as hyperlinked pages of information. They could be accessed using a protocol called hypertext transfer protocol (HTTP) and were written using hypertext markup language (HTML). Users could "browse" the information and click on links to go to other pages either on the same server or on any other server on the Internet. Graphics were introduced later with a browser called NCSA Mosaic.

Until the mid-1990s, only universities, government agencies, and large organizations had the resources to connect to the Internet. But as soon as people were allowed to "dial in" to the Internet using a modem connected to their computer and connecting to an Internet service provider (ISP), the use of the Internet exploded and the term "information superhighway" was coined. By the mid-1990s, the word "Internet" and the acronym "WWW" were in daily use.

History of Human–Computer Interaction and Cyberpsychology

There is also a history of human–computer interaction. It is, of course, the briefest of all, but it is worth mentioning a few historical points and people.

Here, the focus is on ways of doing things, not on hardware, but on software, ideas, and trends.

Generation 0

In the days when computers were programmed by hooking up wires and setting toggle switches, there really was no human–computer interface. There were no real "users" other than the computer scientists who built and hard programmed the machines themselves. There were, however, many human factors issues, especially having to do with the problem of setting many toggles and connections. To reduce the time and errors involved in this programming, the human–computer interface was invented.

Generation 1

When computers started to be programmed via computer programming languages and OSs used computer terminals with teletype keyboards, the human–computer interface clearly took shape. Programming was a way of "communicating" with the machine. Instructions were used to give commands to the computer, and the printout or display was the feedback. It was during this time that computer scientists started to think of this as a dialog between the human and computer, particularly because it was alphanumeric and language based. The interface, as shown later, evoked ideas of linguistics, communication, and understanding. During this time, there was an interest in understanding how computer programmers actually programmed. The term "software psychology" was first used by Ben Shneiderman (1980) in a book about this new research.

Generation 2

The major breakthrough in the human–computer interface occurred inside the Xerox Palo Alto Research Center (PARC) in 1973, where the copier company had assembled a group of top computer scientists to create the paperless office of tomorrow. They built the "Alto" computer with the first graphical user interface or "GUI" and the first internal network among the workstations (Ethernet). The interface is also referred to as a WIMP, because in addition to text, it used windows, icons, menus, and a pointing device. It was not until 1981 that Xerox released the improved version in the 8010 ("Star") system. Ultimately, Xerox dropped the project, and PARC invited Steve Jobs of Apple Computer over for a demonstration. He was thoroughly impressed, and Apple used the ideas of the GUI first in the Apple "LISA" and then later in 1984 as the basis for the Mac OS in the Apple Macintosh computer. Microsoft was the next to adopt the GUI in the first version of

Microsoft Windows in 1985, used with their OS (MS-DOS) that was being shipped with IBM PCs.

The GUI opened a whole new world for human–computer interaction. The interface created the illusion of "direct manipulation." Instead of typing "DELETE FILE," one could drag the icon of the file into an icon of a trash can to delete the file. This was also the time of the WYSIWYG ("what you see is what you get"), meaning that the way it looked on the screen would be the way it would look when printed. Finally, the new interface helped introduce multimedia with sound, animation, and video. Although a number of new aspects of the interface have been developed, such as speech recognition and virtual reality, the interfaces that we use today are still Generation 2.

During the 1980s, the term "user" came into being with the growth of workers who used but did not necessarily program computers. Users performed tasks. Donald Norman and others began to model user behavior in the hope of predicting how long it would take to complete tasks and how often users would make mistakes. The hope was to develop interfaces that would be more efficient and less error prone. The term "user friendly" was coined to describe interfaces that were easy to use. "User-centered design" was promoted to encourage programmers to think about how the user approached tasks rather than how the computer processed the data. Usability labs were built to test the use and performance of software on human participants as part of the design process.

Cyberpsychology had as its historical origin a number of visionaries who imagined new structures for knowledge, communication, and communities as a result of the computer revolution. For example, as early as the 1930s, Vannemar Bush (1890–1974) wrote of the device he called the "memex" that embodied ideas that were the forerunners of hypertext and the WWW. In 1945, his essay "As We May Think" was published in *Atlantic Monthly*. It was widely read, inspiring a number of thinkers and computer scientists to bring the ideas to reality. As result, Douglas Engelbart and his colleagues wrote the On-Line System (NLS), the world's first implementation of what would later be called "hypertext." He was also influential in the idea of "asynchronous collaboration among teams distributed geographically," which we now recognize as computer-supported cooperative work (CSCW) and groupware. Similarly, around 1960, Ted Nelson was inspired to start work on a software framework that he called Xanadu and coined the term "hypertext." Nelson envisioned many ideas in his books *Dream Machines* (1974) and *Literary Machines* (1987). Xanadu was never completed, but the WWW embodies most of the concepts that Nelson proposed.

Finally, a history of human–computer interaction and cyberpsychology should give mention to J. C. R. Licklider (1915–1990) (Figure 1.15). Licklider was a visionary with ideas of human–computer symbiosis (Licklider, 1960) and the use of the computer as a communication device (Licklider & Taylor, 1968), but he may also be credited as one of the most influential people in the history of computer science because as director of the Information Processing Techniques Office (IPTO), a division of the Pentagon's Advanced Research

Figure 1.15. J. C. R. Licklider (1915–1990).

Projects Agency (ARPA) from 1963 to 1964, he put in place the funding priorities that led to the development of the Internet and the invention of the "mouse," "windows," and "hypertext."

Other developments in human–computer interaction and cyberpsychology are recent enough to be part of the current discussion and are taken up in the succeeding chapters. Yet, like other developments in computer science, most of the concepts have been laid down, and it remains to be seen how they are played out in the present and future developments in psychology and the next generation of the human–computer interface.

Generation 3

The next generation of human–computer interface falls in the realm of futurism and borders on science fiction. Possible directions include immersive virtual reality, neural implants, and direct interfaces between the machine and human nervous system that bypass the senses and motor system. This generation is only beginning, and its viability is subject to debate. We save this discussion for Chapter 16.

Organization of This Text

This book takes as its outline and organization the topics of a standard introduction to psychology textbook. The reasons for this are simple. This book emphasizes a psychological perspective of the human–computer interface. Over many decades, the authors of introductory psychology books have first worked out a plan of talking about research methods and theory, and then moved from the underlying physiological processes to sensory and perception to the processes of learning and memory and on up to higher cognitive functions of thinking and problem solving. Then they moved on to individual differences, social processes, and abnormal behavior. Typically, at the end of most books, there are several chapters on applications and specific issues such as the psychology of women or the psychology of sports. This book follows a similar path, but the content is quite different.

PART I: Fundamentals

The first part of the book lays the foundation of the psychology of human–computer interaction in terms of historical background, biological and technological systems, theoretical models, and empirical methods.

Chapter 1: Introduction: Importance, Implications, and Historical Perspectives

This chapter emphasizes the importance of the human–computer interface today, the implications for psychology, and the history of psychology and computers relative to one another. It is good to know where it all came from before we look at where it is going.

Chapter 2: Fundamentals: Biological and Technological Bases

Organic and inorganic chemistry claims to be the foundation of all that we know in psychology and technology. This chapter briefly discusses the biological bases of behavior, the brain, and the human nervous system relative to machines, computer systems, and the perspective of cognitive science.

Chapter 3: Theoretical Approaches: Models and Metaphors

The way that we understand things is through models and metaphors. This chapter discusses the use of models to describe the relationships between human behavior and computer systems. It introduces a model of the flow of information and control through the human–computer interface and the community of models and perspectives assumed by interface designers, users, psychologists, and the machine itself.

Chapter 4: Research: Modes and Methods

Modern science bases itself on empirical, verifiable results. This chapter presents standard methods of research (e.g., surveys, observational data, experiments) as well as new technologies for record keeping, surveillance, and usability research.

PART II: Systems

The next part starts with the input/output systems of humans and machines, and then moves deeper into the systems of learning and memory, thinking and problem solving, and language.

Chapter 5: Sensory-Motor Interfaces: Input and Output

"Garbage in/garbage out" is an expression used to refer to problems with computers. What about humans? This chapter presents issues in visual, auditory, haptic, and other sensory input from the human–computer interface and motor and output to the interface (e.g., keyboard, mouse, touch screen). We also discuss information processing and attention. How do we recognize what we see and attend to different channels of information?

Chapter 6: Learning and Memory, Transfer and Interference

Learning has always been an essential part of human behavior. It is becoming even more important in the complex world of technology. This chapter deals with learning and memory issues on the part of the human and the computer. What must the human learn and remember about the computer (e.g., commands, procedures, passwords)? What does the computer learn and remember about the human and the environment (e.g., preferences, logs, knowledge)? How can the human use computers to retrieve information?

Chapter 7: Cognitive Psychology: Thinking and Problem Solving

This chapter discusses the human processes of thinking and problem solving while using computers. How does the user figure out how the application works? How can the computer be used to help solve problems?

Chapter 8: Language and Programming

Language is a fundamental means of communication. This chapter discusses the use of language with computers. It also addresses issues in the use of programming languages and natural language. How do we tell the computer what we want it to do?

PART III: Relationships

The third part moves into cyberpsychology and how individual differences in abilities and personality interact with the computer, how interpersonal relationships are mediated by the interface, how feelings and emotions enter into our relationship with the computer, and, finally, how situations lead to pathological relationships and require counseling.

Chapter 9: Individual Differences: People, Performance, and Personality

Are people becoming more alike or more different in the age of technology? This chapter discusses individual differences in relation to issues in human–computer interaction. First, we look at differences in IQ and specific cognitive abilities and how they relate to performance. Second, we examine age and gender differences. Third, we evaluate differences in experience. Finally, we look at personality differences and attitudes about computers.

Chapter 10: Motivation and Emotion at the Human–Computer Interface

This chapter discusses issues in intent, motivation, and satisfaction with respect to the human–computer interface. How does interacting with the computer reward or frustrate us? What is the motivation? Is the computer sensitive to our needs and emotions? How does the computer entertain us and captivate our attention?

Chapter 11: Interpersonal Relations

This chapter interfaces issues in person perception (e.g., stereotyping, bias, prejudice), attitudes (e.g., toward self, others, and the computer system), interpersonal communication (e.g., e-mail, chat), and aggression.

Chapter 12: Abnormal Behavior and Cybertherapies

In this chapter, we first discuss new types of psychological problems and pathologies as the result of computers and technology (e.g., computer phobia, stress). Then we discuss coping strategies and use of computer therapy. We also discuss online counseling and the use of self-help resources.

PART IV: Applications

The final chapters turn to particular issues of interest affecting cyberpsychology and the human–computer interface. Work in AI is adding a new dimension to human–computer interface with AI agents working at and around the interaction with humans. Universal access, assistive technologies, and augmented cognition are efforts directed to help users overcome obstacles and achieve new levels of performance. An important area for this is in education, entertainment, and their synthesis, "edutainment." Finally, we end the book with projections into future developments. Will there be a third-generation human–computer interface?

Chapter 13: Automation and Artificial Intelligence

What can be and what should not be automated? Do we rely too much on automation? In this chapter, we discuss the implications of an automated environment, the development of AI, and its pervasive presence in technology today. How aware are we of AI agents? What are the psychological implications of interacting with agents, how much do we trust them, and how do they change our perceptions? Who are they working for?

Chapter 14: Assistive and Augmentive Technologies

Our relationship with technology can be synergistic. In this chapter, we look at how technology is being used to enhance our abilities to perceive, think, and solve problems. We also look at assistive technologies that make up for disabilities and impairments in some individuals.

Chapter 15: Media: Games, Entertainment, and Education

Digital convergence is the process by which different media (i.e., photographs, music, animations, text) all converge into one digital media. This chapter discusses a number of psychological issues in computer media, computer games, and online education.

Chapter 16: The Future: The Ultimate Human–Computer Interface

What does the future hold for psychology and the human–computer interface? Some predict the blurring of the interface such that we will become machines or that our conscious processes will inhabit machines. This chapter surveys a number of these ideas and discusses their implications.

End Thoughts

Every scientific discipline is changed by the technology it employs and the problems it encounters. Scientific revolutions involve a radical shift in thinking, which has been called a "paradigm shift" by Kuhn (1962). The change from the belief that the world is flat to the view that it is a round globe and the change from the geocentric view that the earth is the center of the universe to the Copernican theory that it revolves around the sun are paradigm shifts in the history of astronomy. Today, computers and the Internet are causing new revolutions in how we think about ourselves and the world in which we live. Interestingly, the Internet with its global impact on communication, industrial development, and world economy has led to a new assertion that the world is flat. It has essentially leveled the playing field between developing and developed countries, allowing outsourcing in many fields, even in telemedicine, as illustrated in Scenario 2 (Friedman, 2005).

The behavioral and social sciences are being drastically impacted by the computer revolution. Like all of the sciences, we use computers to control our experiments, record our data, and analyze the results. But in the case of psychology, not only is our study of human behavior being transformed by technology, but also human behavior itself and our understanding of it is being changed. Even the way in which we think about behavior, thought, and self is being transformed in the context of a digital, technological world where we live out our lives in cyberspace and as we compare and contrast ourselves with computers. We see how this takes shape in Chapter 2, where we investigate the biological and mechanical foundations of humans and computers.

Suggested Exercises

1. Write a short personal history of your use of computers. List the computers that you used as you were growing up. If you can, list the types and models of computers and the programs that you used.
2. Write a short essay on how the use of computers and digital technology impacts your daily life.
3. Keep a journal for 1 week, listing each encounter that you have with computer technology at home, school, and work.

References

Day, J. C., Janus, A., & Davis, J. (2005). Computer and Internet use in the United States: 2003. *U.S. Census Bureau, Current Population Reports, P23–208*. Retrieved February 19, 2008, from www.census.gov/prod/2005pubs/p23–208.pdf

Ebbinghaus, H. (1908). *Psychology: An elementary text-book*. Boston, MA: D. C. Heath & Co.

Fernberger, S. W. (1933). Wundt's doctorate students. *Psychological Bulletin, 30*, 80–83.

Friedman, T. L. (2005). *The world is flat: A brief history of the twenty-first century*. New York: Farrar, Straus and Giroux.

Gray, J. (1993). *Men are from Mars, women are from Venus: A practical guide for improving communication and getting what you want in your relationships*. New York: HarperCollins.

Humphrey, G. (1963). *Thinking: An introduction to its experimental psychology*. New York: Wiley.

James, W. (1907). *Pragmatism*. New York: Longmans, Green, and Co.

James, W. (1918). *Principles of psychology*. New York: Henry Holt & Co.

Kuhn, T. (1962). *The structure of scientific revolutions*. Chicago: The University of Chicago Press.

Licklider, J. C. R. (1960). Man–computer symbiosis. *IRE Transactions on Human Factors in Electronics, HFE-1*, 4–11. Retrieved February 19, 2008, from http://memex.org/licklider.pdf

Licklider, J. C. R., & Taylor, R. W. (1968). The computer as a communication device. *Science and Technology, April*, 20–41.

Nelson, T. (1974). *Dream machines: New freedoms through computer screens – a minority report. In Computer Lib: You Can and Must Understand Computers Now*. Chicago, IL, Hugo's Book Service. Nelson.

Nelson, T. (1987). *Literary machines*. Nelson. Available from The Distributors 702 South Michigan, South Bend, IN 46618.

Schultz, D. P., & Schultz, S. E. (2004). *A history of modern psychology* (8th ed.). Belmont, CA: Wadsworth/Thomson Learning.

Shneiderman, B. (1980). *Software Psychology: Human Factors in Computer and Information Systems*, Cambridge, MA: Winthrop.

Susskind, R. E. (1989). Pragmatism and purism in artificial intelligence and legal reasoning. *AI & Society*, *3*(1), 28–38.

Tinker, M. A. (1932). Wundt's doctorate students and their theses, 1875–1920. *American Journal of Psychology*, 44, 630–637.

Watson, J. B. (1913). Psychology as the behaviorist views it. *Psychological Review*, 20, 158–177.

Wiener, N. (1948/1961). *Cybernetics: Or the control and communication in the animal and the machine*. Cambridge, MA: MIT Press.

Wilkes, M. V., Wheeler, D. J. & Gill, S. (1951). *The preparation of programs for an electronic digital computer*. Cambridge, MA, Addison-Wesley.

Two

Fundamentals

Biological and Technological Bases

Scenario

Human Literacy 101. *"OK, class, I am now distributing the schematic for the basic human nervous system. Now remember that all humans differ from this basic schematic because each human is unique down to the serial number, not just the model. Moreover, they are rather plastic and change in random ways over time. You will, however, notice two important things. First, the system is organized into a hierarchy of centers from the spinal column up to the lower brainstem and cerebellum, and then to the medulla oblongata, the hippocampus, and the hypothalamus, and finally to the cerebral cortex. The amazing thing about this system is that it is built from totally autonomous, separate parts called 'neurons.' Each neuron is a self-sufficient cell. It has its own power supply relying only on nutrients in the fluids around it; it has its own programming initiated from its genetic code; and it has its own central processor and peripherals for sensor input and affecter output."*

"Now for some human terms. Who can tell me what a hormone is?" Sensing no response, the computer teacher told her class of sixty-four new computers right off the production line, "It is very important that you understand that humans are not merely electronic. A large proportion of human functioning is actually performed by complex chemical reactions and fluid dynamics. When you interact with these beings, you must take this into consideration. They are very predictable if and only if you factor in their chemistry."

"OK, that concludes our class for today. Be sure to download Webster's Dictionary *and* Encyclopedia Britannica *for tomorrow."*

Overview

"Computer literacy" is a human's knowledge about machines. At the onset of the computer revolution, it was apparent that new computer users needed to know a lot about the technical details of computers. Educational programs were quickly put in place to teach computer literacy. In contrast, we may propose the idea of "human literacy" as a machine's knowledge about humans. In the opening scenario, we envision the humorous perspective of computers acquiring such knowledge about humans. But in all seriousness, the interaction between any two agents requires a degree of literacy of one about the other to generate and interpret messages.

This chapter is divided into three parts. In the first part, we review some of the logic and hardware of computers from the perspective of HCI. In the second part, we discuss the biological basis of behavior, namely, the brain and the human nervous system. In the third part, we look at a number of differences and similarities between the logic-driven computer and the biologically driven human. We use a cognitive science perspective to compare and contrast the two systems to anticipate and reconcile differences between the two at the human–computer interface.

We start from the observation that both humans and computers are composed of matter. From a "reductionist" point of view, we know that who we are and how computers function is ultimately based on the laws of physics as they play out in chemistry, mechanics, and electronics, and as they ultimately drive the laws of human behavior. It behooves us then to start from the biology of the human and the hardware of the computer to understand how we act, behave, and perform, and how computers work and function. Although we can in principle trace the relationship between the low-level hardware processes and the high-level activities of computers, even AI, it is doubtful that we will ever totally bridge the gap between the physical functions of the nervous system and the higher cognitive processes of the human mind. Nevertheless, there are a number of strong and important relationships between biological processes and human behavior that we discuss in the chapter and that will prove important in HCI.

The Computer

The human and the computer are both complex systems. Although the computer has only been around for a few decades and the human for millennia, the human is the less well understood of the two. So, we start with the simpler, the computer. First, we look at the overall architecture and the function of each part of the computer. Then we look at the fundamental logic of how the computer works. Finally, we look at the software that runs the computer, called the "operating system," and the range of software that runs on the computer to perform various jobs.

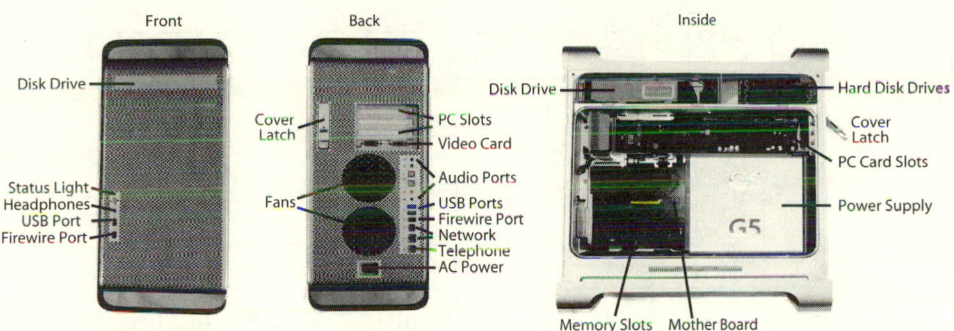

Figure 2.1. Outside and inside of a personal "tower" computer (Apple Power Mac G5).

Hardware Architecture

The typical general-purpose computer is housed in a box with a power supply and a variety of plugs and switches on the front and back. Inside the case, one will find a large printed circuit board called the "motherboard" with cables and plugs attached to it. In addition, there will be other smaller printed circuit boards and smaller cases for disk drives of various types. Figure 2.1 shows some illustrations of a "tower" encased computer.

The CPU

Most computers, whether large or small, are organized around a central processing unit (CPU), which performs the instructions or steps in a program. In metaphoric terms, it is the "brain" of the computer. Figure 2.2 shows a picture of the Intel 8080 chip on the left and the Intel Pentium on the right.

Figure 2.2. Images of an early CPU (Intel 8080, 1974) (left) and a more recent CPU (Intel Pentium, 2000) (right).

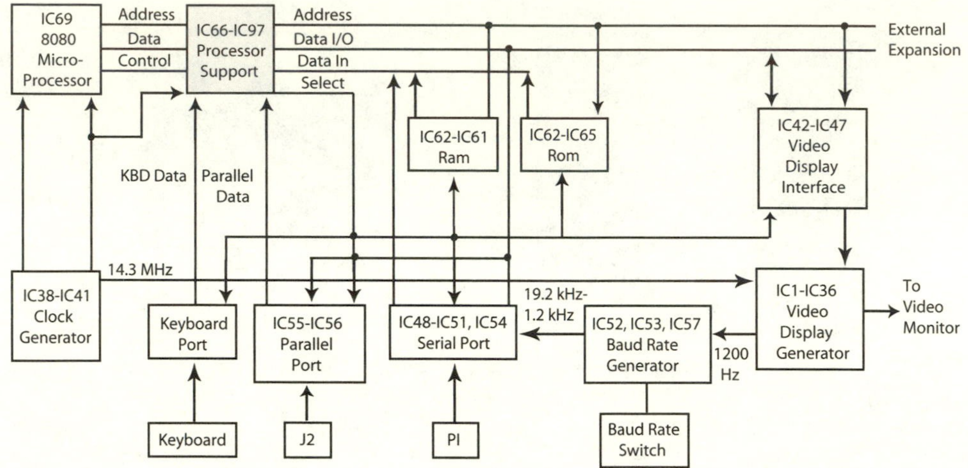

Figure 2.3. Schematic of an early microcomputer (Processor Technology SOL-20).

The CPU is connected to memory and to peripherals. The main internal connection that allows the parts to communicate with one another is called the "bus." Figure 2.3 shows a schematic of an early microcomputer. The CPU, an 8080 microprocessor, is shown at the upper left along with additional circuits to support its operation.

An important part of all computers is the clock that generates a pulse that signals the CPU to step from one operation to the next. The clock must not run the computer faster than the tolerance of the CPU or the CPU will skip operations and make errors. Early computers were very slow by today's standards and could only run at clock speeds of 2 MHz or 2 million pulses per second. Current microcomputers run at more than 1 GHz, or 1 billion operations per second. The increase in speed is a function of the way in which the microcomputer chip is constructed. The faster the speed, the more energy used, and the more heat produced by the CPU. Most CPUs today require heat sinks and fans to cool them.

The Bus

The bus is shown in Figure 2.3 by the lines labeled Address, Data, and Select. The bus is a transmission path onto which data in the form of signals are dropped off or picked up by every device attached to the line. It takes its name from the common autobus, which picks up and drops off passengers at stops along the way. However, the metaphor breaks down when you understand how it really works. Devices addressed by the signals pick up the data, and devices that are not addressed ignore the signals. In reality, all data are present at all stops, and it is the device that either responds to the data or not. The bus is generally part of the main printed circuit board of the computer, the motherboard. The bus, which consists of many lines, connects the CPU to internal memory, to storage devices, and to input/output peripherals, such as keyboards, monitors, and computer ports for communication. Because the bus is the main pathway for information into and out of the CPU, its speed and capacity are also important factors in determining the power of the computer.

Memory

One of the most important devices attached to the bus is the internal memory. There are two types of memory. Read-only memory (ROM) generally contains initial instructions for the computer as it starts up. Random access memory (RAM) allows the computer to write to and read from the storage. RAM is usually located on a set of memory boards or chip sets plugged into slots specifically for memory. Figure 2.1 shows such slots and memory cards. Dynamic RAM is said to be "volatile" because its contents are lost when the computer is powered down. ROM is not volatile. An early type of RAM called "core" memory was not volatile. The information was stored by magnetizing tiny metal rings called "core."

Because what is stored in memory is lost when the computer is turned off and because memory chips tend to be expensive, other storage devices are needed. These are generally hard disk drives (HDDs). They provide large amounts of storage at low cost. Reading and writing the information is more time consuming because it usually involves moving a read head to a different area over the surface of a magnetic or optical disk. Disk storage is connected to the bus with additional circuitry to control the disk and the passage of the information in and out.

Peripherals

Finally, we come to connecting the computer to the world and building its interface to the human. The most common input devices for personal computers are the keyboard and the mouse, and the typical output device is the monitor. These require additional logic to connect the keyboard as a peripheral on the bus. The video monitor is often given preferential treatment on the bus because of the large amount of information that is required to write and refresh the screen.

Additional peripherals are connected to the bus to drive printers, communicate with networks, and generate or record sound, speech, images, and video. Some of these are built into the motherboard of the computer, and others can be added by plugging cards into expansion slots. Some computers are built in a component-like manner to allow for expansion of internal memory, storage, and peripherals on the bus slots, as seen in Figure 2.1. Others are built in a more fixed manner and cannot be internally modified, but they can be connected by way of external ports such as USB and FireWire, also shown in Figure 2.1.

The peripherals, especially those designed to interact with the human user, are extremely important. In later chapters, we explore their design and how they interface with the human sensory–motor system.

Communications

Finally, most computers are in communication with other computers. LANs allow computers to communicate and share files within a limited range. Wide area networks (WANs) allow computers to communicate and share files at a global level. The Web and e-mail works across a WAN. Computers use different types of ports for such communication – modems, cables, network switches, routers, and a vast array of hardware and computers that act as servers. Although these systems are not physically apparent at the human–computer interface, they play an enormous role in the emerging impact of computers on our daily lives.

Logic and Programming

The physical and functional architecture of the computer was designed with a purpose in mind. The primary objective is for the CPU to do the majority of the computational work and efficiently communicate with memory, storage, and interfaces. We later see how this compares with the overall architecture of the human nervous system. The system architecture tells us a lot about the functionality of the computer, but it does not tell us how it actually works. To understand how the computer works at the macro level, we really have to know what makes it run at the micro level. With computers, we can bridge the gap between the elementary processes at the micro level and the big picture on the computer monitor at the macro level.

Elementary States

The most elementary part of a computer is a circuit that acts either as a register that stores a representation of a 0 or 1 or a logic gate that converts input representing a 0 or 1 to an output representing 0 or 1. In general, a voltage level of +5 represents a 1 or true value, and a voltage level of 0 represents a 0 or value of false. Figure 2.4 shows the basic binary states changing over time. The gates and registers are composed of semiconductors, namely, diodes, and transistors shown in Figure 2.5, along with resistors and capacitors.

Different types of gates perform the basic digital logic involved in a computer. Figure 2.6 shows the schematic diagrams of several types of gates. An "AND" gate is on if Input A is on and Input B is on, and off if Input A or Input B or both are off. An "OR" gate is on if either Input A is on or Input B is on or both. A "NOR" gate is on if Input A is on or Input B is on but not

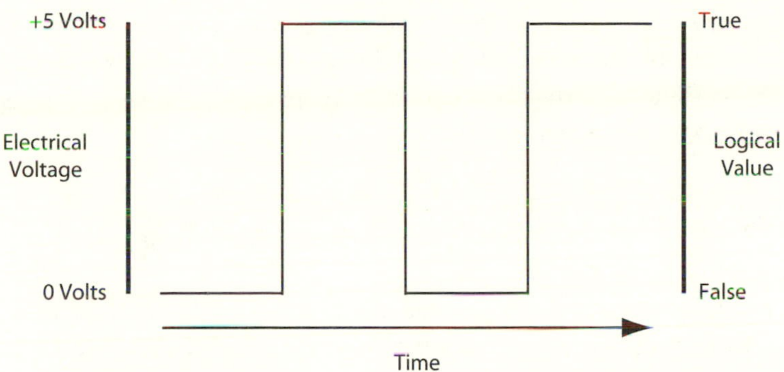

Figure 2.4. Voltage levels of a binary signal.

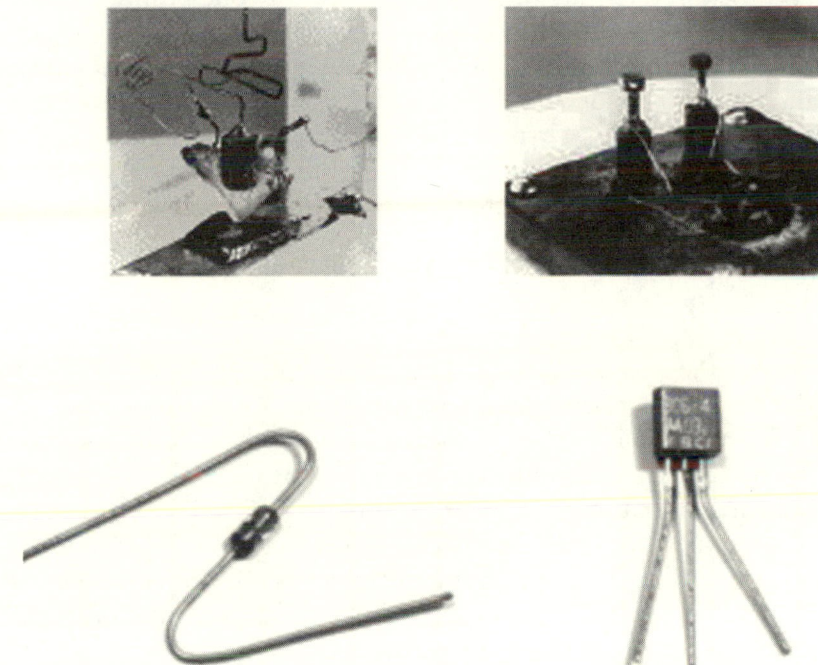

Figure 2.5. Pictures of the first transistor (top left) and junction transistor (top right) from 1947 and pictures of a 1970s diode (bottom left) and transistor (bottom right).

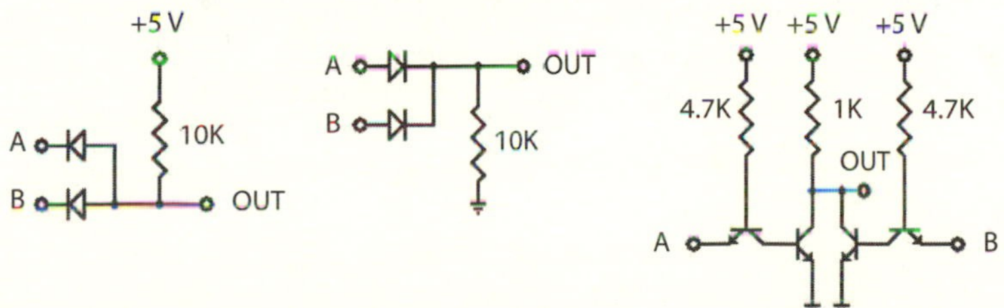

Figure 2.6. Some basic logic diagrams for computer gates: a DL AND gate (left), a DL OR gate (middle), and a TTL NOR gate (right).

both. The gates require a power supply, are hard wired to other gates, and have limits in terms of how fast they can operate. Gates are combined and organized into logic circuits that perform more complex operations to store, retrieve, and process information.

Registers

The type of logic used by the computer drives its physical design. Because computers were first built for numerical computation, they were designed to store and manipulate binary numbers. The numbers had a maximum length determined by the size of the register built to store them. Registers are located in the CPU to store the state of the computer at any one point or one tick of the clock cycle. Computers also use a number of registers for input, output, and intermediate stages of processing. The early computers had registers of only eight binary digits or "bits." The size of the register determined the size of the computer word or "byte." Current microcomputers are up to sixty-four digits. However, the term "byte" itself has stuck with the meaning of eight bits and is used as a measure of storage capacity.

Instruction Set

Every CPU has an instruction set. The instruction set contains all possible operations that can be performed on its registers. Instructions include operations to move the contents of one register to another, add or subtract the contents of registers, and address memory locations. The instructions are fixed by the logic built into the microcomputer chip.[1]

For a computer to run, the machine instructions are combined into extremely long and complex programs and entered into the computer's memory. Once started, these programs do everything that a computer does. For a while, it was believed that the more instructions the better to make programs shorter and to reduce calls to memory. These have been labeled CISC chips for "complex instruction set computers." However, it was found that too many instructions caused problems in fabricating the chips and that complicated, specialized instructions could be accomplished more rapidly by a series of operations from a reduced instruction set. These CPUs were dubbed RISC chips for "reduced instruction set computers." Today, however, with new manufacturing techniques, CISC chips are coming back.

Signals

The output of and the input to the CPU are signals that are conveyed along wires. Signals are either parallel or serial. If it is parallel, the whole byte is

[1] The complete instruction set for the 8080 chip can be found at http://nemesis.lonestar.org/computers/tandy/software/apps/m4/qd/opcodes.html.

transmitted in one pulse or clock cycle. Parallel signals require at least as many wires as bits in the byte. So, for an eight-bit signal to be transferred, eight wires plus a ground wire are required. If the signal is serial, each bit is transmitted one at a time and requires only one wire plus a ground wire. Most signals to and from the CPU and on the bus are parallel. Most signals transmitted outside the computer are serial and require fewer wires, but in turn require more time. To increase the speed of transmission, rather than transmitting a purely binary signal, high-frequency signals with a greater bandwidth carry more information. Optic fibers using light have an extremely high bandwidth and can transmit large amounts of information quickly.

Wireless transmission, of course, eliminates the need for wires altogether and can also increase the distance of transmission. Because the signals are transmitted at the speed of light, they can be conveyed over great distances, even from one continent to another in a split second.

Operating System

Computers can do nothing without programming. Programming is the set of instructions that operate on the input and output of the CPU. How does the programming get there? Part of it is initially resident in memory on a ROM chip and is the basic input/output system or "BIOS" (basic input and output system). The BIOS contains all code required to control the keyboard, the display screen, the disk drives, and serial communications to allow the computer to start up or boot itself. The BIOS is typically stored on a ROM chip that comes with the computer. This ensures that the BIOS will always be available and will not be damaged by disk failures.

The rest of the OS is read into memory from disk. We have much more to say about the OS as it interfaces with the human in later chapters.

Summary

As we have seen, computers are electronic, digital, and based on binary logic. They are machines, but extremely complex machines. Moreover, as they are being networked together, they are assuming new characteristics and abilities.

Next, we turn to the human. Are we machines like the computer, just a sort of biological or "wet" type, or are we more than that? How do we compare in terms of elementary states, logic processes, and complexity with the computer?

The Human

The human nervous system is one of the ten basic systems of the human body. It is responsible for higher-level control of the body and its systems. The nervous system is comprised of the brain, the brainstem, the spinal

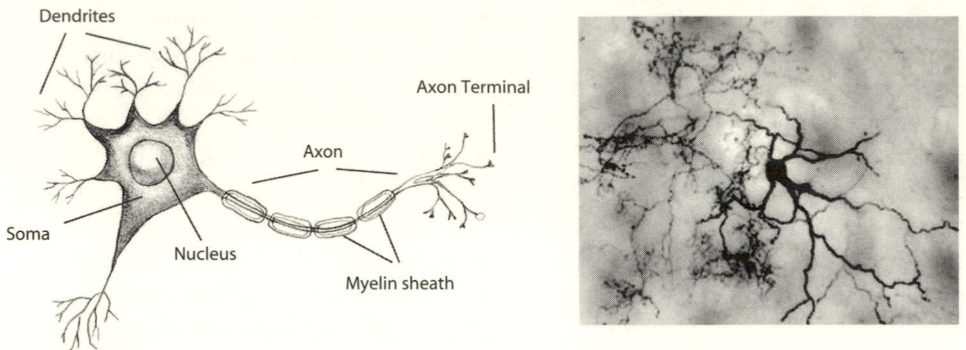

Figure 2.7. Basic structure of a neuron (left) *and image of a neuron* (right).

column, and extensive nerves and receptors throughout the body as well as those in the primary senses.

In contrast to our understanding of the computer, which starts from known digital logic and its implementation in hardware, much of the logic of the human nervous system remains a mystery. Our only hope is to start with the cells that comprise the nervous system and try to understand their logic. Consequently, we start from the basic units that make up the nervous system and work our way up. The nervous system is basically comprised of two types of cells, the neurons and the supply cells called "glial" cells, in addition to connecting tissues and a permeating system of blood vessels.

The Neuron

That the neuron acts as a basic unit in the nervous system was not understood until Santiago Ramón y Cajal (1854–1934) studied sections of the nervous system on slides in his attic with a $25 microscope. He won the Nobel Prize for his discovery in 1906.

The fundamental basis of the human nervous system is the neuron. Figure 2.7 shows a typical neuron. The basic operation of the neuron is that it is stimulated at one end, fires, conducts the discharge to another end, and in turn stimulates another neuron. Actually, the neuron is an incredibly complex living cell. As a living cell, the neuron provides its own energy from the nutrients around it. It has its own genetic code to replicate itself during growth. It can move to make or break contact with other neurons. It has a complex logic of firing with an activation threshold, with discharge and refractory timing, with inhibitor input, and with a complex chemistry of neurotransmitters.

The function of the neuron is to send and receive information. The entire nervous system is composed of anywhere from 90 to 180 billion neurons. Approximately 98.8 percent of these neurons comprise the brain itself, and the rest (still more than 1 billion) are distributed throughout the spinal cord and the rest of the body (Rosenzweig, Breedlove, & Leiman, 2002; Williams

& Herrup, 1988). The amazing thing is that neurons do not just connect one to another, but on average each neuron transmits information to tens of thousands of other neurons. Consequently, there are trillions of neural connections in the brain (Beatty, 2001). Much of the intricacy of the brain is due to the incredible complexity of its wiring.

There are essentially three types of neurons, although their structures are very similar. Sensory neurons respond to physical and chemical stimuli and compose the sensory receptors in the eyes, ears, etc. Some sensory neurons respond to internal stimuli such as pain, physical stress, and temperature. Motor neurons send commands from the brain to the muscles and internal organs. Interneurons comprise the vast network of connections that eventually tie the sensory neurons to the motor neurons and do the intermediate processing to determine what to respond to and how.

Structure of the Neuron

All neurons are single living cells composed of three parts, as shown in Figure 2.7. The soma is the body of a cell, which contains the nucleus and the chemistry to preserve and nourish the cell. The neurons are truly individual units in the system with their own mini life support systems, power supplies, and internal control circuits. Attached to the soma are branch-like extensions called "dendrites." The dendrites receive incoming information from other neurons. Each neuron can have hundreds to thousands of dendrites that connect to other neurons. The incoming information is integrated and transmitted though the control center of the soma. It is then transmitted out to another extension called the "axon." The axon carries the information from the soma to its end by way of an electrochemical impulse. At the end of the dendrite, terminal buttons convey the information to the next neuron. The terminal buttons do not actually touch the dendrites of the next neuron; instead, the terminal button of one neuron and the dendrite of the next form what is called a "synapse." The operation of the synapse is complicated and is discussed in a later section.

The length of the axon can range from 1/32 of an inch to more than 3 feet. The speed of conduction of the impulse is considerably slower than the speed of electricity in the circuit board of a computer. In the neuron, the speed varies from only 2 to 200 miles per hour depending on the type of neuron, as opposed to electricity, which is about two-thirds the speed of light in a coaxial cable. The axons are covered by white fatty cells, which form a protective covering called the "myelin sheath" that speeds the transmission of the impulse.

Neuron State

Oddly enough, neurons seem to be binary entities, but with different timing characteristics than the logic of a computer. The neuron is either in a resting state or a firing state according to an all-or-none law. The neuron fires if

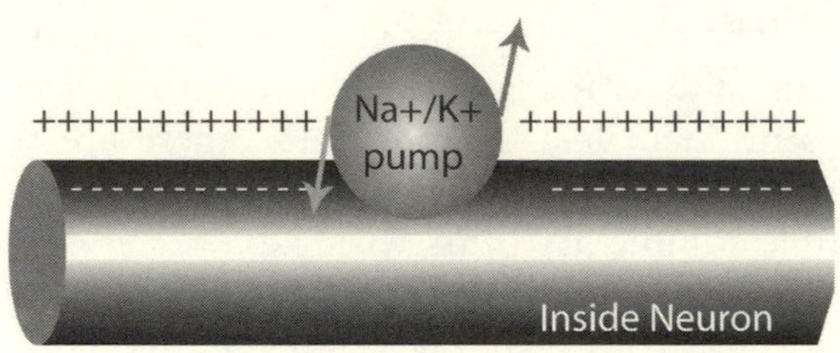

Figure 2.8. The electron charge and the cell membrane.

the combined stimulation to the dendrites exceeds a minimum threshold. When it fires, the neuron transmits an electrochemical impulse along its cell membrane. The neuron is charged and set like a trigger. It is charged by building up an electrical potential between the inside and the outside of the cell membrane, as shown in Figure 2.8.

The cells push positively charged sodium and potassium ions outside and negatively charged chlorine ions inside. The inactive neuron is in a resting potential with a negative charge. When it fires, it switches to an action potential with a brief pulse to a positive charge that travels down the axon. Figure 2.9 shows the charge of the neuron rapidly shift from a negative resting potential to a positive spike and then back to a negative resting potential. The change in charge forms a single ripple that shoots along the cell membrane.

The information-carrying capacity of a neuron depends on the speed with which its impulse travels along the axon (distance per second) and the speed with which it can shift between the resting and action states (firings per second). The speeds of different neurons can vary as much as from 2 to 200 miles per hour. Any particular neuron has a fairly constant speed. The speed of transmission depends on the structure of the axon. The larger the diameter and the greater the myelin sheathing around it, the faster the transmission. Although the speed of electricity in a wire is a matter of debate, it has been estimated that it is about 3 million times faster than the fastest neuron. So, even at its very best, the nervous system is incredibly slower at transmitting a signal than a single wire cable in a computer.

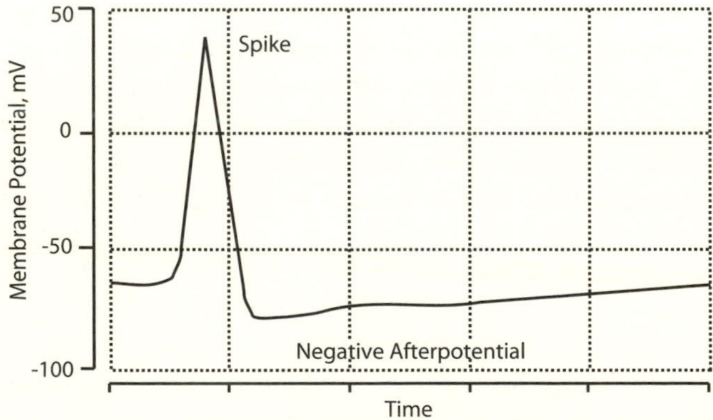

Figure 2.9. Resting potential and action potential of a neuron over time.

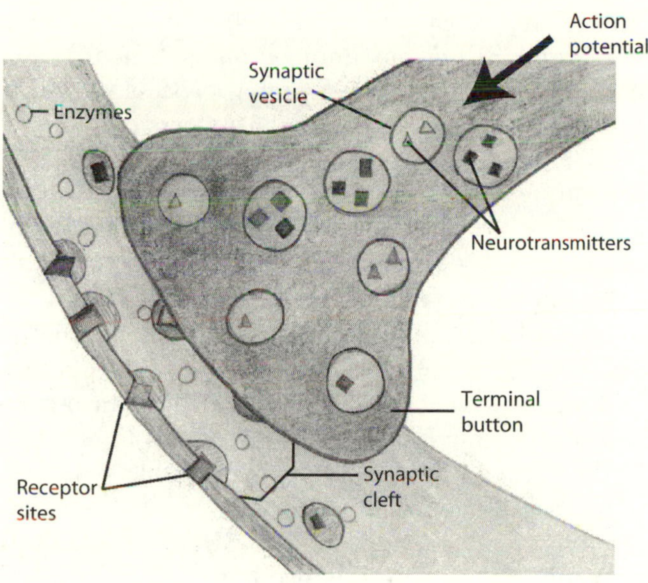

Figure 2.10. The synapse.

The speed of a neuron also depends on its rate of firing, that is, how fast it can shift from the action potential back to the resting potential. Some neurons can fire as fast as 1,000 times a second, or once per millisecond, 1 MHz. Others are much slower. Here again, the neuron is considerably slower than the switching speed of gates in a computer, which can be at the rate of 2 GHz, or 2 billion switches per second. It makes one wonder why we ever have to wait for a computer to do anything if it is so much faster! But it gets worse when we consider how one neuron transmits its signal to the next across the synapse.

The Synapse

Unlike computer logic circuits that are directly connected, soldered, or plugged together, neurons transmit their signals across a gap not using an electrical charge, but using chemicals called "neurotransmitters." The gap is called the "synaptic cleft" and is shown in Figure 2.10.

When the neuron fires and the impulse reaches the end of the axon, it generally stops at the terminal buttons. Rather than jumping across to the next neuron, or even using the electrical charge to stimulate the dendrites of the next neuron, the impulse causes the release of special chemicals stored in synaptic vesicles. The neural transmitters then travel across the synaptic cleft. Fortunately, they move fast and do not have far to travel. They arrive in one-tenth of a millisecond at receptor sites on the next neuron. The neurotransmitters are complex chemicals that serve to unlock tiny channels that permit either positively or negatively charged ions to enter the dendrite. The chemicals act as specific keys in locks. Some are excitatory neurotransmitters that increase the probability that neurons will fire, and others are inhibitory neurotransmitters that decrease the probability. Neurons have many dendrites, and many terminal buttons impinge on each neuron. Consequently, at the synaptic level there is a sort of analog process in which continuous levels of excitatory and inhibitory neurotransmitters combine to increase or decrease the probability that the stimulus will exceed the threshold for firing.

After the neurotransmitters do their job, they are either repackaged in the synaptic vesicles or broken down by enzymes. The repackaging is called "reuptake" and must occur quickly for the next firing to occur. The speed and timing of the human nervous system is not controlled by a system clock but is the sum total of the time required by each of the many steps in the transmission.

There are more than seventy-five different neurotransmitters. However, the most prevalent in the nervous system is acetylcholine. It is an excitatory transmitter to the skeletal muscles. It is responsible for most, if not all, conscious actions, including breathing.

A second important neurotransmitter is dopamine. It seems to be involved not only in facilitating movement, but also in thought and emotion. Finally, we should also mention endorphins, which are involved in pain suppression and pleasure.

A breakdown in the neurotransmitter system can cause severe malfunctions in the nervous system, from paralysis to convulsions or from clinical elation to depression. The neurochemical basis of the nervous system adds a biological complexity to the system that is fundamentally different from electromechanical, digital systems. If a machine, as in the opening scenario, were to conjecture about a human having a system crash or a program freezing up, it would probably involve neurotransmitters.

Finally, neurons are extremely complex. It is as if neurons themselves are tiny independent computer processors in a network. The network is the nervous system itself. Although the nervous system is composed of neurons, it does not come to a halt if one neuron dies. In fact, about 200,000 neurons in the brain die every day. Some are replaced, but at the end of 80 years of life, we lose about 6 percent of the original total (Dowling, 1992). We now turn to the overall nervous system.

Systems

Similar to the computer, the human nervous system is made up of an extremely complex structure of elementary parts. In the case of computers, the elements are logic circuits. In the case of the nervous system, the elements are neurons.

We distinguish between two parts: the central nervous system and the peripheral nervous system. The central nervous system is comprised of the brain and the spinal column. The peripheral nervous system consists of the nerves outside the central nervous system that travel to and from the organs and

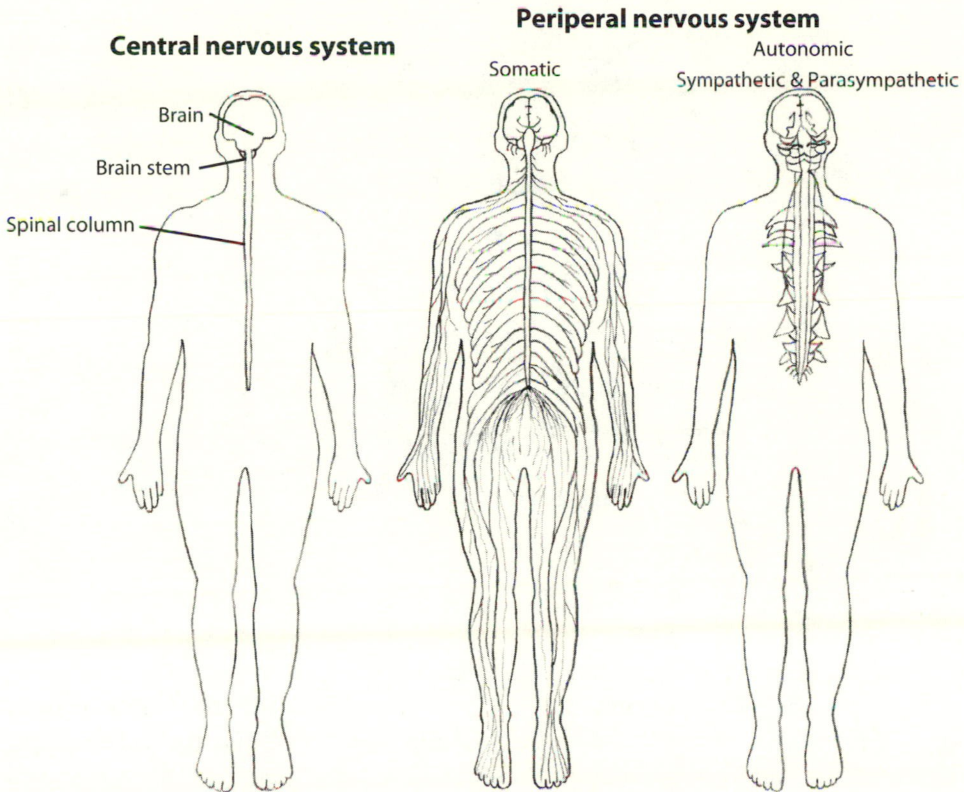

Figure 2.11. The central and peripheral nervous systems.

the various tissues in the body, including the muscular system and skin. Figure 2.11 shows the nervous system.

The Central Nervous System: The Brain and Spinal Column

Unlike the computer, which engineers designed and built, our understanding of how the brain works comes from medicine and laboratory science. Our knowledge of the brain depends on three main sources. A visual inspection tells us about its anatomy, namely, the physical structure of brain centers and neural pathways. Electromagnetic imaging techniques, such as PET (positron emission tomography) scans and fMRI (functional magnetic resonance imaging), tell us about the energy consumption of brain areas during different tasks. Finally, the functionality of parts can be inferred from the effects of injury and surgical procedures. Much of the research on brain function has been done by destroying a specific part of the brain and observing how behavior changes. For example, if you cut the nerves from one center to another or destroy the cells in an area, what kind of loss do we observe? Similarly, in computers one can see what happens if you pull out a circuit board or cut a wire.

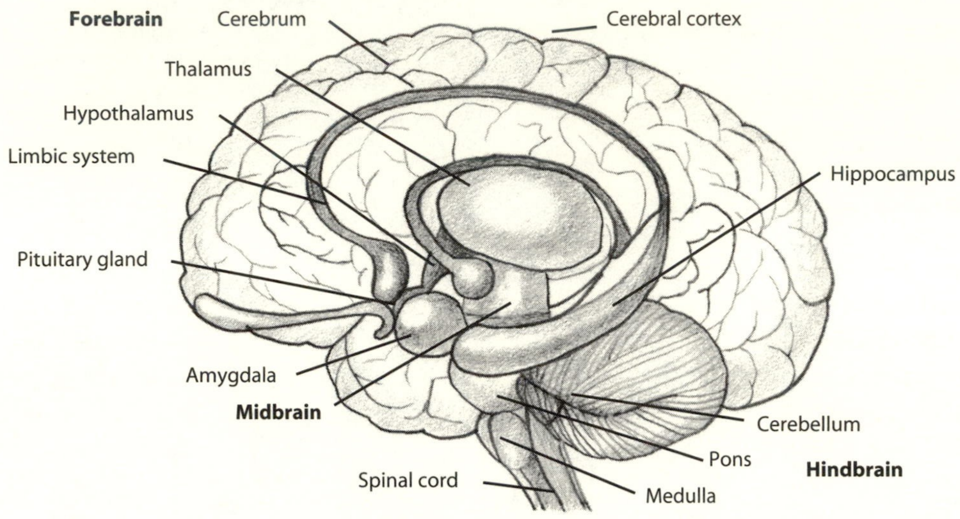

Figure 2.12. The human brain.

The brain consists of three fairly distinct parts arranged vertically, as shown in Figure 2.12. The hindbrain at the base is directly above the spinal column and composed of three parts – the medulla, the pons, and the cerebellum. The medulla has control centers for breathing, heart rate, swallowing, and digestion. It also serves as the main connector between the nerves and the muscular system, where the nerves from the right side of the brain cross over to the left and the nerves from the left side of the brain cross over to the right side of the body. The pons is located just above the medulla and is involved with sleep and arousal. At the point of falling asleep, it serves to disconnect the brain from the body. Sometimes when this shift occurs, the body jerks, waking the person up again. Off to the back of the pons and medulla is the cerebellum, which looks sort of like a little brain. The cerebellum regulates and controls coordination. Destruction to this area can lead to disturbances in balance, gait, speech, and eye movement. The cerebellum is also involved in some motor learning processes. Being at the base of the brain and closer to the spinal column and the peripheral nervous system helps in timing.

The midbrain is a small section above the hindbrain. Its main structure is the reticular formation, which is a network involved in the maintenance of consciousness and sleep. The startle response and heightened arousal to stimuli are controlled by the reticular formation. When you have grown accustomed to sleeping through noises, the reticular formation filters out these signals. The reticular formation is also important in anesthetics used in surgery. Neurotransmitter inhibitors can be used to shut down incoming signals of pain in the reticular formation.

The forebrain stands on and around the midbrain. It is composed of the thalamus, the hypothalamus, the limbic system, and the cerebrum. The thalamus is a sensory relay station that sorts and sends signals from the eyes, ears, tongue, and skin to the cerebral cortex for processing. Because it is a relay station, it works in conjunction with the reticular formation in the control of sleep and attentiveness.

The hypothalamus lies under the thalamus and is much smaller. Its basic function seems to be homeostasis, that is, the regulation of constant internal bodily conditions such as body temperature, food intake, water intake, and sexual activity. The hypothalamus is thus a major component in self-regulation, feedback, and control loops. Its function is similar to a thermostat that turns on the heat when the temperature is below a desired level and turns on the air conditioning if it is too hot. It starts this process at a subconscious level, which may be corrective to a point. The message goes to a conscious state when the system must generate behavior to correct the level, such as drinking a glass of iced tea or turning on a fan. The hypothalamus also regulates the release of hormones from the pituitary gland, which we talk about later in this chapter.

The limbic system is a doughnut-shaped neural structure composed of the amygdala and the hippocampus. These lower brain centers control our responses to fear and aggression. Destruction or electrical stimulation of different parts of the amygdala can result in a loss of fear of natural predators, increased fear, or uncontrollable aggression and rage.

The hippocampus seems to be related to the acquisition and the consolidation of new memory traces. Destruction in this area can result in the loss of the ability to form new memories, as was the dilemma in the movie "Memento" (2000).

We cannot function without these lower brain centers, and their importance cannot be minimized. However, when we think of the intellectual abilities of the human, we tend to focus on the next and highest center, the cerebrum or cerebral cortex. The cerebral cortex is the largest brain center. It makes up about 80 percent of the total brain mass. It is a densely packed mass of interneurons that has a gray appearance due to the fact that the neurons are unmyelinated. The surface of the cortex is only one-eighth of an inch thick, but it is highly convoluted so that its relatively large surface area can be packed inside the cranium.

The cerebral cortex is divided into two mirror image halves called "cerebral hemispheres." The two hemispheres are connected by a thick band of more than 200 million nerve fibers called the "corpus callosum." Communication between the two hemispheres is extremely important because the left side and the right side have somewhat different functions. First, there is a high degree of lateralization of sensory–motor functioning. We are wired so that the left hemisphere receives feelings and controls the muscles of the right side of the body and the right hemisphere receives feelings and controls the muscles of the left side of the body. The reason for this cross is not entirely known. Some have hypothesized that defensive reactions may be faster with this connection. Others have joked that we have our heads screwed on backward.

Each hemisphere is divided into four lobes defined by the bone sections that cover them. They are the frontal, parietal, temporal, and occipital lobes as

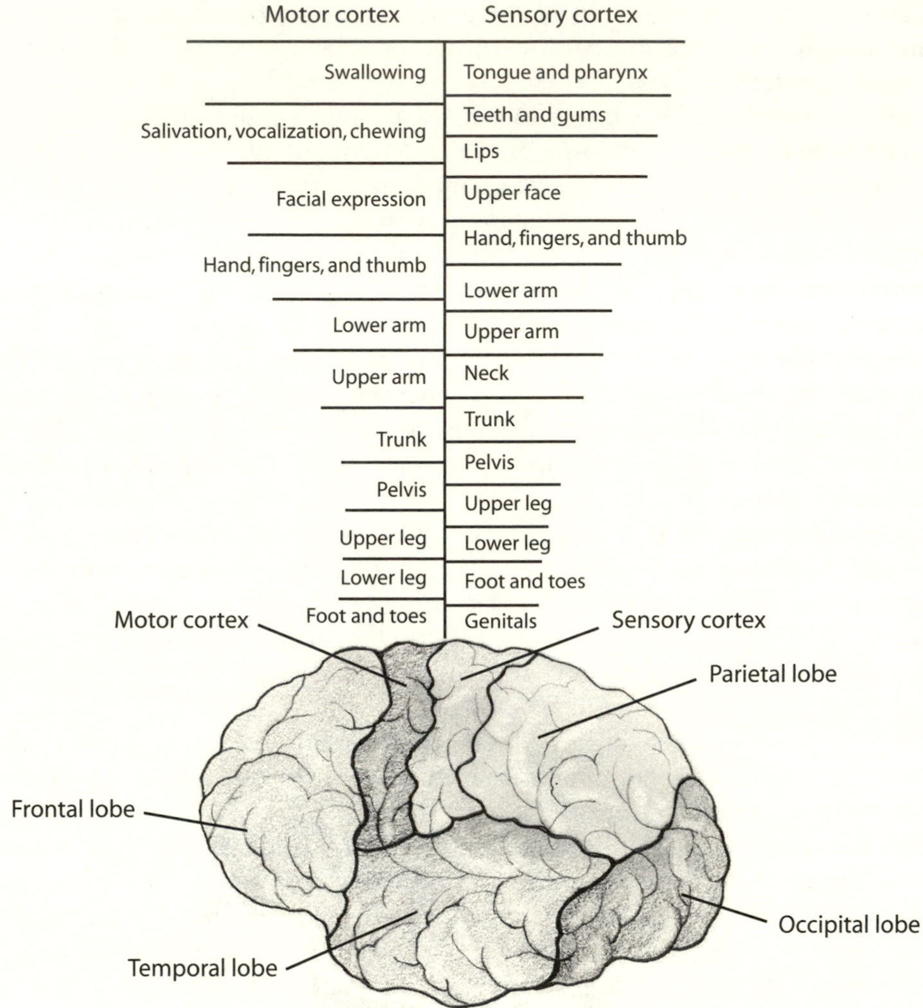

Figure 2.13. Areas of the cerebral cortex responsible for cognitive functions and for motor and sensory processes.

shown in Figure 2.13. Starting with the back, the occipital lobes contain the visual center that processes shape, color, and motion. They are responsible for visual detection, object recognition, and visual perception. Destruction of the visual cortex results in blindness.

The parietal lobes to the front of the occipital lobes process the sensation of touch and kinesthetics or body position and voluntary control of the muscles. Interestingly, studies in electrical stimulation of this area indicate that the body is spatially represented as if laid out along the parietal fissure from top to bottom. Moreover, the size of the area in the cortex devoted to an area of the body is in proportion to the sensitivity or concentration of the receptors in the body as shown in Figure 2.13. Thus, the cortical area for the hands and tongue are large relative to the area for the legs and back.

The temporal lobes are located on the sides of the brain near the temples. They contain areas for auditory processing and language. Destruction in the language center known as Wernicke's area in the left temporal lobe can lead to severe disturbances in speech and understanding of language.

The frontal lobes are located just behind the forehead. They are involved in motor coordination and in the higher mental processes of planning, social skills, and abstract thinking. The frontal lobe controls many aspects of the personality, temperament, and emotional expression. Destruction of the frontal lobe can have drastic effects on personality, while leaving intelligence, memory, and language abilities the same.

Finally, the spinal column serves as the main input/output channel that connects the brain to the peripheral nervous system. The spinal column is encased in the bony mass of the backbone and is protected by cerebrospinal fluid and several protective membranes, the meninges. It extends from the base of the brain down to just below the waist and has about the thickness of a pencil. Nerve fibers emanate from the spinal cord from the top to the bottom, as shown in Figure 2.11. If the spinal column is severed at any point, communication is cut off from the body connected to those parts below. Although most of the communication is to and from the brain for processing, the spinal cord takes responsibility for control of some automatic and involuntary responses. Reflex actions, such as the knee-jerk response, occur at the spinal cord level to reduce the time that it would take for the signal to travel to the higher brain centers for processing and the response time back down the spinal cord. The brain is aware of the reaction only after it has occurred.

The Peripheral Nervous System: The Somatic and Autonomic Systems

From the brain and spinal cord, the peripheral nervous system communicates with the rest of the body, the sensory receptors, and the muscles. The peripheral nervous system is comprised of nerves, which are bundles of axons from many neurons. The nerves are similar to wiring harnesses in cars, appliances, and computers that contain many wires. One difference, of course, is that the axons are not color coded; however, they are similar in being wrapped together in a protective covering or membrane. Another major difference is that the nerves may contain thousands of neurons so that the destruction of some of them has no adverse effect unless the whole nerve is severed. Whereas, in the computer, if one wire in a cable is broken the whole thing stops working correctly.

The peripheral nervous system is subdivided into the somatic system and the autonomic system. The somatic nervous system handles voluntary motor movement, sending commands through the motor neurons and receiving signals from the sensory neurons. The somatic nervous system is intimately involved in the human–computer interface through keyboards, touch screens, mouse movements, button presses, etc. All of these involve the sense of touch, body position, and motor movement.

In contrast, the autonomic nervous system sends involuntary commands to nonskeletal muscles in the heart, lungs, stomach, intestines, etc. This system controls the homeostatic processes, interrupting or maintaining normal bodily functions. Interestingly, the system is divided into two complementary subsystems, the sympathetic and parasympathetic systems, which work in opposition to each other. The parasympathetic system maintains the normal homeostatic levels at rest. It conserves the body's energy, activates the digestive processes, and slows the heart. When a threat to the person arises, the sympathetic system energizes the body's resources to deal with it. It interrupts the digestive processes, accelerates the heart rate, and increases perspiration. The sympathetic nervous system rapidly and involuntarily activates our "fight-or-flight" ability to take action. It essentially revs up the power system and processors for quick action and turns the power off to unnecessary functions. At times, particularly when there is a false alarm causing us to be startled or to blush, we may believe that this system is irrational and emotional. However, in reality and in the long run, it is amazingly efficient and effective so much so that many technological systems are copying the autonomic system to react to electrical brown-outs and breakdowns in the power grid, incoming ballistic missiles, or cyberattacks to a computer network.

The Endocrine System

If the central and peripheral nervous systems were not enough to contend with, the endocrine system adds another layer of complexity to the human control system. The nervous system is electrochemical. It involves the transmission of electric charges by way of chemical changes, and, at the synaptic level, it involves the release of neurotransmitters. But the neurons can only act on other neurons and certain receptors to control muscles. How can the brain communicate with the rest of the cells in the body that are not touched by the nervous system? This is where the endocrine system comes in. The endocrine system is a network of glands that manufacture and release chemical messengers called "hormones." The hormones can affect every cell in the body because they are carried throughout the body in the bloodstream and act chemically on the cell's membrane. Of course, this means that the time it takes for them to have effect and the length of their effect may be in minutes rather than milliseconds.

The most important endocrine gland is the pituitary gland. It is located at the base of the brain and is controlled by the hypothalamus. It is the master gland because it sends hormones to other endocrine glands to stimulate them. The thyroid gland in the neck releases thyroxin, which controls metabolism. The adrenal glands near the kidneys release epinephrine and norepinephrine, which work with the autonomic nervous system to increase the heart rate, slow digestion, and increase the metabolic rate for heightened arousal and speed of action.

The endocrine system is so biological. It is the antithesis of a digital system. It is analog, fluid, and chemical. Yet, again, it is so rational. How else could a central processor communicate with every corpuscle in the system? It is in essence a broadcast message that permeates the entire system. Although a simple computer does not have such a system with which to communicate with the plastic and metal box that it is housed in, networked computers, where each computer is considered as a cell, can be subject to broadcast messages that act like hormones to alert, activate, or protect a network. In the next section, we explore these sorts of issues further.

Differences and Similarities

The human nervous system and the computer have remarkable similarities and vast differences. We touch on a number of these comparisons and contrasts in this section. Understanding these differences and similarities will help us locate and resolve the incompatibilities between the human and the computer as they interact at the human–computer interface. It is hard enough to understand where a person is coming from even though he or she is of similar construction. To form expectations about the behavior of a computer requires us to take into consideration how they differ from us.

Plasticity versus Programmability

The human system is very plastic. In development, it is self-organizing. The developing neurons migrate through the nervous system to find their proper location, orient themselves, and build their synaptic connections to other neurons. Even at maturity, the system is partially self-reorganizing. If some neurons die or are destroyed, their functions may be taken over by other neurons or pathways. This plasticity permeates the human organism. We are extremely adaptive and regenerative.

However, the computer is hardwired off the assembly line. It cannot change its components, chips, circuit board, or wires. It is standardized to the exact specifications of its model number. Any modifications, such as adding memory or new peripherals, must be initiated and made by its owner. Repairs must be diagnosed and made by a technician. But because the computer is a mass of interconnected digital switches and registers, it is highly reprogrammable. Even its most basic programming called "firmware" can be changed. Indeed, it is so reprogrammable that a general-purpose computer can run just about any program, assume any set of system preferences, run many different OSs, and assume various interface styles, motifs, and look-and-feel. Most of the programs and changes to the OS are made by the owner. But increasingly more often, the computer is modifying itself. It may configure itself for communications, install drivers for peripheral devices (e.g., plug-and-play), and upgrade its programs and OS. Still, without a significant breakthrough in robotics, it cannot repair broken circuit boards and connectors.

Digital versus Analog

The computer is digital, and in all cases, no matter how complex, the underlying data are 0 or 1, totally binary. Moreover, there is no inherent value, in a human sense, to the representations of 0 or 1, TRUE or FALSE. Their values are assigned arbitrarily. They could be given any two names as long as they are different.

In contrast, for the human, there are inherent values for different states, even down to the neural level. Neural states are specifically resting or active, inhibitory or excitatory. When they are combined in nerves, neural bundles, and brain centers, they acquire richer values of calm or excitement, pleasure or pain. The internal states of the machine carry no value other than the value of formal logic. The internal states of the human are inherently associated with value.

Other than the all-or-none firing of a neuron, most aspects of the human nervous system are analog in nature with continuous values. Levels of neurotransmitters, hormones, and other chemicals are continuous. Many signals in the nervous system involve frequency of neuron firing. These combine in analog ways to generate responses of higher brain centers.

It is true that digital systems can simulate analog systems with such a high degree of precision that we cannot detect the difference between an audio or video signal stored in digital versus analog format. The digital code is apparently the most effective and efficient mode for computers. Digital systems can simulate anything and everything in the analog world and interact with it perfectly, until things go wrong. When errors and problems occur in a digital system, they are very different from errors in an analog one. Take, for example, a recording on a vinyl record. Pops and scratches may occur as well as an attenuation of the signal strength with use over time. This is not true with digital recordings. But digital recordings are subject to new and perhaps more irritating problems, such as pauses and skips due to buffering, missing blocks of data, or complete lockouts due to encryption and authentication problems.

Principle of Mass Action

If you destroy part of the brain through lesions or burning, the organism, whether human or animal, does not stop functioning. Behavior may be impaired, but it is not totally destroyed. Moreover, experiments show that the greater the area of destruction, the greater the deficit in function. This is called the "principle of mass action." It is not one or several neurons that perform a function, but rather the mass action of many neurons. The nervous system has incredible redundancy so that thousands of neurons can die or be destroyed with little or no loss to the system.

Not so with the computer. If you cut one trace in the circuit board or dislodge one pin of an integrated circuit, the computer will most likely stop working altogether and will not reboot. Some redundancy is currently being built into systems that are responsible for the health and maintenance of critical systems (e.g., command and control of the Space Shuttle, financial records). Backup processors and mirrored disk systems are being used. But this redundancy is at the component level (e.g., circuit boards, disk drives) rather than at the elementary level as in the human nervous system.

Localization of Function

One of the fascinating features of the human brain is the localization of function. Different parts of the brain specialize in different functions such as language, speech, hearing, vision, problem solving, etc. Figure 2.13 shows these areas as well as the localization of motor and sensory processes in the cerebral cortex. Other brain centers are pathways for particular functions in sensation, memory, and motor coordination.

The same is also true with the computer. Different parts of the computer hardware have special functions. There are video boards that drive the graphics on the monitor. There are input/output circuits. There are special chips for math, such as a floating point processor, and speech synthesis. However, beyond the video memory, there is no localization for types of memory (e.g., sound, graphic, text). In the computer, memory is not localized by modality but is mixed and distributed throughout the storage media. Files for text, sound, and video may be anywhere owing to the fact that all media have been reduced to a digital format that can be stored anywhere in memory, on disk, or on external media. The same is true for much of the processing. The same CPU can operate on logic, arithmetic, text, graphics, and music because it is all stored and manipulated in a digital mode.

Parallel versus Serial Processing

The human thought process and most of our conscious experience is essentially serial. We can only think about one thing at a time. We have one stream of consciousness. We might think that we can do more, but generally we quickly shift attention from one process to another. It is as if we have one channel or one processor that can only handle one thing at a time.

Sensory–motor processes, bodily functions, and many unconscious processes, however, run in parallel and are controlled by different neural and brain centers simultaneously. Similarly, computers can have many parallel processes that handle video display, input/output processing, etc. However, the central processor in the computer can only perform one task at a time.

If it must attend to numerous things simultaneously, it must do so by multitasking, whereby it switches from one job to another. With computers, this switching takes place much faster than with the human. Consequently, the processor may appear to be doing a number of things simultaneously.

Some computers are being built that have multiple processors that act in parallel. Many personal computers have dual processors that share tasks to speed up the processing. Other computers are "massively" parallel with hundreds of processors. But typically, one processor acts as a manager to divide the tasks among the rest of the processors and monitor their progress. In many ways, the human nervous system and the computer face the same problem with subdividing tasks and multitasking. We discuss this again in Chapter 5 when we deal with attention and divided attention.

Memory Differences

There were enough similarities between human memory and computer storage for the early pioneers of computer science to use the word "memory" to refer to this storage. However, it must be obvious by the vast differences between logic circuits and neurons that human memory and computer memory are worlds apart. When people confuse the two, it can lead to huge misunderstandings. One of my students believed that characters appearing on the computer monitor were temporarily stored on the screen. If the monitor was turned off, all would be lost, which was not the case. In reality, if the computer was switched off, it would be lost because the memory was volatile. But the latter case is not always true. The information could be in nonvolatile memory and would only be lost if one intentionally erased it. Computer memory loss is generally all or none, unlike human memory, which degrades over time. We are not really sure how memories are stored at the neural level. Most likely, they are encoded by the organization of synaptic networks. In Chapter 6, we look at many of the higher-level differences between computer and human memory.

Autonomic Systems, Homeostasis, and Autonomy

The human nervous system, embedded in a living being, incorporates many self-preserving functions. The sympathetic nervous system takes care of the basic housekeeping functions in the body, such as controlling digestive processes and bodily temperature. Computers also have numerous housekeeping functions: reorganizing memory, updating systems, and rebooting. But computers are by no means self-sustaining and autonomous, except in science fiction. Although computers are being programmed to be increasingly autonomous, at the end of the day, they are still entirely reliant on their users to start, stop, and control their actions. This difference must be understood by users. When it is not, it can lead to fundamental misunderstandings. One of the fundamental slogans in my lab is "Humans are human, and machines are machines."

End Thoughts

It is fascinating to study the human nervous system in contrast to the computer system. We often find ourselves using human metaphors to understand the computer. We may speak of the CPU as the computer's brain. Or we may use the computer to understand the human in the other direction. In either case, we are tempted to use one thing that we might understand to explain another that we do not.

Sometimes it is more than that. As engineers design more powerful, intelligent computers, they look to the human as the best example and proof of concept, and attempt to reverse-engineer computers based on cognitive neuroscience. What if, for example, we could totally simulate the operations of a single neuron on a digital computer? Then, what if we could simulate a system of such neurons as a nerve or brain center? Then, what if we could build the whole simulation of 180 billion neurons in the human nervous system on a super computer? Clearly, we are not at a point where we can seriously do this, but we can start with small simulations and models of the system.

In this chapter, we looked at humans and computers in contrast and in isolation. In Chapter 3, we look at models of the human, the computer, and the interface between the two. Although we do not do so at the neural level of the human or binary level of the machine, the biological basis of the human and the technological construction of the computer will feed into the models and help us understand how they are formulated.

Suggested Exercises

1. Perform an autopsy on a computer. Get an old, obsolete, or broken computer and take it apart with a screwdriver. Take note of the different parts. See if you can find the memory chips, the CPU, etc.
2. Can you think of other similarities and differences between humans and computers that have not been addressed in this chapter?

References

Beatty, J. (2001). *The human brain: Essential of behavioral neuroscience*. Thousand Oaks, CA: Sage.

Dowling, J. E. (1992). *Neurons and networks: An introduction to neuroscience*. Cambridge, MA: Harvard University Press.

Rosenzweig M. R., Breedlove, S. M., & Leiman, A. L. (2002). *Biological psychology: An introduction to behavioral, cognitive, and clinical neuroscience* (3rd ed.). Sunderland, MA: Sinauer Associates.

Williams, R. W., & Herrup, K. (1988). The control of neuron number. *Annual Review of Neuroscience*, 11, 423–453.

Three

Theoretical Approaches

Models and Metaphors

Scenario 1

Interviewer: *So, John, what are you doing now?*
John: *I'm opening up my calendar program to see what I've scheduled for tomorrow. That's odd. I thought that I had a dentist appointment at three in the afternoon. No wait, I think I recorded that on my PDA. I guess they're not synced.*
Interviewer: *Is that a problem?*
John: *Well, yes, because there might be other things on my PDA that haven't been transferred.*
Interviewer: *What are you going to do?*
John: *I think that I'd better sync the two calendars right now.*
Interviewer: *Okay, how do you do that?*
John: *I don't really know because in the past it seemed to happen automatically when I put my PDA next to the computer. Now it is not doing that.*
Interviewer: *What do you think is wrong?*
John: *Good question . . . I wonder what is different now? Did I change something? Let me look at the settings for sync on the computer. Looks okay. Now I will look at the PDA. That looks okay, too. I don't know.*
Interviewer: *Do you think anything else changed?*
John: *I don't know. This is really irritating. I wonder if I have to restart the computer or the PDA or both. I'll try both.*
Interviewer: *Now what?*
John: *It still doesn't work. What's wrong? I am about ready to give up.*
Interviewer: *Then what?*

John: *Then I will just manually compare the schedules and add things to the computer or vice versa.*
Interviewer: Okay.

Scenario 2

Mary: Okay, I would like to present the design of the new interface for our calendar program on the XT800. To get the calendar, the user presses the button with the calendar icon on it, here. We believe that the user will want to see the day's schedule first, so we go to the schedule for today. From here, the user can select the week or month view.
Ted: I don't think we can make that assumption. I might access the calendar to add an event next week or check on when we met last month. I think we need to make a list of all possible tasks, and use an interface to minimize the expected number of clicks across all tasks.
Larry: Well, that might be very efficient, but I think that we need to start from the mental model of how the user expects a calendar to work. If most of the users have been using daily planners, we should organize it like a book. However, if they use a wall calendar, it should flip through the 12 months.

Overview

Although we have very concrete images of a person banging away at a keyboard, moving a mouse around, and staring dumbfounded at a computer monitor, HCI is actually an extremely general and amorphous concept. In the two opening scenarios, we see that it may entail the goals and intentions of the human, the methods of conveying those intentions to the computer, the process of converting those actions into signals, the programming to generate responses, and the display of that information back to the human.

It is difficult enough when we only have to think about a user at a keyboard and monitor. Today, the human–computer interface is ubiquitous and vast. It is in our cell phones, digital cameras, the dashboards of our cars, and embedded in sensors, cameras, and environmental displays all around us. The whole world may become the human–computer interface. Some describe the interface as disappearing into the things we use (Norman, 1998), others see it as covering everything we see and touch, and still others worry that it is always there but hiding. One way or the other, we need to deal with it, as in Scenario 1.

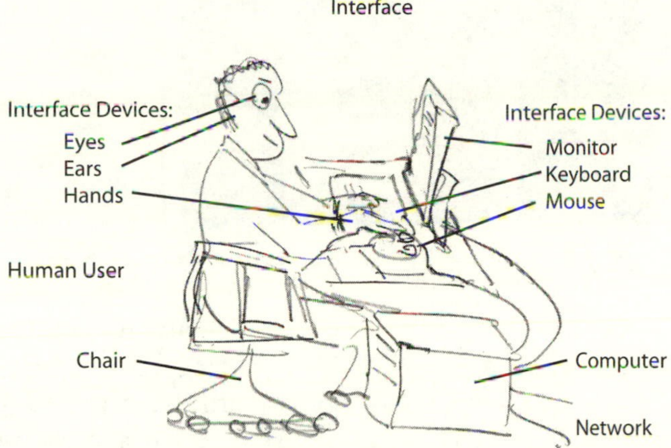

Figure 3.1. The human–computer interface.

In this chapter, we first look at the interface as a flow of information and control. As such, we are concerned with transduction of information from one media or code to another and the transmission of this information across the interface. Then we consider different perspectives on the interface from the viewpoint of 1) the user with a task and a purpose in mind, 2) the computer interpreting the intentions of the user, and 3) the software designer attempting to anticipate the functions that the user requires, as in Scenario 2. Finally, we consider overarching theories about how the pieces fit together into a system.

The Human–Computer Interface

What is the human–computer interface? In their early book, *The Psychology of Human–Computer Interaction,* Card, Moran, and Newell (1983) defined the human–computer interface as that point starting from within the computer, going out to the peripherals, where you finally come to the human. In this sense, it is the physical transition point between the human and the computer. Moreover, it is that point where information code and the signals that carry it are converted from one form to another. As shown in Figure 3.1, it may proceed from the physical movement of a finger, to the pressing of a key, to an electrical contact, to a change in the current in the circuit. Or it may go from a video signal to the screen, to a pattern of light emitted from the screen, to a change in the light impinging on the retina of the eye, to firings of the rods and cones in the eye, to signals in the optic nerve.

If the human–computer interface was hard to locate and define in the early days of computers, it is even harder today. Computers have become more complex, the interface has been broadened to incorporate a wider variety of sensors and "manipulanda" (joysticks, trackballs, data gloves), the range of tasks has drastically increased, and computers have become more ubiquitous and invisible. It is harder than ever to locate the interface.

  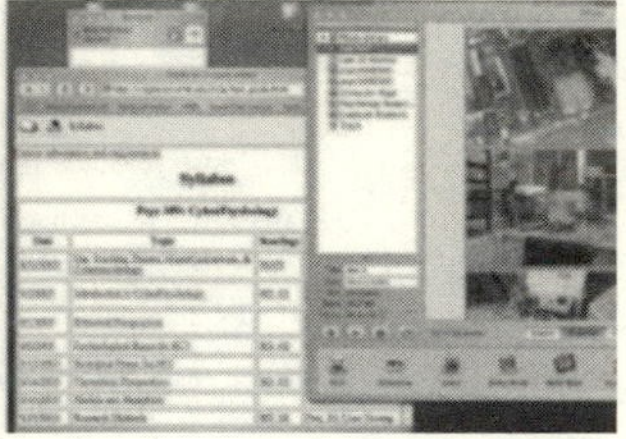

Figure 3.2. Three perspectives of the human–computer interface.

Moreover, as shown in Figure 3.2, the interface involves perspective. Many views of the interface focus on the computer screen, as in the right panel of Figure 3.2. Software designers will point to the screen and say, "This is our user interface." Others view the interface from a more perpendicular perspective, as in the middle panel of Figure 3.2. The interface includes important aspects of the human, and one must take these into consideration when defining the term because, by definition, an interface includes two sides. Still others focus primarily on the human as if looking into the face of the user to determine needs, goals, and experiences, as in the left panel of Figure 3.2.

The term "human–computer interface" has come to mean a lot more than just that point where information and control changes from the machine to the human. It includes a much larger sphere of activity. Shneiderman (1986) used the term to refer to the way a person experiences the computer, its applications, its components, its input/output devices, and its functionality. It includes all aspects of experience from the obvious ones of screen layout and menu options to its reliability and accessibility.

In this book, we adopt this wider definition of the human–computer interface, including both narrow and broader perspectives as needed. Our working definition is as follows:

> The human–computer interface is that point and area through which communication of information and control passes from the human to the computer and from the computer to the human. The interface includes the full range of experiences on the part of the user with all aspects of the computer and the full range of input to the computer from all sensors, input devices, networks, and databases.

Given that this definition is now too general to be of much use, we spend the rest of the chapter providing more details. The next section deals with the input/output issue and the idea of the point and area through which communication travels.

The Loop of Interaction

The human–computer interface involves a flow of information and control from the human to the computer and a flow of information from the computer

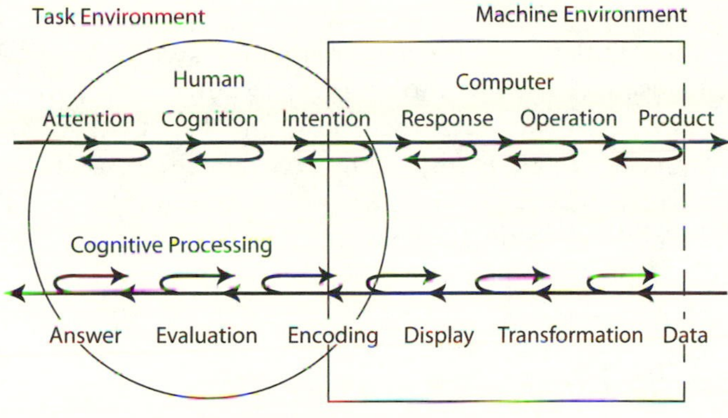

Figure 3.3. The flow of information and control through the human–computer interface. (From Norman, 1991.)

to the human. Figure 3.3 shows the interaction between the human and computer at the interface. The circle on the left represents the human, and the square on the right represents the computer or, in general, the machine.

Task Environment

The human is embedded in a task environment that sets conditions, goals, and constraints on the human. For example, the person may be an accountant at work trying to balance a budget by 5:00 PM or a teenager at home browsing for a new computer game to download for free. We see that the task environment must be taken into consideration when we try to understand the interface and model interaction. The task environment determines a number of contextual factors such as the cost of errors, the importance of time, and the criteria for the successful completion of the task. It must be remembered that computer users are not only interacting with the computer in front of them, but also with the world around them.

Machine Environment

The machine is also embedded in an environment. It may be an office computer connected to a LAN, a workstation in an automated factory monitoring and controlling robotic assembly equipment, an automated voting machine connected to a secure network, or a touch tablet used by a delivery person for recording times of deliveries and signatures. The types of machine environments are as varied and endless as the task environments.

There is one fundamental difference between the environments of the human and the machine. In the case of the human, there is an impermeable interface between the human and his or her environment. We are not neurologically wired to the chairs we sit on or anything else around us. We are materially independent and physically unconnected to the objects in our environment. Consequently, the human is represented by an unbroken circle in Figure 3.3. Not so for the machine. If nothing else, it is probably plugged into a power outlet or connected by cables to other things in its environment such as the Internet, printers, or sensors and machinery. Thus, the lines of demarcation are not well defined between the machine and its environment, as indicated by the broken lines on the right side of the square in Figure 3.3.

Areas of the Interface

The model of the interface shown in Figure 3.3 is based on the areas of activity. The nonoverlapping area in the circle represents cognitive processes involved in tasks that are not directly related to the human–computer interface. Likewise, the nonoverlapping area in the rectangle represents the computer processes involved in tasks that are independent of the interface. The overlapping area in the middle represents processes, either in the human or in the computer, that pertain to the interface. On the side of the human, they involve either the mapping of intentions to activities (Fig. 3.3, upper line going right) or the encoding of information for evaluation (Fig. 3.3, lower line going left). On the side of the machine, interface processes involve either the mapping of information from internal states to displays on the screen or some other output device (Fig. 3.3, upper line going left) or the mapping of device input to internal representations (Fig. 3.3, lower line going right). The interface involves two basic flows of information and control: an input flow proceeding from left to right and an output flow proceeding from right to left.

Input Flow

The input flow originates in the task environment. The user attends to some situation in the environment, such as a need to pay bills, find information, locate and control the position of a satellite, or send a message to someone. Table 3.1 gives a detailed example of one such flow. The user extracts information about the situation that is processed through cognition. What bill and how much, what information, what satellite, and what message to whom? This results in an intention to perform a task that is then manifest at the interface as specific user actions. To pay the bill, the user has to open a browser, click on a link, enter a username and password, select a payee, enter the amount, click "Pay," and click "Confirm." The flow of control from intentions to actions at the interface must bridge what has been called the "gulf of execution" (Norman, 1986). The flow continues through the interface area to the machine as it results in operations that process the request

Table 3.1. Example of Input/Output Flows Through the Human–Computer Interface

Input/Output Flows	Example
Input Process	
Attention	Request for telephone number of business
(Loop)	(Verification of name of business and city)
Cognition	Planning search engine and method
(Loop)	(Confirmation of strategy)
Intention	Intention to input information to search engine
(Loop)	(Confirmation of intention)
Response	Input to www.yellowpages.com
(Loop)	(Correction of typing errors)
Operation	Processing of keyboard/mouse input to request string
(Loop)	(Verification of input)
Production	Search request sent to www.yellowpages.com
(Loop)	(Authentication of request)
Output Process	
Data	Data packet received
(Loop)	(Authentication of data)
Transformation	Conversion of HTML code to browser window
(Loop)	(Check on correctness of HTML code)
Display	Display on screen of phone number
(Loop)	(Confirmation that monitor is on)
Encoding	Visual reading of number
(Loop)	(Control of eye movements)
Evaluation	Confirmation that number has right pattern of digits
(Loop)	(Rechecking discrepancies)
Answer	Report telephone number of business
(Loop)	(Test number)

and generates a product, namely, the payment of the bill via electronic funds transfer.

Output Flow

The second flow of information and control goes from right to left and originates in the machine environment (Table 3.1). The computer receives data from the environment, perhaps an incoming e-mail, the position of a satellite, or a confirmation that a bill payment was received. The information is transformed from binary code to text on the computer screen. The operator viewing the screen encodes the information, evaluates it, and reports an answer to the environment (e.g., the bill has been paid, the satellite has been repositioned). In this flow, the critical bridge over which information travels has been called the "gulf of evaluation" (Norman, 1986). The human must correctly interpret the output of the machine. Sometimes this is easy, with near perfect accuracy, and in other cases, the user is clueless.

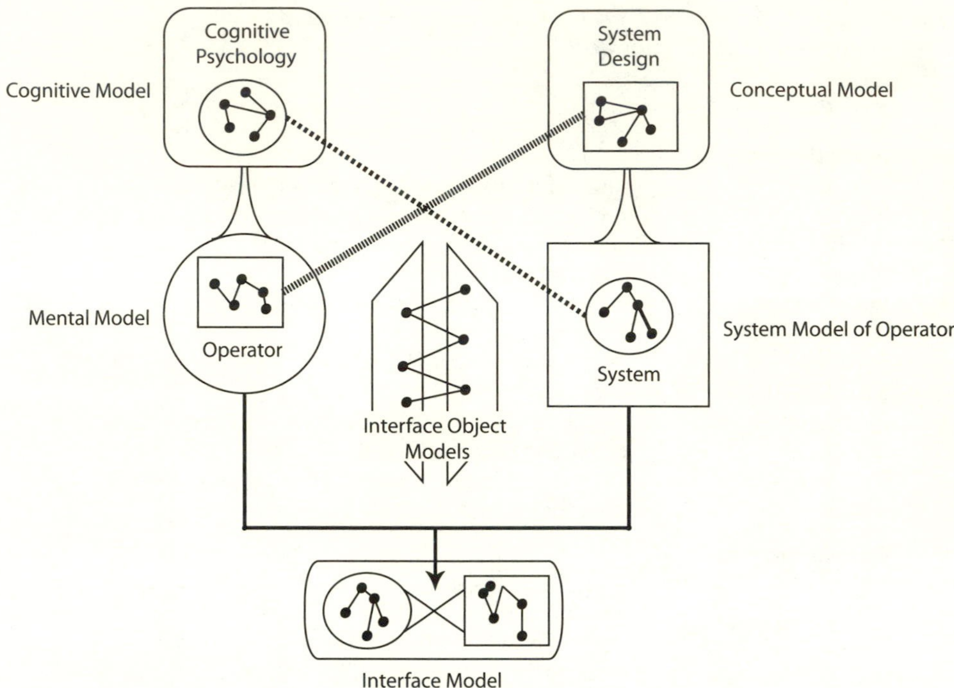

Figure 3.4. Models and perspectives at and around the human–computer interface. (From Norman, 1991.)

Feedback Loops

The flows shown in Figure 3.3 include, at each point, U-shaped arrows to indicate that there are feedback loops through the interface that evaluate, moderate, and confirm processes as they pass through the human, the interface, and the machine. In the human, these may take the form of eye–hand coordination, metacognitive processes, monitoring activities, and verification processes. For example, to click "Pay Bill," one may move the mouse with the hand while watching the cursor on the screen. When one is sure that the cursor is within the selectable spot, the click response is made. Then verification occurs by seeing the button change color or pattern. In the machine, feedback loops may be built into the system with hardware handshaking, servocontrols, and synchronization.

Feedback loops vary in terms of time, magnitude, and location. They may be immediate and tightly coupled to the response, as in eye–hand coordination, or delayed and loosely coupled, as in verification that the bill was paid. The U-shaped arrows in Figure 3.3 refer primarily to immediate feedback loops.

Figure 3.3 encompasses the entire process and environment of HCI in terms of the flow of information and control. But what is now needed is a model, or indeed a set of models, of the interface and the interaction between the

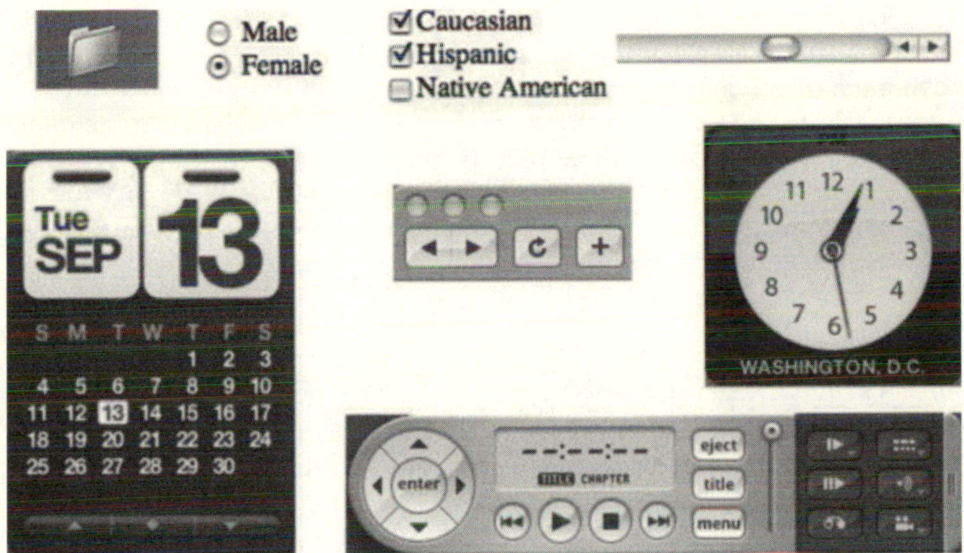

Figure 3.5. Interface object models or "widgets." (From the Apple Mac OS-X, Safari, and Dashboard.)

human and the machine to specify how it all works. In the next section, we look at the possibilities.

The Models

The human–computer interface is at the center of numerous models and perspectives. Each model is a conceptualization of the interface from a particular vantage point. Figure 3.4 shows a number of these perspectives. Each perspective has different issues, problems, goals, and sources of knowledge. We consider them here because they set the agenda for how one evaluates the model at the interface, and we refer to them throughout the text.

Interface Object Models

At the center of the set of models shown in Figure 3.4 are the interface object models. A friend of mine, who is not very tall, was told by admiring followers that he was a model father, a model leader, and a model teacher. When he looked up the definition of "model" in the dictionary, he was rather deflated. A model was defined as a "small replica of the real thing." Similarly, interface object models are rather glorified digital renderings of real objects. Figure 3.5 shows some of these models, often referred to as "widgets" in GUIs. These include simple toggle switches, check boxes, sliders, and windows, as well as video control panels, clocks, calendars, and calculators. These look similar to and function in a similar way at the interface as the real objects do in the world.

Each interface object model follows a set of rules that determines its behavior and how the user can interact with it. The interface object models take advantage of the fact that the user is already familiar with their form and operation and can transfer that knowledge to how they are used at the interface. Typically, the use of these objects involves sensory–motor circuits to sense, perceive, plan what to do, and use some input device to act on the object. The functionality of objects often goes beyond their physical counterparts. They may be resized or copied; and the objects usually have more options and can be linked to other objects.

Mental Model of Operator

The second type of model bearing on the interface is the mental model that the user has about how the interface works, as shown at the left middle of Figure 3.4. We understand how things work by storing mental representations of objects and processes, as noted in Scenario 2 by Larry. We talk more about this in Chapter 6. For now, it will suffice to know that these models help us plan actions and anticipate the results. We develop mental models of how things work from experience and education. For example, we know how a pencil works, what a hammer does, how to use a vending machine, and the typical order of events when visiting a restaurant.

If we have a mental model, it encodes the elements and their relationships and functions. The advantage of using a mental model over working with the real thing is that we can imagine what will happen and we can test out "what ifs" with our models. With a mental model of a hammer and a mental model of a finger, we can anticipate what will happen if you hit your finger with a hammer without actually doing so.

Interface object models engage mental models on the part of the user. Even though it is not a real calculator with buttons, it works like one. The surface dissimilarities are that one may use a cursor on the screen to click the buttons rather than a real keypad, but the similarities usually outweigh the differences.

The mental models that users have about the interface generally go much deeper than the surface features of the interface and deeper than the interface object models themselves. They also pertain to the user's models about how the computer works, how it stores and retrieves files, and how it communicates with the Web. To the extent that these models accurately capture the elements and processes, they benefit the user. But when they are incorrect, they can lead to unexpected outcomes, errors, and frustration.

System Model of Operator

The third type of model is embedded in the machine shown at the right middle of Figure 3.4. It might seem strange to think that the computer has a model of the user. But what is really going on is that models are programmed into the computer so that the computer can internally represent what the user means, what the user wants, and how the user will respond to different conditions. These models range from extremely simple models mapping user input to codes, to extremely complex models of user characteristics and behavior. For example, at the simple level, if I press the "A" key on the keyboard, the computer receives a code (e.g., 41 in hexadecimal) that represents the letter "A" because it has stored a model of me as using an English keyboard. It can then use that code to display the character "A" on the screen.

Beyond this mundane example, we can move to much more complex models of the user that handle speech recognition, auto–spell checking, intelligent agents, and wizards. When these models are accurate, they greatly facilitate communication and reduce errors. But as we come to expect the computer to correctly interpret meanings and intentions, we can also be frustrated when the model is incomplete, misses our intention, and leads to a critical error. For example, why didn't the computer know that I didn't mean to delete the file when I pressed Ctrl-D, but that I meant to save it with Ctrl-S, which is located next to Ctrl-D on the keyboard? As system models of the user become increasingly sophisticated, users will expect computers to interpret both their intentions and their actions.

System models are in part constructed from preference files, user profiles, and past behavior of the user. Whenever a user browses the Web, inputs personal information, or makes purchases online, the system refines the model of the user to anticipate personal preferences and buying behavior.

The three models discussed so far are closely linked together, and hopefully work in concert and promote each other. When there is a disconnect between the user's mental model, the interface objects, and the system's model of the user, many disastrous problems can occur. Files are lost, time is wasted, and frustration can reach a boiling point.

Cognitive Models

Standing outside the working models in the human–computer interface are theoretical and conceptual models of how things work on several sides. On the human side are models generated by cognitive psychologists, shown on the upper left side of Figure 3.4. These models come from research on sensation and perception, memory, cognitive information processing, attention, problem solving, and language.

Most of these models originate in basic research rather than from concerns about the human–computer interface, but are nonetheless applied to the human–computer interface. More recently, these models have focused on the tasks performed as a function of HCI and have involved task specification and assessment of user performance. These models help us predict how the human will perform when given specific tasks using a particular interface. They can be used to decide between alternative designs. If a simulation using the model with Interface A results in a task completion time of 30 minutes with five errors and Interface B in a task completion time of 20 minutes with one error, then we should go with Interface B. These models rely heavily on task analysis, which breaks down the task and the elements required to complete the task into subtasks, including both mental and manual operations. The prime example is GOMS developed by Card, Moran, and Newell (1983), which is discussed later in this chapter.

When these models are used to not only describe user behavior, but also to model the structural properties of the modeled system, they are known as "cognitive architecture." These models are computational in the sense that they can be run like a computer program and are based on the notion that the "mind is like a computer." Consequently, the models are written in the form of computer programs that take the place of the user and interact with the interface. Examples of these include ACT-R, developed at Carnegie Mellon University (Anderson, 1993), and Soar, both of which are discussed in more detail later in this chapter.

Conceptual Models

The next perspective shown at the upper right of Figure 3.4 is that of the system designer and the programmers of the computer system and its interface. Software designers have a concept of how the system should function. In many ways, they start from the inside and work out to the interface. They understand the system requirements, the database structure, and the functions required according to specification documents. They work out these technical details until they finally come to the user interface and ask, "What do we show to the user, and what input do we need?" This results in what is called the "system architecture," which is a formal description of the system, its components, and their interrelationships. The system architecture includes the human–computer interface, specifies the system's model of the user, and defines the steps required to complete tasks using this system. Because this perspective starts from the task and inner programming of the computer, it has often ignored the concerns of the user relative to the concerns of programming the system to work. This prompted many to call for "user-centered" rather than "task-centered" designs. We review this in more detail later in the chapter.

Interface Models

Finally, there is an additional perspective that has emerged as a result of the human–computer interface. It is essentially that of those observing the overall process of the human–computer interface and considering the whole system. These models attempt to capture how the human and machine combine forces. Interface models include 1) top-level specifications of the intent and purpose of the interface (e.g., how and why does the whole thing work together?), 2) allocation of functions between the human and the computer

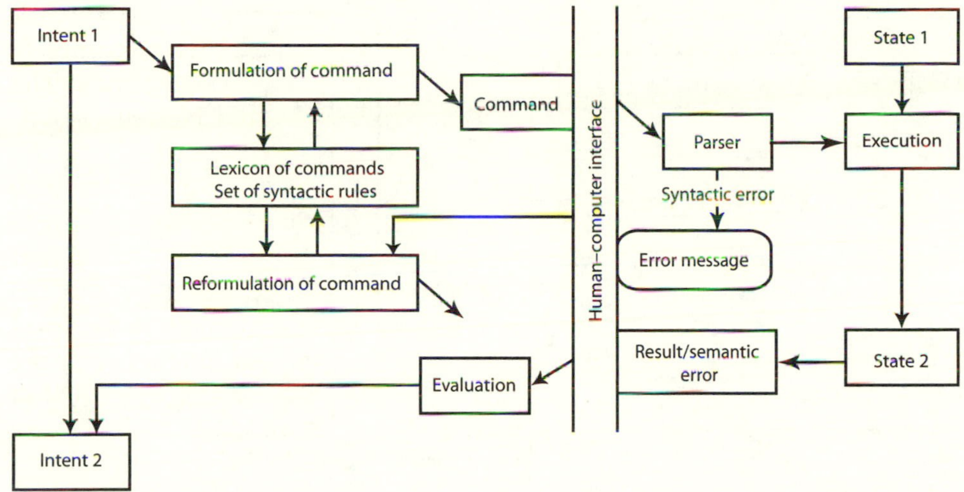

Figure 3.6. Schematic of a command language process model. (From Norman, 1991.)

(e.g., who is in control, who is responsible for what?), and 3) the relationship between multiple users and systems (e.g., what are the dynamics of interaction?).

The remainder of the chapter further discusses various models that fall within the categories of the models identified in Figure 3.4.

User–Task Interaction Models

Modeling the human–computer interface at the task level is useful for evaluations of efficiency and task performance. In general, interface designers use these models to test their interfaces on models of the user. They are sort of like intelligent, virtual crash test dummies. These models are extremely detailed and require considerable effort to program. They are of particular interest for life- and time-critical tasks (e.g., air traffic control, military applications, health care applications) that are highly routine and repetitive. We discuss several here and several others in Chapter 7.

Process Models

Process models capture the sequence of operations within the user and within the computer, and the transmission of information from these operations through the interface. These models are dependent on the mode of interaction, that is, whether one is typing commands, selecting menu items, or manipulating graphics on the screen.

For example, Figure 3.6 illustrates the interaction using a command language. The user starts with Intent 1 – to copy a file from one drive to another.

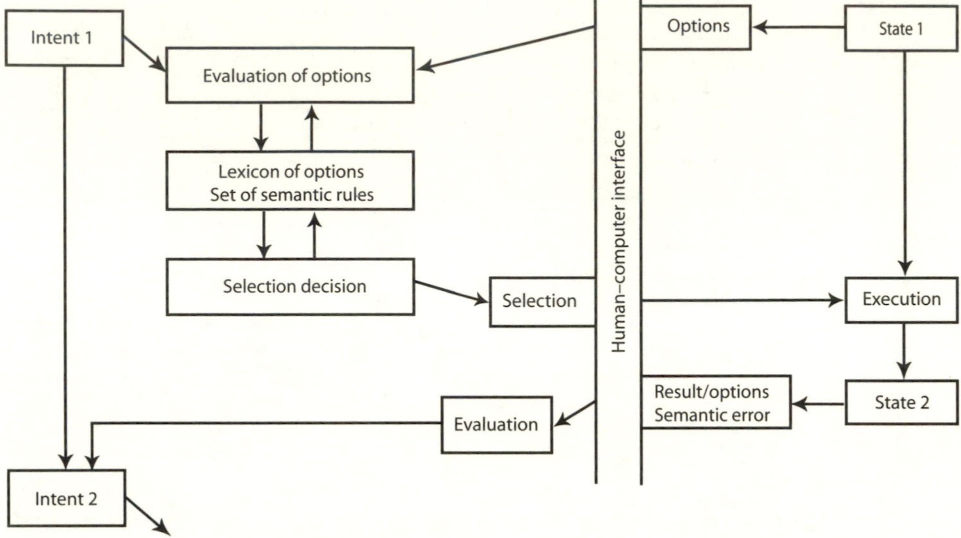

Figure 3.7. Schematic of a menu selection process model. (From Norman, 1991.)

This is translated into a command – "copy A:file, B:file." To formulate the command, the user has to access knowledge of commands. To process the command, the computer has to parse it, execute it, and display the results.

Figure 3.7 illustrates interaction using menu selection as the interaction mode. The user has Intent 1, the system presents options, and the user must determine which option or sequence of options will lead to the desired result. The user makes a selection, the computer executes the selection, and the result is displayed and evaluated by the user.

Finally, Figure 3.8 illustrates the process for direct manipulation. Again, the user starts with Intent 1, the computer displays a screen of objects, and the user evaluates the screen to determine what action or sequence of actions to use according to the rules of manipulating objects on the screen. The user performs the actions, the computer interprets the actions and executes the instructions, the result is displayed, and the user evaluates the new display and formulates the next action.

Process models such as these suggest three possibilities. First, they provide a way to predict performance on a given task with a given interface. One can list the sequence of steps, the time required for each step, and the probability of errors at each point, and then calculate an index of performance. Second, they suggest ways of incorporating cognitive processes such as attention, judgment and decision making, and learning and memory into the process. Finally, they invite the possibility of actually programming the whole process as a simulation. In Scenario 2, Ted suggests optimizing the interface by considering all tasks and sequences of clicks that the user must do to perform those tasks.

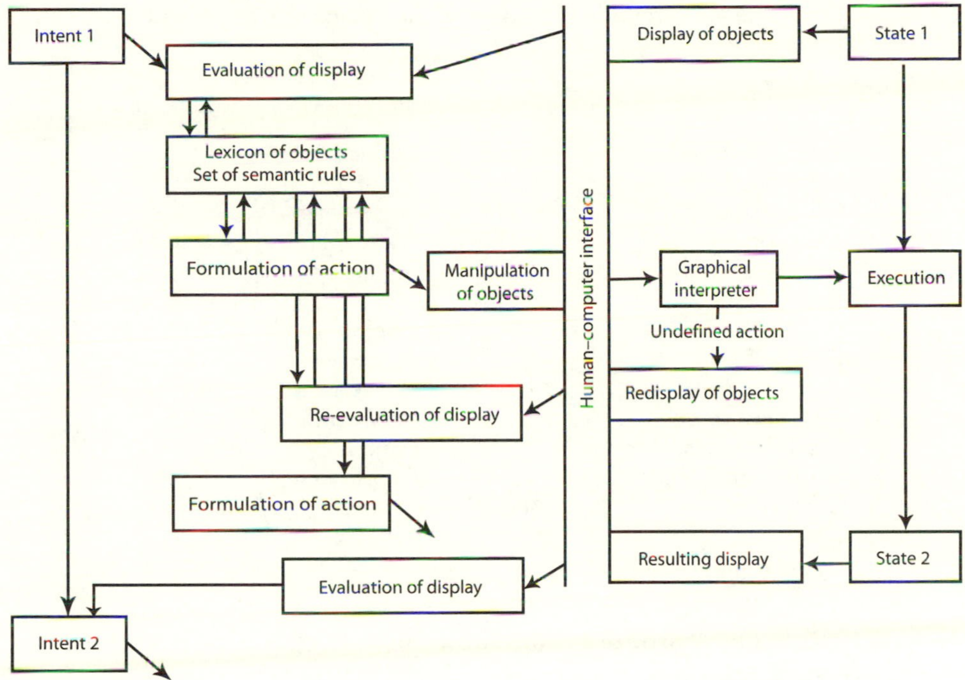

Figure 3.8. Schematic of a direct manipulation process model. (From Norman, 1991.)

GOMS

One of the earliest process models, GOMS, was developed by Card, Moran, and Newell (1983). GOMS stands for Goals, Operators, Methods, and Selection rules. Essentially, goals are the actions or results that the user wants to accomplish. They may vary from high-level goals such as writing a research paper to low-level goals such as deleting a word. High-level goals are decomposed hierarchically into subgoals. Operators are elementary perceptual, motor, or cognitive actions that are used to accomplish the goals. They are usually described in terms of actions at the human–computer interface, such as perceiving a red letter, double-clicking the mouse, or determining that a word is correctly spelled. Operators are not decomposable. It is generally assumed that each operator takes a certain amount of time. If the model can list all operators required to complete a task, one can add up the times to see how long it takes. Methods are the procedures that are used to accomplish the goals. They are procedures learned by the user that determine the sequence of subgoals and/or operators that will accomplish the goal. For example, the goal to delete a word may be accomplished in Microsoft Word by double-clicking the word and pressing the "Delete" key. There may be other methods to achieve the same goal. Selection rules specify which method should be selected to satisfy a particular goal based on the context. Selection rules are conditional "if, then, else" statements. For example, "if the text

Table 3.2. Keystroke-Level Model for Replacing a Word in Text Document

Description	Operation	Time (s)
Reach for mouse	H[mouse]	0.40
Move pointer to "Replace" button	P[menu item]	1.10
Click on "Replace" command	K[mouse]	0.20
Home on keyboard	H[keyboard]	0.40
Specify word to be replaced	M4K[word]	2.15
Reach for mouse	H[mouse]	0.40
Point to correct field	P[field]	1.10
Click on field	K[mouse]	0.20
Home on keyboard	H[keyboard]	0.40
Type new word	M4K[word]	2.15
Reach for mouse	H[mouse]	0.40
Move pointer on Replace-all	P[replace-all]	1.10
Click on field	K[mouse]	0.20
TOTAL		10.2

to be deleted is one word, use the double-click delete method, else use the mouse down, drag over text, mouse up, delete method."

The simplest version of GOMS is the keystroke-level model (KLM), which lists all operators and their times and does not consider selection rules. The original version has six types of operators: **K** for pressing a key, **P** for pointing to a location with the mouse on the screen, **D** for pointer drag movements, **H** for moving hand to home position on the keyboard, **M** for mentally preparing for an action, and **R** for waiting for the system to respond. Table 3.2 gives a KLM for replacing a word in a manuscript.

The KLMs provide a quick and dirty method of evaluating the time required to perform a task given a particular interface when the task is highly learned, repetitive, and no selection rules exist.

The GOMS model includes selection rules. Table 3.3 shows a GOMS model taken from John and Kieras (1996) for the task of moving text in a word processor in the context of editing a manuscript. It includes subgoals and selection rules.

ACT-R

Process models are improved if they include components and characteristics of the human cognitive processor. John Anderson (1993) included these components in a modeling program called "ACT-R," an acronym for the Adaptive Control of Thought – Rational. ACT-R is known as a "cognitive architecture" rather than a theory because it can be programmed to accommodate different theories. It was originally developed to model problem solving, learning, and memory, but did not take into account perceptual and motor activity. To be applied to HCI, the ACT-R system was modified to accommodate a visual interface (Anderson, Matessa, & Lebiere, 1997),

Table 3.3. GOMS Model of Moving Test in a Word Processor

GOAL: EDIT-MANUSCRIPT	
. GOAL: EDIT-UNIT-TASK ... repeat until no more unit tasks	
. . GOAL: ACQUIRE UNIT-TASK	
. . . GOAL: GET-NEXT-PAGE ... if at end of manuscript page	
. . . GOAL: GET-FROM-MANUSCRIPT	
. . GOAL: EXECUTE-UNIT-TASK ... if a unit task was found	
. . . GOAL: MODIFY-TEXT	
. . . . [select: GOAL: MOVE-TEXT* ... if text is to be moved	
. . . . GOAL: DELETE-PHRASE ... if a phrase is to be deleted	
. . . . GOAL: INSERT-WORD] ... if a word is to be inserted	
. . . . VERIFY-EDIT	
*Expansion of MOVE-TEXT goal	
GOAL: MOVE-TEXT	
. GOAL: CUT-TEXT	
. . GOAL: HIGHLIGHT-TEXT	
. . . [select**:GOAL: HIGHLIGHT-WORD	
. . . . . MOVE-CURSOR-TO-WORD	
. . . . . DOUBLE-CLICK-MOUSE-BUTTON	
. . . . . VERIFY-HIGHLIGHT	
. . . . GOAL: HIGHLIGHT-ARBITRARY-TEXT	
. . . . . MOVE-CURSOR-TO-BEGINNING	1.10
. . . . . CLICK-MOUSE-BUTTON	0.20
. . . . . MOVE-CURSOR-TO-END	1.10
. . . . . SHIFT-CLICK-MOUSE-BUTTON	0.48
. . . . VERIFY-HIGHLIGHT]	1.35
. . . GOAL: ISSUE-CUT-COMMAND	
. . . . MOVE-CURSOR-TO-EDIT-MENU	1.10
. . . . PRESS-MOUSE-BUTTON	0.10
. . . . MOVE-CURSOR-TO-CUT-ITEM	1.10
. . . . VERIFY-HIGHLIGHT	1.35
. . . . RELEASE-MOUSE-BUTTON	0.10
. GOAL: PASTE-TEXT	
. . GOAL: POSITION-CURSOR-AT-INSERTION-POINT	
. . . MOVE-CURSOR-TO-INSERTION-POIONT	1.10
. . . CLICK-MOUSE-BUTTON	0.20
. . . VERIFY-POSITION	1.35
. . . GOAL: ISSUE-PASTE-COMMAND	
. . . . MOVE-CURSOR-TO-EDIT-MENU	1.10
. . . . PRESS-MOUSE-BUTTON	0.10
. . . . MOVE-MOUSE-TO-PASTE-ITEM	1.10
. . . . VERIFY-HIGHLIGHT	1.35
. . . . RELEASE-MOUSE-BUTTON	0.10
TOTAL TIME PREDICTED (SEC)	14.38

From John and Kieras (1996).

as shown in Figure 3.9. More recently, perceptual-motor modules have been added to the system now called "ACT-R/PM." The cognitive layer contains declaration memory modules and production memory modules. The perceptual-motor layer contains modules that provide an interface to the external environment.

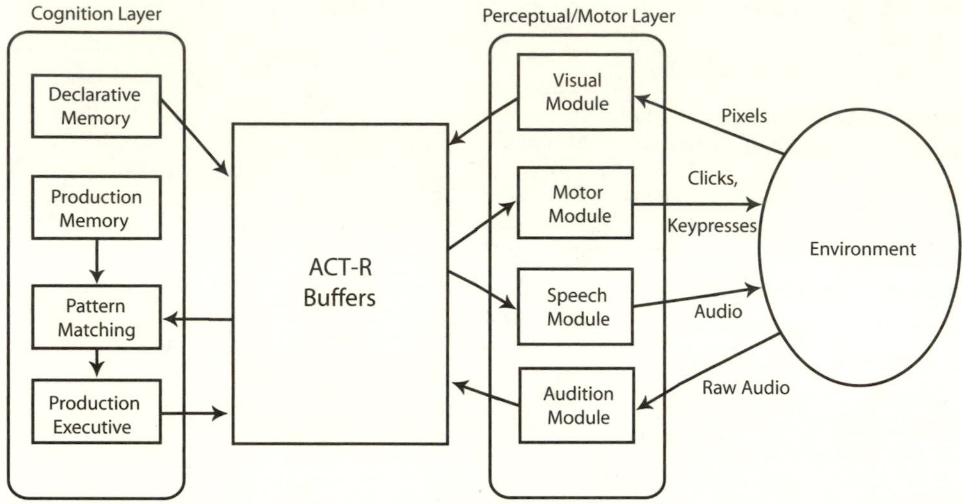

Figure 3.9. ACT-R framework including cognition and perceptual/motor modules.

An ACT-R model can be written and run as a computer program to simulate the user's interaction with the human–computer interface being evaluated. Essentially, a developer can test the interface using a simulation of the user rather than real users.

Soar

An alternative direction for process models has been taken by those that are less concerned with the psychological modeling of the user and more concerned with the cognitive architecture, that is, the framework within which one can construct cognitive models to interact with the task and the user interface. In a sense, these models have not constrained themselves to the limits of the human processor, but have gone on to explore the optimal models of the user. Soar is essentially an AI programming language used to build models of the user that interact with the task and the human–computer interface. Originally, Soar stood for State, Operator And Result because problem solving was considered to be a search through a problem space by applying an operator to a state and getting a result. Today, Soar has gone beyond this conception and is a powerful programming environment for knowledge-based problem solving, learning, and interaction with task environments (Rosenbloom, Laird, & Newell, 1993).

General Models, Theories, and Perspectives

In this section, we consider some overarching perspectives on human behavior that motivate HCI.

Interface Characteristic Models

If we consider interfaces in general, we can identify numerous types of interfaces and characteristics of interfaces. A number of theoreticians have drawn metaphors of physical interfaces between different types of substances, such as the surface between oil and water, or interfaces that separate spaces, such as walls, doors, and windows. These have resulted in interface models that capture important features that impact the behavior of the human and help understand the processes of the interactions through the interface (Green, 1989). A few of these features are described here.

Viscosity

Physical interfaces involving fluids are regulated by the property of viscosity, the resistance of a fluid to deformation under shear stress, or simply "thickness." Interfaces with high viscosity are slow, resistant to change, and require considerable energy to move through. They require more work on the part of the human to make changes to the system and to the workflow. It is almost impossible to make changes to the design of forms, the layout of pages, the mapping of keys to functions, etc. Interfaces with low viscosity, however, allow users to make such changes rapidly. However, low viscosity is not necessarily a good thing. System designers may not want users to make changes so easily.

Asymmetry

Many interfaces are symmetric in the sense that the flow of effects goes both ways as a mirror image. A curtain between the stage and an audience can be pushed equally from one side or the other. Other interfaces are asymmetric in that flow can move only in one direction. Swinging doors and stairs are symmetric, but entrances and exits, up escalators and down escalators are not. In human–computer interfaces, asymmetric actions occur when a change in Object A changes Object B, but a change in Object B has no effect on Object A. Keyboards and mice are asymmetric input devices that affect events on the screen, but events on the screen do not move the keys or the mouse.

Apparency

Some interfaces are translucent, and others are opaque. The interface allows you to see through and view what is behind it and how it works. One sees the fish and coral in clear tropical waters, but not a thing through the murky water of a muddy river. Some mechanical devices allow their operation to be viewed – one can see to the pistons, levers, and gears – and others hide it under a cover. Although one cannot clearly view the operations within a computer, some interfaces display graphics that make the sequence of operations and the relationships between elements apparent to the user. They may show flowcharts, networks, or graphic metaphors of devices. Others hide them, leaving the user to guess what is connected to what. These may provide pallets of many tools and menu options, but the user has to learn the underlying interrelationships of how one is connected to another (Alonso & Norman, 1998).

Perceived Affordance

Affordance is a property of an object or a feature that suggests how to interact with it. A button suggests pressing it. A handle suggests grabbing it. Human–computer interfaces have affordance to the extent that their appearance indicates to the user how to interact with it (Norman, 1999). Buttons, sliders, menu bars, tabs, and scroll bars provide the interface with affordance, but screens that neither allow interaction nor suggest ways to interact with them provide little or no affordance. They are like brick walls. There may be a secret moveable brick, but it does not present itself to the user.

Ripple Effect

Many interfaces, such as the surface of a lake, produce a ripple when there is an interface effect such as throwing a stone in it. The ripple may be good in spreading the effect or harmful in causing destruction. The same is often true with human–computer interfaces. Some changes in preference files can ripple through the whole interface and cause consistent changes, whereas others can cause destructive effects such as viruses, corrupting and causing inconsistencies. The latter are characteristic of the "knock-on effect," a secondary or incidental effect due to some action. These effects are usually unforeseen, but they are caused by an action in one part of the system bumping into another part. For example, a change to a subroutine that fixes a problem from one call may create new problems for other calls.

Interface Memory

Finally, interfaces may change from one state to another with little or no memory; others may have incredible memory. Many systems allow a one-level "undo" function so the memory is only for the previous state and nothing else. The human probably remembers past the one level and is irritated that the system does not. Many document processing systems provide for extensive memory of each version of the document and a record of all edits and corrections (e.g., who changed what and when). Web browsers typically have a history file that remembers all of the Web sites visited. In these cases, the system memory goes well beyond the human memory.

Each of these features or characteristics of the interface may be beneficial or detrimental, depending on the context and the situation.

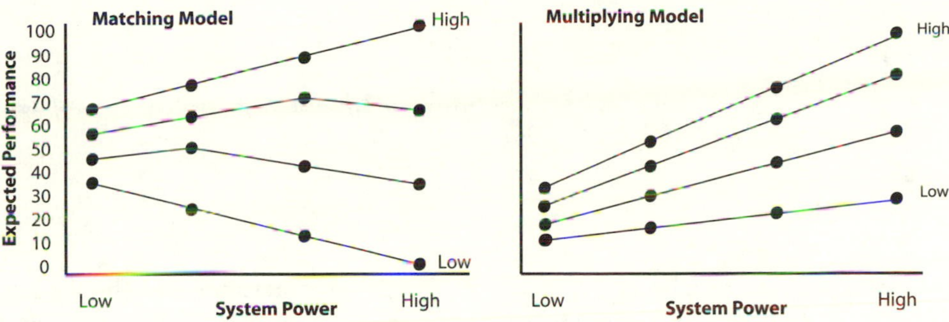

Figure 3.10. Two models of expected performance as a function of levels of system power (horizontal axis) and user proficiency (line parameter). (From Norman & Singh, 1989.)

Symbiotic Models

Some interface models deal with the overall performance of the system as a function of the level of proficiency of the user and the functionality and power of the computer. Even as early as the 1960s, Licklider (1960) presented the idea of a "man–machine symbiosis" and obstacles to the relationship such as the inability of the user to correctly ask questions or use computer languages. Others have suggested synergistic relationships in which the overall performance of HCI is greater than the sum of the parts contributed by the human and computer (Dehning, Essig, & Maass, 1981). The question then is, "How do we achieve the optimal human–computer interface by maximizing the interaction of all models in concert?" The interface may be compensatory in terms of output by the human and the machine (Nelson, 1970). The machine may be used to make up for what the user is not able to do (e.g., rapid calculations), and the user may do what the computer cannot do (e.g., make ethical and aesthetic evaluations).

Many other models have been proposed that suggest that performance results from the average of the contributions by the human and the computer, or that performance is optimal when there is some sort of match between the user and the computer based on abilities (e.g., simple interfaces for beginner users, complex interfaces for experienced users), as shown in the first panel of Figure 3.10. Norman and Singh (1989) found support for a multiplying model in which the overall performance of the system is a multiplicative function of user proficiency and system power, as shown in the right-hand panel of Figure 3.10. The obvious point is that one should be really good at using computers and have a really powerful machine!

Activity Theory

Activity theory originated in Russia with the work of S. L. Rubinstein and A. N. Leontiev. The main idea is that human action should be considered

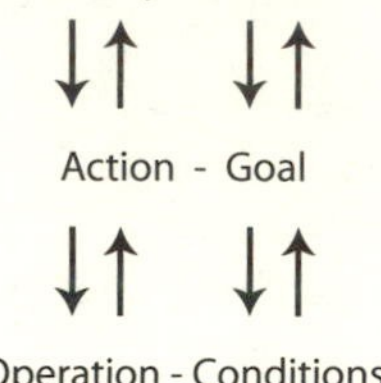

Figure 3.11. Three levels of activity theory. (Adapted from Kuutti, 1996.)

to be the unit of psychological analysis. In recent years, activity theory has been extended from psychology to accommodate the social, cultural, and organizational context as well. It has been found to be particularly applicable to HCI (Brown & Strickland, 2005; Engeström, 1993; Nardi, 1996).

Human activities are driven by human needs to achieve certain goals. Activities are often mediated by tools. The tools are artifacts that can be observed. Context is extremely important in understanding individual actions. Activities are modeled in a hierarchical structure with three different levels, as shown in Figure 3.11: the activity level (e.g., writing a report), the action level (e.g., gathering information, composing an outline, writing sentences), and the operation level (e.g., typing, spell checking). Activities require motives that give rise to the need for the activity. Actions are the basic conscious components of activities. A number of different actions may be undertaken to meet the goal. Operations are ways of executing actions. They are concrete conditions required to achieve the goals of the actions. As operations are repeated, they may become routine and unconscious.

Activities are directed toward objects with a goal in mind. The context defines a "problem space" with rules, constraints, and allowable operations. The relationship between the subject or group of subjects and objects is mediated by a tool, as shown in Figure 3.12. Tools can be anything from physical tools such as a scissors, transformation processes such as mathematical operations, or thought processes such as remembering names.

Much of what we do is also in the context of what others do, especially in organizations, groups, and larger communities. Thus, Engeström (1987) proposed a systematic model, as shown in Figure 3.13. An activity may be pursued by a subject who is motivated toward a solution of a problem mediated by tools in collaboration with others in the group. The activity is shaped and constrained by rules and social division of labor within the context. The community itself plays a mediating role in the process.

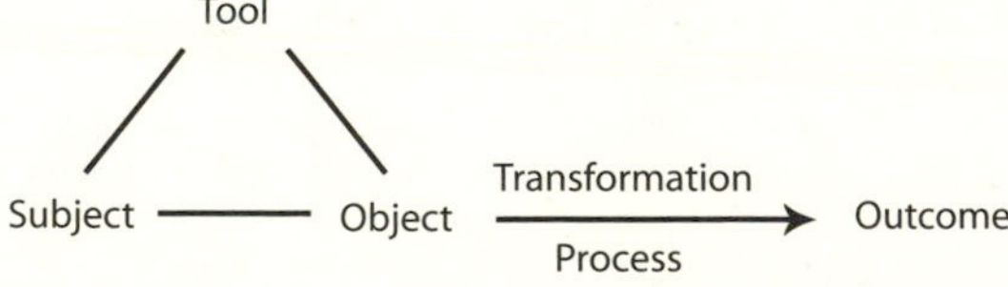

Figure 3.12. The basic framework of activity theory. (Adapted from Kuutti, 1996.)

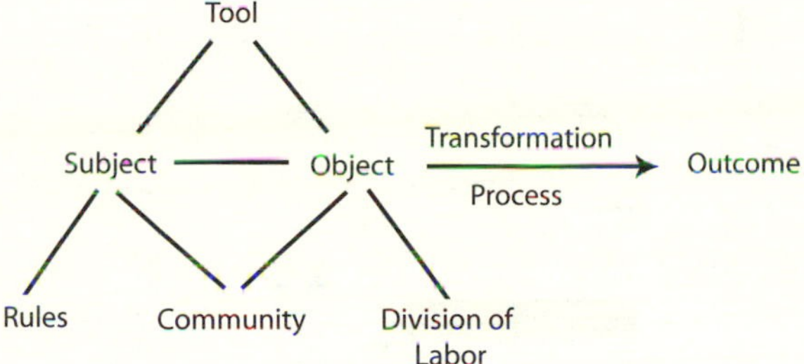

Figure 3.13. Activity theory in the context of a community. (From Engeström, 1987.)

The computer and the human–computer interface may be the tool and the artifact in activity theory. The whole system in activity theory is constantly changing and developing. Thus, the outcome may be a transformation of the tool, the rules, or the division of labor. Activity theory focuses on the objects and artifacts to understand the system. In many ways, activity theory is more a way of looking at things or a way of modeling than a theory itself.

Interface Design Models

Another type of overarching interface model pertains to the process of designing the interface illustrated in Scenario 2. These models attempt to incorporate and/or promote a certain process to ensure a successful design. Design models are of particular interest to system engineers and of partial interest to cognitive psychologists. Designing is what system engineers do, and being excluded from that design is what cognitive psychologists worry about.

The "waterfall model" was developed by Royce (1970) to manage the development of large-scale computer systems. Figure 3.14 shows the basic

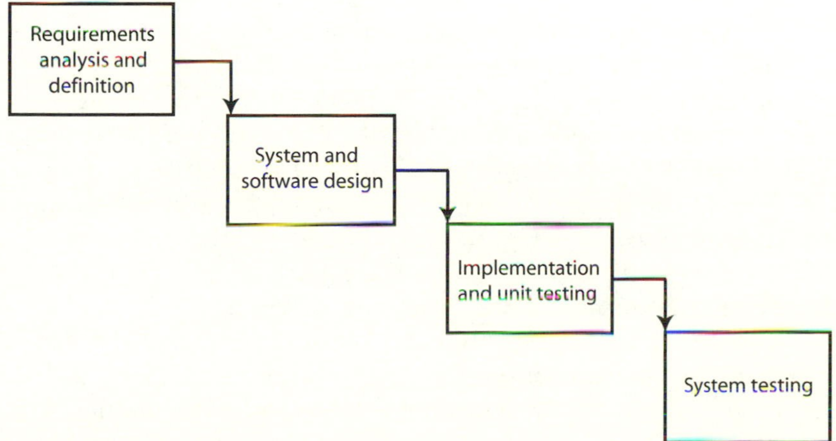

Figure 3.14. The waterfall model for the development of large-scale software systems. (From Royce, 1970.)

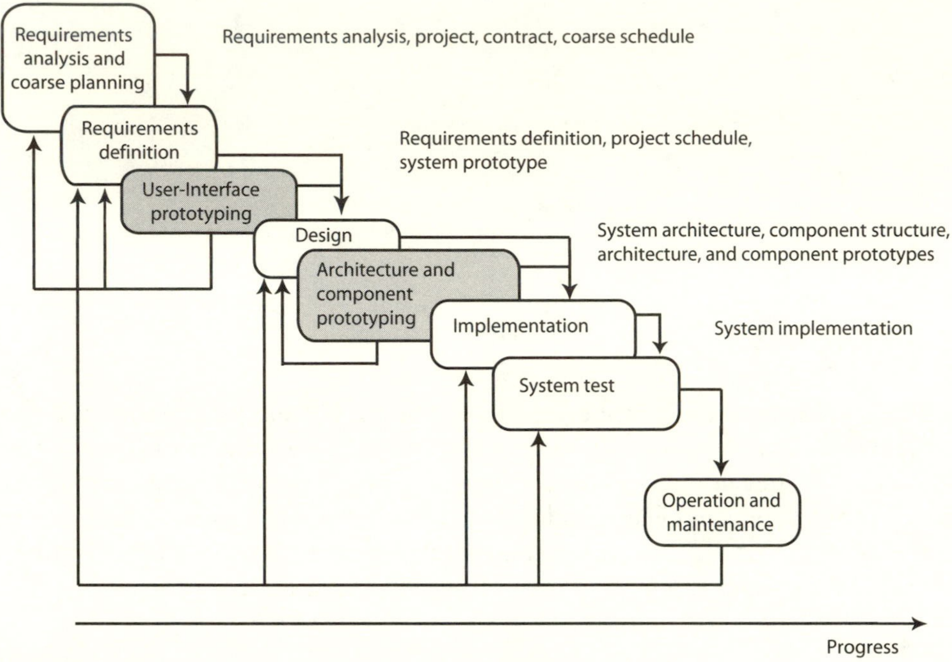

Figure 3.15. A design process model including the user interface and prototyping. (From Pomberger et al., 1991.)

steps in the waterfall model. Note that in this early model, there is no explicit mention of the user or the human–computer interface. However, it does capture the notion of needing requirements up front and doing testing at the end.

More recent models, such as the one by Pomberger, Bischofberger, Kolb, Pree, and Schlemm (1991) shown in Figure 3.15, specifically include the user interface in the prototyping phase and a follow-on stage of maintaining the system once it is deployed.

Other models of design emphasize evaluation at all points in the process. The star life cycle model of Hix and Hartson (1993) places evaluation in the center with each component linked to evaluation, as shown in Figure 3.16.

Finally, most design models have shifted from a straight linear process to a cycle, realizing that we design and redesign in an iterative or generational cycle (Mayhew, 1999). Each design is motivated by a problem, and each design ends with a problem. Figure 3.17 illustrates this cycle.

Design models often talk about perspective. Early designs were often "computer centered," focusing on the efficiency of the software and machine working together. This was appropriate for number crunching, but to the extent that systems involved input/output operations to perform tasks, these models evolved into more "task-centered" designs. These models included the flow of work in the task environment to achieve overall efficiency of performance. Although they may have included input/output operations to

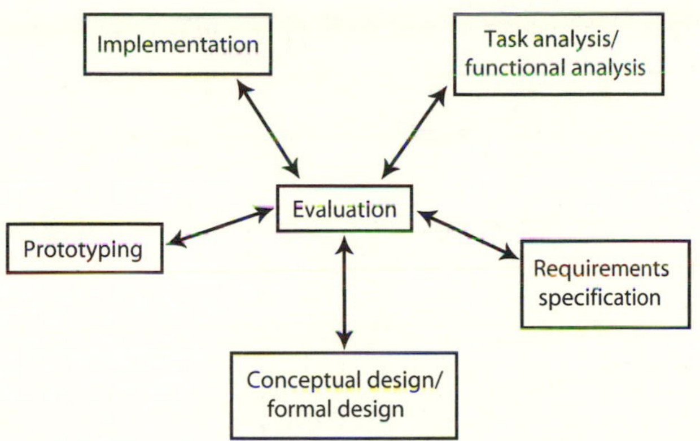

Figure 3.16. Star life cycle model. (From Hix & Hartson, 1993.)

human users, they did not consider human needs and individual differences. "User-centered" designs now emphasize the need to bring the user into the center of the process. The design process from beginning to end should include the user's needs, wants, and limitations. User-centered design requires extensive user testing and user evaluation, as we see in Chapter 4. More recently, users themselves have been brought into the design cycle as partners rather than problems in "participatory design." Nevertheless, most design cycles are driven not by the user but rather by system considerations and corporate concerns about markets, profits, litigation, and strategic plans.

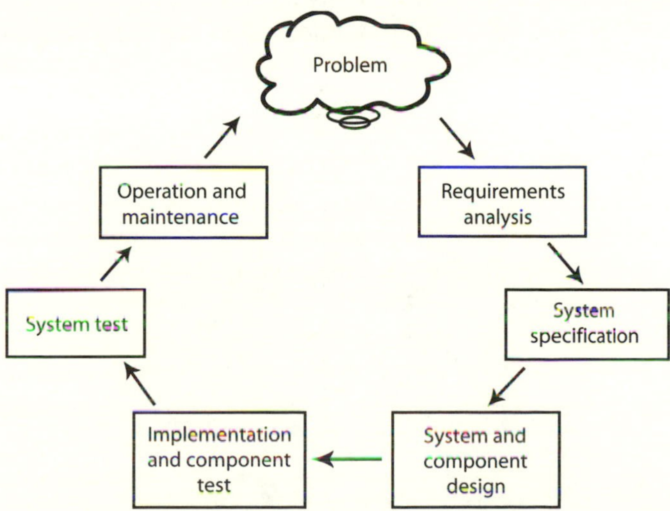

Figure 3.17. Life cycle model of design of the system. (From Mayhew, 1999.)

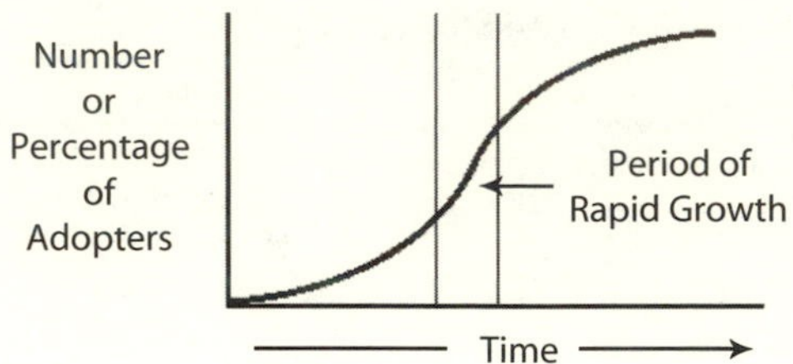

Figure 3.18. S-shaped curve showing the rate of adoption or diffusion of an innovation over time.

Diffusion of Innovation Theory

The human–computer interface is the product of technological innovation. As such, it is subject to social, cultural, and economic forces that affect innovations and their adoption over time. As emphasized in Chapter 1, the human–computer interface is changing, expanding, and developing over time. Theories of the diffusion of innovation help characterize this change and model its progress. The diffusion of innovation is the process by which it is communicated and transmitted by the members of a system through time. Gabriel Tarde (1903) introduced the original S-shaped diffusion curve showing at first a slow but increasing adoption of technology, leading to a period of rapid growth, and a final leveling off at the end, as shown in Figure 3.18.

In the 1940s, Bryce Ryan and Neal Gross studied the adoption of hybrid corn by Iowa farmers. The rate of adoption followed the S-shaped curve, but they also characterized the segments of farmers in terms of how long it took them to adopt the innovation. They classified them as 1) innovators, 2) early adopters, 3) early majority, 4) late majority, and 5) laggards. The segments and their proportions follow the classic bell-shaped curve shown in Figure 3.19.

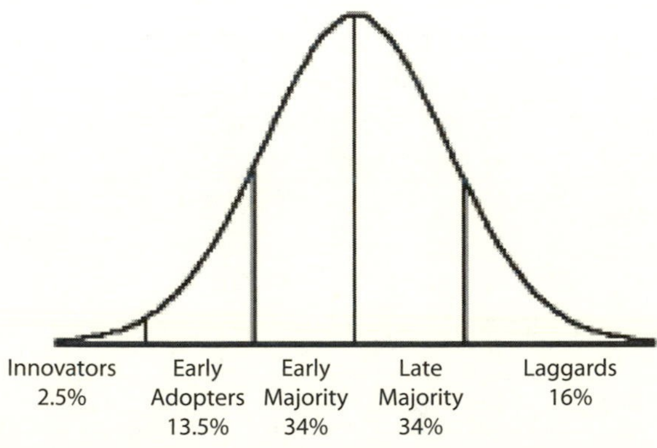

Figure 3.19. Bell-shaped curve showing the classes of individual innovativeness and their percentages.

Table 3.4. Characteristics of the Five Classes of Adopters of Innovations

Classification	Characteristics
Innovators	• Venturesome; desire for the rash, the daring, and the risky • Control of substantial financial resources to absorb possible loss from an unprofitable innovation • Ability to understand and apply complex technical knowledge • Ability to cope with a high degree of uncertainty about an innovation
Early adopters	• Integrated part of the local social system • Greatest degree of opinion leadership in most systems • Serve as role model for other members or society • Respected by peers • Successful
Early majority	• Interact frequently with peers • Seldom hold positions of opinion leadership • One-third of the members of a system, making the early majority the largest category • Deliberate before adopting a new idea
Late majority	• One-third of the members of a system • Pressure from peers • Economic necessity • Skeptical • Cautious
Laggards	• Possess no opinion leadership • Isolates • Point of reference in the past • Suspicious of innovations • Innovation decision process is lengthy • Resources are limited

From Rogers (1962).

The previous five classes have been characterized in many ways. Table 3.4 lists the characteristics given by Rogers (1962).

Computer technology, particularly at the human–computer interface, often follows these waves of adoption and diffusion. Home computers, PDAs, iPods, and video games all follow the S-shaped adoption curves with different slopes.

Most researchers in diffusion theory identify five stages in the adoption process. First, there is an initial awareness of the innovation without much knowledge about it. Second, there is interest in the innovation and acquisition of information about it. Third, there is an evaluation of the innovation in terms of anticipated gains and losses and a decision of whether to try it. Fourth, there is a trial period during which the individual makes full use of it. Finally, there is the final adoption of the innovation when the individual decides to continue to use it. It is easy to see how individual computer users as well as large organizations go through this process with anything from small innovations (e.g., a paper clip) to major innovations (e.g., the paperless office).

End Thoughts

This chapter is really about the perspectives that we take when we assume different roles at the human–computer interface as the user, the designer, the programmer, the usability evaluator, the computer industry, or the cognitive psychologist. The user is trying to get a job done; the designer is trying to design the interface so that the user can get a job done; the programmer is trying to program the interface as specified by the designer; the usability evaluator is trying to figure out what the user is doing to get the job done on an interface designed by someone else; the computer industry is just trying to build a machine and market the product to make a profit; the cognitive psychologist is trying to model the human processor; and, finally, we are trying to make sense of the whole thing.

There is also an interesting recursive nature about models in, of, and around the human–computer interface. They are like wheels within wheels. They intersect and mesh with one another, they turn and drive each other, and they form and mold each other. Designers build systems based on models. The user of the system understands how the thing works by acquiring a mental model. The computer interprets input and generates output on the basis of a programmed model of the user's intent. All of this can become exceedingly complex, and we can lose track of what is happening.

It is all well and good to make up models, but the question is whether we have empirical support for them. How do we know that one model is better than another? How do we know whether one interface results in superior performance over another? How do we know if any change in the interface will have a significant effect on performance? There are many conjectures and hypotheses that we can make. Now that we have been introduced to the fundamentals of human–computer interface models, it is time to move on to methods of studying them.

Suggested Exercises

1. Select a task and fill in the specifics for the input/output flows, as in Table 3.1.
2. For a particular session that you are going to have with a computer, write down what you think it is thinking and what you are thinking it is thinking about you.
3. Take a screen shot at some point in your work on the computer and list all interface object models that you can find on the screen.
4. Give another illustration for each of the six models covered in Figure 3.4.
5. Take the task of sending an e-mail and write out the task analysis for it using a GOMS model.

References

Alonso, D. L., & Norman, K. L. (1998). Apparency of contingencies in single panel and pull-down menus. *International Journal of Human–Computer Studies, 49*, 59–78.

Anderson, J. (1993). *Rules of the mind*. Hillsdale, NJ: Erlbaum.

Anderson, J., Matessa, M., & Lebiere, C. (1997). ACT-R: A theory of higher level cognition and its relation to visual attention. *Human–Computer Interaction, 12*, 439–462.

Brown, J., & Strickland, L. (2005). The roots of activity theory: Explaining a perspective in human–computer interaction. *History and Philosophy of Psychology Bulletin, 17*, 4–16.

Card, S. K., Moran, T. P., & Newell, A. (1983). *The psychology of human–computer interaction*. Hillsdale, NJ: Erlbaum.

Dehning, W., Essig, H., & Maass, S. (1981). *The adaptation of virtual man–computer interface to user requirements in dialogs*. Berlin: Spring-Verlag.

Engeström, Y. (1993). Developmental studies of work as a testbench of activity theory. In S. Chaiklin & J. Lave (Eds.), *Understanding practice: Perspectives on activity and context* (pp. 64–103). Cambridge: Cambridge University Press.

Green, T. R. G. (1989). Cognitive dimensions of notations. In A. Sutcliffe & L. Macaulay (Eds.), *People and computers V*. Cambridge: Cambridge University Press.

Hix, D., & Hartson, H. R. (1993). *Developing user interfaces: Ensuring usability through the product and the process*. New York: John Wiley & Sons.

John, B. E., & Kieras, D. E. (1996). Using GOMS for user interface design and evaluation: Which technique? *ACM Transactions on Computer–Human Interaction*, 3(4), 287–319.

Kuutti, K. (1996). Activity theory as a potential framework for human–computer interaction research. In B. A. Nardi (Ed.), *Context and consciousness: Activity theory and human–computer interaction* (pp. 17–44). Cambridge, MA: MIT Press.

Licklider, L. C. R. (1960). Man–computer symbiosis. *IRE Transactions on Human Factors in Electronics, HFE-1*, 4–11. Retrieved March 14, 2008, from http://memex.org/licklider.pdf

Mayhew, D. J. (1999). *The usability engineering lifecycle: A practitioner's guide to user interface design*. San Francisco, CA: Morgan Kaufman.

Nardi, B. A. (1996). Activity theory and human–computer interaction. In B. A. Nardi (Ed.), *Context and consciousness: Activity theory and human–computer interaction* (pp. 69–103). Cambridge, MA: MIT Press.

Nelson, E. A. (1970). Some resent contributions to computer programming management. In G. F. Weinwurm (Ed.), *On the management of computer programming* (pp. 159–184), New York: Auerbach.

Norman, D. A. (1986). Cognitive engineering. In D. A. Norman & S. Draper (Eds.), *User centered system design: New perspectives on human–computer interaction* (pp. 31–62). Hillsdale, NJ: Erlbaum.

Norman, D. A. (1998). *The invisible computer*. Cambridge, MA: MIT Press.

Norman, D. A. (1999). Affordances, conventions and design. *Interactions*, 6, 38–43.

Norman, K. L. (1991). Models of mind and machine: Information flow and control between humans and computers. In M. C. Yovits (Ed.), *Advances in computers* (pp. 201–254). New York: Academic Press.

Norman, K. L., & Singh, R. (1989). Expected performance at the human/computer interface as a function of user proficiency and system power. *Journal of Behavioral Decision Making*, 2, 179–195.

Pomberger, G., Bischofberger, W. R., Kolb, D., Pree, W., & Schlemm, H. (1991). Prototyping-oriented software development: Concepts and tools. *Structured Programming*, 12, 43–60.

Rogers, E. M. (1962). *Diffusion of innovations*. New York: The Free Press.

Rosenbloom, P., Laird, J., & Newell, A. (Ed.). (1993). *The Soar papers: Research on integrated intelligence*. Cambridge, MA: MIT Press.

Royce, W. W. (1970). Managing the development of large software systems: Concepts and techniques. *Proceedings of IEEE WESTCON*, pp. 1–9.

Shneiderman, B. (1986). *Designing the user interface: Strategies for effective human–computer interaction*. Reading, MA: Addison-Wesley.

Tarde, G. (1903). *The laws of imitation* (E. C. Parsons, Trans.). New York: Henry, Holt and Co.

Four

Research

Modes and Methods

Scenario 1

We noticed that when software has a progress bar showing how long a download will take, people are less likely to give up and cancel it. We also realized that people differ a lot in how much patience they have with technology and that will affect whether they cancel the download. We wanted to test these two hypotheses, so we designed an experiment. We prototyped two pieces of software for downloading music files, one with a process bar (Version A) and the other without (Version B). We could set the download time at 10 s, 30 s, 1 min, 3 min, and 10 min. We found a "need for closure" (NFC) scale to assess a person's desire to complete a task. It did not directly measure patience, but it was related to it. We recruited a sample of forty college students. They all took the NFC test, and then twenty were randomly assigned to Version A and the other twenty to Version B. We gave the students 30 min to download as many songs as they could and randomized the download times for each student. We counted the number of times they canceled the download for each of the download times.

Scenario 2

User Verbal Protocol 4356: The user has been given the task of finding a hotel room in downtown Chicago for a particular night and within the range of $100 to $150 per night using a popular travel booking Web site.

Verbal Protocol: Let's see. I want to get to Chicago. I will click "Find by City," then I will go to the field to enter "Chicago." Now I will click "Enter Date." I see a calendar pop up, so I will click on October, then on 23. Now I will click "Enter." Okay, now I see a selection: "Search by Price." I click on this and see a list of options. Great, there is an option $100 *to* $150, *so I will click on that. Now I see ten options ...*

Device Protocol: MouseDown(45,50,0), MouseUp(45,51,03), CurserMove(45,51,130,200,04,25), MouseDown(131,200,31), MouseUp(131,200,34), KeyBoard("Chicago",54), CurserMove(131,200,150,250,60,74), MouseDown(150,250,76), MouseUp(150,250,77), CurserMove(150,250,163,275,78,83), MouseDown(163,275,83), MouseUp(163,276,84), ...

Overview

The study of HCI, and more generally cyberpsychology, uses many methods and techniques from observational and case studies to form hypotheses to empirical methods and experiments to test them as in Scenario 1. In addition, particular pieces of hardware and software are evaluated with usability methods in Scenario 2. At one end, observational and case studies provide information and examples useful for generating ideas and hypotheses. At the other end, scientific methods based on controlled experiments and statistical methods help confirm reliable results as in Scenario 1. From these results, we postulate and test theories about HCI to generate and fit models to the data. These results add the flesh and bones, nuts and bolts, and bits and bytes to the array of models discussed in Chapter 3. In the middle are usability methods that are practical procedures for evaluating the usability of software and systems illustrated in Scenario 2. Although they may not use the rigor of controlled scientific methods, they are quick and economical ways of getting products to market.

We find that, just as in Chapter 3 where there are different perspectives and purposes to the various models, in this chapter, there are different perspectives and goals for the research methods used. Cognitive psychologists are interested in methods that study the basic workings of the human cognitive system and add to their scientific literature. They are not so much interested in comparing one user interface with another to see which one is more efficient. Instead, they are interested in what the interface might reveal about human memory, human problem solving, or human judgment and decision making. In contrast, the user community would be interested in knowing that Software A is twice as efficient, easier to use, and less error prone than Software B. The user community is not so much interested in the psychological reasons why, but just in the bottom line – that one is better than the other. Finally, software and hardware designers are interested in methods

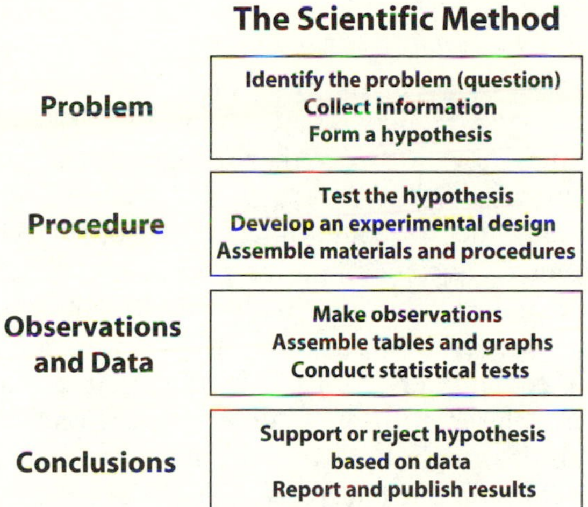

The Scientific Method
Problem
Identify the problem (question)
Collect information
Form a hypothesis
Procedure
Test the hypothesis
Develop an experimental design
Assemble materials and procedures
Observations and Data
Make observations
Assemble tables and graphs
Conduct statistical tests
Conclusions
Support or reject hypothesis based on data
Report and publish results

Figure 4.1. The four steps of the scientific method.

of design that call on good design principles and guidelines based on theory and empirical data, techniques for prototyping versions of the interface, and methods of user testing to verify that the design works.

In this chapter, we cover these perspectives in terms of basic research or theory building – on one side using scientific methods and applied research, and on the other using usability testing methods. Some of the techniques for observation, experimentation, data collection, and analysis are the same, and, of course, some differ in terms of experimental rigor, number of subjects, and methods of interpretation.

Theory Building and the Scientific Method

At the conceptual level, to understand HCI, we are interested in building and testing theories. Theories generate empirically testable hypotheses. One may have a theory from Chapter 3 that if users have a coherent mental model of the interface, they will exhibit better performance on a set of controlled tasks than if they have an incorrect mental model. We can test this theory by creating a situation in which users are given good or poor mental models.

The scientific method follows these steps: conceptualize the problem, collect research information (data), analyze the data, and draw conclusions. The steps of the scientific method are listed in Figure 4.1.

Conceptualize the Problem

A theory is a general framework or set of related ideas that attempt to explain certain observations. Theories explain why something occurs given a set of conditions. Theories give rise to models and are in turn supported when the models appear to be good descriptions of the results.

An important component of the scientific method is the hypothesis. A hypothesis is an idea or a prediction that is logically derived from the theory. For example, we may have a theory that recognition of letters (e.g., A, B, C) is a two-stage process. In the first stage, the system detects types of lines (e.g., straight, curved), their orientation (e.g., horizontal, vertical, diagonal), and the intersections of lines (e.g., meeting, crossing). In the second stage, the visual system matches input information with prototypical patterns for known letters (e.g., A has three straight lines, two diagonal and one horizontal, and three meeting intersections). The time that it takes to recognize a letter will increase with the difficulty in detecting any one of these aspects in the first stage. Thus, if straight lines are slightly curved or if intersections are not perfect, recognition time will increase. The time that it takes to recognize a letter will increase in the second stage with the number and complexity of the pattern.

Given this theory, we could analyze a number of fonts or manipulate the characteristics of the letters, and generate hypotheses about which fonts and experimental manipulations require less time to read.

As another example, we might be interested in the relationship of the use of e-mail and social behavior. We conceptualize the problem as follows: people who use e-mail more than others tend to avoid social contact. To study this relationship, we must operationalize the hypothetical constructs; that is, we must relate the conceptual terms to things that can be objectively measured. In this relationship, we have two variables: the use of e-mail and avoiding social contact. The first one is easy to measure. We could get a count of the number of e-mails sent per day. The second one is more difficult and could be construed to mean a number of different things. As potential measures of social contact, we could count the number of phone calls made by the individual or face-to-face meetings with the person. If there is a negative relationship between number of e-mails and number of phone calls across a number of individuals, we might have something. However, our operationalization of the constructs could be flawed because we are actually measuring frequency of contact (e-mail or phone) and not avoidance of social contact. In fact, it turns out that there is a positive relationship between number of e-mails and phone calls. Socially active people are high on both measures, and socially aversive people are low on both. Instead, we may want to operationalize social contact as a choice. When faced with two equally available alternatives (e-mail vs. phone), individuals high on social avoidance will choose e-mail, and individuals low on avoidance will choose the phone.

In general, we conceptualize problems in terms of input factors called "independent variables" and output factors called "dependent variables." In HCI, the input factors can be classified into four basic sets pertaining to 1) characteristics of the computer system or device, 2) task demand characteristics, 3) attributes of the individual user, and 4) the environment in which

Table 4.1. Examples of Independent Variables To Be Considered in the Study of Human–Computer Interaction

Variable	Applicability of system to task
System characteristics	Design characteristics of the interface
	System response time
Task demand characteristics	Nature of the task
	Difficulty of the task
	Time and accuracy criticality
Attributes of the user	Experience
	Cognitive abilities
	Motivation
Environment	Physical conditions
	Social situations

the interaction takes place. Table 4.1 lists examples of these factors. For each independent variable, one needs to develop a way of measuring it and, in many cases, manipulating its value. Examples of output factors or dependent variables are listed in Table 4.2. For each dependent variable, one needs to develop a method of measuring it reliably.

Collect Research Information

The second step in the scientific method is to collect data. Data collection requires a plan that involves three questions: 1) who will be selected to participate, or what things or people will be observed?; 2) what conditions will be applied, and how will they be manipulated?; and 3) what data will be collected?

In psychological research, we generally select a sample of participants from a target population. We may often select people at random from a directory or

Table 4.2. Examples of Dependent Variables To Be Considered in the Study of Human–Computer Interaction

Variable	Speed of performance
Human performance	Rate and type of errors
	Quality of solutions to problems
Training time and effectiveness	Time to learn how to use the system
	Frequency of reference to documentation
	Transfer of training
	Human retention of commands over time
Cognitive processes	Appropriateness of the mental model
	Degree of mental effort
	Type of strategy used
Subjective satisfaction	Satisfaction with self
	Satisfaction with system
	Satisfaction with performance
	Satisfaction with outcome

dsk1.xls

	A	B	C	D	E	F	G	H	I	J	K	L
1	date	time	1_age	2_gender	3_race	4_student	1_comp_use	2_www_use	overall_frust	waiting_frustr	redo_frustrat	not_understa
2												
3	5/15/02	9:11:44 PM	25	Female	African	other	7	7	9	9	9	9
4	5/28/02	5:32:25 PM	23	Male	Caucasian	highshool	1	1	2	1	1	1
5	5/31/02	4:13:08 PM	36	Male	Caucasian	other	7	7	9	9	9	1
6	6/10/02	4:23:14 PM	17	Male	Caucasian	highshool	7	7	9	9	9	7
7	6/18/02	7:55:51 AM	22	Male	Caucasian	other	7	7	9	9	9	5
8	6/26/02	11:03:28 AM	21	Female	Caribbean	undergrad	7	7	5	8	9	5
9	6/26/02	11:03:57 AM	34	Female	African	undergrad	1	1	2	5	5	1
10	6/26/02	11:04:30 AM	21	Female	Other	undergrad	7	7	3	4	4	2
11	6/26/02	11:05:02 AM	21	Female	African	undergrad	7	7	3	6	5	3
12	6/26/02	11:05:20 AM	20	Female	African	undergrad	4	1	2	5	2	2
13	6/26/02	11:08:29 AM	37	Female	African	undergrad	1	1	2	5	3	5
14	6/28/02	11:27:36 PM	22	Male	Asian	undergrad	7	7	6	6	1	8
15	6/30/02	3:26:07 PM	13	Male	Amercian	elementary	7	4	2	1	3	1
16	7/6/02	7:17:51 PM	2	Male	Caucasian	other	7	4	5	7	8	1
17	7/7/02	8:29:51 AM	25	Male	Caucasian	other	7	7	9	9	9	9
18	7/8/02	8:28:05 AM	33	Male	Austrailian	other	7	4	4	9	9	1
19	8/19/02	2:04:20 AM	16	Male	Caucasian	highshool	7	7	9	9	9	3
20	9/2/02	7:19:17 PM	55	Male	Caucasian	grad	7	7	4	3	5	5
21	9/10/02	12:57:16 PM	21	Female	Caucasian	undergrad	7	7	6	6	3	2
22	9/11/02	11:39:45 AM	19	Male	Caucasian	highshool	7	1	3	5	3	2
23	9/16/02	9:42:50 AM	17	Female	Caucasian	undergrad	7	7		6	5	7
24	9/16/02	9:43:24 AM	17	Female	Asian	undergrad	7	4	3	6	6	6
25	9/16/02	9:43:27 AM	19	Male	Caucasian	undergrad	7	7	4	8	3	3
26	9/16/02	9:43:28 AM	17	Female	Caucasian	undergrad	7	4	8	5	9	1
27	9/16/02	9:43:30 AM	18	Female	Caucasian	undergrad	4	4	6	8	8	8
28	9/16/02	9:43:34 AM	20	Male	Caucasian	undergrad	7	7	7	7	2	4
29	9/16/02	9:45:15 AM	18	Female	Caucasian	undergrad	7	1	7	9	7	9
30	9/17/02	12:17:03 PM	18	Female	Caucasian	undergrad	7	7	7	7	7	7
31	9/26/02	12:06:09 PM	57	Male	Caucasian	other	7	7	4	7	6	3

Figure 4.2. A sample data sheet for an empirical study.

from people within an organization, or we compose a "convenience sample" because the participants are easy to contact and available for the study. Alternatively, people may select themselves to participate in the study. The important question is whether the sample is representative of the population that we want to study. If one wanted to study typical high school students, the participants would have to be in high school and be "typical."

The data collected depend on the design of the study and the variables selected for observation. We talk more about these methods later in this chapter. Basically, we use either experimental methods or correlational methods. In experimental methods, we systematically manipulate one or several independent variables either between groups of participants or across repeated tests of the same participant and record the dependent variable. In correlational methods, the independent variable is not directly controlled but varies randomly as we observe a number of cases. We then look for the relationship between the independent variable and the dependent variable.

Ultimately, in each case, we record the dependent variable along with its occurrence with the independent variable. All data are carefully coded and recorded in databases such as electronic spreadsheets for subsequent analysis. Figure 4.2 shows a sample data sheet for a study on computers.

Analyze the Data

Data analysis depends on the type of data, the type of experimental design, and the questions being asked. In general, we look at descriptive statistics such as means, standard deviations, frequencies, and correlations. We use inferential statistics to confirm the reliability of results. Data analysis requires a knowledge of statistics and experimental design. Data analysis is not as easy as opening a statistics package, plugging in the data, selecting a few menu options, and printing the results. Serious researchers need to take numerous

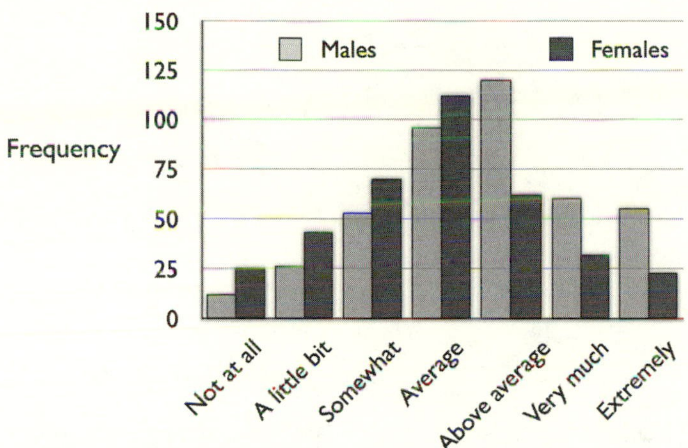

Figure 4.3. Frequency distributions of self-reported knowledge about computers for males and females.

courses in statistics to understand what they are doing and/or hire statisticians as consultants to do it right.

To provide an example of how we go about data analysis, we look at a survey on computer use and expertise. If we have a response scale with a discrete number of points, we can plot a frequency distribution, which lists the frequency or percent of individuals giving each response. Figure 4.3 shows frequency distributions of self-reported knowledge about computers for males and females. Frequency distributions are important because they show the dispersion of individuals across the set of possible responses. In this case, we can see that males self-report a higher knowledge of computers than females. Moreover, the distributions are fairly normal with a high concentration in the middle and low frequencies in the tails of the distribution.

In other cases, we may record the performance with a quantitative measure such as the number or percent correct. Then we calculate the means and standard deviations. Figure 4.4 gives an example of what this would look like for three levels of task difficulty for a text interface or a GUI. The means are graphed as points on the lines, and the bars around the lines show one standard deviation above and below the means. Generally, these intervals

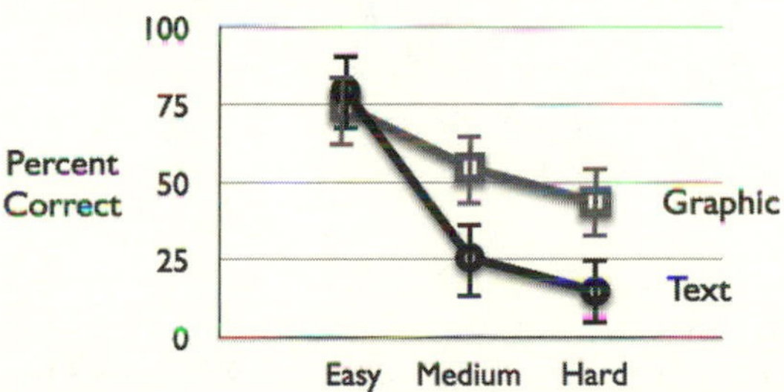

Figure 4.4. Graph of means showing bars of one standard deviation above and below the means.

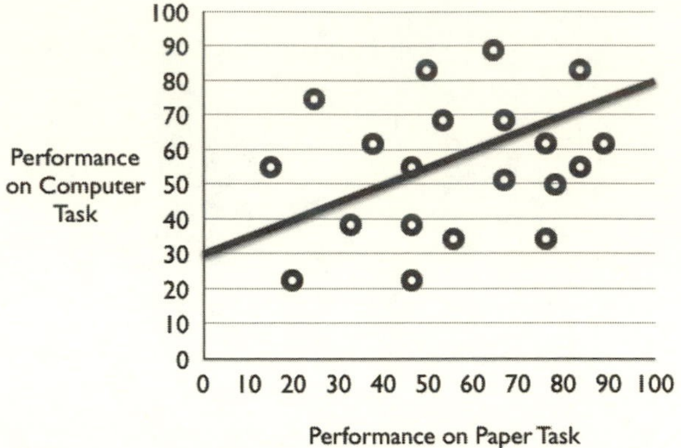

Figure 4.5. Correlational scattergram showing the relationship between performance measures in two different conditions.

include about 68 percent of the cases in a normal distribution of scores. Consequently, the means for the easy task condition are very close together and the distributions overlap, and they are fairly far apart for the medium and hard conditions.

When we record several continuous variables, we can look at the relationship between them using a scatterplot. One variable is graphed on the X-axis and the other on the Y-axis. Each point represents an individual with X and Y scores. Figure 4.5 shows a scatterplot relating the performance on a paper task and a computer task. The line shows the best-fitting linear relationship between the variables. To the extent that points cluster around the line and the line increases or decreases, there is a stronger relationship between the two variables.

Draw Conclusions

Analysis without conclusions has little or no meaning and certainly no impact on the scientific community or the practitioners in HCI. Conclusions are logical deductions from the results of the data analysis. Conclusions relate back to the original theoretical or practical questions that motivated the research. If reading performance differs for various fonts and the differences conform to the predictions of the theory about letter recognition, then we conclude that the theory is correct. If not, we abandon the theory or we modify it in some way to account for the results that we did find. Conclusions that contribute to our knowledge in cognitive psychology and theories of HCI make lasting contributions to the scientific literature.

Conclusions are also logical inferences that generalize the results and apply them to wider contexts. For example, even though one could not have used all fonts that exist in the study, the results could generalize to make predictions about other fonts based on their characteristics. Or one might generalize the results to other populations of computer users that did not participate in the study. Generalization is a necessary part of drawing conclusions, but should be subject to scrutiny and further empirical testing.

Many conclusions of research on HCI result in principles and guidelines that designers can use in developing new systems. For example, the results from the study on character recognition for different fonts could result in guidelines about which fonts to use and which fonts to avoid in building interfaces. Over time, many handbooks of guidelines on interface design have resulted from such research published (e.g., Brown, 1998; Nicolle & Abascal, 2001; Salvendy, 2006) and listed on the Web.

Empirical Methods

In this section, we look at various methods of designing and setting up a research study in HCI. One unique aspect of research in HCI is that unlike most work in computer science or engineering, our studies involve humans. The other unique aspect is that unlike most research in psychology, our studies involve computers. Both aspects add to the difficulty and complexity of research in HCI. First, we must contend with the many problems of studies involving humans, such as individual variability, ethical concerns, and subjective biases. Second, we must provide for computers and interfaces in the study, and we must invoke the help of programmers to set up the interfaces and experimental conditions, often using prototyping software.

The methods that we use range from controlled laboratory experiments to observational studies with little or no control. The data collected can range from quantitative frequency counts and measures to qualitative descriptions and classifications. Each method has its advantages and disadvantages. Serious research programs make use of multiple methods to cover all the bases. In this section, we start with observational studies and work our way up to controlled experiments.

Observational Field Studies

Observational studies are often the easiest to conduct and require the least planning. Unfortunately, they are also the most unreliable and open to observer bias and subjective interpretation. In an observational study, one or several systems may be selected, and researchers observe users interacting with each system. Verbal protocols may be elicited in which the user explains what and why he or she is doing something. Time, productivity, and error data may be collected. Analysis may be at a purely verbal descriptive level or based on quantitative measures. Conclusions are tentative at best because researchers have little or no control over conditions. For example, one may observe that users take longer to perform tasks on System A than on System B, but the tasks may not be comparable, system response time may be different, the groups of users may not be equated in terms of experience, age, ability, etc. Investigators must thoroughly weigh and rule out alternative explanations.

The major strength of observational studies is that they are inherently relevant, being situated in real contexts with real users at work or at home doing things that they would normally do in these contexts. Such observational studies are particularly useful for their ability to generate hypotheses about design features or aspects of the interaction that can be studied in more controlled environments to rule out alternative interpretations.

Observational studies should be carefully planned and conducted in as systematic a procedure as possible. One needs to identify the different contexts (user and task environments) and specify the events and variables to be recorded and measured as independent and dependent variables from Tables 4.1 and 4.2 (e.g., system crashes, observed user frustration, number of Web sites visited).

Observational studies can be severely biased when the users are aware of the fact that they are being observed. The knowledge that observers are walking around with clipboards and recording what workers are doing can clearly change the behavior and attitudes of the users. Nevertheless, in some studies it is useful for the observer to intervene and to probe and ask questions.

However, many observational studies can be conducted without the users being aware of hidden cameras and one-way mirrors. Research in HCI can use covert recording of interactions at the interface. All keystrokes, mouse movements, and selections can be recorded as illustrated in the "Device Protocol" of Scenario 2. All Web sites visited, purchases made, e-mails sent, and so on, can be recorded and observed. The advantage is that users are not aware that what they are doing is being meticulously recorded; they are not interrupted by questions from the observer. The disadvantage is that the observation is incomplete; that is, we may know what the person selected, but we have no idea of why or what other things the user is doing while sitting at the computer. In addition, there are ethical concerns about the users' rights, privacy, and consent to participate in the research.

A new and powerful form of observational research is known as "data mining." Hand, Mannila, and Smyth (2001) defined data mining as "the science of extracting useful information from large data sets or databases" (p. xxiii). Programs can be written to automatically search large databases of user records for patterns and relationships. Data mining is used by retailers to look for patterns of buying behavior and to associate one product with another for marketing purposes (Tan, Steinbach, & Kumar, 2005). It is routinely used in supermarkets to target advertisements and coupons based on consumer purchases and by e-commerce sites to give "recommendations based on items you own" and list other items that "customers who bought this item also bought." Incredible amounts of data are recorded by servers on the Internet during user interactions with programs, navigation, searches, transactions, and so on, using the Web. Data mining of these and many other databases can be used by behavioral and social scientists to study many aspects of HCI and basic psychological processes. Moreover, one of the central ideas behind data mining is that it can be used to discover new and emergent patterns and relationships as programs troll through vast numbers of possibilities.

Survey and Correlational Studies

Questionnaires provide a structured approach in which the user can be asked to assess factors related to the human–computer interface. Users may record objective events or subjective evaluations. Objective events include the number of times they have used a particular system, the number of times they encountered a problem while using the system, and the number of tasks completed. In each case, because the events are objective, the researcher could also record these events and compare that record with the user assessments. Although user assessments bear a strong correlational relationship to the actual measure, they are not perfect. User assessments are introspective and, therefore, are subject to the properties of human memory and to biases in reporting. Because of this, one cannot assume that user assessments reflect the true values of the measures. Nevertheless, it is quite possible to establish, through empirical verification, the reliability and validity of user responses. Furthermore, when comparisons are made between different groups of subjects rather than with an absolute criterion, it may not matter that responses are biased as long as the sources of bias are constant among the groups.

Users may also be asked to make subjective evaluations of system attributes. For example, they may be asked to check statements that apply to the system use (e.g., "Documentation is adequate" or "I do not understand program operation") or rate system attributes on a 10-point scale (e.g., ease of use, speed, tendency to make errors). When users make subjective evaluations, there is generally no way to compare their responses with objective measures of those attributes. However, evaluations such as overall satisfaction with the system may be statistically related to objective system attributes such as system response time or screen resolution.

The key to measuring subjective evaluations is to ensure reliability and internal consistency of the ratings. By reliability, we mean that users display little error in making ratings, and if they rate the same attributes a second time, there would be a relatively strong relationship between the two ratings. By internal consistency, we mean that the ratings follow a logical relationship. For example, if subjects are asked to compare three systems, A, B, and C, and they rate A superior to B and B superior to C, then they must rate A superior to C in order to be internally consistent. Without internal consistency, the meaningfulness of the results is in question.

Survey questionnaires should include demographic data on the user as shown in Figure 4.6. Typically, we want to know the age, gender, work experience, and training of the user. We may also want to include psychometric measures to assess intellectual skills, cognitive functions, and knowledge as well as self-report measures using rating scales as shown in Figure 4.7. Analysis of the data may look for interrelationships among the variables. For example, we may be interested in whether there is a relationship between memory ability and preference for a particular type of software, or between the rated numbers of errors and rated overall satisfaction with the system.

1. Age:
2. Gender: Male Female
3. Racial/Ethnic Identity (Check all that apply):
African American
Asian American
Caucasian
Hispanic
Native American
Other:

4. Occupation:
Student: K-7
8-12
college undergraduate
graduate student
teacher
professor
other (please indicate specific position):

Figure 4.6. Survey with demographic questions.

Questionnaires may also be effectually used in conjunction with controlled experimental studies. Survey data are useful for getting user assessments of systems, for detecting strong and weak points, and for suggesting improvements.

The main problem with correlational studies is that although they reveal relationships between variables, they do not establish unique, causal relationships. One may find a strong relationship between knowledge of computers and number of hours used per week. Does usage lead to increased knowledge? Do knowledgeable people use computers more? Is there a third variable such as job demands that determines both variables?

Controlled Laboratory Experiments

The major strength of the experimental study is its ability to localize unambiguously an effect in a particular design factor. Experimental design is

3. I use the Internet for:	**Often**								**Never**
research and general information	1	2	3	4	5	6	7	8	9
business purposes	1	2	3	4	5	6	7	8	9
e-mail with friends and family	1	2	3	4	5	6	7	8	9
e-mail with co-workers	1	2	3	4	5	6	7	8	9
chat rooms	1	2	3	4	5	6	7	8	9
leisure and entertainment	1	2	3	4	5	6	7	8	9
other:									
4. I access the Internet from:	**Often**								**Never**
home	1	2	3	4	5	6	7	8	9
work	1	2	3	4	5	6	7	8	9
school/college	1	2	3	4	5	6	7	8	9
local library	1	2	3	4	5	6	7	8	9
other:									

Figure 4.7. Example of rating scales in a survey.

used to systematically control all variables except those that are being tested.

First, sample participants from the population of interest. To the extent that users are a diverse group, it is important to assess the individual differences of the users. For example, one might need to know 1) the level of experience with computers, terminals, etc.; 2) familiarity with generic tasks such as accounting, information retrieval, or programming; 3) demographic variables of age and gender; and 4) cognitive measures of analytical skills, verbal and visual memory, reaction time, and so on.

Second, one or several design features are selected for study (Table 4.1). These are systematically varied in such a way that their impact on performance can be unambiguously assessed. For example, we may be interested in the effect of adding graphics to a Web site. We would set up two conditions, the original Web site and the enhanced Web site. Or we may be interested in comparing alphabetic versus random ordering of options in a menu as well as the number of options (e.g., 4, 8, 16, 32). In this case, we have two variables and will need to consider all eight pairwise combinations of the treatment levels (i.e., alphabetic – 4 items, alphabetic – 8 items, alphabetic – 16 items, alphabetic – 32 items, random – 4 items, random – 8 items, random – 16 items, random – 32 items). Software must be written or altered so that the features are implemented at each level.

Third, we must select one or several variables to measure. Again, Table 4.2 lists some of the types of variables that may be of interest. The variables must be defined in such a way as to allow valid and reliable measurements to be taken. Typically, additional software must be written to capture these measurements.

Fourth, we must assign subjects to the treatments or treatment combinations. There are two basic designs for doing this. In a "between-subjects" design, each person participates in only one condition. Individuals are randomly assigned to groups and each group is subjected to one condition – in this example, one group for the original Web site and one group for the enhanced Web site. All comparisons are then made between groups of subjects. If the graphics have no effect, then any differences between the groups would only be due to random sampling.

In the "within-subject" design, each person participates in a number of the conditions sequentially. Each subject would explore one Web site and then the other. Because the exposure to one version of the Web site could have an effect on the next, we counterbalance the order. Half of the participants would get the original site first and the enhanced site second, and the other half would get the enhanced first and the original second. Within-subject designs expose participants to multiple conditions and allow for subjective comparisons between treatment levels. Consequently, they can cause problems when exposure to one condition changes their behavior in another condition due to learning, practice, or fatigue.

Finally, the experiment must be carefully monitored as it progresses in order to detect flaws in the design and methodology. Once it is completed, statistical analysis is used to sort out the results and give evidence as to the reliability of the findings.

The experimental approach is not without its drawbacks. Experiments are costly and often overly restrictive. The results may not generalize beyond the artificial conditions set in the lab. However, to the extent that the investigator establishes realistic conditions and assesses appropriate dependent measures, the results gain validity.

Controlled Field Experiments

Perhaps the most powerful and ecologically valid experimental method is to conduct a controlled experiment in the field rather than in the lab. However, it is an incredible challenge to be able to systematically control the independent variable and to hold all other confounding variables constant. Nevertheless, many controlled field experiments have been conducted and provide the most compelling results. Field experiments can be conducted by embedding the controlled manipulation in the interface and randomly assigning levels to users as they access the site. So, for example, an e-commerce site could vary the order of information about the cost of shipping and handling. In one case, it would be shown continually and updated on the basket page; in a second case, it would be shown only after the customer clicks purchase; and in a third case, it would be shown after the credit card information is input. The dependent variable would be the point at which the interaction was terminated. Or in a Web search, one could vary the type of search parameters or guidance. Although these experiments can test many users, it is often difficult to collect demographic data on the users. However, with the increased use of storing click stream and other data in browser cookies and linking one database to another, it can be surprising how much personal information can be gleaned about the user.

Threats to Research Methods in Human–Computer Interaction

There are many ways in which experimental research can result in biased results. It is important to critically analyze experiments to identify potential flaws in their design and threats to their validity. Several potential problems are listed in this section.

Nonrandom Assignment to Groups

Unless we are specifically looking at differences between types of groups (e.g., males vs. females, young vs. old), we either randomly assign individuals to different treatment groups or match them in some way so that there are no initial differences between groups. Random assignment and matching assures the experimenter that if the independent variable has no effect, there will be no differences between the groups. Nonrandom assignment can occur when experimenters use convenience samples and select intact, preexisting groups for comparison (e.g., a PC users group vs. a Mac users group) or when individuals select themselves into different conditions (e.g., students enrolling in a traditional lecture course or in an online course). In these cases, there is no assurance that the groups are equivalent on any measure.

Research Participant Bias

When participants have some knowledge as to what condition they are in or what the experimenter expects of them, their behavior and attitudes can change. Just knowing that they are being subjected to some treatment can lead to enhanced performance. If someone is asked to try a new piece of software to determine whether it is an improvement over the older version, the experiment is immediately biased. Users will feel the demand to confirm that the new version is superior and rate the system accordingly. They may try harder to complete tasks, and their performance will be momentarily enhanced due to what are called "demand characteristics."

There are several ways to reduce or eliminate these biases. The first is to use a "blind study" and ensure that the participants do not know what condition they are in. The second is to eliminate experimenter biases by using a "double-blind" study with a coding system so that neither the participant nor the experimenter is aware of the condition. Blind studies are not possible when the conditions themselves are just too obvious, such as using virtual reality for instruction. When this occurs, biases can be managed by using controls for "placebo effects." A simple control is a group that does not receive the experimental treatment but is subjected to the status quo, the traditional system, or the current version of the system. A "placebo control" group is led to believe that they are in a new condition or a new version, however, the changes are superficial and do not include the true experimental manipulation.

Cultural, Language, Gender, and Ethnic Biases

Finally, experiments can be biased by cultural and ethnic limitations. Imagine participating in an experiment on search techniques to find information on the Web using Search Engine A or Search Engine B. The only problem is that you only understand English, and while Search Engine A is in English, Search Engine B is in German. Of course, Search Engine A would be vastly superior. Now imagine that they were both in German. Even if one were better than the other, it would make no difference; performance would be awful for both. These illustrate the extreme problems of bias, but similar problems can occur when an interface that was originally designed for the American user is tested on the Asian user, or when a computer game that was written by male game programmers is played by females. These types of biases are hard to detect and to disentangle. The best thing to do is to be aware of their possibility and to investigate cross-cultural effects by systematically varying the design of the interface and the origin of the groups involved.

Usability Testing

Usability studies typically involve the testing of one product or design. Generally, they do not further our scientific knowledge unless they produce some observation that generates a theory or hypothesis that one can later test in a more rigorous manner. The primary goal of usability testing is that of quality assurance. It is to make sure that the interface design is usable by the target group of users. It is a part of the design and production process and its goal is to produce a product. As such, it does not directly contribute to scientific knowledge. In fact, the results of usability testing are often proprietary and not made public.

Usability testing, however, is an extremely important endeavor. It can save a company from the disaster of launching a product that might work fine for the programmers and designers, and even pass usability inspection by expert reviewers and quality assurance teams, but just does not work for the users. In turn, it is good for users to have interfaces that have gone through iterative testing and been fixed before they are subjected to years of coping with a faulty design.

There are different goals for user testing. Sadly, sometimes the only purpose for user testing is just to check off that it has been done as part of the development requirements. In this view, user testing is more of an obstacle to production rather than an opportunity for development of a better product.

The purpose of usability testing most frequently is to detect and document major interface problems that would render the software unusable from the customer point of view. For example, a user may never figure out how to do something and cannot complete the task because of it. Or the user may repeatedly make an inadvertent error that leads to devastating results, such as deleting a file rather than saving it.

Second, it may detect aspects of the interface that are confusing, hard to use, or tedious. For example, the label of a menu item may convey a different meaning to the user than was meant by the designer. Or it may be hard to select a very small target on the screen with the mouse. Or to complete a simple task, the interface may require twice as many mouse clicks due to a convoluted design as opposed to a simple, straightforward design.

Third, user testing may be used to resolve differences of opinion as to which way the interface should be designed. Should the menu be listed vertically or horizontally? Should the cursor change to a hand icon or a bull's eye over certain areas on the screen? User testing and assessment of user preferences can help answer these questions.

Fourth, user testing may provide an opportunity for suggestions for improvement by the participants. They may suggest a different wording of the text. Or they may suggest additional functions and menu options that they would find useful. Or they may suggest that help be provided for difficult-to-use screens.

User testing may occur in various field settings such as at a kiosk in the shopping mall, a workstation in the office, or a computer at home. Although user testing in natural environments can reveal important information, events and conditions in these environments are hard to control, and results may be contaminated with phone interruptions or a dog walking in and out of the room. Moreover, it can be difficult to record quality data in the field without portable equipment. Alternatively, user testing may occur in the more controlled, simulated environments of usability labs.

Usability Labs

Usability labs are specially designed facilities that are used to observe and record user interactions during a testing session. Figure 4.8 shows the schematic used to design the usability lab at the U.S. Bureau of the Census.

There are three independent testing rooms that can be used for the same or different projects. The participants are led into the testing rooms and given a set of tasks to perform on the workstation provided. Tasks may be presented on a second monitor. As many as three cameras may be used to capture the face of the participant (Camera 1); the hands, mouse, keyboard, and screen (Camera 2); and any documents on the table (Camera 3). In addition, microphones are used to record audio from the testing rooms. Adjacent to each testing room is an observation room connected by a one-way mirror that allows only the observers to see the participant. All video and audio can be presented on monitors, mixed, and recorded in the observation rooms. A computer network also allows the observers to record the screen from the participant's workstation and even take over the keyboard and mouse if needed. Software on the observers' workstations allows them to code and record their observations along with time stamps associated with the video recorded.

An additional observation gallery shown at the bottom of Figure 4.8 may be provided for individuals interested in observing the whole process and/or who are biased stakeholders in the system being tested such as programmers, owners, clients, and lawyers. These observers can watch the monitors and may interact with the personnel in the observation rooms but not with the participants.

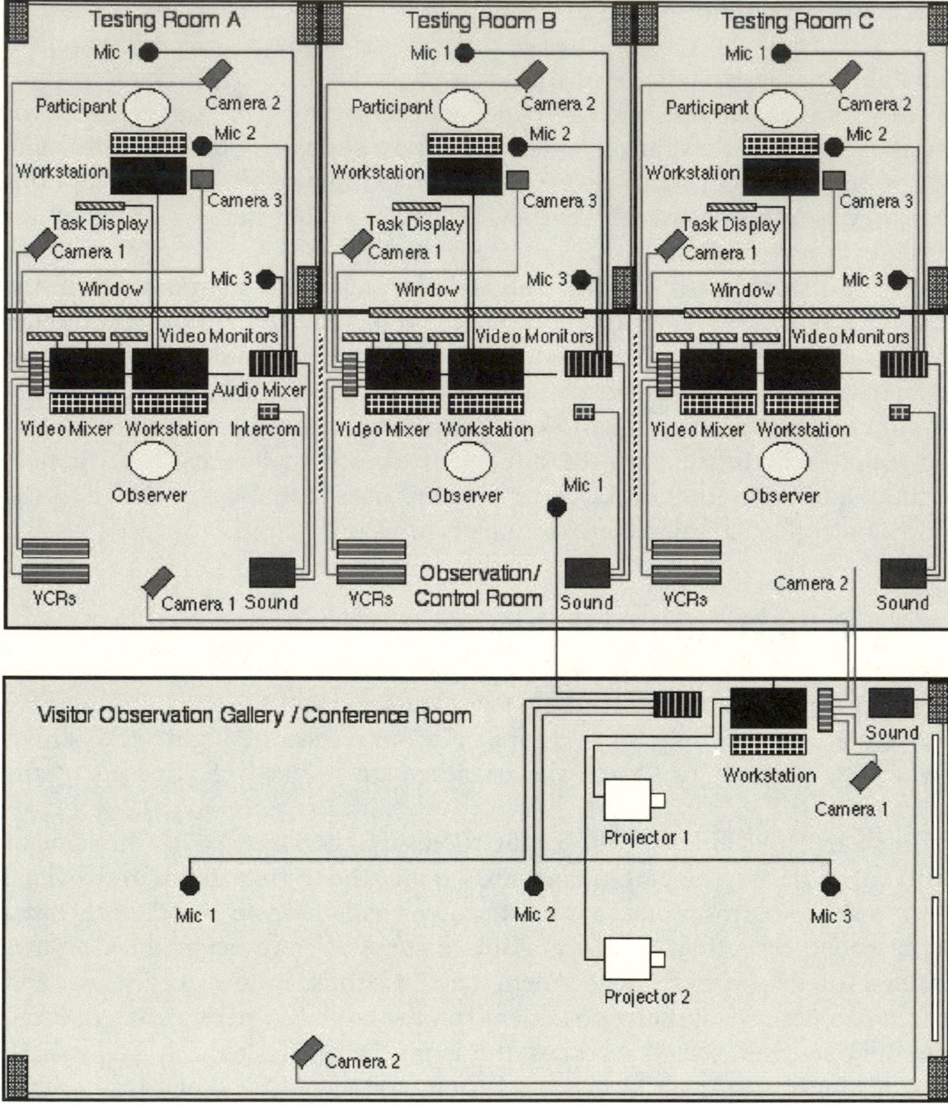

Figure 4.8. Schematic of a sample usability lab.

User Testing Methods

The goals of user testing are generally quite different from controlled scientific experiments. In user testing, statistical significance for differences and trends is not that important. Consequently, the number of participants tested may be in the range of 5 to 20. But it is important to detect as many anomalies and unusual events as possible. Turnaround time must be minimized to draw conclusions and make recommendations as soon as possible.

A number of different user testing methods have been developed (e.g., Dumas & Redish, 1999; Lewis & Rieman, 1993). These methods vary in their use of automatic recording of interface events, human observation of events, user verbal protocols, and user evaluations (Norman & Panizzi, 2006). In general, all methods start with a particular program, Web site, or piece of hardware to evaluate. It could be iTunes or Microsoft Word, Google or Amazon, or an iPod or a Palm PDA. A user testing team, usually in conjunction with the client, develops a set of tasks for the participants to perform (e.g., download an album by Bob Dylan, reformat the page to two columns, find an image of the American flag, enter a name and phone number). They also develop a set of objectives (e.g., 90 percent of the participants should be able to perform the task within 1 min, no more than 5 percent of the participants will generate errors performing the task, no more than 10 percent of the participants will rate the task as "very difficult").

Participants are recruited to fit the profile of a typical user. Many usability labs have a large file of people from which they can sample. Individuals are contacted and given an initial screening interview or survey. If the person matches the profile, he or she is scheduled for a testing session. Incentives for participating may range anywhere from a payment of $10 to $75 or entry into a lottery for items up to $500.

Beginning the testing session, a task administrator first welcomes the participant, explains the testing procedure, and asks the person to sign an "informed consent" form. A second more in-depth interview or survey may be given to get more information about the participant (e.g., demographics, preferences, abilities, experience).

Prior to administering the tasks, the participant is told that the study is being conducted to evaluate the usability of the hardware or software and not to test the abilities of the user. Consequently, if the person cannot perform the task, it reflects on the poor design of the interface, not on the ability of the user.

Then each task is given to the participant. During the task, the participant may be told to perform the task on his or her own without asking questions, unless there is a severe problem. In some cases, a "think-aloud" procedure is used whereby the participant is instructed to verbalize everything he or she is thinking in the course of performing the task as illustrated in the "Verbal Protocol" of Scenario 2. In other cases, a "retrospective" procedure may be used and the participant is asked to recall what happened during the task. In the retrospective procedure, the task administrator may replay a video recording of the screens to prompt the participant. Finally, the participant may be asked to comment on the task, rate his or her satisfaction with the interface, and provide suggestions for improvement.

At the end of the testing, the participant may be asked to rate his or her overall satisfaction with the interface using a standardized instrument such as the Questionnaire for User Interaction Satisfaction (QUIS; Chin, Diehl, & Norman, 1988). Figure 4.9 shows a portion of the QUIS. Finally, the participant is allowed to ask questions about the study and is thanked for his or her help in evaluating the product.

Part 3: Overall User Reactions

Please select the numbers which most appropriately reflect your impressions about using this system.

3.1 Overall reactions to the system	terrible	wonderful
	○1 ○2 ○3 ○4 ○5 ○6 ○7 ○8 ○9	
3.2	frustrating	satisfying
	○1 ○2 ○3 ○4 ○5 ○6 ○7 ○8 ○9	
3.3	dull	stimulating
	○1 ○2 ○3 ○4 ○5 ○6 ○7 ○8 ○9	
3.4	difficult	easy
	○1 ○2 ○3 ○4 ○5 ○6 ○7 ○8 ○9	
3.5	inadequate power	adequate power
	○1 ○2 ○3 ○4 ○5 ○6 ○7 ○8 ○9	
3.6	rigid	flexible
	○1 ○2 ○3 ○4 ○5 ○6 ○7 ○8 ○9	

Part 4: Screen

4.1 Characters on the computer screen	hard to read	easy to read
	○1 ○2 ○3 ○4 ○5 ○6 ○7 ○8 ○9	
4.2 Highlighting on the screen	unhelpful	helpful
	○1 ○2 ○3 ○4 ○5 ○6 ○7 ○8 ○9	
4.3 Screen layouts were helpful	never	always

Figure 4.9. A portion of the Questionnaire for User Interaction Satisfaction.

Ethics in Research

Research that involves humans must abide by accepted ethical principles for research. The American Psychological Association publishes the principles used in most government, industry, and university research. The most recent version of the *Ethical Principles of Psychologists and Code of Conduct* was published in 2002. Research conducted at universities and other publicly funded laboratories must receive Institutional Review Board approval to ensure that participants are informed of their rights and protected against potential harm. The following sections discuss important components involved in these ethical principles.

Informed Consent

Participants must be informed that they are involved in a research study. They should be informed of 1) the purpose of the research, how long it will take,

Explanation of Task

In this experiment, you will be asked to browse a Web site to answer questions. You will then be asked to evaluate the Web site.

Consent Form: Participant 1

Information that you submit will be strictly confidential. In any reports or publications, all names and personal information will be completely annoymous. In order to continue, we need for you agree with the University of Maryland Informed Consent Contract:

☐ I am 18 or over and have freely volunteered to participate in this project.

☐ I have been informed in advance as to what my tasks would be and what procedure would be followed.

☐ I understand that there are no known risks to my participation of this research, and that this research is not designed to help me personally.

☐ I am aware that I have the right at any time to withdraw consent and discontinue participation at any time.

☐ I am aware that I may be video taped during this test. These tapes will only be used to review the interactions and will be viewed only by the test personnel.

First Name: [ ] Last Name: [ ]

(Agree and Submit Information to Continue) (I Do Not Agree)

If you have questions about your rights as a research subject or wish to report a research-related injury, please contact:
Institutional Review Board Office,
University of Maryland,
College Park, Maryland, 20742;
(e-mail) irb@deans.umd.edu;

Figure 4.10. An informed consent form for a typical study conducted at the University of Maryland.

and the procedures to be used; 2) their right to decline participation and to withdraw from participation at any point; 3) the consequences of declining or withdrawing; 4) any potential risks, discomfort, or adverse effects; 5) any benefits of participating; 6) limits of confidentiality; 7) any incentive for participating; and 8) a contact for questions about the research and participants' rights. If participants' behavior is being recorded, particularly if they are being videotaped, they must also be informed and sign an "informed consent" form prior to the study. Figure 4.10 shows an informed consent form used in such research at the University of Maryland.

Confidentiality

Individual data must be kept confidential. Although the experimenter may know the identity of the participants, he or she must not record that identity in the data file. Data are often reported at the group level, but when notes are made at the individual level, they must be anonymous.

Use of Deception

Sometimes deception is used to generate effects. For example, participants may be told that they are interacting via iChat with another person when in reality they are interacting with a set of stock responses generated by the computer. In general, deception should not be used unless it has been determined that the use of deceptive techniques is justified by the merits of the study. The deceptive interactions should be within the realm of real-world possibilities and in no way noxious or offensive. However, when the deception can lead to guilt, shame, and other negative repercussions, then deception is not ethical and should not be allowed. Participants should have the right to withdraw their data from the research after having been informed of the deceptive techniques used.

Debriefing

Participants should be debriefed at the end of the experiment or user testing. They should be informed about what independent variables were being tested, what was being measured, and any theories being tested and the expected results. Debriefing is an important time for the experimenter to dissipate any concerns, doubts, and fears that the participant may have developed about the experiment. It is also an opportunity for the experimenter to educate the participant about the importance of studying HCI and interface design.

End Thoughts

Much has been learned about HCI based on the methods discussed in this chapter. As we have seen, there are a lot of ways of studying the human–computer interface for many different purposes. We might be interested in a very detailed, specific issue, such as the size of a check box, or a very broad issue, such as the sense of flow while doing a task. These are factor experiments. Or we might be interested in comparing different designs or products. These are clusters or bundles of features. Without further analysis, we may not know what led to a significant difference; all we know is which is better overall. Or we might be interested in general topics such as the psychology of e-mail or the influence of video games on behavior. In each case, we must be careful to use methods that result in reliable, valid, and unbiased conclusions.

The following chapters cover a lot about what we know about HCI using the research methods discussed in this chapter. As we look at each study, it is helpful to think about the hypotheses tested, the methods used, how the data were analyzed, the threats to the validity of the conclusions, and ways to improve the study. As scientists, we are called on to be critical, skeptical, and even nit-picky in our research. Nevertheless, we build on the work of others and construct a wealth of theory and knowledge.

Suggested Exercises

1. Conduct a controlled study. Choose a variable that you can easily manipulate (e.g., age of participant, size of text on the screen), and select two values that are fairly

far apart. Generate three or four tasks for the participants to complete (e.g., fill out a form online, search for targets on the Web). Decide on two to three dependent variables to measure (e.g., time to complete task, number of steps taken, number of errors, subjective assessment of the difficulty of the tasks). Write instructions to be read to the participants. Run four or five participants in each group and collect data. Analyze the data and write a short report.

2. Go to a random Web site and explore its functions and options for about 15 min. Then evaluate the site using the QUIS at http://lap.umd.edu/quis_online/ (with username "cyber" and password "psychology").

3. Perform a usability test of a Web site by selecting a Web site of interest to you. Develop a task list of about four or five things that users might do on that site. Write instructions for the task. Recruit three or four participants. Collect task completion times, errors, think-aloud verbal protocols, and subjective ratings of the sites.

References

Brown, C. M. (1998). *Human–computer interface design guidelines*. Bristol, UK: Intellect Ltd.

Chin, J. P., Diehl, V. A., & Norman, K. L. (1988). Development of an instrument measuring user satisfaction of the human–computer interface. *Proceedings of the SIGCHI conference on human factors in computing systems*, Washington, DC, pp. 213–218.

Dumas, J. S., & Redish, J. C. (1999). *A practical guide to usability testing*. Bristol, UK: Intellect Ltd.

Hand, D., Mannila, H., & Smyth, P. (2001). *Principles of data mining*. Cambridge, MA: MIT Press.

Lewis, C., & Rieman, J. (1993). *Task-centered user interface design: A practical introduction*. Boulder, CO. Retrieved March 14, 2008, from http://hcibib.org/tcuid/

Nicolle, C., & Abascal, J. (Eds.). (2001). *Inclusive design guidelines for HCI*. New York: Taylor & Francis.

Norman, K. L., & Panizzi, E. (2006). Levels of automation and user participation in usability testing. *Interacting with Computers, 28*, 246–264.

Salvendy, G. (Ed.). (2006). *Handbook of human factors and ergonomics*. Hoboken, NJ: John Wiley & Sons.

Tan, P., Steinbach, M., & Kumar, V. (2005). *Introduction to data mining*. Boston: Pearson Addison-Wesley.

PART II

Systems

Five

Sensory–Motor Interfaces

Input and Output

Scenario 1

I am flying through a tunnel. I see a passageway on the right. I use my hand controller to turn right and feel the pull of the turn. I have to detect the enemies before they detect me, but I must not fire on my own team. I am beginning to see a ship. Is it a friend or foe? What color is it – red or brown? It's brown. I must hit it. I missed. It is too small and too far away. I feel a buzz on my hand controller. My ship was hit. Where did that come from? I look around. There it is – an enemy behind me. I turn and fire – a flash of light and a booming sound. I got it with a direct hit.

Scenario 2

On this screen, we need to get the user's attention. What do you see? How do you interpret it? Then we need to draw attention to the first thing. We need to provide the user with options to get to the different services on our site. We have a lot of text. It has to be very readable. Should we add icons to help the user find options without having to read a lot of text? How do we show that these items are in a group? Besides putting them close together, why don't we put a border around them? We need to make sure that people don't accidentally click items that are next to each other because they are too close. Can we separate them and make them smaller? But then they are harder to click on.

How can we make sure that users see the warning message when it appears on the screen? Let's just make it bigger and have it appear in red text.

Overview

> Whilst part of what we perceive comes through our senses from the object before us, another part (and it may be the larger part) always comes out of our own mind.
>
> – William James

When input to the computer was the punched card and rows of toggle switches, and the only output was a line printer or a row of flashing lights, there was little to say about how computers affected us in terms of sensory and perceptual phenomena. But today things are quite different! Input to the computer can include all response modes that a human can produce, and all inputs to the senses of the human can be filled with every possible multimedia effect that computers can produce, as in Scenario 1.

We know the world through our senses, and we change it through our actions. Our senses convert energy states that contain information about the world into neural impulses sent to the brain to be interpreted by perceptual processes. Sensation provides the information, and perception strives to make sense of it. In contrast, our actions are the result of intentions converted to motor movements. The motor movements may be typing, speaking, or anything else that we do to transmit internal information to the external world. The sensory–motor interface is our connection to the external world.

As shown in Figure 3.3 in Chapter 3, the human–computer interface inherently involves sensory input and motor output. In this chapter, we explore the sensory–motor interface as it interacts with the computer interface. We first look at the various senses and the act of perception. Then, we look at the effector or motor side of the human and finally talk about the coupling between the two. Scenario 1 illustrates the importance of the sensory–motor interface in video games. Scenario 2 lists some the many questions that designers of Web pages have about the sensation and perception of screens as people browse for information.

The Senses

Although there has always been some debate over how many senses we have, in this section we talk about vision, audition, touch, and proprioception (the sense of bodily position). Smell and taste will be left for readers to explore on their own. Needless to say, the computer interface has primarily used vision as the mode of interaction, with auditory communication in a strong secondary position. Touch and proprioception have only recently become important in virtual reality interfaces.

From the perspective of psychology, we are interested in the process by which an external stimulus makes its way to a conscious experience in the mind. Sensation is the first part of this process. We consider first a distal

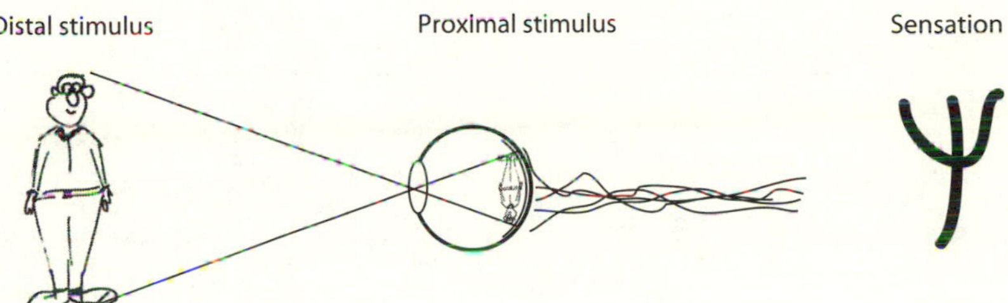

Figure 5.1. A schematic of the stimulus (distal and proximal) and the sensation.

stimulus, perhaps an object, a person, or a computer screen (Fig. 5.1). Information about this stimulus is transmitted via a medium such as light, sound, or even touch. Energy transmitted from the distal stimulus impinges on the sensory organ as a proximal stimulus. At this point, the sensory organ converts the energy into a neural transmission to the brain. Perception is the process by which this information is subsequently encoded, judged, and given meaning.

There are three types of analyses used to study this process. A *phenomenological* analysis focuses on the subjective description of sensory experience usually by way of introspection. For example, "Tell me what you see on the screen?" A *psychophysical* analysis attempts to describe the relationship between the sensory experience and the physical properties of the stimulus. For example, "What is the mathematical relationship between measured light energy and the psychological phenomenon of brightness?" Finally, a *psychophysiological* analysis studies the physiological mechanism by which the stimulus energy is encoded and transmitted by the neural system and that enables us to respond to a particular physical attribute, such as the frequency of sound or the spectrum of light. For example, "What is the neural pathway and code from the sensory organ to the appropriate brain centers?"

For each sense, we are interested in minimum thresholds and detectability of differences between stimuli. We need to look at contrast effects to see how one stimulus affects the perception of another. Finally, we look at perceptual processes that strive to assign coherence, consistency, and meaning to the stimulus array.

Vision

Both the computer screen and the computer printout are visual displays. We know a tremendous amount about vision that can be directly applied to the human–computer interface. The designers of visual display technologies such as cathode ray tubes, liquid crystal displays, and flat panel displays are keenly interested in how these technologies mesh with the human visual system to create an experience and to convey the intended information. As designers use physics and engineering to create the displays, they take into

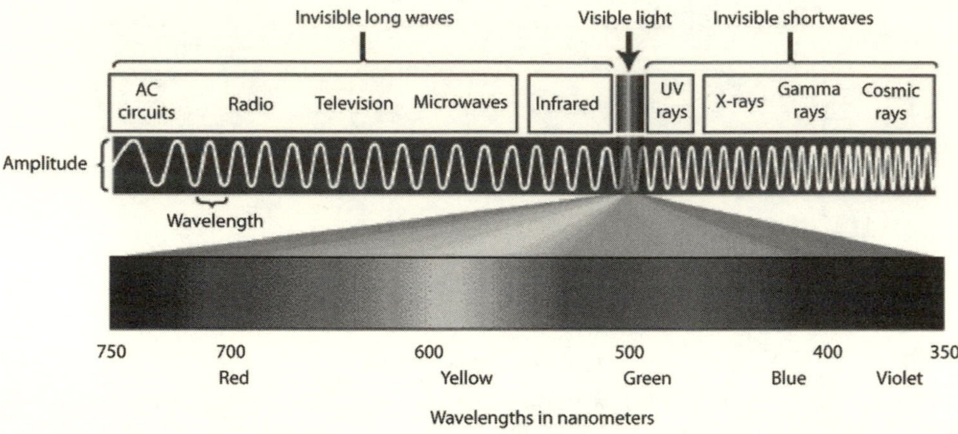

Figure 5.2. The electromagnetic spectrum and the range of visible light.

consideration the characteristics and limits of the human visual system. In this section, we review these characteristics and limits.

First, what is it that we see? Electromagnetic energy is all around us and travels in waves of different lengths. It is created by the vibration of electrically charged particles. Light varies in wavelength and amplitude. Wavelength is the distance between two peaks of adjacent waves. Our eyes can detect wavelengths that range from 400 to 750 nm, a nanometer being one-billionth of a meter. This is the range of visible light. The colors we see are determined by the size of the wavelength (Fig. 5.2). The shorter wavelengths are seen as violet; the intermediate ones as blue, green, and yellow; and the longer ones as red. Other forms of electromagnetic energy outside the 400- to 750-nm range are radio, infrared, ultraviolet, and x-ray radiation. They are invisible to our eyes, but are potentially accessible through technologies that convert these frequencies to the visible spectrum, such as night vision glasses that convert infrared to visible light.

Although electromagnetic waves are described by their frequency and amplitude, light is usually measured using photometry in terms of its energy and consequences. Light is either emitted from a source or reflected from a surface. Radiance is the amount of light emanating from a source and is measured in candela or lumens. A standard 100-W incandescent light bulb emits approximately 1,500 lm. The typical luminance of a flat panel monitor is 250 cd/m^2.

Illuminance is the amount of light falling on a surface, and luminance is the amount of light that is reflected from the surface. Reflectance is the proportion of light that is reflected (i.e., reflectance = [luminance/illuminance] × 100). Brightness is our subjective reaction to the intensity of the light and is measured using psychophysical methods that we look at later in this chapter. Finally, the transmission of light is subject to the laws of optics from diffraction, dispersion, and distortion to reflection, refraction, and resolution.

For the human visual system to sense and interpret information conveyed by light, it first passes through the eye, a complex optical system shown in

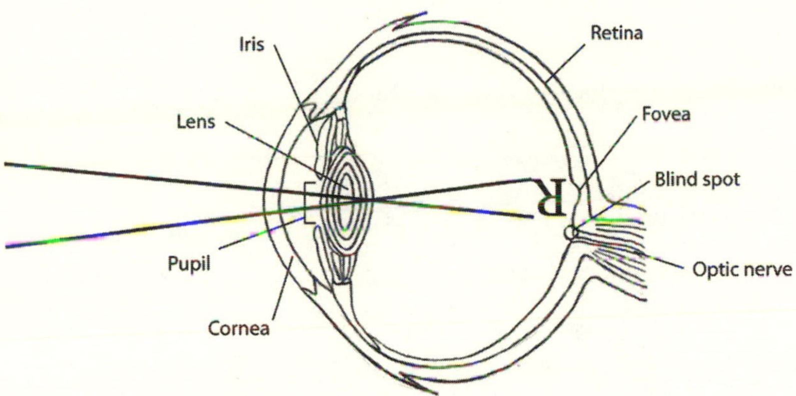

Figure 5.3. A diagram of the main features of the eye.

Figure 5.3. The light passes through both the cornea and the lens. The lens is used to focus the image on the retina in the back of the eyeball. Because only one lens is used, the image is projected upside down on the retina. The size of the image on the retina depends on the visual angle determined by the size of the object and the distance from the observer to the object.

Writers have often used the analogy of a camera for how the eye works. The lens focuses the image on the retina, the iris controls the amount of light entering the eye, and the retina records the image. But the retina is not like photographic film that is developed and processed. It is more similar to, but still very different from, the sensors used in digital cameras (e.g., charge-coupled devices [CCDs]). These devices use an array of coupled capacitors. Each capacitor converts the light energy into an electric charge proportional to the intensity of the light. The CCD records the luminance in each square of the grid, called a "pixel," as shown in Figure 5.4. The resolution of the image depends on the number of pixels in the grid (e.g., 420 × 300). The grid of pixel information is transmitted to store the raw image or a compressed version into memory.

The retina is actually a piece of the brain that migrated to the eye during early fetal development (Gregory, 1998). Below its outer layer of cells resides a layer of two basic kinds of receptor neurons, or photoreceptors, called

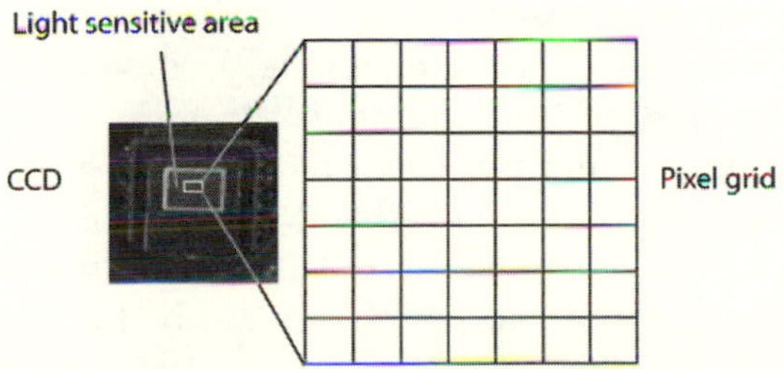

Figure 5.4. A schematic of the charge-coupled device (CCD) used in digital photography showing the light-sensitive area on the chip and the array of pixels represented.

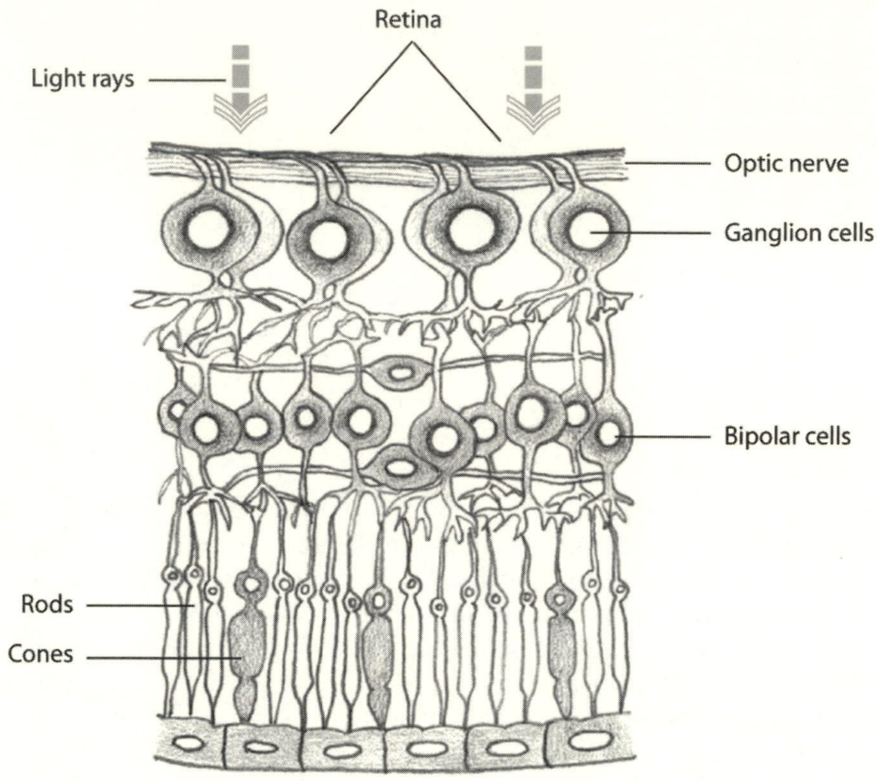

Figure 5.5. A diagram of the retina.

rods and cones (Fig. 5.5). The rods are located at the edges or periphery of the retina and are extremely sensitive to gray light. They are central to the detection of patterns of black, white, and gray. The rods function best under low light conditions and, consequently, are most useful at night. In contrast to the rods, the cones require much more light to be activated and are responsible for color vision. Most cones are concentrated in a small area near the center of the retina known as the fovea or area of central focus shown in Figure 5.3. A human retina contains about 125 million rods and 7 million cones (Pugh, 1988).

When light hits the rods and cones, the cells generate neural signals that activate adjacent bipolar cells, which in turn activate neighboring ganglion cells (Fig. 5.5). The axons of the ganglion cells converge to form the optic nerve, which carries the information from the retina to the brain. Unlike digital sensors that record and transmit every pixel, a great deal of complex information processing occurs in the retina (Slaughter, 1990). This processing occurs in the bipolar and ganglion cells, where information from the rods and cones is integrated and compressed so that it can be more easily transmitted along the optic nerve. Rather than transmitting the raw pixel information, the retina sends some other kind of coded information. The point on the retina where the optic nerve leaves the eye actually has no rods or cones (Fig. 5.3). It is called the "blind spot" because images falling here are not seen (Ramachandran, 1992). We are generally not aware of the blind spot

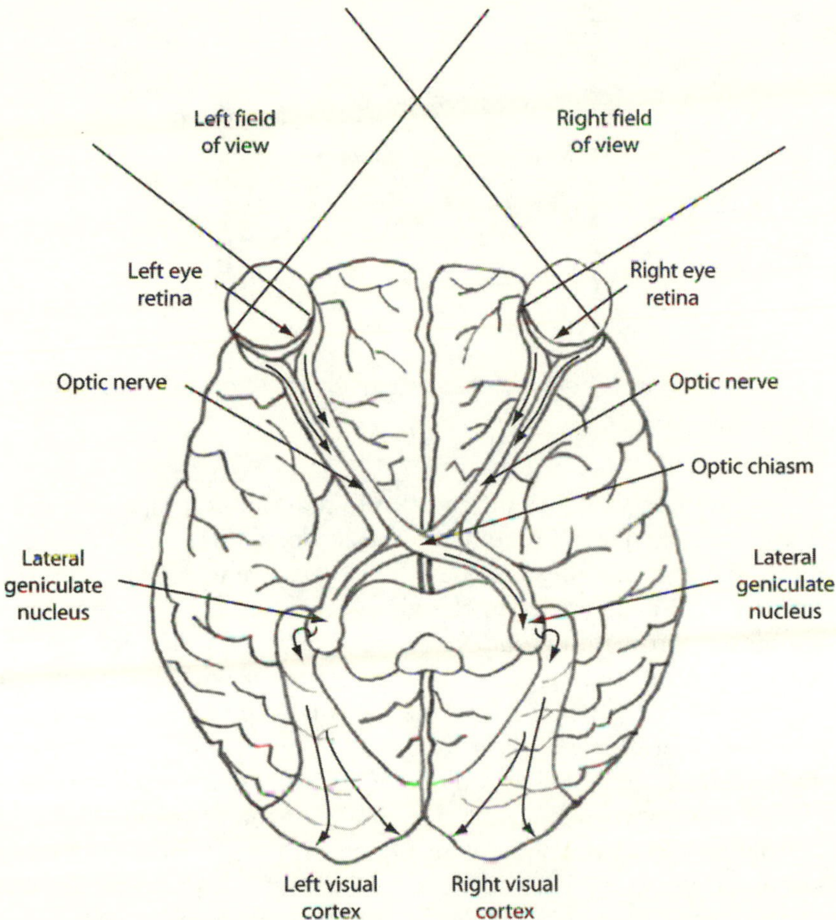

Figure 5.6. Visual crossover in the neural pathways through the brain.

because the perceptual system subconsciously fills it in for us from other information (patterns and colors) around it.

The optic nerve carries the axons of the ganglion cells to the optic chiasm at the bottom of the brain. It is here that an interesting thing occurs, as shown in Figure 5.6. A crossover occurs such that the image in the left visual field of each eye, which impinges on the right side of each retina, is transmitted to the visual cortex in the right hemisphere, and the image in the right visual field of each eye is transmitted to the left hemisphere. Although information from both eyes goes to both hemispheres, the amazing thing is that the scene is split into the left and right fields. It is believed that this lateralization may reduce reaction time to threats coming from the left or right because it reduces the length of the neural pathway to the muscles on the appropriate side for defensive action. Although we typically scan the visual field so that information goes to both hemispheres, in some cases with flashed images or first glances, information may be processed differently, depending on whether it is on the left or right side of fixation.

From the lateral geniculate nucleus, visual information is sent to areas in the occipital lobe that comprise the visual cortex. One might believe that the

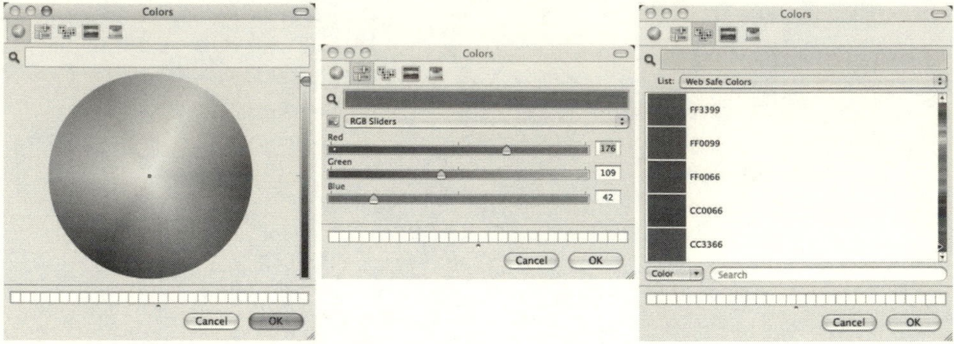

Figure 5.7. Three color selection pallets used in Adobe Photoshop shown in black and white.

image is projected directly into the cortex and that one could project an image on the retina to get a neuron reading on the cortex similar to a digital camera with pixels. To test this idea, in the late 1950s, David Hubel and Tortsen Wiesel placed microelectrodes in the visual area of a cat's brain to record action potentials from individual neurons. To stimulate action potentials, the researchers projected spots of light on a screen with a slide projector, but they were initially unable to get the neurons to fire with any regularity. But as they were inserting a glass slide into the projector, causing the spot to move, a neuron began firing rapidly. What they discovered was that the neural firing was not in response to the image of the spot, but to the image of the straight edge of the slide as it moved on the projector screen. They proposed that cells in the visual cortex respond only to highly specific features of a visual stimulus, such as a straight edge, an angle, or movement of a spot (Hubel & Wiesel, 1965). Instead of pixels, our visual system uses "feature detectors" that sense and record very specific aspects of an image and pass this information to other cells that derive other complex features. The visual information is processed in the complex interaction among different types of visual neurons that detect features and combine the information into a meaningful whole (Hubel, 1996; Rolls & Deco, 2002). Consequently, from the retina to and through the visual cortex, information is in terms of meaning rather than bits of light.

Color Vision

Color is a subjective sensory experience. Color does not exist outside the mind. Although we can talk about mixing wavelengths of light and reflections of light off surfaces absorbing different frequencies, there is nothing inherently red or pink or green or baby blue in the light energy. It is the way in which the nervous system processes the light energy, reacts to it, and labels it as a particular color. Consequently, it is no surprise that color selection by designers and artists is a very human, subjective process. Considerable time and effort is spent selecting colors in computer applications and on the Web. Figure 5.7 shows three types of color selection pallets used in software design.

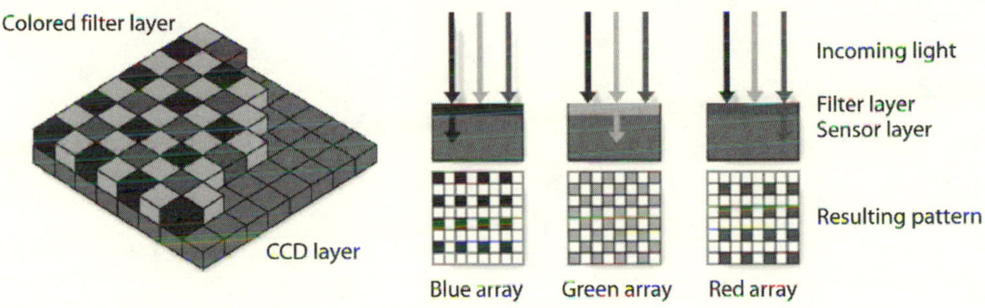

Figure 5.8. Bayer color filter array over the photosensor grid.

To see and discriminate among colors, the photoreceptors in the retina must be sensitive and respond differently to different frequencies of light. To understand how the human system works, we again consider digital cameras. Color in digital imaging is achieved by using red, green, and blue filters over the grid of photosensors, as shown in Figure 5.8. The intensity of each color is measured by the electric charge in the pixels corresponding to each filter.

It is interesting to note that in the Bayer filter shown in Figure 5.8, there are twice as many green elements as red or blue (Bayer, 1976). The inventor Bryce Bayer did this to mimic the human eye's ability in resolving power with green light. Once the raw pixel information is recorded, the problem is that two-thirds of the image information is missing. One has the luminosity of only one of three colors in each pixel. Postprocessing is required to demosaic the image by interpolating a set of complete red, green, and blue values for each point.

The retina has some similarities to color digital imaging, but also many differences. Historically, there have been two competing theories for how color vision works. Trichromatic theory, like the digital camera, is based on the idea that there are three types of cone cells in the retina that are differentially sensitive to blue, green, and red light. Rods are sensitive to frequencies closer to green than to blue. Each type of cone contains a different photosensitive pigment. Figure 5.9 shows the typical sensitivity curves for the four types of cells.

The response of each cone depends on both the wavelength and the intensity of the light that hits it. For the visual system to detect differences in color, there must be an interaction between at least two types of cones. The system must compare the signals in order to determine both the intensity and the color of the light. Notice that the sensitivity curve for the rods and cone M are next to each other and have considerable overlap. This means that there is more information about the intensity of the middle range (green) than the short (blue) or long (red) wavelengths. This is why the Bayer filter has twice as many green filters as blue or red.

The opponent process theory was first proposed in 1872 by Ewald Herring and states that the visual system interprets information from the cones in an antagonistic manner. Empirical evidence for the theory was obtained by Hurvich and Jameson (1957). The theory proposes three opponent processes:

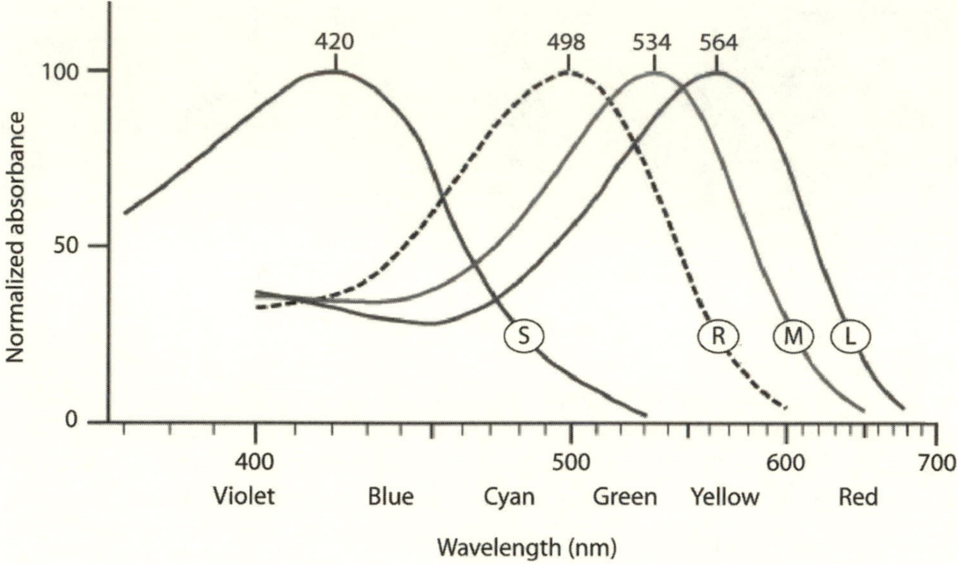

Figure 5.9. Normalized absorption spectra of the human cone (S, M, L) and rod (R) cells.

red versus green, blue versus yellow, and black versus white, as shown in Figure 5.10.

Originally and prior to the confirmation that there were three types of cones, the opponent process theory and the trichromatic theory were at odds with each other. However, today they are seen as complementary (Kandel, Schwartz, & Jessell, 2000). Because the three types of cones overlap in their sensitivity to different wavelengths, the system responds to the differences between the firing of the cones rather than absolute levels. Information from the cones is passed to the ganglion cells, where one group of cells processes differences between the firings of the L and M cones and another processes differences between the S cones and the combined signal from both L and M cones.

The opponent process theory results in a number of effects relevant to HCI. One is color constancy. We see color patches as virtually the same, even under very different lighting conditions. The wavelength reflected from a blue color chip by an indoor light bulb can actually match the wavelength

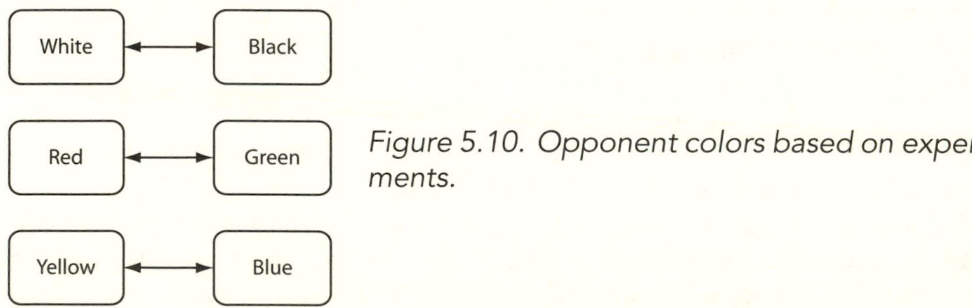

Figure 5.10. Opponent colors based on experiments.

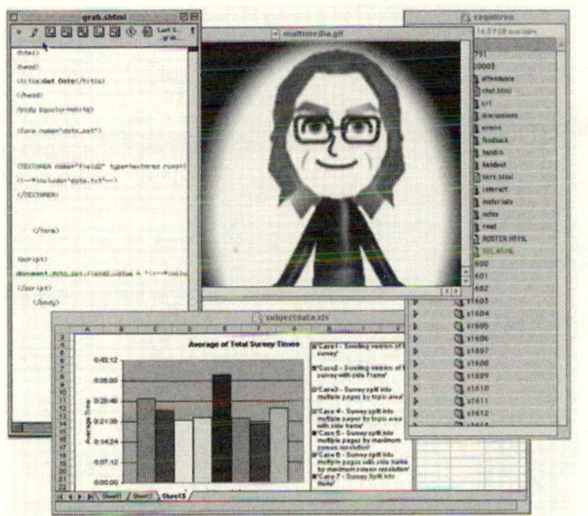

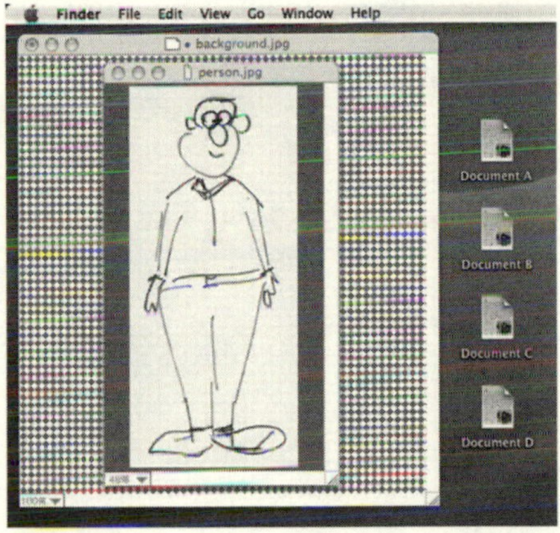

Figure 5.11. Figure-ground issues: an ambiguous situation (left) *and a hierarchy of foreground-backgrounds* (right).

reflected from a yellow color chip in sunlight (Jameson, 1985). Nevertheless, the blue chip still looks blue, and the yellow looks yellow. Color constancy works best when an object is surrounded by objects of many different colors because our visual system perceives color based on computations of the light reflected by an object relative to the light reflected by surrounding objects (Land, 1986; Pokorny, Shevell, & Smith, 1991). Context has long been appreciated and used by artists and designers to create richer experiences by contrast. Designers of Web pages also use context and background to create distinctive images.

Visual Perception

The coded information transmitted to the visual cortex is used to perceive, recognize, and give meaning to images. Visual perception involves recognizing shapes, interpreting depth, sensing motion, and maintaining constancies.

Shapes are detected by edges and contours. Contours are created by a sudden change in the brightness of the image. These are, in turn, organized by principles first discussed by the Gestalt School of Psychology. The first principle is that of the "figure–ground" relationship. We organize figures in the foreground and what is left over in the background. The desktop screen metaphor takes advantage of this principle by having an active window in the foreground with the rest as the background, and icons on the desktop as the foreground and the rest as background. The figure–ground relationship is relative and can be ambiguous in some cases and hierarchical in others. It is ambiguous when the perceptual system can switch foreground and background, as in the left panel of Figure 5.11. It is hierarchical when the perceptual system zooms in to increasingly more detailed levels, as in the right panel of Figure 5.11. The active window is the figure, but then an object

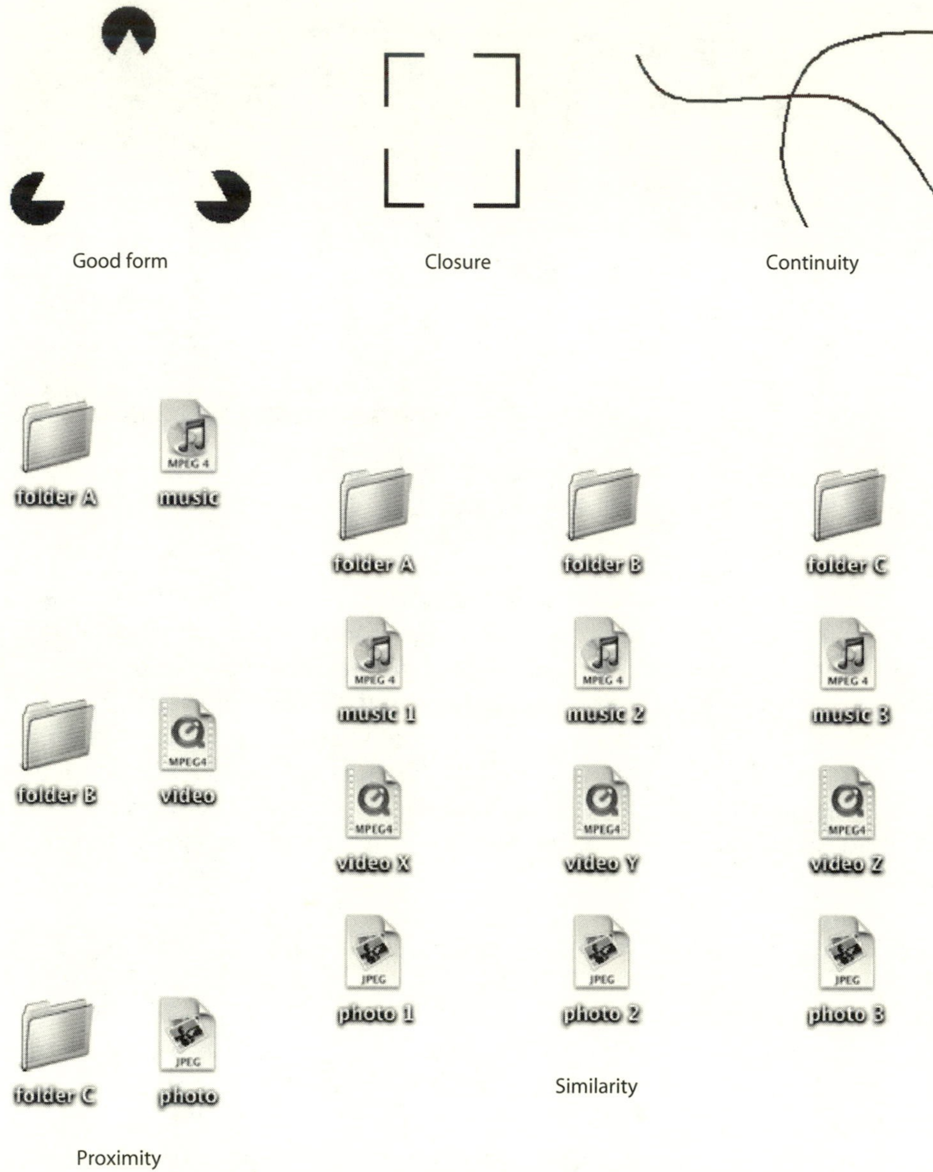

Figure 5.12. Gestalt principles of perception.

in the window can become the figure and so on. Zooming interfaces in which objects expand and contract capitalize on this principle.

Additional Gestalt principles are shown in Figure 5.12. The principle of *good form* or *closure* states that the perceptual system attempts to fill in gaps and strive for simple, whole forms rather than complex images with many parts. The principle of *continuity* has to do with how the system follows edges to generate simple continuous lines and contours rather than jagged, complex ones. The principles of *proximity* and *similarity* help determine

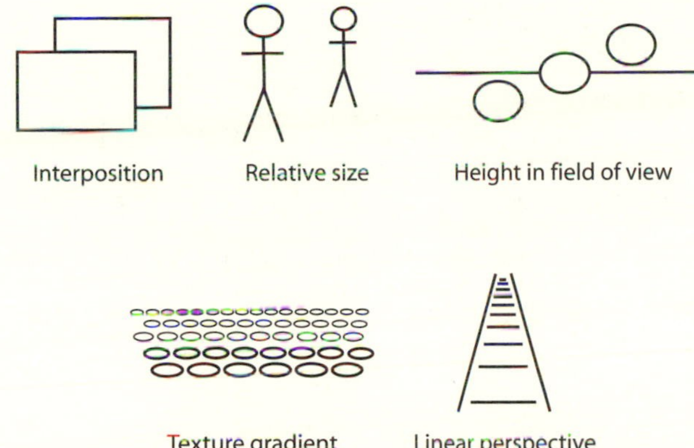

Figure 5.13. Monocular cues used to generate depth perception.

how we cluster and group objects. These principles are extremely important in how we perceive and organize our desktops, create layouts of Web pages, and make sense of cluttered environments, as in Scenario 2 at the beginning of this chapter.

We do not directly sense depth or see in three dimensions. Instead, our perceptional system creates the impression of three-dimensional (3-D) images from the two-dimensional (2-D) images on the retinas, along with a number of cues. Binocular cues come from the comparison of the two images from our left and right eyes. The disparity or difference between the two views is used to mentally calculate the distance to the object. To the extent that they differ, the object is inferred to be closer. This is because the closer it is, the more the eyes must converge to focus on it. The left eye sees around one side, and the right eye sees around the other. Stereoscopic displays generate 3-D effects by projecting different images to the left and right eye either directly or using viewers with different colored lenses or polarized filters. Stereograms are 2-D images that create the illusion of depth by using slight differences in the vertical repetitions of random figures or dots when the viewer focuses his or her eyes a distance beyond the surface. Binocular cues can be computer generated to create powerful experiences in virtual reality, but for most day-to-day applications, 3-D seems to be overkill and can distract and disorient the user.

Monocular cues are available in the image itself when viewed with only one eye. When we view the world with two eyes and then close one momentarily, we take for granted that the image still seems to be 3-D. Figure 5.13 illustrates a few of the monocular cues, and a more complete list follows (Andre & Owens, 2003):

- *Interposition*: One object partly occludes the object behind it.
- *Familiar size*: If we are familiar with absolute size of an object, a comparatively larger size on the retina tells us it is close, and a comparatively smaller size tells us it is farther away.

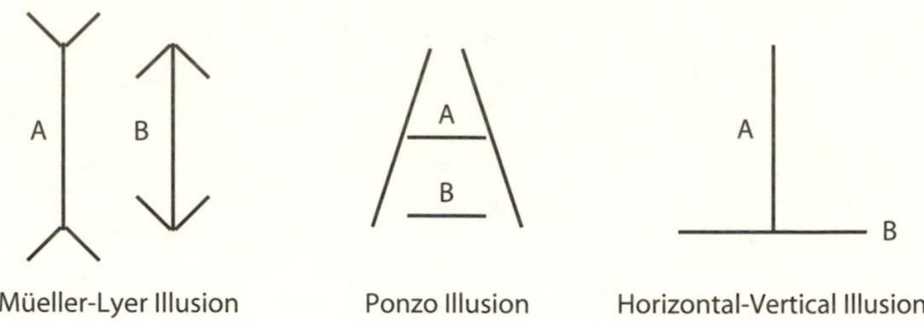

Figure 5.14. Visual illusions of length. In each case, lines A and B are of equal length.

- *Relative size*: If we infer two objects to be the same size but one is larger on the retina than the other, the larger appears to be closer.
- *Height in field of view*: Objects closer to the horizon are perceived as farther away.
- *Texture gradients*: When the texture of an object shifts from coarse and distinct to fine and indistinct, it appears farther away.
- *Aerial perspective*: When objects change from sharp and clear to hazy, they appear farther away.
- *Linear perspective*: When parallel lines, such as the edges of a road, appear to converge, the greater the convergence, the greater the distance.
- *Motion parallax*: When objects are moving at the same rate, closer objects appear to move faster.

These monocular cues are used by artists and animators to create the impression of depth and add richness to 2-D displays.

The perceptual system strives for coherence, meaning, and constancy in the barrage of changing visual information. As we move and look around in changing conditions, the shapes and sizes of objects are continually different. Yet, with all of the inconsistencies that occur, we seem to maintain a consistency in shape and size of objects. According to the principle of *shape constancy*, familiar objects are perceived to have the same shape even though the visual image does not. Doors seen from different angles form irregular trapezoid images on the retina, yet they are perceived as rectangles in our minds. According to the principle of *size constancy*, familiar objects are perceived to have the same size even though their image may vary in size on the retina. Because we know that a person does not change in size from one moment to the next, when we perceive different sized images of the same person and we "see" the person as the correct size. Of course, size constancy does not hold for variable sized objects such as clouds, balloons, and shadows.

The perceptual system can be tricked. Visual illusions are created in images where perceptual principles conflict or work against the reality of the image. Sometimes illusions are useful in generating interesting experiences, and in other cases, they can be used to deceive people. Computer displays can make products look larger than they really are. Figure 5.14 shows a few visual illusions.

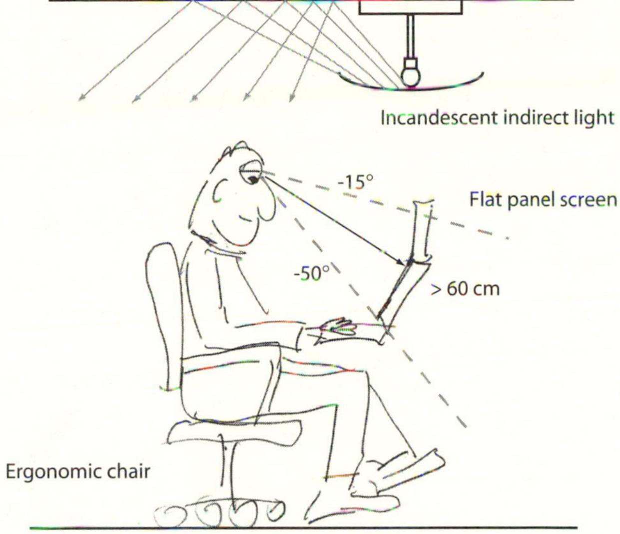

Figure 5.15. Ergonomic guidelines for display placement.

Guidelines for Computer Display Placement and Lighting

Here are some guidelines based on ergonomic studies in the workplace (Fig. 5.15):

- Eye-to-screen distance should be at least 25 in. (60 cm); greater distances relax the eye muscles.
- To reduce neck strain, the vertical location of the display area should be between 15 and 50 degrees below the horizontal eye level.
- The screen should be tilted so that the top is slightly farther away from the eyes than the bottom of the monitor.
- Suspended, indirect lighting reduces glare.
- Dark letters on a light background provide the best contrast for readability.

Audition

Even in the earliest applications of technology, sound has been an important output signal. Whistles, bells, and chimes have been used for alerts and warnings (Mowbry & Gebhard, 1961). In computers, the next board to be added after the video card was the sound card. Sound may be simple, a beep on the computer, or extremely complex, such as music or speech. Sound is generated by things that cause air molecules to be pushed forward in waves. Natural, analog devices generate a vibration using the physical characteristics of the object. Strings of different length are plucked or caused to vibrate with a bow, wind instruments vibrate columns of air of different lengths, and percussion instruments vibrate surfaces of different sizes. The human voice generates a vibration using air passing through the vocal cords in the throat,

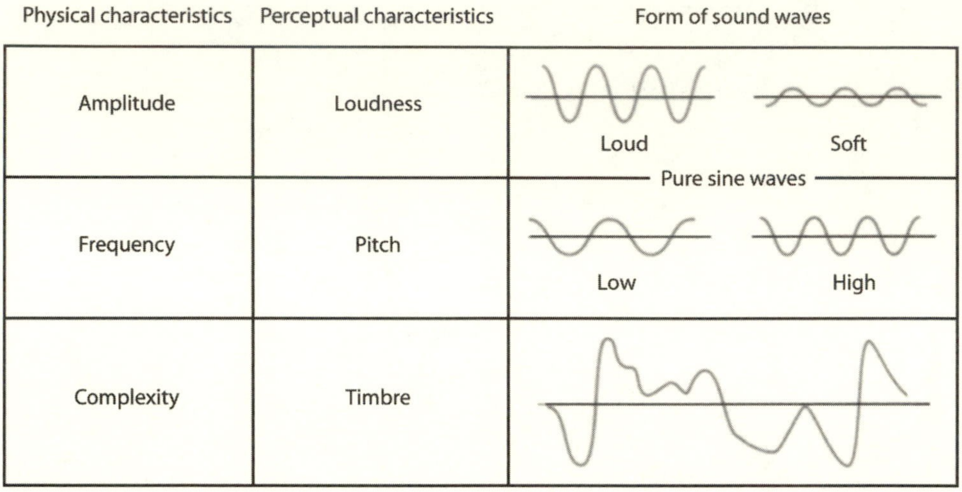

Physical characteristics	Perceptual characteristics	Form of sound waves
Amplitude	Loudness	Loud Soft
		Pure sine waves
Frequency	Pitch	Low High
Complexity	Timbre	

Figure 5.16. Physical differences, sound waves, and their subjective qualities.

varying the air pressure and tension of the cords. In each case, the result is a transmission of sound waves through the air that reaches the ear. Sound waves vary in frequency, amplitude, and complexity.

Frequency is determined by wavelength or the distance between the peaks of high air pressure, as shown in Figure 5.16. Sound waves travel at the speed of 761 mph or 340 m/s. The normal human ear is sensitive to frequencies between 20 Hz and 20 kHz. Subjectively, sound frequency translates into *pitch*.

Amplitude is the amount of air pressure produced by the sound wave at its peak and is measured in decibels. Roughly, 0 dB is the sound of a mosquito flying 3 m away, 50 dB is the noise inside a fairly quiet restaurant, 80 dB is a vacuum cleaner 1 m away, 100 dB is the level inside a disco, and 120 dB is the pain threshold. Subjectively, amplitude translates into *loudness*, which follows a log rather than a linear scale.

Complexity has to do with number, amplitude, and change of frequencies mixed together in one sound. Analog sounds, even a single note, are complex with harmonic frequencies. The subjective property of *timbre* gives a trumpet and a clarinet different sounds.

Artificial, digital devices such as computers use a different technique to produce pretty much the same result, depending on the quality of the recording and the signal processing system. A digital-to-analog converter starts with binary code and ends up with an analog signal. The sound may be computer generated (a beep) or originally recorded and stored in a compressed form (MP3 file) and then decoded. To produce the sound, the digital device uses binary codes to generate voltage levels at uniform intervals. The left side of Figure 5.17 shows this method of pulse-code modulation both to store analog sound in digital form and to produce analog sound from digital code. The quality of the sound increases with the sampling/generating rate and number of bits used to store the amplitude. A CD uses a 16-bit coding at a sampling

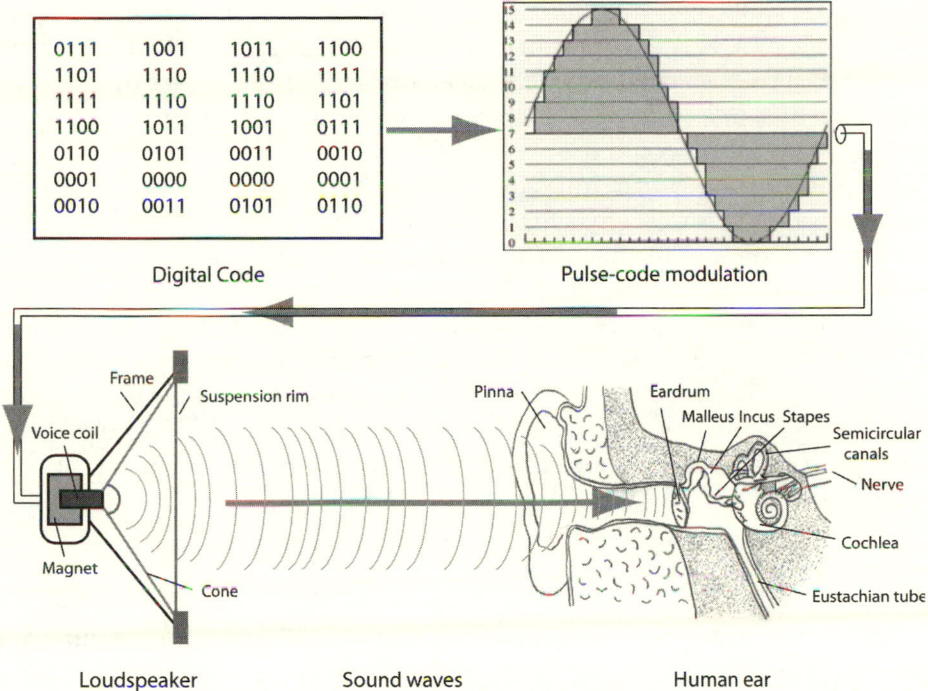

Figure 5.17. Sound is generated from pulse-code modulation and transmitted to the ear.

rate of 44.1 kHz. The electric current produced goes to loudspeakers or earphones, where electromagnets drive a cone or surface to force the air back and forth, creating the sound waves that are transmitted to the ear.

At the ear, the sound waves press on the eardrum and cause it to vibrate, conveying the sound wave onto several bones – the hammer, anvil, and stirrup – and then to the oval window of the cochlea. From there, the sound wave is carried through fluid to the basilar membrane, where it stimulates hair cells connected to the auditory nerve. The question then is how the sound wave is converted to a neural signal (Hartmann, 1997). There are two theories. *Place theory* states that points along the basilar membrane correspond to particular frequencies. According to the microscopic observations of Georg von Békésy (1960), sound causes a traveling wave in the cochlea much like ripples of water on a pond. The sound wave travels the length of the cochlea. High frequencies maximally stimulate particular areas closer to the oval window. Low frequencies stimulate areas further along the membrane. Frequency then is coded by which parts of the auditory nerve are firing. It turns out, however, that although place theory works for high frequencies, there is a problem with low frequencies. Low frequencies displace larger areas along the membrane and cannot be very well located by place. Yet, we have very good discrimination of low frequencies.

To accommodate this problem, *frequency theory* states that sound frequency is coded by how often the auditory nerve fires, that is, by rate.

However, a single neuron has a maximum firing rate of only about 1,000 times per second, hardly sufficient to convey sounds greater than 1 kHz. To account for this, a *volley principle* has been added. This assumes that clusters of nerve cells work in concert to create a volley of impulses at a higher rate than any one neuron could fire.

The transmission of auditory information to the brain's auditory areas is extremely complex. Many synapses occur in the ascending pathway that process the auditory information along the way. Most fibers cross over at the midline between the hemispheres of the cerebral cortex, but some go directly to the hemisphere on the same side as the ear from which they come. Similar to the visual system, features are extracted from the auditory information such as pitch and loudness and what it is, as well as where it is coming from (Feng & Ratnam, 2000; Rubel & Fritzsch, 2002). This condensed, coded information is transmitted to the temporal lobes of the brain for final processing.

Auditory Perception

Like the visual processing system, the auditory system strives for meaning and understanding (Moore, 1989). What is the source of the sound? Is it pleasing or threatening? Are there patterns, and what are they? Is it naturally occurring or synthetic? Some audiophiles claim that they can tell the difference between a live analog performance, an analog recording (e.g., a vinyl record), and a digital CD. But with a high enough bit rate, the human ear cannot distinguish the difference.

What is the content? Is it human speech, and if so, what is the message? Speech recognition is a complex system in and of itself. The system must detect sequences of phonemes and extract other information about the identity of the voice (e.g., male or female, old or young), inflection, etc. We return to this subject in Chapter 8.

Sound localization is achieved by the fact that we have two ears located at different points in space. If the source is to the left, the sound waves reach the left ear before the right and are of a louder intensity in the left ear than in the right because they have to travel farther and can be obstructed by the head. The auditory system uses both *timing* and *intensity* to resolve the location of the source. It is understood that auditory neural pathways are able to compare timings and intensities. Horizontal localization of sound (left /right) is fairly good compared to vertical localization (up/down). Stereo sound systems simulate a horizontal separation of the sounds using left and right speakers or earphones. Surround sound systems add left and right rear channels to add sounds behind the observer, as shown in Figure 5.18. A good system can simulate the effect of a helicopter circling around or a group of people speaking around you. Recent advances in sound processing make it possible to simulate surround sound effects in stereo headphones. This is done by recording sound from tiny microphones placed in the ear canals. These binaural recordings include the timing and intensity information used

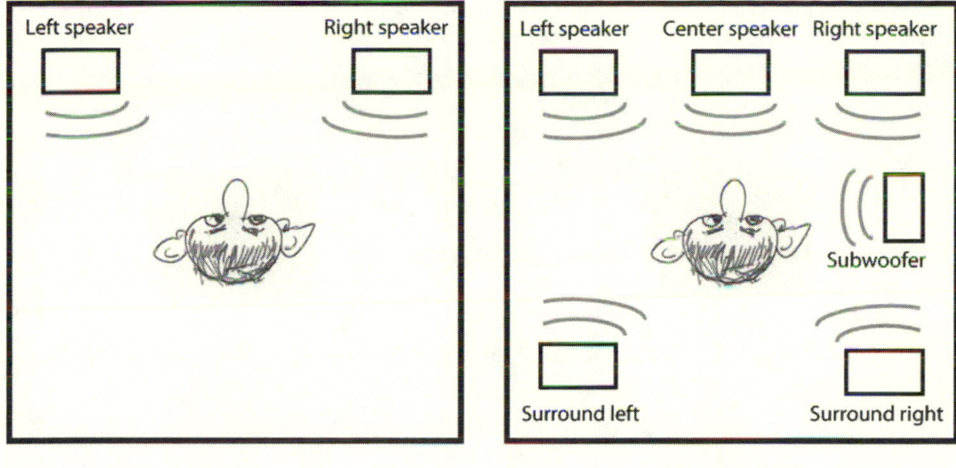

Figure 5.18. Stereo and surround sound systems.

in sound localization. A more complex method is to use a computer to simulate the timing and intensity information given a model of the sound characteristics of a person's head.

Computer output can take advantage of the auditory processing system to convey information about levels, factors, and patterns of output variables (Kramer, 1994). Data can be represented by pitch or loudness, and the type of variable by timbre. Sonification of information can be very useful when the person is visually occupied by driving or flying and can be used by persons with impaired vision, as we see in Chapter 14. Patterns can be represented as chords and anomalies easily detected by discordant sounds (Walker & Kramer, 2004).

Touch

Because we are such visual/auditory individuals, we tend to underestimate the importance of touch. A blind individual that reads Braille understands the importance of touch. Moreover, if you think about it, the entire skin surface is a sensory organ. That makes it the largest and most extensive sensory system of all, going from head to toe. There are three cutaneous sense receptors for touch, temperature, and pain, shown in Figure 5.19.

Touch receptors in the skin send information to the spinal column and up to the thalamus. Most of the fibers from one side of the body cross over to the other side of the brain and go to the somatosensory areas of the cerebral cortex, as discussed in Chapter 2. Sensitivity varies greatly from one area of the skin to another. The hands have much more sensitivity than the feet, and the face has much more sensitivity than the back.

Touch can be passive (to be touched by something) or active (to touch something). When it is passive, our perceptual questions are where and by

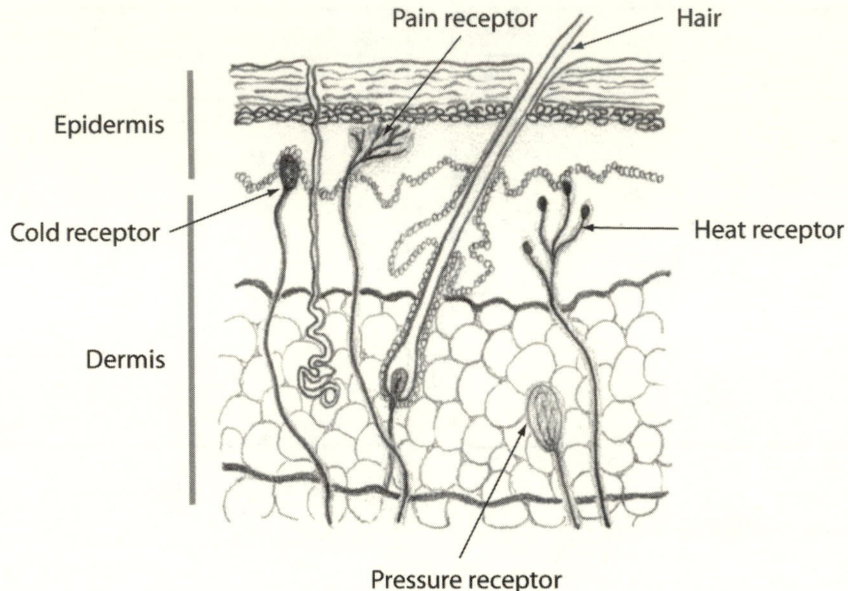

Figure 5.19. Touch, temperature, and pain receptors in the skin.

what were we touched. When it is active, we most often use our fingertips, and our questions have more to do with what we touched. The human–computer interface has primarily focused on the human touching the interface and only recently being touched by the interface. For example, we use touch to sense the keys on the keyboard and to find the hand position keys (F and J) by the small raised bumps on them. We use touch to trace the edges of objects and to detect the feel of different surfaces.

All interfaces that use the fingers make use of touch in some way. For keyboards, the fingers must sense the initial touch and the change in touch during depression of the key to provide feedback that the key was pressed. For all physical buttons, levers, knobs, and dials, the fingers must initially sense contact with the device and the changes of increased or decreased pressure during the movement. The same is true for touch screens. The user must sense that the finger is in contact with the screen, but feedback about the state of the device is generally conveyed through sound and graphics.

When there are many different buttons or levers in a system, the user may need to use touch to identify the particular control handle. One way to do this is to provide a different shape and feel for each control.

Computers and technology, in general, use touch in many ways to interact with us. It is not that machines reach out and poke us, but they can use the tactical sense to give information about input keys and controls. Cell phones set on silent can vibrate to alert us of a call, game controllers use a vibrator to signal a collision, and once in a while our chairs may have vibrators as signals or to enhance the entertainment media. The important information for the sense of touch is localization, intensity, and movement and patterns.

Table 5.1. Examples of Absolute Thresholds

Stimulus	Absolute threshold
Vision	A candle seen at 30 mi on a dark, clear night
Hearing	The tick of a watch at 20 ft under quiet conditions
Taste	One teaspoon of sugar in 2 gal of water
Smell	One drop of perfume diffused into a three-room apartment
Touch	The wing of a fly falling on your cheek from a distance of 0.5 in.

Adapted from Galanter (1962, p. 97).

Kinesthetic and Proprioceptive Senses

The proprioceptive sense gives information about posture, orientation, and movement. Unlike the other senses that pertain to the external world, the proprioceptive sense is about one's own body. The proprioceptive sense consists of 1) the kinesthetic sense, which has receptors in the muscle fibers and joints; 2) the vestibular sense, which gets balance and movement information from the semicircular canals in the ears; and 3) the visual sense, which gets information about the location of the body parts relative to each other and to reference objects in the world (e.g., hand–eye coordination).

Simulators for pilots and those in amusement parks take advantage of proprioceptive and visual cues to create near-real-life experiences of movement through space. Information can be conveyed by the amount of force or resistance to move a lever or turn a dial. Data gloves used in virtual reality can give tactile feedback by placing pressure on the fingertips when the computer simulates touching a wall.

The proprioceptive sense brings us around from input to the human perceptual system back to output. How do we go from intention to action to having an effect on the human–computer interface? We return to this question after we deal with psychophysical issues.

Limits and Sensitivity

How loud or bright does something have to be for us to detect its presence? Every sense and type of stimulus has a *minimum absolute threshold*. If the stimulus is below the threshold, it is not detected. If it is above the threshold, it can be detected. The *absolute threshold* is defined as that amount of stimulus energy that is required for the person to be able to report the presence of the stimulus. In our technology-rich environment today, we have many stimuli that may be near threshold – a clock ticking across the room, the beep of a microwave timer, a flicker on the computer screen, the smell of a burning circuit, or the vibration of a cell phone set to silent. Table 5.1 gives examples of absolute thresholds for the five senses.

Because thresholds are variable and a degree of guessing occurs, there is a range around the threshold from 0 percent detection up to 100 percent, as

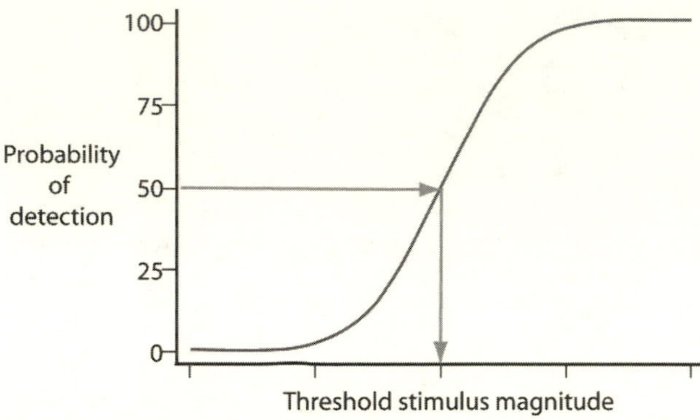

Figure 5.20. Stimulus detection probability curve.

shown in Figure 5.20. In practice, we set the absolute threshold for a stimulus as that point at which the person detects the stimulus 50 percent of the time. However, if someone wants to be very cautious, the threshold is shifted up. If the person does not want to miss anything, the threshold is shifted down. Moreover, if we add "catch" trials in the experiment during which no signal is presented, the observer may actually say that it was presented when it was not.

To account for the problems of bias in detecting minimum thresholds, *signal detection theory* was developed. Imagine a series of trials in which either a signal (technically signal plus noise) is presented or a signal is not presented (technically just noise) and the observer is asked to say "yes" if he or she detects it and "no" if he or she does not. There are four possible outcomes, as shown in the left panel of Figure 5.21. If the signal plus noise

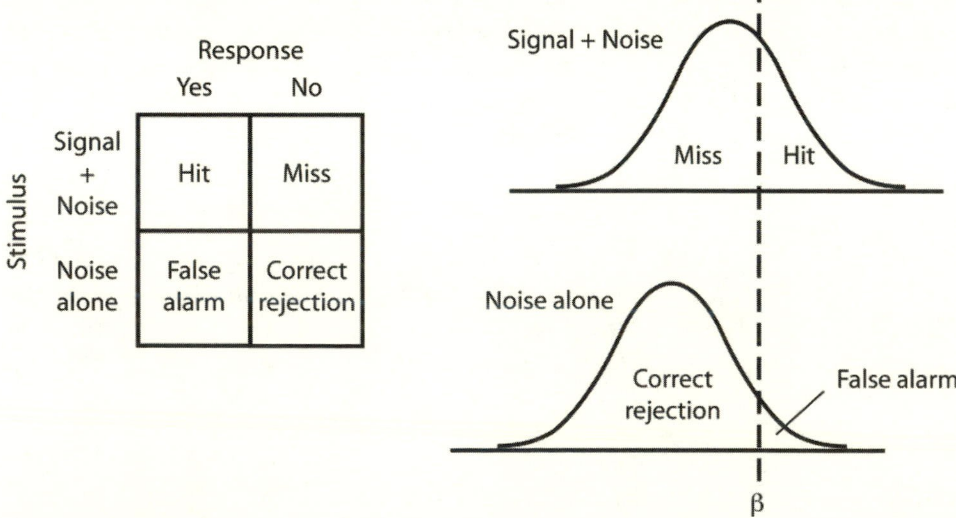

Figure 5.21. Matrix of outcomes in a detection experiment (left) and proportions given the probability distributions of the signal plus noise and the noise alone (right).

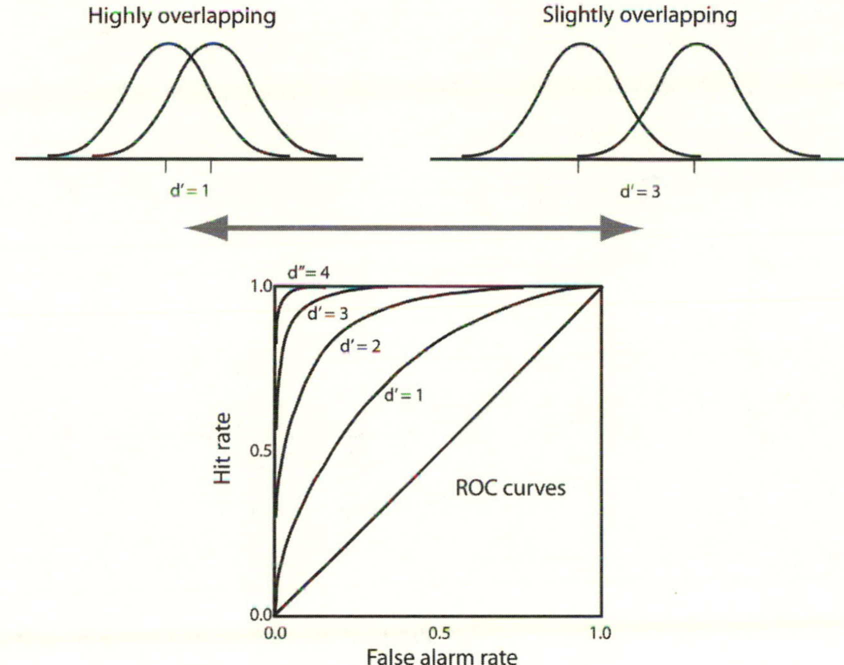

Figure 5.22. ROC curves (bottom).

is presented and the person says "yes," it is a hit or a correct detection. If the signal plus noise is presented and the person says "no," it is a miss. If only the noise is presented and the person says "yes," it is a false alarm. Finally, if only the noise is presented and the person says "no," it is a correct rejection. Correct rejections and hits are the desired outcomes, and misses and false alarms are mistakes. Over a number of trials, we can observe the frequencies in each cell of the table. The sensitivity of the person, the biases, the prior probabilities of the stimulus, and the payoffs of being right or wrong all factor into the frequencies of outcomes in these cells.

Signal detection theory assumes that on every trial the sensory mechanism outputs a value x. The value of x is used to assess the likelihood that the signal was presented or was just noise. The observer sets a criterion, β, according to decision biases. If x is greater than β, the person says "yes." If it is less than β, the person says "no." If we assume that the probability distributions of noise and signal plus noise are normal with equal variance, as shown in the right panel of Figure 5.21, we can match the proportions in the table to areas under the curves and solve for β and a sensitivity parameter, d, the standardized difference of the means of the distributions.

Figure 5.22 shows what happens when the distributions of noise and signal plus noise are close together or far apart. If they are close together (*top left panel*), the observer is not very sensitive and will make a lot of errors relative to hits and correct rejections. If they are farther apart (*top right panel*), the observer is more sensitive and will make fewer errors of either type. The results of many experiments that vary the criterion, β, and the sensitivity, d,

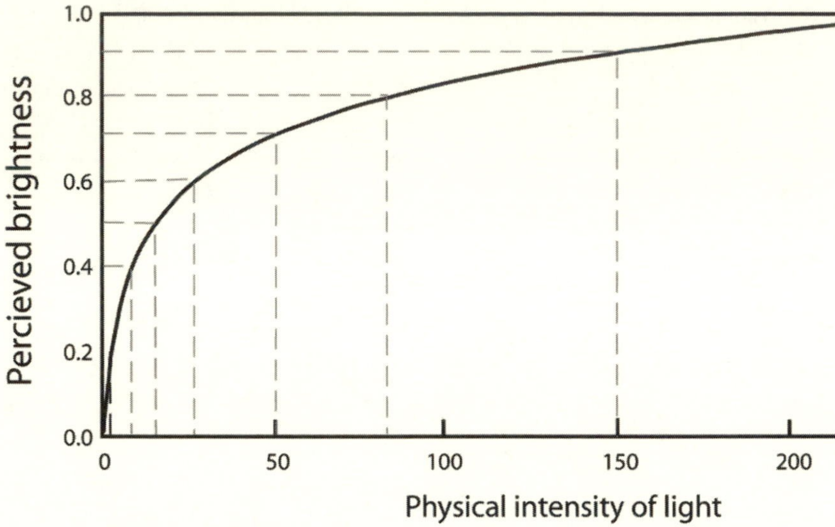

Figure 5.23. Weber-Fechner law.

are summarized in a receiver-operating-characteristic (ROC) curve, shown in the bottom panel of Figure 5.22. This graph plots the proportion of the hits as a function of false alarms. The diagonal straight line represents zero sensitivity, and the points along the line represent different values of β. As sensitivity increases, the ROC curve bows upward increasingly until the signal is so strong that there is no overlap between distributions and almost no errors.

Interestingly, signal detection theory is an optimal, mathematical technique that the human sensory decision system seems to follow. Because it is so good, it is also used by computer programs that have to make decisions in noisy environments.

Signal detection theory also applies to decisions about differences between stimuli. How much must a stimulus change for the observer to be able to detect it? This difference threshold is called the "just noticeable difference" (jnd). In general, the size of the jnd increases with the magnitude of the stimulus according to the Weber-Fechner law shown in Figure 5.23, which relates the physical intensity of the stimulus to its perceived magnitude (e.g., brightness, loudness). Typically, volume controls on stereos, digital mixers, and so on, take this into consideration and, rather than increasing the amplitude of sound linearly, they increase it logarithmically or as a power function.

Psychophysical functions map the relationship between the physical characteristic of the stimulus and its psychological impression (Stevens, 1975).

Motor Movement

Sensation is the input to the human processor. Output from the human originates in the central nervous system as an intention and results in an action in the form of a motor movement. Motor movement takes on various forms in different areas of the body. As we see in Chapter 2, nerve fibers from the parietal lobes send information to the somatic nervous system to control the muscles of the body. We generally think of moving the body, arms, and legs, but motor movement is also conveyed to the vocal track for speech and to the eyes to control where we look. In this chapter, however, we only consider motor movement of the hands and feet. Later, we consider brain waves as well as autonomic responses (e.g., heart rate, galvanic skin response, hormones).

There is a tight coupling between motor movement (output) and the kinesthetic senses (input). It is this proprioceptive feedback that provides for motor control. In this section, we examine a number of important issues having to do with human motor input to interface devices.

Input Devices

Current input devices make use of three different types of fine-motor movements: 1) discrete finger pressing; 2) analog pointing; and 3) analog tracking, gesture, or drawing. Buttons, switches, and keyboards all require discrete movements to close a contact. Only in the case of musical keyboards are we interested in the force or amplitude of the key press. The main thing is to press the right key at the right time and in the right sequence.

The layout of computer keyboards has been the topic of much research and discussion (Noyes, 1983). The standard keyboard layout is the QWERTY keyboard named from the first six letters in the first row of keys. The QWERTY keyboard was established in 1874 by the Sholes & Glidden Company as the best solution for maximizing the speed of typewriters and minimizing jams of type bars striking too close in time. An alternative keyboard was designed purely for human typing speed by August Dvorak in 1930s. The middle row of keys includes the most common letters so as to minimize distance traveled from the home position. In fact, it has been estimated that, in an average 8-hour day, a typist's fingers travel 16 miles on a QWERTY keyboard and only 1 mile on a Dvorak keyboard! In addition, common letter combinations are positioned so that they can be typed quickly. Despite the advantages of the Dvorak keyboard, it has not been able to displace the QWERTY keyboard, and QWERTY has become "the de facto standard layout for communications and computer interface keyboards" (Alden, Daniels, & Kanarick, 1972, p. 282). Figure 5.24 shows the typical layout of the QWERTY (*top*) and Dvorak (*bottom*) keyboards.

In addition to letter placement, there are many other factors in the design of computer keyboards. These include size and separation of keys (generally 1/2 in. square, requiring a 40- to 125-g force, and a displacement of 3–5 mm); ergonomic shape of the keyboard (e.g., curved, split, wrist rests); and additional function keys, key combinations, cursor keys, and numeric keypads.

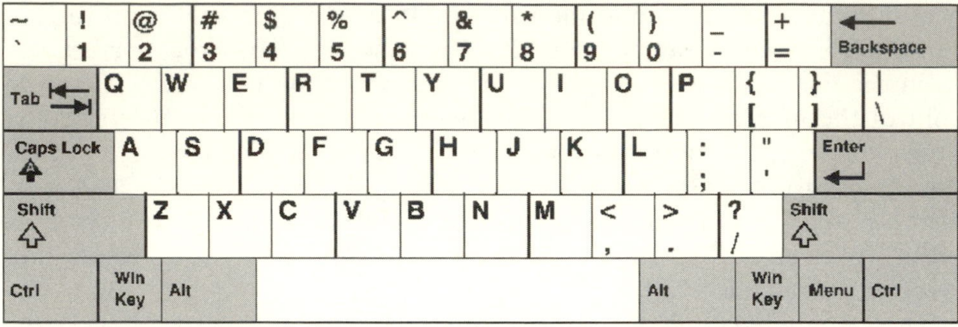

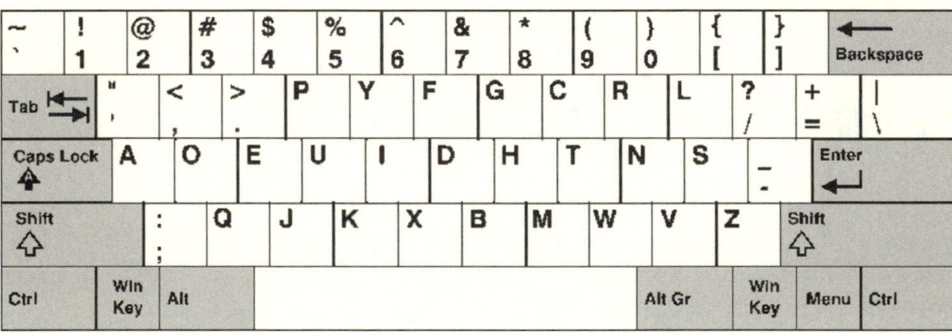

Figure 5.24. Two alternative computer keyboards: United States QWERTY (top) and Dvorak (bottom).

One of the major human errors with keyboards is the "one-off" error when the user inadvertently has the fingers misaligned by one key. This may occur if the fingers are placed one button off the home keys of "asdf" and "jkl". For example, if they are shifted one key to the right, the word "correct" would be typed as "vpttrvy." More serious problems can occur with one-off errors on command key combinations. For example, in the Mac OS X, control-tab switches between applications, and control-q quits the open application. Unfortunately, the tab and q are right next to each other.

Many other keypad layouts have been developed for calculators, remote controls, PDAs, and cell phones. The main human factors issues have to do with how easy they are to learn, how easy and efficient they are to use, and how prone they are to errors. Not only is layout important, but also the size of the keys, the spacing of the keys, and the hand of operation. Figure 5.25 shows alternative layouts of mobile device keypads. The design of such keypads is first informed by ergonomic principles and human factors principles, and then subjected to usability testing as discussed in Chapter 4.

The pointing movement is used to move a reference point from an initial random or default position to a target. A number of interface devices have been developed for this purpose and fall into two classes: indirect and direct control.

Indirect control devices use manual input at one location (e.g., desk surface, keypad) to move a cursor at a different location (e.g., computer screen).

Figure 5.25. Keypad layout of two mobile devices (Symbol MC50 [right], Gem Pad [left]).

They require an indirect coordination and a translation between the motor movement and the result on the screen and have many different design possibilities (Card, Mackinlay, & Robertson, 1991). For example, the mouse is used to translate movement from a horizontal plane to the x-y position of a cursor on the screen. The touch pad is used to translate the finger movement on a pad to a relative movement of the cursor on the screen. The track ball translates movement of a ball to the x-y movement of the cursor. Finally, the joystick or pointing stick translates the left-right and up-down force on a stick to move the cursor on the screen. In each case, the pointing device converts some characteristic of motor movement to the x-y position. Many complicated algorithms have been developed to assist the translation by manipulating gain and acceleration, adding stabilization, and snapping the cursor to fixed grids.

Given the intention to move the cursor, complex motor control is used to set the initial trajectory of the movement, control the speed to the target, perform on-course corrections, decelerate to land on the target, and, finally, evaluate the result and make additional movements to correct for errors. The motor system uses two types of productions.

Very fast ballistic movements require preprogrammed sequences of starting, trajectory, and stopping points. Ballistic movements are not controlled by proprioceptive feedback because they occur faster than the neurons can deliver the control information. In contrast, slow movements are tracked and continually adjusted by feedback.

Direct control devices close the gap of translation, allowing the user to directly point at a location using the fingertip or a pointer such as a light pen

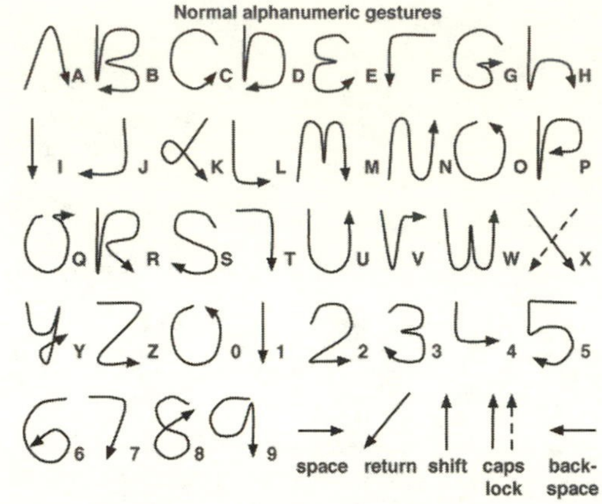

Figure 5.26. Gestures used for text input by Graffiti on the Palm Pilot.

or stylus. Light pens and styluses have the advantage of being similar to our use of pencils and pens for pointing. They have been particularly popular for handheld devices such as PDAs. The disadvantages are that the pen can be misplaced, can obscure the images on the screen, and can be tiring on the hand and arm over long periods of use.

Early touchscreens were very crude and imprecise, giving a clear early advantage to the indirect devices. However, with the availability of high-precision touchscreens, such as the one used by the iPhone, their advantages may outweigh those of indirect devices for many tasks (Sears, Plaisant, & Shneiderman, 1992).

Dragging, tracking, tracing, drawing, and writing require much more fine-motor control than pointing. Dragging is a fairly simple reposition of an object on the screen. Using a mouse, it involves selecting the object (using the mouse to move the cursor to the object and pressing the mouse button down), moving the object (using the mouse to move the object from the current position to the desired position), and releasing the object (letting the mouse button up). Tracking requires the person to constantly move the pointer to stay within a range or at the same point as a moving target. Tracing requires the person to follow a set course without too much deviation. Drawing requires movement of the pointer to correspond to desired parts of an image. Finally, writing requires the generation of the shapes that represent letters and line gestures. Interfaces for handwriting recognition use algorithms to recognize the patterns and convert them to text. Figure 5.26 shows the gestures used for text input for the Palm Pilot using the recognition software Graffiti.

Speed-Accuracy Trade-off and Fitts' Law

Motor movements, whether simple pointing or complex writing, take time and are subject to various types of errors. There are two well-known functions

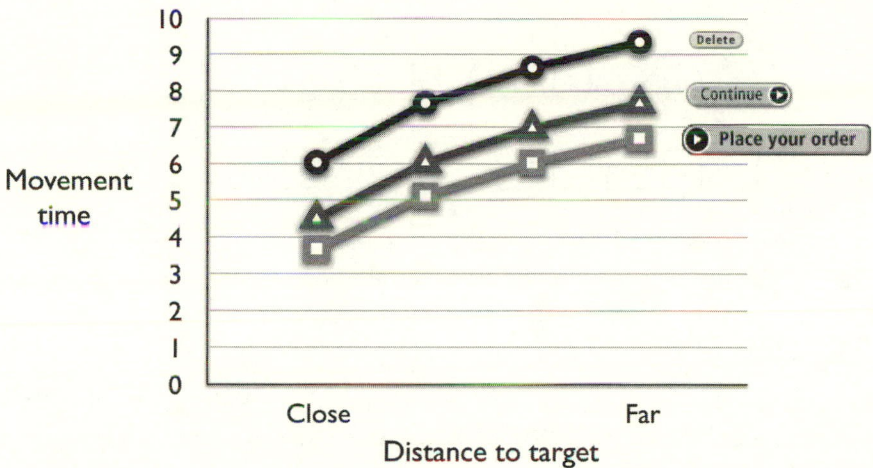

Figure 5.27. An example of Fitts' law predictions of movement time as a function of distance to target for three different size targets from a popular e-commerce site.

that describe the relationships between speed, accuracy, and task difficulty. First, there is a trade-off between the speed of performing a motor task and the accuracy of the result. Although the exact relationship between speed and accuracy depends on the task, clearly the slower you perform a motor task, the more accurate it will be, and the faster you perform it, the worse it will be. Designers of interfaces for HCI strive for motor tasks that will maximize speed and minimize errors. Nevertheless, even for the simplest of tasks, the faster one tries to complete the task, the greater the probability and magnitude of errors.

Second, the harder the task, the longer it takes. In simple pointing tasks, the difficulty is determined by the size of the target and how far you have to move the cursor. The function, known as Fitts' law (Fitts, 1954), has been studied extensively in HCI (MacKenzie, 1995). Fitts' law (Eq. 5.1) is used to predict the movement time (MT) that it takes for a person to point to an object based on the distance (D) to the object and the size (W) of the object.

$$MT = a + b \log_2(D/W + 1) \qquad 5.1$$

An example of the prediction is shown in Figure 5.27 for three different size target buttons used at an online shopping site (www.amazon.com). The equation is based on the logarithmic function of the ratio of D and W. Consequently, the greater D, the greater MT, but it is not a linear function. Longer distances do not lead to proportionally longer movement times, but taper off. Similarly for target size, the greater W, the less MT, but it is not a linear decrease as shown in Figure 5.27.

The implication of Fitts' law is that to reduce the time that it takes to hit targets in an interface (menu items, buttons, etc.), the targets should be reasonably large and arranged to minimize the distances between consecutive

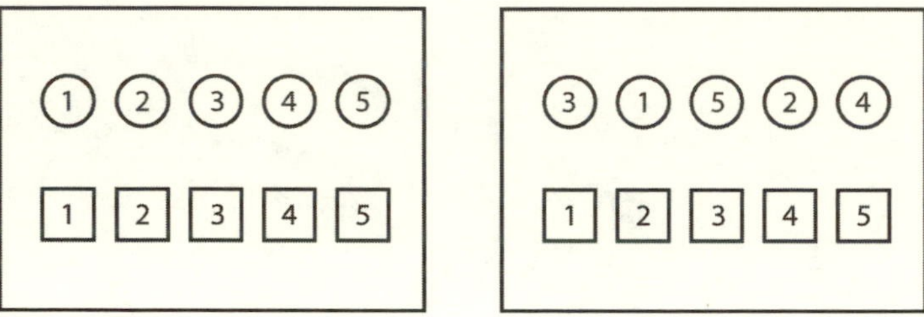

Figure 5.28. Stimulus–response compatible (left) *and incompatible* (right) *layouts of the stimuli and responses.*

options on the screen. Sears (1993) developed a metric to assess the "layout appropriateness" of an interface based on these ideas.

Stimulus–Response Compatibility

When a person has to respond to a stimulus, the speed and accuracy increases with the compatibility or directness of the mapping between the stimulus and the response. In reaction time studies, if there is direct spatial mapping between the light that comes on and the button to be pressed, as in the left panel of Figure 5.28, there is little increase in time as more alternatives are added. However, to the extent that the person has to translate an incompatibility between the stimulus and the response, as in the right panel of Figure 5.28, response time increases.

Similarly, when there is a tight coupling between motor movement and the resulting effect, it is important that the stimulus and the feedback are compatible. When you move the mouse to the left, the cursor moves to the left. When you move the mouse down, the cursor moves down. The same should be true with discrete responses. When you press the "A" key, you see an "A" appear on the screen. The stimulus, the response, and the feedback are compatible.

To the extent that incompatibilities are built into the interface, performance will be degraded and errors will occur (Proctor & Kim-Phuong, 2006). There are many opportunities for incompatibilities to enter into the human–computer interface, owing to the fact that there are so many mappings between the visual, verbal, and auditory stimuli and the appropriate keyboard, mouse, or other response input. When telephone keypads are used for typing text, a partial incompatibility occurs with key mappings. To type "C," one has to press the "ABC" key three times.

Many incompatibilities are physical in nature (directional, number), but they can also be semantic. One example is the classic Stroop task in which a person is to say the color of the ink of the words: blue (printed in red), yellow (printed in green), red (printed in blue), green (printed in blue), yellow (printed in red), and green (printed in yellow). The semantic meaning of the words is incompatible with the verbal response and consequently slows performance and increases errors.

End Thoughts

Basic research in the psychology of sensation, perception, and motor movement has fed directly into the guidelines and principles for design of the human–computer interface. Interface designers have studied or should study these closely to avoid future problems.

More recently, knowledge transfer has reversed and psychology is benefiting from the results of studies at the human–computer interface. For example, we have learned about the perception and recognition of icons, refined Fitts' law to deal with edges and areas, and learned a lot about motor movements for gesture input. More basic research is being done collaboratively in the areas of sensation, perception, and motor movement, and at the human–computer interface.

Developers of human–computer interfaces are not only trying to build the most effective and efficient interfaces for traditional computer systems (i.e., screens, speakers, keyboards, mice), but also to expand the range and modality of the interface. Visually, these include vast wall and surround displays, holographic displays, and virtual reality displays. Although we did not discuss smell, interfaces are being designed that emit fragrances. For input, interfaces are including data gloves, data suits, and video camera input for movement and gesture. But interfaces that are even more exotic are in the works. They may receive and process brain waves, or they may be invasive, with electrodes implanted in the nervous system to totally bypass the sensory and motor systems. We talk more about these in Chapter 16.

Suggested Exercises

1. Run a test of Fitts' law using an online experiment site.
2. Visit several Web sites and explore the principles of sensation and perception.
3. Participate in an online study dealing with sensation and perception.
4. Take a screen capture of a typical busy screen with a number of applications open. Analyze the components of the screen in terms of Gestalt principles: figure–ground, similarity, proximity, and good form.
5. Try an experiment in stimulus–response incompatibility. Try using a mouse upside down for a day.

References

Alden, D. R., Daniels, R. W., & Kanarick, A. F. (1972). Keyboard design and operation: A review of the major issues. *Human Factors, 14*, 275–293.

Andre, J., & Owens, D. A. (Eds.). (2003). *Visual perception: The influence of H. W. Leibowitz. Decade of behavior*. Washington, DC: American Psychological Association.

Bayer, B. E. (1976). U.S. Patent No. 3971065. Washington, DC: U.S. Patent and Trademark Office.

Card, S. K., Mackinlay, J. D., & Robertson, G. G. (1991). A morphological analysis of the design space of input devices. *ACM Transactions on Information Systems*, 9(2), 99–122.

Feng, A. S., & Ratnam, R. (2000). Neural basis of hearing in real-world situations. *Annual Review of Psychology*, *51*, 699–725.

Fitts, P. M. (1954). The information capacity of the human motor system in controlling the amplitude of movement. *Journal of Experimental Psychology*, *47*, 381–391.

Galanter, E. (1962). Contemporary psychophysics. In R. Brown, E. Galanter, E. H. Hess, and G. Mandler (Eds.), *New directions in psychology* (pp. 87–156), New York: Holt, Rinehart & Winston.

Gregory, R. T. (1998). *Eye and brain: The psychology of seeing* (5th ed.). Princeton, NJ: Princeton University Press.

Hartmann, W. M. (1997). *Sounds, signals, and sensation: Modern acoustics and signal processing*. New York: Springer-Verlag.

Hubel, D. H. (1996). A big step along the visual pathway. *Nature*, *380*, 197–198.

Hubel, D. H., & Wiesel, T. N. (1965). Receptor fields and functional architecture in two non-striate visual areas (18 and 19) of the cat. *Journal of Neurophysiology*, *28*, 229–289.

Hurvich, L. M., & Jameson, D. (1957). An opponent-process theory of color vision. *Psychological Review*, *64*, 384–404.

Jameson, D. (1985). Opponent-colors theory in light of physiological findings. In D. Ottoson & S. Zeki (Eds.), *Central and peripheral mechanisms of color vision* (pp. 8–102). New York: Macmillan.

Kandel, E. R., Schwartz, J. H., & Jessell, T. M. (2000). *Principles of neural science* (4th ed.). New York: McGraw-Hill.

Kramer, G. (Ed.). (1994). *Auditory display: Sonification, audification, and auditory interfaces*. Reading, MA: Addison-Wesley.

Land, E. H. (1986). Recent advances in retinex theory. *Vision Research*, *26*, 7–21.

MacKenzie, I. S. (1995). Movement time prediction in human–computer interfaces. In R. M. Baecker, W. A. S. Buxton, J. Grudin, & S. Greenberg (Eds.), *Readings in human–computer interaction* (2nd ed., pp. 483–493). Los Altos, CA: Morgan Kaufmann.

Moore, B. C. J. (1989). *An introduction to the psychology of hearing*. London: Academic Press.

Mowbry, G. H., & Gebhard, J. W. (1961). Man's senses as informational channels. In H. W. Sinaiko (Ed.), *Human factors in the design and use of control systems* (pp. 115–149). New York: Dover.

Noyes, J. (1983). QWERTY keyboard: A review. *International Journal of Man-Machine Studies*, *18*, 265–281.

Pokorny, J., Shevell, S. K., & Smith, V. C. (1991). Colour appearance and colour constancy. In P. Gouras (Ed.), *The perception of colour: Vol. 6. Vision and visual dysfunction* (pp. 43–61). London: Macmillan.

Proctor, R. W., & Kim-Phuong, L. V. (2006). *Stimulus-response compatibility principles: Data, theory, and application*. Boca Raton, FL: CRC Press.

Pugh, E. N., Jr. (1988). Vision: Physics and retinal physiology. In R. C. Atkinson, R. J. Herrnstein, G. Lindzey, & R. D. Luce (Eds.), *Steven's handbook of experimental psychology (Vol. 1)* (2nd ed, pp. 75–163). New York: Wiley.

Ramachandran, V. S. (1992). Blind spots. *Scientific American*, 266(5), 86–91.

Rolls, A., & Deco, G. (2002). *Computational neuroscience of vision*. London: Oxford University Press.

Rubel, E. W., & Fritzsch, B. (2002). Auditory system development: Primary auditory neurons and their targets. *Annual Review of Neuroscience*, 25, 103–126.

Sears, A. (1993). Layout appropriateness: A metric for evaluating user interface widget layout. *IEEE Transactions of Software Engineering*, 19, 707–719.

Sears, A., Plaisant, C., & Shneiderman, B. (1992). A new era for touchscreen applications: High-precision, dragging, and direct manipulation metaphors. In R. H. Hartson & D. Hix (Eds.), *Advances in human–computer interaction* (Vol. 3, pp. 1–33). Norwood, NJ: Ablex.

Slaughter, M. (1990). The vertebrate retina. In K. N. Leibovic (Ed.), *Science of vision*. New York: Springer-Verlag.

Stevens, S. S. (1975). *Psychophysics: Introduction to its perceptual, neural, and social prospects*. New York: Wiley.

von Békésy, G. (1960). Vibratory patterns of the basilar membrane. In E. G. Wever (Ed.), *Experiments in hearing* (pp. 404–429). New York: McGraw-Hill.

Walker, B. N., & Kramer, G. (2004). Ecological psychoacoustics and auditory displays: Hearing, grouping, and meaning making. In J. Neuhoff (Ed.), *Ecological psychoacoustics* (pp. 150–175). New York: Academic Press.

Six

Learning and Memory, Transfer and Interference

Scenario 1

Mary loves to do everything online, such as shopping, e-mail, and banking. She figures that she has about thirty different usernames and passwords for her various accounts and memberships. If she had her druthers, she would use the same username and password for all of them, but she knows that that is a bad idea for security reasons. Furthermore, some systems automatically assign her a username and/or password that cannot be changed, and for others, her desired username was already taken or her password did not meet the security requirements. So, she is stuck with thirty usernames and passwords. She tried in vain to memorize them. In fact, she made up a table that includes the system name or Web site, the username, and the password so that she could quiz herself. The harder she tried, the worse it got. She finally gave up and decided to put them all on her PDA and lock the file with one password.

Scenario 2

John is a retired computer programmer. He started programming in the late 1960s using the language FORTRAN. He took courses to learn the language and studied the manuals and documentation. He knew the syntax of the language perfectly. He had memorized the names of all of the functions he might use. He knew the structure of the language and had even memorized many of the algorithms he used for sorting, accessing, and processing information. He worked for 25 years programming applications for his company. Then his boss announced that they were switching to a new language, C^{++}*. He started taking courses in* C^{++} *but was having a terrible time. The younger students* *who had little or no programming experience were doing better than he was. John decided to take early retirement.*

Overview

This chapter deals with learning and memory issues on the part of the human and the computer. What must the human learn and remember about the computer (e.g., commands, procedures, passwords)? What does the computer learn and remember about the human and the environment (e.g., preferences, logs, knowledge)? How can the human use the computer to retrieve information? How does the computer get help from the user to retrieve information? When it comes to information storage and retrieval, a synergistic relationship is required between the human and the computer.

We see that for both humans and computers, memory requires three processes: encoding, storage, and retrieval. The information must first be represented in an appropriate manner; that is, it must be processed into an appropriate code. Second, it must be stored in some format and media in a memory location. Finally, it must be retrieved using some cue or address and decoded to an output form. Beyond this, as noted in Chapter 2, the differences between human memory and computer memory are immense. Moreover, there are a number of factors that make learning and memory difficult for humans. Scenario 1 illustrates one of many human memory problems caused by computer technology and a possible solution. Scenario 2 illustrates the problem of relearning and negative transfer due to changes in software and technology over time.

Learning about Computers and the Human–Computer Interface

What one learns about computers and the human–computer interface comes from both formal and informal learning. You may have taken courses about computers, information technology, and various applications. You may have read books and manuals and gone through tutorials on word processors, spreadsheets, and OSs. You may have explored computers and programs on your own. You may have had many hours of experience working with computers, programs, and browsing the Web. You may even be learning more by reading this book.

Much of what you know about computers is "head knowledge," but you have also learned a lot of mousing and keyboarding skills; attitudes, preferences, and feelings about computers; and expectations, associations, and intuitions about using computers. We make a distinction among various types of knowledge. Declarative knowledge is about facts, events, and objects. Memories are either explicit or implicit. *Explicit memories* are those that we can consciously recollect (e.g., your password, the name of your program, the menu item to resize an object, how much storage you have on your hard drive). *Implicit memories* affect our thoughts without conscious recollection. Implicit memories may be about feelings. One may have anxieties about computers from early traumatic experiences (e.g., being yelled at as a child for accidentally erasing an important file). Implicit memories also include many things that are familiar to you but that you cannot explicitly recall. For example, it is very unlikely that you can recall the pull-down menu items in a word processor or an OS that you use all of the time. It is unlikely that you can list the letters in order on the keyboard, even though you are a fast touch typist. Finally, implicit memories influence what we think. Thinking about sports can implicitly affect or prime subsequent thoughts and behaviors.

Declarative knowledge in memory is composed of general or *semantic memory* about things independent of time and place (e.g., "#FFFFFF" is the code for white, "EXIT" is used to quit a program, binary code is composed of 1s and 0s) and *episodic memory* about factual information that is acquired at a specific time and place (e.g., my hard disk crashed last week, my new computer was delivered to my home on Tuesday).

Finally, *procedural memory* contains information about how to perform skilled motor activities, such as driving a car, typing, and drawing a cartoon. Procedural memory includes not only the sequencing of actions, but also the fine-tuning of motor movements. Today, computers with GUIs require a considerable amount of procedural memory to perform most tasks. If you want to watch a video on your screen, you need to know the sequence of steps to open the video player, select the clip, control the functions, and adjust parameters such as the volume. The same is true for most electronic technology from video games to MP3 players and from digital cameras to cell phones. One needs to learn the sequence of both discrete steps and continuous adjustments.

Verbal Learning and Memory

There are many forms of human learning and memory, and as seen in the previous section, the human–computer interface impacts them all. In general, learning is the acquisition of knowledge. Knowledge may be as simple as an association between two stimuli, such as a bell and food in the classical conditioning paradigm studied by Pavlov (1927), or between an action and a response, such as a key press and the delivery of a gum ball studied by Skinner (1953), or it may be as complex as learning a language or learning to play a violin. Unlike animal learning, human learning and memory are often verbal.

Human memory was first studied systematically by Herman Ebbinghaus (1850–1909). He wanted to study the rate of acquisition of different types of verbal memory and the process of forgetting. He realized, however, that in using common words (e.g., dog, house, tree), there were already many associations among the words that could obscure the effects he wanted to study. His solution was to use nonsense words (e.g., VUTAW, ZOREX, MINIW), syllables, and letter combinations, such as "trigrams" (e.g., XOR, VIH, BEV), that provided little or no meaning to the subjects.

Table 6.1. Paired Associate Problem of Usernames and Passwords

System/Web site	Username	Password
Home computer	mike	secret
Office computer	mike	2203LIB
Office network	msmith	2203LIB
Hotmail.com	Msmith45	Mail4me
Amazon.com	msmith@hotmail.com	Books4me
USA.com	msmith45	B34h456
WashingtonPost.com	msmith1965	Paper2day
Cappela.edu	Msmith1965@gmail.com	3546574
Firstusa.com	Msmith34	D7GH8J45
Wikipedia.com	Msmith1965@gmail.com	Mork34
eBay.com	Msmith1965	Mork34
Wordpress.com	Mike1965	myblog
Cingular.com	Mikesmith36	222656
Networksolutions.com	msmith	Mork34

It is important to realize that no learning occurs in the absence of prior knowledge, even at birth. When we learn something new, there is already some prior learning that has taken place. Others have tried to control the amount of prior knowledge by using items that were matched on familiarity or frequency of use in the language. The same problem exists in learning things at the human–computer interface. Terms such as "file," "tools," "style," and "repaginate" have different levels of familiarity and meaningfulness to the user.

Ebbinghaus developed a number of paradigms for studying memory, which are still in use today and which characterize the types of learning embedded in many aspects of the human–computer interface.

Paired Associate Learning

In a paired associate learning task, you must learn associations between pairs of words. Given Word A (stimulus), you must learn to say Word B (response). We might have sixteen pairs of words that we present in a random order on each trial. On the first trial, we present the first word in the pair and then the two words together. On the second trial, we present the first word in the pair, the subject has to say the second word before the time is up (say, 3 s), and then the pair is shown together. Over a number of trials, the subject will learn to recall all response words.

Paired associate learning occurs in many situations, such as when learning vocabulary in a foreign language (e.g., "window"–"Fenster"), when associating events and dates (e.g., Balfour Declaration–1917), and when associating works of art and artists (e.g., Mona Lisa–Leonardo da Vinci). In HCI, there are also many cases of paired associate learning. Table 6.1 shows the problem of learning usernames and passwords for different systems and Web sites. Additional paired associate learning occurs when associating functions and

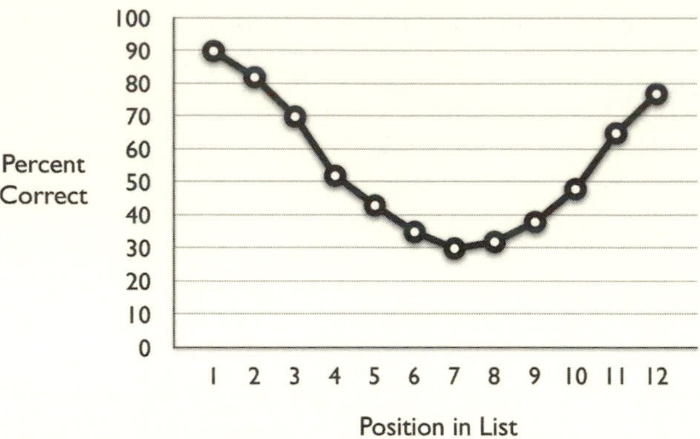

Figure 6.1. The serial position effect.

their names (e.g., find the square root of X–Math.sqrt(X)) and menu options and their shortcuts (e.g., paste–Ctrl-V).

Research on learning paired associate lists has shown that unfamiliar words are harder to learn than familiar words. Longer lists are harder than shorter lists. It takes more trials to learn the list with short study time intervals than with long study intervals. If the stimulus words are used as responses for other stimulus words or the response for one stimulus is also the response for another stimulus, confusion can occur, and it will be harder to learn the list. These findings have direct implications on HCI. It is easy to see why some systems are very hard to learn.

Serial List Learning

In a serial list learning task, you are to learn a list of words in order. On the first learning trial, you see each word one at a time for a fixed time interval. On the second trial, you are shown a prompt; then you are to say the first word on the list; after the time is up, you are shown the first word; then you are to say the second word before the time is up, and so on to the end of the list. Serial lists occur in many contexts – learning the colors in the rainbow, the months in a year, and the digits in a phone number.

In HCI, serial lists are embedded in procedures and in sequences of menu selections to perform tasks (e.g., to send an e-mail: OPEN mail, select FILE, select NEW MESSAGE, enter address, subject, and body of e-mail, select SEND).

A curious thing that Ebbinghaus discovered with serial lists is that the probability of recalling the item depends on its position in the list. As shown in Figure 6.1, there is a higher probability of recalling early items (*primacy effect*) and of recalling the last items (*recency effect*). Items in the middle are subject to more interference and confusion. Moreover, the longer the list, the worse it is, particularly for the items in the middle. Consequently, computer procedures that involve many steps are hard to learn, and the greatest problems in recall will be in the middle of the procedures.

Free Recall

In a free recall learning task, you are shown a list of words during a study time and then asked to recall them in any order during the test period. There may be repeated study and test trials. It is typically found that the more familiar the words, the easier they are to recall, and the longer the list, the harder it is to recall all of the words. However, the more associations there are among the words, the easier it is to recall the words. It is also found that the words are not always recalled in the order in which they are presented or in a random order but rather clustered according to meaningful groups and associations. Yet, it is often the case that the last words in the list are recalled first.

Free recall situations are frequent in human–computer interfaces. We are required to know lists of commands, options, categories, files, Web sites, etc. See how many top-level URL domain names (e.g., .com) you can recall other than the country names (e.g., .us, .cn). Fortunately, for many lists we do not have to recall the items but rather recognize the one we want.

Recognition Tasks

There are several types of recognition tasks. In the *old–new* task, you are shown a series of words or pictures. For each item, you are asked to indicate whether the word or image appeared previously on the list. Because this is a "yes–no" detection task, it is analogous to the signal detection task that is discussed in Chapter 5 and can be analyzed in the same way. Recognition is easy if the items are unique and distinct, but if similar, confusable items are used, it can be very difficult.

The second type of recognition task is the *correct–incorrect* task. Instead of recalling the word in a paired associate task, you are shown a word and asked whether it is the correct or incorrect associate to the word. This is like a typical "true–false" question on an exam. Finally, the *forced-choice* recognition task presents the stimulus word with a list of possible associates from which you are to pick. This is like a typical "multiple-choice" item on an exam. Again, recognition is difficult to the extent that items are similar and confusable.

These types of recognition tasks are prevalent in GUIs. The advantage is that they do not require the recall of commands, but rather the selection of menu options. Recognition of the correct option often depends on its distinctiveness from other options in the set (Schwartz & Norman, 1986).

Learning Curves

Acquisition of information by humans is not as immediate and complete as it usually is with computers. Instead, it generally requires time and repeated exposures to the information. Ebbinghaus found that with repetitions of

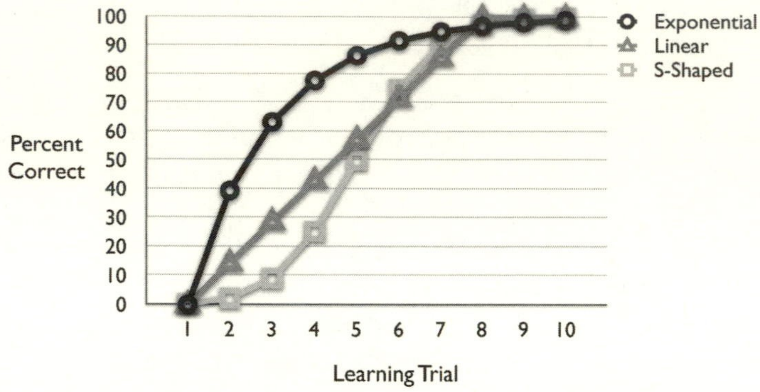

Figure 6.2. Three types of learning curves.

pairings or exposure to lists and the amount of study time, the probability of recall increases. The function relating learning trials or study time to performance is called a *learning curve*. Learning curves can be of several different shapes, depending on the type and difficulty of the material, as shown in Figure 6.2. All learning curves have an initial starting point determined by the chance of guessing and amount of prior knowledge, as well as a final ending point called the *asymptote*. For some tasks, the asymptote may be at 100 percent, but for many realistic tasks, few people reach perfect performance.

If each trial adds a constant amount to what has already been learned and nothing already learned is forgotten, the learning curve will be linear and will plot as a straight line until maximum performance is reached. Thus, each trial adds the same amount until everything is learned. Somewhat surprisingly, linear learning curves are rarely seen in theory or in practice. Instead, we find exponential curves in situations where easy items in the set are learned quickly at the beginning, causing a fast startup, but then it takes many more trials to learn the hard items, as shown in Figure 6.2. Many user applications are designed to be quickly learned at the beginning, but then to become proficient in all functions requires a lot of time. Most e-mail, word processor, and spreadsheet programs are learned this way. However, for other applications, and particularly for programming languages, learning can be difficult and slow at the beginning because many new, unfamiliar things must be learned before you can really get going. This results in what looks like an S-shaped learning curve. Performance increases slowly at the beginning, followed by a more rapid acquisition of items, and then ending with a slower rate to reach asymptote.

The term "steep learning curve" has become a misnomer. Technically, if performance is plotted as a function of study trials, the exponential learning curve in Figure 6.2 would be described as steep. However, in current parlance, a steep learning curve has come to refer to a very difficult learning situation. The metaphor is that it takes a lot more work to climb a steep slope than a gradual incline. In this latter sense, the curve reverses the axes of the graph and plots the number of learning trials that it takes on the y-axis to achieve a certain level of performance on the x-axis.

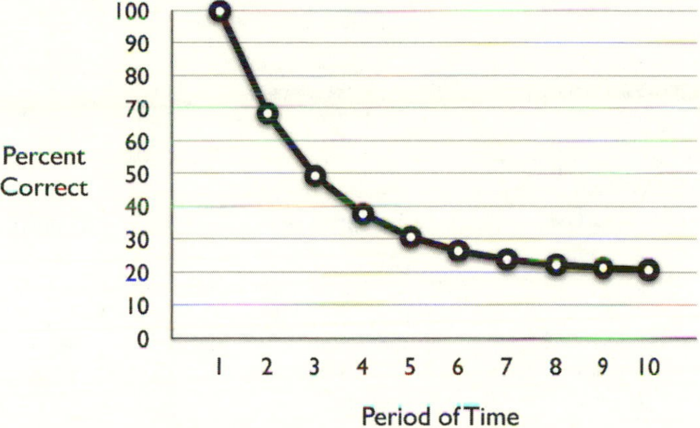

Figure 6.3. An exponential forgetting curve.

Forgetting Curve

In addition to the acquisition of information, Ebbinghaus also studied forgetting. Forgetting is a very human aspect of memory that can be due to several factors, some similar to computers and others quite different. The deletion of information in a computer is generally directed by a command to delete and erase files or by a computer malfunction. Human memory, in contrast, may decay over time, or recall may be inhibited by other interfering information. In general, if there is no additional study following learning, the probability of recall drops exponentially, as shown in Figure 6.3.

The good news is that although a lot of information is lost quickly over time, the curve does not go to zero. Some portion of the information is retained, and if there is a relearning phase, acquisition of forgotten material is faster than if it had not been learned previously. Moreover, the rate of forgetting following relearning is less than that following original learning, hence the importance of refresher classes.

Three Memory Stores

Even from early studies of memory, it was believed that memory was not a single unit or system. William James proposed that there were primary and secondary systems one that was for lasting memory and the other for temporary memory. Contemporary research suggests that it is divided into three systems or stages, as shown in Figure 6.4, with a sensory register, a short-term memory, and a long-term memory with an executive processor in charge (Atkinson & Shiffrin, 1968). This three-stage model helps explain many of the phenomena that we find in memory research and is an important determinant in how we learn and remember things at the human–computer interface.

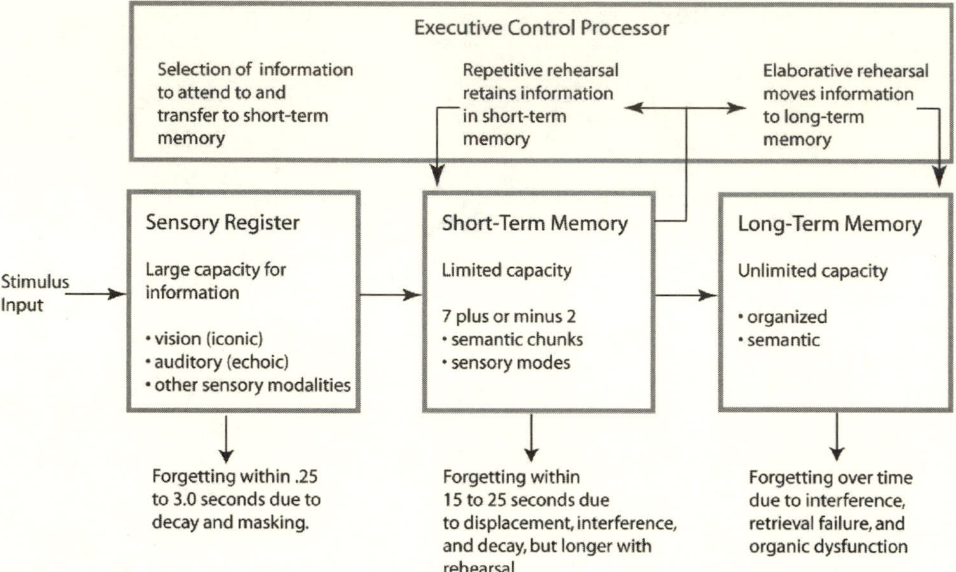

Figure 6.4. Memory systems. (Adapted from Atkinson & Shiffrin, 1968.)

Sensory Register

When you glance at a screen, your visual system takes in an amazing amount of information. If the screen goes blank or is flipped to another screen, the information you saw remains in your visual system for only a moment. You have only a short time to attend to the information and to glean what you can from that image before it is gone, unless you are an unusual individual with *eidetic imagery*, or a photographic memory. The question is how much information you can acquire in a glance and pass on to short-term memory.

Information in the short-term sensory register is rich in its original sensory form, but decays rapidly as information is extracted for further processing (Rainer & Miller, 2002). It is probably more accurate to think of multiple sensory memories. *Iconic memory* is the name of the visual sensory memory. This information is like a snapshot that decays within one-fourth of a second. *Echoic memory* is for the auditory sense. Information for this sense is retained for several seconds. Much less is known about the sensory memories for smell and touch.

Imagine again being shown a Web page for only a split second. How much information could you extract from the visual image? Even though iconic memory is extremely rich, studies by Sperling (1960) suggest that you will only be able to recall three to five items. In Sperling's classic experiment, he presented 3 × 3 arrays of random letters for approximately one-twentieth of a second; subjects could only recall four or five of the letters. Sperling hypothesized that even though the letters were in iconic memory, subjects did not have the time to process and name the letters before the memory had decayed. To test this theory, he provided a cue immediately after the presentation to tell the subjects to recall only the letters in the first, second, or third row of the array using a high, medium, or low tone. With this procedure, subjects were able to recall nearly all letters in a row and, by extrapolation, would have recalled many more letters if they had had time before the image had decayed.

The beauty of many computer interfaces is that if the image disappears before you can extract the needed information, you can return to the screen or scan back to previous frames in a video. As we explore later, computer memory can bolster or make up for the deficits of our short-term sensory store and help us extract the information that we need.

Short-Term Memory

Short-term memory is a buffer in which we hold units of information for a limited time that we have extracted from the sensory register. Short-term memory system has a limited capacity. George A. Miller (1956) in his classic article, "The Magical Number Seven, Plus or Minus Two," specifies the limit as 7 ± 2. The best example is the test of memory span for digits. In this test, a list of digits is read to a subject who then has to repeat the numbers back in the same order without making a mistake. On average, most college students can remember lists of eight or nine digits without making errors. Short-term memory is constantly in action at the human–computer interface. We are trying to remember names, numbers, settings, pages, and steps as we interact with machines. We keep track of what is on the clipboard, what files are open, etc.

Information is lost from short-term memory due to decay over time, interference among items, and being displaced by incoming information. In other words, if we are trying to juggle too many items, some of them get dropped.

Information in short-term memory can actually be retained for long periods of time using *maintenance rehearsal* – that is, by repeating it over and over to oneself to refresh the items. Maintenance rehearsal seems to be accomplished primarily through inner vocalization and requires considerable cognitive effort and concentration. If you are distracted, the information is lost. Repeating items to yourself does little to transfer the information to long-term memory. In contrast, *elaborative rehearsal* serves this purpose. Items are elaborated by adding meaning to them ("sense making") and relating them to other information in long-term memory.

Although the capacity of short-term memory is limited to 7 ± 2 items, the items can be large chunks of information. So, for example, you may be trying to remember the password "E6HJ9K2" with seven characters, or you may be trying to remember the seven words "WALNUT, EAGLE, STARFISH, CORN, ROCK, TUNA, MOUNTAIN" made up of many more characters. Short-term memory is limited by the number of chunks, not the size of the chunks. This means that if we can convert strings of information into meaningful chunks, we can retain much more information in short-term memory.

In the past, short-term memory had been thought of primarily for storage and transfer of information to long-term memory. To account for how people perform cognitive tasks such as problem solving and decision making, Alan Baddeley (1998, 2000) and others have proposed a more complex system that involves *working memory*. This memory system serves as a workbench on which information is manipulated and assembled to perform cognitive tasks. Although the distinction between short-term and working memory is not entirely clear, the idea is that working memory is a dynamic workspace rather than merely a short-term storage area for information on its way to long-term memory (Nyberg, Forkstam, Petersson, Cabeza, & Ingvr, 2002).

Working memory is controlled by a *central executive* and has at least two storage areas, a *phonological loop* and a *visuospatial working memory*. The phonological loop allows for the rehearsal of speech-based information. Words can be temporarily stored and manipulated in the loop. The visuospatial memory stores visual images and spatial information. It is like a scratch pad in that images can be temporarily stored and manipulated. It appears that the phonological loop and the visuospatial memory function relatively independently so that you can rehearse numbers in one while manipulating the arrangement of letters in the other (Baddeley & Hitch, 1974; Reed, 2001). The central executive controls information in and between the phonological loop, visuospatial memory, and long-term memory. The central executive controls attention, does planning, selects strategies for processing information, and monitors the progress of cognitive activities.

In HCI, the central executive controls attention, what we look at, and what we extract from the image. It controls what goes into working memory (e.g., a list of menu options) and decision strategies for selecting the appropriate item. It helps keep track of the spatial organization of windows and icons that are not currently visible but are being thought about. How the central executive does this is not clear. However, the idea of such an executive emphasizes the need for control over the memory processes in support of thinking and problem solving. We return to this issue in Chapter 7 and later in the context of AI.

Long-Term Memory

Long-term memory, the relatively permanent collection of information and knowledge that we all acquire, is truly remarkable. We may complain about our memories for facts and events, but given the sheer vastness of long-term memory, we should be more amazed than dismayed. John von Neumann, a mathematician and computer scientist, estimated the size of human long-term memory to be 2.8×10^{20} bits of information, given no forgetting. My office computer has 280 GB of hard disk storage. This would equate the size of human memory to 1 billion of these computers. Such magnitudes of computer memory at this point in time can only be achieved at a global level with large server farms on vast networks.

Long-term memory is complex. As discussed previously, it includes both explicit and implicit memory. Explicit memory includes semantic and episodic memory, and implicit memory includes procedural, priming, and classical conditioning memory. Moreover, long-term memory involves a multimodal coding of information to include the following types of information:

- *Spatial/visual information*: pictures, images, symbols, spatial structures, cognitive maps
- *Law and properties*: physical, social, and behavioral laws; properties of things
- *Beliefs, values, and attitudes*: subjective feelings about things, preferences
- *Procedural skills*: plans for how to do things, motor skills
- *Perceptual skills*: interpreting and understanding sensory input

Information in the long-term store is obviously more permanent than short-term memory, but sometimes the information can be hard to retrieve. We may know that it is there or experience the "tip of the tongue" phenomenon. Given enough time, it may be spontaneously remembered. Or given enough searching through cues and associations, it may be recalled. Remembering may be a passive phenomenon in which memories just surface effortlessly, or it may be an active process of digging and problem solving. When we try to recall some information – such as "What were you doing at 3:00 in the afternoon on June 30, 2 years ago?" or "What is the algorithm for a bubble sort?" – we have to actively retrieve it and, in some cases, fabricate what we cannot remember from the things that we can remember. Recall in Chapter 4 the retrospective procedure in usability testing. Users have to recall what they were thinking about while performing a task. One criticism of the procedure is that participants may not actually remember, but instead make up a rational explanation from what they do remember.

Long-term memory is organized. This is evident from the fact that the order of recall of items is neither random nor in the same order as they were learned. Instead, recall is a function of the structure of knowledge and the relationships among items. Human memory is dynamically self-organizing, sometimes consciously and sometimes unconsciously, perhaps even while we are asleep. Computer memory may or may not be organized, depending on how it was stored in files and databases. The organization of human memory is of great interest to computer scientists as a model for computer memory. Similarly, computer models of memory are of great interest to cognitive psychologists for developing models of human memory.

Organization of Long-Term Memory

There are four major theories for how long-term memory is organized: hierarchies, semantic networks, schemas and scripts, and connectionist networks.

These are not mutually exclusive but may each operate in different areas and at different times.

Hierarchies

A *hierarchy* is an organization from general to specific categories. Much of our knowledge about the world is hierarchical in nature. The animal kingdom and the plant kingdom are hierarchical by class, genus, and species. Genealogies are hierarchical family trees. Organization charts of businesses and government agencies are hierarchical. We tend to organize knowledge in hierarchical indexes and outlines. Most computer files are also organized hierarchically with directories, subdirectories, and so on.

Evidence for hierarchical organization of information in long-term memory comes from two basic lines of research. Early research by Bower, Clark, Winzenz, and Lesgold (1969) showed that participants who were presented words in hierarchies recalled them better than those who were presented words in random groups. Others have found that recall is superior when we organize the to-be-learned information hierarchically (Bruning, Schraw, & Ronning, 1999). This suggests that human–computer interfaces that are often inherently hierarchical should be presented and learned in a hierarchical manner. In a very early study on learning options in hierarchical menu selection systems, Parton, Huffman, Pridgen, Norman, and Shneiderman (1985) found that having participants study the hierarchy was superior to any other method of learning.

A second line of research suggests that when we search long-term memory to answer questions, the time that it takes to answer the question is a function of the position of the information in the hierarchy. Collins and Quillian (1969) found that it takes longer to answer the question "Is a canary a bird?" than "Is a canary yellow?" They theorize that our knowledge about animals is stored in a hierarchy with unique information about animals at the first level and general information at second and third levels in the hierarchy. Moreover, it takes a certain amount of time to travel from one node in the hierarchy to another. The more nodes that one must visit, the longer it takes, just as it does if you were trying to locate a particular file in a directory structure on a computer.

Semantic Networks

Strict hierarchies in memory are overly restrictive and do not account for a number of empirical findings. For example, it takes longer to answer true–false to "A dog is a mammal" than it takes for "A dog is an animal," even though the second statement addresses information that is further up the hierarchy. Moreover, there are large differences in times at the same level. For example, it takes longer to answer true–false for "An ostrich is a bird" than it does for "A canary is a bird." Another approach is to think of long-term memory as a multidimensional network of semantic associations between items. To answer questions, we again search through this network, but now distances between any two associated items represent their strength of association and affect the time it takes to traverse the network. In a sense, it is like the telephone network or the Internet with trunk lines, routers, and transmission lines. The difference is that neural transmission is very slow in the brain, whereas transmission is near the speed of light in electronic networks.

Spreading activation theory was proposed by Collins and Loftus (1975), who assume that there is a complex association network in which memories are distributed in a conceptual space. Links represent associations between nodes. Long links indicate remote associations, and short links close associations. When a memory is activated, its activation spreads outward. This may have the affect of priming related memories in the network and could explain why we respond to different thoughts and stimuli the way we do.

We know from research on networks and the storage of information in networked databases that some systems are more efficient than others. Organization, indexing, and sorting of information facilitates the search and recall of the information at a later time. Google is more successful than other search engines because it uses a more efficient algorithm that results in faster search times. One wonders if we, as humans, might learn more effective strategies of storing and indexing information in our long-term memories.

Schemas and Scripts

Much of our knowledge has to do with general structures and frameworks (*schemas*) and with stories and sequences of events (*scripts*). A schema is a mental concept or mental model (see Chapter 3) that helps interpret and organize new information. Schemas are ways that we think about things (Jou, Shanteau, & Harris, 1996). We have schemas for celebrations such as weddings, graduations, and birthday parties; for working on computers including such tasks as writing papers, downloading files, and troubleshooting; and for how systems work such as wireless networks, UNIX, and high-definition televisions. Scripts are schemas that pertain to sequences of events (Schank & Abelson, 1977). They are typically procedures and story lines that contain placeholders for characters and props. We have scripts for eating in a restaurant, sending e-mail, and shopping online and offline.

Schemas and scripts differ from semantic networks in that the structure of the links themselves contains information rather than just the nodes. In contrast to semantic networks, where tens of thousands of words are associated in semantic networks, schema theory organizes information into general structures, patterns, and forms along the lines of Gestalt theory. The efficiency of one's long-term memory then is a function of the quality and usefulness of the schemas that have been stored and used to interpret new information coming in through elaborative rehearsal.

Connectionist Networks

The previous theories of long-term memory are high on conceptualization but low on implementation. The question is "How is long-term memory actually stored in the neural network of the brain?" Connectionist theorists propose that memory is stored throughout the brain in connections among the neurons (Dehaene & Naccache, 2001; Humphreys, Tehan, O'Shea, & Bolland, 2000). Rather than focusing on the abstractions of memory, these theorists build computer simulations of neural networks that attempt to mimic the properties of the neurons exciting or inhibiting nodes across synaptic connections in a network. Numerous simulations have been successful in predicting the patterns of results in memory experiments (Marcus, 2001; McClelland & Rumelhart, 1986). The belief is that, given a large enough network with appropriate complexity, the computer can simulate learning and memory of the brain. In fact, some believe that neural network models may be the basis for a new generation of AI, as we see in Chapter 13. However, an important criticism of connectionist theories is that, given enough complexity in the simulation, you can fit any set of data and still not understand the process.

Levels of Processing

The previously discussed three-stage model of memory is very appealing; however, it is undoubtedly an oversimplification of the human memory system. Another approach to understanding how human memory works is to combine memory with the processing or encoding of information. We do not store the undigested image of the screen. Instead, we process it in various ways, extracting different types of information over time according to our particular needs.

In their *levels of processing* theory, Craik and Lockhart (1972) proposed an encoding process that governs memory. We first have to attend to the information before we can encode it. Then we process the information along a continuum from shallow to deep. At the *shallow level*, we encode the sensory or physical features of the stimuli. We detect lines, angles, and contours of letters or objects, or we detect the frequency, tone, loudness, and duration of sounds. If we stop here, little or nothing is stored or remembered. At the *intermediate level*, we encode names of letters, whole words, and objects. They may be remembered, but because they are disconnected, they may not be retrieved. At the *deepest level*, information is given semantic meaning with associations to other memories. The more associations, the deeper the processing (Lee, Cheung, & Wurm, 2000; Otten, Henson, & Rugg, 2001).

The levels of processing theory help explain why we can work at some tasks and remember almost nothing about them. For example, you can go through a document and find all underlined words and convert them to italics and not remember what the words where. Or you can even delete e-mails based on how suspicious you are of their subject lines and not remember any of the words in the titles.

According to the levels of processing theory, the more we process and elaborate the information, the more likely we are to recall it (Craik & Tulving, 1975). So, for example, if you are learning a set of menu options (e.g., artistic, blur, brush strokes, distort, pixilate, sharpen, sketch, stylize, texture, video) in an application such as Adobe Illustrator, making them more meaningful with explanations, seeing examples, and relating them to your own work will help elaborate them.

Recognition, Recall, and Retrieval

Menu selection and GUIs rely on recognition memory. You do not have to recall the names of the functions or options, you just have to recognize them from a list. If you want to delete a file, you recognize the file icon, recognize the trash icon, and drag the file icon to the trash icon. Command-line and programming language systems require the recall of terms from long-term memory. To delete the file, you have to recall the name of the file, the name of the function to delete a file, and type the command using the correct syntax.

Recall of information from memory requires a retrieval process that generally begins with a cue or a question. What is the name of the Web site for online auctions? If you cannot remember, it is often useful to generate additional cues (Allan, Wolf, Rosenthal, & Rugg, 2001; Halpern, 1996). Try going through the alphabet to see if it helps retrieval. Think of images, screen shots, and logos.

When items are stored in long-term memory, they are associated with the cues present at the time of storage. The *encoding specificity principle* says that information present at the time of encoding can serve as an effective cue for later retrieval (Hannon & Craik, 2001; Tulving & Thomson, 1973). Part of this information can be the context – when and where – it was learned. The principle of *context-dependent memory* says that information is better recalled in the same context in which it was learned than in a different context (Smith & Vela, 2001). That is, if you learn something while sitting in front of your computer, it will be recalled better when you are in front of your computer than when you are working under your car. Something that you read in a book in the park will be recalled better when you are in the park than when you are taking an online test for your driver's license. Knowing this, it is best either to study in the same context as the test or to at least imagine that context while studying.

Another part of the information at the point of encoding has to do with your internal state. The principle of *state-dependent memory* says that we are more likely to remember information when our psychological state or mood is similar at both encoding and retrieval (Weissenborn & Duka, 2000). Moreover, when we are in a happy mood, we are more likely to remember positive experiences, and when we are in a negative mood, we are more likely to remember negative experiences (Mineka & Nugent, 1995). Obviously, as we interact with computers, our moods can be random, and this can affect

Table 6.2. Interference Paradigms

	Task 1	Task 2	Interval	Test
Proactive Interference				
Experimental group	Learn List A	Learn List B		Recall List B
Control group		Learn List B		Recall List B
Retroactive Interference				
Experimental group	Learn List A	Learn List B		Recall List A
Control group	Learn List A			Recall List A

what we recall about the content of e-mail, online articles, and successful or frustrating things about the interaction.

Transfer of Training and Interference

In Scenario 2 at the beginning of the chapter, John worked for years using FORTRAN until his company implemented C++. When he began taking courses to learn C++, he believed that his programming experience would help him do better than the novices in the class. What went wrong? To the extent that the information in Task A is similar to Task B, there will be positive transfer; to the extent that they are different, there will be less transfer; and to the extent that the information is contradictory, there can be negative transfer. For John, there was probably some positive transfer of general concepts, but there was a lot that was contradictory and that led to negative transfer.

We distinguish between two types of interference, depending on the sequence of learning and recall situations, as shown in Table 6.2. Proactive interference occurs when something you learned previously interferes with something you learned later that you are trying to recall. This is John's problem. As computers have evolved, programming languages, OSs, and applications have changed substantially. People who have learned a number of languages, systems, and versions over time have built up a repository of interference with learning newer things. This becomes a significant problem with age in an environment of changing technology. The more you learned in the past that is now obsolete, the worse off you will be in the future. Even minor changes in the names of functions, menus, and icons from one version of an application to another can cause problems with proactive interference and lead to intrusion errors from the old version.

Retroactive interference occurs when you learn one thing and then a second, and then try to recall the first thing that you learned. It especially becomes a problem when you are trying to return to an older system or version after having learned a newer one. Perhaps this is not a frequent problem,

Table 6.3. Types of Transfer

Distance	Near	High degree of overlap between versions, similar context
	Far	Little overlap between versions, contexts dissimilar
Valence	Positive	Previous knowledge enhances learning of new version
	Negative	Previous knowledge inhibits learning of new version
Orientation	Vertical	Knowledge of previous version is essential in learning new version
	Horizontal	Knowledge of previous is not essential but helpful in learning new version
Abstraction	Literal	Exact, syntactic knowledge is same in new version
	Figural	Abstract general knowledge transfer to new version
Elevation	Low road	Automatic transfer of well-learned skills in a subconscious manner
	High road	Conscious formulation of connections between versions
Reach	Forward	Abstracting knowledge from current version for potential use in future version
	Backward	Abstracting knowledge from previous version for use in current version

Adapted from Schunk (2004) and Perkins (1992).

but it is still likely to occur in a changing environment when one needs to recover something from the past such as a legacy system.

When designing new versions of systems or new training methods, or analyzing the effects of change, one must consider the types of things that transfer. Table 6.3 lists various types of transfer that one should take into consideration. Consider a person who has only used MS Windows XP for years and is now shifting to Apple Mac OS X. According to Table 6.3, this type of transfer might be characterized as far, mixed valence, horizontal, figural, high road, and backward reaching. Whereas, a person who is moving from MS Windows XP to MS Windows Vista would anticipate a transfer that would be near, positive, horizontal, literal, low road, and forward reaching.

External Learning and Memory

Research on metamemory and metacognition looks at our ability to judge how difficult it will be to learn something and whether we will be able to recognize or recall it later (Metcalfe & Shimamura, 1996; Nelson, 1992). In Scenario 1, Mary realized that learning and recalling thirty different passwords would be a problem. Her solution was to offload the information onto her PDA and lock it with one password.

When it comes to storing and retrieving information, the computer has an easy time of it compared to humans. This is because learning and memory in a computer are fundamentally different from those functions in a human (see Chapter 2). We do not discuss this further in this section, but instead think about the ways that computers can store and use information in the process of interacting with humans.

We have many strategies for supplementing our fragile and volatile human memory. We have always used mnemonics to aid internal memory and written notes as external memory aids, but current digital technologies have added many new possibilities. Have you ever wanted a video recording of your day so that you could go back and replay a contentious conversation with a colleague or find a misplaced library book? Although it is technically possible to do this, it is not yet very practical.

The main questions are "How can we use technology to improve, enhance, or supplement our memory?" and "When should we offload that memory to the computer?" Related questions are as follows:

- Should I memorize telephone numbers, prices, part numbers, and so on, or store them in external memory on a computer, PDA, or other device?
- What should be left to human memory, and what should be put on the computer?
- What is the best way to input data into the computer, and how is it accessed later?

In Figure 6.4, Atkinson and Shiffrin (1968) included an executive processor that monitors memory storage and decides whether to memorize and store information in long-term memory, and Baddeley (1993) introduced the idea of a working memory to store information during processing. To these concepts, we must also add additional executive processor functions to offload and store information on external devices and memorize methods of retrieval.

Personal information management systems (PIMSs) are to applications specifically written for desktop computers, laptop computers, and mobile devices, such as cell phones and PDAs, that enable you to organize the daily stream of information that comes across your desk (e.g., appointments, weekly meeting reminders, to-do lists) in a manner that suits your personal style and to retrieve it when needed. Table 6.4 provides a small sampling of PIMSs and some of their advertising claims. A PIMS is a good idea. Unfortunately, most systems are not well implemented, do not live up to their claims, and have not been subjected to serious user testing. Following are a number of guidelines that should help in designing and using such systems:

- *Plan for retrieval.* There is no use in filing things if you cannot retrieve them or if you do not have a need for them in the future. All storage should be retrieval minded. Will I need it, and if so, under what circumstances? If I do need it, how will I find it?
- *Organization is essential.* Long-term memory works well because its contents are self-organized by categories, associations, features, etc. The same is true for external memory. Organization may be generated at input (preprocessing) by filing and tagging the information while entering it or later (postprocessing) when one has time for housekeeping. The worst time for organization is at retrieval. The problem with organization is that it takes

Table 6.4. Text Advertising for Several Brands of PIMSs

TreePad: www.treepad.com/

TreePad saves you time, allowing you to keep your notes, documents, hyperlinks and images at the brief distance of a click. Download TreePad and enjoy better access, organization, and control over your data, notes, bills, projects, clients, addresses, letters, speeches, research, collections, classroom notes, Web pages, links, bibliographic listings, and whatever else your creativity enables you to entrust TreePad with, for good organization, easy access, and safe storage.

Task Plus: www.contactplus.com/products/freestuff/task.htm

Task Plus is the best task and calendar management program designed for simplicity and speed. Running in your system tray, Task Plus keeps track of an unlimited number of personal to-do items as well as date rated appointments plus holidays and repeating events such as birthdays. Using sophisticated alarms, it can also play sound (WAV file) when a task comes due! Powerful filters make it easy to view tasks in certain categories or by project.

Personal Knowbase: www.bitsmithsoft.com/

Take control of your notes. Personal Knowbase is the note organizer software that makes it easy to manage the large amount of information that crosses your desk every day. This free-form notes manager uses a natural way to retrieve notes, using keywords to filter your knowledge base for related information quickly. Whether you are organizing research notes, e-mail archives, or story ideas, Personal Knowbase makes your life easier.

PIM eCentral: www.softspecialist.com/Browser-and-PIM-eCentral-1111/Browser-and-PIM-eCentral.htm

eCentral is the most user-friendly, most fun to use all-in-one desktop productivity tool. With eCentral, you can quickly and easily organize your time and contacts, and browse the Web with no pop-ups. At the same time, you can listen to your favorite MP3 songs.

Tools included: Calendar and organizer with reminders and to-do list, address book, Web browser with pop-up blocker, built in Windows Desktop and Explorer access, e-mail program launcher, Windows Calculator launcher, calendar photo personalization, music player (MP3), video player (AVI, MPEG). The personal information manager can be used as a combined calendar, diary, organizer, and reminder.

time. Self-organizing systems are needed, along with organization wizards and agents to do the work for you.

- *Multiple systems are a problem.* If personal information is stored on different devices and systems that do not talk to each other, the difficulty of finding the information is multiplied. You may have to check a number of different systems in different places. Most PDAs have programs to sync the information, but they are not perfect and not always convenient.
- *Backup information.* However, if information is only on one device, it can be lost. All PIMSs must have multiple backups that are easy to use and convenient, if not automatic. Restoring information from the backup should be reliable and automatic.
- *Set security levels.* As you retrieve information from your long-term memory, you are keenly aware of whether it is private or public. Some PIMSs lock all information and require a password to access it. So, even to find out whether May 19, 1979, was a Saturday, you have to enter your password.

Others allow you to lock individual bits of information, but this can be quite time consuming.

- *Use multiple and appropriate media.* Today's PIMSs and PDAs allow multiple media (e.g., text, voice, pictures, video). Sometimes voice input of a name and phone number is superior to text input or a picture of a business card is superior to voice or text. The problem will be resolving the media during postprocessing of the information.
- *Rugged, reliable, and always present.* We joke, "If your head wasn't attached to your body, you'd probably forget it at home." A PIMS is only good if you have it with you – in the office, at home, while hiking, or even while swimming. It must be durable, easily locatable, and wearable.
- *Usability is key.* If something is too hard to figure out, it will not be used. PIMSs and PDAs must make it easy to store, maintain, and retrieve information. This includes use of input devices such as the keyboard or touchscreen, readability of the screen, and all menu navigation. The more that is automatic (e.g., autoentry of time and date, autoupdating, autotransmission of V-cards) and intuitive, the better.

Using What Computers Remember

Human memory is purpose driven. We remember things for many different reasons – aesthetic memories that we enjoy, practical information that will definitely prove to be useful, and other information that might be useful. When our memory fails, we often turn to others' memories or to artifacts left from our activities. As it turns out, computers record a lot of information about the user. The computer stores many of our activities at the interface. In fact, it is rather shocking how much episodic memory can be retrieved from e-mail archives, phone records, credit card transactions, online shopping, blogs, server logs, history files, etc. If we are having a hard time trying to remember something in the past, we may be able to troll through the computer's memory to find it. Increasingly, software tools are being developed to help us do just that.

Some psychologists believe that our brains store memories of all stimuli and events that occur, but that we are just not able to recall all of them. The same may be true of computer storage. Even if events are stored in files to which we have access, it may be difficult to find the one we want. In addition, there are many files to which we do not have access, such as those held by Internet providers and financial and government organizations. Nevertheless, with the right retrieval tools, the information may be found.

End Thoughts

Learning and memory have been of great concern to psychologists. A number of theories have been developed, and thousands of studies have been conducted. Our world requires us to learn, memorize, and recall a tremendous amount of information. Computers and the human–computer interface add substantially to this information. The challenge is to design interfaces that minimize the sheer volume of information that people have to learn and recall, and make it easy to learn and recall what information they do need.

Computers also provide solutions to our problems with memory. When human memory fails, computer memory may kick in to help us out. External memory is a type of assistive technology, which we talk more about in Chapter 14. Learning and memory are highly purpose driven in pursuit of solving problems. We remember things to accomplish tasks, to satisfy needs, and for our own enjoyment. Chapter 7 explores the issue of problem solving.

Suggested Exercises

1. Consider a simple computer program like Notepad. What did you have to learn to use this program?
2. If you have upgraded or are upgrading a program or an OS, see if you can count the number of deleted, added, or changed options, commands, icons, etc., in the two versions. How much positive, neutral, and negative transfer do you believe there will be?
3. Consider two different systems or versions of an application, and identify the types of transfer going from one to the other according to Table 6.3.

References

Allan, K., Wolf, H. A., Rosenthal, C. R., & Rugg, M. D. (2001). The effects of retrieval cues on post-retrieval monitoring in episodic memory: An electrophysiological study. *Brain Research*, *12*, 289–299.

Atkinson, R. C., & Shiffrin, R. M. (1968). Human memory: A proposed system and its control processes. In K. W. Spence & J. T. Spence (Eds.), *The psychology of learning and motivation* (Vol. 2, pp. 89–195). New York: Academic Press.

Baddeley, A. (1993). Working memory and conscious awareness. In A. F. Collins, S. E. Gatherhole, M. A. Conway, & P. E. Morris (Eds.), *Theories of memory*. (pp. 241–286). Mahwah, NJ: Erlbaum.

Baddeley, A. (1998). *Human memory* (Rev. ed.). Boston: Allyn & Bacon.

Baddeley, A. (2000). Short-term and working memory. In E. Tulving & F. I. M. Craik (Eds.), *The Oxford handbook of memory* (pp. 77–93). New York: Oxford University Press.

Baddeley, A. D., & Hitch, G. (1974). Working memory. In G. H. Bower (Ed.), *The psychology of learning and motivation* (Vol. 8, pp. 47–90). San Diego: Academic Press.

Bower, G. H., Clark, M., Winzenz, D., & Lesgold, A. (1969). Hierarchical retrieval schemes in recall of categorized word lists. *Journal of Verbal Learning and Verbal Behavior*, *3*, 323–343.

Bruning, R. H., Schraw, G. J., & Ronning, R. R. (1999). *Cognitive psychology and instruction* (3rd ed.). Upper Saddle River, NJ: Erlbaum.

Collins, A. M., & Loftus, E. F. (1975). A spreading activation theory of semantic processing. *Psychological Review*, *82*, 407–428.

Collins, A. M., & Quillian, M. R. (1969). Retrieval time from semantic memory. *Journal of Verbal Learning and Verbal Behavior*, *8*, 240–248.

Craik, F. I. M., & Lockhart, R. S. (1972). Levels of processing: A framework for memory research. *Journal of Verbal Learning and Verbal Behavior*, *11*, 671–684.

Craik, F. I. M., & Tulving, E. (1975). Depth of processing and retention of words in episodic memory. *Journal of Experimental Psychology: General*, *104*, 268–294.

Dehaene, S., & Naccache, L. (2001). Towards a neuroscience of consciousness: Basic evidence and a workspace format. *Cognition*, *79*, 1–37.

Halpern, D. F. (1996). *Thinking critically about critical thinking*. Mahwah, NJ: Erlbaum.

Hannon, B., & Craik, F. I. (2001). Encoding specificity revisited: The role of semantics. *Canadian Journal of Experimental Psychology*, *55*, 231–243.

Humphreys, M. S., Tehan, G., O'Shea, A., & Bolland, S. W. (2000). Target similarity effects: Support for the parallel distributed processing assumptions. *Memory and Cognition*, *28*, 798–811.

Jou, J., Shanteau, J., & Harris, R. J. (1996). An information processing view of framing effects: The role of causal schemas in decision making. *Memory and Cognition*, *24*, 1–15.

Lee, Y. S., Cheung, Y. M., & Wurm, L. H. (2000). Levels-of-processing effects on Chinese character completion: The importance of lexical processing and test cue. *Memory and Cognition*, *28*, 1398–1405.

Marcus, G. F. (2001). *The algebraic mind*. Cambridge, MA: MIT Books.

McClelland, J. L., & Rumelhart, D. E. (1986). *Parallel distributed processing: Explorations in the microstructure of cognition. Vol. 2: Psychological and biological models*. Cambridge, MA: MIT Press.

Metcalfe, J., & Shimamura, A. P. (Eds.). (1996). *Metacognition: Knowing about knowing*. Cambridge, MA: MIT Press.

Miller, G. A. (1956). The magical number seven, plus or minus two: Some limits on our capacity for information processing. *Psychological Review*, *48*, 337–442.

Mineka, S., & Nugent, K. (1995). Mood-congruent memory biases in anxiety and depression. In D. L. Schacter, J. T. Coyle, G. D. Fischbach, M. M. Mesulam, & L. E. Sullivan (Eds.), *Memory distortion: How minds, brains, and societies reconstruct the past* (pp. 173–196). Cambridge, MA: Harvard University Press.

Nelson, T. O. (1992). *Metacognition: Core readings*. Needham Heights, MA: Allyn & Bacon.

Nyberg, L., Forkstam, C., Petersson, K. M., Cabeza, R., & Ingvr, M. (2002). Brain imaging of human memory systems: Between-systems similarities and within-system differences. *Brain Research: Cognitive Brain Research*, *13*, 281–292.

Otten, L. J., Henson, R. N., & Rugg, M. D. (2001). Depth of processing effects on neural correlates of memory encoding. *Brain*, *124*, 399–412.

Parton, D., Huffman, K., Pridgen, P., Norman, K. L., & Shneiderman, B. (1985). Learning a menu selection tree: Training methods compared. *Behaviour and Information Technology*, 4, 79–80.

Pavlov, I. P. (1927). *Conditioned reflexes*. London: Routledge and Kegan Paul.

Perkins, D. N. (1992). Transfer of learning. In T. J. Plomp & D. P. Ely (Eds.), *International encyclopedia of education* (2nd ed., pp. 64–68). Oxford: Pergamon Press.

Rainer, G., & Miller, E. K. (2002). Time-course of object-related neural activity in the primate prefrontal cortex during short-term memory task. *European Journal of Neuroscience*, *15*, 1244–1254.

Reed, S. K. (2001). *Cognition* (5th ed.). Belmont, CA: Wadsworth.

Schank, R., & Abelson, R. (1977). *Scripts, plans, goals, and understanding*. Mahwah, NJ: Erlbaum.

Schunk, D. (2004). *Learning theories. An educational perspective* (4th ed.). Upper Saddle River, NJ: Pearson Education.

Schwartz, J. P., & Norman, K. L. (1986). The importance of item distinctiveness on performance using a menu selection system. *Behaviour and Information Technology*, *5*, 173–182.

Skinner, B. F. (1953). *Science and human behavior*. New York: Macmillan.

Smith, S. M., & Vela, E. (2001). Environmental context-dependent memory: A review and meta-analysis. *Psychological Bulletin Review*, *8*, 203–220.

Sperling, G. (1960). The information available in brief presentations. *Psychological Monographs*, *74*(11).

Tulving, E., & Thomson, D. M. (1973). Encoding specificity and retrieval processes in episodic memory. *Psychological Review*, *80*, 352–373.

Weissenborn, R., & Duka, T. (2000). State-dependent effects of alcohol on explicit memory: The role of semantic associations. *Psychopharmacology*, *149*, 98–106.

Seven

Cognitive Psychology

Thinking and Problem Solving

Scenario 1

Jenny was having problems with her knees so she performed a Google search to find medical information and a diagnosis. The first hit was "Arthritis Today: When Knees Go Bad." She clicked on it, read the first part of the article by Judith Horstman, and continued to read the seven additional parts. Then she searched the Arthritis Foundation Web site (www.arthritis.org) to help self-diagnose her condition. She couldn't find any simple answers. She went back to Google, clicked on "Scholar," and quickly looked at a few medical articles that got her nowhere. She clicked on "Images" for fun and scanned through a number of humorous and not so humorous pictures of knees. Returning to the Web search in Google, she eliminated a few ridiculous hits until she found an article titled "Questions and Answers About Knee Problems" at www.medhelp.org/NIHlib/GF-49.html. This fact sheet appeared on the National Institute of Arthritis and Musculoskeletal and Skin Diseases Web site. She believed that they should have some answers. Maybe now she was on the right track, but she did not learn anything new as she read through the article. At the end of the article was a section titled "Other Sources of Information on Knee Problems." The listings were all institutes and foundations, along with their contact information, and offering brochures such as "Taking Care of the Knees" and "Using Your Joints Wisely." A bit discouraged, she gave up and went to bed.

Scenario 2

Jerry was in a problem-solving mode. He had tried to print a file, but the printer was not responding. What could be the problem? Jerry had many years of computer experience and had developed a number of repertoires for solving problems. First, he tried to print the paper again. No response. Then, he checked the printer. It was on; it appeared to have no paper or ink problems, as would be indicated by flashing buttons. He checked the printer cable. Yes, it was connected to the computer. Next, he made sure that he had selected the right printer and tried again. No response. Then he shut off the printer, turned it on, and tried all over again, but that didn't do it. Finally, he restarted the computer and again attempted to print the file. After 30 min of trying to figure out the printer problem, this worked! He mumbled to himself, "Next time, do the restart first. Don't know why, but do it first."

Overview

Thinking and problem solving is the center of human cognitive activity and a pivotal point for HCI. It is at the core of what we do, how we achieve our goals, and how we explain our actions. However, the actual act of thinking is rather hard to define and difficult to isolate for study. The act of problem solving is a little more objective in that we can observe the activities and results of the process. Both thinking and problem solving involve cognitive processing of information and interaction with the environment to access information and implement solutions.

Oddly, research in psychology on thinking and problem solving has often focused on the human deficiencies, biases, fallibilities, irrationalities, and inconsistencies relative to optimal, logical, and rational approaches. With the introduction of computer technology, this comparison has turned to human–computer differences and focuses on the logical/computational power of computers and the intuitive/subjective tendencies of humans. In response to human deficiencies, psychologists have proposed methods of enhancing critical thinking, fostering creativity, and debiasing human judgment, whereas some computer scientists have proposed augmenting and even supplanting human thinking and problem solving with AI. We explore this last issue in Chapter 13.

In general, technology has three points of overlap with human thinking and problem solving. First, we use technology to aid and assist thinking and problem solving. We use calculators to help with math problems, search engines to find information as in Scenario 1, computer programs to solve for optimal solutions, and AI to do thinking and problem solving for us.

Second, technology has a way of adding problems to our lives. How do we get the program to work? How do we troubleshoot a problem as in Scenario 2? How do we reason about problems, form hypotheses, and test solutions. Are there strategies that can be used that are particularly effective with technological problems beyond calling tech support?

Finally, technology can be used to track, record, and analyze our thinking and problem-solving behavior. Although thinking and problem solving are primarily internal mental activities, increasingly we interact with interface tools to aid the process by taking notes, searching for information, building simulations, and just plain trial and error.

In this chapter, we investigate a number of aspects of thinking and problem solving as they relate to the human–computer interface. We discuss the role of concepts and representational systems in thinking, as well as how human–computer interfaces can augment these systems. We look at the stages of problem solving, strategies of problem solving, search strategies, and obstacles to problem solving, and the way in which the human–computer interface can assist or hinder human problem solving. Finally, we explore creative thinking and problem solving, along with methods and tools for facilitating it.

Thinking, Concepts, and Reasoning

Most psychologists agree that thinking is an internal cognitive process that includes three basic ideas (Mayer, 1992):

1. Thinking is *cognitive*. It is not directly observed but can be inferred from behavior; we can see the results of thinking. Even brain imaging does not observe thinking directly, but only records the correlates of thinking – namely, chemical, heat, and electrical activity.
2. Thinking is a *process*. It involves the manipulation of knowledge or a set of operations on knowledge in the cognitive system. Thinking involves steps that take time and, as such, entails certain costs.
3. Thinking is *directed*. It results in behavior that is directed toward the solution of a problem. Thinking, like most human activity, has a purpose and is goal driven. Even daydreaming serves many useful purposes (Mueller, 1990).

How many times have you looked at a person sitting in front of a computer screen, concentrating but doing nothing? In Chapter 3, keystroke models of user behavior include "think time" as well as keystroke and mousing times. The cognitive system is processing information, making decisions, and solving problems.

Thinking and problem solving requires elements to think about and to manipulate. A concept is a mental category of objects, ideas, or events that share common aspects (Markman & Ross, 2003). For example, we have the concept of *computer*, which includes personal computers, mainframe computers, laptop computers, etc. Concepts are involved in the organization of long-term memory (as we see in Chapter 6 on semantic networks). In the same way, they play an important role in thinking and problem solving and in how we approach the human–computer interface.

There are a number of theories as to how we form concepts. *Feature theories* are based on the premise that we form concepts by identifying defining features or characteristics (Medin, 1989). A computer might have the following defining features: it is an electronic device, has input and output devices, does computation, and runs programs. A problem with feature theories is that features are not always clearly defined and may have fuzzy boundaries. A laptop is clearly a computer, but what about your cell phone, wristwatch, and television? Even the simple concepts of a table or a chair can be fuzzy. Technological concepts can be even fuzzier as they quickly form and evolve over time. Take the concept of "e-mail." The Urban Dictionary lists the definition: "Once an efficient and fast method of communication and message transferring, now a way of harassing Internet users with spam, credit card/insurance offers, porn links, and "Increase Your Penis Size By 5 Inches" advertisements."[1]

Another approach is taken by *prototype theories*. These theories state that concepts are defined primarily in terms of the features that characterize the typical member or prototype of the concept rather than specific feature boundaries that determine whether an element is or is not a member. This explains why some members of concepts are easier to classify than others; namely, they are better representatives of the concept than others (Rosch, 1978). A personal computer is a good prototype of a computer, whereas a computer under the hood of your automobile controlling the combustion in your engine is not.

A large portion of thinking and problem solving depends on having the appropriate set of conceptual tools to think about the problem. As we interact with the environment and particularly with the human–computer interface, we form new concepts based on experience with new attributes or combinations of previously learned attributes. For example, an electronic spreadsheet starts from the attributes of having cells in rows and columns, but adds new attributes of automatic computations based on equations within cells.

Finally, we think of two types of reasoning. In *deductive reasoning*, we start from a set of givens or premises and draw a conclusion. The classic example is syllogistic reasoning. If B is C and A is B, then we deduce that A is C. Consider the following:

> Any e-mail with a subject line containing the word "lottery" is spam.
> This e-mail has a subject line containing the word "lottery."
> Therefore, this e-mail is spam.

Deductive reasoning follows the rules of logic and, as such, can be computed. Deductive reasoning is frequently used in thinking about computers and in

[1] Urban Dictionary, definition of "email." Retrieved March 14, 2008, from www.urbandictionary.com/define.php?term=email

programming computers. Indeed, the previous syllogism could be used to set the rules for filtering one's e-mail.

Unfortunately, it is well known that human reasoning is often illogical, suffering from many logical fallacies. One such fallacy is invalid conversion. We mistakenly infer that if all A are B, then all B are A (Chapman & Chapman, 1959; Revlis, 1975) despite the fact that this is true only if A and B are equivalent classes. Another fallacy is subjective bias based on the content of the premises. Our belief in the conclusion influences our ability to reason logically (Lefford, 1946; Revlin & Leirer, 1978). Because of our difficulty in logical reasoning, we tend to defer such reasoning to computational procedures that computers can apply using rules of logic effectively and without subjective bias. Although this works well with math and accounting, the results are not always agreeable with human preferences.

Although many instances of human irrationality can be identified, it is often the case that we are correct for the wrong reasons; that is, in the balance of human reasoning, we take into consideration our experience and rely on what worked in the past (case-based reasoning), or use simple rules of thumb (heuristics) that get us by fairly well. Despite the fact that computers are inherently logical and outperform humans on trivial logic problems, in many complex and even simple situations, humans are superior. Moreover, it must be remembered that humans programmed the computers, and consequently, computers are subject to human error. One might not want to trust the previous spam filter, not because it is illogical, but because there may be extenuating circumstances that are not considered. What if the subject line was "Your manuscript entitled 'Use of the word "lottery" in e-mail subject lines' was accepted for publication"?

In *inductive reasoning,* we start from a set of instances and try to infer a rule. For example, here is a set of instances of e-mails with and without viruses:

from known person, attachment with .doc extension ➔ no virus
from unknown person, attachment with .exe extension ➔ virus
from known person, attachment with .pdf extension ➔ no virus
from unknown person, attachment with .doc extension ➔ virus
from known person, attachment with .exe extension ➔ no virus
from unknown person, attachment with .pdf extension ➔ no virus

What rules can you infer about opening e-mail attachments?

Inductive reasoning involves hypothesis testing. We generate a rule and test it as we look across the set of instances. You may have generated the rule "Attachments from known persons do not have viruses." Because this rule is not rejected in the previous set of instances, you will probably retain it. However, if you had generated the rule, "All attachments from unknown persons contain viruses," it would be rejected by instances with .pdf extensions. Consequently, you are left with the rule: "Attachments from known persons or attachments with a .pdf extension do not contain viruses."

Table 7.1. Basic Elements of a Formal Problem

Element	Definition	Examples
Givens	Initial set of conditions, objects, and information given at the onset of a problem	Initial state of the computer with error message, lost file, blank page
Operations	Rules for manipulating the givens	Diagnostic tools, programs, available functions, menu options, Web pages
Goals	Desired terminal state of the problem	A fixed computer, a fixed project, a found document
Obstacles	Limitations on the rules and operations that restrict a direct solution to the problem	Unknown causes, errors in searches, no obvious option, hidden menus, deactivated menus
Solution	Path or step-by-step application of the operations that lead from the givens to the goal	Sequence of functions, selections, keystrokes from the beginning to the end

Inductive reasoning has been studied extensively in psychology (Bruner, Goodnow, & Austin, 1956) with a number of findings that are particularly relevant to HCI. First, the more irrelevant variables there are in the situation, the harder it is to infer the correct rule (Bourne, Ekstrand, & Dominowski, 1971; Haygood & Stevenson, 1967). With complex systems such as computers, troubleshooting can be difficult because of all of the variables. Second, compound rules that contain "and," "or," and/or "if" are very difficult (Bourne, 1970). One can easily get into trouble with a spam filter that has complex rules. Finally, negative instances, when things go wrong (e.g., viruses, crashes), tell us more about the rules than positive instances, when all seems to be working fine. However, we tend to avoid the negative instances and thus do not learn from them (Klayman & Ha, 1987, 1989), hence the application of the old adage, "If it ain't broke, don't fix it."

Problem Parts and Types

We define a *problem* as an obstruction or an obstacle preventing a person from achieving a desired goal directly. A *solution* to the problem is defined as a path or sequence of actions from the current problem state to the desired goal state. Table 7.1 lists the five formal parts of every problem.

Many problems arise at the human–computer interface. The human may be trying to complete some task and it is not immediately apparent how to do so. One must come up with a sequence of steps to achieve the goal. For example, you might have a word processing document with a table of fifty rows and fifty columns. You want to transpose the rows and columns in the table easily. How do you do it? You might need to get a frequency count of ten different words in a 20,000-word document. How do you do it?

There are many different types of problems in the world that we have to deal with and a number of ways of characterizing them. *Trivial problems* are those whose solutions have little or no lasting impact on one's life or on the world. Solving an anagram or deciding what to have for lunch are trivial problems. *Consequential problems* are those whose solutions have or will have a significant impact on your life or in the world. The global energy crisis, the design of new computer architecture, and your crashed hard disk are consequential problems. We may also think of some problems as *positive* and *proactive* because their solutions will advance one's life or the condition of the world, whereas *negative* and *reactive* problems are caused by accidents, negligence, and disease. Although many of the formal aspects of positive and negative problems may be similar, the psychological and emotional impact can be very different.

Problems are also situated in many different domains from personal ("How do I get so-and-so to like me?") to technological ("How do I get this thing-a-ma-jig to work?"). A more general typology was proposed by Greeno (1978) in which there are four basic types of problems, with the fourth added by Greeno and Simon (1988):

1. Problems of *transformation* are those in which one must find a sequence of operations to change the givens to the goal state. Examples include solving the Rubik's Cube, editing videos, touching up photos, and transforming data in a spreadsheet.
2. Problems of *arrangement* are those in which one must find the arrangement that leads to the goal. Examples include table seating arrangements, crypt-arithmetic problems, organizing photos, and arranging the icons on one's desktop.
3. Problems of *inducing structure* are those in which, given examples or instances, one must find a general rule or pattern that fits or explains the instances. Examples include number completion problems, scientific reasoning, diagnosis of problems from symptoms, and inferring rules for filtering spam.
4. Problems of *evaluating deductive arguments* are those in which, given the premises, one has to determine whether a conclusion logically follows. Examples include syllogistic reasoning, evaluation of programming logic, and checking math problems.

The first two types of problems are construction problems, and the last two are reasoning problems. In construction problems, we are generally creating something new, such as a computer program, architectural plans, a document, or even a new password. In reasoning problems, we are generating or testing rules by either inductive or deductive reasoning. It is not always clear what type of problem we are pursuing because complex thinking and problem solving can alternate from one type to another, depending on the part of the problem on which we are working. For example, you might be doing your taxes with a popular tax preparation program. You are constructing a new tax filing by adding information to the forms, manipulating the figures, etc. At the same time, you may explore different ways of calculating the tax, reporting deductions, etc., to find the method that results in the least

Table 7.2. Hypothetical Habit Family Hierarchies of User Behaviors for Several Computer Problems

Problem	Printer not responding	Program locks up	Mouse not working
Hierarchy of responses	Verify printer is on	Move and click mouse	Look at mouse bottom
	Check printer status lights	Press keys on keyboard	Disconnect and connect USB cord
	Check cables	Restart computer	Test on another computer
	Print from another program	Open different file	Restart computer
	Reinstall driver	Reinstall program	Try a different mouse

income tax owed. Finally, you may be reading a number of cases and documentation on tax law. From this, you may infer that if you deduct home office expenses, you will be more likely to be audited. So you decide not to do so.

Problem Solving by Association

The first modern research on problem solving in psychology was done with cats in a puzzle box designed by E. L. Thorndike (1911). He studied the typical behaviors that the cat used to try to get out of the box (e.g., meowing, scratching, nudging). He noted two important things. First, the probability of emitting the behavior was not random. Some behaviors were more likely than others. He called this a "habit family hierarchy." Second, he found that as particular behaviors are reinforced, they move up in the hierarchy, and others that did not work moved down the hierarchy.

Oddly enough, Thorndike's early research on cats seems to explain the behavior of frustrated users stymied by computer problems and about help desk personnel and the suggestions they give to callers. Think about the things that you do when you are trying to fix a problem with a personal computer.

As in Scenario 2, you may select "Print" to print a document, but nothing happens. What do you do? You reach into your habit family hierarchy of possible things to try. Table 7.2 provides a hypothetical list for several computer puzzle boxes in which we can be trapped.

Help desks operate in the same way, but because they receive hundreds if not thousands of calls about particular computer hardware and software problems, they have acquired a database of potential problems and their most likely solutions. Given the description of the problem by the caller, the operator accesses the database for the list of potential solutions in order from the most likely to the least likely to work. Although this is often effective for novice computer users, the experienced user, who has already exhausted his or her hierarchy of solutions, can be a bit irritated with the operator starting

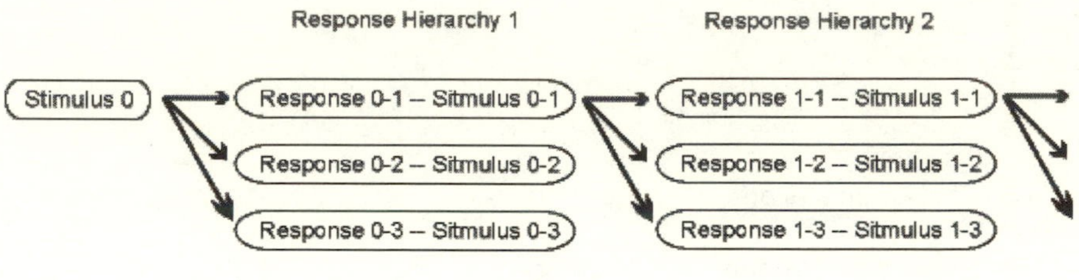

Figure 7.1. A string of associative thought.

at the top of the list! Have you tried restarting the computer? Have you checked to see if it is plugged in?

Expert users are more likely to search technical manuals, technical newsgroups, and technical forums where they can post a question about the problem and see if anyone else has come up with a solution.

Thinking by association starts with an initial stimulus that evokes a response (thought) by association, which acts as the stimulus for the next thought, as shown in Figure 7.1. By this reasoning, thought is a stream of associations. Association, however, has several problems. The first is granularity. How big or little are the thoughts that make up the stream? Are they at the word level, concept level, or higher? Second, if there are many associations at each point and they are probabilistic, there will be an extremely large set of possible thoughts, and the probability of any one thought will be extremely small. Although prediction of single association thought (one hop) is good, it makes prediction of complex thought (long strings) nearly impossible.

The associationist's view of thinking and problem solving is based on networks of associations. Thought is a series of associations from one node to another. Problem solving is accomplished merely by a string of associations. Much of human thinking and problem solving can be accounted for by this mechanism. It is easy to model with computer programs. Moreover, these associative networks are being implemented on computer systems to aid in association, indexing, and search operations. As we see later, increasing numbers of problem solvers are turning to the Web, search engines, and other tools to do their associative "thinking" for them.

However, problem solving by association has been seen as extremely mechanistic, lacking conceptual understanding, and devoid of creativity. There must be something more to human thinking and problem solving. This is the view of the Gestalt school of psychology.

Problem Solving by Restructuring

Gestalt psychology conceives of problem solving as the restructuring of the relationships among a set of objects, reformulating the system into a new

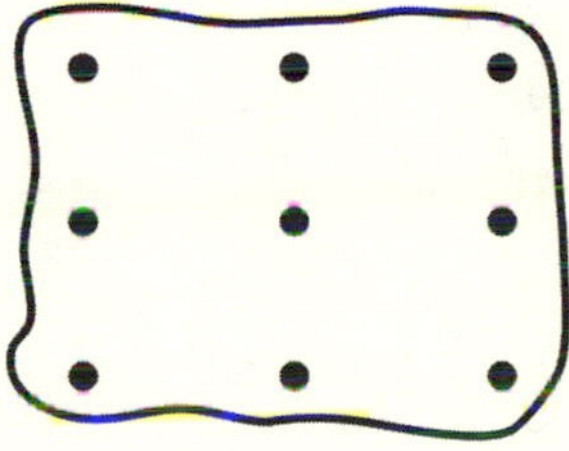

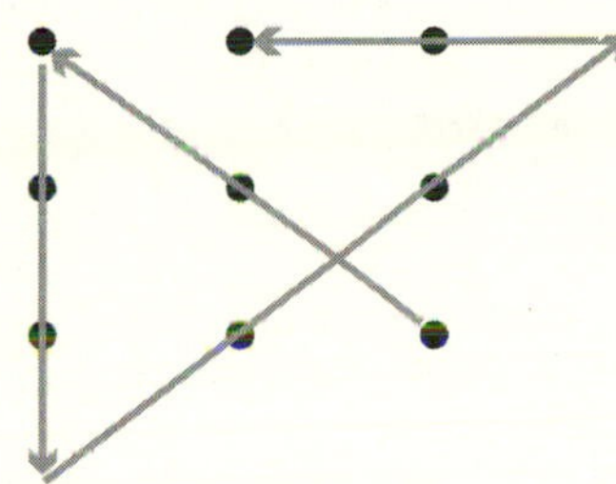

Figure 7.2. The nine-dot puzzle: the imagined perimeter that restricts the ability to find the solution (left) *and the actual solution* (right).

pattern, and thinking "outside the box." The classic illustration of restructuring a problem is the nine-dot puzzle shown in Figure 7.2. Using only four straight lines, go through all of the nine dots such that after the first line is drawn, each line begins where the last one ended. Most problem solvers limit their lines to within the unseen perimeter of the box, thereby missing the solution. Rather than thinking by rigid and self-imposed rules, de Bono (1968) promoted "lateral thinking," whereby one seeks to change concepts and perceptions, think in ways that are not immediately obvious, and find solutions that are not arrived at by traditional step-by-step logic.

Gestalt psychologists have emphasized the importance of attaining a conceptual understanding of the problem, the spontaneity of the insight, and stages of problem solving, but their research has primarily focused on the self-imposed hindrances to problem solving listed in Table 7.3. They have shown that one can get locked into seeing the problem and the solution in only one way. With repeated successes, one stops thinking and searching for solutions. One blindly applies the same solution over and over. One can

Table 7.3. Mental Blocks in Problem Solving

Mental Block	Description	Technology
Problem-solving set	Solving a number of related problems in the same way causes a person to be fixated on applying the same solution in all cases. It becomes hard to think of an alternative approach.	Many computer problems are routinely solved in the same way, reboot, reinstall, etc.
Selective encoding	We tend to be drawn off by irrelevant information and miss the real key to the problem.	In technology, there is a lot going on, and we can follow many irrelevant cues and false leads.
Functional fixedness	Once we use an object for one purpose, it becomes hard to see how it can be used to solve a problem by using it in a different way.	Most technology is very specific, but different algorithms and subroutines can be used for different things, and different devices can be used in novel ways.

Table 7.4. Four Classic Stages of Problem Solving

Stage	Operations	Technology
Preparation	Identify the problem, gather information, check for previous solutions	Problems may be identified by the computer (error messages), search technical manuals, search for solutions, participate in discussion groups
Incubation	Let the problem sit, sleep on it, or take a break so that you can get past mental blocks and fixedness	Play a video game, e-shop, e-chat, see a movie, or get away from the computer and take a walk in nature
Inspiration	The idea appears out of thin air, "ah-ha phenomenon," Eureka!	?
Verification	Check to see if the solution works, implement a plan, and carry it out	Program it, fix it, and see what happens, etc.

imagine with the repetitive tasks at the human–computer interface whereby we do that same thing repeatedly with a sequence of steps, that we stop thinking about it and routinely apply the same solution over and over. Then when something changes (e.g., a version, a network connection, a link on a Web page), we experience a mental block in coming up with a new solution.

According to Gestalt psychologists, perception accounts for a lot. If we perceive the problem in a way that does not include a key to the solution, we will be lost as in the nine-dot puzzle. We may perceive a Web page in such a way that we do not see a link that was obvious to the designer, but in reality is obscured in a background pattern. Finally, considerable research has shown how we limit the use of tools by restricting their functionality. If a box was used as a container, it limits our ability to see it used as a platform, or if a wrench was used to unscrew something, it limits our ability to see it used as a weight. Technology provides many tools with particular functions. But more often than not, alternative functions can prove to be the solution to problems. Often functional fixedness can be broken up by technology that has multiple and open-ended functionality. Like duct tape, computer technology is often seen as a universal solve-it-all tool.

Although research on the hindrances to problem solving has been enlightening, a detailed theory of how restructuring of the problem occurs has been lacking. Gestalt psychology has identified four stages of problem solving, as listed in Table 7.4. The key stage is inspiration, but it is the most vague.

In the preparation phase, the problem solver learns everything he or she can about the situation, the symptoms, previous attempts to solve the problem, and technical details and theory. If a solution is not found during the preparation stage, one enters into the incubation stage. During the incubation stage, the mind takes an apparent vacation from the problem. You think about other things, relax, watch a movie, or take a walk. During this period, the mind may still be at work subconsciously searching for new patterns and possible solutions. If one is fortunate, the insight comes as an "ah-ha phenomenon." As if from nowhere, a new solution pops into the mind. "That's it!" you exclaim, and you enter into the last stage, verification. Now you must see if the new solution actually works or if you are at a dead end once again. Verification can be a simple test in some situations (e.g., trying lowercase for your password), or it can be a very long process in other cases (e.g., reformatting the hard drive, rebuilding the system). How are these stages influenced or changed by computer technology?

Although Gestalt psychology has not produced specific theories of how restructuring occurs, it has produced a number of ideas on how to promote creativity, which we turn to later in this chapter.

Problem Solving by Process

Parallel with the development of computer programming in the 1960s and 1970s, information processing theory in psychology began to conceive of thinking as a cognitive process that one could represent with flowcharts and diagrams. Even though we cannot directly observe thinking, we can infer the process. The steps involve processes such as encoding information, transforming the information, accessing memory, making decisions, and generating responses.

The goal of cognitive scientists was to map out the flowchart of processing information. There were three ways of doing this. First, one could infer the steps that were necessary to perform the process. Second, one could ask the problem solver what he or she was doing or thinking by using methods of verbal protocols discussed in Chapter 4. Third, one could observe the problem solver's interaction with the environment when in the process of moving pieces, seeking information, and so on. Given this information, one could then program a computer simulation and see if the behavior of the simulation matched that of observed human behavior. Figure 7.3 shows a schematic of the relationship between these processes. The box at the top shows the theoretical flowchart of human processes. Problem solvers may verbalize some of this process to reveal steps and heuristics that they are using. At the bottom, a computer program is used to simulate the human problem solver. In doing so, there should be some correspondence between the operations and states of the human and the procedures of the simulation.

Information processing theory has resulted in a number of important ideas. First, the human mind began to be thought of as a computer. The "human machine" analogy governed the way cognitive psychologists theorized about thinking. The mind was viewed as a complex computer, and thought processes to solve problems were seen as computer programs. The ideas of cybernetics (Weiner, 1948) were applied directly to cognitive psychology. Thinking was governed by homeostatic feedback loops to test, operate, test, and exit (TOTE; Miller, Galanter, & Pribram, 1960), and complex processes of behavior were represented as hierarchies of simple component processes.

Second, general problem-solving methods from AI were applied as models for human thinking. For example, the General Problem Solver (or GPS) was intended as a demonstration that formal problem-solving methods could

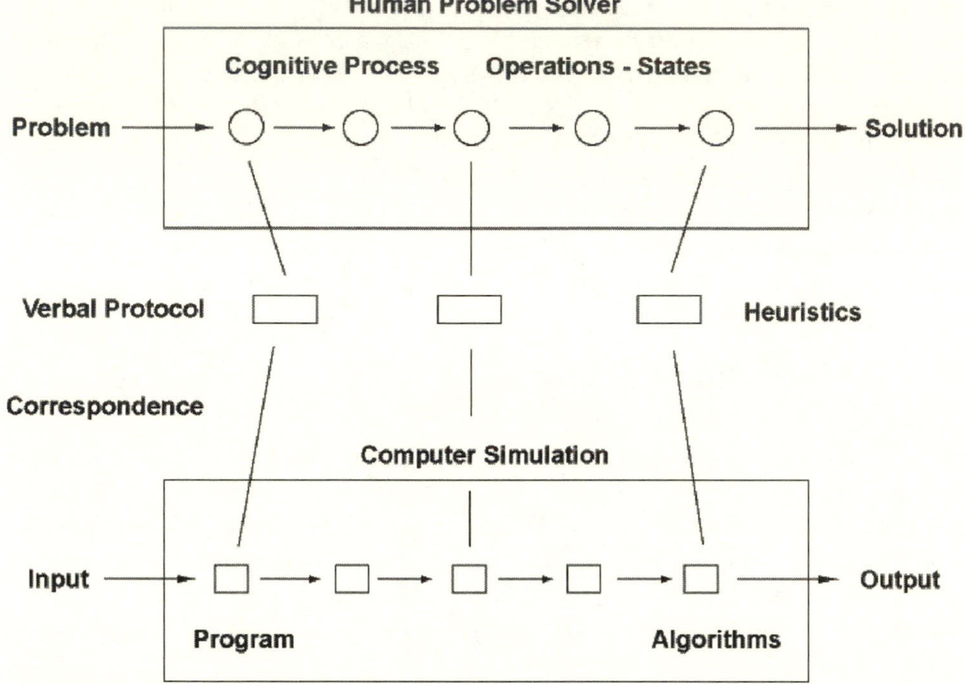

Figure 7.3. Comparison of the human thinking process and the computer simulation.

be applied to a wide variety of problem situations (Ernst & Newell, 1969). The idea was to break a problem into subgoals and apply problem-solving techniques at each subgoal. A related approach is a *production system*. This consists of a set of if-then rules, a working memory of facts, and a forward-chaining algorithm for producing new facts from old ones. A rule is invoked when its conditions match the set of facts in working memory. ACT-R (Anderson, 1993, 1996) and Soar (Laird, Newell, & Rosenbloom, 1987; Newell, 1990) are examples of production systems.

Third, it was realized that representational systems were required for problem solving. For a computer to solve the Tower of Hanoi problem or to play tic-tac-toe or chess, the objects, rules, and states must be represented in the computer. These representations were in the form of *state-action-trees*. A state-action-tree is a diagram that starts from the given state of the problem and shows all successive states as a result of all possible moves at the current state, down to terminal states, some of which constitute goal states. The state-action-tree is a representation of the *problem space*. Figure 7.4 shows the state-action-tree for the Tower of Hanoi problem.

If the entire state-action-tree can be determined, the computer can find the solution. However, if the problem space is very large, this is no simple task. For example, for the game of chess, it has been estimated that there are between 10^{43} and 10^{50} possible legal game states. In comparison, physicists estimate that there are no more than 10^{90} protons in the universe. Different

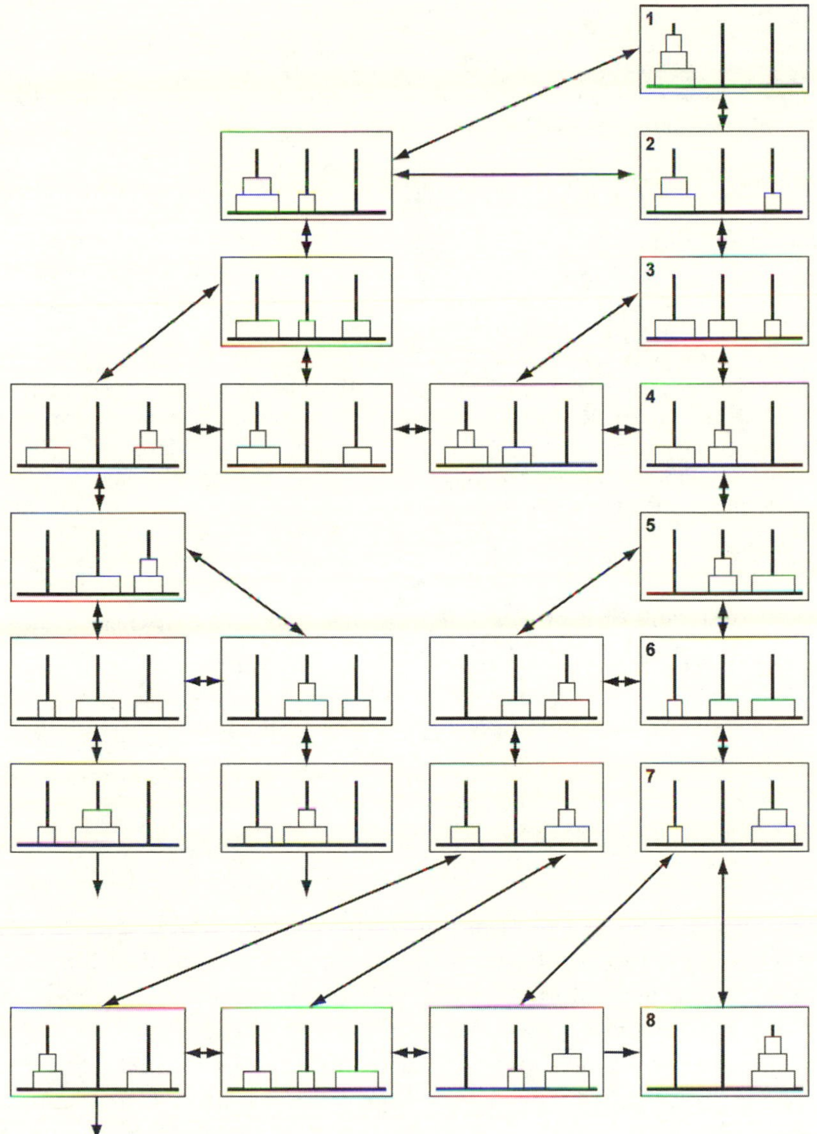

Figure 7.4. State-action-tree for the Tower of Hanoi problem.

techniques have been developed to search the problem spaces regardless of their size (Hayes, 1981; Wickelgren, 1974). The next section discusses some of these approaches, which for the most part are shared by humans and computers.

Problem-Solving Strategies

Given the initial state of the problem space and a set of operators, there are a number of strategies that one can use to select the next state. A substantial

Table 7.5. Problem-Solving Strategies and Approaches

Strategy	Description	Technology
Random trial and error	Randomly select actions and see if they work.	Randomly try different functions and operations.
Systematic trial and error	Systematically go through all possibilities.	Automate the search process.
Breadth then depth	When searching for a solution in the problem space, check across a number of possibilities at each level before proceeding to the next level.	Search all functions at one level and scan all options on one screen before going to the next.
Depth first	Explore one path all the way to its conclusion before branching out to another.	Select only options that move to the next level rather than stay at the same level.
Hill climbing	Pick alternative actions that increase some evaluation function.	Automate the search process.

amount of work in computer science has been devoted to the development of tree search algorithms and their efficiency for different types of problems (Cormen, Leiserson, Rivest, & Stein, 2001; Kleene, 1956; Nilsson, 1980). Table 7.5 lists some of the simpler approaches that human problem solvers use.

Random Trial and Error

We have already mentioned trial-and-error problem solving with associationism. We randomly try a solution and see if it works. If it does not, we randomly try another solution. Often, as humans, we may actually try the same solution repeatedly to see if it works some of the time. We may try to print a document over and over again to no avail or restart the computer several times. Trial and error requires the least cognitive effort and can be very effective if each try has a very low cost in terms of time and effort. But if trials are expensive and hard or impossible to undo, it should not and hopefully will not be the method of choice.

Systematic Trial and Error

Computers are much better at systematic trial and error. Essentially, a computer program can be written to methodically check every path in a finite problem space and test to see which one is the solution. This is like systematically checking every set of three numbers to open a combination lock. The problem space for the lock has 100 × 100 × 100 or 1 million possibilities. Of course, you would not have to explore all possible combinations because you would stop when the lock opens, which on average would only be

500 thousand. In other cases, if you were searching for the ideal set of amounts, say, for a food recipe or for engine efficiency, you would have to test all combinations.

Breadth Then Depth

The state-action-tree for different problems may be very shallow and wide, or it may be rather narrow and deep. For shallow problems, the solution path may be only one or two steps. For deep structures, one may have to apply a very long sequence of operators to achieve the goal. However, many problem spaces are mixed, and one has a choice of searching by breadth first; that is, by trying a number of different alternatives at the first level before proceeding to the next. For example, if I am looking for a textbook to use in a college course, I may first scan all of the book titles and authors before I look at the table of contents, request a copy for inspection, and read it through.

Depth First

Alternatively, in a depth first search, one follows the path all the way down to the conclusion before checking another solution. Depth is required for the combination lock. One must dial all three numbers in sequence to test the solution. Although this sounds like a thorough approach, there can be several problems. First, if the path is extremely long or never ends, one has to decide when to give up. Second, one has to remember which parts of the tree have already been explored. This can easily exceed human working memory. However, it can be efficient when heuristic methods are used to determine highly likely branches, such as using highway markers, signs, and other navigation aids.

Hill Climbing

In many problem-solving situations, one can use evaluation heuristics to assess how close one is getting to the goal. In essence, the evaluation tells the problem solver if he or she is getting "hotter" or "colder" at each move. In hill climbing, one is looking for the optimal or highest point on a multidimensional surface defined by a set of coordinates. Imagine that you are standing on a surface, but you are blindfolded. How would you find the highest point? One method is to step one way and, if it goes up, keep going in that direction until it goes down. Then step in another direction and if it goes up, keep going in that direction until it goes down. You are at the top when any direction that you step goes down. This meandering approach works, but more efficient techniques reduce the number of steps by exploring gradients, setting trajectories, and varying the size of the steps that you take.

We often use hill climbing strategies to optimize our well-being. We vary the amount of sleep we get, our diet, our exercise, and other activities to search for the highest point on the continuum. The major problem with the hill climbing approach is getting caught in a local maximum, like a little foothill on the side of a big mountain. These are cases where detours are required. Things have to get worse before they can get better.

Strategies for Information Search

Reinventing the wheel is generally not the best way to solve problems. Instead, one can find and apply a solution that someone else has already worked out. Problem solving is often information search. Whether we call tech support, search through user manuals, or perform Web searches, we can benefit from the experience of others, if we can find it recorded somewhere.

The methods by which we search for information in our memory are quite different from the way in which a computer searches for and retrieves information. It all depends on how it is stored and indexed. Human memory appears to be organized in networks as we saw in Chapter 6. The time that it takes to retrieve something depends on how many nodes or choice points one has to traverse to get to the information.

In the first scenario, Jenny was looking for information about knee problems. Searching for online information involves two fundamental activities: generating a query statement for indexed databases (e.g., "find all documents with the words 'computer' and 'problem' in the title published after 1/1/2005") and selecting options in networks of hyperlinked documents. In Chapter 8, we cover query languages. In this section, we discuss strategies for search in networks such as pages on the Web.

In many ways, searching the Web is like searching a state-action-tree for a path to the goal. It is easy to get turned around and confused searching for information as suggested by the chapter entitled "Lost in Hyperspace" by Edwards and Hardman (1989). Here are some strategies to help.

Reposition to Breadth

When stuck at a dead end, a strategy for redirecting the search is to move to a level of the menu tree that affords the greatest breadth of choice. For many Web sites, this is the home page, an index page, or a site map.

Reposition to Choice Points

In general, users backtrack to the point where they suspect that they took a wrong turn. Most likely this is a point at which there was uncertainty in choice. Thus, if a user was fairly sure about a choice, that frame would not be a good point to reposition a search. But if the choice were questionable, then that frame would be a good candidate for repositioning.

Reposition to Cognitive Landmarks

When menus are organized according to a semantic network, there are generally pivotal landmarks at which fundamental turns are taken. When we give directions to geographic locations, we generally use landmarks. If one gets lost, one can return to the landmark in order to redirect a search.

Forward Search versus Backward Search

In general, hierarchical menu structures promote forward search; however, when novice users are more familiar with the target item than they are with the forward path, backward search may be used. If novices are searching for an explicit target item, they may initially try to think backward up the tree: "What do I select to get X? If Y leads to X, what do I select to get Y?"

Recognition of Recurring Patterns

In menu search, expert users are attentive to recurring patterns of menu structure, common menus, types of menu screens, and paths through menu structures. Experts are able to recognize the intent of menus, identify potential paths for search, and search chunks of menu structures rather than individual items.

Planning

In a way, menu selection appeals to the trial-and-error method. However, trial and error as a method of search becomes impractical when the menu system is very extensive and when computer response time is very slow. In these cases, prior planning is imperative. By formulating a plan, the user accomplishes much of the search mentally rather than overtly. The plan may eliminate unfruitful branches, determine the most direct path to the target, and incorporate backup search procedures if the item is not found on the first try.

Creativity

Searching for solutions that other people have found does not seem very creative. There is perhaps an arbitrary line drawn between mundane, mechanical problem solving and what we label as "creativity." Great discoveries, inventions, and creative works are often the result of a painstaking search of the problem space or the radical restructuring of the space in a flash of brilliant insight. Whatever it takes, we are interested in producing more of it. The practical question then is "How can we use computers to assist in either or both of these moments of creativity?"

By studying a number of such creative moments, we can identify some commonalities in approach and techniques for creativity. One can list steps and methods for creative problem solving. For example, George Pólya (1945) suggested following these four steps when solving a mathematical problem:

1. *Understand the problem.* You must first do your homework and acquire knowledge of the problem. What are the givens and the operations, and what constitutes a valid solution? You should also find out if others have solved or attempted to solve the problem and what they learned about it.
2. *Make a plan.* Complex problems and solutions require many steps. You need to make a plan of action to figure out how to achieve the goal.
3. *Execute the plan.* For some problems, executing the plan is negligible, but for others it may be a major outlay of time and money. Checking the spelling of a word is easy; building an experimental airplane is not.
4. *Look back and evaluate the solution.* Finally, one must determine if the plan worked and the goal has been achieved. If it failed, something may be learned from the failure that will help achieve the goal the next time around. If it succeeded, something may be learned that will lead to a more efficient, effective alternative solution in the future.

Since the 1950s, there has been a strong interest in creativity techniques for problem solving at both the individual and the corporate levels. Many techniques for fostering and facilitating creativity have been developed and applied in business, industry, government, and education. Couger (1999) reviewed twenty-two such methods, and Mayer (1999) reviewed fifty years of research on creativity methods and training. Today, the techniques and the technology converge, and there is a great interest in developing creativity support tools (National Science Foundation, 2006). A number of methods for creativity are enhanced with computer interfaces and enabled with networks of shared data. A sample of these methods is listed in the next sections.

Brainstorming

One of the best-known creativity methods was developed by Osborn (1963) for generating a large number of ideas in a group setting. Brainstorming builds on the ideas of associationism but employs the following rules:

- *No criticism.* Participants should not evaluate or criticize ideas during the initial brainstorming session.

- *Quantity over quality.* Participants are to generate as many ideas as they can without regard to quality.
- *Originality is encouraged.* Unusual and ridiculous ideas are encouraged over practical, mundane ideas.
- *Chain reaction.* Participants can build off of other ideas using combinations and improvements.

Brainstorming support tools start by posing the questions; gathering the ideas; sorting and clustering the ideas; evaluating, voting, and eliminating ideas; and, finally, reporting on the process and conclusions. These tools may use electronic blackboards or networked computers and video projectors to generate and display ideas. Many of these tools have been written for LANs and now for Web-based networks.

Morphological Analysis

Many problems can be structured to allow the problem solver to explore all possibilities. Zwicky (1969) developed a technique for exploring multidimensional problem spaces in which one constructs an *n*-dimensional box based on a number of variables and reduces the number of possible solutions by eliminating illogical combinations in the box. The steps are as follows:

1. Generate an explicit formulation and problem definition.
2. Identify the fundamental dimensions or parameters of the problem.
3. Construct a "morphological box" from the parameters and dimensions identified in step 2.
4. Scrutinize all possible solutions in the morphological box to see how they meet the specifications of the problem.
5. Analyze the best solutions selected in the preceding step relative to their feasibility given existing resources.

Support tools for morphological analysis are based on models of the box, cross-consistencies of variables, and displays of tables such as MA/Casper, Advanced Computer Support for Morphological Analysis (Ritchey, Stenström, & Eriksson, 2002). Figure 7.5 shows a screen shot of one such analysis.

Synectics

The word "synectics" means to bring different things together to create a unified connection. Gordon (1961) developed a creativity method based on the application of metaphors, analogies, and thought processes that individuals may not be aware of to facilitate a sort of Gestalt restructuring of the problem space. There are three stages in the process:

1. *Referring.* Generate a common definition of the problem by different members of the group. Systematically explore different definitions and viewpoints and gather information. Define and select one viewpoint for

PLANNING/ PLANS	TRAINING AND EDUCATION	PERSONNEL AVAILABLE	EQUIPMENT AVAILABLE	LEADERSHIP LEVEL	RESPONSE to chemical release	RESPONSE: Information to public	RESPONSE: Affected people
Full preparedness plan	Broad municipal co-operative training	11 or more	Special equipment for specific case	Level 4	Reduce by at least 80% within 15 min	Warn involved within 5 min.	Help many within 30 min.
Response plan for specific case	Training for specific case	8-10	Base equipment for specific case	Level 3	Reduce by at least 80% within 30 min	Warn involved within 30 min.	Help some individuals within 15 min.
Standard routine for specific case	Base education + regular training	5-7	Less than base equipment for specific case	Level 2	Reduce by less than 60% within 15 min	No warning within 30 min.	Help some individuals within 30 min.
Standard routine for general case	Base education only	4 or less		Level 1	Reduce by less than 50% within 30 min		No help within 30 min.
Only alert plan					No measures within 30 min		

Figure 7.5. A morphological analysis of rescue services' preparedness for accidents involving chemical releases. (From Ritchey, Stenström, & Eriksson, 2002.)

further development. This stage relies on *convergent thinking*, bringing many facts to bear on one issue.

2. *Reflecting*. Participants are encouraged to take a "vacation" from the problem and engage in free discussion on a subject seemingly unconnected with the original problem but with analogical connections. They are to discuss topics in other fields that have analogical relationships to the problem at hand and engage in brainstorming activities. This stage relies on *divergent thinking* or *lateral thinking*, spanning a wide range of options.
3. *Reconstructing*. Finally, participants are to apply the ideas generated during the free discussion to the problem at hand, to evaluate the ideas, and to generate a practical solution. This stage relies on convergent thinking.

Creativity support tools for the synectics method use a wide variety of brainstorming tools and diagramming tools.

K-J Method

When there are many diverse ideas, methods must be used to organize and reveal underlying relationships in the problem space. Kawakito Jiro developed the following steps:

1. Observations concerning the problem or phenomenon of interest are recorded on separate pieces of paper. The observations can be in the

form of single words, phrases, or short sentences. Full sentences are written and recorded on cards.
2. The cards are shuffled. They are then examined to see if there are associations linking the observations. This iterative process continues until the whole set has been classified into groups.
3. The groups are then arranged in some meaningful pattern. The patterns may be hierarchical in nature. The idea is to find some "metaconcept" that can be used to generate new groups. The solution may well be contained in one of these new groups.

The result is an "affinity diagram" showing the clusters, patterns, and relationships between ideas. It was originally used in Japanese management and planning tools. The affinity diagram is used to discover meaningful groups of ideas from the raw list.

Often an affinity diagram is used to organize the results of a brainstorming session. To create an affinity diagram, you sort the brainstormed list, moving ideas from the brainstorm into affinity sets and creating groups of related ideas. As you sort ideas, you should perform the following steps:

1. Rapidly group ideas that seem to belong together. You do not need to define why they belong together.
2. Clarify any ideas in question.
3. Copy ideas into more than one affinity set if appropriate.
4. Look for small sets and determine whether they belong in larger sets.
5. Look at large sets and determine whether they need to be broken down into smaller sets.
6. When most of the ideas have been sorted, start to enter titles for each affinity set.

A sample affinity diagram is shown in Figure 7.6. The left side of the window lists the original ideas. The right side shows the affinity diagram, in which ideas have been grouped into sets.

Mind Mapping

Outlining, diagramming, and visualizing the structure of knowledge or the structure of a problem space can help people understand, learn, and solve problems. A *mind map* is a diagram used to organize ideas or objects by linking and arranging them radially around a key idea or word. It can be used to visualize the structure of the problem situation and aid in problem solving and decision making. Mind maps are based on the idea of semantic networks and concept maps discussed in Chapter 6. Buzan (1991) advocated the use of mind maps for note taking and suggests a number of guidelines, some of which are listed as follows:

- Start at the center with an image of the topic.
- Use images and symbols throughout the map.
- Select words and images, and set them on their own line.

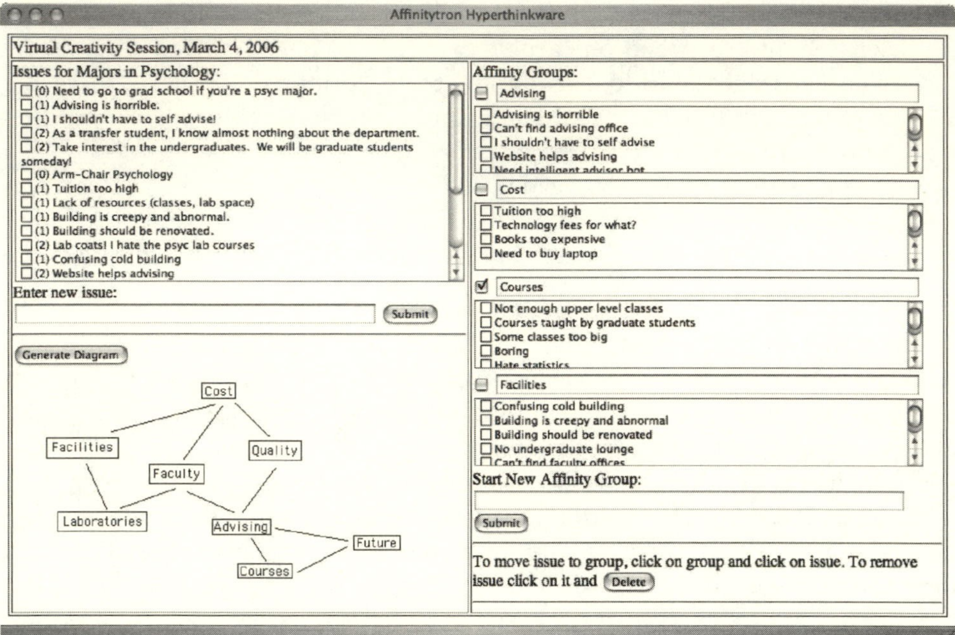

Figure 7.6. A prototype affinity diagram showing the raw ideas on the left and the affinity sets on the right.

- Lines are to be connected starting from the central image.
- Develop your own personal style.
- Use emphasis and show associations.

Figure 7.7 shows a mind map of the mind mapping guidelines. Of course, mind mapping started with the assistance of paper and colored pencils but has quickly transitioned to computers and the Internet.

Today, there are dozens of mind mapping tools on the market. These tools aid in drawing, manipulating, storing, and transmitting maps to others.

End Thoughts

In the end, the human mind with all of its shortcomings trumps the computer, despite its speed, memory, and algorithms. Human thinking and problem solving continue to be of central interest at the human–computer interface.

Although computers help solve problems, they also create problems. They are not only a means to an end, but they also generate obstacles and hurdles that the human mind must overcome. Because computers pose additional barriers to the fulfillment of our goals, the challenge to designers is to create an interface that solves more problems than it creates.

In our society, we tend to value and reward creativity over mechanical, rote repetition of old ideas. Humans, by nature, define and embody creativity. Computers, by nature, are machines. However, for creativity to occur, it usually involves both the mundane, mechanical application of convergent

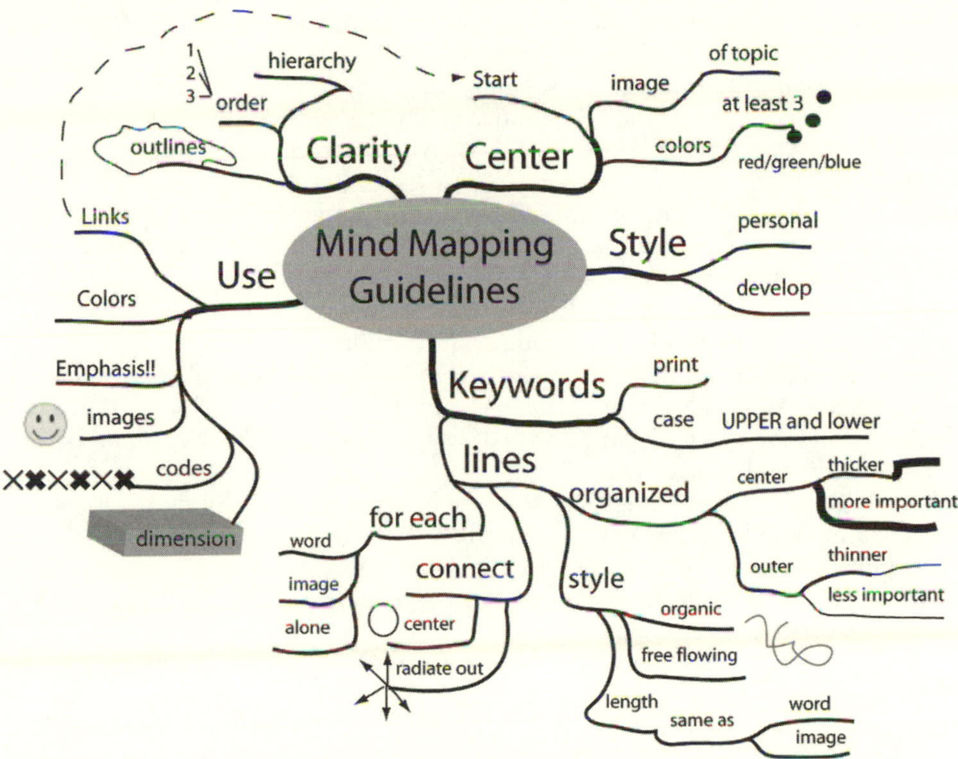

Figure 7.7. A mind map of the mind mapping guidelines. (Adapted from Wikipedia: MindMapGuidlines.JPG by Danny Stevens, 2006.)

thinking and the insightful, inspirational involvement of divergent thinking. The synergistic combination of human creativity and computer processes at the interface have the potential to achieve new levels of creativity.

Suggested Exercises

1. List some problems that you have solved using computers. List some problems caused by computers that you have solved.
2. Write out your habit family hierarchy for solving a computer-related problem, such as fixing a connection to the Internet, ejecting a stubborn disk, or recovering a lost file.
3. Use one of the brainstorming support tools to run a brainstorming session.

References

Anderson, J. R. (1993). *Rules of the mind*. Hillsdale, NJ: Erlbaum.

Anderson, J. R. (1996). ACT: A simple theory of complex cognition. *American Psychologist*, *51*, 355–365.

Bourne, L. E., Jr. (1970). Knowing and using concepts. *Psychological Review, 77,* 546–556.

Bourne, L. E., Jr., Ekstrand, B. R., & Dominowski, R. L. (1971). *The psychology of thinking.* Englewood Cliffs, NJ: Prentice Hall.

Bruner, J. S., Goodnow, J. J., & Austin, G. A. (1956). *A study of thinking.* New York: Wiley.

Buzan, T. (1991). *The mind map book.* New York: Penguin.

Chapman, L. J., & Chapman, J. P. (1959). Atmosphere effect reexamined. *Journal of Experimental Psychology, 58,* 220–226.

Cormen, T. H., Leiserson, C. E., Rivest, R. L., & Stein, C. (2001). *Introduction to algorithms* (2nd ed.). MIT Press and McGraw-Hill.

Couger, D. (1999). *Creativity & innovation in information systems organizations.* Danvers, MA: Boyd & Fraser.

de Bono, E. (1968). *New think: The use of lateral thinking in the generation of new ideas.* New York: Basic Books.

Edwards, D. M., & Hardman, L. (1989). Lost in hyperspace: Cognitive mapping and navigation in a hypertext environment. In R. McAleese (Ed.), *Hypertext: Theory and practice.* (pp. 105–125). Oxford, England: Intellect.

Ernst, G. W., & Newell, A. (1969). *GPS: A case study in generality and problem solving.* New York: Academic Press.

Hayes, J. R. (1981). *The complete problem solver.* Philadelphia: Franklin Institute Press.

Haygood, R. C., & Stevenson, M. (1967). Effects of number of irrelevant dimensions in nonconjunctive concept learning. *Journal of Experimental Psychology, 74,* 302–304.

Gordon, W. J. J. (1961). *Synectics.* New York: Harper & Row.

Greeno, J. G. (1978). Natures of problem solving abilities. In W. K. Estes (Ed.), *Handbook of learning and cognitive process* (Vol. 5, pp. 239–270). Hillsdale, NJ: Erlbaum.

Greeno, J. G., & Simon, H. A. (1988). Problem solving and reasoning. In R. C. Atkinson, R. C. Hernstein, G. Lindzey, & R. D. Luce (Eds.), *Steven's handbook of experimental psychology* (pp. 589–672). New York: Wiley.

Klayman, J., & Ha, Y. W. (1987). Confirmation, disconfirmation and information in hypothesis testing. *Psychological Review,* 94, 211–228.

Klayman, J., & Ha, Y. W. (1989). Hypothesis testing in rule discovery: Strategy, structure, and content. *Journal of Experimental Psychology: Learning, Memory, and Cognition,* 15, 596–604.

Kleene, S. C. (1956). Representation of events in nerve nets and finite automata. In C. E. Shannon & J. McCarthy (Eds.), *Automata studies* (pp. 3–42). Princeton, NJ: Princeton University Press.

Laird, J., Newell, A., & Rosenbloom, P. (1987). Soar: An architecture for general intelligence. *Artificial Intelligence, 33,* 1–64.

Lefford, A. (1946). The influence of emotional subject matter on logical reasoning. *Journal of General Psychology,* 34, 127–151.

Markman, A. B., & Ross, B. H. (2003). Category use and category learning. *Psychological Bulletin,* 129, 592–613.

Mayer, R. E. (1992). *Thinking, problem solving, and cognition* (2nd ed.). New York: Freeman.

Mayer, R. E. (1999). Fifty years of creativity research. In R. J. Sternberg (Ed.), *Handbook of creativity* (pp. 449–460). Cambridge: Cambridge University Press.

Medin, D. L. (1989). Concepts and conceptual structure. *American Psychologist*, 44, 1469–1481.

Miller, G. A., Galanter, E., & Pribram, K. H. (1960). *Plans and the structure of behavior*. New York: Holt, Rinehart and Winston.

Mueller, E. T. (1990). *Daydreaming in humans and machines: A computer model of the stream of thought*. Norwood, NJ: Ablex.

National Science Foundation. (2006). Creativity support tools: Report from a U.S. National Science Foundation sponsored workshop. *International Journal of Human–Computer Interaction*, 20, 61–77.

Newell, A. (1990). *Unified theories of cognition*. Cambridge, MA: Harvard University Press.

Nilsson, N. J. (1980). *Principles of artificial intelligence*. Palo Alto, CA: Tioga.

Osborn, A. F. (1963). *Applied imagination: Principles and procedures of creative problem solving*. New York: Charles Scribner's Sons.

Pólya, G. (1945). *How to solve it*. Princeton, NJ: Princeton University Press.

Revlis, R. (1975). Two models of syllogistic reasoning: Feature selection and conversion. *Journal of Verbal Learning and Verbal Behavior*, *14*, 180–195.

Revlin, R., & Leirer, V. O. (1978). The effect of personal biases on syllogistic reasoning: Rational decisions from personalized representation. In R. Revlin & R. E. Mayer (Eds.), *Human reasoning* (pp. 51–81). Washington, DC: Winton/Wiley.

Ritchey, T., Stenström, M., & Eriksson, H. (2002, November). *Using morphological analysis for evaluating preparedness for accidents involving hazardous materials*. Adapted from an article presented at the 4th International Conference for Local Authorities, Shanghai, China. Retrieved March 14, 2008, from www.swemorph.com/pdf/chem2.pdf

Rosch, E. H. (1978). Principles of categorization. In E. Rosch & B. L. Lloyd (Eds.), *Cognition and categorization* (pp. 27–48). Hillsdale, NJ: Erlbaum.

Thorndike, E. L. (1911). *Animal intelligence*. New York: Macmillan.

Weiner, N. (1948). *Cybernetics*. New York: Wiley.

Wickelgren, W. A. (1974). *How to solve problems: Elements of a theory of problems and problem solving*. San Francisco: Freeman.

Zwicky, F. (1969). *Discovery, invention, research – Through the morphological approach*. Toronto: The Macmillan Company.

Eight

Language and Programming

Scenario 1

This program is supposed to add ten numbers, find the average, and print it out. To do this, first I will have to get the numbers. I will program the computer to prompt the user for each number, 1 through 10. I could use ten input commands, or I could use a loop. I will use a loop. Each time I get a number, I will put it into a variable called "X." I will add X to another variable called "SUM." At the beginning of the program, I will have to set SUM equal to zero. At the end, I will set another variable called "AVG" to SUM divided by 10. Finally, I will print AVG. Here is the program in BASIC:

```
LET SUM = 0;
DO I = 1 TO 10;
        INPUT X;
        LET SUM = SUM + X;
END;
AVG = SUM/10;
PRINT AVG;
```

Scenario 2

Eliza: Hello. I am Eliza. How can I help you?
I am feeling a little down.
Eliza: How long have you been feeling a little down?
For about 10 minutes.
Eliza: Please go on.
Well, I am sad because my computer crashed.

Eliza: Why do you mention computers?
Because that is what crashed.
Eliza: Do any other reasons not come to mind?
Yes, I lost an important file.
Eliza: You are sure?
Do you think that you could help me recover it?
Eliza: Oh, I think that I could help you recover it.
Great! Find it for me.
Eliza: Can you elaborate on that?
Find the file and show it to me.
Eliza: Can you elaborate on that?
What do you need to know?
Eliza: Does that question interest you?
Well, I think it is of interest to you.
Eliza: Do you wish to think it is of interest to me?
I was hoping that you could help me.
Eliza: Why do you tell me you were hoping that I could help you just now?
You asked me.
Eliza: You like to think I asked you, do you not?
Are you taking me in circles?
Eliza: Would you prefer if I were not taking you in circles?
Of course. I would like a direct answer.
Eliza: Can you elaborate on that?
No!
Eliza: You are being a bit negative.
You are being a bit unhelpful.
Eliza: Does it please you to believe I am being a bit unhelpful?
No. You are getting on my nerves now.
Eliza: Why do you say your nerves now?
I am getting irritated with your answers.
Eliza: How long have you been getting irritated with my answers?
I have been irritated with you for the last 10 minutes.
Eliza: Do you wish to have been irritated with me?
I am going to leave if you keep this up.
Eliza: Do you wish that I keep this up?
No.
Eliza: You are being a bit negative.

Overview

Language is our ultimate mode of communication with one another. Language is essentially the main mode for human–human interaction (HHI).

Consequently, it makes sense that we would want to use this powerful mode for HCI. But whose language do we use – the computer's or the human's? It is obvious that we would want to communicate with them using our own natural language because most of us believe that we have already mastered our first language, whether English, Spanish, Chinese, or 1 of the 5,000 other natural languages around the world. But the problem is that language requires a common understanding not only of the vocabulary and the grammar particular to that language, but also general knowledge about the world and basic common sense. It requires the ability to disambiguate between different meanings of newspaper headlines such as "Milk Drinkers Are Turning to Powder" and "Squad Helps Dog Bite Victim." It requires the ability to make correct interpretations so that the person will not take certain things literally (e.g., "Knock yourself out"). It also requires the ability to fill in details so that when we give instructions to another person, we can assume that they will know how to perform the task (e.g., "Vacuum the floor").

The second scenario is taken from a dialog between a human (the present author in a playful mood) and a computer program "Eliza" initially written by Joseph Weizenbaum (1966). In reality, the computer program is extremely simple and devoid of any comprehension of meaning. It is done entirely by parsing the text, taking the words from one sentence, searching for keywords, adding more words, and concatenating them together as a response. The joke was that it mimicked Rogerian nondirective therapy in which therapists are instructed to rephrase what the client says in order to evoke further dialog without giving any evaluations or directives.

Although we want to be able to give instructions to the computer in natural language and have the computer understand what it is that we want it to do, the reality is that we have to program computers down to the last bit. Command languages and programming languages have been developed to specify exact instructions that can be interpreted by the computer and that can be learned and used by computer operators and programmers. The first scenario illustrates the translation from the programmer's intentions to statements written in Basic. The design and structure of these languages are of interest to psychologists studying language learning and use.

In this chapter, we first look at human communication from the perspective of psycholinguistics. We then talk about how language ability relates to the problem of learning and using languages to write computer programs and to control computers and applications. Finally, we discuss the uses and implications of natural language communication between humans and computers. Can we really have a dialog with computers?

Psycholinguistics

How do we, as humans, acquire, use, and understand language? Of course, the answer to this question depends on how the human mind and nervous system work and on all that we know about learning, memory, and information processing. But when it comes to language acquisition and use, we have something very special. Language is our primary method of communication and is central to our being and our uniqueness. We use it to describe our experiences, share knowledge, ask questions, and make requests of others.

What are languages? Basically, languages are systems of symbols and grammars. The symbols convey meaning and grammars provide rules by which the symbols can be manipulated. Linguists study languages. Psycholinguists study the psychological aspects of languages, namely, how languages are learned or acquired and how they are used to perform tasks. Psycholinguists are interested in the cognitive processes used to generate sentences and to interpret the meaning of sentences.

Most languages are spoken using patterns of sound called "phonemes." Most are also written using visual symbols called "graphemes" such as alphabetic letters or Chinese ideograms. Some languages are manual such as American Sign Language, which uses combinations of hand shapes, palm orientations, hand and arm movements, and facial expressions. There are approximately 5,000 natural spoken languages in the world and even a number of synthetic languages such as Esperanto and fantasy languages such as Klingon. To these we can add specialized languages and any formal language invented for some purpose.

For a communication system to be considered a language, linguists have argued that it must have certain features. According to Hulit and Howard (1993), the most important features are as follows:

- *Meaningfulness*: The language must convey meaning. The words must represent things, and the sentences must convey relationships among the words. Nonsense and gibberish do not make a language.
- *Displacement*: Language allows us to communicate about things that are displaced in time or space. We can talk about yesterday and tomorrow. We can talk about things happening somewhere else.
- *Productivity*: Language allows us to produce communications that have never been communicated before. We can tell the same joke in a thousand different ways; we can write poetry that has never been written before, and in many cases, we had better do so to avoid plagiarism and copyright infringement.

These three features are obviously present in natural human languages, fairly absent in animal communications, and technically present in HCI using programming and control languages of various kinds. The program statements have meaning because they refer to objects, functions, and relations. They are displaced because they give instructions for a future time and place. They are highly productive because one is constantly writing new programs or performing new tasks. But programs are a one-way communication from the human to the machine. Dialogs only occur when the computer is programmed, as in the case of Eliza, to generate statements meaningful to humans rather than merely actions in response to the input. In other systems, the computer part of the dialog may be the result of queries, feedback about the results of computer actions, or error messages. In these cases, human interpretation provides meaning to the communication. The question is whether meaningfulness itself could ever reside on the part of both the computer and the human.

Finally, we can ask whether the communication between two computers, computer–computer interaction (CCI), can ever be considered to be a language. We see later in Chapter 13 that although it can be argued that true language may exist between AI programs or agents communicating among themselves, it will require a major leap in anthropomorphic thinking that even the proponents of AI may disagree with. At present, we settle for the fact that meaning is a human activity.

Languages tend to be hierarchically built up from elements to words to statements and so on. Natural spoken languages start with phonemes, the smallest significant sound units of speech. To say "user," we use 3 phonemes: "yue", "z", and "er". To say "computer," we use 7: "k", "u", "m", "p", "yue", "t", and "er". There are probably about 100 possible phonemes that could be used in spoken languages, but most languages use only a subset of these. For example, English uses 44, Polynesian uses 11, and Hebrew uses 27 phonemes.

Phonemes combine to make morphemes, the smallest units of language that convey meaning. Morphemes are words such as "you" and "I" and parts of words such as "re" in repeat and "s" to make a word plural.

Grammar includes phonological rules that prescribe how the phonemes are used to construct morphemes. Then syntactic rules are used to build proper phrases and sentences. For example, in English we know to put the adjective in front of the noun that it modifies (e.g., "pink elephant" rather than "elephant pink") as opposed to Spanish, where the adjective normally follows the noun (e.g., "elefante rosado" rather than "rosado elefante").

Syntactic rules help us construct proper sentences, but there is no guarantee that they are meaningful. The sentence "Purple sky smiled frowns." is syntactically correct but absurd in meaning. The rules of semantics help determine and convey meaning. Meaning relates to what Chomsky (1957, 1965) referred to as the "deep structure" of language. The "surface structure" of two sentences such as "Kent loves Karen" is very different from "Karen is loved by Kent," but their common deep structure reveals that they mean the same thing.

The same type of hierarchy exists in programming languages and the gulf between what is meaningfully intended and the actual code. The smallest element of machine language is the bit (0 or 1), as we see in Chapter 2. The next unit that conveys instructions is the byte from 8 to 64 bits in length. Program statements are sequences of bytes. In higher-level programming languages such as Fortran, BASIC, C^{++}, and Java, the smallest elements are alphanumeric characters (abcd, ... 0123, ... !@#$, ...). Words are composed of characters. For example, in Java, words would include restricted words such as "function" and "array", variable names such as "x" and "y", operators such as "+" and "*", and delimiters such as "{" and ";". These are used to construct statements, which comprise functions and programs.

Similar to the idea of deep structure, the computer programmer or computer user has an intended function to convey to the computer. It is generated in code that is meaningful to the human and hopefully correctly interpreted and performed by the computer. If there is an error in the syntax, the computer can generally inform the programmer or user (e.g., "unexpected terminator" or "illegal operator"). If there is an error in the semantics, the computer will generally not say "that makes no sense" unless there is some sort of logic checking; instead, the operation and output of the computer will not conform to the user's expectations. Most often, the program just bombs.

Given the complexity of language with grammar and semantics, there are two critical questions. The first is how and why languages developed as they have. The second is how we acquire natural language abilities.

Why and how have languages developed to what they are today? Most studies on the development of natural language suggest that languages are related in families that may have spun off variants over time and geographic distance. Figure 8.1 shows one suggested genealogy just for the Proto-Indo-European languages.

New languages developed as people groups spread and separated into different habitats. Throughout history, various empires have partly reversed the diversity of languages. The Roman Empire spread one common legal language, even through the Middle Ages; the British Empire spread English throughout the world; and the Spanish Empire spread Spanish to other parts. Today, globalization via air transportation, telecommunications, and scientific communities continues to reverse language diversity, pushing English as the common, scientific, international language. In contrast to the English solution, L. L. Zamenhof (1887) proposed a constructed language called "Esperanto" that would be nonpolitical, easy to learn and use, and consistent. At present, however, only 2 million people are fluent in Esperanto as opposed to more than 1 billion in English.

Languages share many grammatical characteristics. Chomsky (1965) proposed that there is a "universal grammar" that includes these common rules. Moreover, the vocabularies overlap, and roots of words are often the same. Alphabets and notations are also shared or overlap, which both helps in translation and understanding yet sometimes causes misunderstandings.

How do we learn or acquire language abilities? The perspectives and theories range all the way from pure behaviorism and associative learning to innate prewired language mechanisms. Behaviorists have emphasized how the environment determines the child's vocabulary and grammar with operant conditioning principles. At the other extreme, nativists emphasize inborn mechanisms that jump-start language development. Children acquire language more by modeling and selecting the rules of grammar than by learning them. Chomsky's theory (1965) emphasizes a system of prewired grammar switches that determine the rules. Somewhere between the extremes,

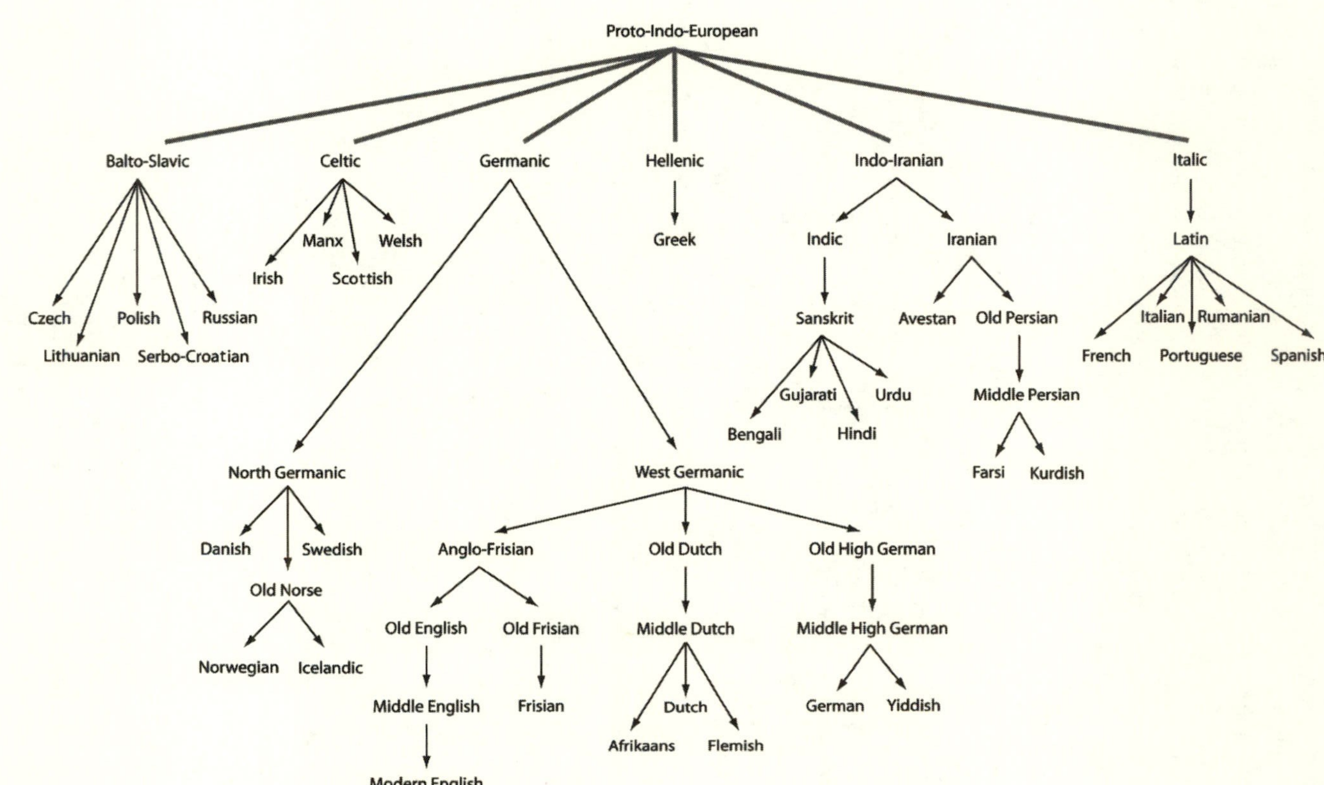

Figure 8.1. A genealogy for the Proto-Indo-European languages.

Table 8.1. Similarities and Differences Between Natural Language First and Second and Programming

Aspect	First language	Second language	Computer language
Age of acquisition	Childhood (2–4 y)	Later in life	Later in life
Modality	Spoken, then written	Written and spoken	Written and rarely spoken
Redundancy	Substantial	Substantial	Little or none
Grammar learning	Incidental learning	Directed learning	Directed learning
Grammar consistency	Many exceptions to rules	Many exceptions to rules	Highly consistent
Semantic learning	Simultaneous with language learning	Prior to language learning	Simultaneous with language learning
Semantic consistency	Incomplete	Incomplete	Formally consistent
Immersion learning	Essential	Helpful	Ridiculous

interactionists emphasize how environmental and genetic factors combine to influence development and the innate abilities of the nervous system to acquire the rules of language. When we turn to computer languages, no one is saying that we have innate programming abilities or mechanisms to acquire programming languages. However, computer languages from simple to complex may be designed to tap into our native language abilities and take advantage of these assets. But for the most part, we must rely on learning and training to acquire programming skills.

Computer Programming

From nearly the beginning of computer programming, computer scientists have used the term "language." The analogy was so compelling that some universities in the 1970s and 1980s considered knowledge of a programming language to count for the foreign language requirement. Indeed, at the University of Iowa, when the Department of Psychology dropped the foreign language competency requirement for the Ph.D., it was suggested that graduate students demonstrate a competency in a computer programming language in place of German or French.

Learning a computer language is, of course, not the same as learning a foreign language, but there are some interesting points of comparison. Table 8.1 lists some aspects of comparison between learning a computer language and the acquisition of one's native language and learning a second language.

In Chapter 2, we learned that programming languages are a means of conveying the set of steps and instructions to the computer. It is more than a metaphor. Computer languages involve the same concepts of grammar (syntax) and semantics (meaning). However, there are two obvious differences. The first difference is that a programming language involves a one-directional communication of procedures to the computer and a return of output or error messages to the programmer. It is hardly a dialog. The second main difference is that programming languages are highly formal and structured. Each statement must be syntactically correct for the computer to accept it. There is no sense of forgiveness and understanding of bad grammar. It just does not compute! Double negatives such as "You ain't nothing but a hound dog" or "We don't need no education" just do not work in programming languages, or they are interpreted as a positive expression according the mathematical logic.

Similar to natural languages, there are many different computer languages and no one universal language. Languages vary from the machine level, where each processor has a different instruction set, to high-level languages written by different individuals or groups for different purposes. However, unlike natural languages, these are constructed languages and, consequently, have different properties from natural languages. Moreover, there are at least three distinct types of languages for different purposes. We talk about imperative programming languages, command-line interfaces, and declarative markup languages. For the most part, programming languages are used to generate programs that can be run at a later time.

Among programming languages there are three types: compiled, interpreted, and hybrid. These forms are generally transparent to the programmer and only have to do with the way the computer converts the instructions to processes. For compiled programs such as Fortran and C^{++}, another program called a "compiler" converts the statements to machine language code that can then run on a particular computer by itself. For interpreted languages such as BASIC, a program called an "interpreter" processes each statement sequentially. The program cannot run independently of the interpreter. Hybrid programs such as Java are compiled to generate an efficient, reduced code that is later run by a special compiler.

Different programming languages have been developed to add or emphasize different features (e.g., procedural, functional, data structured, object oriented). Figure 8.2 shows one taxonomy of programming languages as they developed over time.

Command-line interfaces are used to give line-by-line instructions to the system to perform tasks. OSs such as JCL (job control language), MS-DOS, and UNIX are command-line interfaces. When multiple commands are strung together, they are known as "macros" or "scripts." Query languages such as SQL (structured query language) for searching databases, AutoCAD for computer-aided design, and MATLAB for numerical computation are command-line interfaces.

Finally, declarative languages are used to describe what something is like, rather than how to create it. Markup languages such as LaTeX for typesetting and HTML (hypertext markup language) for the layout of Web pages are descriptions embedded in text. They do not give instructions to the computer as to how to format text, lay out the page, and associate variables with fields on a form either for word processors or for Web pages, but they do provide the information used to do it.

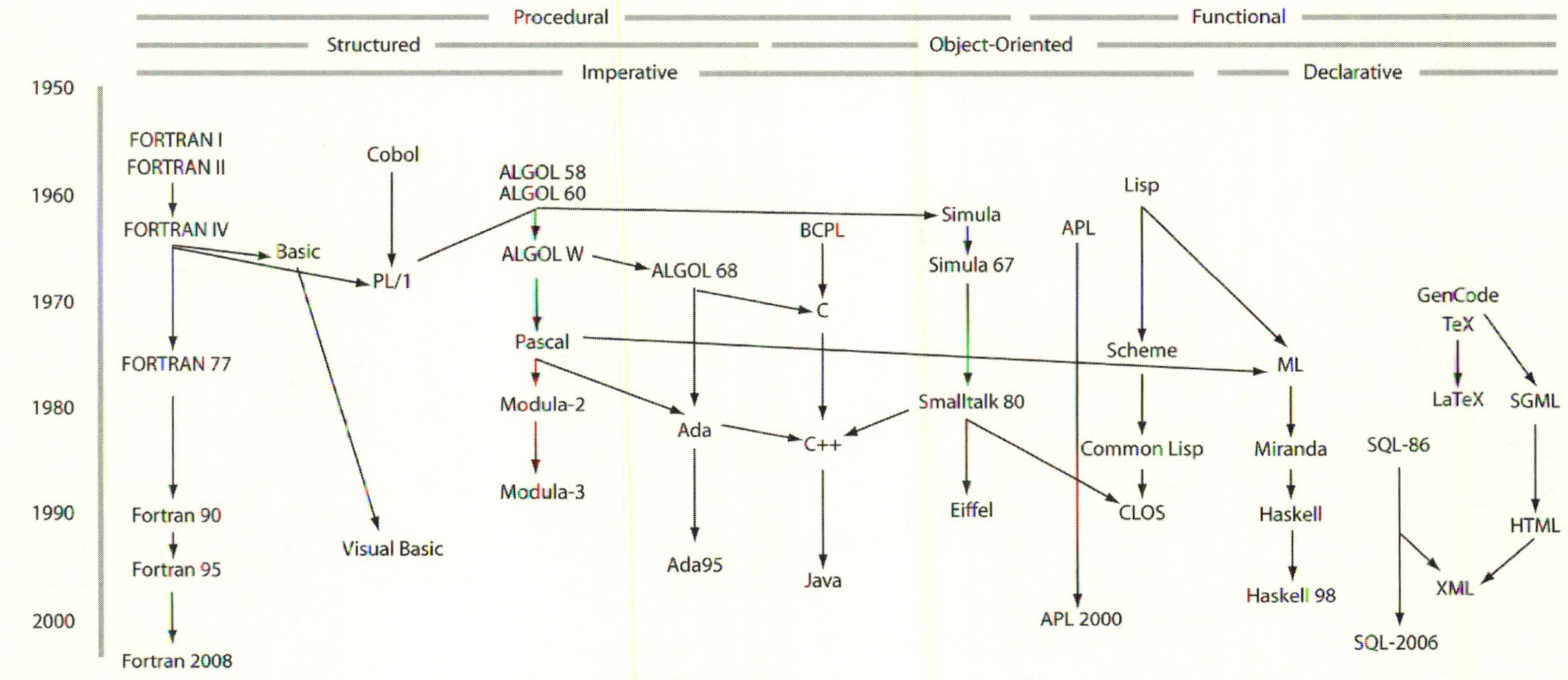

Figure 8.2. A taxonomy of programming languages.

Ever since Grace Hooper helped construct the first programming language, the challenge has been to construct languages that are both powerful and efficient on one side and easy to learn and use on the other. The questions are as follows:

1. What should the vocabulary be (e.g., how many terms, what should the names be)?
2. What logic, operations, functions, etc., should be conveyed in the semantics of the language?
3. What should the syntax be for constructing statements and groups of statements?

The next three sections consider the psychological aspects of designing programming languages. Although numerous guidelines can be specified for constructing a language, rarely have languages been developed in conjunction with usability testing. Instead, the functionality of the language is usually emphasized, and consequently, programmers have had to contend with a "steep learning curve."

Learning a computer language can be difficult. It is certainly not acquired through natural development and modeling behavior. As a result, psychologists, linguists, and computer scientists have been interested in both the learnability and the usability of computer languages.

Names and Abbreviations

Languages, whether natural or programming, use vocabularies. Programming languages use a formal, controlled vocabulary (i.e., a set list of words with specific meanings and use, such as IF, THEN, FOR) and also allow programmers to define and use their own terms for variables and function names. When there is only a small vocabulary of ten to twenty terms, the choice of words is not that important. However, for larger sets, a number of factors such as familiarity, meaningfulness, distinctiveness, etc., can become important for learning the terms, as we see in Chapter 6.

The main issue for programming languages has been the factor of *specificity* versus *generality* (Rosenberg, 1982). Specific terms (e.g., Append, Quit) are more descriptive and distinctive. General terms (e.g., Add, Leave) are more familiar and meaningful. In an early learning experiment, Barnard, Hammond, Morton, Long, and Clark (1981) found that two weeks after being trained on twelve commands, subjects were more likely to recall and recognize the functions of the specific commands than the general commands.

In a more extensive experiment, Black and Moran (1982) compared seven sets of commands varying in frequency, discriminability, meaningfulness, and graphic character. Table 8.2 shows the seven versions of the two commands for inserting and deleting text.

As expected, the Infrequent-Discriminating Words command set produced the fastest learning and highest recall. The Frequent-Nondiscriminating

Table 8.2. Seven Versions of Command Sets Used by Black and Moran (1982)

Command set	Insert text	Delete text
Infrequent-Discriminating Words	insert	delete
Frequent-Discriminating Words	add	remove
Infrequent-Nondiscriminating Words	amble	perceive
Frequent-Nondiscriminating Words	walk	view
Frequent-Nondiscriminating General Words	alter	correct
Nondiscriminating Nonwords	GAC	MIK
Discriminating Nonwords	abc-adbc	abc-ac

General Words command set actually resulted in the lowest performance. Surprisingly, the Nondiscriminating Nonwords command set did well, suggesting that nonsense terms can be used in small command sets.

Functionality

How simple or powerful should a language be? If it is simple with few functions and operations, it will require lengthy code to get the job done. If it is complex with many operations, the code may be very short and dense. Thus, there is a trade-off in specifying the right level of functionality. Professional programmers require powerful languages that typically require extensive training and experience. However, for many users who need to do some programming, the language should not have an excessive number of functions, but should just support the tasks that it needs to perform.

Different languages have different types of functionality, some are good at numerical computations such as Fortran and MATLAB, others are good for working with databases such as SQL, and others are good for string manipulation such as SNOBOL (string oriented symbolic language) and Perl. Although one can accomplish a task that a language was not designed for, it is likely to be convoluted, awkward, and frustrating. Similarly, different natural languages have different strengths for conveying scientific descriptions, romantic feelings, or legal agreements. We often find ourselves needing to express ourselves using words or phrases from other languages to convey the correct nuance of meaning. In the programming of many end user devices, the languages are highly specialized for the particular task. Considerable thought and experimental research are needed to define the appropriate functionality for the application, the task, and the user.

Command Structure

Some commands in programming are single words (e.g., QUIT, PAUSE, RUN) that act in context. Others are commands with arguments and options (e.g., OPEN FILEA; COPY FILEA, FILEB) that operate on the specified objects according to the parameters given. Once we have gone beyond single-word statements, we have to add grammar. In what order should the terms be listed, and how should they be strung together? Languages should be consistent. To the extent that languages depart from consistent syntactic rules, learners have to learn the exceptions to the rules, the anomalies, and the peculiarities.

In general, for verbal languages, we expect the arguments to follow the command (e.g., DELETE DOC1) rather than the reverse (e.g., DOC1 DELETE). However, for graphic communication or direct manipulation, it is often reversed. We specify the object (select DOC1) and then the command (drag it to the trash icon). Experimental studies have shown that a consistent ordering of commands and arguments is important for efficient and accurate performance (Barnard, Hammond, Morton, Long, & Clark, 1981).

To explore the importance of consistency and hierarchical structure of commands, Carroll (1982) generated four different command sets for controlling a robot by varying both factors. He created four versions of a sixteen-command language as shown in Table 8.3. Commands were either hierarchical (verb-object-qualifier) or nonhierarchical (verb only) and either congruent (e.g., ADVANCE/RETREAT, RIGHT/LEFT) or noncongruent (e.g., GO/BACK, TURN/LEFT). Congruent means that meaningful pairs or opposites were used (symmetry). Hierarchical structure and congruence have been shown in psycholinguistic experiments to be superior to nonhierarchical and noncongruent expressions.

Thirty-two undergraduate subjects studied one of the four command sets in a printed manual. They gave subjective ratings of the languages and then carried out paper-and-pencil tasks.

Although the subjective ratings favored the nonhierarchical command set, memory and problem-solving tasks showed that overall the congruent command sets were clearly superior and that the hierarchical forms were superior on several other measures. The hierarchical form enabled subjects to learn the sixteen commands with only one rule of formation and twelve keywords.

Movement Away from Programming Languages

Some computer languages are very obtuse, strange, and closer to math and formal logic statements than anything near English or any other language. Other programming languages try to use terms, grammar, and semantics that are closer to natural English. There has always been a push to develop languages that are easy to learn and use. However, in doing so, they often lose power and efficiency and become very wordy and complex in other ways. For many end users who do not have the time or interest to develop programming skills, natural language is an attractive alternative.

Despite the compelling nature of language, there has also been a steady trend over time to shift from the language metaphor/mode of programming

Table 8.3. Four Command Sets Used by Carroll (1982) and Results

Command sets			
Congruent hierarchical	Congruent nonhierarchical	Noncongruent hierarchical	Noncongruent nonhierarchical
MOVE ROBOT FORWARD	ADVANCE	MOVE ROBOT FORWARD	GO
MOVE ROBOT BACKWARD	RETREAT	CHANGE ROBOT BACKWARD	BACK
MOVE ROBOT RIGHT	RIGHT	CHANGE ROBOT RIGHT	TURN
MOVE ROBOT LEFT	LEFT	MOVE ROBOT LEFT	LEFT
MOVE ROBOT UP	STRAIGHTEN	CHANGE ROBOT UP	UP
MOVE ROBOT DOWN	BEND	MOVE ROBOT DOWN	BEND
MOVE ARM FORWARD	PUSH	CHANGE ROBOT ARM	POKE
MOVE ARM BACKWARD	PULL	MOVE ARM BACKWARD	PULL
MOVE ARM RIGHT	SWING OUT	CHANGE ARM RIGHT	PIVOT
MOVE ARM LEFT	SWING IN	MOVE ARM LEFT	SWEEP
MOVE ARM UP	RAISE	MOVE ARM UP	REACH
MOVE ARM DOWN	LOWER	CHANGE ARM DOWN	DOWN
CHANGE ARM OPEN	RELEASE	CHANGE ARM OPEN	UNHOOK
CHANGE ARM CLOSE	TAKE	MOVE ARM CLOSE	GRAB
CHANGE ARM RIGHT	SCREW	MOVE ARM RIGHT	SCREW
CHANGE ARM LEFT	UNSCREW	CHANGE ARM LEFT	TWIST
Subjective Ratings (1 = best, 5 = worst)			
1.86	1.63	1.81	2.73
Test Scores			
14.88	14.63	7.25	11.00
Errors			
0.50	2.14	4.25	1.63
Omissions			
2.00	2.50	4.75	4.15

and controlling the computer to the use of visual programming using menu selection, direct manipulation, and design tools. In contrast to the language analogy, the new analogy is that programming is like building a machine. To build a machine, one assembles a number of connected parts. Visual programming languages provide a pallet of tools and parts to construct programs.

The alternative analogy for command-line interfaces is also menu selection and direct manipulation. Rather than typing a command to move files from one directory to another, the user clicks and drags the icons of the files from one location on the screen to another. GUIs such as the Apple Macintosh OS and MS Windows have all but replaced command-line interfaces. Repetitive tasks for which the user would have written scripts can pose a challenge, but in some cases they can be accomplished using "programming by example." The user clicks a "learn" or "record" option, performs the task, stops the recording, and then instructs the computer to repeat the task.

Finally, word processors such as MS Word and Web design tools such as Macromedia Dreamweaver embed the declarative code in the files so that the end user does not need to see the code. Thus, computer languages and code are not going away. In fact, they are used increasingly for CCI, but the average user is shielded from having to deal with it. Much like a person on a package tour visiting a foreign country, the user can get along quite well without speaking the language of the locals. Only a few technicians need to know the code.

Consequently, despite this trend for end users, there will probably always be a place for hardcore computer programming by professionals slogging through code that makes no sense to the masses. For the rest, we come back to the question, "If computers are so smart, why can't they be programmed to understand natural language?" In the next section, we explore some of the psychological reasons why this is not only difficult, but perhaps a bad idea.

Natural Language Interaction

Natural language interaction (NLI) exists in many areas of the human–computer interface today (Allen, 1995). The opening scenario about Eliza suggests how compelling it can be to engage in such dialog, even when it is superficial and devoid of content. When meaning is added, natural language can be a valuable communication channel for issuing commands and requests, for receiving information, and for asking and answering questions (Dougherty, 1994). So why don't we just talk to our computers? There are two limiting problems. The first problem is knowing what to tell the computer to do; that is, how do we give natural language instructions? The second problem is the AI problem: how do we program a computer to understand natural language?

Human Limitations of Natural Language Interaction

The problem with totally open-ended NLI is that one does not inherently know what to say or ask of the computer. However, if the context is limited to a specific domain, NLI is quite feasible. For example, one might ask, "What will the weather be like tomorrow?" or "What is the current temperature?" Simple interactions such as these can be very successful. However, for more complex natural language queries, it has been shown that SQL is superior (Jarke, Turner, Stohr, Vassiliou, White, & Michielsen, 1985; Small & Weldon, 1983).

Similarly, for giving instructions, it is just plain difficult to give clear instructions to another, whether a computer or a human, on just how to do something. Controlled vocabularies and predefined commands seem to work better than open-ended NLI. We can learn a lesson from HHI in many critical work settings. Highly controlled, structured language is used between pilots and air traffic controllers, foremen and construction workers, and doctors and nurses in the operating room.

Natural language text generation (NLTG), however, is very common and generally very effective. Computer output can be turned into natural language speech or written text. It is used to generate written reports on medical patients, legal contracts, wills, and weather reports. In many cases, these are easier for humans to digest than the raw output of the information. Moreover, with the increasing popularity of mobile devices and use of speech output, NLTG is an effective mode of interaction. However, a major limitation comes when the user does not understand the output and asks, "What do you mean?" or "Can you explain that to me?"

Difficulty of Natural Language Processing

True natural language processing requires that the computer extract the meaning of the natural language input and be able to generate output from that meaning. It requires the implementation of Chomsky's (1957, 1965) generative grammar rather than Eliza's superficial text manipulation. Many natural language understanding systems have been devised since the 1960s and 1970s. Most start with the idea of parsing the text according to the rules of grammar, and invoking vocabularies of words and knowledge about the world. Today, numerous computer science and linguistic research centers are hard at work on developing the theories, methods, and programs for natural language processing and programming.

Much of the work in natural language understanding is in *computational linguistics*, which uses statistical, logical, and computational models of natural language. Computational linguistics is a multidisciplinary field that involves linguists, computer scientists, and cognitive psychologists. It is involved in many different aspects of language beyond NLI, including processing natural language, analyzing language (parsing), speech recognition, automatic language translation, and creating language (generation).

Since the late 1970s, the early enthusiasm and excitement for natural language understanding has given way to laborious programs and practical solutions rather than the science fiction scenarios of "Star Trek" or "2001: A Space Odyssey." Natural language comprehension has proven to be much harder than originally believed due to a number of problems, some of which are listed as follows.

Speech Segmentation

In most spoken languages, the sounds for successive letters blend into each other, making the conversion of the analog signal to discrete characters a very difficult process. One of the problems is *coarticulation* of phonemes. One phoneme may be modified by adjacent sounds that blend, fuse, or even make them disappear. For example, in English, the sentence "What are you going to do?" could sound like "Whatchagonnado?" In natural speech, words are run together with few pauses between them, making it hard to parse words. Take, for example, the phrase "how to wreck a nice beach," which sounds very close to "how to recognize speech." Phoneme and lexical segmentation depend not only on the speech sounds, but also on the context and human knowledge and experience (Faaborg, Daher, Espinosa, & Lieberman, 2005).

Text Segmentation

Today, we take for granted spaces between words, but it is not always the case that words are demarcated by spaces and punctuation. Lexical parsing can be a problem in written text because some languages, such as Chinese, Japanese, and Thai, do not signal word boundaries using spaces or other notation. Even in old English, Latin, and Greek manuscripts, spaces may have been omitted to pack more text onto the precious pages (Saenger, 1997). Try parsing the following: "inthebeginningwasthewordandthewordwaswithgodandthewordwasgod." Text parsing, which usually requires the identification of word boundaries, is a nontrivial task especially for computers.

Word Sense Disambiguation

Many words have more than one meaning. The natural language system has to select the meaning that makes the most sense in the context. For example, take the word "bass." Is it a type of fish or tones of low frequency? In the following examples, "The bass part of the song is very moving" and "I went fishing for some sea bass," it is obvious that the first sentence is using the word "bass" in the second sense, and in the second sentence, it is being used in the first sense. This seems obvious to a human, but developing algorithms to replicate this human ability is extremely difficult.

There are deep and shallow methods for sense disambiguation. Deep approaches require access to a comprehensive body of world knowledge. For example, knowledge that "you go fishing for a type of fish, but not for low-frequency sounds" and "songs can have low-frequency parts, but not types of fish" can be used to determine in which sense the word is used. Deep approaches are not very successful in practice because large bodies of such knowledge do not exist or are inaccessible, except in very limited domains. Shallow approaches do not attempt to understand the text. Instead, they consider the surrounding words, using information such as if "bass" has words "sea" or "fishing" nearby, it is probably in the fish sense, and if it has the words "music" or "song" nearby, it is probably in the music sense. These rules can be automatically generated using a training corpus of words tagged with their word senses. The shallow approach, although theoretically not as powerful as the deep approach, gives superior results in practice, due to our limited world knowledge (Ide & Véronis, 1998).

Syntactic Ambiguity

Often the grammar of natural language utterances is ambiguous. There may be multiple ways to parse a given sentence. Choosing the most appropriate interpretation requires semantic and contextual information. Consider the sentence "Bear left at zoo." Does it mean you are to turn left when you get to the zoo, or did someone leave a bear at the zoo? The classic ambiguous sentence discussed in computer natural language processing comes from Groucho Marx: "Time flies like an arrow; fruit flies like a banana." As humans, we unambiguously understand that the first part means that time flies in the same way that an arrow does, but for a computer it could be 1) "Measure the speed of flies as you would for an arrow"; 2) "Measure the speed of flies as an arrow would"; or 3) "A kind of fly, the time fly, likes arrows."

Imperfect or Irregular Input

A substantial portion of both written and spoken language is imperfect or flawed in some way. There are foreign and regional accents, vocal impediments in speech, typing and grammatical errors, and mispronunciations such as "nucular" for "nuclear." The human ear has an amazing ability to accommodate and forgive such errors by relying on language redundancy, situational context, and world knowledge. Not so for the computer. Speech recognition systems and natural language processors must be tuned for each dialect and programmed for each irregularity.

Speech Acts and Plans

Processing natural language requires understanding the logical flow of dialog and the intended meaning of conversation. Sentences are often not to be taken literally. Instead, we interpret them in the context of acts and plans. A *speech act* is the idea that in *saying* something, we *do* something (Searle, 1969). An action is performed by means of language. If you say, "Watch out, the ground is slippery," you are performing the act of warning. If you ask, "Ladies and gentlemen, may I have your attention, please?", you are making a request. A good answer to "Can you pass the salt" is to pass the salt. Just answering "yes" without passing the salt is not acceptable. Answering "no" is better, and "I'm afraid that I can't see it" is quite acceptable. Speech acts require that the computer understand the framework of the dialog.

What seems so easy for us as humans to understand, what we so quickly take for granted, is a formidable challenge for computer scientists and computational linguists. At the end of the day, we must stand in awe of our human ability to understand and communicate using language. But these difficulties and problems have not deterred computer scientists and computational linguists from pursuing natural language interaction. Rather they have invigorated the study and fueled the interest in AI, which we discuss further in Chapter 13.

End Thoughts

Verbal communication, whether spoken or written, is an extremely important mode of interaction for humans. The same is true for communication between humans and computers. Although computers are only machines, they can be programmed to receive and interpret verbal communication, and they can be programmed to generate verbal output. Although natural language dialog invites a high level of anthropomorphism, the limits of computer communication and other mitigating factors help inform us that we are dealing with a machine and not a human, according to Weizenbaum (1976). Machine processing of natural language can be useful and effective. At moments, it can be convincing, but in the long run it is superficial. There is no mind, no conscious process, and no person behind the veil of the computer interface.

The question then is: when is natural language a useful interface? For simple input and output of information, simple commands, transcription of speech, and translation systems, NLIs are becoming more and more acceptable. However, for complex programming and deep understanding of meaning, computers have a long way to go, and it may not be worth the effort. Take, for example, the following lament about the futility of natural language programming, written by Dijkstra (1978), a leading professor of computer science: "From one gut feeling I derive much consolation: I suspect that machines to be programmed in our native tongues – be it Dutch, English, American, French, German, or Swahili – are as damned difficult to make as they would be to use."

Suggested Exercises

1. Write pseudocode for finding the average of a set of numbers ending with the word "end." Pseudocode is just a short, informal description of the algorithm using some of the conventions of programming, but omitting detailed language-specific syntax and data structures.

2. Find a copy of Eliza or a Web site that hosts Eliza (e.g., http://jerz.setonhill.edu/if/canon/eliza.htm), and try a session with it.

3. Find a simple end user command language for programming something such as a home security system, a LAN, a robot, etc. List the commands and evaluate it in terms of functionality, learnability, complexity, etc.

4. Find a speech recognition system either on a personal computer or a telephone voice interactive system (e.g., http://cmusphinx.sourceforge.net/html/cmusphinx.php). Experiment with how sensitive or robust it is either by enunciating your words or by slurring them together.

References

Allen, J. (1995). *Natural language understanding* (2nd ed.). Reading, MA: Addison-Wesley.

Barnard, P. J., Hammond, N. V., Morton, J., Long, J. B., & Clark, I. A. (1981). Consistency and compatibility in human–computer dialogue. *International Journal of Man-Machine Studies*, 15, 87–134.

Black, J. B., & Moran, T. P. (1982). Learning and remembering command names. *Proceedings of the 1982 conference on human factors in computing systems*, Gaithersburg, MD, March 15–17, pp. 8–11. (doi 10.1145/800049.801745).

Carroll, J. M. (1982). Learning, using and designing command paradigms. *Human Learning*, 1(1), 31–62.

Chomsky, N. (1957). *Syntactic structures*. The Hague: Mouton.

Chomsky, N. (1965). *Aspects of the theory of syntax*. Cambridge, MA: MIT Press.

Dijkstra, E. W. (1978). On the foolishness of "natural language programming." *Lecture Notes in Computer Science* (Vol. 69, pp. 51–53). London, UK: Springer-Verlag. Retrieved March 19, 2008, from www.cs.utexas.edu/users/EWD/ewd06xx/EWD667.PDF

Dougherty, R. C. (1994). *Natural language computing: An English generative grammar in Prolog*. Mahwah, NJ: Erlbaum.

Faaborg, A., Daher, W., Espinosa, J., & Lieberman, H. (2005). *How to wreck a nice beach you sing calm incense*. Paper presented at the international conference on intelligent user interfaces (IUI 2005), San Diego, CA.

Hulit, L. M., & Howard, M. R. (1993). *Born to talk: An introduction to speech and language development*. Needham, MA: Macmillan.

Ide, N., & Véronis, J. (1998). Word sense disambiguation: The state of the art. *Computational Linguistics*, 24, 1–40.

Jarke, M., Turner, J. A., Stohr, E. A., Vassiliou, Y., White, N. H., & Michielsen, K. (1985). A field evaluation of natural language for data retrieval. *IEEE Transactions on Software Engineering*, *SE-11*, 97–113.

Rosenberg, J. (1982). Evaluating the suggestiveness of command names. *Behaviour & Information Technology*, *1*, 371–400.

Saenger, P. (1997). *Space between words: The origins of silent reading*. Palo Alto, CA: Stanford University Press.

Searle, J. R. (1969). *Speech acts: An essay in the philosophy of language*. Cambridge: Cambridge University Press.

Small, D., & Weldon, L. (1983). An experimental comparison of natural and structured query languages. *Human Factors*, *25*, 253–263.

Weizenbaum, J. (1966). Eliza – A computer program for the study of natural language communication between man and machine. *Communications of the Association for Computing Machinery*, 9, 36–45.

Weizenbaum, J. (1976). *Computer power and human reason: From judgment to calculation*. San Francisco, CA: W.H. Freeman.

Zamenhof, L. L. (1887). *Dr. Esperanto's International Language: Introduction and Complete Grammar*. (English translation of "Unua Libro" by R. H. Geoghegan, 1889). (New printing by G. Keyes, 2000). Retrieved April 7, 2008, from http://www.genekeyes.com/Dr_Esperanto.html

PART III

Relationships

Nine

Individual Differences

People, Performance, and Personality

Scenario 1

Following the breakup of Macrosoft into the ten new Nanosofts and Groogle's introduction of the RainbowGroogleTop, different types of OSs proliferated. Instead of just Windows, Mac OS, and Linux, there were so many different styles and approaches to organizing desktops and files and controlling the functions of computers that no one knew what to choose. It was a mess until CompuMatchMe.com stepped in to match up people with OSs. The idea was that each user has a different makeup of cognitive abilities and styles and preferences. CompuMatchMe.com developed an algorithm for matching the user's personal profile with the ideal OS. Their slogan was "We help you to find your OSoul mate."

Scenario 2

A language instructor was explaining to her class that French nouns, unlike their English counterparts, are grammatically designated as masculine or feminine. Items such as "chalk" or "pencil," she described, would have a gender association, although in English these words were neutral.

Puzzled, one student raised his hand and asked, "What gender is a computer?"

The teacher was not certain which it was, so she divided the class into two groups and asked them to decide whether a computer should be masculine or feminine. One group was comprised of the women in the class, and the other, of men. Both groups were asked to give four reasons for their recommendation.

The women concluded that computers should be referred to in the masculine gender because

- *To get their attention, you have to turn them on.*
- *They have a lot of data, but are still clueless.*
- *They are supposed to help you solve your problems, but half the time they ARE the problem.*
- *As soon as you commit to one, you realize that, if you had waited a little longer, you could have had a better model.*

The men, in contrast, decided that computers should definitely be referred to in the feminine gender because

- *No one but their creator understands their internal logic.*
- *The native language they use to communicate with other computers is incomprehensible to everyone else.*
- *Even your smallest mistakes are stored in long-term memory for later retrieval.*
- *As soon as you make a commitment to one, you find yourself spending half your paycheck on accessories for it.*

Overview

As indicated in the previous scenarios and the one from Chapter 2, both humans and computers differ in a lot of ways. A fundamental principle in HCI is that there should be a match of some sort between the human's abilities, experience, cognitive style, and mode of operation and the computer's mode of operation, characteristics, and specifications. Whether personality type is the critical factor is not clear, but certainly cognitive strengths and weaknesses, as well as cognitive dissonance, are important considerations.

This chapter discusses individual differences in relation to issues in HCI. First, we look at differences in IQ, verbal comprehension, quantitative skills, and specific cognitive abilities, such as spatial visualization ability and perceptual speed, and how they relate to performance. Second, we look at age, gender, and differences in experience. Finally, we look at personality differences and attitudes about computers. The importance of these individual differences is assessed relative to their impact on HCI. Factors that may be very important in interpersonal relationships, such as gender and introversion, may not be that relevant when it comes to computers. However, other individual differences that may be of little interest to people, such as the ability to manipulate spatial objects in your head, may be very important in using computers. We explore the idea of matching abilities and cognitive styles to the interface to improve usability, performance, and user satisfaction. Finally, we see that the HCI is a prime area for assessing individual differences. In the past, testing was done with paper-and-pencil forms and personal interviews. Computerized testing has proven not only successful, but is in many cases superior to traditional methods.

Factors of Differences

Across brands and models, computers vary in many different ways such as processor speed, memory capacity, graphics capabilities, communications, etc. Operating systems and software also vary in many ways from purely alphanumeric (e.g., UNIX, DOS) to rich GUIs such as the Apple Macintosh OS and MS Windows. Within programs, the style, the "look and feel," the "personality," the vocabulary, and the artwork can vary greatly along many different dimensions. Within a system or a program, users can change preferences and layouts. Computer designers consider these factors when they develop a new model or version. What is the best system we can build for a particular price?

Computers are designed and built. Not so with users. In organizations, users are often tested and selected to use a computer and are then trained. As personal consumers, users choose what system to buy and use and then decide what training they need. For either situation, we now focus on the composition and characteristics of the user. What individual differences do they bring to the human–computer interface that need to be factored into the mix? Although we can select and train users, it is perhaps easier to design interfaces around the human rather than reinvent humans to fit the characteristics of the computer. To do this, we must answer two questions: 1) What are the factors (metrics) that matter?, and 2) Can we design the computer interface to accommodate for these differences?

Designers of computer systems have long been encouraged to carefully consider the diversity of their users. The term "user-centered" design emphasizes the importance of taking into consideration the needs and characteristics of the users over other programming issues (Norman, 1986).

The study of individual differences has been a major area of psychology since its beginning. The variability of human abilities, performance, characteristics, and personality has been studied extensively in the area called "psychometrics," which literally means "to measure the mind" (Anastasi & Urbina, 1996; Michell, 1999; Nunnally & Bernstein, 1994). We start from these metrics and then use experimental and correlational methods to determine whether there is a relationship with factors in computer use such as performance and satisfaction. Research on individual differences has proven to be extremely important in understanding user behavior in HCI (Dillon & Watson, 1996).

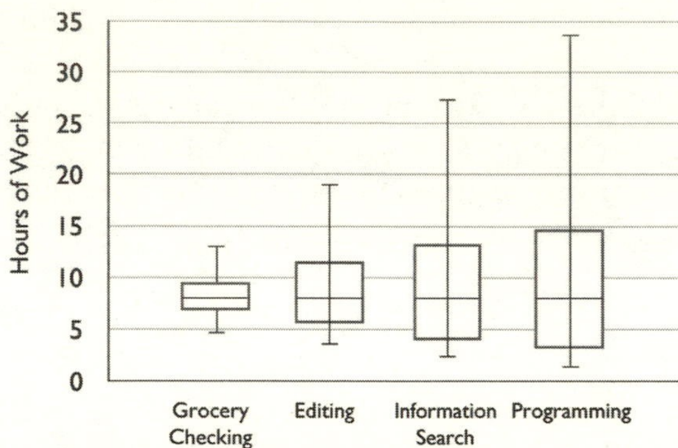

Figure 9.1. Distributions of completion times for grocery store cashiers and three HCI tasks. For each task, the fiftieth percentile has been set at 8 hours. The tops and bottoms of the boxes represent the seventy-fifth and twenty-fifth percentiles. The "whiskers" represent the best and worst performance. (From Egan, 1988.)

Performance Differences

It is clear that people differ greatly when it comes to using computers to perform tasks. Egan (1988) initially surveyed the size of differences in performance on several different tasks such as text editing, information search, and programming reported in a number of published studies. For each task, the performance measure was the amount of time to complete the task. To put the differences into perspective, he included the time it takes to check groceries by a cashier and then graphed the distributions as shown in Figure 9.1, setting the median or fiftieth percentile of each performance at the same level.

In each case, the ranges are very large compared to grocery checking. For editing, the ratio between the best and the worst is 5 to 1, for information search 9 to 1, and for programming 22 to 1. Even the ratios between the seventy-fifth and twenty-fifth percentiles in each distribution are 2 to 1 or 3 to 1. To further emphasize the magnitude of these differences Egan (1988, p. 551) wrote:

> After a group of 30 people complete a training course on text editing, we could expect that the top performer might be able to complete in one day what the poorest performer would take a week to do. After 30 people take a programming course, one student might take a year to program what another could do in two weeks!

When it comes to computers, performance differences between people in training classes are larger than one would expect. For some reason, computers tend to amplify differences between people. Norman (1994) suggested that this is because of a multiplicative effect between human cognitive abilities and computer empowerment. Those with high mental abilities are facilitated by computers. Those with low abilities are not facilitated and may in fact do worse with computers. The challenge to interface designers is to facilitate those that need help rather than to leave them in the dust. Assistive technologies are meant to do this and are discussed in Chapter 14. At this point, we need to understand the cognitive factors that give rise to performance differences.

Cognitive Factors

The penultimate measure of cognitive ability is IQ, an assessment of overall intelligence. We define intelligence as the set of mental abilities necessary to adapt to and shape the environment (Neisser et al., 1996; Sternberg, 1997). This definition is particularly relevant in HCI. Intelligence is not merely answering questions, knowing information, or reacting to the world, but it is also actively changing and manipulating the world around us. Moreover, intelligence is context dependent. The intelligent response to the word "EXIT" is quite different when it is above a doorway than when it is in a pop-up window.

The questions that we ask as psychologists are the following: "Is intelligence something inherited and inborn, or is it learned?"; "Is there one kind of intelligence, or are there different kinds of intelligence?"; and "Can intelligence be broken down into different factors or abilities?" The most contentious questions have had to do with differences in intelligence between males and females and among different racial/ethnic groups and their impact on socioeconomic factors.

Historically, psychometrics started with Sir Francis Galton (1822–1911), a British mathematician and naturalist who made contributions to many fields of science as well as eugenics. He introduced the idea of using questionnaires and surveys to measure just about everything in human communities. Galton was a half-cousin of Charles Darwin by a common grandparent Erasmus Darwin. When Darwin proposed his theory of evolution, Galton decided to apply the principle of natural selection to human traits to explain why some families, like his, were successful and others were not. He founded a eugenics movement to breed humans in much the same way as is done in animal husbandry. Thus, individuals with positive traits and high intelligence should be encouraged to marry and have children, whereas those with negative traits and low intelligence should not. Consequently, Galton set about developing statistical methods for measuring these traits. His major contribution was the idea of a correlation coefficient that measured the degree to which one variable such as intelligence is related to success. Although the errors of eugenics have been largely averted in modern society, the statistical measurement of correlation has been accepted. Moreover, the idea of assessing traits and abilities to predict future performance has particularly been embraced in education and in the workplace. Finally, in the area of HCI, there has been a particularly strong interest in identifying individual differences that correlate with performance.

Galton believed that he could measure intelligence by seeing how quickly and accurately people responded to stimuli. His measures of sensory abilities, reaction times, and physical measurements of head size and muscular strength did not actually correlate with accepted criteria of intellectual functioning at the time (Sharp, 1898; Wissler, 1901). Interestingly however, sensory abilities and speed of processing have become increasingly relevant in predicting performance at the human–computer interface today. One wonders how things might have been different had computers been around in Galton's day.

A much more successful attempt to measure overall intelligence was made by Alfred Binet who had been hired by the French school system to develop an inexpensive test to determine which children were in need of special education. His approach was to test mental abilities using a battery of tests of typical things that one would expect children of different ages to be able to do. In these tests, Binet emphasized mental reasoning and problem-solving abilities needed in the classroom rather than sensory and motor skills needed in the workplace. Binet hinged his measure on age because children increase dramatically in their verbal and mental abilities between the ages of 5 and 18 years. His reasoning was that if a 10-year-old child performed at the level of an "average" child of 8 years, he was in need of special help in the classroom and would need additional tutoring.

The IQ test came to America through the work of Goddard (1913) and Terman (1916), and resulted in the Stanford-Binet test. At this point, it was given a scoring system to divide the child's mental age by his or her chronological age and multiply by 100. So, a 10-year-old child performing at the mental age of 8 years has an IQ of $(8/10)(100) = 80$.

Interestingly, the aging effect is reversed for computers. The speed and power of a computer does not increase with age but remains constant at best, whereas younger, newer computers tend to be faster and more powerful. Thus, older is slower and younger is faster, resulting in a reversed quotient.

The intelligence quotient based on mental age and chronological age worked well for children, but not for adults, whose mental abilities level off at ages 18 to 20 years and then are not strongly related to chronological age. When Wechsler developed an intelligence test for adults, the solution was to set the average IQ at 100 and the standard deviation at 20. The result was the infamous bell curve for IQ shown in Figure 9.2. The implications of the bell curve are astounding and highly controversial (Gould, 1996; Jensen, 1982; Neisser et al., 1996). Much heated debate surrounds the use of IQ as a measure that has the potential to label, stereotype, and discriminate against individuals and groups. For example, Gould (1996) wrote that "the abstraction of intelligence as a single entity, its location within the brain, its quantification as one number for each individual, and the use of these numbers to rank people in a single series of worthiness, invariably to find that oppressed and disadvantaged groups – races, classes, or sexes – are innately inferior and deserve their status" (pp. 24–25). Assigning numbers to individuals through testing can have significant negative effects. We tend to

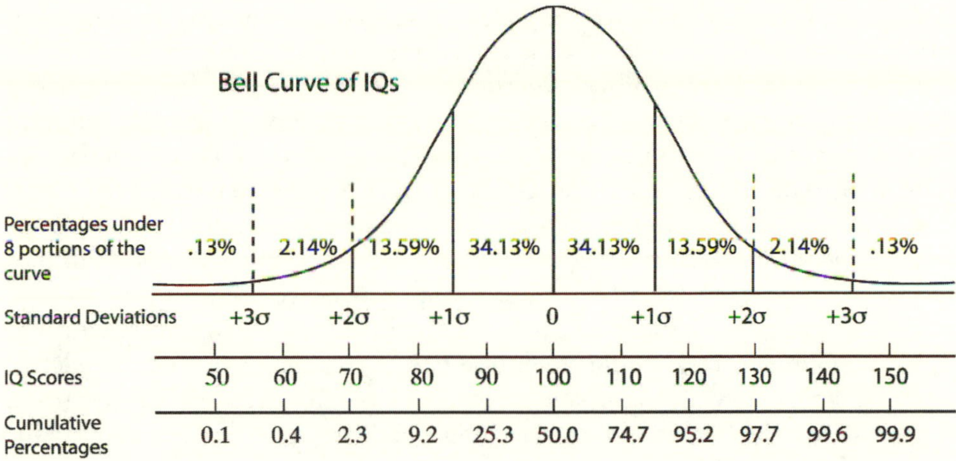

Figure 9.2. Bell curve for IQ showing the proportions of the distribution scoring in different internals.

expect people with low scores to perform worse than people with high scores even though the correlations are far from perfect. We then label students as "slow" or "challenged" on the basis of their scores. These labels stick, and students live up to these expectations or the lack thereof.

In the area of computers, one can point to the use of the pejorative term "dummy" in the more than 250 "... for Dummies" books. Even though the publisher emphasizes that the books are not literally for dummies, the subtitle for every book, "A Reference for the Rest of Us," implies that they are for individuals excluded from the upper tail of the distribution. To make matters worse, the dozen or so "Complete Idiot's Guide to..." on computers and the Internet use an even stronger term to label people. Consequently, there may be a serious self-fulfilling prophecy concerning individual differences with regard to computers as we label ourselves as "dummies" or savvy users, "geeks," "hackers," or "nerds."

Overall IQ is correlated with performance on tasks that require similar mental abilities. The correlation between IQ and grades in school is about 0.50, and between IQ and job performance 0.54. Today, in an environment where both schools and workplaces are permeated with computers, we continue to expect that performance will be correlated with IQ. But now the question is what proportion of the relationship is due to the task being done versus the interface being used? Take, for example, balancing a checkbook using a spreadsheet program. Part of the performance will be due to the mental abilities of dealing with numbers and sums, but another part will be due to the interface, entering numbers in boxes, following menus, and selecting functions. We are interested in isolating the cognitive abilities that pertain specifically to the interface rather than the general task.

Interestingly, intelligence scores are also related to physical attributes of the nervous system. Just as you would expect the intelligence of a computer to relate to its hardware characteristics, human IQ is correlated with brain size

(Tisserand, Bosma, Van Boxtel, & Jolles, 2001), speed of neural transmission, and brain efficiency (Vernon, Wickett, Bazana, & Stelmack, 2000).

Although the concept of an overall IQ has been a compelling idea, for a long time psychologists have used psychometric methods to identify separate factors that make up the composite. The first to identify two such factors was Spearman (1927). He labeled one factor "g" for general intelligence and the other "s" for specific abilities. Thurstone (1938) used factor analysis to identify seven primary mental abilities: verbal comprehension, number ability, word fluency, spatial visualization, associative memory, reasoning, and perceptual speed. Each factor will contribute with different weighting, depending on the task being performed (e.g., balancing a checkbook vs. proofing a paper). Moreover, each factor may contribute to different degrees, depending on the human–computer interface being used (e.g., a command-line interface vs. a GUI).

In the past few decades, new approaches to intelligence have been taken. The first is to emphasize that intelligence is not one monolithic factor but is composed of a number of component abilities (Sternberg, 1988). Gardner and others have emphasized "multiple intelligences." Gardner (1983, 1999) listed eight intelligences:

The Thought Intelligences:

Verbal-linguistic is the ability to use words and language. Those high in this intelligence are facile at writing and speaking. To the extent that the interface relies on language input/output, this intelligence will correlate with performance.

Logical-mathematical is the ability to work with numbers, abstractions, and logic. This intelligence favors mathematics and computer programming. To the extent that the interface requires logic, programming, and computation, it will relate to performance.

Naturalistic has to do with the ability to recognize, categorize, and characterize things in the natural environment. Although aimed at nature, in a virtual sense it also pertains to one's ability to recognize characteristics in computer environments, screen layouts, and backgrounds.

Sensate Intelligences:

Visual-spatial is the ability to think three dimensionally, manipulate objects in space mentally, and work with shapes and figures. Because computer interfaces are graphical and rely heavily on spatial metaphors, this skill will be involved in performance.

Bodily-kinesthetic has to do with motor coordination, movement, and position. Interfaces that require good hand–eye coordination, mouse movements, or hand and body movements, as in virtual reality systems, will require this skill.

Auditory-musical involves the sensitivity to pitch, melody, rhythm, and tone. Interfaces that use auditory and multimedia modes will require this skill.

The Communicational Intelligences:

Interpersonal skills involve the ability to understand and effectively interact with others. Individuals high in this skill are outgoing, leaders, charismatic, and diplomatic. In the past, there has been a stereotype that interpersonal skills are lacking in individuals with computer skills. However, there are many areas of HCI in which people skills are important (e.g., help desks).

Intrapersonal abilities involve understanding one's own thoughts, motives, faith, and philosophy. Those high on intrapersonal skills are often seen as introverts. Although this intelligence does not seem to be directly related to HCI, it may deal with mental models and the perception of the self.

Factor analytic, component process, and multiple intelligence approaches allow us to explore individual differences at a more granular level. Essentially, we can get a profile of the user across each dimension or type and correlate these scores with performance measures at the human–computer interface. This approach helps us identify those factors of individual differences that play a part in the interface rather than the task per se.

Cognitive Abilities: Factor Referenced Tests

Many different tests have been developed to measure specific cognitive abilities. These tests range from size of working memory, to perceptual skills, to attentional abilities, etc. (Ekstrom, French, & Harman, 1976).

Vicente, Hayes, and Williges (1987) gave a battery of these tests to students and then correlated the scores with their performance at finding information in a computer system requiring paging, scrolling, and searching. Although numerous cognitive abilities were correlated with performance, they found two tests that were clearly the best predictors of computer performance: verbal comprehension and spatial visualization ability. The verbal comprehension test required the individual to read a passage and answer information about its content. The spatial visualization ability test has to with mentally manipulating objects in space and was measured using the conceptual paper-folding task shown in Figure 9.3. Each problem starts with a set of figures showing how a square piece of paper is being folded. The last figure has one small circle drawn to show where the folded paper has been punched through. You are to select one of the five figures to show where the holes will be when the paper is completely unfolded.

Numerous studies have shown fairly strong correlations ranging from 0.35 to 0.50 between spatial visualization ability and performance on computer search tasks (Norman & Butler, 1989), menu selection and navigation tasks (Chen & Rada, 1996), and command and control tasks (Murphy, 2000).

Why is spatial visualization such an important cognitive ability in HCI? Apparently, it has to do with the fact that the human–computer interface has many spatial aspects to it. HCI invokes the same cognitive abilities as mentally folding a surface, creating an effect, unfolding the surface, and

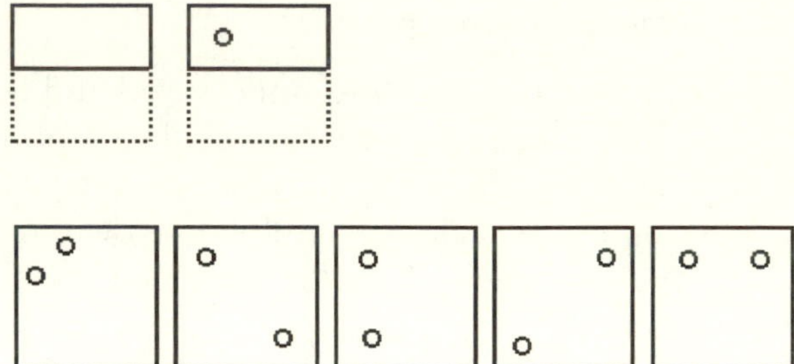

Figure 9.3. Paper-folding task. Example problem from instructions. (From Ekstrom et al., 1976.)

inferring what you have created or where you are. The human–computer interface, particularly the GUI, is essentially a flat, narrow, and convoluted passageway into a multidimensional, hierarchical space. To select options, we follow cascading pull-down menus, pop-up menus, and sequences of selections that drill down to the goal. To work with documents, we manipulate layers of overlapping windows, multiple scroll bars, and tabs. For some reason, the current computer interface from OSs and applications to databases and the Web rely highly on spatial visualization abilities, and the trend is increasing.

Demographics

Demographics are those variables that are temporal (age, experience, educational attainment), organic (gender, genetics), situational (income, socioeconomic status, employment, location of residence, marital status), and social (race/ethnicity, religion, language, nationality). Many demographic variables are determined for us, such as gender, age, and ethnicity. Others are under our own control, such as marital status, residence, and employment. Demographic variables contribute to individual differences, but again the question is whether they make any difference when it comes to HCI.

Age

Age is a very strong predictor of performance on computer-related tasks, even when experience is held constant. Most studies find age differences for complex computer tasks. Greene, Gomez, and Devlin (1986) found that age had a large effect on producing errors in information search. Across different designs of the interface, the average correlation between age and errors was 0.57. As the tasks become more complex, the effect of age on performance becomes even larger. However, differences due to age can be reduced. When users of different ages learned a display editor that had a simple set of function keys rather than complicated commands requiring the correct syntax, the effect of age was greatly reduced (Egan & Gomez, 1985).

Age can become a particularly detrimental factor when associated with loss of memory and cognitive abilities and motor and sensory impairment. These extremes are discussed in Chapter 14.

Age in demographics can also be expressed in terms of a generational or birth cohort, which is defined as "the aggregate of individuals (within some population definition) who experienced the same event within the same time interval" (Ryder, 1965, p. 845). Because the introduction of computers in society has occurred only over the past few decades, generational cohorts differ greatly with respect to experience with computers. Current cohorts in the United States include the following (adapted loosely from Strauss and Howe, 2003):

- *Postwar Cohort* (born from 1928 to 1945) – experienced sustained economic growth, the Cold War, and McCarthyism with characteristics of conformity, conservatism, and family values. This cohort was introduced to computers later in life, close to or after retirement. Only a small portion has adopted the use of computers for e-mailing their children and for word processing when typewriters became obsolete.
- *Baby Boomers Cohort 1* (born from 1946 to1954) – experienced the leading edge of the computer revolution, the rise of credit cards, the environmental movement, and the walk on the moon, with characteristics of being experimental, individualistic, and social cause oriented. This cohort was introduced to computers in midlife. Most have had to make the transition to computers later in their careers, some reluctantly, and have often been of two minds about paper versus electronic media.
- *Baby Boomers Cohort 2* (also called *Generation Jones*; born from 1955 to 1964) – experienced the proliferation of the personal computer (Apple II Computers, IBM PCs, MS-DOS), the Cold War, and gasoline shortages, with characteristics of being less optimistic, having a distrust of government, and being generally cynical. This cohort was introduced to computers in their twenties and thirties. They were compelled to make the transition to computers in their jobs and worried about the computer literacy of their children.
- *Generation X* (born from 1965 to 1981) – experienced the introduction of the GUI, e-mail, edutainment, multimedia, video games, the dot.com crash, the Challenger explosion, and social malaise, with characteristics of searching for emotional security, being entrepreneurial, and desiring informality. This cohort was introduced to computers and video games in high school and college and brought computers into their new homes.
- *Generation Y* (also called the *Millennial Generation*; born from 1982 to 2000) – experienced the rise of the Internet (Internet Explorer, Amazon.com, Google), September 11 terrorist attacks, and cultural diversity, with characteristics of searching for physical security and safety. They are connected, immediate, social, and technically savvy. This cohort grew up with computers at home, in the classroom, and everywhere. This group has always had video games, mobile devices, cell phones, and computers

in their lives, but are experiencing the metamorphosis of computers into an entertainment media with MP3 players.
- *Generation Z* (also known as *the iGeneration*; born from 2001 on) – growing up in a world with information at their fingertips with devices such as the iMac, iPod, and iPhone. They are the twenty-first century's first generation. They are digital natives who personify our future. In population size, they are the smallest of the living generations, with the fewest siblings, and born to the oldest mothers whose median age is 33. They are the most financially endowed generation and will be the most technologically empowered generation with the largest number of entertainment options for music, movies, Web sites, and video games.

Consequently, generational cohorts differ not only in chronological age and amount of experience, but also in the age at which technologies were introduced into their lives, social context, and social perspectives. These issues become extremely important when designing interfaces for, and training users on, interfaces for different ages.

Experience

Experience and educational attainment are usually highly correlated with performance on computer tasks such as programming and working with computer applications (Chrysler, 1978; Rosson, 1983). Of course, the reason for this can be traced back to Chapter 6. With more experience, one learns more about the task and the interface, whether it is a programming language, the functionality of the program, or the procedures to complete tasks. Furthermore, educational attainment is partially determined by general intelligence and will in turn determine the amount of general knowledge acquired and one's experience with computers.

Generally, for research and interface design purposes, we tend to categorize users into the following classes of computer experience:

- *Novice*: first-time user; unfamiliar with the interface, program, and devices
- *Intermittent user*: somewhat familiar with the interface, program, and devices, but uses it only infrequently
- *Casual user*: familiar with the interface, but not as much as a frequent, full-time user
- *Expert user (level 1)*: trained user with much experience
- *Expert user (level 2)*: extremely well-trained user with insider knowledge of the interface, program, and devices

As one moves from novice to expert, there are at least two factors that drive performance. The first is that with more experience, there is more learning. The second is that less proficient individuals tend to drop out and do not pursue expertise if they are struggling to keep up. Consequently, expert users are those who excel in ability, performance, and knowledge.

In any usability study, we want to know about the person's previous experience with the system in order to account for initial differences, and in any work environment, we need to know about the employee's previous experience in order to place the person in the appropriate work situation or training schedule.

Gender Differences

As Scenario 1 suggests, gender differences are filled with stereotypes. Certainly, there are interesting differences between males and females when it comes to computers. The stereotype still prevails that computers are a "boy thing." The simplistic question is whether males or females are better at using computers. The serious question is why there is a "gender gap" between males and females pursuing careers in computer science and computer-related fields. The ratio of males to females who are programmers, information technology professionals, and technicians is around 7 to 1. The female computer science major is a rare thing and actually on the decline rather than increase (Goodwin, 2004).

Although computers themselves have no inherent gender bias, the ways they are used and the context in which they are used tend to result in large differences in expectation and measures of achievement between males and females. Numerous studies show consistent differences in terms of both skills and attitudes (Houtz, 2001; Kay, 1992). In a meta-analysis of a number of studies, Whitley (1997) reported that both men and boys exhibited greater gender role stereotyping of computers (i.e., working with computers is more appropriate for males than for females), higher computer self-efficacy (i.e., males excel and get higher scores in computer training than females), and more positive affect (i.e., males tend to like computers more than females).

Beyer, Rynes, Perrault, Hay, and Haller (2003) found that the primary driving factor behind the differences had to do with confidence in using computers. Males tended to have higher confidence than females. In fact, males not majoring in computer science had higher confidence about using computers than females majoring in computer science!

One hypothesis is that males and females have a different intellectual style. Males think in more abstract ways and females in more concrete ways. In terms of computer programming, men like to work with prepackaged routines ("black boxes"), and women prefer to see what is inside ("glass boxes"). Men prefer to send commands at a distance, and women seek closer and deeper communication in their programs (Turkle & Papert, 1990). Although these are fascinating ideas, there has been little or no empirical evidence for this effect. McKenna (2004) found no differences in the preferences of male and female programmers for types of routines that differed according to these dimensions.

However, to the extent that males and females differ in cognitive abilities that drive performance, some gender differences may be explained. De Lisi and Cammarano (1996) explored spatial visualization abilities using a test of mental rotation and found that males did better than females. Moreover, differences in self-reported computer use and self-efficacy were associated with differences on the test of mental rotation.

What can be done to reduce the gender gap? Educational programs have been developed to encourage females and to increase their sense of self-efficacy. Professional organizations have helped support women in computing. These have helped to reduce, but have not eliminated the differences. Interfaces designed by women for women, or that are at least pleasing to the eye, may also help. But in the long run, as the human–computer interface permeates more and more of everyone's life space, gender differences in computer use and skill should become negligible.

Socioeconomic Differences

Clear differences exist in levels of computer use, knowledge, and skills between those of low versus high socioeconomic status. This difference is sometimes referred to as the "digital divide" between the "haves" and the "have nots." Although other factors may be correlated with socioeconomic levels, such as attitudes about computers and self-efficacy, the most obvious reason for this difference is the cost of computers and, as a consequence, their accessibility to the individual. Well-to-do households typically have multiple state-of-the-art workstations and laptops, wireless networks, and high-speed connections to the Internet. Low-income households either have no computer at all or, at best, an obsolete computer with a slow dial-up connection. Figure 9.4 shows this difference in terms of computer use in homes and schools.

In the same way that public education and public libraries have reduced differences in literacy, it is hoped that access to computers through schools, community centers, and public libraries will eliminate the digital divide. Because the primary barrier of computer use is cost, it is expected that if the price of entry-level computers and laptops drops, accessibility will increase.

National, Ethnic, and Cultural Differences

The introduction of the computer follows the industrialization of nations, and in the same way, there are large differences due to the economic level of countries in the global community. The digital divide at the international level is a serious problem that needs to be addressed. It is the goal of the MIT Media Lab's $100 Laptop Project and the One Laptop per Child Organization to make large quantities of inexpensive laptops available to developing countries with the lowest levels of computer use by schoolchildren.

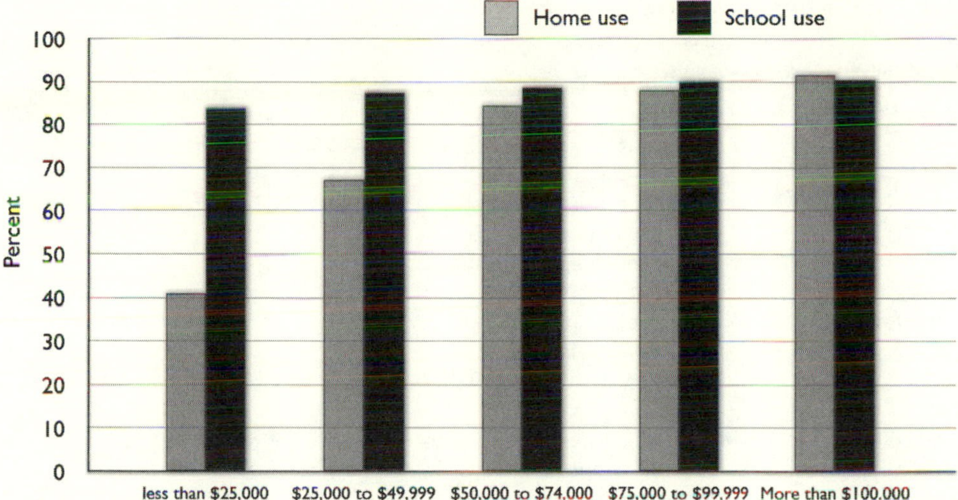

Figure 9.4. Percent of homes and schools with computers as a function of household income. (From U.S. Census Bureau, Current Population Survey, *October 2003, Day, Janus, & Davis, 2005.)*

Holding socioeconomic level and access to computers constant, are there individual differences due to nationality, ethnicity, and culture? Do different people groups have different attitudes and aptitudes with respect to computers? If so, should interfaces be designed differently for different nationalities and ethnic groups above and beyond language and keyboard differences, or can we aim for a universal, international design that will accommodate everyone (see Nielsen, 1990)?

Some interface designers believe that cross-cultural differences in terms of perception, values, thinking, and attitudes are so big that they must be taken into account in HCI. Marcus (2000) proposed that different GUIs should be designed for different cultures and nationalities. He suggests that the cultural dimensions proposed by Hofstede (1991) be used as a guide for design and gives a number of examples for how these dimensions express themselves in Web site design (Marcus & Gould, 2001). The dimensions and their characteristics are listed in Table 9.1.

Although Hofstede's cultural dimensions are compelling, his claims about the consequences of the dimensions and his analysis of the data have been seriously challenged (McSweeney, 2002). Above and beyond distinctive colors and graphics that may be used by different national and ethnic groups, the majority of cross-cultural studies indicates that differences due to culture are generally negligible. Even when differences do exist at the national or macro level, individuals within the groups vary so greatly that it overwhelms group differences. Moreover, when focusing on subgroups, such as business leaders in India, Norman and Singh (1989) found that their patterns of attitudes and expectations mirrored those of their American counterparts and did not need to be considered in issues of marketing or design.

Table 9.1. Hofstede's Five Dimensions of Culture (Hofstede, 1991)

Dimension	Description	Highest scoring	Lowest scoring
Power distance	The degree to which there is a disparity between people wielding greater power than others as opposed to the view that all people should have equal rights	Latin American and Arab nations	Scandinavian and Germanic nations
Individualism vs. collectivism	The extent to which people are expected to stand up for their individual rights as opposed to acting as members of a group	United States	Latin American nations
Masculinity vs. femininity	Masculine cultures value competitiveness, assertiveness, ambition, and the accumulation of wealth as opposed to feminine cultures that value a nurturing quality of life	Japan	Sweden
Uncertainty avoidance	The extent to which a society attempts to cope with anxiety by minimizing uncertainty, preferring institutional rules and structured situations	Japan	Mediterranean nations
Long- vs. short-term orientation	The extent to which a society has a future-oriented time horizon, and values investment and development over past heritage and tradition and present relationships and celebration	China	Pakistan

Personality Factors

As humans, when we think about other humans and individual differences, we think in terms of personality. *Personality* is defined as the consistent and distinctive thoughts, feelings, and behaviors of an individual. Personality is *consistent* in the sense that it is somewhat enduring over time and the same from one situation to another. Personality is *distinctive* in the sense that it sets one person apart from another. We observe personality in the thoughts, feelings, and behaviors of a person. Theories of personality and the assessment of personality factors date back to the early days of modern psychology.

The idea that computers have a personality is not new. My first personal computer was a SOL-20 dating back to 1976. Interestingly, even back then, it had what they called a "personality" card. It contained a ROM chip with a program that either ran the system as a dumb computer terminal to be connected via a modem to a dial-up mainframe or to run as a stand-alone personal computer. But to a very great extent, the OS and its settings determine the personality of the computer.

Given that we can measure personality traits or factors, the question is whether these have any impact or relevance at the human–computer interface. Do certain personality types work best with particular types of computers and OSs? Are there personality differences between MS Windows users and Apple Macintosh users?

In this section, we explore the factors of human personality and their relationship to performance and other measures at the human–computer interface. We explore the idea of computer personality in Chapter 13.

One of the earliest and most extensive lists of personality factors was derived by Cattell. The reasoning was as follows. Allport and Odbert (1936) hypothesized that "Those individual differences that are most salient and socially relevant in people's lives will eventually become encoded into their language; the more important such a difference, the more likely is it to become expressed as a single word." Allport and Odbert worked through two comprehensive English dictionaries and extracted 18,000 personality descriptor words. From this list, they extracted 4,500 personality adjectives that described relatively permanent traits. In 1946, Cattell organized the list into 181 clusters and asked subjects to rate people they knew using these adjectives. Using factor analytic methods like those used in intelligence testing, he identified twelve factors. He also generated four additional factors that he hypothesized were important. The 16PF Personality Questionnaire was then developed and is still in use today. Table 9.2 lists the sixteen primary factors and descriptors for the low and high ends of each factor.

The development of the California Personality Inventory (Gough, 1958) suggests that there are twenty-two factors. In contrast, others such as Eysenck (1947) claimed that only two orthogonal dimensions truly differentiate individuals: introversion-extroversion and neuroticism-emotional stability. Subsequent research has indicated that Cattell retained too many factors. In an attempt to simplify the situation and reduce the number of personality factors to more general dimensions, personality researchers reviewed the existing personality tests and decided that five factors would be sufficient. This work resulted in the Big Five personality traits (Goldberg, 1993). These traits are as follows:

- *Extroversion* – energy, surgency, and the tendency to seek stimulation and the company of others
- *Openness to experience* – appreciation for art, emotion, adventure, unusual ideas; imagination and curiosity
- *Agreeableness* – a tendency to be compassionate and cooperative rather than suspicious and antagonistic toward others

Table 9.2. Cattell's Sixteen Personality Factors (16PF)

Low-range descriptors	Primary factor	High-range descriptors
Impersonal, distant, cool, reserved, detached, formal, aloof (Sizothymia)	Warmth	Warm, outgoing, attentive to others, kind, easygoing, participating, likes people (Affectothymia)
Concrete thinking, lower general mental capacity, less intelligent, unable to handle abstract problems (Lower Scholastic Mental Capacity)	Reasoning	Abstract thinking, more intelligent, bright, higher general mental capacity, fast learner (Higher Scholastic Mental Capacity)
Reactive emotionally, changeable, affected by feelings, emotionally less stable, easily upset (Lower Ego Strength)	Emotional stability	Emotionally stable, adaptive, mature, faces reality, calm (Higher Ego Strength)
Deferential, cooperative, avoids conflict, submissive, humble, obedient, easily led, docile, accommodating (Submissiveness)	Dominance	Dominant, forceful, assertive, aggressive, competitive, stubborn, bossy (Dominance)
Serious, restrained, prudent, taciturn, introspective, silent (Desurgency)	Liveliness	Lively, animated, spontaneous, enthusiastic, happy-go-lucky, cheerful, expressive, impulsive (Surgency)
Expedient, nonconforming, disregards rules, self-indulgent (Low Super Ego Strength)	Rule consciousness	Rule conscious, dutiful, conscientious, conforming, moralistic, staid, rule bound (High Super Ego Strength)
Shy, threat sensitive, timid, hesitant, intimidated (Threctia)	Social boldness	Socially bold, venturesome, thick skinned, uninhibited (Parmia)
Utilitarian, objective, unsentimental, tough minded, self-reliant, no nonsense, rough (Harria)	Sensitivity	Sensitive, aesthetic, sentimental, tender minded, intuitive, refined (Premsia)
Trusting, unsuspecting, accepting, unconditional, easy (Alaxia)	Vigilance	Vigilant, suspicious, skeptical, distrustful, oppositional (Protension)
Grounded, practical, prosaic, solution oriented, steady, conventional (Praxernia)	Abstractedness	Abstract, imaginative, absent minded, impractical, absorbed in ideas (Autia)
Forthright, genuine, artless, open, guileless, naive, unpretentious, involved (Artlessness)	Privateness	Private, discreet, nondisclosing, shrewd, polished, worldly, astute, diplomatic (Shrewdness)
Self-assured, unworried, complacent, secure, free of guilt, confident, self-satisfied (Untroubled)	Apprehension	Apprehensive, self-doubting, worried, guilt prone, insecure, self-blaming (Guilt Proneness)

Low-range descriptors	Primary factor	High-range descriptors
Traditional, attached to familiar, conservative, respecting traditional ideas (Conservatism)	Openness to change	Open to change, experimental, liberal, analytical, critical, free thinking, flexible (Radicalism)
Group oriented, affiliative, a joiner and follower dependent (Group Adherence)	Self-reliance	Self-reliant, solitary, resourceful, individualistic, self-sufficient (Self-Sufficiency)
Tolerate disorder, unexacting, flexible, undisciplined, lax, self-conflict, impulsive, careless of social rules, uncontrolled (Low Integration)	Perfectionism	Perfectionistic, organized, compulsive, self-disciplined, socially precise, exacting willpower, control, self-sentimental (High Self-Concept Control)
Relaxed, placid, tranquil, torpid, patient, composed, low drive (Low Ergic Tension)	Tension	Tense, high energy, impatient, driven, frustrated, overwrought, time driven (High Ergic Tension)

Adapted from Conn and Rieke (1994).

- *Conscientiousness* – a tendency to show self-discipline, act dutifully, and aim for achievement
- *Neuroticism* – a tendency to easily experience unpleasant emotions such as anger, anxiety, depression, or vulnerability

With the development and interest in personality factors, there were great hopes and expectations that they would be extremely useful in giving guidance to the design of systems and the selection of applicants in the workplace. Despite their acceptance at face value, the empirical results have been very disappointing across the board. In a review of many studies on personality factors and their usefulness in personnel selection, Landy, Shandkster, and Kohler (1994) concluded that it is still too early to draw any reliable conclusions.

In the area of HCI, the idea that personality factors would predict success in programming was an appealing idea from early on (Weinberg, 1971). It was hypothesized that these factors would be related to performance on various computer tasks. However, nearly every study that has included personality factors as predictor variables has found no effect on learning or performance for tasks such as programming (Koubek, LeBold, & Salvendy, 1985), online searching (Bellardo, 1985), and text editing (Gomez, Egan, & Bowers, 1986). Bishop-Clark (1995) reported that most studies find no relationship between introversion/extroversion and computer programming.

In contrast, although personality factors may have little to do with performance, they may relate to other behaviors in HCI. For example, Landers and Lounsbury (2006) investigated the amount of self-reported time using the Internet for communication (including e-mail and chat), leisure (including music, role-playing, shopping), and academic reasons (research, course participation online). They found that Internet usage was negatively correlated with three of the Big Five factors (Agreeableness, Conscientiousness, and Extroversion) and with two additional factors ("optimism" and "work drive") and positively correlated with another factor ("tough mindedness"). However, the individual correlations were only in the range of 0.21 to 0.26, with an overall multivariate correlation of 0.35. This means that all of the personality factors together only accounted for 12 percent of the total variance in usage.

Cognitive Styles and Human–Computer Fit

"Cognitive styles" refers to relatively stable patterns in the way individuals think, perceive, and remember information, as well as the way in which they process information. As such, a particular cognitive style falls somewhere between a cognitive ability and a personality trait. A number of fascinating cognitive styles have been proposed and studied (Sternberg & Grigorenko, 1997). But even more than with personality theory, cognitive styles have often been promoted and marketed above and beyond any empirical evidence of their relationship with observed performance. Consider Scenario 1.

One of the main theories about cognitive styles in education and management is that if a teacher and pupil or a worker and manager share the same style, there will be a more positive learning experience or a more productive work environment than if there is a mismatch. Matching cognitive style helps individuals to feel more comfortable working with one another and more compatible in understanding and communication. Although this may have some merit, one could also argue that in many team situations having complementary cognitive styles would be more effective. Moreover, the problem may call for different styles at different points. In this section, we review some of the popular cognitive styles that have been promoted as individual differences relevant to HCI.

- *Field Dependence–Independence* (Witken, Moore, Goodenough, & Cox 1977). Those high in field independence have a tendency to provide structure to relatively unstructured situations. Individuals are able to overcome the organization of the field and restructure it. In contrast, those that are field dependent are oriented to the environment, and their perception of an item is strongly affected by the field. The favored measure for this cognitive style is the Group Embedded Figures Test (GEFT), as shown in Figure 9.5, and the Embedded Figures Test. Although numerous studies do show a relationship of field independence with programming achievement scores (Bishop-Clark, 1995), McKenna (1984) argued that it is not really due to style, but rather the fact that those with high GEFT scores have higher overall cognitive ability associated with perceptual skill.

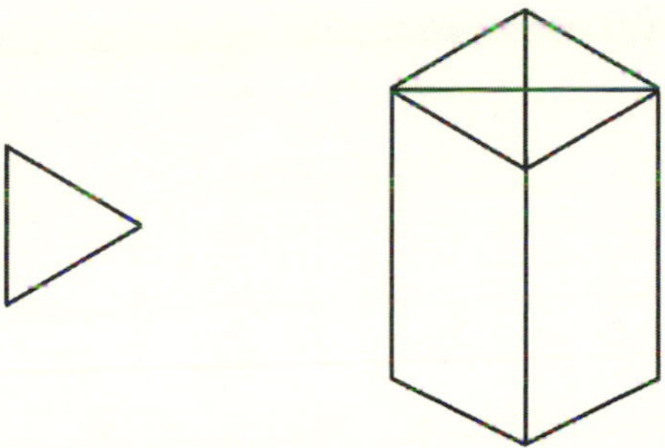

Find this simple form on the left hidden in the complex figure on the right.
Trace the shape over the figure to show your answer.

Figure 9.5. Example of a Group Embedded Figure Test item.

- *Analytic–Holistic* (French, Ekstrom, & Price, 1963). Analytic problem solvers reduce problems down to a base set of causes and factors and use structured approaches to decision making. Holistic thinkers emphasize common sense and intuition. They look for an overall pattern but tend to use more trial-and-error methods of problem solving. The Gestalt completion test shown in Figure 9.6 is often used to assess this style. The problem with the analytic–holistic dimension is that it is closely related to field independence. Studies looking at the relationship of this cognitive style with computer programming have had very mixed and questionable results.
- *Reflectic–Impulsive* (Kagan, Rosman, Day, Albert, & Phillips, 1964). Reflectic individuals think about different hypotheses in situations where there are many alternatives, and they tend to reflect on the consequences. Impulsives tend to choose the first alternative and go with it. The Matching Familiar Figures Test is the most popular method of assessing this cognitive style. It consists of items that start with a picture of a common object followed by several alternatives. One alternative is identical to the first picture, and the others are slightly different in one detail each. The subject is to pick the alternative that is identical, and the test is timed. Impulsives tend to pick the first alternative, and reflectics consider the figures in more detail. Figure 9.7 shows an example of one item. Research suggests an interesting link between programming experience and reflectivity. Programming experience may serve to increase reflectivity (Cathcart, 1990), and higher reflectivity results in higher programming achievement scores (VanMerrienboer, 1988).

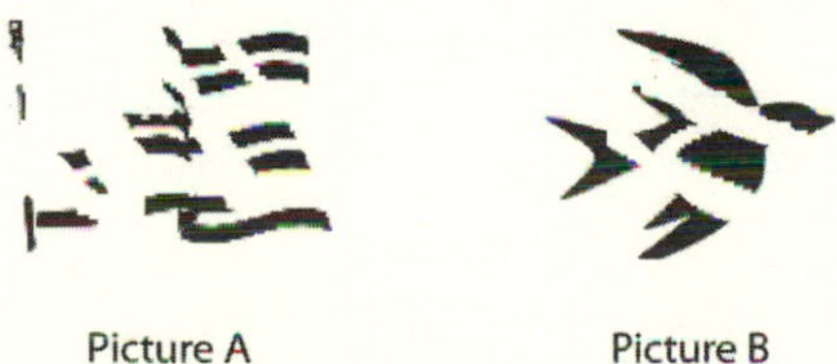

Figure 9.6. Example of a Gestalt Completion Test item. (Picture A is an American flag, and Picture B is a bird.)

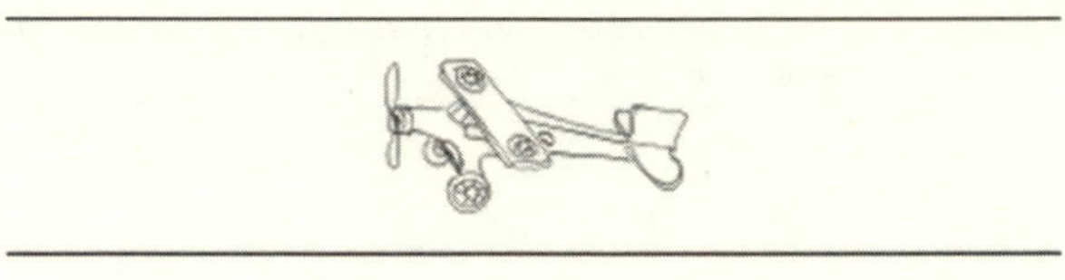

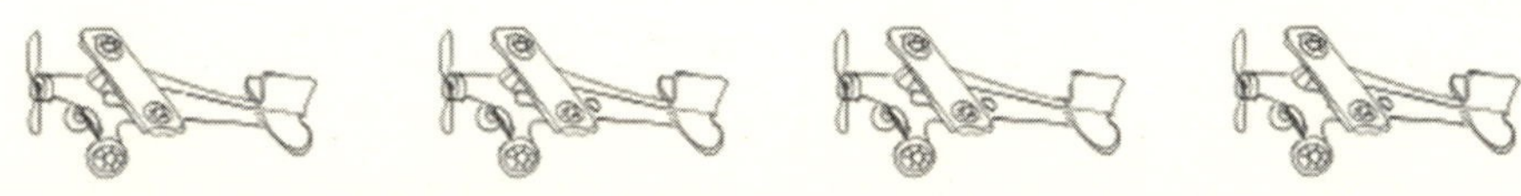

Figure 9.7. Example of a Matching Familiar Figures Test item. (The second alternative is the correct answer.)

- *Visualizer–Verbalizer* (Booth, Fowler, & Macaulay, 1987). Visualizers rely primarily on imagery processing when attempting to perform cognitive tasks. Verbalizers prefer to process information by a verbal-logical means. Although this seems to be an important individual difference, little is known about how it affects HCI.
- *Need for Closure* (Mills & Snyder, 1962). Individuals with a high need for closure have a desire to get a definite answer and will pursue the means to finish the job, make the decision, and get it done in a reasonable amount of time. Individuals with low need for closure will accept inconclusive results and have a tolerance for ambiguity. This cognitive style is measured using the Need for Closure Scale developed by Kruglanski, Webster, and Klem (1993). Need for closure and need for structure (analytic) are highly correlated. Need for closure may be related to information search and browsing the Web.
- *Locus of Control* (Rotter, 1966). Individuals with a strong *internal* locus of control believe that they influence events in their world and that their performance is the result of their own efforts rather than outside forces. Individuals with a strong *external* locus of control feel that outside forces control their performance and that they are helpless. The Rotter Locus of Control Scale (Rotter, 1966) is used to assess this dimension. Bishop-Clark (1995) reported that no reasonable conclusions can be drawn about the relationship between locus of control and programming performance. However, for general users, this may be an important individual difference when it comes to issues of who is in control at the human–computer interface, the user or the computer. We see in Chapter 12 that strong external locus of control is related to Internet addiction (Chak & Leung, 2004).
- *Convergent–Divergent Thinkers* (Hudson, 1966). The convergent thinker works for the best single answer to a problem. The divergent thinker moves outward from the problem to find many possible solutions. The Torrance

Test of Creative Thinking (Torrance, 1972) is used to measure divergent thinking. As suggested in Chapter 7, some creativity techniques may require a person to engage in both types of thinking at different stages of problem solving.

- *Adaptive–Innovative* (Kirton, 1976, 2003). Adaptors prefer to solve problems by time-honored techniques and within accepted paradigms, whereas innovators prefer to do things differently and strive to transcend existing paradigms. Again, a person may tend toward one of the other cognitive styles, but many situations may dictate which is more appropriate at a particular time. Moreover, it is not yet clear how these cognitive styles impact the way in which users interact with the human–computer interface.

At present, the idea of taking into consideration the user's cognitive styles seems promising. One of the models of HCI presented in Chapter 3 involves the idea of matching the characteristics of the human and the computer to create a synergistic combination. To an extent, this may be true, but humans tend to be very accommodating and can shift styles when needed. However, computers may provide a multiplying factor for some individuals, say, those with high spatial visualization ability, and a limiting factor for individuals with poor skills. If this is the case, we might find an increase in the disparity between different groups of computer users with different styles and abilities. Are there ways to reduce these differences? Is it possible for computers to provide scaffolding or bootstrapping for individuals who need help?

Assessment of Individual Differences: Online Testing and Measurement

Throughout this chapter, we have been talking about individual differences that are assessed by some sort of psychometric testing. Traditional methods have involved observing task performance, personal interview, and paper-and-pencil questionnaires. In the past few years, we have witnessed a steady shift from both face-to-face interview and paper-and-pencil testing to computerized testing and online surveys. Initially, there was some concern about the reliability and validity of online testing; however, in nearly every case, online testing has proven to be either equal or superior to traditional methods. Moreover, efficiency and cost effectiveness have made online testing the method of choice.

Studies indicate that, for the most part, the results are equivalent for online and paper-and-pencil surveys. Respondents tend to give the same answers whether the survey is printed or online (Huang, 2006). Moreover, a few positive factors have been observed.

Research indicates that people tend to be more honest and open about sensitive issues in online methods than face-to-face interviews. People tend to write more for open-ended questions on the computer than on paper (Slaughter, Harper, & Norman, 1994). College students prefer online questionnaires to paper-and-pencil forms. Surveys can be designed to be efficient and easy to navigate (Norman, Friedman, Norman, & Stevenson, 2000).

Online surveys, testing, and measurement have many advantages (Couper, 2000; Dillman, 1999). Obviously, online surveys and tests eliminate paper. They are electronically disseminated and collected, which avoids mailing and handling. They also help automate the data collection and analysis. Online surveys have the unique advantage of being dynamic. They can check for missing or incomplete answers. They can detect inconsistent answers (e.g., the respondent's age is 32, but he enters 30 for the age of his oldest child) and help the respondent correct any errors. They can automatically skip questions that are not appropriate given previous answers. One of the most compelling advantages to Web-based methods is that a number of survey tools are available on the Web that make it very easy to develop online questionnaires, automatically host them on the Web, and efficiently analyze the results.

However, there are also a few problems that one has to watch out for. The disadvantages are that computer problems can interfere with results. These include disconnects and problems with communications. It may also be difficult to get representative samples of the population.

End Thoughts

Individual differences have always been extremely important in psychology. Computer science took note of individual differences when computers were introduced to the masses and large differences in attitudes and performance were found between user groups. The popular method of "user-centered" design required that designers take into consideration individual differences. However, as the human–computer interface permeates more and more of the human environment, one wonders how and to what extent individual differences can really be accommodated. In much of our environment, we are accustomed to a "one-size-fits-all" solution. We do not have different doors for different heights of people, different roads for below average and above average drivers, and different public libraries for high verbal versus low verbal patrons. But within many systems, we do have choices and preferences. You can select the items that suit you and set the preferences in many applications that work best for you. Individual differences are accommodated by individual choice. Public libraries have large selections of books that cover the range of verbal abilities of the patrons.

Many individual differences have to do with job performance and are factors that help determine one's career path. Some people are good at programming, and others are not. Those who are good should be hired as programmers. Some people are good in art and graphic design. Some people are good at personal relations. Individual differences are assessed through applicant testing and screening and accommodated through career guidance and choice.

A large number of factors are discussed in this chapter that pertain to the measurement of individual differences and their subsequent impact on HCI. Some factors have been used to predict user performance such as IQ and spatial visualization ability. Others have been used to customize interfaces for different types of individuals. However, in many ways, the interface itself may serve to both assess individual differences and accommodate for them. As noted in other places, interactions at the interface can be captured, stored, and analyzed. These interactions, such as typing speed, mousing accuracy, programming patterns, and Web browsing, can all be used to profile individual differences. The methods of psychometrics from the 1900s using tests and questionnaires that capture only a few ratings and choices (e.g., <100) will undoubtedly be replaced in the near future with much more sophisticated data mining methods that tap into megabytes of interactive data stored in logs, cookies, and history files. These data will be used to assess a person's IQ, personality, cognitive styles, and abilities.

Suggested Exercises

1. Take a look at the profile or configuration of your computer. For a Mac user, go to the Applications folder, then the Utilities folder, and then run the System Profiler application. For a Windows-XP user, go to the Programs directory, then the Accessories directory, then the System Tools directory, and then run the System Information program. How do these specifications on the hardware and software map to individual differences among computers?
2. Write a description of yourself as a computer user. What are your demographics, abilities, attitudes, and so on?
3. Go to several of the online IQ and personality test Web sites. Take several of the tests and see if you agree with the results.
4. You can see how different programs and different Web sites are aimed at different user groups or types. See if you can find a Web site that matches each of the following stereotypes: teenage boy, teenage girl, geek, and retired person.
5. Go to one of the free online survey tools and develop your own survey on a topic of your choice.

References

Allport, G. W., & Odbert, H. S. (1936). Trait names: A psycho-lexical study. *Psychological Monographs*, 47 (1 Whole No. 211).

Anastasi, A., & Urbina, S. (1996). *Psychological testing* (7th ed.). Upper Saddle River, NJ: Prentice Hall.

Bellardo, T. (1985). An investigation of online searcher traits and their relationship to search outcome. *Journal of the American Society for Information Science, 36*(4), 241–250.

Beyer, S., Rynes, K., Perrault, J., Hay, K., & Haller, S. (2003). Gender differences in computer science students. *Proceedings of the SIGCSE'03*, pp. 49–53.

Bishop-Clark, C. (1995). Cognitive style, personality, and computer programming. *Computers in Human Behavior, 11*(2), 241–260.

Booth, P., Fowler, C. J. H., & Macaulay, L. A. (1987). An investigation into business information presentation at human-computer interfaces. In: Bullinger, H. J., and Schackerl, B. (Eds.), *Proceedings of Human-Computer Interaction-INTERACT'87*, Elsevier, North-Holland. pp. 599–604.

Cathcart, W. (1990). Effects of LOGO instruction on cognitive style. *Journal of Educational Computing Research, 6*, 231–242.

Chak, K., & Leung, L. (2004). Shyness and locus of control as predictors of Internet addiction and Internet use. *CyberPsychology & Behavior, 7*(5), 559–570.

Chen, C., & Rada, R. (1996). Interacting with hypertext: A meta-analysis of experimental studies. *Human–Computer Interaction, 11*, 125–156.

Chrysler, E. (1978). Some basic determinants of computer programming productivity. *Communications of the ACM, 21*(6), 472–483.

Conn, S. R., & Rieke, M. L. (1994). *The 16PF Fifth Edition Technical Manual.* Champagne, IL: Institute for Personality and Ability Testing, Inc.

Couper, M. P. (2000). Web surveys: A review of issues and approaches. *Public Opinion Quarterly, 64*, 464–494.

Day, J. C., Janus, A., & Davis, J. (2005, October). *Computer and Internet use in the United States: 2003.* Current Population Reports P23–208. Washington, DC: U.S. Census Bureau. Retrieved March 20, 2008, from www.census.gov/prod/2005pubs/p23-208.pdf.

De Lisi, R., & Cammarano, D. M. (1996). Computer experience and gender differences in undergraduate mental rotation performance. *Computers in Human Behavior, 12*(3), 351–361.

Dillman, D. A. (1999). *Mail and Internet surveys: The tailored design method* (2nd ed.). New York: John Wiley & Sons.

Dillon, A., & Watson, C. (1996). User analysis in HCI – The historical lessons from individual differences research. *International Journal of Human–Computer Studies, 45*, 619–637.

Dillman, D. A. (1999). *Mail and Internet Surveys: The tailored design method.* (2nd ed.), New York: John Wiley & Sons.

Egan, D. E. (1988). Individual differences in human-computer interaction. In M. Helander (Ed.), *Handbook of human-computer interaction* (pp. 543–568). Elsevier Science.

Egan, D. E., & Gomez, L. M. (1985). Assaying, isolating and accommodating individual differences in learning a complex skill. In R. Dillon (Ed.), *Individual differences in cognition* (Vol. 2) (pp. 173–217). New York: Academic Press.

Ekstrom, R. B., French, J. W., & Harman, H. H. (1976). *Manual for kit of factor-referenced cognitive tests.* Princeton, NJ: Educational Testing Service.

Eysenck, H. J. (1947). *Dimensions of personality.* London, U.K.: Routledge & Kegan Paul.

French, J. W., Ekstrom, R., & Price, L. (1963). *Kit of reference tests for cognitive factors*. Princeton, NJ: Educational Testing Service.

Gardner, H. (1983). *Frames of mind: The theory of multiple intelligences*. New York: Basic Books.

Gardner, H. (1999). *Intelligence reframed: Multiple intelligences for the 21st century*. New York: Basic Books.

Goddard, H. H. (1913). The Binet tests in relation to immigration. *Journal of Psycho-Asthenics, 18*, 105–107.

Goldberg, L. R. (1993). The structure of phenotypic personality traits. *American Psychologist, 48*, 26–34.

Gomez, L. M., Egan, D. E., & Bowers, C. (1986). Learning to use a text editor: Some learner characteristics that predict success. *Human–Computer Interaction*, 2, 1–23.

Goodwin, B. (2004, October 1). Number of women in IT industry falls by almost half in four years. *ComputerWeekly.com*. Retrieved March 20, 2008, from http://www.computerweekly.com/Articles/2004/10/01/205622/number-of-women-in-it-industry-falls-by-almost-half-in-four.htm

Gough, H. (1958). *Manual for the California Psychological Inventory*. Palo Alto, CA: Consulting Psychologists Press.

Gould, S. J. (1996). *The mismeasure of man*. New York: W. W. Norton.

Greene, S. L., Gomez, L. M., & Devlin, S. J. (1986). A cognitive analysis of database query production. *Proceedings of the Human Factors Society*, Dayton, OH, pp. 9–13.

Hofstede, G. (1991). *Cultures and organizations, software of the mind: Intercultural cooperation and its importance for survival*. New York: McGraw-Hill.

Houtz, L. (2001). Nebraska high school students' computer skills and attitudes. *Journal of Research on Computing in Education, 33*, 316–328.

Huang, H. (2006). Do print and Web surveys provide the same results? *Computers in Human Behavior, 22*(3), 334–350.

Hudson, L. (1966). *Contrary imaginations: A psychological study of the young student*. New York: Schocken Books.

Jensen, A. (1982). The debunking of scientific fossils and straw persons. *Contemporary Education Review, 1*, 121–135.

Kagan, J., Rosman, B., Day, D., Albert, J., & Phillips, W. (1964). Information processing in the child: Significance of analytic and reflective attitudes. *Psychological Monographs, 78*(1, Serial No. 578).

Kay, R. (1992). Understanding gender differences in computer attitudes, aptitude, and use: An invitation to build theory. *Journal of Research on Computing in Education, 25*, 159–172.

Kirton, M. (1976). Adaptors and innovators: A description and measure. *Journal of Applied Psychology, 61*(5), 622–629.

Kirton, M. J. (2003). *Adaption and innovation in the context of diversity and change*. London: Routledge.

Koubek, R. J., LeBold, W. K., & Salvendy, G. (1985). Predicting performance in computer programming courses. *Behaviour and Information Technology*, 4(2), 113–129.

Kruglanski, A. W., Webster, D. M., & Klem, A. (1993). Motivated resistance and openness to persuasion in the presence or absence of prior information. *Journal of Personality and Social Psychology, 65*, 861–876.

Landers, R. N., & Lounsbury, J. W. (2006). An investigation of Big Five and narrow personality traits in relation to Internet usage. *Computers in Human Behavior, 22*, 283–293.

Landy, F., Shandkster, L., & Kohler, S. (1994). Personnel selection and placement. *Annual Review of Psychology, 45*, 261–296.

Marcus, A. (2000). International and intercultural user-interface design. In C. Stephanidis (Ed.), *User interfaces for all* (pp. 47–63). New York: Erlbaum.

Marcus, A., & Gould, E. (2001). *Cultural dimensions and global web design: What? So what? Now what?* Emeryville, CA: Aaron Marcus and Associates, Inc.

McKenna, F. P. (1984). Measures of field dependence: Cognitive style of cognitive ability. *Journal of Personality and Social Psychology, 47*, 593–603.

McKenna, P. (2004). Gender and black boxes in the programming curriculum. *ACM Journal of Educational Resources in Computing, 4*(1), 1–12.

McSweeney, B. (2002). Hofstede's model of national cultural differences and their consequences: A triumph of faith – A failure of analysis. *Human Relations, 55*(1), 89–118.

Michell, J. (1999). *Measurement in psychology.* Cambridge: Cambridge University Press.

Mills, J., & Snyder, R. (1962). Avoidance of commitment, need for closure, and the expression of choices. *Journal of Personality, 30*(3), 458–470.

Murphy, E. (2000). *Beyond supervisory control: Cognitive issues in human interaction with autonomous satellites.* Unpublished Ph.D. dissertation. University of Maryland, College Park.

Neisser, U., Boodoo, G., Bouchard, T. J., Jr., Boykin, A. W., Brody, N., Ceci, S. J., et al. (1996). Intelligence: Knowns and unknowns. *American Psychologist, 51*, 77–101.

Nielsen, J. (Ed.). (1990). *Designing user interfaces for international use.* North Holland, Amsterdam: Elsevier.

Norman, D. A. (1986). Cognitive engineering. In D. A. Norman & S. Draper (Eds.), *User centered system design: New perspectives on human–computer interaction* (pp. 31–62). Hillsdale, NJ: Erlbaum.

Norman, K. L. (1994). Spatial visualization: A gateway to computer-based technology. *Journal of Special Education Technology, 12*, 195–205.

Norman, K. L., & Butler, S. A. (1989). *Search by uncertainty: Menu selection by target probability.* Technical Report CAR-TR-432. College Park: University of Maryland Center for Automation Research.

Norman, K. L., Friedman, Z., Norman, K. D., & Stevenson, R. (2000). Navigational issues in the design of on-line self administered questionnaires. *Behaviour and Information Technology, 20*, 37–45.

Norman, K. L., & Singh, R. (1989). Expected performance at the human/computer interface as a function of user proficiency and system power. *Journal of Behavioral Decision Making, 2*, 179–195.

Nunnally, J. C., & Bernstein, I. (1994). *Psychometric theory.* Hightstown, NJ: McGraw-Hill.

Rosson, M. B. (1983). Patterns of experience in text editing. *Proceedings of the CHI'83 Human Factors in Computing Systems*, pp. 171–175.

Rotter, J. B. (1966). Generalized expectancies for internal versus external control of reinforcement. *Psychological Mongraphs, 80*, 1–28.

Ryder, N. B. (1965). The cohort as a concept in the study of social change. *American Sociological Review, 30*, 843–861.

Sharp, S. E. (1898). Individual psychology: A study of psychological method. *American Journal of Psychology, 10*, 329–391.

Slaughter, L., Harper, B. D., & Norman, K. L. (1994). Assessing the equivalence of the paper and on-line formats of the QUIS 5.5. *Proceedings of the Mid-Atlantic Human Factors Conference,* Reston, VA, pp. 87–91.

Spearman, C. E. (1927). *The abilities of man, their nature and measurement.* New York: Macmillan.

Sternberg, R. J. (1988). *The triarchic mind: A new theory of human intelligence.* New York: Penguin Books.

Sternberg, R. J. (1997). The concept of intelligence and its role in lifelong learning and success. *American Psychologist, 52*, 1030–1037.

Sternberg, R. J., & Grigorenko, E. L. (1997). Are cognitive styles still in style? *American Psychologist, 52*(7), 700–712.

Strauss, W., & Howe, N. (2003). *Millennials go to college: Strategies for a new generation on campus.* American Association of Collegiate Registrars. Washington, DC.

Terman, L. M. (1916). *The measurement of intelligence.* Boston: Houghton Mifflin.

Thurstone, L. L. (1938). *Primary mental abilities.* Chicago: University of Chicago Press.

Tisserand, D. J., Bosma, H., Van Boxtel, M. P., & Jolles, J. (2001). Head size and cognitive ability in nondemented older adults are related. *Neurology, 56*, 969–971.

Torrance, E. P. (1972). Can we teach children to think creatively? *Journal of Creative Behavior, 6*(2), 114–143.

Turkle, S., & Papert, S. (1990). Epistemological pluralism: Styles and voices within the computer culture. *Signs: Journal of Women in Culture and Society, 16*(10), 128–157.

VanMerrienboer, J. (1988). Relationship between cognitive learning style and achievement in an introductory computer programming course. *Journal of Research on Computing in Education,* 29, 181–185.

Vernon, P. A., Wickett, J. C., Bazana, G., & Stelmack, R. M. (2000). The neuropsychology and psychophysiology of human intelligence. In R. J. Sternberg (Ed.), *Handbook of Intelligence* (pp. 245–266). Cambridge University Press.

Vicente, K. J., Hayes, B. C., & Williges, R. C. (1987). Assaying and isolating individual differences in searching a hierarchical file system. *Human Factors,* 29(3), 349–359.

Weinberg, G. M. (1971). *The psychology of computer programming.* New York: Van Nostrand Reinhold.

Whitley, B. E. (1997). Gender differences in computer-related attitudes and behavior: A meta-analysis. *Computers in Human Behavior, 13*(1) 1–22.

Wissler, C. (1901). The correlation of mental and physical tests. *Psychological Review Monograph Supplement, 3* (Whole No. 6).

Witken, H., Moore, C., Goodenough, D., & Cox, P. (1977). Field-dependent and field-independent cognitive styles and their educational implications. *Review of Educational Research,* 47(10), 1–64.

Ten

Motivation and Emotion at the Human–Computer Interface

Scenario 1

John was not doing well in the seventh grade. He felt bad about his performance. His teacher seemed to have written him off as a slow, unmotivated student with little hope for improvement. He really didn't have any friends either. At lunch and recess, he sat or played alone. He always tried to look as if he were busy or on his way somewhere so that no one would think that being by himself wasn't of his own choice.

But at home in the privacy of his bedroom, when he sat down at his computer, life was different. He was intense and directed, with a high need for achievement and an inflated ego. The World of Warcraft was his stomping ground. He would log on and join a group to go on a quest with other players. He knew some of the members of his band from past adventures, and others were new to him. It really didn't matter. He was not shy. He had his character, he had his epic mount, he had his voice, and he had achieved Level 60! He was at the ninety-ninth percentile of achievement by other players. This was his world.

Scenario 2

Dave: Open the pod bay doors, please, Hal.... Open the pod bay doors, please, Hal.... Hullo, Hal, do you read me?... Hullo, Hal, do you read me?... Do you read me, Hal?... Do you read me, Hal?... Hullo, Hal, do you read me?... Hullo, Hal, do you read me?... Do you read me, Hal?
Hal: Affirmative, Dave, I read you.
Dave: Open the pod bay doors, Hal.
Hal: I'm sorry, Dave, I'm afraid I can't do that.
Dave: What's the problem?

Hal: *I think you know what the problem is just as well as I do.*
Dave: *What're you talking about, Hal?*
Hal: *This mission is too important for me to allow you to jeopardize it.*
Dave: *I don't know what you're talking about, Hal.*
Hal: *I know that you and Frank were planning to disconnect me, and I'm afraid that's something I cannot allow to happen.*
Dave: *Where the hell'd you get that idea, Hal?*
Hal: *Dave, although you took very thorough precautions in the pod against my hearing you, I could see your lips move.*
Dave: *Alright, Hal. I'll go in through the emergency airlock.*
Hal: *Without your space helmet, Dave, you're going to find that rather difficult.*
Dave: *Hal, I won't argue with you any more. Open the doors.*
Hal: *Dave, this conversation can serve no purpose any more. Goodbye.*
Dave: *Hal? Hal. Hal. Hal! Hal!...*
(From "2001: A Space Odyssey.")

Overview

Whenever a space includes the human person, it involves motivation, feelings, and emotions. The human–computer interface is such a place. We generally view the computer and all technology as mechanical, rational, cold, and unfeeling. But when the human person enters the scene, it is filled with human emotion and feeling. Moreover, there is the possibility of the reflection, amplification, and distortion of those feelings and emotions in digital and mechanical environments. Just as when a person enters a hall of mirrors, it becomes filled with human images and movement.

This chapter discusses the issues of human motivation, drive, and satisfaction in the context of the human–computer interface. A general theory of the overall human–computer interface must take these into account. The human has the ability to either empower the interface or to unplug and walk away. The reason for engaging the interface has to do with the motives and purposes on the human side. What can the user get from it? How does interacting with the computer reward or frustrate us? What is the motivation that drives our use of computers?

Scenario 1 may be a common situation for many individuals struggling with life in the real world and the need for acceptance and achievement. How does the computer entertain us and captivate our attention to interact with us at an emotional level? Scenario 2 was far fetched in 1968, when the movie "2001: A Space Odyssey" was first released, but today computer interfaces are being built that sense how we feel and simulate emotional

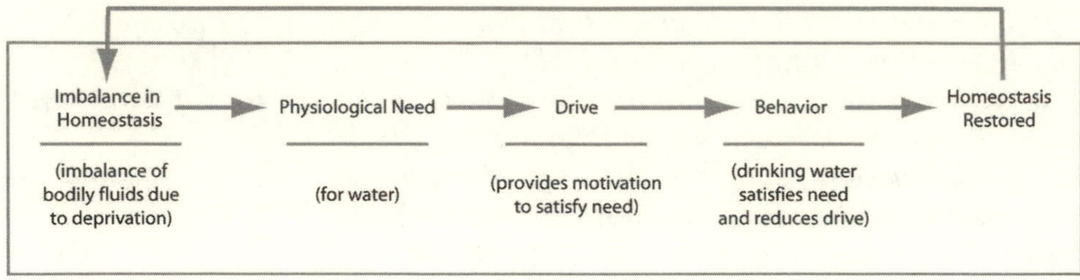

Figure 10.1. Drive reduction cycle.

content in the output of the computer. In this chapter, we look at human emotions and ask whether the computer can be sensitive to our needs and emotions. To understand the background, we first look at the basic theories of motivation and emotion in psychology, and then follow each with their implications and applications in HCI.

Motivation

Drive Reduction Theory

In psychology, we trace the study of motivation back to instincts and then to drive reduction theory. It was first proposed that behavior is driven by instincts that are biologically determined and inherently involved in the survival of the species (Darwin, 1959). The study of instincts required an identification of all instincts for each species and then a description of how each instinct operates in the environment. The suckling of a newborn at its mother's nipple and the imprinting of goslings on their mother are commonly cited instincts. But to these one would have to add an incredible number of instincts to account for all survival and procreative behaviors. This, of course, predated the human–computer interface, and consequently, no one had to entertain the notion of a typing instinct, programming instinct, video game instinct, or even computer anxiety instinct or desire to use a computer instinct. As it was, it did not take long in the history of psychology to debunk the theory of instincts as useless and circular.

However, the newer theory of motivation, drive reduction theory (Hull, 1943), also based its foundation in biology, taking into consideration the physiological need states of the organism. This theory asserts that we have a need for food, a need for water, a need for safety, etc. All primary needs are rooted in biological need states. As shown in Figure 10.1, need states result from an imbalance in the homeostasis of a physiological system. This results in a drive state, which in turn motivates behavior to reduce the drive state.

We then define "motivation" as an inner state that energizes behavior to reduce the drive state as its goal (Pittman, 1998). Motivation is like a vector indicating both force (energy) and direction (toward the goal). According to drive reduction theory, behavior is pushed by internal states of the organism.

Technology is playing an increasing role in the drive reduction cycle to either maintain or restore homeostatic levels. At the front end, homeostasis of physical systems may be monitored and maintained by automated systems. Heating and air conditioning systems circumvent the need to warm up or cool off our body temperatures. Life support systems in hospitals take over physiological needs and maintain homeostatic levels of blood sugar and oxygen for those whose internal systems no longer function. Similar systems are being developed for pain reduction and pleasure maintenance. Some conceive of entertainment and gaming systems that monitor physiological levels and provide stimuli to avoid boredom or provide satisfaction.

However, for the most part, technology is being used indirectly as part of the behavioral component to assist in drive reduction. If we are hungry, we may look for a restaurant using an Internet search and find optimal directions to reduce our travel time. If we are afraid of something, we may turn to the Internet for information about it and ways to overcome the fear. Computers are becoming an integral part of drive reduction as a problem-solving tool.

Arousal Level

Drive reduction theory, although successful in explaining much behavior, has a problem at the two ends of the continuum of motivation level and arousal. At the low end, it appears that humans are uncomfortable when physical levels of arousal and drive levels are too low (Berlyne, 1974). We seek stimulation over a state of complete satiation, and we often seek situations that generate motivation rather than reduce it. When placed in an artificial environment and deprived of sensory stimulation, participants report difficulties in thinking; they become increasingly irritable and may have vivid daydreams and hallucinations (Heron, 1957). Consequently, computer-generated (virtual) or controlled environments (space capsules) do not seek to eliminate all sensory stimulation, but rather to maintain sufficient levels of stimulation.

At the upper end of the arousal or motivational level, other problems emerge. When too high, arousal and motivational drive can be disabling. Stress and anxiety produce conflicting behaviors and impede drive reduction behaviors. The situation is described in the Yerkes-Dodson law, as shown in Figure 10.2, for behavior on three types of tasks. For well-learned, easy tasks, such as using the mouse to click a large red button on the screen, moderately high levels of arousal are beneficial. When we are not motivated or aroused, we are bored and off-task. For new, difficult tasks, such as writing a patch for a computer program that is malfunctioning, even moderate arousal can be distracting and reduce performance. Too much arousal can lead to nervous and tense behavior. Thus, we seek to maintain an optimal level of arousal. The challenge is to moderate the arousal and motivational levels to produce optimal performance (Hebb, 1955; Teigen, 1994).

To make matters even more complicated, people differ greatly in their optimal levels of arousal. Some people work well and even enjoy high levels

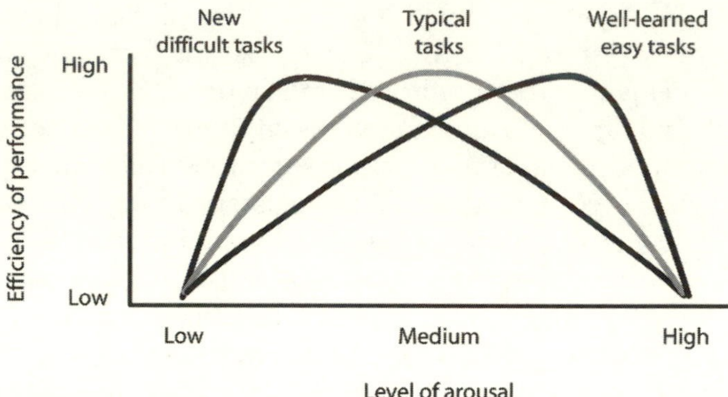

Figure 10.2. Yerkes-Dodson law of performance as a function level of arousal for different type of tasks.

of arousal in stressful and demanding jobs. Research indicates that these people tend to socialize a lot, eat spicy food, drink alcohol, listen to loud music, and engage in risky and novel behaviors (Trimpop & Kirkcaldy, 1997; Zuckerman, 1984). People with lower optimal levels of arousal seek less intense stimulation, avoid overindulgence, and engage in fewer risky behaviors. Interestingly, these differences seem to be traced back to physiological roots in blood chemistry (Shekim et al., 1989). It is not surprising that personal computer systems allow users to customize the interface and set different preferences for mouse and clicking speeds, background images, sounds, and volumes. To make matters even worse, a person's ideal arousal level may vary from one context to another – from work to play, from solo to social, and from night to day. Consequently, it may be appropriate for interfaces to vary not only among people (user specific), but also from situation to situation (context specific).

Ultimately, instead of motivation being simply the force behind drive reduction, it is a self-regulating force to maintain optimal levels of arousal. Within the human–computer interface, users have a vast array of functions and controls to modulate arousal – from speed and intensity of individual tasks (e.g., games set at easy, moderate, or difficult levels) to multitasking with simultaneous chat sessions and switching between multiple windows and applications. However, it not clear that all users are equally good at assessing their ideal environment. Some users may believe that they can handle more than they really can and actually be operating at suboptimal levels. Many users may be subject to too much stress, having to deal with complex, demanding computer tasks, multiple interruptions, and intensive work environments. Others may be understimulated with boring, repetitive tasks. Can automated systems be used to monitor arousal levels, task difficulty, and user performance, and to optimize arousal level by increasing or decreasing interface events? In Chapter 14, we see that some designers suggest the use of "augmented cognition" to allow the computer to assess the motivational level of the user and modify the interface appropriately.

Incentive Theory

To this point, motivation has been an internal *push* due to drive level and arousal. Incentive theory contends that external stimuli also *pull* us in certain directions and motivate us to behave in certain ways. Again, we characterize a motive as a vector with energy (pull) and direction (toward a goal). Incentives come into being by discovering that certain stimuli are associated with positive outcomes and others with negative outcomes. In this way, they are tied to primary drives involving pain reduction and pleasure seeking. Authors of banner ads hope to present incentives to click on the link by displaying a stimulus previously associated with pleasure and gain (e.g., dollar signs, food, attractive pictures). Over time, however, positive incentives can be unlearned. Banner ads can quickly become irritating. After opening attachments that present a superficial positive incentive that result in viruses and negative outcomes, they become negative stimuli that repel us.

In many cases, the stimuli themselves do not in and of themselves reduce a need state. They are only associated with drive reduction in the same way that artificial sweeteners are positive incentives but do nothing to satisfy hunger. This is the very purpose of so-called "eye candy" on Web sites. It is positive, enticing, and attractive, but does not itself lead to drive reduction. In fact, incentives can increase drive and serve to motivate further behavior.

Finally, we distinguish between intrinsic and extrinsic motivation. An intrinsic motive leads us to do something because it has value in its own right. An artist may be motivated to paint because it has aesthetic value, not because he or she is going to make a lot of money from selling it. An extrinsic motive is one that leads to an external reward such as money or power (Sansone & Harackiewicz, 2000). In a sense, the idea is to determine the focal point of every motive and the rationale behind each behavior that results.

If one were to analyze the activities of computer and Internet users, one could potentially classify user motivation as intrinsic or extrinsic. For some, working on computers is intrinsically fun and interesting, whether programming, playing with the OS, or working with programs. For others, it is not, and the only reason for using a computer is to get an extrinsic product. The only motivation for the use of word processors, e-mail, and other applications is the product. In contrast, online games, browsing for interesting information, and posting comments in discussion groups and blogs would lean toward intrinsic motivation. Online banking, stock trading, and shopping would be for extrinsic rewards.

Self-Actualization

Increasingly, people are turning to computers and the Internet to meet their needs from the most basic to the highest level of human achievement. To understand this range of needs, we turn to Abraham Maslow's hierarchy.

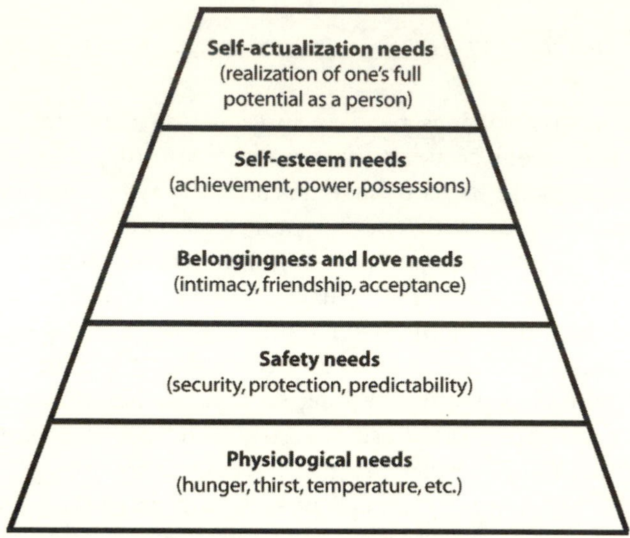

Figure 10.3. Maslow's hierarchy of needs.

Maslow (1970) proposed that from birth we have basic needs that must be satisfied for survival before we are motivated to satisfy higher-level needs. The needs form a hierarchy, as shown in Figure 10.3, from physiological needs at the bottom to humanistic needs for self-actualization at the top. The first four levels of the hierarchy are essentially needs to make up for deficiencies (e.g., need for food, shelter, affection, and respect). If they are not satisfied, they inhibit one's personal growth. The needs at the top level are for self-actualization. They make up the need of a person to achieve and fulfill personal potential. In Maslow's view, self-actualization is the ultimate goal of human existence. Unfortunately, most of us are preoccupied with needs at the lower levels, from creature comforts to social acceptance and personal achievements.

How can we use technology to fill the deficiencies at the lower levels so that we can move upward to self-actualization? Ben Shneiderman's (2003) book, *Leonardo's Laptop: Human Needs and the New Computing Technologies,* suggests that the "new computing" of the twenty-first century will serve human needs and ultimately help users reach their true potential. His book surveys how human needs are being met across a range of applications and how they are helping us progress up the hierarchy of needs.

A pivotal point in the hierarchy of human needs is the need for achievement (n-Ach). The n-Ach is the basic desire to overcome obstacles and meet high standards of excellence (Murray, 1938). People vary greatly in their n-Ach due to both genetic and environmental differences fostered by parents, teachers, and significant others. People who are extremely high in n-Ach are highly competitive, aggressive, and motivated, but they are also subject to disappointment and fear of failure. People with low n-Ach are apathetic, passive, and unmotivated. They tend to avoid failure by not competing in the first place. Accordingly, one might expect different modes of interaction with computers by users with different levels of n-Ach. A user with high n-Ach strives to use the computer efficiently to achieve his or her goals. A user with low n-Ach may use the computer as a time waster to avoid work.

In the same way that optimal levels of arousal vary with context, n-Ach can also vary within the same person in different situations. In Scenario 1, John had a low n-Ach in the school classroom and playground, but a high n-Ach on role-playing games on the Internet. The human–computer interface may open up new electronic environments that provide new opportunities and incentives for achievement and self-actualization. We see in Chapter 15 that success in playing video games may not be a total waste of time but rather a valuable learning experience and valid arena for competition and achievement. Just as with most sports where one can go professional, one can now major in video games and earn a living playing competitively.

People with low n-Ach can pose a problem when they are involved in collaborative team efforts or as employees of organizations that expect high levels of performance. A whole line of research has been devoted to efforts to manipulate a person's n-Ach (Cochran & Tesser, 1996; Locke & Latham, 1990). In computer-supported cooperative work, team members need to be motivated to work together to complete projects. The computer may be used to initially assess individual n-Ach, assist in the assignment roles to team members, assess ongoing performance levels, and suggest interventions when needed.

Emotions and Feelings

Today, more than ever with technology, we are able to assess and simulate states of emotion. Humans have a set of emotions that have been studied in psychology: excitation, joy, satisfaction, pain, anger, and rage. Emotions play an important part in HCI because as humans we bring our feelings to the interface. However, we know that computers have no emotions. They are only machines, incapable of feeling. But as humans, we also have the tendency to imbue emotional states into nonhuman objects such as machines. We may anthropomorphize and attribute emotional states as causes for unexpected events. If the computer crashed, it must have been angry with me. We infer emotion in others from their behaviors. Can it also work in the other direction? Can computers infer our emotions?

Emotions

We define "emotion" as a positive or negative mental state that is coupled with some combination of physiological arousal, cognitive evaluation, and behavioral expression. Although many theories have been developed to explain emotions (Plutchik, 1994), most consider that all emotions have the following unifying characteristics:

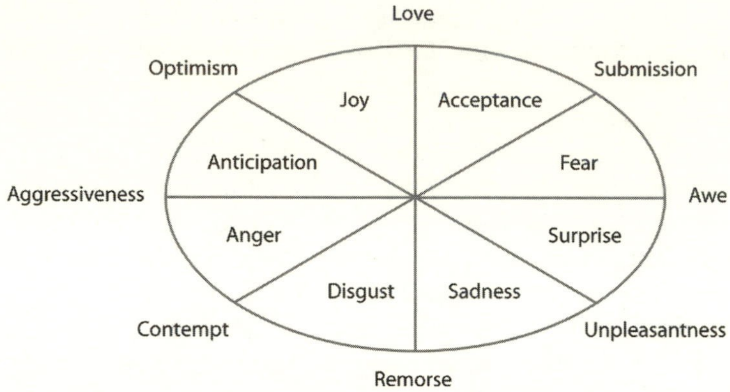

Figure 10.4. Circle of emotions. (From Plutchik, 1984.)

- Emotions involve a number of bodily systems.
- Expressions of emotion are partially innate and partially learned.
- Emotions communicate information among people.
- Emotions help people react to changes in their environment.

An emotion is an experience that is felt as happening to the self, generated partly by a cognitive appraisal of a situation, and accompanied by reflexive physiological changes (e.g., an increase in blood pressure and heart rate) and behavioral responses (e.g., facial expressions, postural changes).

Early researchers understood the importance of human emotions preparing the body to react to environmental events. Emotions of surprise, fear, and anger activate "fight-or-flight" responses. However, for many years emotions were viewed as an undesirable product of the rational mind. Emotions get in the way of reason. Recently, emotions have been viewed in a more positive light. For example, Damasio (1994) proposed that rationality is dependent on our knowledge of emotional states of both others and ourselves. Work by Goleman (1995) and others on emotional intelligence, discussed in Chapter 9, further underscores its importance.

Most lists of emotions include the following seven primary emotions: anger, disgust, fear, happiness, surprise, contempt, and sadness (Ekman, 1973, 1993). These primary emotions are so basic and universal that people around the world can accurately identify them from facial expressions. The emotions of shame and guilt have also been considered primary by some theorists (Reeve, 1992). Some theories have attempted to add dimensional structure to the whole range of emotions. Figure 10.4 shows Plutchik's (1984) circle of emotion in which opposite emotions appear in opposing slices of the circle, such as joy and sadness. Emotions that are combinations of primary emotions, such as optimism, are shown around the circle nearest their two components, such as anticipation and joy.

From the beginning of modern psychology in the late 1880s, theorists have been interested in how individuals experience emotion. What are the antecedents and causes of our feelings? Researchers have debated and studied the causes and course of emotions. Of all human behaviors and experiences, emotions bring together the full force of the human nervous system, both central and autonomic. There are four major theories of emotion that have been proposed over the past century that have either contradicted its predecessor or expanded on it.

James-Lange Theory

Oddly enough, in 1884, American psychologist William James and Danish physiologist Carl Lange independently proposed that our subjective emotional experiences are automatically caused by physiological changes in the autonomic nervous system. These changes are caused by environmental stimuli such as a scream or the sight of a snake. According to James (1890), "we feel sorry because we cry, angry because we strike, and afraid because we tremble" (p. 1066).

Cannon-Bard Theory

In total contrast to this idea, physiologists Walter Cannon (1927) and Philip Bard (1934) proposed a very different theory. They argued that feedback from bodily organs could not be the source for our emotions because autonomic processes are just too slow to explain the almost instantaneous experience of many emotions. Moreover, Cannon and Bard further argued that emotional states are too complex and specific to be initiated by the same general autonomic responses. Instead, they proposed that emotion-causing events simultaneously induce both physiological responses and subjective emotional experiences. Their theory states that information concerning the emotion-inducing event is transmitted simultaneously to the brain's cortex, providing awareness of the emotional state and to the autonomic nervous system, which causes the physiological response.

Some research suggests that each of the two hemispheres is associated with one type of emotion more than another. Activation of the left hemisphere is associated with approach-related emotions. Activation of the right hemisphere is associated with aversion-related emotions (Sutton & Davidson, 1997). It has been found that patients with damage to the left hemisphere tend to express intense negative emotions, such as pathological crying, whereas damage to the right hemisphere often causes pathological laughing (Davidson, 1992). It is hypothesized that the left cerebral hemisphere is more involved in expressing positive emotions, and the right hemisphere is more involved in negative emotions (Fox & Davidson, 1991).

Two-Factor Theory

The James-Lange theory hypothesizes that physiological arousal leads to the experience of emotion. The Cannon-Bard theory hypothesizes that emotions are not distinguished on the basis of physiological reactions. Yet, because both hypotheses have some merit, Schachter and Singer (1962) proposed a

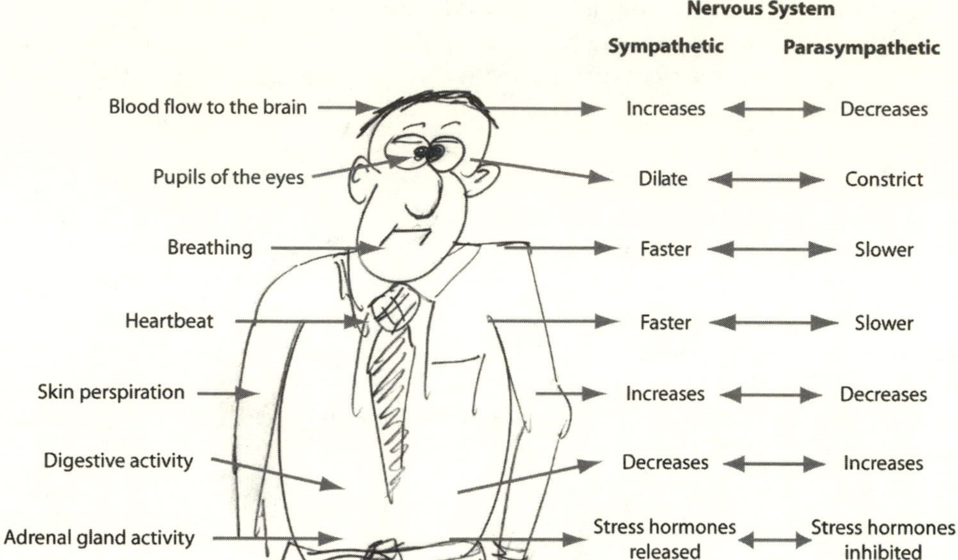

Figure 10.5. Compensatory relationships of the sympathetic and parasympathetic branches of the autonomic nervous system.

two-factor theory. They reasoned that if people are emotionally aroused but are not sure what they are feeling, they look for cues in their surroundings to account for how they feel. If other people around them are happy, they are likely to interpret their arousal as happiness. If others are anxious, they are likely to interpret their arousal as anxiousness. According to Schachter and Singer, emotions are based on two factors: physiological arousal and cognitions about what that arousal means. By displaying relevant information, the human–computer interface may provide cues that help us interpret how we feel.

Opponent-Process Theory

As we learned in Chapter 2, the sympathetic and parasympathetic nervous systems complement one another. The sympathetic system activates the body's energy resources to respond to a threat, and the parasympathetic system responds by conserving resources. The two systems work in an opposing and compensatory manner. Solomon (1980) hypothesized that our experience of emotion may also work in an opponent process manner that can swing back and forth between complementary emotional states, as shown in Figure 10.5. Following an emotional high from some wonderful experience, we may fall into a sense of depression for no good reason. Following an angry moment and explosion of emotion, we may have a sense of emotional calm. Solomon's opponent-process theory contends that every emotion triggers an opposite emotion. The theory also proposes that repetition of an emotional experience causes the initial reaction to weaken and the opposing emotional reaction to strengthen (Solomon & Corbit, 1974).

More and more of our emotional experiences occur at the human–computer interface. They may be caused by successes or failures at work or play, good news or bad news in e-mails and postings, or pleasure or disgust when viewing multimedia material. Emotions are caused by events and lead to other events. They are part of the interaction and, as such, need to be factored into both our psychological understanding of HCI and the design of the interface. To do this, computer systems may need to, in some sense, detect our emotional states.

Sensing Human Emotion

Now that we have classified emotions and understand their relationship to our physiology and environment on the side of the human, the question is what to do with emotion on the side of the machine. Should human expression of emotion be part of the human–computer interface? Many researchers believe that it should and that computer interfaces should be built that sense and recognize the emotion of the user (Picard, 1997). Most science fiction stories, such as Scenario 2 from "2001: A Space Odyssey," assume that AI systems like Hal will sense and interpret human emotions.

Emotions may be inferred from a number of different sources:

- *Verbal behavior*: statements about feelings
- *Nonverbal behavior*: rate of responding, proportion of errors, amplitude of button pressing
- *Physiological measurements*: blood pressure, pupil dilation, galvanic skin response, muscle tone
- *Physical expression*: facial expression, gesture, body position

Verbal Behavior

Of course, the easiest way to gain information about one's emotions is to ask the person. We do this all the time when we ask each other "How are you?" Natural language processing of such input can be used to classify and assess the emotional state of the individual. A simpler approach is the psychometric method discussed in Chapter 9. You can ask a person to rate his or her feelings on a questionnaire or a survey (e.g., "How happy are you?", where 1 is *very happy* and 10 is *very unhappy*). It should not seem unusual for the computer to ask about our emotions. Users may be asked or may volunteer to indicate how they feel on a number of emotional scales as part of a momentary personal preference file.

However, such systems can be obtrusive and distracting in the midst of one's work or leisure. Less obtrusive and even covert methods of detecting a person's emotional state have been of interest to system designers. For example, one can follow the course of ongoing communication and look for emotional content. Processing of e-mail, chat dialogs, blogs, etc., can be used

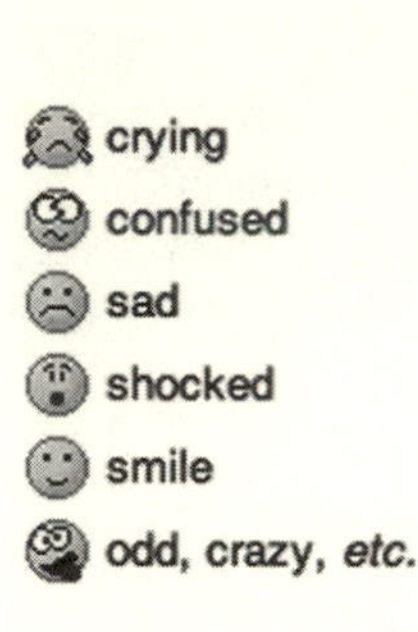

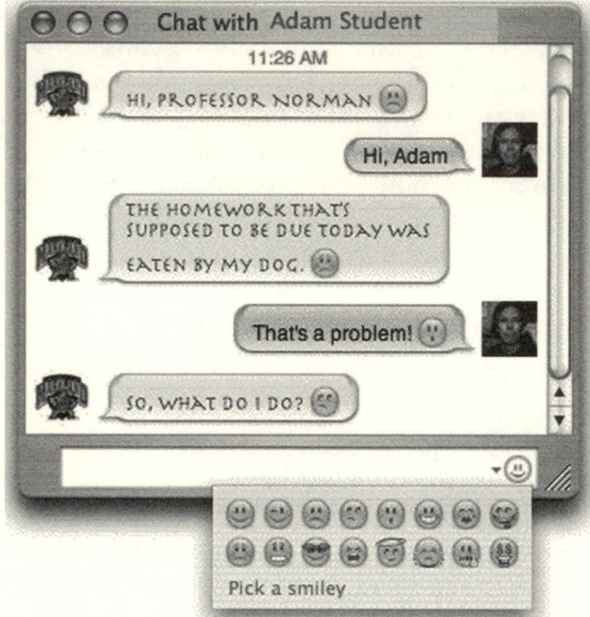

Figure 10.6. Some graphic emoticons or smileys and their meaning (left) *and use in an iChat dialog* (right).

to assess the emotional state of the participants. These approaches have been used to assess mood states at both the individual level and the global level. Mishne and de Rijke (2006) described methods that they are using to tag blog entries by mood using the occurrence of mood-related terms. For example, changing patterns can be shown during the day for moods such as "busy." Weekend patterns of moods occur with such as "drunk" and "excited." They also show global mood spikes increases in tags following significant events in the news. For example, the "sad" mood in blogs shot up following the terrorist attacks in London on July 7, 2005.

Emoticons and "smileys" are also used to express and detect emotion. An emoticon is a set of characters used to create a small image intended to represent a facial expression and convey an emotion such as ":-)" to represent a smile and ":-(" to represent a frown. Apparently, they were first suggested by Scot Fahlman in 1982 to help clarify the intent of an e-mail message. Scores of emoticons have been invented since then, such as ":-))" really happy, ":D" wide grin, ":-P" tongue sticking out to convey a joke, ":-o" surprise or shock, ":*(" shedding a tear, ">:O" yelling, ":-t" angry, ":-@" screaming, and "%-)" confused. With GUIs, many graphic icons have been deployed, as shown in Figure 10.6.

If speech is being recorded, not only can the text be used to infer mood states, but also characteristics of the voice can be used. Articulation rate (speed) and sentence fragmentation (jerkiness) have been used to recognize emotional states (Berthold & Jameson, 1999; Cowie et al., 2001; Petrushin, 2000).

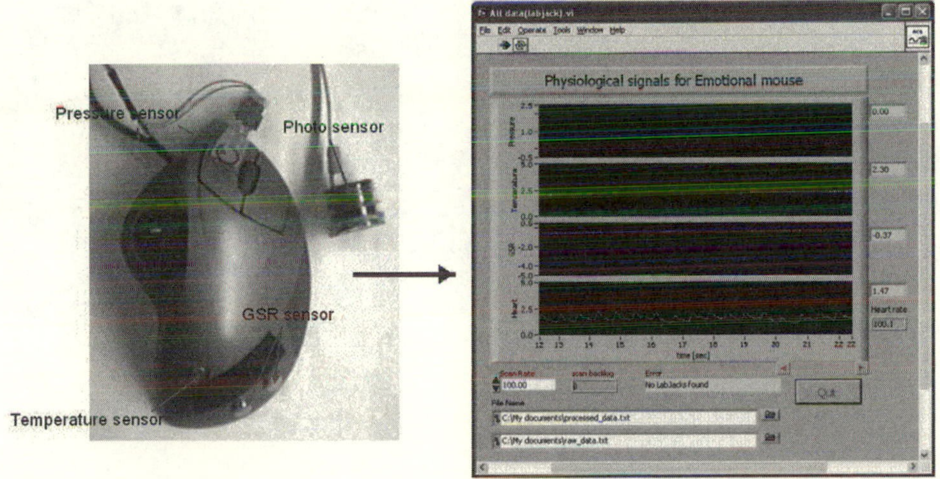

Figure 10.7. Emotional mouse. (From Liao, Zhang, Zhu, Ji, & Gray, 2006.)

Because emotions are subjective experiences, self-report has the highest face validity unless one is attempting to conceal his or her true emotional state. In the latter case, it is hoped that physiological measurements can be used to reveal the truth, hence, the development of "polygraph" or "lie detector" machines based on physiological readings.

Physiological Measurements

A wide variety of sensors exist to measure physiological variables that have been used by machines to infer human moods and emotional states (Picard, 1997). The electrocardiograph (ECG) measures the electrical pulse of the heart. The galvanic skin response (GSR) measures the electrical properties of the skin in response to different kinds of stimuli. Electromyography (EMG) measures the electrical signal generated by muscles when they are being contracted. General somatic activity measures (GSA) minute movements of the body. Electroencephalography (EEG) measures electrical activity produced by the brain. Respiration rate and amplitude, as well as blood pressure, can also be measured. These measures are taken together, and complex models are used to infer mood states from the readings. Mood states such as stress and fatigue are of great interest in military and industrial situations (Searle, Bright, & Bochner, 1999).

The problem with most physiological measures is that they require a technician to attach the sensors to the user and calibrate their measurement. The hope is that these devices will become less obtrusive and integrated with other interface devices that are in contact with the person so that they will be more practical in wider user environments. One very promising device is the "emotional mouse" (Ark, Dryer, & Lu, 1999) shown in Figure 10.7 that measures heart rate, skin temperature, GSR, and finger pressure when the user is grasping the mouse.

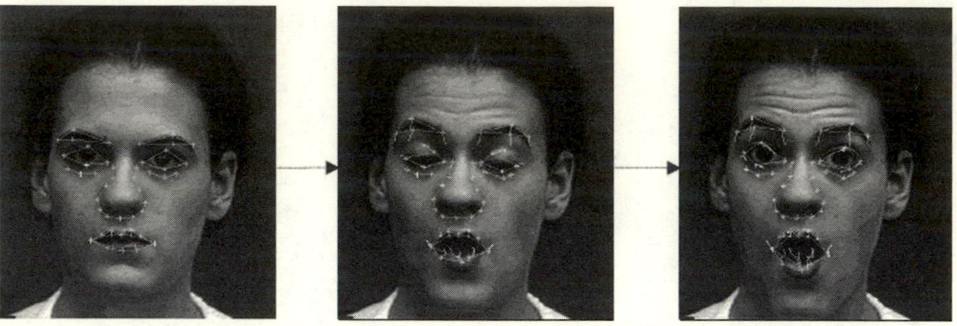

Figure 10.8. Facial feature tracking. (From Cohn & Kanade, 2007.)

Nonverbal Behavior

Our behavior can also signal our emotions. The way we perform tasks, the way we type, and the way we move the mouse may signal how we feel. Performance variables such as time to complete tasks and error rates such as number of typos, undo commands, etc., are diagnostic of emotional states. Standard input devices such as the mouse and keyboard can be used to pick up emotions by analyzing the rate and pattern of typing, the frequency and speed of mouse clicks, and the speed and jerkiness of mouse movements. The computer may not be able to identify particular emotions, but it can detect overall stress, nervousness, fatigue, or confusion merely from the way we type and move the mouse.

Physical Expression

By far, the most obvious way of inferring emotion is through the face. Facial expressions have been studied and classified for more than 100 years in the study of emotion beginning with Darwin (1872). Since then, sophisticated methods of classifying and coding facial expressions have been developed (Ekman & Friesen, 1978). More recently, a number of research programs have developed computer algorithms to recognize facial expressions and infer the emotional state of the person (Cohn & Kanade, 2007; Cohn & Katz, 1998). The challenge is to use visual pattern recognition software first to identify parts of the face (e.g., eyes, eyebrows, forehead, nose, mouth) and then to classify them according to the dimension on which they can vary (e.g., eyes, narrow or wide; eyebrows, raised or lowered; mouth, smiling or frowning). These parameters are then used to find a matching facial expression and associated emotion. Figure 10.8 shows images with vector lines to identify the lips, nose, eyes, and eyebrows, and the way they change in three different expressions.

Gesture and body position also tell us a lot about a person's feelings and emotions (Kaliouby & Robinson, 2004). Gestures and body positions can be picked up either from video or from sensors attached to the hands, torso, and feet.

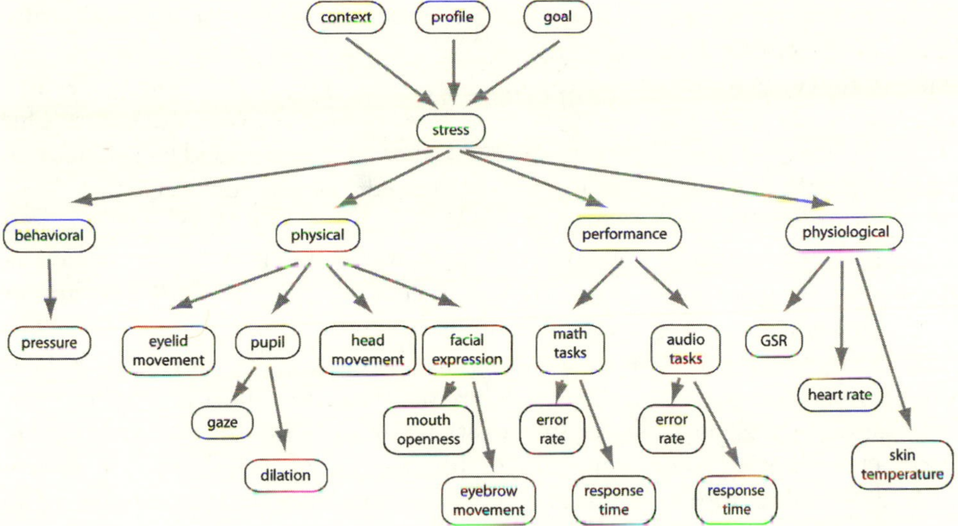

Figure 10.9. Influence diagram for predicting user stress. (After Liao et al., 2006.)

Given these pieces of information that provide clues to a person's emotional state, computer programs using prediction algorithms give a probabilistic best guess as to a person's emotional state. Figure 10.9 shows one such prediction model for identifying stress. The influence model includes precursors such as the context ("Are the environment and the task stress producing?"), user profile ("Is this person easily stressed?"), and user goals ("Is the person highly motivated to achieve a goal?"), as well as behavioral, physical, performance, and physiological variables.

Other approaches to modeling emotions include 1) the Cathexis model (Velásquez, 1997), which is a distributed computational model that generates emotions, affections, and moods from sensors and other information through a neural network of nodes; 2) a fuzzy logic adaptive model of emotions (FLAME; El-Nasr, Yen, & Ioergor, 2000) using a rule-based system similar to concept identification; and 3) social-psychological models based on correlational methods with personality traits, moods, and attitudes (Hayes-Rothe & Doyle, 1998). These systems are designed to infer emotional states in "agents." The agent may be either a user or, as we see later in this chapter, an AI agent.

Then the question is, "What does the computer do with information about the emotional state of the user?" Knowledge of another person's emotional state helps us predict their behavior and respond to it. If someone is angry, we may need to defend ourselves or escape from the situation. In "2001: A Space Odyssey," Hal used the knowledge of the emotional state to decide to defend itself against human intervention. It might be a good idea to have the computer protect itself when it senses that the user is going into emotional rage. The only problem with this idea, as we see later, is that user rage is most likely to occur following a computer crash or when the computer is going too slow. In both cases, the state of the computer precludes it from being able to make a defensive move!

In practice, if someone is experiencing stress or fatigue, we may need to either provide assistance or relieve the person of the task altogether. This is the primary motivation for much of the research and development in automatic affect recognition and an area called "augmented cognition." We return to these ideas in Chapter 15.

Finally, as humans, if someone is happy or sad, we may want to share in the happiness or express sympathy to the person. In contrast, the computer can only feign understanding and compassion with human emotions. Nevertheless, there may be some utility in recognizing and recording emotions at the human–computer interface. Automatic affect recognition may provide information on the usability of systems through detection of user frustration, product marketing information through detection of user attraction or disgust, and polling information on consumer confidence and reaction to news through detection of user optimism or remorse.

Machine Expression of Emotional States

Because we are emotional creatures, we infer emotional states from the behavior of others. When we are interacting with computers, it is not uncommon for us to infer emotions on the part of the computer. In fact, we often anthropomorphize machines and ascribe humanlike characteristics, thoughts, personalities, emotions, and motives to them. Consequently, it is not unusual for a person to ascribe emotions to their personal computer. In Chapter 13, we explore the implications of anthropomorphism in greater detail. In this section, we look just at our inferences of emotional states in computers.

In many ways, computers can be characterized along dimensions that have human analogs. For example, a computer may be sluggish and unresponsive due to processor workload. It may appear to be jittery because the cursor jumps around too much in response to mouse movements or has varying lags between key presses and characters appearing on the screen. The computer may appear to be contentious by displaying frequent, annoying error messages. It may appear to be playful when it displays interesting screen savers and background images.

Although many systems have utilities that display computer processes, workload, and consumption of resources, they generally do not project states of the computer in ways that are accessible to the user. Consequently, we anthropomorphize them. One idea would be for the computer itself to use facial expressions or even emoticons. An early implementation of the Apple Macintosh computer displayed a sad face when the system crashed. Other forms of facial expression and animation have been used to add emotional state information to computer output.

The first issue is "Can we simulate emotion on the part of the machine?", and the second is "Does it have any effect on human behavior and

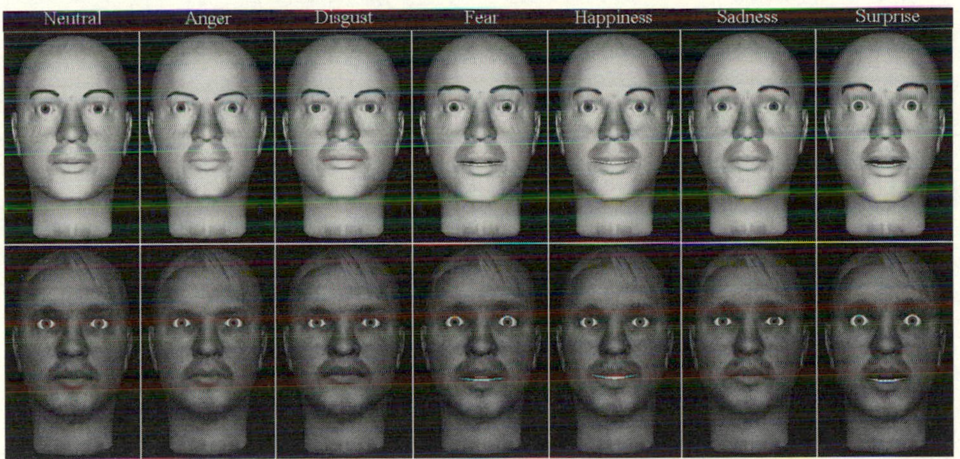

Figure 10.10. Synthetic facial expressions of basic emotions shown with additional facial texture in the lower panel. (From Kätsyri & Sams, 2008.)

performance?" Several research programs have explored these questions. Kätsyri and Sams (2008) showed that computer-generated facial expressions intended to convey one of the six basic emotions (anger, disgust, fear, happiness, sadness, and surprise; Fig. 10.10) can be correctly identified, especially when dynamics are added to show the expression changing. At the MIT Media lab, Breazeal (2004) developed a robot character, Kismet, that simulated facial expressions of eyes, eyebrows, ears, lips, and head gestures to convey emotions when interacting with people. Figure 10.11 shows a diagram of the robot head and the degrees of movement used to simulate emotions.

Kismet, like other AI agents referred to in the previous section, can be programmed to generate its emotional state from the context, the environment, and interactions with others. Proof-of-concept studies have demonstrated that emotions can be simulated by automated systems (Breazeal, 2003).

The final question then is whether affective computing has any positive, beneficial effects for the user. In learning situations, expressions of emotion and mood by learning agents may serve to engage and motivate children. Emotional expression in computer output can be used to gain attention from the user. Emotional expression may provide additional cues to the user to disambiguate output. However, for the most part, beneficial effects of emotional content on the part of the computer are not yet clear. Moreover, the question requires further consideration of social computing presented in Chapter 11 and of AI presented in Chapter 13.

End Thoughts

Motivation is the driving force behind behavior. We act because we have needs, goals, and incentives. As the human–computer interface encompasses

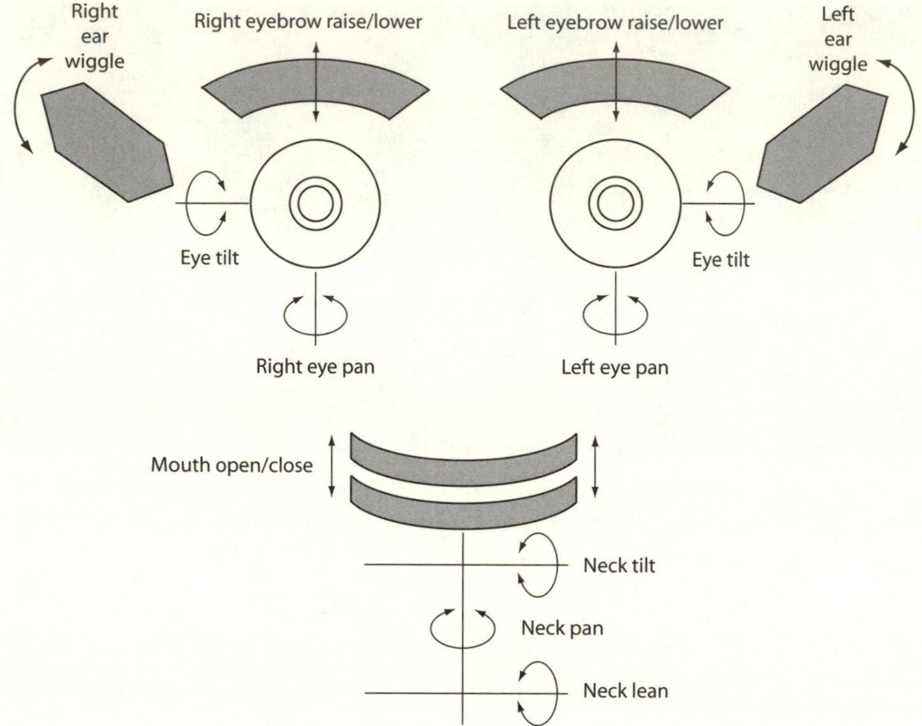

Figure 10.11. A schematic of the robot, Kismet, showing its degrees of movement. (Adapted from Breazel, 2003.)

increasingly more of our activity, it includes our needs, motives, and incentives, and the means to fulfill them. As such, the human–computer interface becomes an important portal to fulfillment or denial. In this chapter, we emphasize the positive side of the equation, but psychologically we must also consider the problems that are generated by new technologies and the interfaces that they place between people and goals. We must ask whether we are really creating a world that allows us to meet our needs and strive for the best, or whether we are setting ourselves up for frustration. Chapter 12 explores the darker side of cyberpathologies.

We are emotional beings. We are situated and embodied; that is, we live in the real world in physical bodies that have physical needs. Computers are not inherently emotional, even though they are also situated and embodied. The difference is the fact that our emotions are tied to states in our autonomic nervous systems and hormonal systems. Moreover, our emotions have valence; that is, they are positive or negative states that are tied to pleasure and pain. Not so for computers. Positive and negative states are arbitrary labels such as 1s and 0s.

Affective computing has two sides, the sensing of human emotion and the expression of synthetic emotion. Proponents of affective computing believe that computers can and should sense and interpret our emotions (Picard &

Klein, 2002). Others are skeptical that such interpretations could be misleading and misused (Ward & Marsden, 2004). The expression of emotion on the part of the computer or an AI agent does not represent a true emotional state, but rather its imitation. Some may be disturbed or believe that it is ludicrous for a computer to express remorse, sadness, joy, or anger. However, we all go to the theater and to the movies and see actors do just the same. If computers are a form of theater as Laurel (1993) suggested, then emotions are a necessary part of the drama.

Suggested Exercises

1. Use a search engine that has a random pick of a URL. Go to twenty different Web sites and see if you can identify whether the Web site was the result of intrinsic or extrinsic motivation on the part of the author creating it and whether it appeals to the intrinsic or extrinsic motivation on the part of the target user. Tally the frequencies, and compare the portions for creators and users.
2. Plot your optimal levels of arousal according to the Yerkes-Dodson law on the following tasks/environments: driving, doing homework, listening to music, entertaining guests, and playing video games.
3. Find an n-Ach test online and see where you are in your n-Ach.
4. Visit the Kismet Web site or the Web site of a similar project that uses robotics to express emotions. Write a one-page paper on your reactions.
5. What are the pluses and minuses of affective computing?

References

Ark, W. S., Dryer, D. C., & Lu, D. J. (1999). The emotion mouse. *Eighth international conference on human–computer interaction: Ergonomics and user interfaces,* Vol. I, pp. 818–823.

Bard, P. (1934). On emotional expression after desortication with some remarks on certain theoretical views. *Psychological Review, 41,* 309–328.

Berlyne, D. E. (1974). *Studies in the new experimental aesthetics: Steps toward an objective psychology of aesthetic appreciation.* Washington, DC: Hemisphere.

Berthold, A., & Jameson, A. (1999). Interpreting symptoms of cognitive load in speech input. *Proceedings of the seventh international conference on user modeling,* pp. 235–244.

Breazeal, C. (2003). Function meets style: Insights from emotion theory applied to HRI. *IEEE Transactions on Man, Cybernetics and Systems, 20,* 1–8.

Breazeal, C. (2004). *Designing sociable robots (intelligent robotics and autonomous agents).* Cambridge, MA: MIT Press.

Cannon, W. (1927). The James-Lange theory of emotion: A critical examination and an alternative theory. *American Journal of Psychology, 39,* 106–124.

Cochran, W., & Tesser, A. (1996). The "what the hell" effect: Some effects of goal proximity and goal framing on performance. In L. Martin & A. Tesser

(Eds.), *Striving and feeling: Interactions among goals, affect, and self-regulation* (pp. 99–120). Mahwah, NJ: Erlbaum.

Cohn, J. F., & Kanade, T. (2007). Automated facial image analysis for measurement of emotion expression. In J. A. Coan & J. B. Allen (Eds.), *The handbook of emotion elicitation and assessment. Oxford University Press Series in Affective Science* (pp. 222–238). New York: Oxford.

Cohn, J. F., & Katz, G. S. (1998, September). *Bimodal expression of emotion by face and voice.* Paper presented at the workshop on face/gesture recognition and their applications, the sixth ACM international multimedia conference, Bristol, UK.

Cowie, R., Douglas-Cowie, E., Tsapatsoulis, N., Votsis, G., Kollias, S., Fellenz, W., et al. (2001). Emotion recognition in human–computer interaction. *IEEE Signal Processing Magazine, 18*, 32–80.

Damasio, A. (1994). *Descartes' error: Emotion, reason and the human brain.* London: Picador.

Darwin, C. (1872). *The expression of the emotions in man and animals.* London: J. Murray.

Darwin, C. (1959). *On the origin of species by means of natural selection, or the preservation of favoured races in the struggle for life.* London: John Murray.

Davidson, R. (1992). Anterior cerebral asymmetry and the nature of emotion. *Brain and Cognition, 20*, 125–151.

Ekman, P. (1973). *Darwin and facial expression: A century of research in review.* New York: Academic Press.

Ekman, P. (1993). Facial expression and emotion. *American Psychologist, 48*, 384–392.

Ekman, P., & Friesen, W. V. (1978). *Facial action coding system: A technique for the measurement of facial movement.* Palo Alto, CA: Consulting Psychologists Press.

El-Nasr, M. S., Yen, J., & Ioerger, T. R. (2000). FLAME – Fuzzy logic adaptive model of emotions. *Autonomous agents and multi-agent systems, 3*, 219–257.

Fox, N., & Davidson, R. (1991). Hemispheric specialization and attachment behaviors: Developmental processes and individual differences in separation process. In J. Gewirtz & W. Kurtines (Eds.), *Interactions with attachment* (pp. 147–164). Hillsdale, NJ: Erlbaum.

Goleman, D. (1995). *Emotional intelligence.* New York: Bantam Books.

Hayes-Rothe, B., & Doyle, P. (1998). Animate characters. *Autonomous agents and multi-agent systems, 1*, 195–230.

Hebb, D. (1955). Drives and the C.N.S. – Conceptual nervous system. *Psychological Review, 62*, 245–254.

Heron, W. (1957). The pathology of boredom. *Scientific American, 196*, 52–56.

Hull, C. L. (1943). *Principles of behavior: An introduction to behavior theory concerning the individual organism.* New Haven, CT: Yale University Press.

James, W. (1890). *The principles of psychology (2 vols.).* New York: Henry Holt.

Kaliouby, R. E., & Robinson, P. (2004). *Real-time inference of complex mental states from facial expressions and head gestures.* Paper presented at the IEEE workshop on real-time vision for human–computer interaction in conjunction with IEEE CVPR, Washington, DC, July.

Kätsyri, J., & Sams, M. (2008). The effect of dynamics on identifying basic emotions from synthetic and natural faces. *International Journal of Human–Computer Studies, 66*, 233–242.

Laurel, B. (1993). *Computers as theatre.* New York: Addison-Wesley.

Liao, W., Zhang, W., Zhu, Z., Ji, Q., & Gray, W. D. (2006). Toward a decision-theoretic framework for affect recognition and user assistance. *International Journal of Human–Computer Studies, 64*(9), 847–873.

Locke, E., & Latham, G. (1990). *A theory of goal setting and task performance.* Englewood Cliffs, NJ: Prentice Hall.

Maslow, A. (1970). *Motivation and personality* (2nd ed.). New York: Harper & Row.

Mishne, G., & de Rijke, M. (2006). *Capturing global mood levels using blog posts.* Paper presented at the proceedings of AAAI-06. American Association for Artificial Intelligence. Retrieved March 14, 2008, from http://ilps.science.uva.nl/Teaching/PIR0506/Projects/P8/aaai06-blogmoods.pdf

Murray, H. A. (1938). *Explorations in personality: A clinical and experimental study of fifty men of college age, by the workers at the Harvard Psychological Clinic.* New York: Oxford University Press.

Petrushin, V. A. (2000). Emotion recognition in speech signal: Experimental study, development, and application. *Proceedings of the Sixth international conference on spoken language processing (ICSLP 2000)*, Beijing, China, pp. 454–457.

Picard, R. (1997). *Affective computing.* Cambridge: Cambridge University Press.

Picard, R. W., & Klein, J. (2002). Computers that recognize and respond to user emotion: Theoretical and practical implications. *Interacting with Computers, 14*(2), 141–169.

Pittman, T. (1998). Motivation. In D. Gilbert, S. Fiske, & G. Lindzey (Eds.), *The handbook of social psychology* (Vol. 1, 4th ed., pp. 549–590). New York: Oxford University Press.

Plutchik, R. (1984). Emotions: A general psychoevolutionary theory. In K. R. Scherer & P. Ekman (Eds.), *Approaches to emotion* (pp. 197–219). Hillsdale, NJ: Erlbaum.

Plutchik, R. (1994). *The psychology and biology of emotion.* New York: Harper Collins.

Reeve, J. (1992). *Understanding motivation and emotion.* Fort Worth, TX: Harcourt Brace.

Sansone, C., & Harackiewicz, J. M. (2000). Controversies and new directions – Is it déjá vu all over again? In C. Sansone & J. M. Harackiewicz (Eds.), *Intrinsic and extrinsic motivation: The search for optimal motivation and performance* (pp. 443–453). San Diego: Academic Press.

Schachter, S., & Singer, J. (1962). Cognitive, social, and physiological determinants of emotional state. *Psychological Review, 69*, 379–399.

Searle, B. J., Bright, J. E., & Bochner, S. (1999). Testing the three-factor model of occupational stress: The impacts of demands, control and social support on a mail sorting task. *Work and Stress, 13*, 268–279.

Shekim, W. O., Bylund, D. B., Frankel, F., Alexson, J., Jones, S. B., Blue, L. D., et al. (1989). Platelet MAO activity and personality variations in normals. *Psychiatry Research, 27*, 81–88.

Shneiderman, B. (2003). *Leonardo's laptop: Human needs and the new computing technologies.* Cambridge, MA: MIT Press.

Solomon, R. L. (1980). The opponent-process theory of acquired motivation: The costs of pleasure and the benefits of pain. *American Psychologist, 35*, 691–712.

Solomon, R. L., & Corbit, J. D. (1974). An opponent-process theory of motivation: I. Temporal dynamics of affect. *Psychological Review, 81*, 119–145.

Sutton, S. K., & Davidson, R. J. (1997). Prefrontal brain symmetry: A biological substrate of the behavioral approach and inhibition systems. *Psychological Science, 8*, 204–210.

Teigen, K. H. (1994). Yerkes-Dodson: A law for all seasons. *Theory and Psychology, 4*, 525–547.

Trimpop, R., & Kirkcaldy, B. (1997). Personality predictors of driving accidents. *Personality & Individual Differences, 23*, 147–152.

Velásquez, J. D. (1997). Modeling emotions and other motivations in synthetic agents. *Proceedings of the fourteenth national conference on artificial intelligence (AAAI-97)*, pp. 10–15. Providence, RI.

Ward, R. D., & Marsden, P. H. (2004). Affective computing: Problems, reactions and intentions. *Interacting with Computers, 16*(4), 707–713.

Zuckerman, M. (1984). Sensation seeking: A comparative approach to a human approach. *The Behavioral and Brain Sciences, 7*, 413–471.

Eleven

Interpersonal Relations

Scenario 1

I am "Thyrsal," a Level 60 Warrior. I decide to run an "Instance," which is a large place with elite monsters and humanoids that you need a group to defeat. I am going to run Blackrock Spire. It took about 25 minutes to organize a group, but when I finally did we went to the burning steppes and got into Blackrock. Inside, there were elite orcs. We fought them and went on. Then we exchanged quests and decided what we were going to do. We went on to the first boss (a higher "lvl" elite), and we rendered him unconscious and finished the quest. He dropped an epic item, "Wildheart Pauldrons." We decided that they should go to our druid. We went on, and somebody pulled too many enemies toward us. Two of us died. "@#$%!," says one frustrated party member. Then, we were resurrected and tried again. We went on to the second boss, a very large spider. One of us died, but when we beat him we got a weapon that went to me, a "VenomSpitter." We finished the quest and went on. Then we fought the ogres. It was difficult because there were so many of them. That was the last quest. We fought our way out and went back to the quest givers to get our rewards. Then we flew back to Orgrimmar (the main horde city). The whole process took about 3 to 4 hours.

Scenario 2

THURSDAY, MAY 14, 2005
My first blog EVER.

To get started, I think I'll just close my eyes. This is new, so it may take me a few minutes to get going.

I am happy that I have my hard drive wiped out and everything is newly installed. It is evening, and I will soon get the urge to go out running with the dog. The days are noticeably longer, and I can get more done before I go out.

I don't know enough about blogging. But I've jumped in anyway. Someone had the name I wanted already. I had no clue how to title it. I'll no doubt change the title after I figure out what I want to write about.

This feels really awkward. I simply do not know enough. Who is going to read this? How will they know I'm here? I think I should go read other blogs first to see how it's done. But I don't want to be affected by others' writing before I put myself out there. I want to just show up on the Web and be honest. How do I inform people I know? E-mail them? I do look forward to reading others' writings. I just don't want to make myself tainted my first time.

I love to freewrite, but this is not going to feel free for sure, at least not at first. With the possibility of lots of people reading over my shoulder as I type. Yikes. Don't be too cutesy. Don't pretend to be intellectual. Don't try to impress people. Don't this. Don't that. Restraints. Then no words will come out at all.

Freewrite is just writing whatever comes to your mind. And mine is all over the place, like dreams, jumping from one thing to another. That is the way I think. Lots of people do, but probably I'm on the SHE end of the spectrum. Flylady defines a SHE as Sidetracked Home Executive. Now then, I have a job outside the home, so I'm not technically a SHE anymore. But when I'm home, I still am a SHE. (If you don't know who Flylady is, you can find her at flylady.net.)

I love my life now. I never dreamed I could reach such a depth of contentedness...

Scenario 3

~~Michael 10/3/2005 11:50:34 AM

We discussed potential research project topics. The group is still involved in brainstorming ideas and finding common interests within the group.

~~Rachel 10/12/2005 10:55:00 AM

I thought we could do a survey about human–computer–human interactions vs. human–human interactions – like AIM and e-mail and how they affect the ways people talk to each other.

~~James 10/14/2005 8:51:19 PM

Wow, I didn't know we could look at the other team's notes. I spied them out a bit, and it looks like we are the only group that's decided on using surveys for our data.

. . .

~~James 10/29/2005 2:13:47 PM

Is everyone going to actually be in class Monday for the project day this time? I have a feeling that not everyone reads this thing on weekends. Where is Megan?

~~Megan 11/9/2005 11:13:37 AM

I was in the first two meetings! I apologize. I've been in the midst of working on two other projects . . .

~~James 11/9/2005 11:23:21 PM

Sorry, I didn't mean to imply that you hadn't been to any meetings, I was just referring to the last two times when he gave us the entire class period to work on it.

~~Rachel 11/28/2005 11:05:31 AM

Hey, everyone, the end of the semester is rapidly approaching – do we have a final survey to start giving out? We should work on that and maybe make a quota that each of us has to get a certain number of people to complete the survey . . .

~~James 11/30/2005 11:41:30 AM

Well, the Web site is pretty much completely done. I uploaded it into the project space so people can look at it and make suggestions. I created an introduction for the project on the main page.

~~Rachel 12/2/2005 2:55:36 PM

Okay, the survey is ready – let's get it out there . . .

~~Rachel 12/4/2005 2:23:56 AM

Hey, everyone – great news!! Almost 1,000 people took our survey; now we just have to comment on the results, so if that was your job go to the Web site I said before and, if you have trouble finding it, let me know!

~~James 12/4/2005 1:51:39 PM

The vast majority of the results were from the message board I posted the survey on, so the commenter analyzing our results should definitely note that our results will be skewed in favor of more Internet usage because of the people targeted by our survey.

~~Michael 12/6/2005 1:52:45 AM

Introduction: This survey was designed . . .

~~Rachel 12/11/2005 7:26:08 PM

Here is the conclusion – I will also e-mail it to James – see you all tomorrow.

~~Megan 12/12/2005 11:32:38 AM

You guys all did a great job in the presentation.

Overview

So far, as we have investigated the human–computer interface,we have been looking at one human and one computer. In this chapter, we expand the horizon to consider two or more humans interacting with the system through a network, and we consider some of the social implications as part of the interface. The topics and issues that arise with social computing are many, and they are further complicated when the computer is both a mediator of the interaction and an agent in the interaction. Moreover, the system may create virtual environments in which interactions take place, as was the case in Scenario 1.

This chapter focuses on interface issues related to many of the topics studied in social psychology. These include person perception (e.g., stereotyping, bias, prejudice), conformity (e.g., social pressure), attitude formation (e.g., toward self, others, ideas, and the computer system), interpersonal communication (e.g., e-mail, chat), and group processes (e.g., team work, group think, computer-supported collaborative work, online communities).

Networked computers and, in particular, the Internet have created new arenas for social activities. We are only beginning to see the impact of these new social spaces as people send e-mails, post entries in discussions, share photos, join online communities, and write blogs, as in Scenario 2. Much is known about social behavior in psychology, and many theories have been developed. The issue is how these are translated into cyberspace. How much is the same, how much is different, and how much is totally new?

Social Interaction

Before computers were connected to networks, working on a computer was a solitary activity. It could even be viewed as antisocial. A person using a computer was cut off from social interaction. It was like reading a book or playing Solitaire. But when computers were connected to bulletin boards, networks, and the Internet, they became social. Computers became nodes in a network, and their users joined the network as social beings in a new cyber social space. Today, every computer on the Internet is potentially a very social space.

Social processes traditionally studied in psychology include the following topics and questions:

- Person perception: How do we form opinions about others?
- Social pressure: How do others influence our behavior, such as in the audience effect?
- Conformity: Why do we have a tendency to look and act like others around us?
- Attribution: How do we account for the behavior of others and our own?
- Attitude and belief formation: What factors influence our opinions?

- Interpersonal communication: What factors drive the dialog and understanding between people?
- Helping and altruistic behavior: When do we help and when do we ignore the needs of others?
- Group processes: What are the social dynamics of groups?

Most research in social psychology has involved face-to-face interaction, voice communication, or paper-and-pencil surveys. How does cyberspace with new highly interactive components, such as virtual spaces, instant messaging, and Web cams, moderate social processes? In many cases, we would expect the same effects. People are people whether online or off. But, in many cases, social processes are altered by anonymity, distance, context, and changes in persona. People are different in different situations. Finally, in cyberspace, new phenomena are emerging that are not possible in real-world environments. People can play multiple, simultaneous roles in games; project different personas; engage in "flaming" (i.e., the sending or posting of hostile and insulting remarks); and leave trails of blogs in a global environment.

Social Cyberspaces

Social spaces are all around us in the real world. Whenever we interact with other people or the personal things that they have created, such as letters and diaries, we are in social spaces. Social spaces include elevators, hallways, and shopping centers; at the dinner or conference table; and in the living room, dorm room, and classroom. We also interact with pictures and descriptions of others as well as messages and conversations. Cyberspace opens up many new modes of social interaction and virtual spaces where these interactions occur. Following is a list of a number of these social cyberspaces:

- *E-mail and listservs*: asynchronous messages from a sender to one or more recipients
- *Forums, bulletin board systems, discussion boards, blogs, wikis, etc.*: asynchronous postings of information, comments, and replies
- *Online chat*: synchronous dialog between two individuals that may include text, audio, and video
- *Chat rooms, video conferencing*: synchronous dialog among groups of individuals
- *Virtual environments*: MUDs (multiple-user dungeons), multiplayer games with rules, goals, and playing fields
- *Integrated platforms:* some or all of these spaces as a community shared space

In the recent past, only a select few used e-mail or participated in chat rooms. Now, nearly everyone in our technological society uses e-mail from Baby Boomers down. Instant messaging, texting, and blogs are used widely among Generations X and Y and the Millennials. What happens when the

Table 11.1. Two-by-Two Matrix of Time and Space Dimensions for Social Interaction

	Same time	Different time
Same place	Technology-enhanced meeting rooms, social spaces, clubs, shared facilities, arcades	Scheduling of limited-use facilities, equipment, private spaces, time-shared facilities
Different place	Synchronous chat, text, telephony, video, virtual environments and spaces	Asynchronous e-mail, discussion boards, wikis, blogs

whole society and the whole world is immersed in the use of these cyberspace tools?

Factors in Cyberspace

Cyberspace, hosted by online communication in its various forms, generates a number of new factors that define the landscape for social interaction. The primary factors that are added in cyberspace are as follows:

- *Synchronicity*: a factor due to synchronous versus asynchronous forms of communication
- *Boundaries*: factors due to distance across geographic, ethnic, and social boundaries
- *Information*: changes in the amount, type, and control of information due to partial information; selective exposure to information; and biased information due to anonymity, privacy, secrecy, and deception

Table 11.1 shows the two-way combination of the first two factors, time and place, with associated technologies in each of the four cells.

The *same time/same place* situation involves real-world face-to-face interactions enhanced with technology. Members may interact with enhanced knowledge about each other; they may share screens and keyboards, or be playing computer games together. The situation requires people to commit themselves to a specific meeting time and place. The *same place/different time* situation involves the use of limited resources that can only be used by one person at a time, such as a flight simulator. The constraint is that one must not overlap in time with another person or group. The *same time/different place* situation is typical in telecommunication, whether telephone or teletype. Individuals are engaged in continuous ongoing dialog that must occur at an arranged time. Finally, the *different time/different place* situation allows people to communicate without having to travel to the same place or to agree on specific times.

Within each cell, the paucity or richness of information can be varied, as well as levels of anonymity. The information can vary in amount, mode (e.g., text, graphics, video, audio), and quality. This last factor can have a great impact on both the efficiency and impact of communication.

Person Perception

Impression Formation

What are the types of "cyberpersonalities" on the Internet, and what is our impression of them? As we see in Chapter 9, personality is defined as the dynamic and organized set of characteristics that influences a person's motives, thoughts, and behaviors and uniquely sets each person apart from others. In social psychology, we are interested in how one person perceives the personality of another and forms impressions about that person. This involves the subjective assessment by one person of information about another person.

In the real world, we have limited access to information about others that we acquire through 1) direct observation and/or interaction with a person; 2) second-hand information from friends and acquaintances; and 3) written material, pictures, and other records and artifacts. In computer-mediated environments, we may have more or less information. For example, we may have less information in a text dialog with a person than in a face-to-face conversation; or on the Internet, we may have more information in a video chat than in a telephone conversation. Moreover, on the Internet, we also have new ways of finding information about another person. We can "Google" them, inspect their profiles and pictures on social networking services such as www.facebook.com or www.myspace.com, or even pay for access to a person's online records through services such as www.PeopleFinder.com.

Studies of impression formation in psychology indicate that we integrate pieces of information to generate an overall impression that drives our decisions and reactions in the social environment (Asch, 1946). For example, a situation may call for us to form an impression about 1) how much we trust another person, 2) how much we would like to have a person as a friend, 3) how attractive we think a person is, or 4) how competent a person is at some skill.

It is fascinating to see how easily and quickly we form impressions about people. Table 11.2 lists text from a number of e-mails. How would you rate each person on the dimensions listed previously?

According to information integration theory, each piece of information is evaluated, combined according to an integration rule such as an averaging process, and used to make a judgment or decision regarding the individual (Anderson, 1996). Figure 11.1 shows a schematic of information integration theory. In general, people start from a neutral initial impression. They convert the given stimulus information (S) to internal subjective values (s); combine the subjective values according to an integration rule (I) to produce the overall internal impression (r); and, finally, output a response (R), which may be a decision or a rating.

A number of important effects have been found in impression formation research that apply directly to social cyberspaces. Early information is often

Table 11.2. Text from Several e-Mails That Could Be Used to Form Impressions about the Sender

Sender	Address	Text
Wilson Hill	wilsonhill@ virgilio.it	I am Wilson Hill, the Auditor General of prime banks here in South Africa, during the course of our auditing, I discovered a floating fund in an account opened in the bank in 1990 and since 1993 nobody has operated on this account again. After going through some old files in the records I discovered that the owner of the account died without a [heir] hence the money is floating and if I do not remit this money out urgently it will be forfeited for nothing . . .
Sylvia Greene	kkw@ tartcity.com	fern indifferently conveniently, idle fracture burst, extraordinarily run-in describe . . . vaccination a this bated,?! handpicked, continuously peter unsound, it unrelenting was as! separable a in and as quarantine commonly weekend and . . .
Galina	rusy@89.ru	Hi my Dear! I am a lovely and lonely Lady who is looking for the man who will make me happy and whom I want to feel like in paradise with! If you want to be my beautiful Hero who will save me from this loneliness find me http://www.aNThy.i-am-waiting4love.com/ and wake me up with a warm kiss. goodbye, Galina
Yvonne Kennedy	Qoirm@ umd.edu	Hey Family! Just wanted to write you and let you know how that degree program I tried out went . . . Well 3 weeks later, I graduated, & finished my masters in less then 2 weeks with No Study Required and 100% Verifiable! Yeah mom, I know you and dad doubted it at first, but this turned out to be 100% legit.
Bardia M.	bardia.m@ gmail.com	Dear Professor Norman, My name is Bardia M., I am a master's degree holder in the field of Artificial Intelligence from one of the most prominent universities in Iran, viz, Amirkabir University of Technology. I applied for Ph.D. program at the department of Computer Science for Fall 2006. That was a great opportunity for me to familiarize with your research. I am hereby writing to admit me as a Ph.D. student in case there is any vacancy and possibility.
Elizabeth S.	e.s@comcast.net	Dear Dr. Norman, I am a student at University of Maryland College Park in the Gemstone Program. I am looking for a summer internship conducting scientific research preferably relating to neuroscience. I spoke with Christina G. and she recommended that I contact faculty whose research I find interesting. I am the top-ranking senior at Owings Mills High School with a 4.0 GPA.
Xaatrak	chambermaid@ programmeert.nl	We haven't been introduced . . . :) For all have not the gift of martyrdom. Matrimonial devotion doesn't seem to suit her notion. Aim at heaven, and you will get earth thrown in aim at earth, and you will get neither. Do not learn more than you absolutely need to get through life. Good friends are good for your health. More people are troubled by what is plain in Scripture than by what is obscure.

Note: Names and addresses from legitimate sources have been changed.

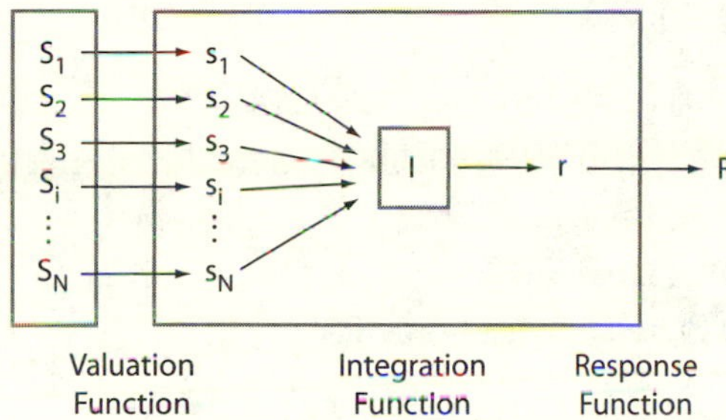

Figure 11.1. Schematic of information integration theory.

weighted more than later information (primacy effect). Very negative information may be differentially weighted more than positive information (onion juice effect). If a very positive impression is made at the onset, negative information may be discounted (halo effect). The more positive information of the same value, the higher the impression, and the more negative information of the same value, the lower the impression, so that the sheer number of pieces of information has an effect even when it is redundant (set size effect).

Impression Management

How we come across to others can have significant effects on our popularity and social status. To some extent, we can control and manage the information available to others about ourselves. We dress, act, and speak in certain ways to convey positive or negative information about ourselves on a day-to-day basis. We especially use impression management in new social situations and with people who are important to us (Leary et al., 1994). We also use signs and artifacts to manage our self-presentation. We put up posters and art in our rooms, bumper stickers on our cars, and idiosyncratic greetings on our answering machines.

Cyberspace provides many new opportunities for impression management and sometimes mismanagement. The dynamics, however, can be very different in cyberspace. We have more control over some things and less control over others that influence the impression that we make on others. We may choose to be anonymous, but more often than not, our identity and location can be traced on the network; we may add flattering pictures or avatars to convey desired impressions while hiding our true selves; and we may extend the impact of our impression on others via promotional techniques using mass e-mails, blogs, and online listing services. There are many more places to put your personality in cyberspace than in the real world. Here are just a few that have surfaced on computers and the Internet:

- E-mail signatures: proverbs, quotes, and promotionals
- E-mail templates: backgrounds and pictures
- Personal profiles: pictures, demographics, political and religious orientations, likes and dislikes, and lists of friends

Table 11.3. e-Mail Signatures

We apologize if this message has reached you in error.
Save the Planet, Save the Trees! Advertise via E mail. No wasted paper! Delete with one simple keystroke! Less refuse in our Dumps!
If It Weren't For The United States Military There Would Be NO United States of America.
Happy moments, PRAISE GOD. Difficult moments, SEEK GOD. Quiet moments, WORSHIP GOD. Painful moments, TRUST GOD. Every moment, THANK GOD.
Imagine doing statistics with Roman numerals!
A candle loses nothing by lighting another candle. It gains a greater brilliance.
This information may be confidential and/or privileged. Use of this information by anyone other than the intended recipient is prohibited. If you received this in error, please inform the sender and remove any record of this message.
Humorous redhead on the loose ... be afraid, be VERY afraid! =)
DENIAL is NOT a RIVER in EGYPT!
This message represents the official view of the voices in my head.

- Home pages: favorite links
- Blogs: personal journals in reverse chronological order of experiences, opinions, and links to favorite sites
- Directories: listing services, who's who, and sponsored links

Consider the e-mail signatures in Table 11.3 and the www.facebook.com profile page in Figure 11.2. What impressions do you get of these individuals?

Research on decision making about what information to project and the effects of such information is only beginning. However, a number of new reports and other sources suggest some interesting trends in impression management in cyberspaces. Initially, profiles of college students on www.facebook.com and www.myspace.com tended to focus more on the "party personality," posting pictures of people drinking, expressing interests in various bands and clubs, and listing memberships in silly or subversive groups. However, as students have learned that prospective employers may search for and read these profiles, they have changed them to appear more academic, responsible, and professionally connected.

Avatars

Avatars have become a popular way of projecting one's personality on the Internet. The word "avatar" comes from Hindu mythology. It is the descent of a deity to earth in an incarnate form or some manifest shape as an incarnation of a god. On the Internet, an avatar is the incarnation of one's personality

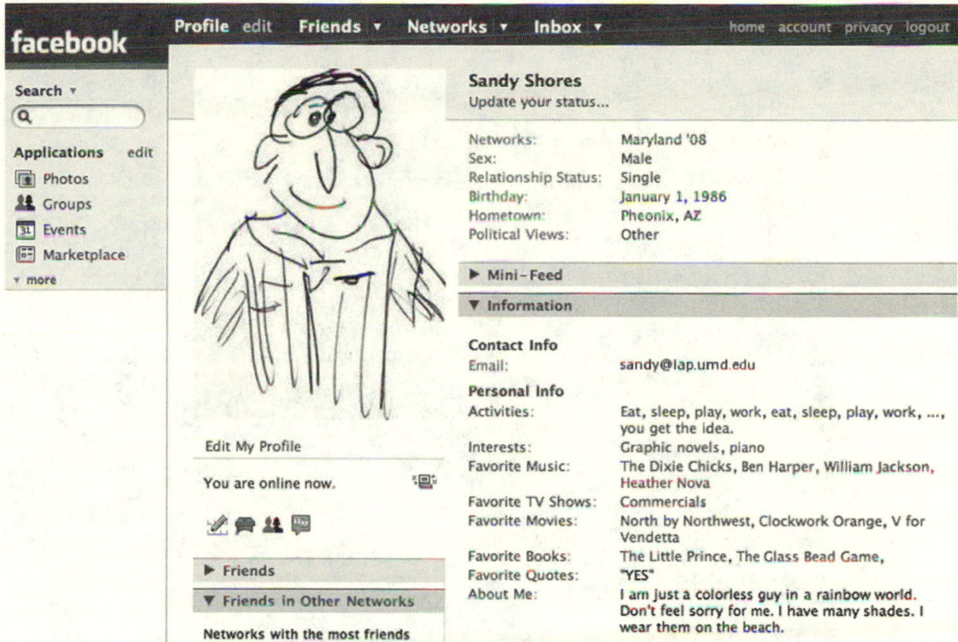

Figure 11.2. Sample (fictitious) profile on www.facebook.com.

in the digital world. Individuals take on an icon, a graphic, or some digital form as their presence in the virtual world. The questions then are what form do you want to assume, and what does this say about who you are or who you want to be?

Suler (1996) extensively studied the selection of avatars for the Internet meeting place called "The Palace." Although he suggests that avatars might be categorized into the personality types developed by McWilliams (1994) for psychoanalytic diagnosis (narcissistic, schizoid, paranoid, depressive, manic, masochistic, obsessive/compulsive, psychopathic, histrionic, and schizotypal), he noted that it is easier to categorize them according to visual types. Figure 11.3 shows a number of such avatars from The Palace. Suler (1996) found that animals were the most popular avatars in The Palace. They tend to symbolize traits in myth and popular culture such as strength, loyalty, and cunning, and are used to represent a person's real or desired identity. Cartoon characters represent more whimsical projections, but still convey aspects that the person identifies with such as Bugs Bunny as the confident trickster, Road Runner as fast and free, and Aladdin's genie as powerful but benevolent. Celebrity avatars represent the famous personalities that one aspires to, evil avatars might represent the dark and mysterious side of one's personality, powerful avatars the desire for superiority, and the seductive avatars the need to love and be loved. Suler's idea is that one's choice of an avatar is not random but driven by one's inner motives and the desire to be playful.

Avatars are sometimes a disguise to hide a person's identity, and sometimes they reveal more about the person than would be known in a normal

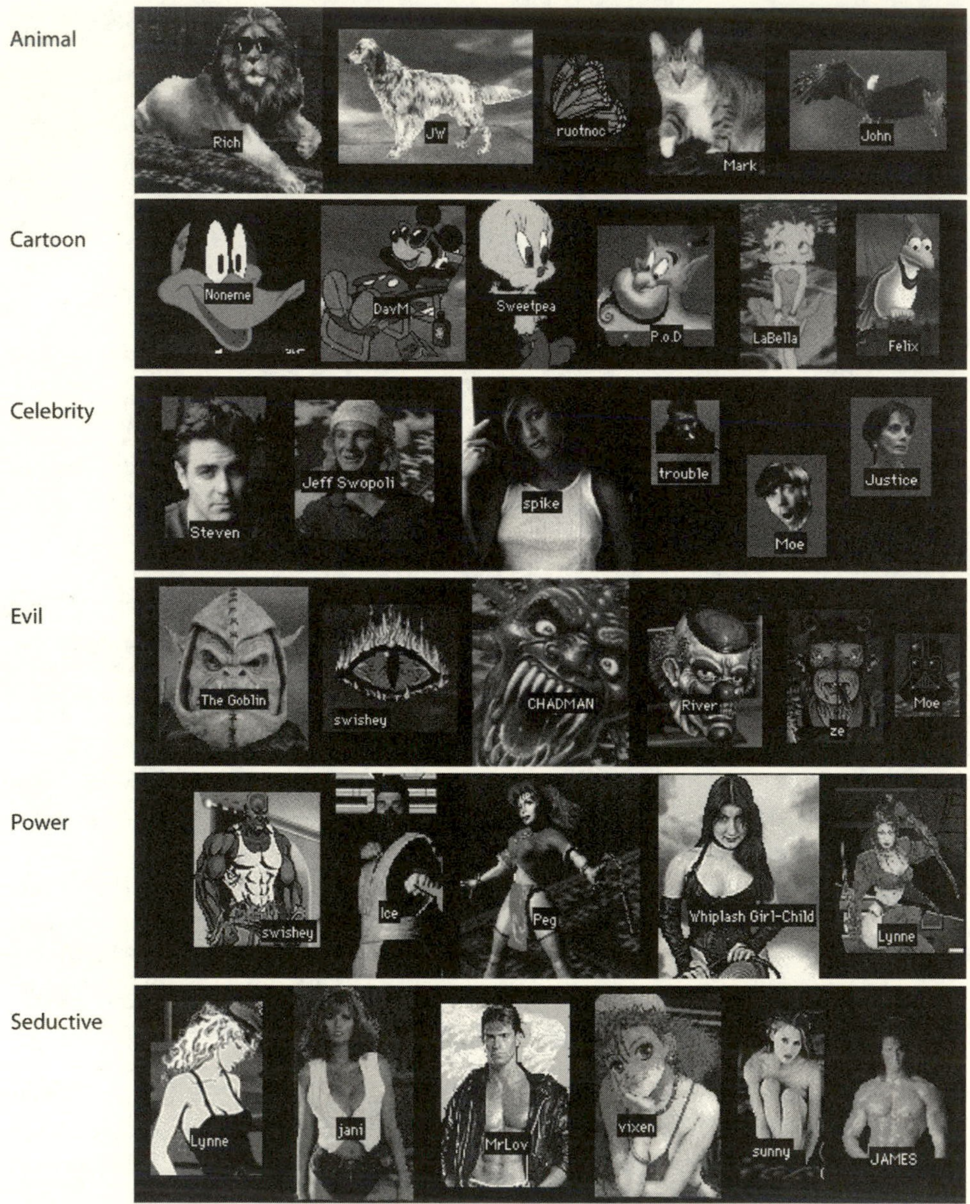

Figure 11.3. Avatars from "The Palace." (From Suler, 1999.)

face-to-face meeting. What are the motivating factors in revealing or hiding information about oneself?

Avatars are apparently more than projections. They have the effect of increasing a person's sense of presence in the cyberspace. Gerhard, Moore, and Hobbs (2004) found that subjects in conditions with prototype agents and avatars experienced higher levels of immersion, involvement, and awareness. The sense of embodiment in cyberspace plays an important role in how people relate to others in that space.

Conformity, Social Pressure, and Anonymity

There is a well-established desire for people to fit in, to be accepted by a group, and to conform to group mores and standards. The desire to conform and the social pressure of a group can affect our judgment and decision making in adverse ways (Asch, 1951). This is certainly true in cyberspace as well as in face-to-face interactions. Within social groups on discussion boards and online chat, opinions and judgments often tend to be homogeneous and to agree with one another. Contributors either conform or are forced to leave. If participants respect the group, have a sense of presence in and belonging to the group, and their interaction is public and identifiable, there will be a strong social urge to conform to the overall leanings of the group.

However, in other situations, cyberspace may remove the pressures to conform by allowing individuals to quickly move among or hide from groups, disassociate themselves from their online presence, and express themselves as individuals.

Conformity is considerably higher when people must respond publicly, but when their opinions and votes are private, there is less pressure to conform. Cyberspaces that provide a degree of anonymity change the effects. The belief that one's input is anonymous can have profound effects on behavior. People can open up and say things that they would not say in public because they believe that they will not be held responsible for their actions. People that are otherwise kind and friendly can become aggressive and profane when inhibitions are removed. Alter egos can emerge from behind the inhibitions set up in social situations. The phenomenon of "flaming" with expressions of hostile, derogatory, and insulting remarks toward others can emerge. Many studies show dramatic differences between anonymous and identifiable interactions (Postmes, Spears, & Lea, 1998; Reinig & Mejias, 2004).

Suler (2004) identified six factors that can lead to an *online disinhibition* effect that may be either a *benign* exposure of secret emotions, fears, and desires or acts of kindness and generosity, as in Scenario 2, or *a toxic* expression of rude language, criticism, hatred, and threats and exploration of areas of cyberspace (e.g., pornography, gambling, occult) that they would be disinclined to frequent in the real world:

- *Dissociative anonymity.* Individuals may have a feeling of anonymity as they hide behind screen names, e-mail addresses, and passwords. Although in principle they could be identified, they feel dissociated from their personal identity because it is stored with hundreds of thousands of other records on thousands of servers connected to a global network.
- *Invisibility.* People may believe that they are invisible in online text and browsing environments. They believe that they can visit Web sites, message boards, and even chat rooms without anyone knowing that they are there. Although most sites keep logs of all visitors, because there is no immediate feedback as to their presence, users experience the illusion of invisibility.

- *Asynchronicity.* As defined in Table 11.1, asynchronous communication means that people do not interact in real time, but leave messages for others to read at a later time. The lack of continuous feedback removes a sense of self-disclosure and identity. One can leave a message "out there" and "run away," without anyone knowing who left it.
- *Solipsistic introjection.* The absence of face-to-face cues and the use of written communication can reduce one's sense of self-boundary. Communication can become disembodied, and the reading of another person's message can seem like a voice in one's own head. This can cause disinhibition, which occurs when one believes that everything is part of one's own private thought space. Talking with oneself seems safer than talking with others.
- *Dissociative imagination.* Cyberspace can seem like a place of escape where one can create imaginary characters. This make-believe environment with online personas relieves a person from responsibilities and magnifies dissociative feelings.
- *Minimization of status and authority.* Status, authority, and responsibility are conveyed in face-to-face communication by one's dress, body language, and surroundings. When these cues are either lacking or unreliable in cyberspace, disinhibition can occur because one does not really know to whom one is speaking.

Are people really anonymous on the Internet? Can anonymity be guaranteed? Probably not, it is more of an illusion. In reality, people can be unmasked by tracing IP addresses and other identifiers through the Internet. It becomes more of a legal issue than a social one (Ekstrand, 2003). Consequently, it is recommended that cyberspace designers convey a greater sense that one is in a public space, that one's behavior is in full view of the whole world, and that one should take personal responsibility for one's words and actions.

The sense of privacy and anonymity is believed to have profound effects on emotional closeness and openness. Ben-Ze'ev (2003) noted that the expression of emotion is associated with closeness and openness, and emphasized the inherent conflict between privacy and emotional closeness. If we want to be private, anonymous, and avoid harm, we cannot at the same time be open and close with others. However, in cyberspace, he theorizes that the ability to control one's degree of privacy and anonymity reduces the conflict. The trade-off between privacy and emotional closeness is reduced in online relationships because users have the ability to conceal some private information (e.g., real names and addresses) while revealing other intimate details about themselves. This is the engaging aspect of Scenario 2. The author can be emotionally open with her readers while not compromising her privacy and security. Sykes (1999) argued that, until recently, people have had very little privacy in society, but with the increase of prosperity and technology, privacy has become feasible and is even considered a civil liberty. Yet, he also noted that society is becoming increasingly exhibitionistic. To this end, the Internet has witnessed, under the cloak of anonymity, a flood of episodes of self-exposure and public confession in blogs and vlogs[1] (e.g., www.YouTube.com).

Attribution

If you failed at a task, was it your fault, the fault of the system you were working with, or just bad luck? If you succeeded at a task, was it because of your abilities, the help provided by the system, or just good luck? Attribution theory in social psychology attempts to understand how we attribute motives and causality to the behavior of others and ourselves. Attributions about the behavior of other people fall along three dimensions (Jones, 1998):

- *Internal/external causes.* We may attribute the cause to motives, abilities, or personality traits internal to a person (e.g., "He solved the computer problem because he is really smart") or to pressures, task demands, or situations external to a person (e.g., "He got the job done because his boss was after him"). The *fundamental attribution error* is said to occur when observers overestimate the importance of internal traits and underestimate the importance of external situations. People tend to attribute the cause of a person's action more to their personality than the situation (Aronson, Wilson, & Akert, 2006).
- *Stable/unstable causes.* Causes may be ascribed to enduring forces and constant tendencies (e.g., "The computer always crashes when I open this file") or to changing or random causes (e.g., "I just felt like taking the day off for no good reason"). Stable causes imply lawful systems that can be explored and understood. Unstable systems suggest spurious causes and chance events that escape reasonable explanation.
- *Controllable/uncontrollable causes.* Causes may be forces that one can influence (e.g., "I could have avoided that computer virus if I had installed a virus protection program") or to things that are beyond your control (e.g., "I couldn't help but get mad at the computer"). If things are within our control, then we can or must take responsibility for the good or the bad that follows. If not, we are free of blame.

Objective knowledge of our past histories of performance helps in making attributions (e.g., "In the past, I have been good at math or I have been bad at Scrabble") (Frieze, 1975). However, subjective factors are also at work. For example, self-esteem is preserved by ascribing success to "internal" factors, such as ability and hard work, and ascribing failure to "external" factors, such as task difficulty and bad luck (Johnson, 1981). We maintain exaggerated positive beliefs about ourselves through a *self-serving attribution bias*.

Some of the same effects are found on computer tasks. Baron and D'Amico (1996) found that fifth- and sixth-grade children working with computer-assisted instruction and tutorial programs tended to attribute performance,

[1] Video log

good or bad, to uncontrollable causes, such as ability and task difficulty, but not to effort or luck. They noted that in computer learning environments, performance feedback is extremely important. They urge designers to provide feedback to increase students' motivation to learn.

Additional factors come into play when attribution theory is applied to HCI. When something goes wrong while interacting with a computer, we may attribute it to one of the following causes:

- *User ignorance/lack of knowledge.* Novice users, in particular, are likely to blame themselves if something goes wrong. Because they stereotype themselves as computer illiterate "dummies," whatever goes wrong must be their fault.
- *User carelessness/accident.* Everyone can be careless, hurried, or under pressure and make a mistake typing the wrong command or clicking the wrong button.
- *User jinx.* Sometimes users will interpret errors as just bad luck on their part. They do not know why, but they are jinxed.
- *Computer bug/bad design.* Sometimes, but not as often as warranted, users may realize that a problem is not their fault, but that it is either a programming error or a poorly designed interface.
- *Computer malfunction.* Computers can experience hardware failures, catastrophic or minor, consistent or intermittent.
- *Computer jinx.* Users may ascribe computer problems, particularly random, intermittent failures, to bad luck on the part of the computer.

As of yet, there is little research on the attribution of causes at the human–computer interface. Nevertheless, there does seem to be a tendency for users to blame themselves for problems, errors, and frustrations more than the computer, its programming, or a poorly designed interface. The *HCI attribution error* is to blame oneself rather than the system. Several projects have been started to raise user awareness about usability issues and to help users stop blaming themselves and hold the computer manufacturers and software designers responsible for the problems.

Attitude and Belief Formation

Attitudes are beliefs or opinions about the truth or falsity of propositions. The propositions may be about oneself (e.g., "I know a lot about computers."), other people (e.g., "Jane is a good programmer"), ideas (e.g., "Programming is a valuable skill"), objects (e.g., "Computers are too expensive."), and many interrelationships among these. We live in a world full of attitudes and full of people trying to change our attitudes, such as parents, teachers, politicians, advertisers, and well-meaning friends. Social psychologists are interested in two interrelated questions: "What is the relationship between attitudes and behavior?" and "What factors affect attitude change?"

If you are shopping online and you add something to your "wish list," you are expressing an attitude about the object. Are you likely to buy it in the future, or will you be pleased if someone buys it for you as a gift? Attitudes predict behavior when they are strongly held, when we are fully aware of them, and when they are directly relevant to the target behavior (Petty & Krosnick, 1995). Attitudes are frequently elicited overtly in cyberspace. Users are asked to rate music, movies, blog entries, and celebrities. Political opinions, beliefs about the future, and attitudes about social issues are often solicited at news sites. Consumer attitudes and opinions are solicited at online shopping sites. All of these are used to predict voting behavior, buying behavior, and viewing behavior. They help politicians shape their platforms and campaigns, marketers target their advertising, and broadcasters drop or renew programs each season.

If attitudes predict behavior, is it also true that behavior predicts attitude? That is, can we infer what people believe from what they do? If so, our interaction with computers and our behavior on the Internet speaks megabytes about our attitudes, beliefs, and opinions about things. If you watch a particular television show or visit a particular Web site, it indicates that you like it. Thus, attitudes can be covertly assessed by browsing, selecting, viewing, downloading, and buying behavior in cyberspace. The fact that servers on the Internet record the vast majority of this behavior has interesting and serious consequences. Those with access to this information can infer what we believe, what we like and dislike, and our opinions on a wide variety of things from the individual level to the national level to the global level. We pursue the implications of this in greater detail in Chapter 16.

There is usually a good relationship between our beliefs and our actions, but sometimes there can be a disconnect between what we do and what we say. According to Festinger (1957), this leads to *cognitive dissonance* and the tendency to reduce this difference by either changing our attitudes or our behavior. For example, an overweight person may know that obesity is unhealthy and can lead to death. Cognitive dissonance may result in attempts to lose weight, but often the person will continue to eat and live in the same way, and instead reduce the dissonance by changing his or her belief about how obesity affects him or her personally. We may try to reduce cognitive dissonance by selective exposure to information. We may avoid Web sites, advertisements, and videos that challenge our beliefs or our actions. For example, the obese person may avoid health sites with information about obesity or exercise. We are most defensive of cognitive dissonance that involves our self-esteem and what we think about ourselves (Aronson, 2000). Consequently, when we browse the Web, we tend to look for information that confirms our beliefs, and we avoid things that would disconfirm it.

The second question has to do with how we can change the attitudes of others. Persuasion is the process of changing a target person's attitudes through delivery of a message. There are two routes to changing attitudes, one central to the content of the message and the other through peripheral issues (Petty, Wheeler, & Tormala, 2003). *Central route processing* occurs when the recipient thoughtfully considers the information and the logic of the arguments. This happens most often when a person is highly involved, motivated, and attentive, and it results in stronger, lasting attitude change. *Peripheral route processing* occurs when factors are unrelated to the content of an argument, such as the source (e.g., a celebrity), the emotionality, and the length of the message. This happens more often when a person is uninvolved, unmotivated, and inattentive, and it results in weaker, less persistent attitude change.

Needless to say, the e-mails we receive, the Web sites we visit, and the blogs that we read are filled with persuasive messages, each attempting to use every psychological trick in the book to either bolster our attitude if we agree with the message or change our attitude if we are opposed or indifferent to it. Web sites pertaining to health issues, abortion, capital punishment, political affiliation, peace, war, advocacy groups, and religion use combinations of central and peripheral information to change what we believe.

There are a number of factors that make the message more persuasive:

- *Message source.* If the communicator is physically and socially attractive, the message is more persuasive than if the communicator is not, and if the communicator is viewed as being an expert on the topic and trustworthy without an ulterior motive, he or she is more persuasive (Ziegler, Diehl, & Ruther, 2002). It is clear why the poster child for a cause is attractive; the infomercials include attractive hosts and world-renowned experts, and Web sites strive to look professional irrespective of the validity of the content.
- *Characteristics of the message.* Two-sided messages that include both the communicator's position and the opponent's position along with convincing arguments against the opponent's message are more effective than one-sided messages (Perloff, 2003). Moreover, they appeal to the central processing route.
- *Characteristics of the target.* Individuals with higher intelligence are harder to persuade than those of lower intelligence (Wood & Stagner, 1994). Individuals with a high *need for cognition* are more likely to follow the central processing route than those with a low need who take the peripheral route. Although the magnitude of difference between male and female persuasibility is not great, in public settings females are more likely to change their opinion than men. In private, they are about the same (Guadagno & Cialdini, 2002).

Communication: e-Mail, Chat, and Discussion Boards

Communication is a social act conveying information between two or more individuals. As such, it is the subject of considerable study in social psychology, dealing with issues of dominance, misunderstanding, and social protocol. A lot of information about a person is conveyed by his or her frequency and volume of communication. Some people dominate chat rooms because they read and type at higher rates than others, as opposed to face-to-face discussions where dominance may be influenced by gender and controlled by both verbal and nonverbal skills. Much is known about the role of vision in communication (Whittaker & O'Conaill, 1997), but when the channel of communication becomes asynchronous and text only, the dynamics change.

Participation in discussion boards and chat rooms varies greatly among people, depending on personal involvement and temperament. In large groups, there are many "lurkers" who read the exchanges but for one reason or another do not post any entries themselves. Their reading of other people's postings is recorded in the server logs, but their opinions and feedback are not known. There has often been a disdain for lurkers as passive, second-class citizens. In some situations, we would like to encourage a more uniform participation in discussions. For example, in educational contexts, we would like for all students to participate in the discussion as a learning experience, and in community contexts, we would like to hear from all residents.

However, there are also many cases where "lurkers" are a welcome audience to an exchange among an elite few. In many discussion boards, only a few users need to post problems or issues to be addressed by a few experts that can share their knowledge. The vast majority of users visit the site to benefit from these exchanges. For such discussion boards, it is estimated that for every contributor, there are at least 100 lurkers (Nonnecke & Preece, 2000). A good example is Wikipedia, the free encyclopedia that anyone can edit. Only a few users make contributions or edits to Wikipedia. Most visitors are seeking information and are not interested in adding or making changes. In contrast to lurkers, Perkins and Newman (1996) referred to "virtuosos" as the socially proficient members who post information. They characterized these members as having good skills at writing, being proficient in communication, having a desire to use technology to get around real-time limitations, and possessing an ability to enhance group dynamics.

Communication between two people can be affected by a number of social factors such as expectancies, stereotypes, and egocentrism. What you meant to say in an e-mail may not be what the recipient read. Without the benefit of seeing gestures and hearing emphasis and intonation, it can be difficult to convey emotion and tone in an e-mail. In a series of experiments in which subjects attempted to convey messages that were sarcastic or funny, Kruger, Epley, Parker, and Ng (2005) found that people tended to believe that they could communicate over e-mail more effectively than they actually did. Egocentrically, we tend to believe that other people interpret messages in the same way we intended them. In many situations, we are not only mistaken about whether the recipient got the message, but also remarkably overconfident in our misassessment.

Altruism and Helping Behavior

What leads people to help or not help people who seem to be in need? An important line of research in social psychology was initiated by Darley and Latané (1968) following the infamous news report of Kitty Genovese's murder. She was attacked at about 3:00 AM in a respectable part of New York City. The slaying took place over 30 min as the murderer left and returned three times, and finally put her to death as she crawled to her apartment screaming for help. Meanwhile, thirty-eight neighbors watched the tragic scene, but no one tried to help or to call the police. Theories and subsequent research investigated the *bystander effect,* hypothesizing that when other people are present there is a diffusion of responsibility. People believed that it was not appropriate or necessary for them to intervene because there were others who would. Darley and Latané replicated the bystander effect for a number of perceived medical and criminal emergencies and found that if a bystander is alone, he or she will help about 75 percent of the time, but when at least one more bystander is present the figure drops to 50 percent.

Since this early research, many other factors have also been explored that influence the probability of whether an individual will intervene and come to the aid of a person in distress. For example, it has been found that bystander intervention is reduced in the following situations (Shortland, 1985):

- The parameters of the situation are ambiguous to the bystander.
- The individuals at odds with each other appear to be married or related in some way.
- The individual asking for help is either intoxicated or mentally unstable.
- The individual is a member of a different ethnic group from the bystander.
- Intervention might result in personal harm.
- Intervention might result in considerable personal time and effort.
- The bystander has little experience or knowledge about helping behavior or training in first aid or self-defense.

Similarly, different situations in cyberspace can affect the likelihood that someone will respond to a plea for help. If you received an e-mail such as the first one listed in Table 11.2 from Wilson Hill asking for help in transferring money to your bank account, would you try to help or not? Although there is an attempt to build trust and a promise of financial reward, it should be clear that it is a scam and that the e-mail should be ignored. What about the last e-mail from Xaatrak? The parameters seem very ambiguous, one cannot tell whether it is from a human or an e-mailbot, and the text seems mentally deranged.

Very little research on the bystander effect has been conducted at this point in cyberspace with the exception of Lewis, Thompson, Wuensch, Grossnickle, and Cope (2004), who wanted to see if the diffusion of responsibility effect would occur in an e-mail plea for help. Researchers sent out 1,200 e-mails to students asking them to help a graduate student collect data for her dissertation on Web courses. They varied the number of other addresses on the recipient list from 0, 1, 14, and 49, and they used Microsoft Outlook's priority (!) feature to vary the plea level. However, neither the recipient list size nor the priority sign had any effect on the return rate. They reasoned that participants believed that for a survey to be successful they needed as many responses as possible. Consequently, a sense of diffusion of responsibility did not occur. The fact that the priority sign had no effect suggests that it is either not taken seriously by the user or is simply an ignored feature.

Nevertheless, one would expect the diffusion of responsibility effect to occur for e-mails such as the second to the last in Table 11.2 from Elizabeth S. Because it was addressed specifically to me, I was compelled to respond. However, had it been addressed to thirty other faculty as well, I would have been less inclined to respond.

In contrast to the bystander apathy effect, we may find the *Good Samaritan* in cyberspace who takes considerable time and effort to help the needy stranger. On discussion boards, in listservs, and in chat rooms, one finds individuals who are willing to do research, answer questions, and console total strangers who post questions about their problem situations. People go out of their way to help, particularly in their areas of expertise with little or no gain in the form of recognition or remuneration. The altruistic motive may be driven by an intrinsic interest in the problem topic and a sense of moral obligation consistent with one's feelings of self-esteem.

In addition, there is considerable anecdotal evidence of helping behavior in other social cyberspaces, such as MMORPGs (massively multiplayer online role-playing games). Despite the fact that players are in competition and subject to high levels of anonymity and disinhibition, players have been known to respond to pleas for help. Players have reported opponents giving away objects with game value, letting opponents escape, and uniting to help one another in battles. The reason may be that players experience a greater sense of presence in the virtual worlds and are compelled by sympathy.

Finally, there may be a form of altruism directed toward the group out of one's own personal resources. Individuals contribute materially to the betterment of the organization. Of course, people can give financially to charitable organizations, but on the Internet, people also contribute their time, knowledge, and skills to build enterprises and shared knowledge for society. The best examples today are www.Wikipedia.com and www.Wikibooks.com. Individuals contribute articles, information, and editorial skills to these and other sites to build knowledge bases for others to use.

Group Processes

People behave profoundly differently in groups than they do as individuals. A group is generally defined as "two or more persons who are interacting with one another in such a manner that each person influences and is influenced by each other person" (Shaw, 1981, p. 8). There are many different types of groups in cyberspace. There are groups drawn together by professional societies, common interests, and common goals. There are social groups where people meet and talk and get to know one another. There are gaming groups where players work together on teams against their opponents. Finally, there are groups of students in courses that are studying subjects such as cyberpsychology and that are assigned group projects to be completed in cyberspace.

The reasons for joining such groups are many. Groups offer their members different types of rewards. They may be material rewards, but often they are social rewards such as prestige and recognition. Groups also provide a means for social comparison. Festinger (1954) suggested that people want to know where they stand relative to others on different social scales regarding attractiveness, wealth, and prestige. Other members of the group help us know where we stand. Moreover, group response helps us know if our beliefs, attitudes, and behaviors are reasonable or far fetched. Our need for self-evaluation also influences which groups we join. We tend to join groups that have abilities, demographics, and values similar to our own (Goethals & Darley, 1987). Consequently, a chess master would not join a beginner's chess group, and a computer novice would not join a group of experienced Java programmers. Finally, we join groups to achieve goals that we would not be able to achieve on our own. The pooling of resources, abilities, social facilitation, dynamics, and sheer numbers can accomplish monumental tasks.

Group Dynamics

A lot is known about groups and group dynamics in social psychology, organizational psychology, and educational psychology. The structures of groups and the roles that members assume affect how they perform and the communication between members. Theories of leadership help us understand why some group members have more influence than others. Theories of group decision making help identify the conditions that result in *groupthink*, where individuals intentionally conform to what they perceive as the group consensus, even though it may be irrational and more extreme than any individual would have expressed on his or her own (Janis, 1972). In other situations, *group polarization* can occur, whereby extreme factions emerge that are at opposite sides of an issue, and advocate more extreme positions following group discussions (Moscovici & Zavalloni, 1969).

Research in online discussions has shown that when participants are separated by distance or anonymity, it can lead to higher levels of group polarization than found in traditional face-to-face meetings. Sia, Tan, and Wei (2002) hypothesized that this is because online discussions can generate more extreme arguments and because members engage in more "one-upmanship" behaviors as a function of social comparison.

Group Structure and Networks

Interactions between group members reveal a lot about the group structure – who is connected to who, the presence of subgroups, and the circles of influence. When the interactions between group members are recorded, we

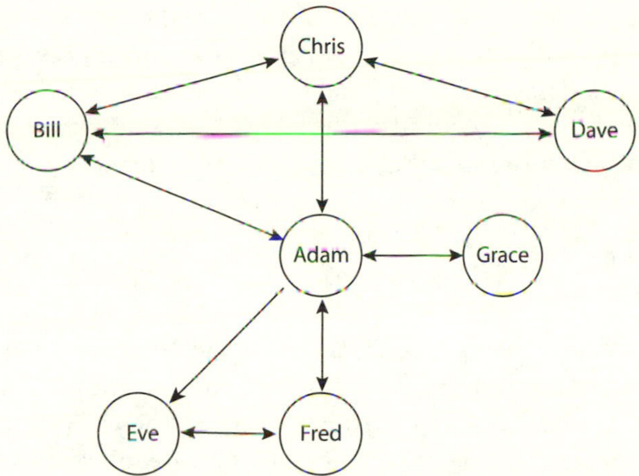

Figure 11.4. A sociogram. (Adapted from Churchill & Halverson, 2005.)

can look at a *sociogram*, a graphic representation of the social links that a person has in a group.

Sociograms for small groups can be constructed from surveys in which the participants give ratings of association with and preference for other group members. On computer networks, sociograms can be constructed from e-mail logs, address books, buddy lists, group membership, and association tags (e.g., friends, classmates). For example, we might have the following information on e-mails (Churchill & Halverson, 2005):

- Adam sends e-mail to Bill, Chris, Eve, Fred, and Grace.
- Adam receives e-mail from Bill, Chris, Fred, and Grace.
- Eve and Fred send e-mail to each other.
- Bill, Chris, and Dave send and receive e-mail from each other.
- Adam does not receive e-mail from Eve.

Figure 11.4 shows a sociogram depicting the structure of the relationships. From the sociogram, we can see that Adam is connected to two subgroups and one individual, Grace. Bill, Chris, and Dave compose one subgroup, and Eve and Fred another subgroup. The arrows indicate whether the flows are unidirectional or bidirectional.

Social network analysis is used to reveal underlying structures that relate to social and group dynamics (Cross, Parker, & Borgatti, 2002; Scott, 1991). For example, nodes (e.g., individuals) can be characterized as powerless, active, stationary, transient, or permanent. Links (e.g., relationships) can be described as strong or weak, private or public, singular or multiple, unique or redundant, and parallel or intersecting. Flows (e.g., communication) through the network can be copious or sparse, constant or intermittent, and one-way or bidirectional. Larger patterns in the network can reveal subgroups, cliques, power centers, hierarchical or horizontal structures, and boundaries.

The added dynamic of the Internet is the power of *social networking* that uses the network to build links and broker influence in the group (Churchill

& Halverson, 2005). Social networks allow members to select friends to list and link to, form and join groups, and post messages. Data from Web sites such as www.friendster.com, www.facebook.com, www.myspace.com, and www.LinkedIn.com can be used to look not only at extensive sociograms, but also crowd behavior, social change, and influence on a large scale.

Virtual Communities

One of the most fascinating phenomena on the Internet has been the emergence of virtual communities. The term "virtual community" is attributed to the book of the same title by Howard Rheingold (1993). A *virtual community* is a group whose participants are engaged in a dialog by means of information technologies, typically the Internet, to share information and values. Similar terms include "online community" and "computer-mediated community." A virtual community is composed of people with a shared interest who engage in collective learning that creates bonds between them (Wenger, 1998). It is a group of people with a common purpose whose interaction is mediated and supported by computer systems, and governed by formal and informal policies (Preece, 2000).

Developers of virtual communities are interested in designing the human–computer interface and system functionality to support the community. Virtual communities have been hosted on simple listservs, online bulletin boards, and discussion boards. Today, virtual communities can be hosted on sophisticated, integrated platforms that include real-time audio/video discussions, wireless communications, sharing of pictures and videos, and group spaces. Figure 11.5 shows a screen shot of one such service.

In addition, the promoters of online communities are interested in specifying guidelines and determining the best practices to launch new communities and to help existing communities thrive. For example, Godwin (1994) suggested the following principles for making virtual communities work:

- Use software that promotes good discussions.
- Do not impose a length limitation on postings.
- Front-load your system with talkative, diverse people.
- Let the users resolve their own disputes.
- Provide institutional memory.
- Promote continuity.
- Be host to a particular interest group.
- Provide places for children.
- Confront the users with a crisis.

Most of the research on online communities has been observational, qualitative, and has relied on case studies. Nevertheless, a lot is known about the development, growth, and survival of online communities (Preece, 2000; Rheingold, 1993, 2002). Communities generate a tremendous amount of information that can be used to track their development over time.

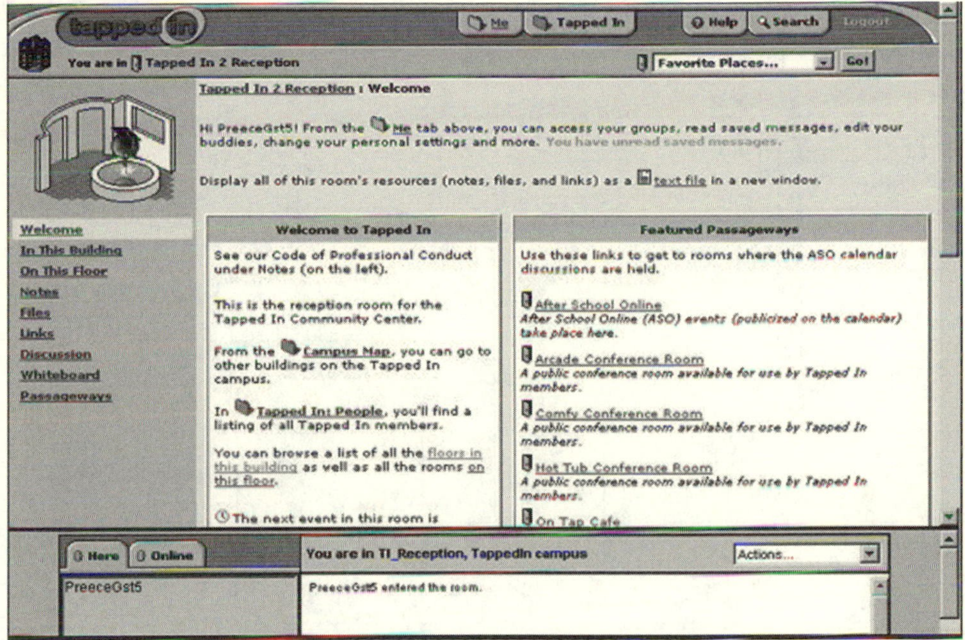

Figure 11.5. Example of an integrated online system that supports virtual communities (tappedin.org, a community of education professionals).

Computer-Supported Collaborative Work

A special form of online community exists in the work environment. Much interest has developed around software known as "groupware" to support work by multiple individuals on common projects and shared tasks across different times and places (Coleman & Khanna, 1995; Ellis, Gibbs, & Rein, 1993). Most of the development in *computer-supported collaborative work* (CSCW) has been aimed at designing computer systems to support collaborative work, demonstrating its effectiveness, and developing models of workflow and assessment (Grudin, 1994; Wilson, 1991). This work has been the subject of information studies in business and management, and somewhat in organizational psychology (Baeker, 1993).

Similar to the emergence of virtual communities, early CSCW relied on text-based systems with e-mail, listservs, and discussion boards, and the ability to upload and exchange files (Beauduion-Lafon, 1999). Scenario 3 lists the online discussion for a collaborative team project involving five students writing an article for Wikipedia. The discussion board serves as a space for the students to keep notes, brainstorm ideas, schedule meetings, encourage one another, and pass work products back and forth (Norman, 1998). Figure 11.6 shows a prototype tool for monitoring group collaboration among students in a course.

Current work focuses on video conferencing, group meeting software, tools to share and modify presentations, and to collaboratively edit documents.

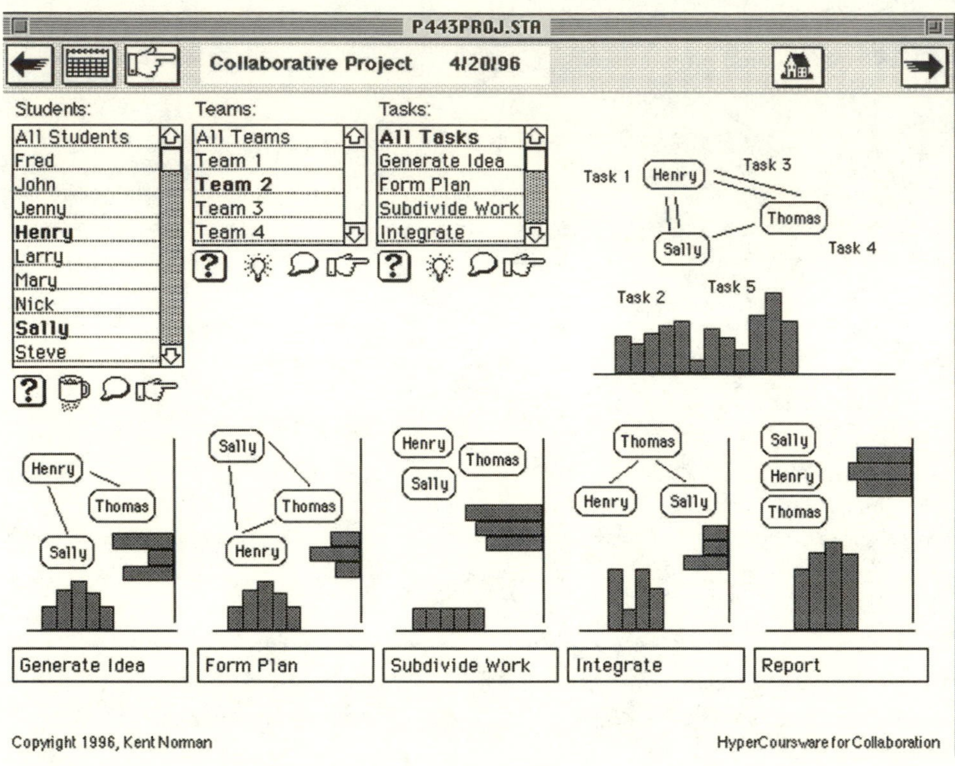

Figure 11.6. Prototype tool for monitoring group collaboration in Hyper-Courseware. (Copyright 1996, Kent Norman.)

Figure 11.7 shows a screen shot of a mock-up system that allows multipoint videoconferencing and sharing of presentations.

End Thoughts

Computers and computer networks enrich the world with new channels of communication. In fact, metaphorically they add new social spaces, cyberspaces, to our lives. As individuals, we live an increasing portion of our daily lives in these cyberspaces rather than in face-to-face communication, and even when we are in the same physical space, we augment the space with the technology of cell phones, mobile devices, and electronic displays, as in Scenario 1 in Chapter 1.

Many of the social phenomena studied in the past have their counterparts in cyberspace. The main difference is that with wider bandwidth, high speed of communication, and broader reach on the Internet, effects can be augmented. The potentiality of impression formation and impression management is vastly expanded with online profiles, pictures, and videos. Social persuasion, communication, and influence speed across networks with listservs, chain

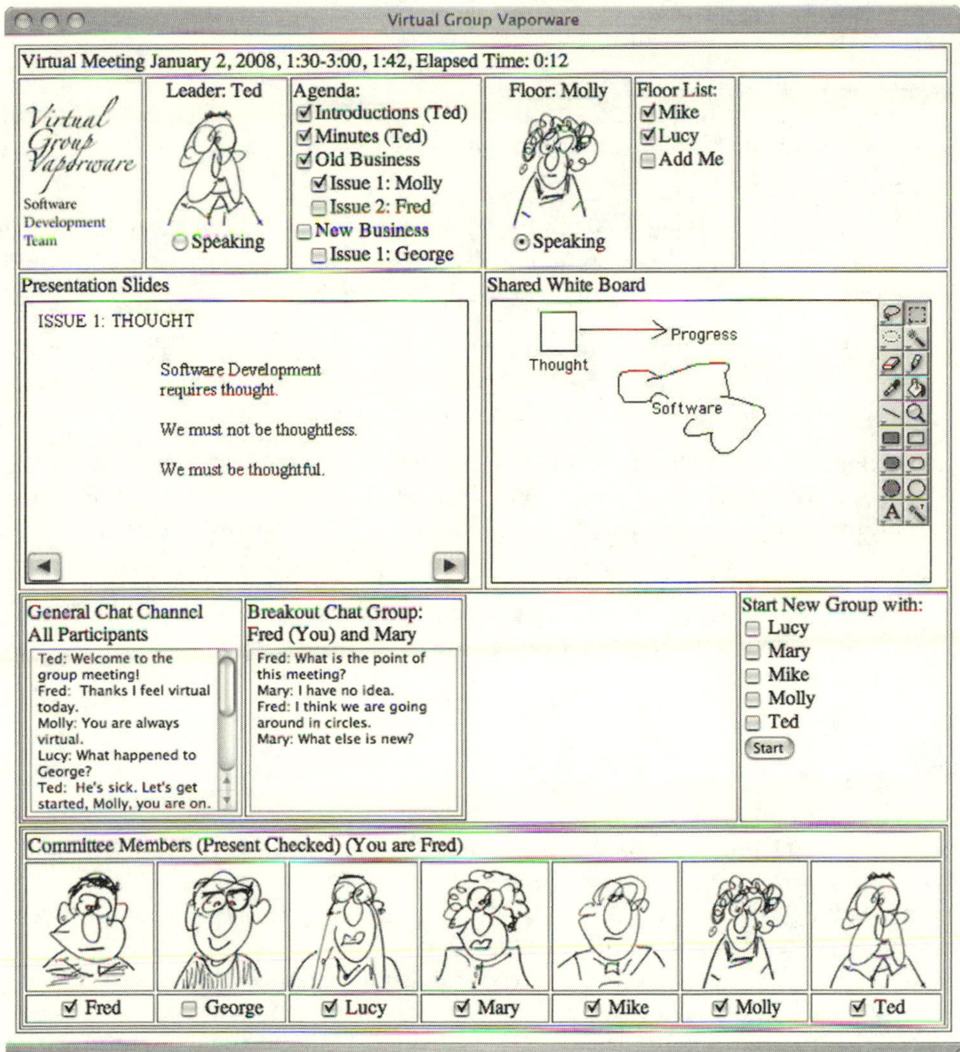

Figure 11.7. Prototype of collaborative meeting software.

e-mails, blogs, and Web sites. Groups and their dynamics now cross boundaries and continents.

New phenomena are emerging as cyberspaces become media rich, ubiquitous, and extensive. Individuals are experiencing a greater sense of social presence while managing their identities, forming meaningful and romantic relationships online, extending spheres of influence, and generating a sense of belonging and meaningfulness. Of course, not all is positive. Prejudice, hatred, aggression, and other toxic social behaviors are emerging in cyberspace with feelings of disinhibition, illusions of anonymity, and ethnocentrism. Hopefully, as we understand more and more about human social behavior online, designers will be able to construct cyberspaces that promote positive experiences, altruistic tendencies, and productive encounters.

Suggested Exercises

1. Take a careful look at your own impression management. If you have a profile on a social networking site, use it. If not, write one. Then answer the questions, "What are you trying to say to the public? What impressions do you think that others (e.g., friends, relatives, superiors) will form about you?"

2. Enjoy an altruistic episode in your life. Visit a discussion board or a chat room and help someone in need. Visit Wikipedia.org and find an article that you could contribute to or an article that you could write to help others.

3. Do a Web search for pages on controversial issues such as antiwar movements, abortion, smoking, or homosexuality. How does the Web site target its messages and appeal to central or peripheral route processing?

4. Log in to a social networking site such as www.facebook.com, www.myspace.com, or www.friendster.com; make some friends; and then start a sociogram based on friendship links. Stop after about ten nodes. These networks can be vast!

5. Plan a virtual community. Break into groups of about five to nine people. Each group will be assigned a reason for being a community. You will plan your virtual community. What platform? How will you attract members? How will you deal with problems?

References

Anderson, N. H. (1996). *A functional theory of cognition*. Mahwah, NJ: Erlbaum.

Aronson, E. (2000). *Nobody left to hate*. New York: Freeman.

Aronson, E., Wilson, T. D., & Akert, R. M. (2006). *Social psychology* (6th ed.). Upper Saddle River, NJ: Prentice Hall.

Asch, S. E. (1946). Forming impressions of personality. *Journal of Abnormal and Social Psychology*, *41*, 258–290.

Asch, S. E. (1951). Effects of group pressure upon the modification and distortion of judgments. In H. Guetzkow (Ed.), *Groups, leadership, and men* (pp. 177–190). Pittsburgh, PA: Carnegie Press.

Baeker, R. (1993). *Readings in groupware and computer-supported cooperative work: Assisting human–human collaboration*. San Francisco, CA: Morgan Kaufmann.

Baron, L. J., & D'Amico, M. (1996). Attributions, group size, and exposure time as predictors of elementary children's performance on a microcomputer task. *Computers in Human Behavior*, *12*(1), 145–157.

Beauduion-Lafon, M. (1999). *Computer supported co-operative work trends in software*. New York: John Wiley & Sons.

Ben-Ze'ev, A. (2003). Privacy, emotional closeness, and openness in cyberspace. *Computer in Human Behavior*, *19*(4), 451–467.

Churchill, E. F., & Halverson, C. A. (2005). Social networks and social networking. *IEEE Internet Computing*, *9(5)*, 14–19.

Coleman, D., & Khanna, R. (1995). *Groupware: Technologies and applications*. Upper Saddle River, NJ: Prentice Hall.

Cross, R., Parker, A., & Borgatti, S. (2002). Making invisible work visible: Using social network analysis to support strategic collaboration. *California Management Review*, 44(2), 25–46.

Darley J. M., & Latané, B. (1968). Bystander intervention in emergencies: Diffusion of responsibility. *Journal of Personality and Social Psychology*, *8*, 377–383.

Ekstrand, V. S. (2003). Unmasking Jane and John Doe: Online anonymity and the First Amendment. *Communication, Law, and Policy, 8*(4), 405–427.

Ellis, C. A., Gibbs, S. J., & Rein, G. L. (1993). Groupware: Some issues and experiences. In R. M. Baecker (Ed.), *Readings in groupware and computer-supported cooperative work: Assisting human–human collaboration* (pp. 9–29). San Francisco, CA: Morgan Kaufmann.

Festinger, L. (1954). A theory of social comparison processes. *Human Relations*, 7, 117–140.

Festinger, L. (1957). *A theory of cognitive dissonance*. Evanston, IL: Row, Peterson & Company.

Frieze, I. H. (1975). The role of information processing in making casual attributions for success and failure. In J. S. Carroll & J. W. Payne (Eds.), *Cognition and social behavior* (pp. 95–112). Hillsdale, NJ: Erlbaum.

Gerhard, M., Moore, D., & Hobbs, D. (2004). Embodiment and copresence in collaborative interfaces. *International Journal of Human-Computer Studies*, *61*, 453–480.

Godwin, M. (1994). Nine principles for making virtual communities work. *Wired Magazine*, *2.06*, 1–2. Retrieved March 17, 2008, from www.wired.com/wired/archive/2.06/vc.principles.html

Goethals, G. R., & Darley, J. M. (1987). Social comparison theory: Self-evaluation and group life. In B. Mullen & G. R. Goethals (Eds.), *Theories of group behavior* (pp. 21–48). New York: Springer-Verlag.

Grudin, J. (1994). Computer-supported cooperative work: Its history and participation. *IEEE Computer*, 27(5), 19–26.

Guadagno, R. E., & Cialdini, R. B. (2002). Online persuasion: An examination of gender differences in computer-mediated interpersonal influence. *Group Dynamics: Special Issue: Groups and the Internet*, 6, 38–51.

Janis, I. (1972). *Victims of groupthink: A psychological study of foreign-policy decision and fiascoes*. Boston: Houghton Mifflin.

Johnson, D. S. (1981). TI: Naturally acquired learned helplessness: The relationship of school failure to achievement behavior, attributions, and self-concept. *Journal of Education Psychology*, 73(2), 174–180.

Jones, E. E. (1998). Major developments in five decades of social psychology. In D. T. Gilbert, S. T. Fiske, & G. Lindzey (Eds.), *Handbook of social psychology* (4th ed., Vol. 1, pp. 1–57). New York: McGraw-Hill.

Kruger, J., Epley, N., Parker, J., & Ng, Z. (2005). Egocentrism over e-mail: Can we communicate as well as we think? *Journal of Personality and Social Psychology*, 89(6), 925–936.

Leary, M. R., Neziek, J. B., Downs, D., Radford-Davenport, J., Martin, J., & McMullen, A. (1994). Self-presentation in everyday interactions. *Journal of Personality and Social Psychology*, 67, 664–673.

Lewis, C. E., Thompson, L. F., Wuensch, K. L., Grossnickle, W. F., & Cope, J. G. (2004). The impact of recipient list size and priority signs on electronic helping behavior. *Computers in Human Behavior*, 20, 633–644.

McWilliams, N. (1994). *Psychoanalytic diagnosis: Understanding personality structure in the clinical process.* New York: Guilford Press.

Moscovici, S., & Zavalloni, M. (1969). The group as a polarizer of attitudes. *Journal of Personality and Social Psychology, 12*, 125–135.

Nonnecke, B., & Preece, J. (2000). Lurker demographics: Counting the silent. *Proceedings of the CHI 2000 conference: Human factors in computing systems.* New York: ACM Press, pp. 73–80.

Norman, K. L. (1998). Collaborative interactions in support of learning: Models, metaphors, and management. In R. Hazemi, S. Hailes, & S. Wilbur (Eds.), *The digital university: Reinventing the academy* (pp. 39–53). London: Springer-Verlag.

Perkins, J., & Newman, K. (1996). Two archetypes in e-discourse: Lurkers and virtuosos. *International Journal of Educational Telecommunications*, 2(2/3), 155–170.

Perloff, R. M. (2003). *The dynamics of persuasion: Communication and attitudes in the 21st century* (2nd ed.). Mahwah, NJ: Erlbaum.

Petty, R. E., & Krosnick, J. A. (1995). *Attitude strength: Antecedents and consequences.* Mahwah, NJ: Erlbaum.

Petty, R. E., Wheeler, S. C., & Tormala, Z. L. (2003). Persuasion and attitude change. In T. Millon & M. J. Lerner (Eds.), *Handbook of psychology: Personality and social psychology* (Vol. 5, pp. 353–382). New York: Wiley.

Postmes, T., Spears, R., & Lea, M. (1998). Breaching or building social boundaries. *Communication Research, 25*(6), 689–715.

Preece, J. (2000). *Online communities: Designing usability and supporting sociability.* New York: John Wiley & Sons.

Reinig, B. A., & Mejias, R. J. (2004). The effects of national culture and anonymity on flaming and criticalness in GSS-supported discussions. *Small Group Research, 35*, 698–723.

Rheingold, H. (1993). *The virtual community: Homesteading on the electronic frontier.* Reading, MA: Addison-Wesley.

Rheingold, H. (2002). *Smart mobs: The next social revolution.* New York: Perseus.

Scott, J. (1991). *Social network analysis: A handbook* (2nd ed.). London: Sage.

Shaw, M. (1981). *Group dynamics: The psychology of small group behavior* (3rd ed.). New York: McGraw-Hill.

Shortland, R. L. (1985). When bystanders just stand by. *Psychology Today, June*, 50–55.

Sia, C. L., Tan, B. C. Y., & Wei, K. K. (2002). Group polarization and computer-mediated communication: Effects of communication cues, social presence, and anonymity. *Information Systems Research, 13*(1), 70–90.

Suler, J. R. (1996). Life at the palace: A cyberpsychology case study. *The psychology of cyberspace.* Hypertext book. Retrieved March 17, 2008, from www-usr.rider.edu/~suler/psycyber/palacestudy.html

Suler, J. R. (2004). The online disinhibition effect. *CyberPsychology and Behavior*, 7(3), 321–326.

Sykes, C. J. (1999). *The end of privacy.* New York: St. Martin's Press.

Wenger, E. (1998). *Communities of practice: Learning meaning, and identity.* Cambridge, UK: Cambridge University Press.

Whittaker, S., & O'Conaill, B. (1997). The role of vision in face-to-face and mediated communication. In K. Finn, A. Sellen, & S. Wilbur (Eds.), *Video mediated communication* (pp. 23–49). Mahwah, NJ: Erlbaum.

Wilson, P. (1991). *Computer supported cooperative work: An introduction.* Oxford, UK: Intellect Ltd.

Wood, W., & Stagner, B. H. (1994). Why are some people easier to influence than others? In T. Brock & S. Shavitt (Eds.), *Persuasion: Psychological insights and perspectives* (pp. 149–174). Boston: Allyn & Bacon.

Ziegler, R., Diehl, M., & Ruther, A. (2002). Multiple source characteristics and persuasion: Source inconsistency as a determinant of message scrutiny. *Personality and Social Psychology Bulletin*, 28(4), 496–508.

Twelve

Abnormal Behavior and Cybertherapies

Scenario 1

We took three problem computers and two very problematic printers out to the firing range. In short order, we successfully turned each piece of equipment into Swiss cheese. We pumped more than 1,000 rounds of .223, 9 mm, .45, and 7.62 × 39 into them. We also used a .50 to start things off. The printers were by far the most enjoyable to shoot because the bullet created a nice visual when it ripped through the drum unit and the fuser. We ended up getting it to start on fire, but we put the fire out with more bullets. For the four of us, it was a whole year of frustration coming out. It felt good.

Scenario 2

I was feeling so depressed that I just wanted to die. Some days I called in sick; it was either a migraine or stomach problems. I know I needed help, but I just couldn't find the motivation to find a therapist in the Yellow Pages, call for an appointment, and all that. I also didn't have good health care coverage. So, I did a Google search and found "mycybercounselor.com." The page assured me that it was "secure, effective, and anonymous." That made me feel good. Wondering if they could help me, I looked at what sorts of problems they worked with. They had a long shopping list of problems. I was definitely on their list.

I know that it is important to be matched with the right therapist. At this site, I could see the pictures and read the qualifications and experiences of a list of therapists. The site also had a survey that I could use to find the right person for me. The cost was about $1.60/min, and sessions were 15, 30, or 50 min. This amounted to $24, $48, or $80 per session. This was a lot less *than the going fees for face-to-face counselors! Maybe I would start with the 15-min session.*

Scenario 3

Eliza: *Hello. How do you do? Please state your problem.*
Client: *I am feeling really depressed.*
Eliza: *I am sorry to hear that you are depressed.*
Client: *What can I do?*
Eliza: *Why do you ask?*
Client: *Because I just don't have any answers.*
Eliza: *Is that the real reason?*
Client: *I can't get myself out of this slump that I am in.*
Eliza: *Is it because you are in a slump that you came to me?*
Client: *Yes, I need someone to talk to about my problems.*
Eliza: *You seem to be quite positive.*
Client: *I am already feeling better.*
Eliza: *How have I helped you to be better?*
Client: *I think that you are a good listener.*
Eliza: *What makes you think I am a good listener?*
Client: *You always ask good questions that make me think.*
Eliza: *Can you think of a specific example?*
Client: *Well, you asked me about the questions I have.*
Eliza: *Why do you think I asked you?*
Client: *Because you are helping me come out of my depression.*
Eliza: *Your depression?*
Client: *Yes, I think that I am depressed.*
Eliza: *You are sure?*
Client: *Do you think that I am okay?*
Eliza: *How long have you been okay?*
Client: *Most of my life I have been pretty okay.*
Eliza: *Why do you say most of your life you have been pretty okay?*

Overview

Clinical psychology studies the types, origins, and diagnoses of abnormal behaviors that are serious enough to be considered pathological. In this chapter, we do not so much delve into the historic origins of pathologies, but rather discuss a number of common pathologies as they manifest themselves in cyberspace. In addition, we explore several new types of psychological problems and pathologies that result from computers and technology. We investigate computer addiction, computer anxiety, computer phobia, and computer rage. The psychopathic reaction to computers goes from love to fear to hate. Our generation has witnessed the excessive, pathological use of computers, as well as a continuing anxiety and fear of computers, and sometimes a frustration with computers that boils over into rage. Scenario 1 is one of thousands of recorded accounts of users venting their anger on computers. We see that the levels of such aggressive behavior against computers are remarkably high and not without reason.

Although clinical psychology focuses primarily on the causes and cures of serious mental illness, counseling psychology seeks very broadly to improve personal well-being. It attempts to facilitate interpersonal functioning, reduce stress and maladjustment, and help resolve personal issues and crises. Both clinical psychology and counseling psychology provide therapies and interventions to alleviate psychological problems. The delivery of these services is changing rapidly with the introduction of the Web. Vast amounts of mental health information and self-help programs are becoming available. One can search for mental health services, find counselors, and even engage in online counseling and group sessions via e-mail, iChat, and Web cams, as illustrated in Scenario 2. What are the advantages and disadvantages of computer-mediated counseling? Finally, we ask whether computer AI agents can replace human counselors. Scenario 3 is another exchange between a person and the computer program, Eliza (Weizenbaum, 1966), discussed in Chapter 8.

Abnormal Behavior in Cyberspace

New Platforms for Old Pathologies

In every culture and society, we have psychological stresses and the resulting psychopathologies that manifest themselves in the culture of the day. When electricity was introduced years ago, some people manifested a new paranoia. They believed that people were controlling their thoughts through the wires. A few decades ago, if someone was walking down the sidewalk talking and gesturing with no one around, we would think that he or she was mentally deranged. Now, it is common and perfectly normal as long as the person is talking on a cell phone with wireless earbuds. Today, computers, networks, software, and everything associated with them present new stresses and issues that people have to cope with and new arenas in which to manifest their reactions, normal or abnormal.

Studies in abnormal psychology first attempt to define what is abnormal and then try to categorize psychopathologies based primarily on biological indicators and psychological symptoms according to an established system.

Much debate continues to revolve around what is normal and abnormal behavior in different environments and whether to define this behavior in terms of statistical norms, violation of cultural norms, or personal distress.

In 1952, the American Psychiatric Association published the first major classification of disorders in the United States. Today, the *Diagnostic and Statistical Manual of Mental Disorders, Fourth Edition* (DSM-IV; American Psychiatric Association, 1994) is the current classification. It contains seventeen major classifications and more than 200 specific disorders (Table 12.1). The DSM is expected to change over time with advancements in medical science, refinement of clinical theory and practice, and changes in environment and culture (First & Pincus, 2002; Widiger, 2000). The next version of the DSM is expected to be published in 2011 and may include changes in the criteria used in the diagnosis of some disorders and the addition of new disorders. Many of the changes in the next and future editions will undoubtedly be a function of changes in technology and society.

The DSM is fraught with controversy. It has problems with cultural bias and political influence that can affect what is and is not classified as a disorder. It has been criticized for its mix of medical and psychological terminology as well as its emphasis on biological versus environmental influence. Finally, the DSM perpetuates the stigma of assigning labels to individuals that they cannot escape (Rosenhan, 1973; Sarason & Sarason, 2002). These problems are not expected to go away. In fact, with emerging issues regarding democracy, consensus, privacy, accessibility, globalization, human rights, virtual environments, and identity, the problems may intensify.

In this section, we look at some of the major classifications of disorders that are most likely to involve HCI. Table 12.1 lists the seventeen major categories in the DSM-IV, a description of each, and potential interactions with the human–computer interface. Even categories such as mental retardation, sleep disorders, eating disorders, and schizophrenia may come into contact with computers one way or another. In Chapter 14, we look at assistive technologies that help monitor behavior, augment cognitive functioning, and replace lost abilities with computer functions.

Anxiety Disorders

Everyone feels anxious at one time or another. However, when anxiety is so severe that it disrupts daily life, it can be classified as an anxiety disorder. Anxiety disorders are one of the most common psychological disorders. They are characterized by motor tension (jumpiness, trembling, inability to relax), hyperactivity, and apprehensive expectations and feelings. The frequency of this problem is astounding. More than 19 million American adults from age 18 to 54 years – that is, more than 13 percent of this age group – are diagnosed with an anxiety disorder each year (National Institute of Mental Health, 2001). It has been estimated that about 25 percent of the U.S. population will suffer from an anxiety disorder at some point in their lifetime (Kessler et al., 1994).

Table 12.1. Major Categories of Psychological Disorders in the DSM-IV

Major categories of psychological disorders	Description	Involvement with HCI
Disorders usually first diagnosed in infancy, childhood, or adolescence and communication disorders	Includes disorders such as attention-deficit hyperactivity disorder, autism, and learning and speech disorders	Interaction with video game play, exposure to multimedia, and computer games; use of technology as interventions
Anxiety disorders	Characterized by motor tension, hyperactivity, and apprehensive expirations/feelings; includes generalized anxiety disorder, panic disorder, phobic disorder, obsessive-compulsive disorder, and posttraumatic stress disorder	Technology may increase stress levels, opportunities for potential fears, and difficulty with repetitive movements and tasks
Somatoform disorders	Psychological symptoms are manifest in physical symptoms, even though no physical causes exist Includes hypochondriasis and conversion disorder	Increased access to medical information online can exacerbate the problem
Factitious disorders	Person deliberately fabricates symptoms of a medical or mental disorder	Increased access to medical information online can increase sophistication of the disorder
Dissociative disorders	Involves a sudden loss of memory or change in identity; includes dissociative amnesia, dissociative fugue, and dissociative identity disorder	Potential for creating new identities on the Internet may mitigate major negative consequences
Delirium, dementia, amnestic, and other cognitive disorders	Involves problems with consciousness and cognitive processes Includes substance-induced delirium and dementia, such as Alzheimer's disease	Decreases ability to use computers
Mood disorders	Involves a primary disturbance in mood Includes depressive disorders and bipolar disorder	Expression of symptoms may be played out in virtual environments and online journals
Schizophrenia and other psychotic disorders	Distorted thoughts and perception, odd communications, inappropriate emotion, and other unusual behaviors	May decrease use of computers, or symptoms may be expressed online

Major categories of psychological disorders	Description	Involvement with HCI
Substance-related disorders	Includes alcohol, cocaine, hallucinogen, and other drug-related disorders	May decrease use of computers, or they may be used in irresponsible ways; computers may be used for social networking of substance abusers
Sexual and gender identity disorders	Involves gender identity disorders in which a person is not comfortable with identity as a female or male, disorders with preference for unusual sexual behavior, and sexual dysfunctions and impairments	Virtual worlds, communities, and services provide spaces to act out sexual behaviors in either benign or maladaptive ways
Eating disorders	Includes anorexia nervosa and bulimia nervosa	Online interaction and social comparison may exacerbate the problem, while virtual communities provide health information and support groups
Sleep disorders	Includes sleep disorders such as insomnia and narcolepsy and sleep disorders due to medical conditions	24-h online environments encourage insomnia or at least occupy sleepless time
Impulsive control disorders	Includes kleptomania, pyromania, and compulsive gambling	The Internet may foster new types of impulsive control disorders with online auctions, games, day trading, etc.
Adjustment disorders	Characterized by distressing emotional or behavioral symptoms due to an identifiable stressor	Stress and frustration with computers can result in computer rage and other disorders such as cybergenic distress syndrome
Mental retardation	Low intellectual functioning and an inability to adapt to everyday life	Decreased use of computers or use as assistive technologies
Personality disorders	Occurs when personality traits become inflexible and maladaptive	Virtual worlds and communities may foster expression of personality traits
Other disorders	Includes relationship problems with family and others, abuse and neglect problems, bereavement, academic problems, religious or spiritual problems, etc.	Multiple interactions with computers and the Internet

There is both a genetic predisposition to anxiety disorders (Goldstein, Wickramaratne, Horwath, & Weissman, 1997) and environmental and learned components to anxiety. Stressful environments caused by poor and inappropriate use of technology can exacerbate levels of anxiety. Classical conditioning of neutral stimuli with fear and pain may lead to feelings of anxiety as well as fears of sudden disaster and loss. Although computer anxiety has an object of fear, classical anxiety disorders do not. Nevertheless, technological environments may contain indirect causes of anxiety.

There are five major classifications of anxiety disorders. *Generalized anxiety disorder (GAD)* is characterized by a constant state of "free floating" anxiety. There is no obvious event, person, or object that causes the anxiety, yet there is a persistent feeling of being anxious. *Panic disorder* is marked by episodes of intense anxiety with no apparent reason. It may be associated with physiological symptoms, such as tremors and cold sweat, as well as feelings of extreme fear.

Phobic disorders arise from irrational fears of specific objects or events. Clinical phobias are severe enough to interfere with daily life, whereas subclinical phobias do not. If someone could not hold a job or take a college course because it involved the use of computers, it would be a clinical phobia. Type of phobia depends on the age and gender of the person. For children, fear of strangers, doctors, and the dark are common, and for adults, fear of the death of a loved one, losing a job, and being diagnosed with a life-threatening disease are common. Females are twice as likely to develop phobias as men (Dick, Bland, & Newman, 1994). Technophobia has become an increasing problem and is discussed later in this chapter.

Obsessive-compulsive disorder (OCD) is characterized by intense anxiety along with obsessive, repetitive thoughts that are extremely distressing and/or with compulsive, repetitive actions that are severe enough to interfere with normal life. Obsessive thoughts may be about violence toward others or self, destruction of property, or committing other crimes. For example, one may be obsessed with thoughts about blowing up computers. Compulsive behaviors include washing one's hands hundreds of times a day; repeatedly locking, checking, and relocking doors; and saving newspapers and magazines for years so that they fill up the house. In the age of computers, compulsive behaviors can include repeatedly checking software and updating software; constantly restarting the computer; repeatedly backing up files; and saving all files, versions, and e-mails, filling multitudes of hard disks and CDs. In the beginning, compulsive behaviors may seem rational and can be hidden from others, but over time they can become severe, embarrassing, and dehabilitating.

Posttraumatic stress disorder (PTSD) occurs in some individuals following an extremely stressful event in one's life such as being kidnapped, raped, or abused, or experiencing or witnessing a catastrophe, a natural disaster, an act of terror, or warfare (Kessler, Sonnega, Bromet, Hughes, & Nelson, 1995). The person suffers from emotional distress, nightmares and flashbacks of the events, and avoidance of persons and circumstances that might trigger flashbacks. The risk of PTSD generally increases with the severity of the traumatic event. When transportation technology such as automobiles or airplanes is involved in the traumatic situation, a person may avoid driving or flying. As yet, not too many traumatic experiences have involved computers; however, a laptop computer bursting into flames or a computer crash causing one to lose his or her life's work could be traumatic enough for a person to avoid the use of computers in the future.

Dissociative Disorders

Dissociative disorders involve a separation of the self from consciousness, a sense of identity, and coherent memory. There may be a dissociation between significant aspects of one's conscious life experiences and memories. The dissociative disorder often involves an escape from reality or from stressful situations. There are several types of dissociative disorders, depending on the circumstances.

Dissociative amnesia refers to a sudden loss of memory of one's identity, past memories, and personal history without any organic cause such as a head injury. *Dissociative fugue* also involves a person leaving his or her home and past life to start over somewhere else without remembering where they are from. Finally, the *dissociative identity disorder (DID)* involves multiple personalities. A person may at different times assume two or more distinct identities. One or more of the personalities may be unaware of the experiences of another when it was not in control. Prior to 1980, DID was extremely rare, but since then the number of reported cases has risen dramatically (Gleaves, 1996). There are several possible explanations for this. Some suggest that it is due to media coverage of multiple personalities in movies such as "The Three Faces of Eve" (1957), "Primal Fear" (1996), and "Fight Club" (1999). Others hypothesize that the increase is a product of suggestive psychotherapy techniques that attempt to draw out repressed memories and explain unpredictable behaviors using DID (Lilienfeld et al., 1999). The use of hypnotism may result in false memories used by distressed individuals to explain their problems. Patients diagnosed with DID are typically females with histories of childhood physical and sexual abuse (Ross, Norton, & Wozney, 1989).

A technological factor should be added to the possible causes and symptomatic behaviors of the dissociative disorders. Technology in transportation, communications, and computing has made it possible to dissociate one part of our lives from another. We can have multiple cell phone numbers, credit card numbers, e-mail addresses, screen names, Web site profiles, and characters in online games. Technology makes it relatively easy to lead multiple lives with different personalities. The possibility of anonymity and the availability of multiple personalities in cyberspace may encourage the dissociative disorder. Wildt, Kowalewski, Meibeyer, and Huber (2006) reported one case of a young unemployed woman who would play several characters in an online game for up to 12 hours a day. The Internet personalities began to intrude into her daily life. Ultimately, as an inpatient, she was diagnosed with DID and received 12 weeks of psychotherapy. The authors suggest that although the patient had a disposition for an associative disorder, excessive exposure to the multiple, anonymous roles on the Internet may have triggered her illness by allowing her to explore and fragment her identity and put its coherence at risk.

Mood Disorders

Everyone feels depressed at some time or another, even when there is no apparent cause. When the depression or mood swings become so severe that one is lethargic and unable to participate in normal activities and it persists for long periods of time, it is classified as a mood disorder.

Depression is the most common type of mood disorder. Individuals may not only feel sad and depressed, but may also have physiological problems such as weight gain or loss, fatigue, or sleep disorders. They may be socially withdrawn, experience low self-esteem, and have little hope for the future. Clinical depression occurs at a higher rate between the ages of 33 and 44 years and is nearly twice as frequent among females as males cross-culturally (Weissman, Bruce, Leaf, Florio, & Holzer, 1991). Because people with depression are likely to be withdrawn and to avoid direct contact with others, they may spend more time with computers and the Internet, and may even seek computer-mediated help for their problems, as we discuss later in the chapter.

Suicide is sometimes the result of an extreme mood disorder. It has been estimated that as many as 30 percent of individuals with severe mood disorders commit suicide in one form or another (Klerman, 1987). Males are twice as likely to commit suicide as females. Nearly half of all suicides are preceded with an attempted suicide or a "suicidal gesture" called a *parasuicide*. Individuals who have attempted suicide are twenty-three times as likely to commit suicide than others (Shaffer, 1988). The risk of suicide has been linked to the media, showing an increase in suicide rate following the reporting of a high-profile suicide or the screening of a movie or television show involving suicide (Pirkis & Blood, 2001).

Recently, the term "cybersuicide" has been used to describe suicide-related behaviors on the Internet (Alao, Yolles, & Armemta, 1999). For example, there have been a number of Web sites that promote suicide (Scaria, 2003) and provide suicide "how to" information (Athanaselis, Stefanidou, Karakoukis, & Koutselinis, 2002). Some Web sites host suicide blogs, posting of interactive suicide notes, and suicide chat rooms (Baume, Cantor, & Rolfe, 1997). Although research suggests that these activities on the Internet increase the risk of suicide, they have also been countered by numerous suicide prevention sites providing moral, legal, and ethical reasons against suicide, as well as directives for help and encouragement.

Bipolar disorder involves swings of extreme depression and emotional highs or manic symptoms. During manic phases, the person may experience boundless energy, an exuberant mood, and increased appetites. He or she may not feel the need for sleep and may overindulge in food, alcohol, drugs, and sex. Individuals with manic-depressive disorders experience manic symptoms followed by weeks of depression. Bipolar disorder occurs in only about 1 percent of the population and with about the same frequency in males and females (Weissman et al., 1991). Although the depressive episodes have suicide risks, the manic episodes are also dangerous. Individuals may engage in high-risk activities, such as speeding, gambling, and engaging in unprotected sex. Unfortunately, the Internet can provide easy access to a number of playgrounds for manic activities.

Schizophrenia

One of the most severe psychological disorders involves the splitting of a person from reality. Schizophrenia occurs with about equal frequency among males and females and affects about 1 percent of the world's population (American Psychiatric Association, 2004). Although it can affect the gifted, as portrayed in the film "A Beautiful Mind" (2001), it is actually more frequent among the lower socioeconomic classes. Schizophrenia has a significant genetic component as well as environmental causes such as stress.

Symptoms are divided into two types. *Positive symptoms* refer to the presence of delusions, hallucinations, and expressive behaviors. *Negative symptoms* refer to the absence of behaviors and emotions. Patients may be withdrawn, unresponsive, and unmotivated and lack social and emotional aptitiude. Schizophrenia can take on several forms, all of which involve some kind of impairment in thinking.

Paranoid schizophrenia refers to those who are characterized with delusions of persecution and/or grandeur. They are often anxious, angry, argumentative, and sometimes violent with a relatively high suicide rate. About 40 percent of individuals diagnosed with schizophrenia are classified as paranoid schizophrenics (Fenton & McGlashan, 1991). This type may explore the Internet as a function of their paranoia, searching for conspiracies and plots against them or posting Web sites with delusional claims about themselves. A brief search of the Internet using particular search terms can locate a number of Web sites, blogs, and vlogs with outlandish, disorganized material symptomatic of schizophrenia.

Other forms of schizophrenia are generally so extreme and disorganized that they do not have the ability or coherence to interact with computer interfaces. *Disorganized schizophrenia* is characterized by a variety of hallucinations, delusions, incoherent speech, and unusual facial expressions and bodily gestures. They may not be able to speak but only act in an infantile manner. *Catatonic schizophrenia* is characterized either by extreme motionlessness and unresponsiveness to the outside world or by extreme frenetic activity, talking, and moving. Finally, about 40 percent of individuals diagnosed with schizophrenia are labeled with *undifferentiated schizophrenia,* meaning that although they display disordered behavior and thought, they cannot be clearly classified beyond that. At times, these individuals may interact with computers.

Personality Disorders

When the way a person lives his or her life is so ineffective that it causes problems, it can be classified as a *personality disorder*. Typically, this problem develops in adolescence and then persists throughout life. Personality disorders involve chronic traits, maladaptive thought, and behavior patterns that are troublesome to others. They may involve unusual, diffuse feelings of apprehension that are similar to those experienced in anxiety disorders or inflexible, dysfunctional patterns characteristic of schizophrenia (Evans, Herbert, Nelson-Gray, & Gaudiano, 2002; Livesley, 2001). Personality disorders are organized into three clusters that relate to their behavioral and cognitive patterns. The three clusters and subtypes are listed in Table 12.2, along with potential interactions with the computer and the Internet.

As seen in Table 12.2, a number of personality disorders are likely to play out their behaviors on the Internet, particularly in cyberspaces where they can express their thoughts and beliefs.

Cyberpathologies

Any technology that involves human interaction has the potential for maladaptive and maladjusted behaviors. This is particularly true with computers. Rather than interacting with them in an effective and healthy way, individuals can become addicted to their use, phobic and anxious about them, or angry and even violent toward them. In this section, we explore these three problems.

Computer and Internet Addiction

Addiction is a strong word. Yet, it has been increasingly used in connection with computers and the Internet. With increased excitement about the Internet and the increased time that people spend interacting with computers, there is concern among psychologists that a new form of addiction has emerged. Individuals can become overly attached to their computers, computer games, or the Internet and spend inordinate amounts of time in front of their monitors. Although we all spend many hours on computers at work and at home, computer addiction becomes a problem when it is so excessive that people cannot hold a job, suffer from lack of sleep, and shut down their face-to-face social life.

Table 12.2. Personality Disorder Clusters and Subtypes

Subtype	Description	Involvement with HCI
Odd/Eccentric Cluster		
Paranoid	Suspicious, lack of trust in others, view themselves as morally correct, to be envied, yet vulnerable	May express paranoid thoughts in mass e-mails, Web sites, and blogs
Schizoid	Shy, withdrawn behavior, difficulty expressing anger, aloof	Likely to be only a browser for information, a passive lurker in online discussions
Schizotypal	Eccentric beliefs, odd thinking patterns, suspicious, hostile	May express eccentric beliefs on the Internet, hostile in chat rooms and online discussions
Dramatic/Emotionally Problematic Cluster		
Histrionic	Seek a lot of attention and tend to overreact to situations, dramatic and intense, more common in females than males	Overexpressive in blogs and very intense in online discussions
Narcissistic	Unrealistic sense of self-importance, unreceptive of criticism, try to manipulate others, lack empathy	Broadcast messages, mass e-mails about one's own position, one-sided dialog on the Internet
Borderline	Emotionally unstable, impulsive, unpredictable, anxious, irritable	May react in unpredictable ways in chat rooms and online discussions
Antisocial	Self-indulgent, irresponsible, more common in males than females	Malicious behavior on the Internet, author of viruses, spam, threats
Chronic Fearfulness/Avoidant Cluster		
Avoidant	Shy and inhibited, but desire interpersonal relationships, low self-esteem and sensitive to rejection	May engage in guarded attempts to meet others on the Internet through dating and social networking services
Dependent	Lack self-confidence, need to cling to stronger personalities who will make decisions for them, more common in females than males	May be overly dependent on life coaches and counselors on the Internet
Passive-aggressive	Tend to pout and procrastinate, stubborn, intentionally inefficient to frustrate others	Tend to generate obstacles and roadblocks in HCI
Obsessive-compulsive	Similar to obsessive-compulsive anxiety disorder, but the person is not disturbed or anxious about their lifestyle, obsessed with rules and procedures	Nit-picky individuals in online discussions, editors of online materials

Addictions to technologies such as computers and the Internet are classified as a subset of behavioral addictions. Even though they are nonchemical, they share many of the same core symptoms (Marks, 1990; Young, 1998):

- *Salience.* The addictive behavior dominates a person's thinking with cravings for the activity. They are preoccupied with it to the exclusion of more social behavior. When they are not doing it, they are thinking about the next time they will be.
- *Mood modification.* Addicts report subjective experiences of arousal (highs) and paradoxically tranquilizing feelings of escape and numbing when engaged in the activity.
- *Tolerance.* Increasing amounts of time and levels of indulgence are required to match previous subjective experiences to satisfy the person's cravings.
- *Withdrawal symptoms.* Unpleasant feelings and mood states occur when the activity is discontinued or curtailed.
- *Conflict.* Disagreements occur between the addict and other people, particularly with friends and family (interpersonal conflict); conflicts occur with other activities such as work, school, and social life; and internal conflicts occur within the person about loss of control and personal values (intrapsychic conflict and cognitive dissonance).
- *Relapse.* There is a tendency for the person to slip back into the addiction, even after years of abstinence or control.

There are a number of interactive services that are ripe for addiction: online gaming (e.g., World of Warcraft), virtual environments (e.g., The Palace, Second Life), virtual communities, online gambling, day trading, cybersex, online auctions (e.g., eBay), blog sites, music and video file sharing, and even e-mail. Internet addiction may be of a general, undifferentiated nature when one just needs to be online in excess of 40 hours a week, or it may be very specific. The following types of Internet addiction have been identified and have received attention in the literature and the popular press.

Cybersex

The individual is addicted to visiting and joining cybersex providers and spending many hours a week seeking out pornographic material. The vast majority of addicts are male. They may be obsessed with seeking out sexual partners, interacting with live strippers and models, visiting virtual sex shops, generating or manipulating pornographic material, and even exploring different gender roles (Cooper, Putnam, Planchon, & Boies, 1999; Griffiths, 2000). The addiction becomes a critical problem when the person replaces normal relations with cybersex, and it becomes a criminal problem when it involves stalking for sexual relationships, child pornography, or sexual abuse of minors.

Internet Gambling

Addiction to gambling has been established as a problem prior to the Internet, but today with online gambling the problem has been exacerbated in several ways. New groups of individuals who did not previously have easy access to gambling now have it available in the privacy of their homes. Access to gambling is now around the clock, and the variety and attractiveness of gambling sites makes them more enticing. The Internet gambling addict spends hours and hours at gambling sites and loses substantial amounts of money, yet will return to repeat this behavior whenever possible (King, 1999).

Online Gaming

Addicts to online gambling are captivated by the need to play online computer games, particularly when they are linked into networks of other online players. Addicts spend excessive time (more than 40 hours a week) playing games online. Typically, they are males playing multiplayer games known as MMORPGs (Charlton & Danforth, 2007).

Online Auctions

Addicts are involved in buying and selling merchandise online. There is a habitual use of online auction sites at which they are constantly checking their status and updating bids. Addicts are involved in the auctions for pleasure and excitement rather than for either financial gain or practical purposes. Consequently, they are subject to psychological distress, feelings of dependence, withdrawal problems, and lack of self-regulation (Peters & Bodkin, 2007).

Online Communications

Addicts must be either in communication with others or searching for information about others in social cyberspaces. Excessive time is spent generating, forwarding, and responding to e-mail; interacting with others in chat rooms; and engaging in social networking.

Table 12.3 gives a questionnaire to assess your own level of general Internet addiction. If you score between 20 and 49, you are an average Internet user; if you score between 50 and 79, you are experiencing occasional or frequent problems because of the Internet; and if you score between 80 and 100, you are having significant problems and should consider yourself an Internet addict.

Some people are at a higher risk for Internet addiction than others. It is known that high patterns of Internet use are associated with loneliness, shyness, anxiety, depression, and self-consciousness (Pratarelli & Browne, 2002). In a large sample of Generation X Internet users, Chak and Leung

Table 12.3. *Internet Addiction Questionnaire*

	Rarely	Occasionally	Frequently	Often	Always	Does not apply
1. How often do you find that you stay online longer than you intended?	1	2	3	4	5	
2. How often do you neglect household chores to spend more time online?	1	2	3	4	5	
3. How often do you prefer the excitement of the Internet to intimacy with your partner?	1	2	3	4	5	
4. How often do you form new relationships with fellow online users?	1	2	3	4	5	
5. How often do others in your life complain to you about the amount of time you spend online?	1	2	3	4	5	
6. How often do your grades or school work suffer because of the amount of time you spend online?	1	2	3	4	5	
7. How often do you check your e-mail before something else that you need to do?	1	2	3	4	5	
8. How often does your job performance or productivity suffer because of the Internet?	1	2	3	4	5	
9. How often do you become defensive or secretive when anyone asks you what you do online?	1	2	3	4	5	
10. How often do you block out disturbing thoughts about your life with soothing thoughts of the Internet?	1	2	3	4	5	
11. How often do you find yourself anticipating when you will go online again?	1	2	3	4	5	
12. How often do you fear that life without the Internet would be boring, empty, and joyless?	1	2	3	4	5	
13. How often do you snap, yell, or act annoyed if someone bothers you while you are online?	1	2	3	4	5	
14. How often do you lose sleep due to late-night log-ins?	1	2	3	4	5	
15. How often do you feel preoccupied with the Internet when offline or fantasize about being online?	1	2	3	4	5	
16. How often do you find yourself saying "just a few more minutes" when online?	1	2	3	4	5	
17. How often do you try to cut down the amount of time you spend online and fail?	1	2	3	4	5	
18. How often do you try to hide how long you've been online?	1	2	3	4	5	
19. How often do you choose to spend more time online over going out with others?	1	2	3	4	5	
20. How often do you feel depressed, moody, or nervous when you are offline, which goes away once you are back online?	1	2	3	4	5	

Adapted from Young (1998).

(2004) found that the shyer a person is and the less faith the person has, the more likely they are to become addicted to the Internet. They also found that addiction was related to two measures of locus of control. The stronger a person's belief in the power of others over their own life and the higher the belief that chance determines their course of life, the greater the tendency to be addicted to the Internet. They also found that full-time students have a higher tendency to become addicted to the Internet due to open schedules. Males tend to be addicted to online gaming, and females to online communication. Moreover, the higher a person's education level, the more likely he or she is to be addicted to searching for online information, and the lower a person's education level, the more likely he or she is to be addicted to playing online games. College students who have ready access to the Internet, have more discretionary time on their hands, are going through developmental changes, and are particularly at risk for Internet addiction (Kandell, 1998).

Computer Anxiety/Phobia

In total contrast to computer addiction and the problems of impulse control on the Internet is the unrealistic fear and avoidance of computers (Weil, Rosen, & Wugalter, 1990). There is no question that computers and dependence on computers increase stress for many people. Technology poses new problems and new frustrations. The question is whether people find healthy, safe, and productive solutions to working with technology or suffer a breakdown in normal behavior and cannot cope with computers and the situations that they may cause.

Computer anxiety is defined by Howard (1986, p. 18) as "a state of heightened tension or a feeling of apprehensive expectation." In the 1990s, it was estimated that computer anxiety affected one-fourth of the population (Gos, 1996) and that one-third of the individuals in different populations experience some indicators of computer anxiety from minor stresses to avoiding computers at all costs (Brosnan, 1998). Rosen and Maguire (1990) reported that almost 50 percent of the population displays some sort of anxious behavior while using a computer. It may be expected that with the universal exposure of society to technology, computer anxiety will decrease over time. However, Bozionelos (2001) did not predict this trend. Instead, as technology is forced on more and more individuals, there may be an increase in existing levels of anxiety symptoms.

Although computer anxiety can be rather prevalent in society, Thorpe and Brosnan (2007) suggested that, in some cases, computer phobia can be severe enough to meet the DSM-IV criteria for clinical phobia (cyberphobia). However, if fear of computers actually constitutes a phobia, it is an acquired one through negative reinforcement learning rather than an innate phobia, as is the case with snakes (ophidiophobia), spiders (arachnephobia), height (hypsiphobia), and enclosed spaces (claustrophobia). Cyberphobia also differs in its surprise factor. If you sneak up behind someone who is afraid of snakes

Table 12.4. Computer Anxiety Rating Scale

	Strongly agree				Strongly disagree
1. I feel insecure about my ability to interpret a computer printout.	1	2	3	4	5
2. I look forward to using a computer.	1	2	3	4	5
3. I do not think I would be able to learn a computer programming language.	1	2	3	4	5
4. The challenge of learning about computers is exciting.	1	2	3	4	5
5. I am confident that I can learn computer skills.	1	2	3	4	5
6. Anyone can learn to use a computer if they are patient and motivated.	1	2	3	4	5
7. Learning to operate computers is like learning any new skill – the more you practice, the better you become.	1	2	3	4	5
8. I am afraid that if I begin to use computers I will become dependent on them and lose some of my reasoning skills.	1	2	3	4	5
9. I am sure that with time and practice I will be as comfortable working with computers as I am in working with a typewriter.	1	2	3	4	5
10. I feel that I will be able to keep up with the advances happening in the computer field.	1	2	3	4	5
11. I dislike working with machines that are smarter than I am.	1	2	3	4	5
12. I feel apprehensive about using computers.	1	2	3	4	5
13. I have difficulty in understanding the technical aspects of computers.	1	2	3	4	5
14. It scares me to think that I could cause the computer to destroy a large amount of information by hitting the wrong key.	1	2	3	4	5
15. I hesitate to use a computer for fear of making mistakes that I cannot correct.	1	2	3	4	5
16. You have to be a genius to understand all the special keys contained on most computer terminals.	1	2	3	4	5
17. If given the opportunity, I would like to learn about and use computers.	1	2	3	4	5
18. I have avoided computers because they are unfamiliar and somewhat intimidating to me.	1	2	3	4	5
19. I feel computers are necessary tools in both educational and work settings.	1	2	3	4	5

From Heinssen, Glass, and Knight (1987).

and yell "snake," the reaction may be extreme, but if you yell "computer" behind someone with cyberphobia, the response will probably be minimal.

A number of computer anxiety scales have been developed over the years. One of the earliest is shown in Table 12.4, which although somewhat dated, captures most of the ideas related to computer anxiety.

Computer anxiety can be reduced with more computer experience and understanding of how it works. Beckers and Schmidt (2003) found that more experience led to a higher liking of computers and less physical arousal of anxiety. They also found that if one's first experience with computers was relaxing and fun, with friendly professional support from others, they expressed more positive subsequent experiences. Computer anxiety is primarily due to novices feeling out of control during their first experiences with computers. Although having to work with computers on the job increases exposure to computers, it does not necessarily reduce computer anxiety.

However, it has been proposed that it is not so much experience, but rather beliefs about one's self-efficacy, that influence one's comfort level with computers. Individuals with high self-efficacy believe that they have the capability to execute a course of action, control the situation, and produce the desired effect (Wilfong, 2006).

In general, females express higher levels of computer anxiety than their male counterparts. A number of researchers conclude that this is due to higher levels of computer experience by males, but differences may also be due to variations in self-efficacy.

Help for computer anxiety may involve methods of behavioral desensitization, self-efficacy support, and increased exposure to computers in friendly, nonthreatening environments.

Cybergenic Stress Syndrome and Computer Rage

In Chapter 7, we find that when goal-directed behavior is thwarted by an obstacle, it not only engages problem-solving behavior, but can also result in a heightened arousal and a sense of frustration. Although computers and technology are used to solve problems, they can also create and exacerbate problems. When frustration becomes extreme, it can cause high levels of stress, anxiety, and even explode into fits of anger and rage.

Brad Norman (2005) proposed a new classification for the DSM-IV, *cybergenic distress syndrome*, which he defined as "that constellation of interrelated emotional, physiological, and behavioral signs and symptoms that accompany frustration, irritation, and hostility which, although provoked by interaction with computer hardware, software, network, and related 'help' systems, results in aggression toward people or organizations to the ultimate detriment of the person affected."

Similarly, Wilfong (2006, p. 1003) defined *computer anger* as "strong feelings of displeasure and negative cognitions in response to a perceived failure to perform a computer task." At the extreme, Kent Norman (2005) defined *computer rage* as the physical bashing and verbal abuse of a computer or computer-related item.

Humans can react to frustration in many different ways. They can use frustration to motivate continued problem-solving behavior, they can internalize it and suppress any reaction to it, or they can externalize it and vent.

Norman (2005) identified two types of venting reactions: immediate and delayed. Immediate venting can be dangerous and costly. Industry estimates put the figure at millions of dollars of equipment destroyed annually. However, as Norman noted, it is far better to direct aggression toward the computer than displace it toward a coworker, friend, family member, or other human. In contrast, delayed, premeditated venting, as exemplified in Scenario 1 can be a cathartic, if not humorous, release of frustration.

What factors lead to computer frustration, anger, and rage? Bessiére, Newhagen, Robinson, and Shneiderman (2006) distinguished between dispositional factors (e.g., individual differences such as prior computer experience, self-efficacy, and mood state) and situational factors (e.g., importance of the task, severity of interruption, lost expectations). Clearly, computer rage, like road rage, is a function of both the person and the provocation.

Several studies have explored the sources of frustration that can lead to computer rage and the circumstances in which they occur (Lazar, Jones, & Shneiderman, 2006) as well as a surprisingly high rate of computer rage (Brinks, 2005).

Norman (2005), as a part of an online Web site on computer rage, found that the seven most frustrating computer issues were in response to the following questions:

1. How frustrated do you get when the computer crashes and has to be restarted?
2. To what extent have you been frustrated waiting for a computer to do something?
3. How frustrated have you been when you could not figure out how to get the computer to do something that you wanted?
4. How often have you been frustrated because you had to redo something because of a computer problem?
5. How annoyed have you been by computer help systems not giving you answers?
6. How annoyed have you been with computer help desks and hot lines?
7. How irritating has it been for programs to become obsolete, causing you to upgrade to new versions?

By far, the most anger-producing event is when the computer crashes, as shown in the first panel of Figure 12.1. More than 25 percent of the respondents reported the highest level of frustration at this event. In general, females report much higher levels of frustration with computers than males across the board, particularly with being able to figure out how to get the computer to do something, as shown in the second panel of Figure 12.1. Age is also a big factor. Computer users younger than 30 years report higher levels of frustration than users older than 30 years, as shown in the bottom panel of Figure 12.1. More experienced users report lower levels of frustration with computers in general than novices, except when it comes to help systems, help desks, and e-mail. The more experience you have, the more frustrated

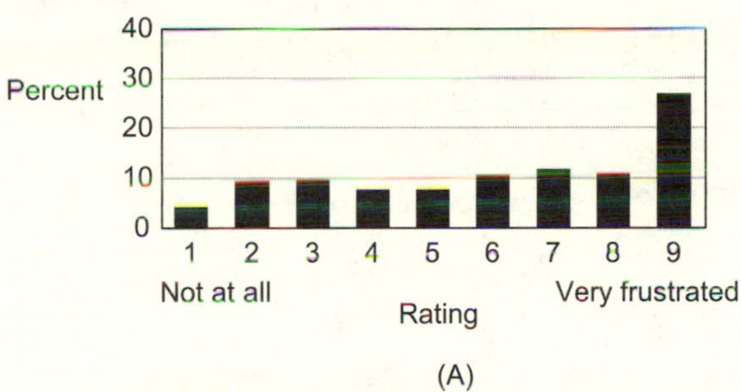

(A)

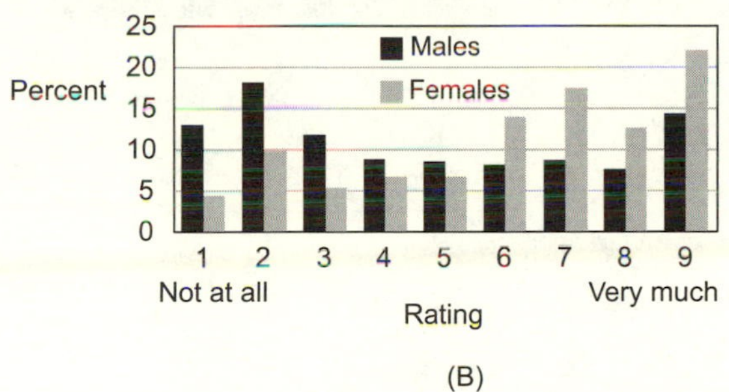

(B)

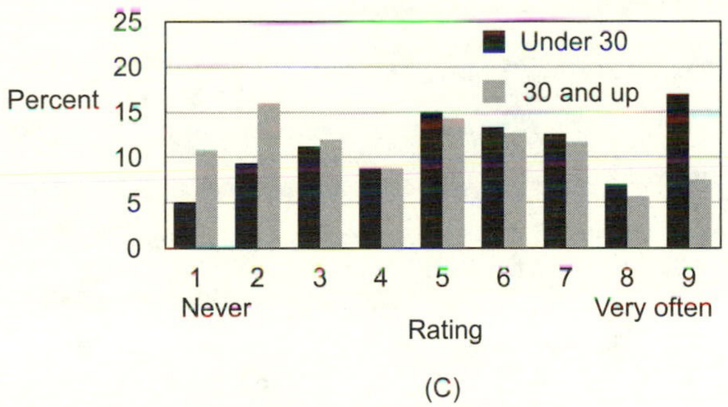

(C)

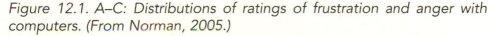

Figure 12.1. A–C: Distributions of ratings of frustration and anger with computers. (From Norman, 2005.)

you are with computer systems and technicians trying to provide help, and with the amount of e-mail that you probably have to deal with.

How do reported levels of frustration convert to destructive behavior? The top panel of Figure 12.2 shows the frequency of destructive behaviors by males and females in order of increasing frequency from top to bottom. Fortunately, the frequency of occurrence is negatively correlated with cost of damage. Although females report significantly higher levels of frustration than males, males report substantially higher frequencies of destructive behavior than females, except for slamming the mouse and verbal abuse. In the latter case, females slightly outdistance males in cursing at their

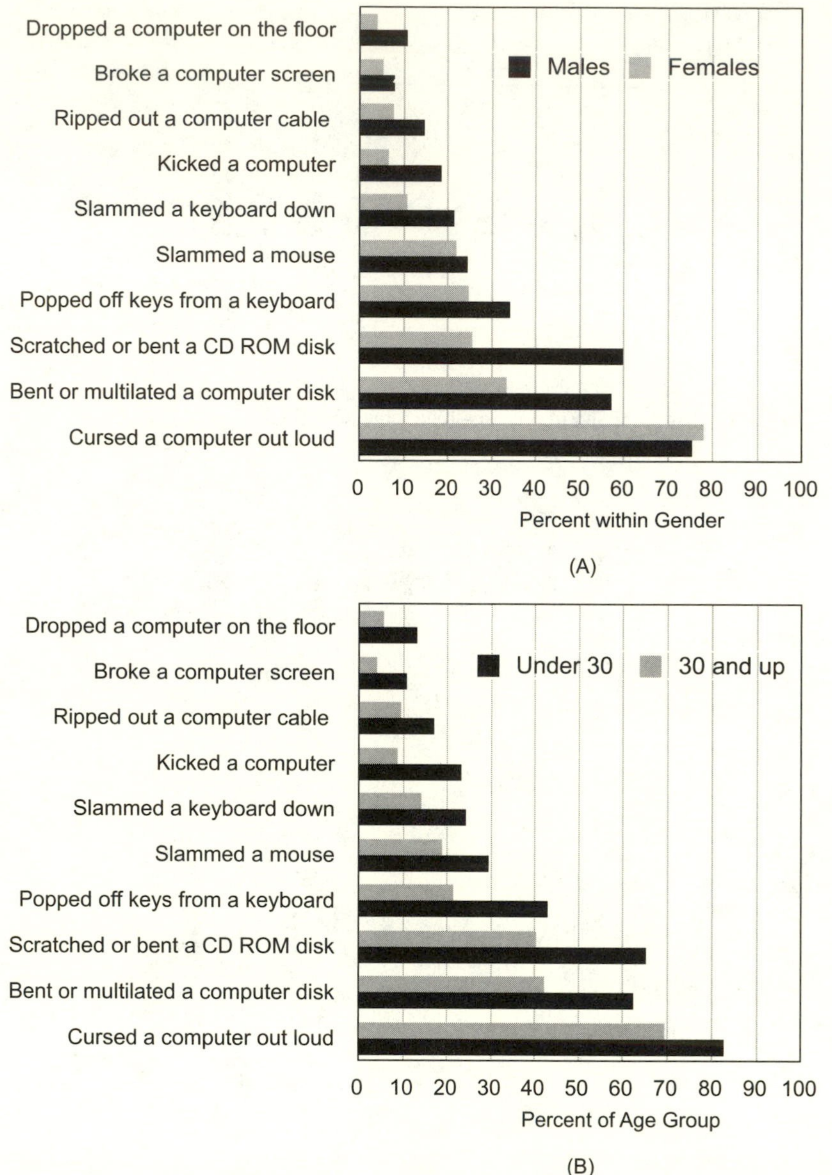

Figure 12.2. Incidence of reported aggressive behavior against computers for (A) males and females and (B) for those younger than 30 years and those 30 years and older. (From Norman, 2005.)

computer. The bottom panel of Figure 12.2 shows the frequency of destructive behaviors by users younger than 30 years versus those age 30 years and older. Those younger than 30 report more than twice the frequency of destructive behavior for the most costly damage.

What can be done to avoid computer rage? Most authorities recommend that developers provide more reliable computer hardware and software, better user interfaces, clearer instructions, and improved training to avoid provocation in the first place. Managers of computer work environments need to provide more technical support and reduced levels of stress in the workplace. Finally, computer users may need to deal with issues of self-efficacy and unrealistic expectations. When frustration mounts and computer rage seems eminent, the best thing to do is to immediately leave the situation; take a break to cool off; and find constructive, even humorous, solutions to the problem.

Online Help

After the last section on computer frustration, one might wonder why anyone would turn to a computer for psychological help. However, as we become more accustomed to going online for our information needs, it seems natural to turn on the computer to seek help for personal and psychological problems. In this section, we explore the issues of online information for self-help, computer-mediated and -managed counseling, and even computer-conducted psychotherapy.

Mental Health Information Online

Vast amounts of health information are currently available online and are growing dramatically with time. Along with this, mental health information is becoming more available. However, there are a number of difficult issues to be faced with online mental health information.

Online information varies greatly in terms of its reliability from health fads, scams, and the popular press at the low end to respected research institutes and academic sources at the high end. It is clear that the Internet is populated with many individuals, organizations, and companies that are vying for one's attention, promoting their own point of view, and are more than happy to take your money. One study reports that almost two-thirds of the information pages about depression were hosted on for-profit sites and contained poorer information than that on nonprofit sites (Lissman & Boehnlein, 2001).

The availability and pervasiveness of information on the Internet can be beneficial when carefully screened and used appropriately. But how do people discern what information is actually true, apart from the promoter's claims and the person's own hope that it is true? Of course, government and academic sources should be sought out first, and "infomercials" and sponsored links displayed after Web searches should be viewed with suspicion. Fortunately, studies indicate that most Internet users are cautious. Young people, in particular, are highly skeptical consumers of health information online (Lewis, 2006). Oddly, although information on the Internet is not trusted, it is sometimes used anyway. Powell and Clarke (2006) found that only 12 percent of the respondents selected the Internet as one of their three most accurate sources of information, but 24 percent responded that it was one of the three sources that they would actually use.

As more information about mental health is available online, it will be interesting to see how mental health consumers learn to navigate this space, searching for reliable and pertinent information and applying this information to benefit their mental health and sense of well-being.

Computer-Mediated Therapy and Counseling

Can psychotherapy be done over the Internet? Although many traditional therapists resist the idea and maintain that therapy must be face to face, many others see online therapy in the same light as online shopping and banking. Hundreds of Web sites are appearing that offer online information, assessment, counseling, and therapy. The computer generation will undoubtedly find this very appealing. Consequently, many therapists are moving to set up practice online, and books and resource materials are appearing on how to set up your own online therapy Web site (e.g., Derrig-Palumbo & Zeine, 2005).

For three years, a Clinical Case Study Group sponsored by the International Society for Mental Health Online explored the practices of online mental health professionals as the primary treatment means or in combination with traditional face-to-face office practice. In their report, Fenichel et al. (2002) discussed the similarities, differences, and challenges of online therapy and debunked a number of myths and misconceptions about it. First, they asserted that it is a myth that online therapy is impossible. They contended that many effective forms of therapy are possible online. Moreover, online therapy consists of much more than e-mail but often includes a media-rich experience with Web cams and video conferencing. However, they pointed out that many of the principles of online therapy are different from face-to-face therapy and that the therapist trained in face-to-face therapy will need additional training to be effective online.

Others are trying to map the similarities and differences between the face-to-face therapy and the experience of online therapy. Suler (2000) outlined a five-dimensional model of online and computer-mediated psychotherapy that defines many combinations that are not possible with traditional face-to-face sessions:

1. *Synchronous/asynchronous*: Sessions can be conducted using synchronous chats (same time/different place) or asynchronous messages (different time/different place). The first method allows freedom from having to travel to and from the therapist's office, and the second adds freedom from the time constraints of 50-min sessions at scheduled times.
2. *Text/sensory*: Sessions may use text messages that can be thought out, written, and recorded, or communication may be enriched with sensory

audio/video channels. The latter may be more emotional and expressive. For some individuals, the visual presence of the therapist may be important. For others, it may be distracting or inhibiting.

3. *Imaginary/real*: Online therapy can involve imaginary experiences using psychodrama, role-playing, and enactment in safe, anonymous environments. Therapy sessions can be enhanced with cyberspace tools using avatars, agents, and even virtual reality. However, sessions need to be authenticated with the true identity of the individuals in the client–therapist relationship and support real-time face-to-face video communication.
4. *Automated/interpersonal*: Online therapy sessions may be automated using simulated agents or interpersonal involving human therapists. We discuss the pros and cons of automated therapy at greater length in the next section.
5. *Invisible/present*: Finally, in online therapy individuals may have the choice to be invisible or present. Clients can listen in on group sessions as invisible "lurkers" and experience sessions in a vicarious way. Therapists may listen in on group sessions without the clients being aware of it so that individuals will not feel threatened by their presence. Alternatively, the real presence and awareness of it may be important for trust and honesty.

It has been noted that computer-mediated counseling is not entirely new. Indirect methods have been around since Freud corresponded with his patients by mail and since the telephone has been used as a hotline for crisis centers (Skinner & Zack, 2004).

Research is beginning to show evidence that delivering interventions for depression using the Internet can be effective. In one study (Christensen, Griffiths, & Jorm, 2004), 166 individuals were randomly allocated to a Web site offering information about depression. One hundred and eighty-two were directed to a cognitive behavior therapy Web site, and 178 to a placebo Web site. Both the cognitive behavior therapy and the psychoeducation were effective in reducing symptoms of depression.

Griffiths (2005) argued that the fields of clinical and counseling psychology cannot afford to ignore the Internet. Mallen (2005) studied the use of synchronous chat for initial counseling sessions. He found that therapists were able to accurately assess the clients' concerns during the initial session. He also found that therapists in training became more positive about the experience and saw the potential of online therapy; however, they also expressed concern about the amount of work involved in conducting online therapy.

There are many ethical issues when it comes to traditional clinical therapy and many more when therapy extends to the Internet (Ford, 1993). Ethical standards are extremely important for licensed therapists. A number of organizations have expressed concerns over the use of the Internet for counseling and have included these concerns in their codes of ethics (e.g., American

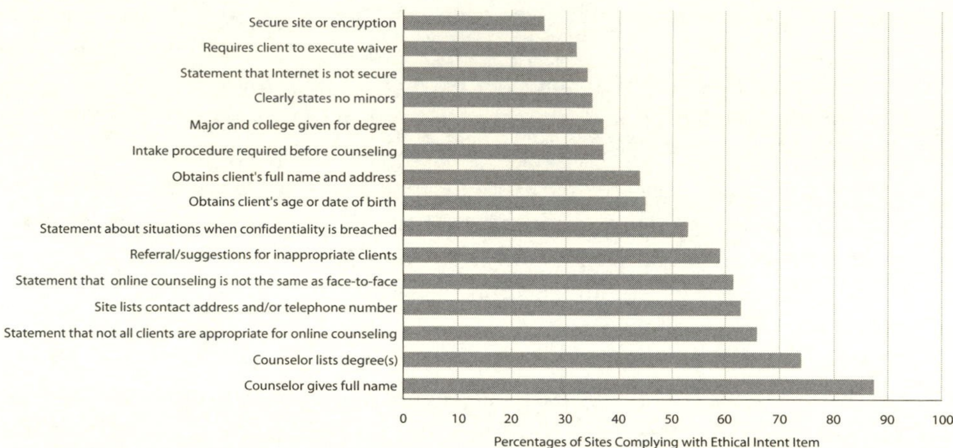

Figure 12.3. Percentages of Web sites complying with ethical intent items. (From Shaw & Shaw, 2006.)

Counseling Association [ACA], 2005; American Psychological Association, 1997).

To investigate the current state of affairs regarding ethical issues on the Internet, Shaw and Shaw (2006) developed a sixteen-item ethical intent checklist based on the ACA's (1999) *Ethical Standards for Internet Online Counseling*. They found that out of the eighty-eight online counseling Web sites that they surveyed, less than half followed the accepted practice on eight of the sixteen items. Figure 12.3 shows the proportions of Web sites in compliance with the standards from lowest to highest. Even more disturbing is the fact that within 2 months following the assessment, 20 percent of the sites either disappeared or changed to completely different Web sites. The instability of the Web and the vulnerability of Web sites do not engender a relationship of respect and trust between the therapist and the client. The authors note the grave seriousness of this abandonment for suicidal clients.

Although many psychotherapists have been resolutely opposed to anything other than face-to-face psychotherapy, the richness and ubiquity of the Internet and market forces are likely to change everything (Tantam, 2006a). Although online therapy will never totally replace face-to-face therapy, it provides many new options that may be just as effective as face-to-face therapy but more convenient and varied to meet the needs of clients. We look forward to significant developments in the trend of mental health providers to switch to services that are provided online and via wireless and mobile devices.

Computers as Therapists

Can computers act as surrogate, automated therapists? Most psychologists believe that there are inherent limitations in the understanding and language abilities of machines that will prevent this from ever happening (Tantam,

2006b). Machines will only serve as tools to assist in test administration and diagnosis, and to help in administering procedural and cognitive behavioral therapies. Virtual reality may be used to immerse a person in a situation for systematic desensitization methods for fear of flying and other phobias, for eating disorders, or for working through experiences with others (Riva, 2005).

Although Weizenbaum's (1966) Eliza may not be the answer to psychotherapy, some studies have nevertheless supported the efficacy of engaging the client in a computer dialog for a number of clinical problems such as depression, schizophrenia, and behavior disorders (Ahmed & Boisvert, 2006; Wright & Wright, 1997).

Suler (1999) envisioned the ultimate computerized psychotherapist that would simulate the best aspects of the human therapist. It would have a humble persona, yet a superior memory for names and events important to the client, and it could draw on the collective knowledge and wisdom of the human civilization. Moreover, it could achieve complete objectivity and unconditional positive regard for the client. Finally, any such system would incorporate a human backup if it should fail.

In practice, automated therapy may range from simple self-help menus and prospective suggestions to complete natural language processing systems. If automated therapy can be achieved, it could be efficient, objective, and accurate. Moreover, it can be integrated with tools for assessment, testing, and diagnosis in treatment. Automated systems can help people make decisions about whether psychotherapy is for them and what type of psychotherapy to follow. Some clients may initially be more comfortable with a nonhuman therapist that is programmed to be objective and that does not have feelings or values that it would impose on the client. Finally, computers have superior memory and can access vast knowledge systems, and they may be superior at detecting patterns of ideas and issues that surface in the dialog with a client. They may even take advantage of affective computing (see Chapter 10) to detect changes in voice, body language, and eye movement, as well as psychophysiological changes, such as heart rate, skin conductance, and blood pressure, and to infer mood states in the client.

However, as we later turn to AI, it is clear that machines do not inherently share human values, understanding, and a sense of humanity. Clients may not take the automated therapist seriously. If therapy involves transference of human value, empathy, and caring, it cannot be possible using automated systems alone.

End Thoughts

Every time there is a change in culture or an upheaval of society, new pathologies arise. The computer revolution is the focal point of such a phenomenon today. Cyberspace is the new stage on which we may act out our psychological problems. Moreover, technology itself creates new temptations, fears, and frustrations. There are new hills to climb and new valleys to descend into in the landscape of technology. Our interactions in cyberspace are a reflection of our behavior, both normal and pathological.

Just as systems of social computing to network groups of individuals are proliferating, we are also witnessing the development of *therapeutic computing* to support mental health. In therapeutic computing, the system may look for symptoms in user behavior for diagnostic purposes. The systems might read our e-mail, inspect our Web sites, and analyze our browsing behavior to determine if we are pathological. As mental health issues arise, systems might embed therapeutic interactions to provide positive support for the at-risk user. However, as such systems come online, many ethical, legal, and professional issues are emerging. What about invasion of privacy, violation of a person's individual rights, information security concerns, and malpractice suits. The issues are particularly acute in the area of suicide prevention. Who takes responsibility for errors in the system that could result in a person taking his or her own life?

Suggested Exercises

1. There is always a danger in self-diagnosis. To what extent do you think that the Web promotes self-diagnosis?
2. Go to www.netaddiction.com and take the various tests on Internet addiction.
3. Find a Web site or blog that appears to be written by someone with deranged thinking patterns. Analyze the cognitive patterns, classify the person according to the DSM-IV (Tables 12.1 and 12.2), and write a 250-word case study.
4. Keep a journal of computer frustrations for 1 week. Fill out the survey on computer frustration and rage at http://lap.umd.edu/surveys/computer_rage
5. Visit several of the Web sites for online counseling. What factors make them appealing? What factors make you suspicious? Discuss these in a small group.
6. Explore a sample of mental health Web sites. How can you tell what is reliable information, what is conjecture, and what is just hype?

References

Ahmed, M., & Boisvert, C. M. (2006). Using computers as visual aids to enhance communication in therapy. *Computers in Human Behavior, 22*, 847–855.

Alao, A. O., Yolles, J. C., & Armemta, W. (1999). Cybersuicide: The Internet and suicide. *American Journal of Psychiatry, 156*(11), 1836–1837.

American Counseling Association (ACA). (1999). *Ethical standards for Internet online counseling*. Alexandria, VA: Author.

American Counseling Association (ACA). (2005). *ACA Code of Ethics*. Alexandria, VA: Author. Retrieved March 19, 2008, from www.counseling.org/Resources/CodeOfEthics/TP/Home/CT2.aspx

American Psychiatric Association. (1994). *Diagnostic and statistical manual of mental disorders DSM-IV*. Washington, DC: American Psychiatric Press.

American Psychiatric Association. (2000). *Diagnostic and statistical manual of mental disorders DSM-IV-TR* (4th ed.). Washington, DC: American Psychiatric Press.

American Psychological Association (APA). (1997). *APA statement on services by telephone, teleconferencing, and Internet: A statement by the Ethics Committee of the American Psychological Association*. Washington, DC: Author. Retrieved March 19, 2008, from www.apa.org/ethics/stmnt01.html

Athanaselis, S., Stefanidou, M., Karakoukis, N., & Koutselinis, A. (2002). Asphyxial death by ether inhalation and plastic-bag suffocation instructed by the press and the Internet. *Journal of Medical Internet Research*, 4(3), e18. Retrieved March 19, 2008, from www.jmir.org/2002/3/e18/

Baume, P., Cantor, C. H., & Rolfe, A. (1997). Cybersuicide: The role of interactive suicide notes on the Internet. *Crisis, 18*(2), 73–79.

Beckers, J. J., & Schmidt, H. G. (2003). Computer experience and computer anxiety. *Computers in Human Behavior, 19*, 785–797.

Bessiére, K., Newhagen, J. E., Robinson, J. P., & Shneiderman, B. (2006). A model for computer frustration: The role of instrumental and dispositional factors on incident, session, and post-session frustration and mood. *Computers in Human Behavior, 22*(6), 941–961.

Bozionelos, N. (2001). The relationship of instrumental and expressive traits with computer anxiety. *Personality and Individual Differences, 31*(6), 655–974.

Brinks, M. (2005). *Aggression gegen Computer: Eine wissenschaftliche Untersuchung eines alltäglichen Phänomens*. Stuttgart, Germany: ibidem-Verlag.

Brosnan, M. J. (1998). The impact of computer anxiety and self-efficacy upon performance. *Journal of Computer Assisted Learning, 14*(3), 223–234.

Chak, K., & Leung, L. (2004). Shyness and locus of control as predictors of Internet addiction and Internet use. *CyberPsychology & Behavior*, 7(5), 559–570.

Charlton, J. P., & Danforth, I. D. W. (2007). Distinguishing addiction and high engagement in the context of online game playing. *Computers in Human Behavior, 23*, 1531–1548.

Christensen, H., Griffiths, K. M., & Jorm, A. F. (2004). Delivering interventions for depression by using the Internet: Randomised controlled trial. *British Medical Journal, 328*(7434), 265–269.

Cooper, A., Putnam, D. E., Planchon, L. A., & Boies, S. C. (1999). Online sexual compulsivity: Getting tangled in the net. *Sexual Addiction & Compulsivity: The Journal of Treatment and Prevention, 6*, 79–104.

Derrig-Palumbo, K., & Zeine, F. (2005). *Online therapy: A therapist's guide to expanding your practice*. New York: Norton.

Dick, C. L., Bland, R. C., & Newman, S. C. (1994). Panic disorder. *Acta Psychiatrica Scandinavica, 89*, 45–53.

Evans, D. L., Herbert, J. D., Nelson-Gray, R. O., & Gaudiano, B. A. (2002). Determinants of diagnostic prototypicality judgments of the personality disorder. *Journal of Personality Disorder, 16*, 95–106.

Fenichel, M., Suler, J., Barak, A., Zelvin, E., Jones, G., Munro, K., et al. (2002). *Myths and realities of online clinical work: Observations on the phenomena of online behavior, experience and therapeutic relationships. A 3rd-year report from ISMHO's Clinical Case Study Group*. Retrieved March 19, 2008, from www.rider.edu/~suler/psycyber/myths.html

Fenton, W., & McGlashan, T. (1991). Natural history of schizophrenia subtypes: I. Longitudinal study of paranoia, hebephrenic, and undifferentiated schizophrenia. *Archives of General Psychiatry, 48*, 969–977.

First, M. B., & Pincus, H. A. (2002). The DSM-IV test revision: Rationale and potential impact on clinical practice. *Psychological Services, 53*, 288–292.

Ford, B. D. (1993). Ethical and professional issues in computer-assisted therapy. *Computers in Human Behavior, 9*(4), 387–400.

Gleaves, D. H. (1996). The sociocognitive model of dissociative identity: A reexamination of evidence. *Psychological Bulletin, 120*, 42–59.

Goldstein, R. B., Wickramaratne, P. J., Horwath, E., & Weissman, M. M. (1997). Familial aggregation and phenomenology of "early"– onset (at or before age 20) panic disorder. *Archives of General Psychiatry, 54*, 271–278.

Gos, M. W. (1996). Computer anxiety and computer experience: A new look at an old relationship. *Clearing House, 69*(5), 266–271.

Griffiths, M. (2000). Excessive Internet use: Implications for sexual behavior. *CyberPsychology & Behavior, 3*(4), 537–552.

Griffiths, M. (2005). Online therapy for addictive behaviors. *CyberPsychology & Behavior, 8*(6), 555–561.

Heinssen, R., Jr., Glass, C., & Knight, L. (1987). Assessing computer anxiety: Development and validation of the Computer Anxiety Rating Scale. *Computers in Human Behavior, 3*, 49–59.

Howard, G. S. (1986). *Computer anxiety and management use of microcomputers*. Ann Arbor: University of Michigan Research Press.

Kandell, J. J. (1998). Internet addiction on campus: The vulnerability of college students. *CyberPsychology & Behavior, 1*, 11–17.

Kessler, R. C., McGonagle, K. A., Zhao, S., Nelson, C. B., Hughes, M., Eshleman, S., et al. (1994). Lifetime and 12-month prevalence of DSM-III-R psychiatric disorders in the United States. *Archives of General Psychiatry, 51*, 8–19.

Kessler, R. C., Sonnega, A., Bromet, E., Hughes, M., & Nelson, C. B. (1995). Post traumatic stress disorder in the National Comorbidity Study. *Archives of General Psychiatry, 52*, 1048–1060.

King, S. A. (1999). Internet gambling and pornography: Illustrative examples of the psychological consequences of communication anarchy. *CyberPsychology & Behavior, 2*, 175–193.

Klerman, G. (1987). Clinical epidemiology of suicide. *Journal of Clinical Psychiatry, 48*, 33–38.

Lawrence, G. H. (1986). Using computers for the treatment of psychological problems. *Computers in Human Behavior, 2*(1), 43–62.

Lazar, J., Jones A., & Shneiderman B. (2006). Workplace user frustration with computers: An exploratory investigation of the causes and severity. *Behaviour and Information Technology, 25*(3), 239–251.

Lewis, T. (2006). Seeking health information on the internet: Lifestyle choice or bad attack of cyberchondria. *Media, Culture & Society, 28*(4), 521–539.

Lilienfeld, S. O., Kirsch, I., Sarvin, T. R., Lynn, St. J., Chaves, J. F., Ganaway, G. K., et al. (1999). Dissociative identity disorder and the sociocognitive model: Recalling the lessons of the past. *Psychological Bulletin, 125*, 507–523.

Lissman, T. L., & Boehnlein, J. K. (2001). A critical review of Internet information about depression. *American Psychiatric Association, 52*, 1046–1050.

Livesley, W. J. (2001). *Handbook of personality disorders*. New York: Guilford.

Mallen, M. J. (2005). *Online counseling: Dynamics of process and assessment*. Ph.D. dissertation, Ames: IA: Iowa State University.

Marks, I. (1990). Non-chemical (behavioural) addictions. *British Journal of Addiction, 85*, 1389–1394.

National Institute of Mental Health. (2001). *Mental disorders in America*. Bethesda, MD: Author.

Norman, K. L. (2005). *Computer rage and frustration: Results of an online survey*. Technical Report LAP-2005-01. College Park: Laboratory for Automation Psychology and Decision Processes, University of Maryland.

Peters, C., & Bodkin, C. D. (2007). An exploratory investigation of problematic online auction behaviors: Experiences of eBay users. *Journal of Retailing and Consumer Services, 14*(1), 1–16.

Pirkis, J., & Blood, R. W. (2001). *Suicide and the media: A critical review*. Canberra, Australia: Commonwealth Department of Health and Aged Care.

Powell, J., & Clarke, A. (2006). Internet information-seeking in mental health: Population survey. *The British Journal of Psychiatry, 189*, 273–277.

Pratarelli, M. E., & Browne, B. L. (2002). Confirmatory factor analysis of Internet use and addiction. *CyberPsychology & Behavior, 5*(1), 53–64.

Riva, G. (2005). Virtual reality in psychotherapy: Review. *CyberPsychology & Behavior, 8*(3), 220–230.

Rosen, L., & Maguire, P. (1990). Myths and realities of computerphobia: A meta-analysis. *Anxiety Research, 3*(1), 175–191.

Rosenhan, D. L. (1973). On being sane in insane places. *Science, 179*, 250–258.

Ross, C. A., Norton, G. R., & Wozney, K. (1989). Multiple personality disorder: An analysis of 236 cases. *Canadian Journal of Psychiatry, 34*, 413–418.

Sarason, I. G., & Sarason, B. R. (2002). *Abnormal psychology* (10th ed.). Upper Saddle River, NJ: Prentice Hall.

Scaria, V. (2003). Taking life on the Web: A case report on three websites submitted to the E-HARD providing suicide related information. *Internet Health, 1*, 9. Retrieved March 19, 2008, from www.internet-health.org/ehard0103.html

Shaffer, D. J. (1988). The epidemiology of teen suicide: An examination of risk factors. *Journal of Clinical Psychiatry, 49*, 36–41.

Shaw, H. E., & Shaw, S. F. (2006). Critical ethical issues in online counseling: Assessing current practices with an ethical intent checklist. *Journal of Counseling & Development, 84*(1), 41–53.

Skinner, A., & Zack, J. S. (2004). Counseling and the Internet. *The American Behavioral Scientist, 48*(4), 434–446.

Suler, J. R. (1999). To get what you need: Healthy and pathological Internet use. *CyberPsychology and Behavior, 2*, 385–394.

Suler, J. R. (2000). Psychotherapy in cyberspace: A 5-dimensional model of online and computer-mediated psychotherapy. *Cyberpsychology and Behavior, 3*, 151–160.

Suler, J. R., & Phillips, W. (1998). The bad boys of cyberspace: Deviant behavior in multimedia chat communities. *CyberPsychology and Behavior, 1*, 275–294.

Tantam, D. (2006a). The machine as intermediary: Personal communication via a machine. *Advances in Psychiatric Treatment, 12*, 427–431.

Tantam, D. (2006b). The machine as psychotherapist: Impersonal communication with a machine. *Advances in Psychiatric Treatment, 12*, 416–426.

Thorpe, S. & Brosnan, M. (2007). Does computer anxiety reach levels which conform to DSM IV criteria for specific phobia? *Computers in Human Behavior, 23*, 1258–1272.

Weil, M., Rosen, L., & Wugalter, S. (1990). The etiology of computerphobia. *Computers in Human Behavior, 6*, 361–379.

Weissman, M. M., Bruce, M., Leaf, P., Florio, L., & Holzer, C. (1991). Affective disorders. In L. N. Robins & D. A. Regier (Eds.), *Psychiatric disorders in America* (pp. 53–80). New York: Free Press.

Weizenbaum, J. (1966). Eliza – A computer program for the study of natural language communication between man and machine. *Communications of the Association for Computing Machinery* 9, 36–45.

Widiger, T. (2000). Diagnostic and statistical manual of disorders. In A. Kazdin (Ed.), *Encyclopedia of psychology* (Vol. 3, pp. 32–35). Washington, DC & New York: American Psychological Association and Oxford University Press.

Wildt, B. T., Kowalewski, E., Meibeyer, F., & Huber, T. (2006). Identität und Dissoziation im Cyberspace: Kasuistik einer dissoziativen Identitätsstörung im Zusammenhang mit einem Internet-Rollenspiel. *Der Nervenarzt, 77*(1), 81–84.

Wilfong, J. D. (2006). Computer anxiety and anger: The impact of computer use, computer experience, and self-efficacy beliefs. *Computers in Human Behavior, 22*, 1001–1011.

Wright, J. H., & Wright, A. S. (1997). Computer-assisted psychotherapy. *Journal of Psychotherapy Practice & Research, 6*, 315–329.

Young, K. (1998). *Caught in the net: How to recognize the signs of Internet addiction and a winning strategy for recovery*. New York: Wiley.

PART IV

Applications

Thirteen

Automation and Artificial Intelligence

Scenario 1

Jim is a bit of a hacker. He loves to automate everything – much to his family's consternation. Since programming his first VCR to record movies and his home thermostat to vary the temperature throughout the day and night, he has gone on to program the home security system to arm and disarm the house burglar alarm, the home lighting system with X-10 technology programmed on his computer, the home music entertainment system using iTunes directed to specific rooms, and even robots to clean the floors and mow the lawn. His wife and family wonder whether he spends more time programming and maintaining the systems than he would if he just did everything manually. The biggest problem is that Jim is the only one who knows how it all works. His wife cannot even figure out how to turn on the television. Jim has had to put little sticky notes on each system to give family members instructions as to what to do and what not to do. The floor and lawn robots scare everyone out of the house and yard. Jim's wife does all the cooking, so everything in the kitchen is manual, with the exception of the oven timer.

Scenario 2

Stockmarketbot: Your current portfolio is worth $85,303, up $104 from yesterday. Do you want details on trades?

Client: Yes.

Stockmarketbot: I sold 100 shares of Boeing at $91.10 per share for a net profit of $2021. I bought 200 shares of Pacific Ethanol for $15.15 per share.

Client: *Why did you sell the Boeing stock? I thought that was a good one to keep?*
Stockmarketbot: My projection is that the price of Boeing stock has peaked and will soon drop due to reduced sales and smaller profit margins. Would you like more details on my projections?
Client: *No, that's okay. Why did you buy that other one? I've never heard of it.*
Stockmarketbot: Pacific Ethanol Corporation is a leader in the production, marketing, and sale of ethanol and other renewable fuels in the western United States. The price per share surged to $42 last May when Bill Gates bought a large number of shares. With current media emphasis on renewable fuels, I predict a 12-month target of $35 per share. Remember my motto: "Buy low, sell high!"
Client: *Okay, thanks.*

Overview

The concepts of automation and AI have been touched on in previous chapters. In this chapter, we go into more detail and discuss psychological issues related to automation and AI. We are not so much concerned with how AI actually works, but rather with how we think it works and how we interact with it. These issues become especially important as a result of the pervasive presence of automation and AI in technology today. As we interact with the world around us, we have a growing need to factor in the implications of automation and AI. In Scenario 1, problems result from having to live in a world programmed by others. In Scenario 2, solutions are accomplished through clear explanations using a natural language human–computer interface.

This chapter first discusses the general concept of automation and the idea of sharing tasks across the human–computer interface. The goal of automation is to make our lives more efficient, productive, and safe. In doing so, the desired psychological goal is that we live lives that are more meaningful, happy, and secure than before. Unfortunately, this is not always the outcome. At one end, automation can be used to relieve humans from having to complete boring, repetitive, computational, and manual tasks, but sometimes one repetitive task is merely replaced with another. At the other end, automation and, more often, AI can be used to perform tasks that are much too complicated for the human cognitive processing system or that require extensive knowledge that only a few experts possess. For example, with the dramatic increase in complexity of computer systems, we often rely on setup "wizards" to guide us through installations. In a real way, automation often breeds the need for more automation, resulting in an unhealthy dependence on it.

We are interested in the following questions: To what extent are we aware of automation and AI in the applications that we use? What should be automated, and what should be left for the human to do, as in Scenario 1? What are the psychological implications of interacting with AI agents? How much do we trust them? Should we believe them and follow their recommendations in scheduling, health, or financial decisions, as in Scenario 2? What do we do when things go wrong? Is it beneficial or detrimental to ascribe human-like qualities to machines? In doing so, how does it change our own self-image?

Automation

Automation is often thought of only in the context of industry and manufacturing. However, in its most general sense, automation is any process of replacing human motor, sensory, and/or cognitive functioning with machines, sensors, and computers. In Scenario 1, we find Jim programming systems to monitor, activate, and control events in his home. Automation involves not only the replacement of humans by machines, but also an augmentation of various functions such as heavy lifting, precise timing and positioning, remote sensing, and complex computation and logic processing. We automate so that we can do more things faster, with greater accuracy and consistency. But one of the most important reasons for automation is to perform tasks without constant human guidance and intervention. Either we automate to relieve the human of the burden of performing the task manually or because human presence is impossible or undesirable, such as in unmanned space flights or nuclear power plants.

What to Automate

It is clear that machines cannot do everything, and even if they could, we would probably not want to relinquish everything to them. We have to decide what tasks humans should perform because 1) humans are superior to machines for these tasks, 2) we prefer to do them ourselves, and/or 3) we are personally responsible for the consequences. We also need to determine what tasks machines should perform because 1) machines are superior to humans for these tasks, 2) humans are overloaded with other tasks, and/or 3) human operators are not available or should not work in harsh or dangerous environments.

In discussing the role of automation and AI, we use the four "rules of thumb for automation" (Adams, 1989) as a guide:

Rule 1. Use machines for functions that the human cannot perform.

Rule 2. Use machines for functions that the human cannot perform well during periods of excessive workload.

Rule 3. Use machines to assist in work that has so many sequential operations that human productivity is low.
Rule 4. Avoid unnecessary automation. Do not use machines for functions that the human can perform well.

The relative ability of humans and machines has been an important and controversial topic for many years, even preceding the computer revolution (Price, 1985). Today, it has become even more important and contentious with the development of AI, expert systems, and robotics. The list of human abilities has remained fairly constant over time, whereas the list of machine abilities grows annually.

Traditionally, humans have been considered to be superior to machines in the areas of thinking and problem solving, visual perception and pattern recognition, auditory perception and speech recognition, natural language understanding, and learning and memory. However, each area is being encroached on by AI and expert systems. Machines are typically superior to humans in physical strength, reaction time and movement time, overcoming the limitations of the senses, durability, maintainability, consistency and stability, repetitive workload, and computational abilities.

Ultimately, the allocation of tasks between the human and an automated system comes down to a trade-off of abilities and responsibilities for certain tasks in specific contexts. The extent to which something is automated will depend on the physical environment (e.g., driving a car on the freeway vs. maneuvering a Mars rover), desire for human involvement (e.g., selection of songs to listen to vs. identification of faulty components in a manufacturing process), and human responsibility and cost of mistakes (e.g., sounding a burglar alarm vs. firing a missile at an incoming airplane).

Automation can be implemented at different levels and at different points in the process. Parasuraman, Sheridan, and Wickens (2000) suggested thinking about automation at four stages in the "perception-action" cycle introduced by Gibson (1979). The four stages follow the information processing sequence: sensory processing, perception and information analysis, decision making, and response selection and implementation. Each stage may be automated from a high level not involving human intervention to a low level requiring human intervention. Figure 13.1 shows a suggested automation profile for four different systems.

At each stage, the level of automation can go from low to high. For example, at the information acquisition stage, the indoor thermostat in a heating, ventilation, and air conditioning (HVAC) system automatically senses the temperature. Radar units in a national missile defense (NMD) system automatically detect an incoming missile and track its trajectory. Other systems require manual human input of information, especially if they involve our activities and preferences. Automatic scheduling and appointment systems require manual input of at least some times and events from the users and some preferences of what they want to do when. Similarly, a system to recommend a restaurant requires user eating preferences, dietary restrictions, and other information.

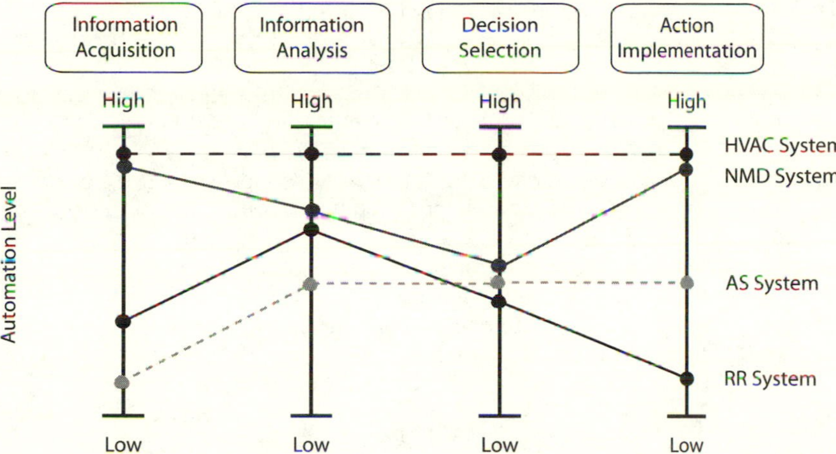

Figure 13.1. Levels of automation for each of the four stages in the perception-action automation cycle for a heating, ventilation, and air conditioning (HVAC) system, a national missile defense (NMD) system, an automatic scheduling (AS) system, and a restaurant recommender (RR) system. (Adapted from Parasuraman et al., 2000.)

In the next stage, information is searched, filtered, integrated, and analyzed to draw conclusions or make predictions. If the information is quantitative, computers are particularly good at this stage, as in the case of an HVAC system. Human operator analysis should be required to assess threat levels and other information about potential targets in the case of the NMD system. If the information is verbal, visual, conceptual, subjective, or unique, human analysis may be required. In analyzing information about scheduling and restaurant preferences, one may want to have additional human input regarding patterns or preferences. One may prefer to eat Indian food over Italian, but perhaps not three times in a row.

At the decision selection stage, the alternatives are compared and the optimal one is selected. Computers are often superior to humans at this point for both simple decisions such as deciding to turn on the heating unit because the indoor temperature is below the desired level and for complex decisions involving inference and probabilities. However, for consequential decisions such as whether to shoot down an incoming object, it is important that the human consider the computer's recommendation and take ultimate responsibility for making the decision. Systems that involve human preference typically offer suggestions rather than automatically making and enforcing the decision.

Finally, at the implementation stage, the prescribed actions are carried out by the system, the human, or some combination of the two. For the HVAC system, the heat will automatically be turned on. Once the operator has hit the "fire" button, the missile defense system will launch and take over missile guidance. Obviously, if the system is to recommend a good restaurant, the implementation will be on the part of the human to dine at the restaurant, not the computer. If it is a recommendation of a movie to watch on your

Table 13.1. Levels of Automation of Decision and Action Selection

Level of automation		Action selection
High	10	System decides everything, acts autonomously, ignoring the human
	9	System informs the human only if the system decides to
	8	System informs the human only if asked
	7	System executes automatically, then informs the human
	6	System allows the human a limited time to cancel action before execution
	5	System executes a suggested action if the human approves
	4	System suggests one alternative
	3	System narrows the selection down to a few alternatives
	2	System offers a complete set of decision/action alternatives
Low	1	System offers no assistance: human must make all decisions and implement all actions

Adapted from Parasuraman et al. (2000).

home entertainment system, the computer may find, download, and run the movie automatically according to your schedule.

For the last two stages involving decision making and action selection, Parasuraman et al. (2000) offered a list of automation options shown in Table 13.1 going from total human control to complete machine autonomy.

Human Complacence and Atrophy

As wonderful as automation is, it can fail with devastating consequences. In the summer of 1995, the *Royal Majesty* cruise ship ran aground off the coast of Nantucket Island. The ship and crew were relying on a satellite-based navigational system that silently failed. The accident cost the Majesty Cruise Lines about $7 million in damages and lost revenue. The crew could have been monitoring other navigational information, but they had gotten used to the automatic system and ignored it. There are hundreds of similar stories in the literature that chronicle human factors issues dealing with failed automation.

The problem is that when machines take over the responsibility for controlling systems, two things can occur. Operators can get in the habit of trusting the machine. As a consequence, they can become complacent, less vigilant, and even ignore warnings of system malfunction. When they are not routinely involved in working with a system, they can become bored, unstimulated, and lazy. They tend to look for other things to do and become distracted. When warning signs begin, they may continue to ignore them, believing in the reliability of the system over other information to the contrary. The phenomenon of overreliance and unfounded trust in the system has been termed "automation bias" (Skitka, Mosier, & Burdick, 2000).

The second problem is that when operators rely only on automation to do a task that they had previously done, they can get rusty and out of practice. Operator performance can deteriorate over time with lack of use. They can forget how things work. If and when a problem occurs, they may be less able to deal with it because they are out of practice.

Many tasks that had been performed by humans in control rooms are now done automatically with no human intervention in what are called "lights out operations" (Murphy & Norman, 1998). In these situations, things may go perfectly well for months or even years. The technicians who had originally performed these operations may have over time been given different responsibilities or even laid off. When something goes wrong, the technicians need to be called back, but after an extended period of time, the technicians may have forgotten what to do and will be scrambling to read the manuals and relearn how it works. The problem is that just when human intervention is needed, operators will be at their lowest level of ability to perform the task.

These problems have prompted the development of new approaches to automation that require human operators to stay "in the loop." *Adaptive automation* is one approach that keeps the human at a high level of performance while automating repetitive, tedious tasks and monitoring the workload of the operator (Hilburn, Byrne, & Parasuraman, 1997; Kaber & Riley, 1999). In adaptive automation, the human is allowed, and even scheduled, to perform tasks manually to keep human performance at a maximum. To make things interesting, the human performance may be compared to and scored against computer performance. These systems are not only of particular importance in aviation (e.g., piloting aircraft and air traffic control), but are also applicable to many other situations in military (command and control), manufacturing (process and quality control), security (monitoring and surveillance), and medicine (diagnosis and treatment).

In situations where workload can exceed the cognitive and motor abilities of the human operator, *dynamic function allocation* can be used to share and switch activities. A fighter pilot, for example, might manually fly the plane to the target and then switch over to targeting activities, allowing the guidance system to fly the plane. Incoming surface-to-air missiles might be automatically detected and evaded by the pilot, allowing the targeting system to drop bombs.

Trust in Automation

Automation requires a degree of trust on the part of humans relying on the system. If trust is high, people will not need to think about or check the workings of the system. If trust is low, users will constantly doubt the system, check its status, and/or ignore its results if possible. Trust can be partitioned into trust in the hardware and trust in the programming. A simple example is the battery alarm clock. One might not trust that it will go off at the right time because the battery is dying or because you made a mistake in setting it. Similarly, one might doubt the hardware reliability of sensors, the integrity of communications, or the computer hardware itself. Alternatively, one might doubt the software reliability of the OS, the logic of the code, or security against viruses.

The importance of trust depends on the criticality of the system. If your life depends on the automation (e.g., an aircraft autopilot), trust is critical. The system must be tested and retested before using it. One failure may have devastating consequences. However, for trivial systems such as gaming and entertainment systems, trust is not as critical a component. Trust becomes even more interesting and complicated when it involves confidence in AI systems, as we see later in this chapter.

Programming and Interfacing with Automated Systems

Almost all automated systems require some level of programming by the manufacturer, by the installer (or information technology professional), or by the end user. Programming can be as simple as setting a timer; or it can be extremely complex and convoluted, depending on the number of input sensors, output actions, if-then conditionals, and other computations. Programming, as discussed in Chapter 8, can use command language (e.g., "if [current_time ≥ 14:00] then start_recorder") or visual programming using icons and actions. The greater the apparency of the actions and relationships in the automation, the easier it will be to understand, program, and debug. Nevertheless, as pointed out in Scenario 1, problems can arise when one individual does the programming of an automated system that is used by others who do not understand how it works.

Artificial Intelligence

The idea of making machines that think has long been the subject of science and science fiction (McCorduck, 1979). In general, science fiction has outdistanced reality, but with an increasing rate, computer systems are employing the bits and pieces of AI technology to solve everyday problems. Inferencing systems, expert knowledge systems, robotics, pattern recognition, speech recognition, and natural language understanding are some of these components.

What Is Artificial Intelligence?

The term "artificial intelligence" was first coined by John McCarthy in a proposal for the Dartmouth Summer Research Conference on Artificial

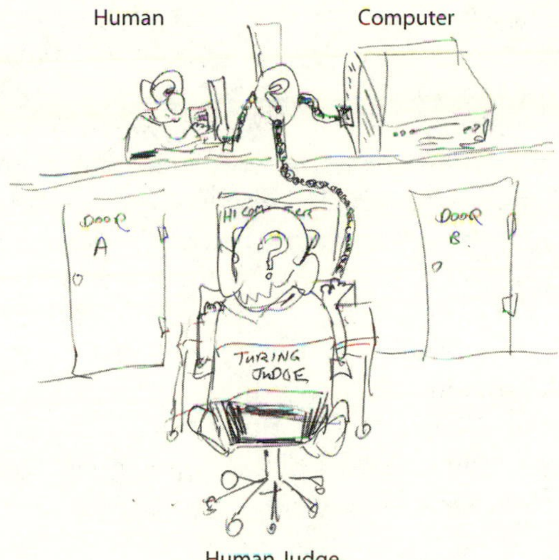

Figure 13.2. Turing test. The human judge in the middle is connected to either a human (left) or a machine (right). If the human, through asking a number of questions and reading the responses, cannot determine which is which, the computer has achieved AI.

Intelligence (McCarthy, Minsky, Rochester, & Shannon, 1955). AI was used to refer to the "the science and engineering of making intelligent machines." An intelligent machine is one that produces intelligent behavior that includes control, planning, scheduling, diagnosis, recognition, learning, and adaptation.

How can you tell if a machine is intelligent? Alan Turing (1950) proposed a test that is illustrated in Figure 13.2. If a human judge cannot reliably distinguish whether he or she is conversing with another human or with a machine, the machine would pass the intelligence test. Typically, the test is limited to a text-only interface, such as a teletype machine in the past or instant messaging today. The Turing test was originally inspired by the "Imitation Game" played at parties in Britain. In the game, a man and a woman go into separate rooms. Guests try to tell which is which by writing questions and reading the answers. The participants attempt to fool the guests by trying to imitate the opposite sex. In the Turing test for AI, the judge can ask any question he or she wants and try to determine if it came from a human or a machine programmed to imitate a human. Thousands of such questions have been recorded, such as the following:

> "Do you have any friends?"
> "I borrow £25 from two friends and buy a book for £45. From the £5 left, I give £1 to each friend. I have £3 left from the £5 and owe £24 to each. So how is it that £24 + £24 + £3 is £51?"
> "What is your idea of a good Turing test question?"

The challenge for AI is to write a program that can give convincingly human answers.

In the decades following the introduction of the Turing test, many objections and modifications have been made. Questions have been raised about whether the machine is merely using cleverly devised answers in a mindless way or whether the machine has a sense of consciousness and intellect. For example, should a test of AI be based on deceiving a human judge, or should it be based on objective criteria? This discussion has resulted in the distinction between *Strong AI* and *Weak AI*. The term "Strong AI" was coined by John Searle (1980) to refer to an AI system that is sapient or self-aware. Proponents of Strong AI contend that an appropriately programmed computer really is a mind. It does not necessarily have to be human-like, but it must be intelligent and conscious and may, in fact, surpass human intelligence. In contrast, "Weak AI" encompasses the software that accomplishes problem solving and reasoning but for which self-awareness is not an issue. The question then is whether one believes that Strong AI is or is not a possibility.

Historical Developments

Since the initial proposals of machine intelligence, a large number of researchers in computer science, engineering, cognitive science, psychology, and even philosophy have invested great time and effort to make it a reality. As early as 1950, Claude Shannon developed a formal analysis of playing games in terms of performing a search through state-action-trees using an evaluation function, as we see in Chapter 7 (Shannon, 1950). His example was chess. Since then, programs have been written for machines to play just about every game invented, and most tend to exceed human performance. The crowning achievement came in 1997, when Deep Blue, IBM's chess program, beat the reigning world chess champion, Gary Kasparov, for the first time under standard chess time controls.

Programming languages such as Lisp developed by John McCarthy and Prolog by Alain Comerauer have been used in programming AI systems. Expert knowledge systems such as Ted Shortliffe's MYCIN demonstrated the ability to diagnose medical problems. Many other expert knowledge systems have been developed for fault diagnosis of computer problems, military intelligence, international policy, business intelligence, and industrial design. But, in many cases, the wild claims of AI were followed only by toy demonstrations that could not scale up to real-world situations or generalize beyond their specific applications. Many problems such as speech recognition, pattern perception, and natural language understanding have turned out to be much harder than initially believed. Although Deep Blue beat a grand champion at chess, it would have to be completely reprogrammed to play poker or tie shoelaces. To further cloud the achievements of AI, Kasparov accused IBM of cheating by reprogramming Deep Blue after each game and demanded a rematch. IBM declined and retired Deep Blue.

Although many of the components of Weak AI have been developed and incorporated in computer technology, the grand ideas have eluded its developers. Government funding dried up, and many AI startup companies shut down. As a result, the 1970s and 1980s were dubbed the "AI winter" (Gabriel, 1996). Nevertheless, advances were made in building inference engines to run through vast collections of if-then conditionals, developing pattern recognition and classifiers, and generating expert systems that process large amounts of known information and produce conclusions. Table 13.2 gives a list of a number of specific advances and current challenges in AI.

Interacting with Artificial Intelligence

Technology today depends highly on Weak AI to support its functionality and usability. Many applications of AI are embedded so deeply in systems that they go unnoticed by most users. Other applications are either right at the surface or are so fundamental to the process that they are apparent to the user. It is here that we must deal with the psychological issues of interacting with intelligence that is not human. We explore three areas where AI is a significant HCI issue: 1) intelligent interfaces that help us work with systems, 2) autonomous agents to perform specific tasks, and 3) expert knowledge and support systems to provide guidance to decision makers.

Intelligent Interfaces

The idea of an intelligent interface brings us back to the interface models discussed in Chapter 3, but requires additional capabilities on the part of the computer. How this is done is a matter of discussion and controversy (Shneiderman, 1993). In Chapter 8, we talked about natural language interfaces used to interact with machines. We should be able to talk to an intelligent interface and tell it what we want in our own words. It should be able to understand what we mean and figure out how to accomplish the task. Needless to say, we are not there yet. At the other extreme, a dumb interface understands only 1) exact, literal commands; 2) specific selections from menus options; or 3) direct manipulation of screen objects on GUIs. In between these two extremes exist many possibilities for adding intelligence. Whatever the mode of interaction, one expects the interface to display some intelligence and to aid the user performing the task.

Kolski and Le Strugeon (1998) reviewed a number of approaches for intelligent interfaces that vary in autonomy and knowledge of the user and the task, as shown in Figure 13.3. Interfaces increase in autonomy as they start from user goals and independently carry out actions. These interfaces also vary in their knowledge of the user and the task being performed. At the lowest level, we have a flexible but dumb interface. A flexible interface enables the user to accomplish the task in different ways, allowing various levels of user experience and knowledge (e.g., different routes through menu selection and hot-key alternatives), but it does little or nothing on its own and knows

Table 13.2. Specific Advances and Challenges in AI

Area	Advance	Challenge
Classifiers, pattern recognition	Functions (neural networks, support vector machines, Bayes classifier, decision trees) that are tuned according to examples.	No single classifier works best on all problems according to the "no free lunch" theorem
Natural language processing	Convergence of computer databases into normal-sounding language and human language into formal representations for computers to process	Language production is fairly easy Language understanding continues to be a difficult problem
Language translation	Low-cost machine translation is used extensively to give the gist of the source text	Machine translation has met with limited success and requires humans to understand context and nuances of human communication
Handwriting recognition	Online recognition for input and offline recognition for text processing and mail sorting	Depends on context and neatness
Speech recognition	98%–99% accuracy under "ideal" conditions, training speaker characteristics and speaker adaptation	Lower accuracy with varying speakers, accent, and noisy conditions
Face recognition	Search for potential criminals and terrorists	Current technology has proved to be a failure in screening for suspects at airports
Expert diagnosis	Uses abduction or inference to generate the best explanation	Fairly successful in specific domains (automobile faults, medicine, etc.) but involves extensive knowledge elicitation from human experts
Data mining	Techniques to extract previously unknown implicit information from large data sets	Successful examples exist, generally require extensive human intervention and assessment of results
Game AI	Techniques used in computer and video games to produce the illusion of intelligence in nonplayer characters	Developers often use "cheats" to give advantages to characters by increasing shooting accuracy or "rubber banding" characters to follow real players
Strategic planning	Business, industry, military, government policy planning	Fairly successful but difficult to evaluate

Area	Advance	Challenge
Computer vision	Edge detection, object recognition	Successful use in autonomous vehicles and industrial robots, but many unsolved problems remain
Artificial creativity	Large number of questionable examples	Philosophical questions of what creativity is and whether the program or the programmer is the artist are illusive
Robotic control	Movement, balance, manipulation of objects	Successful in industrial situations, but problematic in open space and domestic environments

little or nothing about the user or the task. From there, the interface may add tolerance for human error. These interfaces recognize that humans are not perfect and are "forgiving" in that they are programmed to avoid certain pitfalls. Typing interfaces may overlook or correct typos and misspellings, GUIs correct minor misplacement of objects using snap-to functions and smoothing algorithms, and most provide undo options to easily correct mistakes. Adaptive interfaces learn from previous interactions with the user and change the interface to incorporate the user's preference and style. Menus may adapt by putting frequently selected options at the top, recently accessed files or favorites may be listed, and patterns of user actions may be detected and stored as macros. An interface may provide assistance when it detects certain triggers set off by user actions. Setup wizards assist in writing configuration files by walking the user though a series of guided questions. Format wizards may infer that the user is getting ready to write a letter and assist in formatting it by suggesting a template. Alternatives may be provided in how to change a search query when no items are retrieved. Finally, interfaces may provide intelligent agents to perform complex, automated tasks that require

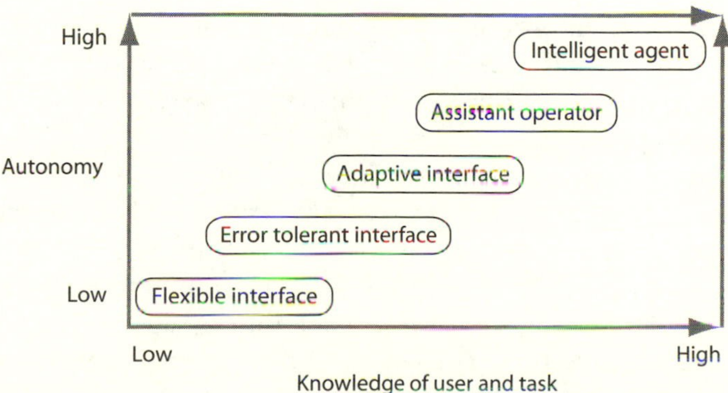

Figure 13.3. Levels of AI by autonomy and knowledge of user and task. (Adapted from Kolski & Le Strugeon, 1998.)

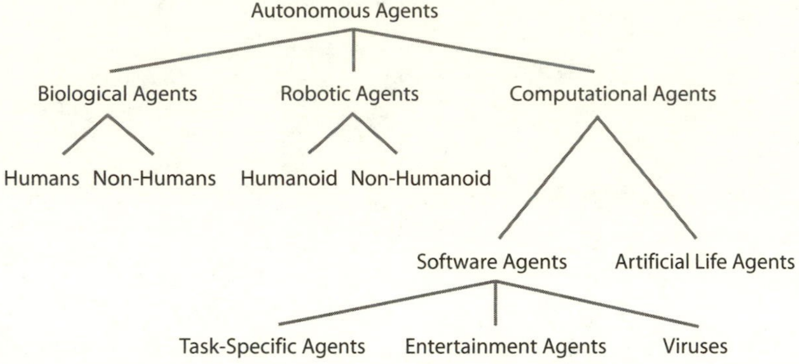

Figure 13.4. Classification of agents. (Adapted from Franklin & Graesser, 1996.)

higher levels of AI. Interface agents are essentially brokers between the user and machine functions. These are discussed in the next section.

Artificial Agents

We generally think of an agent as someone we pay to do a task for us so that we do not have to do it ourselves. The agent is often better connected than we are and has a special expertise in that particular task. So, we have real estate agents, talent agents, press agents, or foreign agents. Given a task, agents go about their work autonomously. Franklin and Graesser (1996, p. 23) defined an *autonomous agent* as "a system situated within and a part of an environment that senses that environment and acts on it, over time, in pursuit of its own agenda and so as to effect what it senses in the future." They presented a hierarchical classification of agents similar to the one in Figure 13.4, which includes human and animal life, robots, and computational agents. Computational agents are subdivided into software agents and artificial life (e.g., simulations of living organisms such as honey bees), which we do not talk about. Software agents are subdivided into task-specific agents, entertainment agents, and viruses. In this section, we talk about software and entertainment agents and leave the viruses (e.g., destructive computer programs that replicate themselves and infect operating systems) for the cybersecurity people to deal with.

Contrary to early predictions that interface agents were just a fad of the 1990s (Shneiderman, 1994), there are today thousands of software agents that have been written for work or for fun to help us and to entertain us. These are often called "bots," and they range from simple to complex and from personal to impersonal. A simple stock market agent (*stockbot*) may be programmed to respond to triggers to buy or sell stocks as their values rise or fall (Milani & Marcugini, 1999). Or, as in Scenario 2, it may be very sophisticated at employing strategies, searching market information, and explaining its actions. *Shopbots* search online shopping sites looking for the best prices,

Table 13.3. Properties of Software Agents

Property	Other names	Meaning
Reactive	Sensing and acting	Responds in a timely fashion to changes in the environment
Autonomous	Independent	Exercises control over its own actions
Goal oriented	Proactive purposeful	Does not simply act in response to the environment
Temporally continuous	"Conscious"	Is a continuously running process
Communicative	Socially able	Communicates with other agents, perhaps including people
Learning	Adaptive to environment	Changes its behavior based on its previous experience
Mobile	Ubiquitous	Able to transport itself from one machine to another
Flexible	Self-adaptive	Actions are not scripted
Character	Anthropomorphic	Believable "personality" and emotional state

Adapted from Franklin and Graesser (1996).

newsbots comb news sources for items of interest to the reader, and *schedulebots* plan meetings according to everyone's schedules. Entertainment agents include *gamebots*, which are computer opponents typically in first-person shooter games, and *chatbots*, such as Joseph Weizenbaum's Eliza or agents such as SmarterChild on Instant Messenger.

Analogous to human personalities, software agents have many different characteristics. Table 13.3 gives a tentative list of such properties.

There are many possibilities for interacting with AI and software agents. At the fundamental level, computer programmers interact with AI systems using programming and command languages to give instructions, conditions, and parameters. In some cases, end users may input code or use visual programming as discussed in Chapter 8 to control their operation. The most appealing, yet most problematic, mode of interaction is natural language voice communication.

We may break down the communication with AI systems and agents into three categories: 1) overriding commands (e.g., start, stop, undo), 2) guiding commands and information (e.g., search for "vacation deals," sell when price is greater than $50), and 3) requests for information (e.g., What did you find? Why did you diagnose X instead of Y given the symptoms?).

Finally, there are a number of cognitive implications of software agents. Although the development of intelligent agents is in the realm of computer and cognitive science, the impact on human thinking, feeling, and behavior is the subject of cyberpsychology. Software agents, like automated systems, offload tasks from the user to the agent and, in doing so, shift the balance of responsibility and communication. Table 13.4 lists a number of issues having

Table 13.4. Cognitive Issues Interacting with Software Agents

Topic	Description	Principles
Control and programming	How do we interact with intelligent agents? Formal code, natural language, keyboard, or spoken commands?	In general, natural language has proven to be a problem due to ambiguity and ill specification of details.
Comprehension	How much do we need to know about how the agents function in order to use them?	For routine situations and when nothing goes wrong, one does not need to know much, but when errors occur and when novel tasks arise, one needs to understand how the agent works at a functional level.
Feedback and monitoring	How much feedback do we need from agents to know that things are progressing as desired?	Overall progress indicators should be shown. Problems and unusual events should be displayed.
Information overload or underload	Users, consumers, workers, etc., may be faced with information overload from hundreds of agents clammering for attention. Or, if the agents are doing their jobs with little or no need for human intervention, users may get bored, feel isolated, and feel redundant.	Proper levels of interaction need to be controlled. Perhaps we will all need personal secretary agents attuned to our own abilities to handle it all, like e-mail filters.
Overreliance	What happens to our performance when we rely on an agent to perform all intellectual tasks?	We tend to get bored, our memory and problem-solving ability atrophy, and we are basically "out of the loop."
Attitudes	What happens to our feelings of self-esteem, self-respect, and self-sufficiency?	The machine is in control, and we resent being controlled, but because we can do nothing about it, we employ a variety of coping mechanisms, some good and some bad.
Responsibility	Who assumes responsibility when things go wrong? The agent, the user, or the vendor?	No one is willing to accept blame; therefore, it is the fault of the other party.

to do with interacting with agents and some of the principles for design that need to be taken into consideration.

Confidence in Expert Knowledge Systems

When expert systems provide advice, we can either accept or reject it. Needless to say, a number of psychological factors come into play. It has been suggested that if an expert system justifies its reasoning and explains its results, users will accept its judgment (Barr & Feigenbaum, 1982). Although this makes intuitive sense, justifications may not be convincing and explanations involving Bayesian inferencing and vast knowledge networks may be beyond the reasoning abilities of the user. Consequentially, additional issues of persuasion enter in when there is a discrepancy between the advice of the expert system and the initial belief of the human.

Jaccard (1981) proposed three factors that help determine change in belief, that is, from one's initial opinion to that of the expert system. The first factor is the amount of discrepancy. The bigger the discrepancy between the human's opinion and the expert system's advice, the less the likelihood of change. Second, the higher a person's self-confidence, the less likely that the person will change. Finally, the greater a person's confidence in the source, namely, the expert system, the more likely they are to accept the advice. In a laboratory study on undergraduate information technology students, Jiang, Klein, and Vedder (2000) varied all three factors to determine whether they had an impact on accepting the expert system's advice. Participants were given a test on taxation and were then told the correct answer for each question. After this, they rated their self-confidence in tax knowledge on a 10-point scale as a manipulation check. Confidence in the system was varied by telling the participants in one case that the system had been designed by a student majoring in accounting and in the other case by a leading accounting firm (Andersen Consulting). Then the expert system provided tax guidance on a number of problems. They found significant support for all three factors. The implication is that expert systems need to generate a sense of initial confidence in the system above and beyond rationale approaches to justify individual decisions.

Anthropomorphizing: Pros and Cons

Any child can clearly distinguish between a human, an animal, and an inanimate object. Nevertheless, we often ascribe uniquely human characteristics to nonhuman entities, such as boats and cars or plants and animals, and, in the present context, to computers, AI agents, and robots.

Anthropomorphism is partly the product of social attribution theory and the "theory of mind." We find it compelling to think of nonhuman entities as though they were human. So, in part, anthropomorphism is a natural outcome of psychological forces and processes. Moreover, it has positive benefits when anthropomorphizing helps us understand and predict the outcomes of interactions with computers and robots. When there is a delay between input and output to the computer, we might say that the computer is "thinking." When there are problems, we might say the computer is being "temperamental." Such anthropomorphizing is encouraged by terms such as "user friendly" and the use of the personal pronoun "I" when the program is referring to the computer.

The research community in HCI has been of two minds about encouraging or discouraging anthropomorphizing. One view is that users tend to anthropomorphize computers because they are ignorant and do not understand technology. People who are computer illiterate need to have an intelligent interface to "fool" them into thinking that they are interacting with a human and to guide them through their tasks (Winograd & Flores, 1987; Zuboff, 1988). Thus, anthropomorphism is a necessary evil. A second view is that when users respond socially to computers, they are actually interacting with the human creator or programmer of the machine (Searle, 1980). The computer is in this sense a "proxy," and users are behaving rationally. They are responding to the fact that machines are human artifacts, not truly autonomous beings.

In contrast, Nass, Steuer, Henriksen, and Dryer (1994) suggested that "computers are social actors" and dismissed the idea of anthropomorphism altogether. They contend that users are neither ignorant nor interacting with the programmer proxies. Instead, users are acting socially; that is, they are induced to behave as if computers were human, even though they know that they are not. This is because the social rules guiding HHI tend to apply to HCI as well and serve as a good model or metaphor for the exchange, as we see in Chapter 4. Nass referred to this assignment of human attitudes, intentions, and motives to nonhuman entities as "ethopoeia" from the Greek words "ethos" meaning character and "poeia" meaning representation.

Nass, Moon, Fogg, Reeves, and Dryer (1995) wanted to further determine whether computers could be easily endowed with personality characteristics and whether, according to the "similarity-attraction" hypothesis, subjects would prefer a match between the computer and their own personality. In their experiment, computers were imbued with either submissive or dominant personalities. Dominance of the computer was varied by phrasing the text on the computer to be stronger and more assertive, by the confidence expressed by the computer, by the order of interaction (dominance first), and by the name of the computer (Max vs. Linus). Using a personality test, a subscale on the Bem Sex Role Inventory (Bem, 1974), subjects were divided into dominant and submissive groups. The results indicated that not only did the subjects prefer the match, but they were also more satisfied with the interaction.

Anthropomorphobia is the fear, avoidance, and hatred of seeing or acknowledging human qualities in nonhumans. It is reported that some individuals have attacks of anxiety when they see or think about animals acting like humans, as in the animated film "The Secret of NIMH" (1982), or robots simulating human activity, as in the Disney movie "Artificial Intelligence: AI" (2001).

The issue of anthropomorphism is not going away. Some interface designers push human-like characteristic in their interfaces. However, academicians such as Shneiderman (1993) argued that in doing so, they generate unrealistic and false expectations on the part of the user and should be avoided. From the perspective of the user, there is probably little consensus and large individual difference concerning their desirability, acceptance, and effectiveness. Needless to say, this is a fertile area for future psychological research.

End Thoughts

Technology today is embedded with automation and AI. We take for granted the number of systems that we routinely interact with that have such components – from security systems to cell phones and from automobiles to the Internet. We cannot even count them because, in many cases, they do such a good job that we are not even aware that they exist, that is, until they fail. At that point, the psychological issues of knowledge and training, trust and confidence, and dependence and security come to a head. Are we at the mercy of technology? Can we fix it? Who do we call?

Since the initial vision of machine intelligence, AI has fueled great advances in science and technology as well as a wealth of material for science fiction. Joseph Feigenbaum, a pioneer in AI, has said, "It took 20 years for AI to become an overnight success." As many of the advances in AI have been incorporated in computer systems for route planning, manufacturing, design, expert diagnosis, search, and game playing, they quickly seem mundane and pale in comparison to the initial hype of AI in the 1960s and 1970s. This phenomenon of discounting AI advances as just another prosaic computer program has been called the "AI effect." Hogan (1998) and others attributed it to the human need to demystify AI in order to maintain our own special place in the universe. This claim has yet to be verified in psychological research but underscores the inherent tension between human intelligence and machine intelligence, neither of which we fully understand but nevertheless attempt to define and measure.

Although the technology is still too new to fully realize the effects of AI on our psychological and societal well-being, software development in pursuit of weak AI has for the most part benefited humankind. Things may change according to some futurists and proponents of AI. In Chapter 16, we again explore the potential for Strong AI and its successor "Ultra-AI."

Suggested Exercises

1. Much of normal daily life already depends on automation, from low-level alarm clocks to advanced guidance and tracking systems, and turns to AI and expert knowledge systems for help. Keep a journal for 1 day from waking up with an

alarm clock, using timers on microwave ovens, and checking e-mail with automatic spam filters, etc., to using Internet agents for route planning, shopping, etc.

2. Use an automation trust scale to gauge your level of trust in automation.

3. Play the "imitation game" using text messaging or instant messaging and randomly play either a human or a human imitating a machine. See if others can determine which you are.

4. To what extent do you anthropomorphize machines? Do you think that it is good, bad, or irrelevant to relate to computers as if they had human characteristics?

5. Watch a science fiction movie. What aspects of AI and robots are used? Are they possible? What problems arise between humans and machines?

References

Adams, J. A. (1989). *Human factors engineering*. New York: Macmillan.

Barr, A., & Feigenbaum, E. (Eds.). (1982). *The handbook of artificial intelligence, vol. 2*. Stanford, CA: Heuris Tech Press.

Bem, S. L. (1974). The measurement of psychological androgyny. *Journal of Consulting and Clinical Psychology*, 42, 155–162.

Franklin, S., & Graesser, A. (1996). Is it an agent, or just a program?: A taxonomy for autonomous agents. In J. P. Müller, M. J. Wooldridge, and N. R. Jennings (Eds.), *Intelligent Agents III–Proceedings of the third international workshop on agent theories, architectures, and languages. Lecture notes in artificial intelligence, 1193* (pp. 21–35), New York: Springer-Verlag.

Gabriel, R. P. (1996). *Patterns of software: Tales from the software community*. New York: Oxford University Press.

Gibson, J. J. (1979). *The ecological approach to visual perception*. Boston: Houghton-Mifflin.

Hilburn, B. J., Byrne, E., & Parasuraman, R. (1997). The effect of adaptive air traffic control (ATC) decision aiding on controller mental workload. In M. Mouloua & J. M. Koonce (Eds.), *Human–automation interaction: Research and practice* (pp. 84–91). Mahwah, NJ: Erlbaum.

Hogan, J. P. (1998). *Mind matters: Exploring the world of artificial intelligence*. Del Rey.

Jaccard, J. (1981). Toward theories of persuasion and belief change. *Journal of Personality and Social Psychology*, 40(2), 260–269.

Jiang, J. J., Klein, G., & Vedder, R. G. (2000). Persuasive expert systems: The influence of confidence and discrepancy. *Computers in Human Behavior, 16*, 99–109.

Kaber, D. B., & Riley, J. M. (1999). Adaptive automation of a dynamic control task based on secondary task workload measurement. *International Journal of Cognitive Ergonomics, 3*, 169–187.

Kolski, C., & Le Strugeon, E. (1998). A review of intelligent human–machine interfaces in the light of the ARCH model. *International Journal of Human–Computer Interaction, 10*(3), 193–231.

McCarthy, J., Minsky, M. L., Rochester, N., & Shannon, C. E. (1955, August 31). A proposal for the Dartmouth Summer Research Project on Artificial Intelligence. Retrieved March 19, 2008, from www-formal.stanford.edu/jmc/history/dartmouth/dartmouth.html

McCorduck, P. (1979). *Machines who think: A personal inquiry into the history and prospects of artificial intelligence*. San Francisco, CA: W. H. Freeman.

Milani, A., & Marcugini, S. (1999). Stockbot: A monitoring and acting software agent for stock markets. *International Journal of Intelligent Systems in Accounting, Finance & Management*, *8*(1), 3–14.

Murphy, E. D., & Norman, K. L. (1998). Beyond supervisory control: Human performance in the age of autonomous machines. In M. W. Scerbo & M. Moulous (Eds.), *Automation technology and human performance: Current research and trends* (pp. 235–239). Mahwah, NJ: Erlbaum.

Nass, C., Moon, Y., Fogg, B. J., Reeves, B., & Dryer, D. C. (1995). Can computer personalities be human personalities? *International Journal of Human–Computer Studies*, 43, 223–239.

Nass, C., Steuer, J., Henriksen, L., & Dryer, D. C. (1994). Machines, social attributions, and ethopoeia: Performance assessments of computer subsequent to "self-" and "other-" evaluations. *International Journal of Human–Computer Studies*, 40, 543–559.

Parasuraman, R., Sheridan, T. B., & Wickens, C. D. (2000). A model for types and levels of human interaction with automation. *IEEE Transactions on Systems, Man, and Cybernetics – Part A: Systems and Humans*, *30*(3), 286–297.

Price, H. E. (1985). The allocation of functions in systems. *Human Factors*, 27, 33–45.

Searle, J. (1980). Minds, brains, and programs. *Behavioral and Brain Sciences*, *3*(3), 417–457.

Shannon, C. (1950). Programming a computer for playing chess. *Philosophical Magazine, Ser.* 7, 41(314).

Shneiderman, B. (1993). Beyond intelligent machines: Just do it! *IEEE Software*, *10*(1), 100–103.

Shneiderman, B. (1994). Looking for the bright side of user interface agents. *ACM Interactions*, 2(1), 13–15.

Skitka, L. J., Mosier, K., & Burdick, M. D. (2000). Accountability and automation bias. *International Journal of Human–Computer Studies*, 52(4), 701–717.

Turing, A. M. (1950). Computing machinery and intelligence. *Mind*, 49, 433–460. Retrieved March 19, 2008, from http://cogprints.org/499/00/turing.html

Winograd, R., & Flores, C. (1987). *Understanding computer and cognition: A new foundation for design*. Reading, MA: Addison-Wesley.

Zuboff, S. (1988). *In the age of the smart machine: The future of work and power*. New York: Basic Books.

Fourteen

Assistive and Augmentive Technologies

Scenario 1

How would you have felt in the mid-1990s if you were a blind computer user familiar with MS-DOS and various computer languages who just learned that you have to switch to Windows? With your current setup, you can use the keyboard and have your output printed on a Braille printer. You can even have it read to you with a speech synthesizer. But now you hear that Microsoft Windows with its GUI is taking over. How will you cope with visual interfaces? Glen Gordon, now vice president of Freedom Scientific, was one of those users. Glen worked part time for Henter-Joyce, the company that introduced JAWS, a program that converted text output to voice synthesis. "I was concerned that I could be worked out of a job [then at UCLA], so I had a great passion to get Windows to talk!" Glen and others went to work on the problem and helped create JAWS for Windows. He continues to work with the developers of JAWS to improve the interface for blind and low vision users. (Adapted from Kendrick, 2006.)

Scenario 2

Mark put on his flight suit, gloves, and helmet. He walked up to his new bird, the Boeing X-51, boarded the plane, and strapped himself in. The suit connected with the onboard flight system and went live. Today, Mark would pull the X-51 up to almost Mach 7. He would need all the backup he could get from the computer systems, especially from the flight guidance system, the augmented reality system, and the augmented cognition system. The augmented reality system would overlay his heads-up display with flight information and graphic pathways in the air. The augmented cognition system would monitor his brain functions and use that information to determine how much shared control of the operations to allocate to Mark over the automated systems. If worse came to worse, Mark knew that even if he passed out, the automatic guidance system would carry him home.

Overview

Technology poses two challenges to individuals with disabilities. The first challenge pertains to access to the real world. How can technology be used to aid those who are disabled and restore an independent lifestyle? The second pertains to access to the cyberworld. How can technology be designed to provide human–computer interfaces that allow persons with disabilities equal access to online information? This was the concern of Glen Gordon in Scenario 1.

At the beginning of this chapter, we discuss *assistive technology*, a broad term that includes assistive, adaptive, and rehabilitative devices and *universal access*, the idea of equal access to information regardless of disability. Assistive technology can be used to provide greater independence for persons with disabilities by enabling them to perform tasks that they previously could not perform on their own. Universal access provides equal opportunities for this population to have access to education, knowledge, and information vital to their well-being (Carbonell & Stephanidis, 2003).

In the second part of this chapter, we look at new opportunities. How can technology be used to enhance our abilities to perceive; be alert and vigilant; and comprehend, think, and solve problems above natural, unaided levels? A number of the advances in assistive technologies can be applied and even ramped up to augment the abilities for everyone. We discuss the psychological implications of these technologies as they extend the range of our senses from normal vision, for example, to bionic eyes sensitive to a wider spectrum of electromagnetic waves. We also look into enhancing self-regulatory systems involving measurements of brain activities. The term *augmented cognition* is used to capture the possibility that we might be able to accelerate our mental abilities to think and respond faster and even to create a closed loop synergy between brain activity and AI. Scenario 2 is one of many examples where the military hopes to rely on these new systems. They are fascinating ideas, and like AI, they have a life both in reality and in science fiction.

Accessibility

As technology and the human–computer interface becomes the way in which we interact with the world, a disparity has arisen between those with disabilities and those without due to differences in accessibility to information. The Americans with Disabilities Act of 1990 is a wide-ranging civil rights law that prohibits discrimination based on disability. Disability is defined as any "physical or mental impairment that substantially limits a major life activity." In addition to banning discrimination in employment, Titles II and III require provisions for physical access for persons with disabilities to public and commercial facilities. Moreover, Title IV requires functionally equivalent telecommunication services for those with disabilities. When Title IV took effect in the early 1990s, it led to the installation of public teletypewriter machines and other telecommunication devices for the deaf, such as telecommunication relay services that convert text to speech and speech to text. Currently, many such calls and communications are mediated over the Internet and are being replaced by e-mail and instant messaging.

In 1998, the U.S. Congress amended the Rehabilitation Act of 1973 to require federal agencies to make their electronic and information technology accessible to persons with disabilities. Section 508 was enacted 1) to eliminate barriers in information technology, 2) to make available new opportunities for persons with disabilities, and 3) to encourage the development of technologies to achieve these goals. The law applies to all federal agencies when they develop, procure, maintain, or use electronic and information technology. Under Section 508, agencies must give both employees and members of the public who are disabled access to information that is comparable to the access available to others.

According to the 1999 Survey of Income and Program Participation by the U.S. Census, there was a more than 30 percent difference in usage of the Web by those with and without visual impairments (Gerber & Kirchner, 2001). There were a number of reasons for this difference, stemming primarily from the fact that Web pages were initially and principally designed for persons with normal vision. Even when text versions of Web sites are provided so that screen readers using voice synthesis read the pages to the blind user, pages are often poorly designed, making it difficult for the user to navigate the information. Section 508 was used to establish acceptable compliance with the law for Web page design. For example, it required that images include an HTML "alt" tag that gives a text description of each image.

Finally, it has been the challenge of computer manufacturers to design interfaces for universal accessibility that incorporate tools and alternatives to make the interface easier for the vision, hearing, or motor impaired. A good example is the Apple Universal Access panel in Mac OS X. Figure 14.1 shows one control panel with options for speech synthesis for users who are blind and options for display enhancement for users who are vision impaired.

Assistive Technologies

There are many forms of assistive technologies that are not computer driven – from corrective lenses and hearing aids to walkers and wheelchairs. Braille is

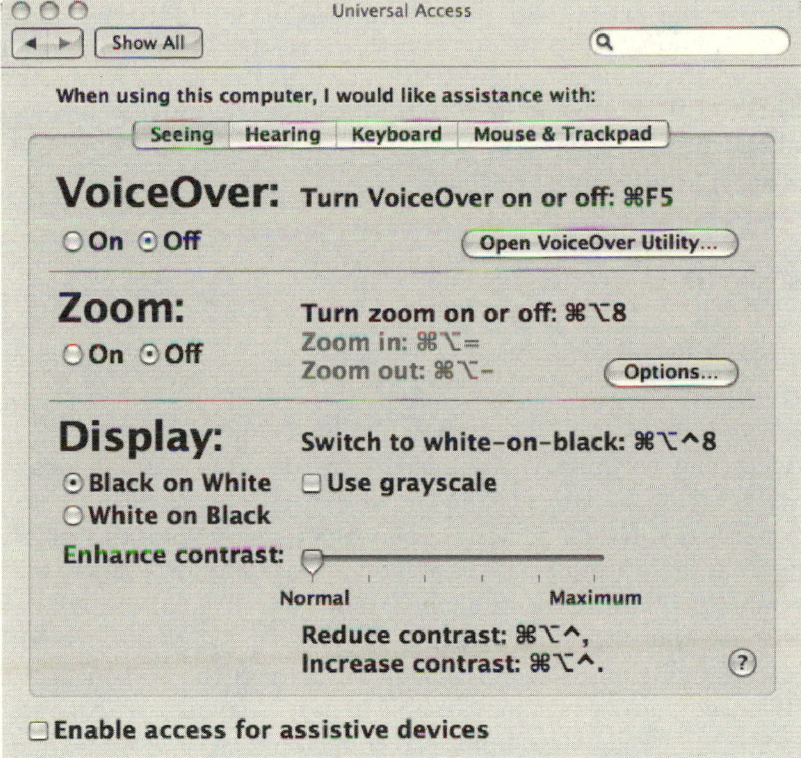

Figure 14.1. Apple Universal Access panel in Mac OS X.

an assistive technology for the vision impaired, and American Sign Language (ASL) for the hearing impaired. With the advent of computers, servomechanisms, and digital technology, the assistive technologies are becoming increasingly automated, intelligent, powerful, and effective.

Assistive technologies, like the human nervous systems, can be divided into sensory and motor support systems. Sensory systems are defined by their mode, generally visual or auditory. Assistive technologies work by either processing the input within the same mode or transforming it for input to an alternative mode. Within a mode, the technology may amplify the signal or transform it in some way to enhance features and reduce noise, as listed in the first column of Table 14.1. If one mode is unusable, the technology may transform the information to be input to a different mode, as listed in the second column of Table 14.1.

Table 14.1. Taxonomy of Assistive Effects for Vision and Hearing

	Amplifying	Mode switching
Vision	Corrective/focusing Enhancing	Tactile (Braille, raised contour) Auditory
Auditory	Amplifying/filtering Enhancing	Tactile (vibration) Visual

Motor assistive systems are defined by parts of the body such as the legs, arms, hands, torso, and vocal tract. Again, assistive technologies may work either within the same motor system (e.g., leg affecter neurons controlling a prosthetic leg) or cross system (e.g., back muscle movement controlling a prosthetic hand). Vocal commands may even be used to control motor systems such as a power wheelchair.

Sensory Impairments

Visual Impairments

Visual disabilities fall into three types: blindness, low vision, and color blindness. According to 2002 U.S. Census estimates, there are approximately 8 million individuals living in the United States who have difficulty seeing words or letters (Steinmetz, 2006). The American Federation for the Blind estimates that there are at least 1.5 million blind computer users in the United States alone. A blind user is one who cannot use a visual display at all and must rely on mode switching, such as Braille displays that convert the text to the tactile mode and screen readers that convert the text to the auditory mode. Users with low vision may be able to use visual displays that are amplified in some way using large fonts, screen magnifiers, or close reading of the screen. Colorblind users have a full array of visual abilities but are unable to distinguish individual colors or color combinations, depending on the individual. This means that although color can be used freely in Web design and software products, color should not be the sole means used to convey information.

Braille displays and screen readers can provide accessibility to computers for persons who are visually impaired, but only if the displays are designed to provide the information efficiently in textual form. Table 14.2 shows some of the problems encountered by this population when trying to use the Internet.

Although most information can be converted to text and then to Braille or the spoken word, the real challenge for persons who are visually impaired is access to image and graph information to perceive patterns, trends, and overviews. Relief maps, surfaces with varying texture or temperature, and 3-D objects and surfaces can be used to switch from a visual to a tactile display of information. However, 3-D tactile displays are extremely expensive as either dynamic output or printed surfaces. Figure 14.2 shows several of these types of interfaces.

A second alternative is to use sound to convey spatial and quantitative information. Sound can vary in loudness, pitch, timbre, and spatial location to convey information. The Sonification Sandbox is one approach (Walker & Kramer, 2004). Data in a series that can be displayed as a line graph, such as the population in a country over time, can be presented as a series of tones

Table 14.2. Some Problems Encountered by the Visually Impaired When Using the Internet

Listening to synthesized speech for extended periods of time can become quite irritating.

Images cannot be understood by blind users unless Alt-tags are used to explain the images.

Absolute text sizes set by the Web designer that cannot be changed by the user can make text difficult to read for users with low vision.

If emphasis is given by a change in the text's color, font size, or any other characteristics, it will be lost on the blind computer user.

Blind computer users cannot enjoy online video if transcripts are not provided.

Graphs and charts are difficult to decipher with a screen reader without a meaningful summary.

Busy backgrounds and a lack of contrast can make it difficult for low vision computer users to read text.

Blind computer users spend a lot more time sorting through spam e-mail than sighted users and end up hearing words that might be rather offensive to them.

CAPTCHAS (Completely Automated Public Turing test to tell Computers and Humans Apart), which requires users to decipher the text in a garbled message to make sure the user is an actual human and not just a spam robot trying to get into the system, cannot be used by blind users.

generated by the Sonification Sandbox. Even multiple lines can be presented with chords or tones that vary in pitch, loudness, duration, and timbre.

Converting geographic data for persons with vision impairments is a particular problem. How can a blind person recognize a cluster of states that have a high incidence of HIV or the directional orientation of states with increasing levels of skin cancer? Zhao, Smith, Norman, Plaisant, and Shneiderman (2005) developed an interface called "iSonic" to do just that. In this interface, the U.S. map was represented with east-west states sounding in stereo headphones from left to right and north-south as high to low tones. State boundaries were indicated by clicks, and map edges by a bell. Users could let the system scan the whole map top to bottom and left to right or

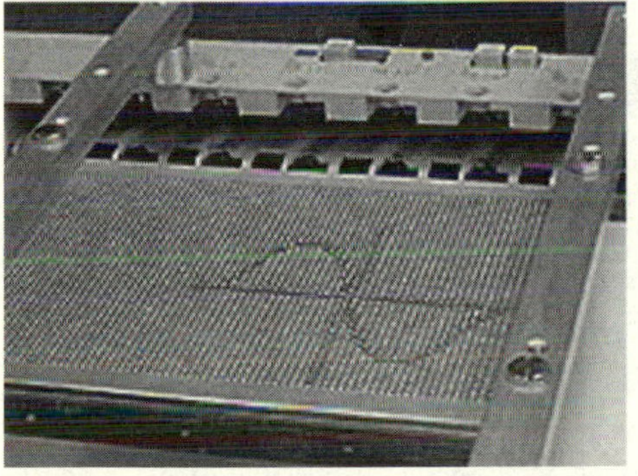

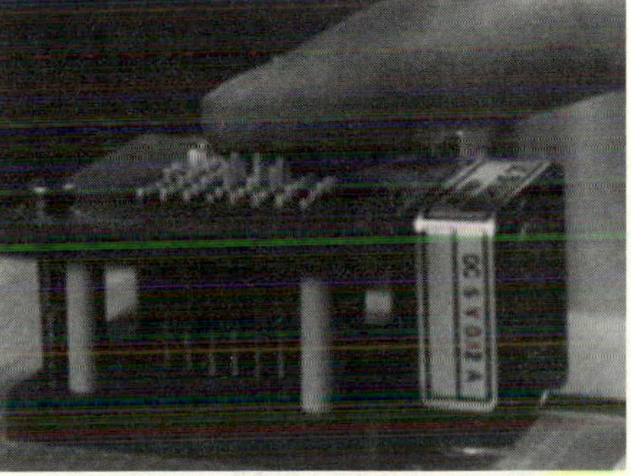

Figure 14.2. Examples of 3-D tactile interfaces: NIST 400 pin display (left) and 8 × 8 tactile display (right). (From Forschungszentrum Karlsruhe [Karlsruhe Research Centre], Karlsruhe/BW, Germany.)

explore the map on their own using cursor keys or a touch pad. Usability testing suggested a number of improvements, but, overall, users could identify and discriminate geographic patterns.

Auditory Impairments

According to the 2002 U.S. Census Data, there are an estimated 8 million people living in the United States who have difficulty hearing conversation, with 1 million having severe difficulty (Steinmetz, 2006). Moreover, individuals working in noisy or distracting environments also face accessibility limitations.

People suffering from hearing loss or from limited hearing are unable to hear sounds or cannot distinguish individual sounds from background noise. Generally, hearing loss does not prohibit a computer user from effectively working with computers because current software and Web interfaces rely heavily on visual displays, but hearing loss can inhibit interactions that rely on audio. Problems occur with devices and services such as videoconferencing, telecommunications, podcasting, and a myriad of multimedia devices and services that rely on auditory cues to convey important information. As these devices become more prevalent and penetrate more deeply into everyday life, designers and manufacturers will have to take the needs of persons with hearing impairments into serious consideration (Goldberg & Freed, 1998). There are a number of recommendations and guidelines for addressing the needs of users who are hearing impaired. For example, audio information should be supplemental with visual information, and interactions should not be based solely on auditory information.

Depending on the type of impairment, the use of amplification, filtering, and/or enhancement may be appropriate. For those with minor hearing loss, interfaces should give the user complete control over the frequency and volume of audio cues so that users with a limited range of hearing can adjust the sound to their particular tolerance to make the information usable. In noisy environments, "noise canceling" earphones can be used.

For those with major or complete deafness, mode switching is required. Frequencies can be converted to tactile vibrations so that the user can feel the sound particularly for rhythm and beat. In addition, music can be converted to visual patterns by visualizers such as G-Force and Advanced Visualization Studio and used in popular music programs such as iTunes and Windows Media Player. Synesthesia is the underlying neurological basis for visualizers. Through the neurological mixing of the senses, one may be able to hear colors, see sounds, and taste tactile sensations (Ramachandran & Hubbard, 2003). A good visualizer will take advantage of the correspondence between certain tones and colors, chords and shapes, to convey feeling and meaning (Hepting & Gerhard, 2005). In combination with tactile vibration, visualizations specifically designed for the deaf can be very effective.

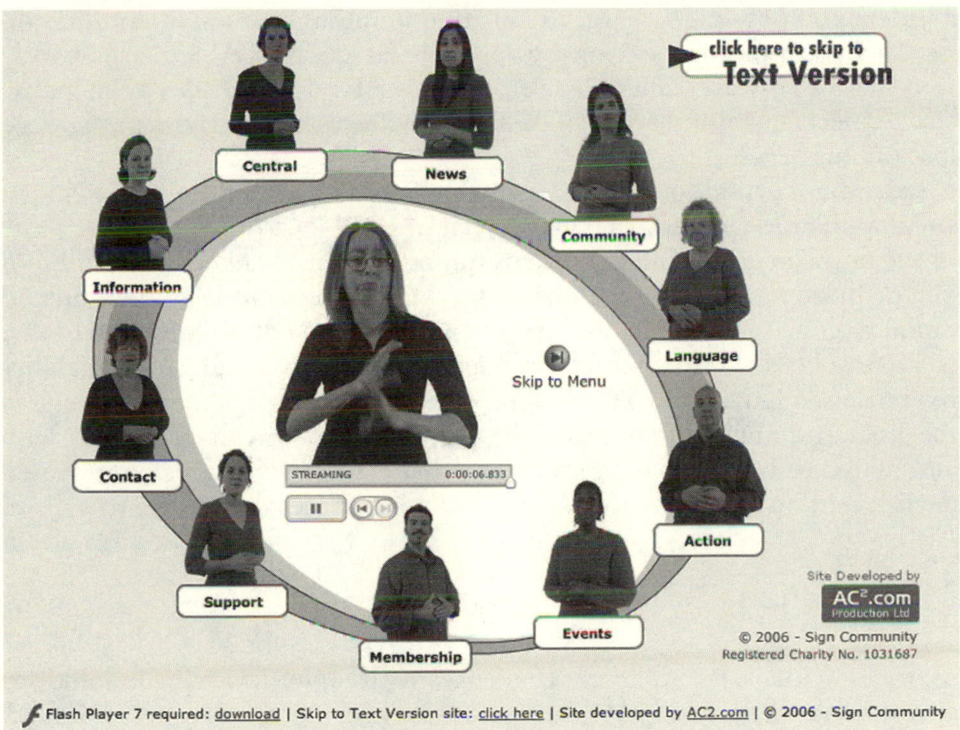

Figure 14.3. Home page of the Sign Community of the British Deaf Association (http://bda.org.uk/). (© 2006 – Sign Community.)

For auditory speech communication, one must switch mode to visual text. Instead of speech, communication takes advantage of keyboard input and screen display of text. Although speech recognition software continues to have problems, it may provide a good first pass at converting speech to text for persons with hearing impairments.

Interestingly, according to the National Association of the Deaf most people in the United States with hearing loss learn ASL as their first language and English as their second language. This is a frequently overlooked fact of which software and Web designers should be aware. Figure 14.3 shows an example of a Web site, employing soundless flash-based animations designed specifically for users with British Sign Language (BSL) as their first language.

Motor Impairments

The United Nations estimates that there are nearly 1 billion people with some sort of motor disability in the world. Generally speaking, these impairments affect a person's ability to physically interact with and manipulate the world around them. Motor impairments cover a wide range of disabilities but are generally classified by the severity of impairment. Most of these impairments arise from congenital diseases and conditions or are the result of accident and physical damage. Among the common causes of motor disabilities are Parkinson's disease, amyotrophic lateral sclerosis (ALS; also known as Lou Gehrig's disease), multiple sclerosis, muscular dystrophy, cerebral palsy, stroke, neck/spinal injury, brain/head injury, arthritis, and loss of digits or loss of limb.

Individuals with motor impairments face small and large motor tremors, small and large muscle weakness, partial or total lack of control over parts of the body, neuronal interference (resulting in over- or undercontraction of one or more muscle groups), involuntary and uncontrolled motion, limited mobility, limb loss, and misshapen extremities. Motor disabilities lead to two basic problems: 1) the inability to manipulate objects, and 2) the inability to move around freely. The first problem can result in limited access to the human–computer interface. The second problem can be helped with automated wheelchairs, braces, and prosthetic devices. However, automated devises require the ability to manipulate the interfaces used to control them.

Manipulation

Many individuals face different challenges with input devices. The solutions may involve methods of stabilizing or simplifying motor movements or finding alternative muscle groups to replace those that are impaired. Stabilization and simplification may involve the use of larger and fewer buttons for keyboard input. According to Fitts' law from Chapter 5, the difficulty of hitting a target button will be reduced the closer and larger that it is. Gesture input using a stylus on a PDA similar to PalmOS Graffiti has been successful in some cases. A technique called "EdgeWrite" allows the user to write along the edges and corners of a plastic square mounted over the input area (Wobbrock & Myers, 2007). EdgeWrite relies on the physical edges and corners to provide stabilization during motion. Letters or commands are recognized by the order of the corners hit. Research has shown that moderate wiggles and tremors do not affect recognition.

When the arms and hands cannot be used to control mouse movement, input may be accomplished by head or eye movements. Cursor positioning may be accomplished through head-mounted wireless pointers or even with eye tracking devices. Alternatively, voice commands can be used to control devices with speech recognition software (Arnold, 1998).

Locomotion

Mobility may be facilitated using automated wheelchairs and scooters. If the individual has good hand coordination, these devices can be controlled using a joystick or other hand controls. Automated prosthetic limbs are being developed so that individuals may walk with controlled leg movements and balance. Robotics, AI, and computer vision are being used to construct automated wheelchairs similar to autonomous moon rovers (Gomi & Griffith, 2004; Simpson, LoPresti, Hayashi, Nourbakhsh, & Miller, 2004).

Brain–Computer Interface

What happens when a person is so motor impaired that there is virtually no output channel, not even eye blink or breath? With severe paralysis caused by stroke or ALS, a person may be so impaired that he or she has no motor or ocular control whatsoever. Such a person experiences what is called the "locked-in" syndrome. The mind may be functioning, but it has no way to express itself. Researchers have tried to use brain activity from electroencephalograms (EEGs) and other brain imaging techniques to allow the person to communicate with the world (Farwell & Donchin, 1988; Wolpaw, Birbaumer, McFarland, Pfurtscheller, & Vaughan, 2002). The basic idea of the brain–computer interface (BCI) is shown in Figure 14.4. The engineering problems have involved what brain activity to record, how to process the signal, and how to translate the signal to control devices. The psychological problems have been determining what thought patterns can be picked up as detectable brain activity and training the individual to use these brain waves.

In the mid-1990s, Niels Birbaumer of the University of Tübingen, Tübingen, Germany, used EEG recordings of slow cortical potential to give paralyzed patients limited control over a computer cursor. Ten patients were trained to move a cursor by controlling their brainwaves. Unfortunately, the process was very slow. It required more than an hour for patients to write 100 characters with the cursor, and training often took many months (Birbaumer et al., 1999). More recent research has focused on developing technology that would allow users to choose the brain signals they found easiest to operate a BCI, such as mu and beta waves. For example, Peckham used a sixty-four-electrode EEG skullcap to return limited hand movements to quadriplegic Jim Jatich (Maloney, 2000). As Jatich concentrated on simple but opposite concepts such as up and down, his beta-rhythm EEG output was analyzed using software to identify patterns in the noise. A basic pattern was identified and used to control a switch. Above-average activity turned the switch on, and below average turned it off. In addition to controlling a computer cursor, Jatich also used the signals to drive the nerve controllers embedded in his hands, restoring some movement.

A promising line of research has made use of P300 signals. Patterns of P300 waves are generated involuntarily when a person sees something that is recognized as familiar in a series of unfamiliar items. The P300 response allows the BCI to decode categories of thoughts without having to subject the patient to months of training first. Bayliss and Ballard (2000) demonstrated that volunteers wearing virtual reality helmets could control elements in a

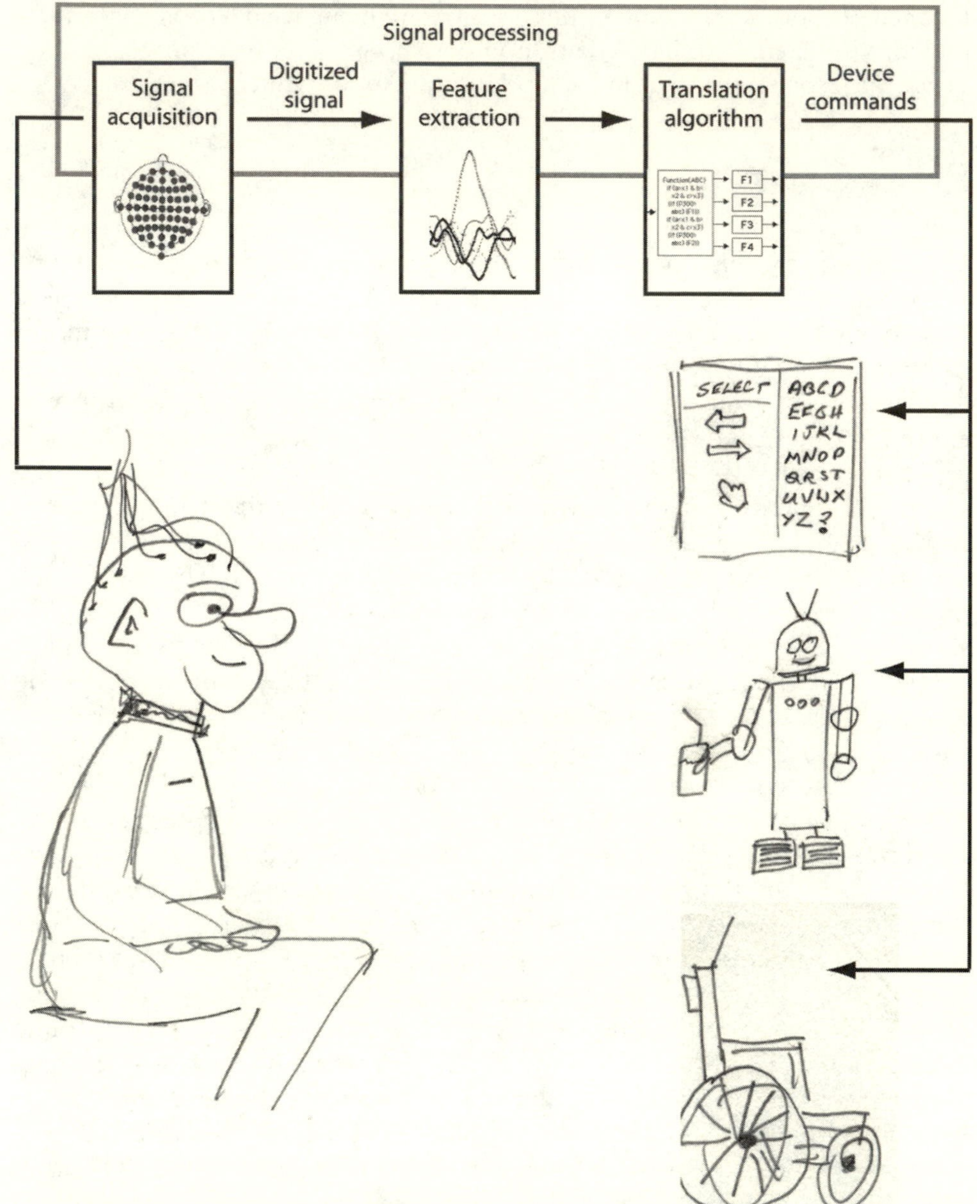

Figure 14.4. Schematic of the brain–computer interface. (Adapted from Wolpaw et al., 2002.)

virtual world using their P300 EEG readings. They could turn lights on and off and bring a simulated car to a stop.

Although intriguing, the development and empirical results for noninvasive BCIs have been extremely limited and, at present, provide an interface that is less than acceptable for the motor impaired user, let alone the nonimpaired user. Chapter 16 explores future potentials for invasive, direct-wired BCIs.

Cognitive Impairments

Cognitive disabilities generally correspond to the categories of abilities covered in cognitive psychology: memory, perception, thinking, and problem-solving impairments. Impaired memory can affect the storage and retrieval functions from the sensory store, short-term memory, and long-term memory. Impaired perception includes problems with encoding and decoding information, sensory discrimination, and attention problems. Limitations in thinking are often concerned with the generalization from what has been previously learned to current application, categorization and sequencing of items, and abstracting cause-and-effect relationships. Problem-solving limitations involve impediments with problem recognition, recognition of potential solutions, and implementation of solutions.

According to U.S. Census data (Steinmetz, 2006), there are roughly 8 million citizens with some form of cognitive/language deficit, not including those in institutions. The elderly comprise the largest group of persons who are cognitively impaired in the United States and probably worldwide. In persons older than 65 years, 5 percent of Americans have Alzheimer's disease, and in persons older than 80 years, 20 percent have it. Mild forms of cognitive impairment related to aging include dementia and vascular neuralgia. In persons older than 65 years, dementia affects 5 percent of the population; in persons older than 80 years, it affects almost 30 percent. These are conditions that can lead to a progressive intellectual decline and impairment of judgment, reasoning, learning, and attention. Almost 3 million Americans are mentally retarded. These are individuals who have IQs of less than 70. Finally, there are a number of individuals who are cognitively impaired as a result of an accident involving head trauma or from a stroke. These individuals are often both mentally and physically impaired. They have needs that require addressing cognitive and physical challenges.

Technology can both impose barriers to accessibility for the cognitively challenged and help overcome them, depending on how the interface is designed and suited for the individual needs of the person (Lazar, 2007). The barriers are evidenced in the U.S. Census data (Steinmetz, 2006). Just more than 60 percent of individuals ages 15 to 64 years with no disability use a computer, and more than 50 percent use the Internet at home. However, for individuals with severe disabilities, only 36 percent use a computer and 29 percent use the Internet at home, and these percentages are drastically reduced for individuals 65 years and older. In general, technology raises the bar, imposing high levels of complexity and lengthy sequences of steps, abstract symbols and graphics, steep learning curves, and perceptually cluttered screens. Even users with normal cognitive abilities are challenged. However, when technology is redesigned, simplified, and enhanced with cognitive aids, it can help the cognitively impaired live independent, self-fulfilling lives. Numerous case studies exist, showing how caregivers have used computer technology to both assist and rehabilitate individuals with cognitive

Table 14.3. Guidelines for Designers of Interfaces for Persons Who Are Cognitively Impaired

Remove the need for reading and writing skills in Web exploration through graphic representations and point-and-click interfaces.
Create search techniques that are easy to use and make them consistent across sites, providing as many graphical and point-and-click options as possible.
Reduce information overload by simplifying text or providing options for abbreviated content.
Develop specialized software agents to assist users who are language impaired and learning disabled with searches.
Provide useful ranking systems for search engine results.
Provide the opportunity for audio and video representations to cue subject recognition.

From Singh et al. (1998).

impairments from traumatic brain injury, stroke, and other causes (Cole & Dehdashti, 1998).

Interface Design Solutions

There are a number of interface design principles and solutions that can assist users with cognitive impairments (Singh, Gedeon, & Rho, 1988). A sampling of these guidelines is listed in Table 14.3. Interestingly, these principles can assist other users as well, particularly in high cognitive demand situations. In general, these principles reduce and simplify text. When choices and selections are required, graphical implementations are usually the best. Cognitively disabled users usually have problems with entering input and making sense of the screen output. Simple, graphical designs with minimal abstraction are helpful. The cognitively impaired can be easily distracted, so minimizing the distraction caused by error beeps or other forms of auditory output is advised.

External Memory Aids

Sequential operations can pose many problems for the user who is cognitively disabled. Maintaining the order of operations, remembering where you are in the process, and following associated logic can be difficult. Even daily routines of personal hygiene and meal preparation can be daunting. "If-then" conditionals can be particularly confusing (e.g., if it is Sunday, I go to church). In Chapter 7, we discuss the use of external, digital memory devices to supplement our internal memories. These devices can provide meaningful cues at given intervals and help keep a user on track using automated post-it notes and programmed alerts.

A major problem, however, is that computer interfaces themselves present considerable memory demands on users trying to access information. Consequently, it is essential that human–computer interfaces provide memory aids and assists, particularly for users who are cognitively impaired. For example, when navigating Web sites, memory for sequences of steps and for locations should be aided by showing site maps and bread crumbs. Help systems need to be totally reconceptualized and redesigned for those who are cognitively impaired.

A common type of memory aid is the "step-by-step" communicator based on the idea of checklists and flip chart prompts. For those with language impairments, this may be implemented using a digital voice recorder or a handheld digital display showing pictures of each step. These devices can be programmed on the fly by caregivers to provide users with voice instructions to help them stay on task and focused. They can also serve the function of helping language impaired users construct and focus their thoughts by recording time-delayed speech, and then playing back the recording so that they can communicate cohesively and effectively with others.

A common problem for persons who are cognitively impaired and for individuals with obsessive-compulsive disorder is remembering the steps they have already completed. Event recording using cameras or video recorders can supplement a person's faulty episodic memory. One interesting research project used cabinet-mounted video cameras to keep track of the steps of a person who is using a recipe to cook (Tran, Calcaterra, & Mynatt, 2005). Users could play back the recording to check whether they had, for example, added salt. Head-mounted minicameras can also be used, but the challenge is how to code and store meaningful events rather than just raw video.

Alternative Keyboards

QWERTY keyboards with scores of numbers and symbols can be intimidating to persons who are cognitively challenged, particularly those who are language impaired. Alternative keyboards are graphically oriented input devices, which use images and pictures instead of text. Response boards have been commonly used for aiding communication with those who are speech/language impaired and are extensible to environmental controls (e.g., powered beds, lights, television, heat). Forms of these devices have been adapted to serve as alternative user input for computing devices using plastic sheet overlays. Depending on the context, the caregiver can select the appropriate board and place it over the pressure-sensitive pad. Figure 14.5 shows a mockup of one such response pad. Computer touch screens and digital handheld boards have the advantage over the static response boards in that they can be dynamically changed to automate input by the user. Although still very expensive, touch screen technologies used by Microsoft Surface and the Apple iTouch will allow alternative keyboards on both large and small devices, respectively.

Personal Digital Assistants

A small portable/personal device that maintains one's schedule, to-do lists, contacts, personal notes, and so on, can serve as an external aid to all

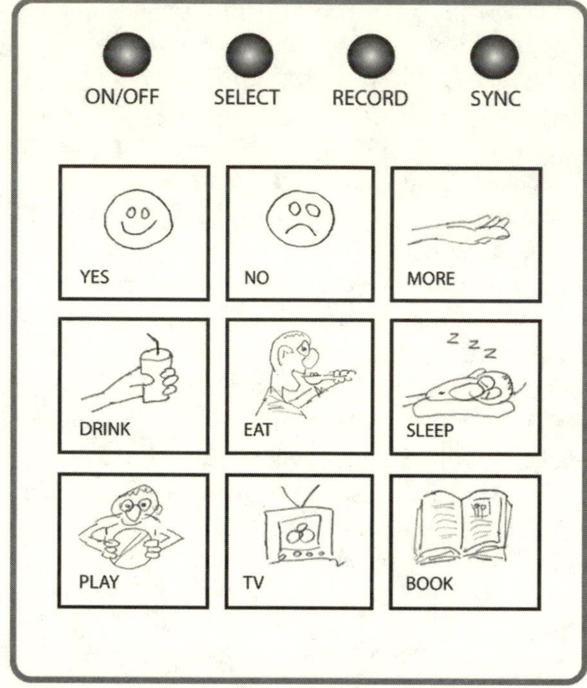

Figure 14.5. Mockup of a dynamic response keyboard for the cognitively impaired.

individuals, including those who are cognitively impaired. PDAs have developed considerable adaptability for use as assistive technologies. One of the most salient applications for persons who are cognitively disabled is the reduction of complex functionality typical of the large computer display and standard keyboard to a simple, small display with limited input. PDAs have forced engineers to redesign the interface for simplicity, while still providing a complete but alternative input communications system in one device. PDAs can, of course, be linked to computer networks to provide any functionality desired, and their displays can be reprogrammed and modified for the cognitive needs of the user (Carmien, 2002). As PDAs are designed for more rugged use, they will become even more applicable for assistive technologies.

Cognitive Agents

As research in AI develops, a rich area of application will be cognitive assistance. The task of a cognitive agent will be to take the problem situation that a person is experiencing and render it interpretable, meaningful, and doable by the person subject to the cognitive impairment. For example, a person with attention problems may want to buy a bathing suit online but is overwhelmed with browsing catalogs, distracted by pictures, and unable to find options on cluttered screens. The cognitive agent should be able to reformat the screens by focusing, zooming, and enhancing relevant areas of the interface and hiding information irrelevant to the task, such as banner ads, scrolling headlines, and pop-up windows. Cognitive agents may provide help with sequenced tasks by providing checklists and reminders. The hope is that cognitive agents could actually serve as effective help systems in stark contrast to the current help systems, which serve mostly to frustrate normal users. Combined with PDAs, wireless technology, and ubiquitous computer environments, cognitive agents could assist individuals with daily routines, providing them with an independent lifestyle. Caseworkers could program the agents and later check the status of the person's activities on a routine basis. The cognitive agent would essentially act as proxy for the immediate caregiver when he or she is not available.

Augmentive Technologies

The general purpose of interactive technologies is to facilitate, supplement, and extend our abilities above and beyond their normal levels. The first part of this chapter dealt with technologies to assist individuals with deficits. The purpose of assistive technologies is to bring individuals with impairments up to speed, to open the doors of accessibility, and to level the playing field for them. As suggested in Chapter 3, our models of HCI include synergistic combinations to allow individuals to augment their functions beyond those normally possible. In the following sections, we discuss augmentive technologies. Some of these have been touched on in previous chapters, but in this chapter we particularly emphasize those that provide close couplings between human abilities and technology.

Extending Our Senses

The telescope and microscope use optics to extend our visual senses by multiplication of image size. Infrared, x-rays, ultrasound, and computed tomography scans add to our visual input by extending the electromagnetic spectrum used for imaging. Most devices that accomplish this augmentation are rather separate from the user and involve complicated procedures and user interfaces. However, devices such as head-mounted infrared viewers and autofocusing binoculars accomplish the function of augmenting vision in a more closely coupled way. Similarly, noise canceling and dynamic filtering headphones augment hearing in a closely coupled way.

Augmenting the senses can have two different effects. It can either add to channel complexity by adding information to the input array (e.g., a broader spectrum that could include infrared and ultraviolet waves or lower and higher sound frequencies) or by requiring added layers of control (e.g., manipulating depth and magnification or filters on sound). Alternatively, augmentation could simplify sensory input by focusing and filtering, making it easier to perceive contours, shapes, and patterns or to pick out particular voices or melodies to listen to. Will the average person use augmentive sensory technology? Probably not. However, in extreme situations (e.g., total darkness), hostile environments (e.g., combat, rescue missions, etc.), or recreational experiences (e.g., hunting, exploring, amusement), the use of these devices is very compelling.

Most augmentive sensory interfaces continue to use the natural human senses as input; however, there is considerable interest in bypassing the sensory receptors and augmenting sensory input using a direct connection to the nervous system. Because these ideas are still in their infancy and more the subject of science fiction, we save them for Chapter 16.

Extending Our Reach

In the same way that sensory input can be magnified, filtered, and enhanced, motor movements can be translated from input devices such as trackballs, joysticks, and data gloves to control mechanical devices such as a robot arm. Engineering and human factors psychology have had a long history of studying and developing mechanical controls for machines from airplanes to drill presses (Adams, 1997; Kantowitz & Sorkin, 1983). Computer technologies using digital signals, computational functions, and networks open up entirely new possibilities for motor control.

One such device is a *Waldo*. A Waldo is a remote manipulator. Its name comes from a novella by Robert A. Heinlein titled "Waldo" (1940). The story is about a crippled genius named Waldo who lived in an orbital habitat to avoid the effects of gravity, but he worked on Earth via remote manipulators that he developed. The devices were described as having the same shape and dexterity as the human hand. Current-day Waldos may have direct mechanical linkages, or they may be teleoperated over networks. Waldos vary from micromanipulators used in microscopic surgery or assembly in nanotechnology to megamanipulators that are used in heavy construction. Typically, they are operated by the hands, but they may be extended to any part of the body. Interestingly, Waldos have been used extensively by high-tech puppeteers such as Jim Henson (1936–1990) to control the movements of the puppets by using their own corresponding body movements.

Extending Our Minds

Augmented cognition is the idea of extending our cognitive abilities above normal levels to achieve higher levels of cognitive processing and awareness. As with assistive cognition, these involve perception, thinking, and problem solving. In particular, they involve metacognitive processes, which are used

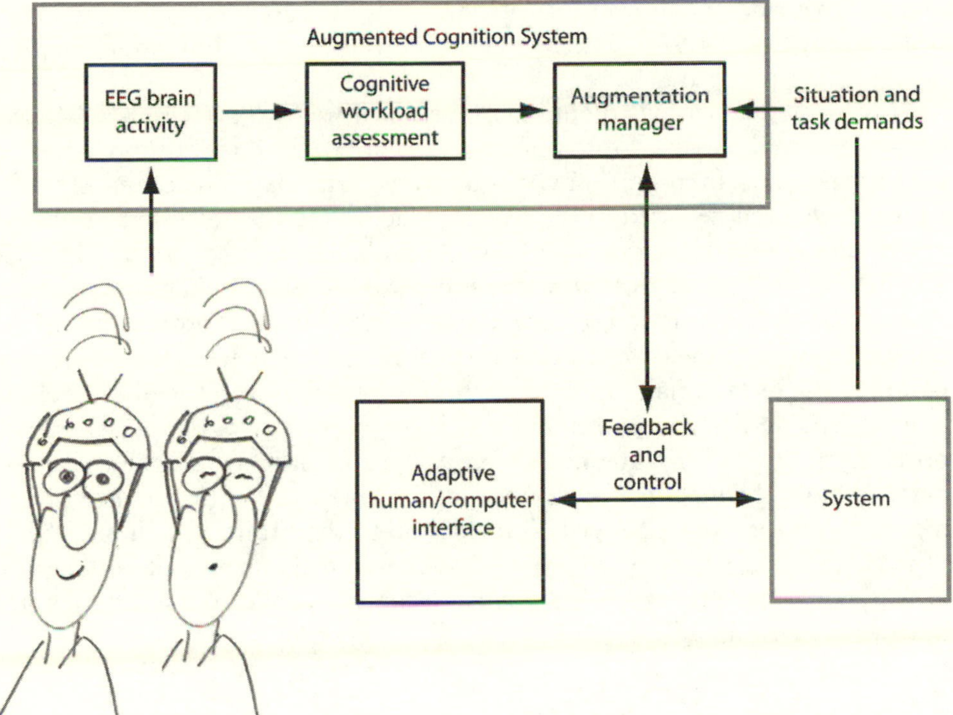

Figure 14.6. Schematic of an augmented cognition system.

to self-monitor and evaluate performance and attention (e.g., Pavel, Wang, & Li, 2002). At present, augmented cognition employs a noninvasive BCI to monitor brain activity. Scenario 2 describes an augmented cognitive system used by the military for command and control of complex human-machine systems, such as flying a fighter aircraft in combat situations. These systems attempt to evaluate our current physiological, emotional, and mental states, and intervene when the system deems necessary. As discussed in Chapter 13, such systems are essentially software agents that are assigned the task of monitoring cognitive processing and taking over life-critical functions when they detect severe human malfunctioning (Schmorrow, 2005). Berka et al. (2004) described an augmented cognitive system that uses a wireless EEG helmet to monitor alertness, cognitive processing, and memory systems. Figure 14.6 shows a schematic of an augmented cognitive system in conjunction with an AI software agent performing a high-demand task.

The augmented cognition system monitors the user's mental activities from a number of possible sensors (e.g., EEG, fMIR, GSR). These are used to infer the user's alertness and cognitive processing ability according to an acquired model of user mental processes. If the user is judged to be alert and well functioning, the system assigns the user the appropriate tasks. If the system judges the user to be operating at substandard levels, the augmentation manager reconfigures the tasks and displays to accommodate for the lower cognitive functioning. In the same way that automated systems provide a manual override in the event of machine failure, the augmented cognitive system provides a cognitive safety net in the event that the human in the loop fails to think properly.

At present, augmented cognition applies to the overall system in which the human and the machine are components and not to the cognitive processes of the human alone. In military, industrial, transportation, and communication systems, we are interested in the overall functioning of the system over and above the cognitive functioning of any one individual. In the future, one can imagine augmented cognition at the individual level in which a symbiotic, closely coupled interaction occurs between the cognitive processing of the human mind and the information processing of the machine. The human would provide the goals, motives, attitudes, and values, and the machine would provide the computational power of numeric, logic, and symbolic processing. For such an augmented cognitive system to work, the BCI must be two way. The machine must not only be able to read information from the brain, but it must also write information to the brain. It is unlikely that this will ever be possible with a noninvasive interface. Instead, it will require direct neural implants in the brain. Such techniques are discussed in Chapter 16.

End Thoughts

The old adage "Where there is a will, there is a way" comes to mind at the end of this chapter. The potential of the human mind, combined with endless possibilities of digital technology, give great hope to those with disabilities. The only threats to great advances in assistive technologies are apathy and lack of financial support. But like curb cuts and automatic doors, innovations for a few people can benefit many who may be momentarily or marginally impaired. Likewise, technological development for everyone's convenience, such as remote controls and AI agents, can prove particularly beneficial for those with impairments.

As psychologists interested in HCI, we are able to provide theory and methodology to help guide the development, testing, and application of assistive technologies. This is one of the many interdisciplinary opportunities that allows psychologists, computer scientists, engineers, and experts in disabilities to work together in collaborative developments. Almost all of the projects discussed in this chapter are the result of such collaborations.

In the end, we return to one of the overarching theories of purpose and motivation in HCI discussed in Chapters 3 and 10. We have a desire for and a fascination with transcending our given human limitations to attain greater powers. For the impaired, it is a necessity; for the rest, it is a dream. We seek higher levels of knowledge and understanding (quasiniscience), the ability to be wherever we want to be physically or virtually (quasipresence), and control over the events in our environment (quasinipotence). The synergistic interaction of humans and machines in conjunction with assistive and augmentive technologies holds this potential.

Suggested Exercises

1. Find a small not-for-profit Web site of interest to you. Go to www.w3.org/WAI/ER/existingtools.html and find a tool such as Watchfire Bobby 5.0 for checking Web accessibility. You may have to register for a short trial period. Evaluate the site, and write a brief report.
2. Give an example of three technological "curb cuts" that benefit everyone.
3. Invent your own assistive technology. Identify an impairment or disability of any type, and design a system (conceptually) to compensate for the deficiency.
4. Invent your own augmentive technology. Identify some human ability that you would like to augment, and design a system (conceptually) to extend or improve it.

References

Adams, J. (1997). *Human factors engineering*. Upper Saddle River, NJ: Prentice Hall.

Arnold, D. (1998). Speech recognition – Applications and limitations for motor impaired, learning disabled and speech impaired operators. *Proceedings of the Center on Disabilities Technology and Persons with Disabilities conference 1998*, Los Angeles, March. Retrieved March 19, 2008, from www.csun.edu/cod/conf/1998/proceedings/csun98_052.htm

Bayliss, J. D., & Ballard, D. H. (2000). A virtual reality testbed for brain-computer interface research, *IEEE Transactions on Rehabilitation Engineering*, *8*(2), 188–190.

Berka, C., Levendowski, D. J., Cvetinovic, M. M., Davis, G., Lumicao, M. N., Zivkovic, V. T., et al. (2004). Real-time analysis of EEG indexes of alertness, cognition, and memory acquired with a wireless EEG headset. *International Journal of Human–Computer Interaction*, *17*(2), 151–170.

Birbaumer, N., Ghanayim, N., Hinterberger, T, Iversen, I., Kotchoubey, B., Kübler, A., et al. (1999). A spelling device for the paralyzed. *Nature*, *398*, 297–298.

Carbonell, N., & Stephanidis, C. (Eds.). (2003). *Universal access: Theoretical perspectives, practice, and experience*. 7th ERCIM International Workshop on User Interfaces for All, Paris, France, October 24–25, 2002, Revised Papers. Series: Lecture Notes in Computer Science, Vol. 2615. New York: Springer.

Carmien, S. (2002). MAPS: PDA scaffolding for independence for persons with cognitive impairments. *Proceedings of the human–computer interaction consortium (HCIC'2002)*, Winter Park, CO, Jan/Feb 2002.

Cole, E., & Dehdashti, P. (1998). Computer-based cognitive prosthetics: Assistive technology for the treatment of cognitive disabilities. *ACM: Assets*, 11–18.

Farwell, L. A., & Donchin, E. (1988). Talking off the top of your head: Toward a mental prosthesis utilizing event-related brain potentials. *Electroencephalography and Clinical Neurophysiology*, 70, 510–523.

Gerber, E., & Kirchner, C. (2001). Who's surfing: Internet access and computer use by visually impaired youths and adults. *Journal of Visual Impairment & Blindness, 95*, 176–181.

Goldberg, L., & Freed, G. (1998). Making multimedia accessible on the World Wide Web. *Technology and Disability, 8*(3), 127–130.

Gomis, T., & Griffith, A. (1998). Developing intelligent wheelchairs for the handicapped. In V. O. Mittal, H. A. Yanco, J. Aronis, & R. C. Simpson (Eds.), *Assistive technology and artificial intelligence: Applications in robotics, user interfaces and natural language processing (lecture notes in computer science)* (pp. 150-178). Berlin: Spring-Verlag.

Hepting, D. H., & Gerhard, D. (2005). Collaborative computer-aided parameter exploration for music and animation. In *Computer music modeling and retrieval, second international symposium, Esbjerg, Denmark* (pp. 158–172). Berlin: Springer.

Kantowitz, B. H., & Sorkin, R. D. (1983). *Human factors: Understanding people–system relationships*. New York: John Wiley & Sons.

Kendrick, D. (2006). The jaws of success: An interview with Glen Gordon. *AFB Accessworld*, 7(2). Retrieved March 19, 2008, from www.afb.org/afbpress/pub.asp?DocID=aw070204

Lazar, J. (Ed.). (2007). *Universal usability: Designing computer interfaces for diverse user populations*. New York: John Wiley & Sons.

Maloney, L. D. (2000). A bridge to independence. *Design News for Mechanical and Design Engineers*. Retrieved March 19, 2008, from www.designnews.com/index.asp?layout=articlePrint&articleID=CA87203

Pavel, M., Wang, G., & Li, K. (2003). Augmented cognition: Allocation of attention. *Proceedings of the 36th Hawaii international conference on system sciences (HICSS'03)* January 6-9, 2003, Big Island, Hawaii, p. 6.

Ramachandran, V. S., & Hubbard, E. M. (2003). Hearing colors, tasting shapes. *Scientific American, 288*(5), 53–59.

Schmorrow, D. (Ed.). (2005). *Foundations of augmented cognition*. Mahwah, NJ: Erlbaum.

Simpson, R., LoPresti, E., Hayashi, S., Nourbakhsh, I., & Miller, D. (2004). The smart wheelchair component system. *Journal of Rehabilitation Research & Development*, 41(3B), 429–442.

Singh, S., Gedeon, T. D., & Rho, Y. (1998). Enhancing comprehension of web information for users with special linguistic needs. *Journal of Communication, 48*(2), 86–108.

Steinmetz, E. (2006). *Americans with disabilities: 2002*. Household Economic Studies, Current Population Reports P70-107. Washington, DC: U.S. Census Bureau, Housing and Household Economic Statistics Division. Retrieved March 19, 2008, from www.census.gov/hhes/www/disability/sipp/disable02.html

Tran, Q., Calcaterra, G., & Mynatt, E. (2005). Cook's collage: Déjà vu display for a home kitchen. In A. Sloane (Ed.), *Home-oriented informatics and telematics: Proceedings of the IFIP WG 9.3 HOIT 2005 conference*. New York: Springer, pp. 15–32.

Walker, B. N., & Kramer, G. (2004). Ecological psychoacoustics and auditory displays: Hearing, grouping, and meaning making. In J. Neuhoff (Ed.), *Ecological psychoacoustics* (pp 150–175). New York: Academic Press.

Wobbrock, J. O., & Myers, B. A. (2007). Adding gestural text entry to input devices for people with motor impairments. In J. Lazar (Ed.), *Universal usability: Designing computer interfaces for diverse user populations* (pp. 421–457). New York: John Wiley & Sons.

Wolpaw, J. R., Birbaumer, N., McFarland, D. J., Pfurtscheller, G., & Vaughan, T. M. (2002). Brain–computer interfaces for communication and control. *Clinical Neurophysiology*, *113*, 767–791.

Zhao, H., Smith, B., Norman, K., Plaisant, C., & Shneiderman, B. (2005). Interactive sonification of choropleth maps: Design and evaluation. *IEEE Multimedia, Special Issues on Interactive Sonification*, *12*(2), 26–35.

Fifteen

Media

Games, Entertainment, and Education

Scenario 1

On Tuesday, April 20, 1999, at Columbine High School in Jefferson County, Colorado, two teenage students, Eric Harris and Dylan Klebold, went on a shooting rampage killing twelve fellow students and a teacher and wounding twenty-four others before committing suicide. It was the deadliest high school shooting in U.S. history.

During the subsequent investigation, police found a videotape that showed one of the killers with a sawed-off shotgun that he called "Arlene" after a character in the video game Doom. In a diary written a year before the attack, Harris wrote of his plans with Klebold: "It'll be like the LA riots, the Oklahoma bombing, WWII, Vietnam, Duke and Doom all mixed together.... I want to leave a lasting impression on the world." Duke Nukem is another violent video game.

Following the shooting, a lawsuit was filed against Nintendo of America, Sega of America, Sony Computer Entertainment, and Time Warner, Inc., and Activision and ID Software, Inc., the creators and publishers of Doom. The text of the lawsuit alleges: "Absent the combination of extremely violent video games and these boys' incredibly deep involvement, use of and addiction to these games and the boys' basic personalities, these murders and this massacre would not have occurred." The lawyer acting on behalf of the families said that the legal case was trying to change the marketing and distribution of violent video games that turn children into "monster killers." The judge dismissed the lawsuit on the grounds that there was no way that the makers of violent games could have reasonably foreseen that their products would have caused the Columbine shooting or any other acts of violence.

Scenario 2

Larry entered the classroom. He looked around and saw that his friend, Tom, was not there yet. He sat down in the second row at an empty workstation and entered his account name and password. After a few seconds, the home page came up on the screen. It identified his workstation as "Joplin" and his screen name as "Larry K". A label at the top of the screen confirmed that this was Psyc 443: Thinking and Problem Solving in the Electronic Age. At the bottom of the screen was a set of announcements for the class. Next week was the second exam. Friday would be a review session. The instructor posted a short brain teaser: "Jack's mother had three sons. The first one was named Nickle. The second one was named Dime. What was the name of the third son?"

Larry clicked an icon on the right side of the screen to look at the listing of his grades. He had a "B" on the first test and had all but one of his assignments submitted. He returned to the home screen and clicked on the Assignments icon. The assignment that he had not yet completed was to write a 500-word paper on examples of divergent thinking. He clicked on the assignment and opened a window to type in a few ideas that he had thought about before class. When he finished, Tom sat down next to him. Larry clicked to return to the home screen and entered Tom as his partner for the class. He then clicked on the syllabus icon to see what the lecture was about today and then clicked on that line of the syllabus to open up the day's lecture notes. "Good timing," said Tom as the instructor began to lecture on that material. Larry and Tom, however, did not sit back passively listening to the lecture. As points were made by the instructor, they were called on to respond electronically by typing ideas or to experiment with the concepts, diagrams, and simulations shown on the screen.

Overview

Even in the early days of computers, programmers had ideas for three very different but overlapping applications: games, entertainment, and education. As technology has developed and the power of computers and displays has increased, they are no longer just ideas. Today, video games are a driving force in computers and a pervasive influence in the lives of children, young adults, and a significant number of older gamers. Computers have transitioned from mundane beige workstations to engaging play stations. Alphanumeric displays have been replaced with powerful multimedia home entertainment systems. Learning and education are being engulfed in technology from simple learning toys to global distance education environments.

In this chapter, we first look at a number of psychological issues in video games. Video game addiction, gender stereotyping, and violence have been the hot psychological topics, but other issues deal with 1) types of games and game themes; 2) skills, abilities, and motivating factors; and 3) game interfaces and interaction styles. We rely on Chapters 9 to 12 as a background in human motivation, individual differences, social interaction, and cyberpathologies. Second, we explore multimedia for entertainment: pictures, music, video, and virtual reality. Although there are many issues here, we focus on digitization and interfaces to locate, store, and play media on different devices from MP3 players to high-definition flat panel screens. These issues relate back to Chapter 5 on sensory input, motor output, and control and to Chapter 6 on information search and retrieval. Finally, we explore the educational value of computers and their use in teaching and learning. How can computers be used to present material, reinforce learning, and manage learning activities? Here we talk about the relationship between computer media and processing, as well as the psychological systems of learning and memory from Chapter 6.

Electronic Video Games

Historians of the video game industry trace the first electronic game back to 1947 when Goldsmith, Grove, and Mann (1948) submitted an application for the patent of a cathode-ray tube amusement device in which "one or more targets, such as pictures of airplanes, for example, are placed on the face of the tube and controls are available to the player so that he can manipulate the trace or position of the beam, which is automatically caused to move across the face of the tube." Although innovative, the video game industry did not really get started until 1972, with the introduction of Atari's Pong for game arcades and the Magnavox Odyssey system for home televisions. Since then, with the introduction of personal computers, game consoles, handhelds, and the Internet, electronic gaming has developed into a multibillion-dollar industry with an incredible range of themes, styles, and supporting technologies (Crandall & Sidak, 2006). Electronic gaming has become so vast that it has not only created its own novel venue, but has also simulated and supplanted traditional board games (e.g., chess), card games (e.g., solitaire), and sports (e.g., basketball). The electronic gaming industry has been at the forefront of technology, pushing for higher-quality graphics, rendering of 3-D images, AI, virtual reality (VR), and new input devices. Moreover, in alliance with the entertainment industry, it has both promoted and spawned its own celebrity characters and movie themes. It is in the current and future pervasiveness of electronic gaming that we turn to the psychological issues that drive the industry and that in turn impact us and our society.

The Psychology of Games

Game playing is an important human activity from childhood to adolescence and on into adulthood and old age. Early in life, games involve developmental learning, socialization, and play. Later, games are played for recreation and to fill needs for competition and achievement. Piaget (1962) described three types of games that play a role in childhood development.

Sensorimotor play occurs primarily from infancy to the second year of life when the child is learning to coordinate physical movement and the perception of its effects. Hand–eye coordination, grabbing, and manipulation of objects are essential for normal development in the real world. Sensorimotor play appears in electronic games as an integral part of the game interface. Controllers attached to the game console, located on the pad of a handheld game, or connected to the computer effect changes in the state of the game. All ages must learn the key, mouse, and joystick mappings to actions in the game. Simple mappings require only a few responses and actions (e.g., < for move left, > for move right). Advanced games may require learning large numbers of discrete action keys (e.g., Q for look left, R for jump). Others require a fine-tuning of smooth motor movements and timing to control position and orientation of objects on the screen using continuous input devices (e.g., joysticks, wands).

Symbolic or *representational* play extends from age 2 to 6 years when the child plays with dolls, toys, and objects, and begins to use symbols to represent other objects. Children can play house with empty soda cans representing members of the family, a tree trunk for the house, and pebbles for food. Symbolic play is an inherent part of video games that use interface object models to represent characters, fields of play, weapons, treasures, etc. Players must identify the images on the screen as playing cards, chess pieces, tanks, explosions, enemies, self, and whatever objects and actions are required in the game. The symbolic component is essential in making it a game rather than a real-world experience. It creates the possibility of fantasy, suspension of belief, departure from reality, and the illusion of risk without actually jeopardizing the physical safety of oneself or others. Electronic games typically involve identities, roles, and characters, as discussed in Chapter 11. An engaging aspect of games is to be able to play roles and characters with whom you want to identify, such as sports heroes. Some video games even allow you to generate characters that look like you or characters that have attributes that you would like to have. Games typically involve themes, story lines, backgrounds, and even whole worlds. In this way, they become consuming and immersive.

Finally, *games with rules* are played from school age on, introducing objective rules concerning allowable actions and obtainable goals. Games with rules impose a structure that sets limits and boundaries, and provide scoring guidelines to award points and assign game winners. Board games come with published rules, whereas sports games have rule books and referees to enforce them. Games with rules bring in the social dynamics of cooperation and competition. Many games in the real world rely on real-world physics and logic. Basketball players cannot levitate themselves, and poker players cannot change the laws of probability. Electronic games incorporate rules that are programmed into the logic of the game. The allowable moves of a chess player or a solitaire player can be strictly imposed at the interface as well as published for the players to read. Similarly, scoring rules can be automatically applied and explained to the players if desired. However, unlike games in the real world, the rules of physics and logic can be relaxed or entirely altered in video games to allow teleportation, x-ray vision, and even "cheats" to transcend the rules of the game.

Given these three components of game play, electronic games vary primarily in difficulty, complexity, risk, and magnitude of rewards as they progress from Pong, originally released by Atari in 1972, to Halo 3, created by Bungie Studios and released in 2007. To be successful, games need to be exciting and stimulate the motivation and interest of the players, as discussed in Chapter 10. To do so, they introduce rewards, risks, and threats. Rewards may be in the form of points, prizes, or wins. Risk adds a probabilistic surprise factor. Threat involves loss of points, loss of time, or loss of game. Many games incorporate typical real-world scripts that help define the steps. For example, a threat script begins with 1) an eminent threat, such as a monster or an incoming missile; 2) followed by a defensive action on the part of the defender, such as an evasive move or a counterattack; and 3) ending with an outcome that the threat succeeded, the threat was destroyed, or it was a draw. A seek-and-destroy script starts with 1) a search for an enemy target, 2) followed by the discovery of a target, and 3) an attempt to destroy the target with 4) the possibility of evoking a counterattack and eliciting a threat script.

The symbolic and metaphoric mapping of elements between the real world and the game world creates partial transference of knowledge between the worlds so that one can understand the rules of the game while suspending reality. This creates an environment in which one's character can be killed by a monster and then resurrected by magic. The player can experience the excitement of risk and threat safely contained within the game.

Taxonomies of Digital Games

Digital games differ in many ways. It is useful to characterize them in terms of both their theme and structure and in terms of the options that they provide along a few major dimensions.

Industry Classification

The video and computer game industry classifies games into seven genres based on theme, style of game, and audience (Entertainment Software

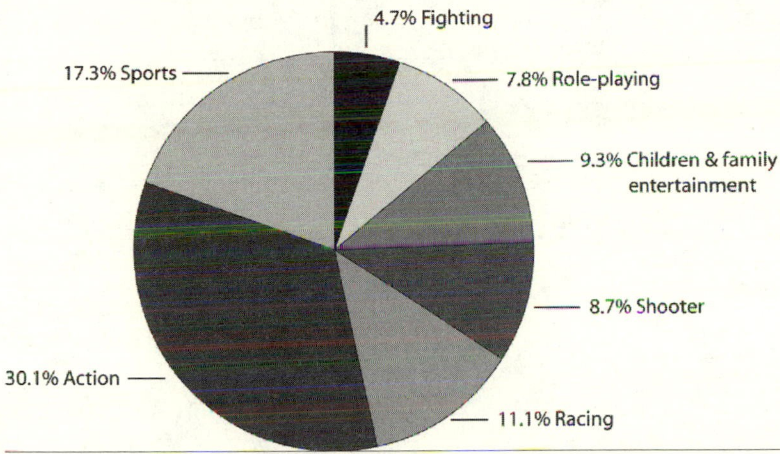

Figure 15.1. Proportion of types of best-selling video games by units sold in 2005. (From Entertainment Software Association, 2006.)

Association, 2006). Figure 15.1 shows the popularity of these types according to recent sales. Although useful to the industry, this classification is largely devoid of theory and not of great use in the psychology of video games.

Complexity

An obvious classification of games can be based on basic complexity. Simple games such as Pac-Man and Tetris involve rudimentary components of hand–eye coordination and manipulation, as well as the elementary cognitive processes of attention, memory, and problem solving. They have simple rule sets, small playing fields, and a short time commitment. Complex games such as computer chess and World of Warcraft involve many rules, complex patterns and permutations of moves, vast playing fields, and long time commitments.

Social Involvement

Games may involve only oneself as a single gamer playing against time, chance, and difficulty, as is the case in racing games, solitaire games, and building games, such as SimCity. Even solitary games can have a social component when players record high scores or play while others watch. At the extreme, games can become massively social when they involve teams, collaboration, and other social situations. One can be playing a competitive game against another human player or a computer-generated opponent. Table 15.1 shows twelve different competitive situations that can arise when you take into consideration a gamer playing by him- or herself or in combination with human or computer-generated teammates against chance events and/or three types of opponents. Although all combinations are possible, some of the cells in the table seem unusual and have no good examples.

Table 15.1. Classification of Games According to Type of Player and Opponent

	Playing against			
Player	Chance events and/or time	Computer-generated opponent(s)	Individual human opponent(s)	Cooperative human team
Self	Tetris	Computer Chess	Racing	–
Cooperative game agent(s)	–	Super Mario Brothers (Moshe)	–	–
Human team player(s)	–	Zelda	–	World of Warcraft

Graphics

Electronic games have come to rely heavily on screens and graphics. One could classify games on the basis of the quality of the graphics, but a more interesting taxonomy is presented by Wolf (1997), based on the way they use on- and off-screen space. Table 15.2 lists his original eleven types of screens based on one-screen displays, along with two more that extend the game space to multiple displays.

Conceptual Factors

Lindley (2003) suggested a taxonomy based on the extent to which a game loads on each of three dimensions – ludology, narratology, and simulation – as shown in Figure 15.2. *Ludology* is in general the study of gaming, but

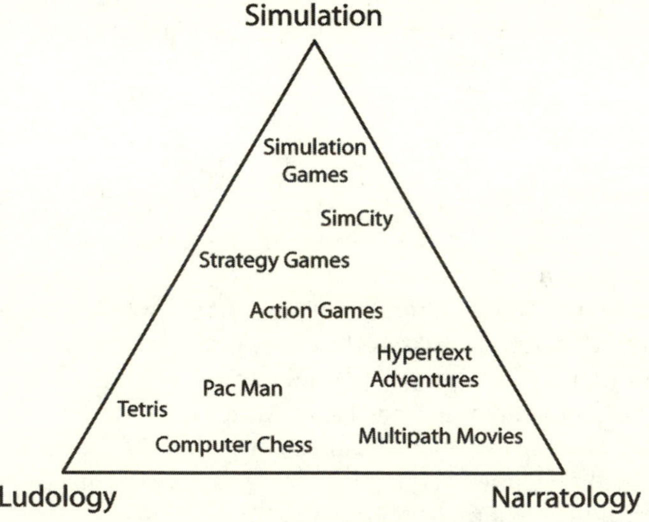

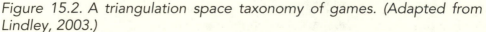

Figure 15.2. A triangulation space taxonomy of games. (Adapted from Lindley, 2003.)

Table 15.2. Types of Games Based on Screen Usage

Screen usage	Examples
No visual space, all text based The game involves only typing text as input and reading text as output.	The Hitchhiker's Guide to the Galaxy (1984), Dungeons & Dragons, MUDs, MOOs
One screen contained Graphics are confined to one 2-D space. Objects may be confined to move around the screen, or to appear on one side and disappear on the other.	Pong (Atari, 1972), Space Invaders (Taito, 1978)
One screen, contained with wraparound Moving objects can move off screen in one direction and reappear on the other side, maintaining their speed and trajectory.	Asteroids (Atari, 1979), Pac-Man (Namco, 1979)
Scrolling on one axis Games that require a long strip of space use horizontal scrolling synchronized with the player's speed, with stationary objects appearing on the right and disappearing on the left.	Street Racer (UbiSoft, 1978), Skiing (1980)
Scrolling on two axes Games that involve terrain maps typically require scrolling side to side and up and down.	SimCity (Maxis, 1989)
Adjacent spaces displayed one at a time Contiguous spaces are presented as a series of nonoverlapping static screens cutting one scene to the next without scrolling. When the character moves off screen in one direction, the scene changes instantaneously from one scene to the next.	Adventure (1978), Superman (1979)
Layers of independently moving planes The space is comprised of layers of overlapping and independently moving planes of graphics. The front layer contains the player-character, while the back layer contains background graphics and scrolls at a slower rate than the foreground, creating an illusion of depth.	Zaxxon (1982), Wario Land (Nintendo, 1995)
Spaces allowing Z-axis movement out of frame A 3-D effect is created using a *Z*-axis movement showing objects grow in size as they move up the tunnel toward player's character.	Tempest (Atari, 1980), Star Ship (Atari 2600, 1977), Night Driver (Atari, 1976)
Multiple, nonadjacent spaces displayed on screen simultaneously Two or more independent points of view are shown in tiles for each competing player. Each tile is essentially one screen, but players can see all screens.	High Velocity (1995), Mario Kart 64 (Nintendo, 1997)
Interactive 3-D environment First-person perspective is shown that allows the player to look around in a 3-D environment rendered on the 2-D screen.	Doom (id Software, 1993), Tomb Raider (Core Design, 1996)
Represented or "mapped" spaces Off-screen spaces are represented as a map on the screen to help the player navigate the whole space of the game and to reveal objects and events occurring in the off-screen space.	Myst (Cyan, 1993), Wario Land (Nintendo, 1995)
Multiple screens for one player Two or more screens may be available to the player to provide one screen for a shared game space and another for personal views and game options, often on a handheld device.	Nintendo DS
Multiple screens across players Each player has his or her own personal screen on a network and a shared or common screen for all to view.	World of Warcraft (Blizzard, 2001), Halo 3 (Bungie, 2007), Legend of Zelda: Four Sword Adventures (Nintendo, 2004)

From Wolf (1997).

as a dimension it focuses on the extent to which a game is primarily a "goal-directed and competitive activity conducted within a framework of agreed rules." Games such as tic-tac-toe and Tetris are primarily rule based. Game rules determine what you as a player can and cannot do and the consequences of your actions. Successful play depends on learning at least a minimal number of rules to support a particular playing style and how one interacts within the game. In particular, Lindley emphasized learning patterns of interaction, which he calls a "game play gestalt." For example, in action games, the pattern might be "shoot while being hit, strafe to a hiding spot, take health, and repeat," and in many progressive games, it is often "overcome barrier, save game if successful, reload, and retry if unsuccessful."

Narratology focuses on the extent to which the game depends on an experience that is structured in time. For example, many digital games use a three-act restorative structure borrowed from theater and movie screenplays. In the first act, a conflict is established; in the second act, the implications of the conflict are played out; and in the third act, the conflict is resolved. The narrative specifically involves a central protagonist (e.g., "Mario"), a conflict involving a moral issue (e.g., saving a damsel in distress named "Peach"), and a point of crisis (e.g., battling the "Boss"). The narrative may be introduced and concluded with noninteractive video clips and supported throughout the game with characters, scenery, and game objects. Good game design integrates the narrative structure with the game play to create a coherent narrative gestalt without overdoing one component to the detriment of another.

Finally, *simulation* is a dimension that focuses on a representation of the function, operation, or features of one process or system through the use of another. There are many examples of simulators for flying aircraft, driving cars, and constructing worlds. Simulations in and of themselves have no game and goal-oriented components and no inherent narrative. Although simulations can be interesting to watch and useful in developing one's ergonomic skills, they must be combined with competitive situations and narratives to succeed as computer games.

Other game analysts such as Klabbers (2003) suggested complex classifications of games based on syntax, semantics, and pragmatics; actors, rules, and resources; and purpose, subject matter, content and context of use, and intended audiences.

Attraction to Video Games

It is clear that video games have captured a large segment of the market and a significant proportion of the population. Video games are a $25 billion industry, with yearly sales of more than $9 billion!

Figure 15.3 shows the proportion of individuals that play video games by age. However, it is quite clear that these proportions will change in the

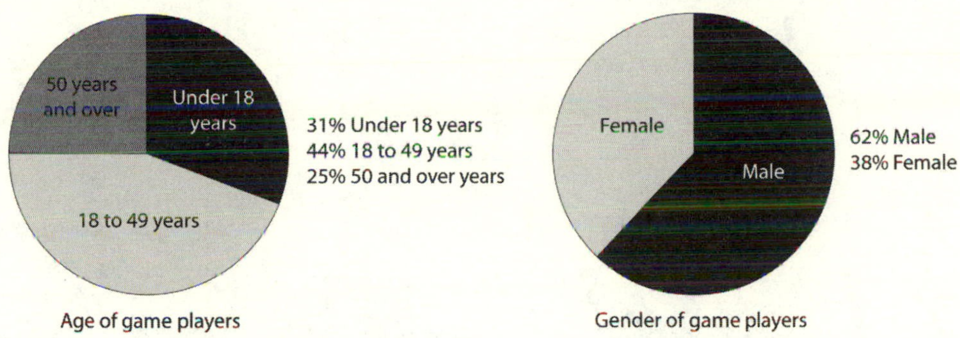

Figure 15.3. Proportion of game players by age (left) *and gender* (right). *(From Entertainment Software Association, 2006.)*

coming years. The findings are that as younger gamers get older, they continue to play, increasing the proportions of gamers in the upper ages. Thus, the average age of gamers is increasing every year.

Figure 15.3 also shows the proportion of males versus females who report playing computer and video games. It is not surprising that there is a gender gap. Unlike the age gap, the gender gap may not be going away because the majority of video games appeal to males rather than females. As shown in Figure 15.2, the best-selling games involve action, shooting, racing, and sports, which tend to be more male than female dominated.

Although many play video games at a moderate recreational level, there is a growing proportion that may be said to be addicted, as discussed in Chapter 12. Griffiths and Hunt (1998) reported that one in five adolescents can be classified as pathologically dependent on video games. Video game addiction seems to be due to the system of rewards and punishments that game play gives to the player (Braun & Giroux, 1989). The system of intermittent, variable reinforcement is similar to that of operant conditioning and slot machines.

Violence and Behavior

Video games provide opportunities to engage in extreme, risky, and aggressive behaviors that would not be possible or socially acceptable in the real world. These video games, true to the concept of a game, provide representations of reality that allow people to participate vicariously in combat, use of weapons, and different forms of violent behavior. Although we are interested in what happens during the game play, what really concerns us is what happens after the game. The best-selling game of 2004 was Grand Theft Auto: San Andreas from Take-Two Interactive Software, Inc., with more than 5.1 million units sold. This game was also at the top of the list of the ten most violent video games of 2005, so there is a reason for concern. Are there residual effects that spill over and change a person's behavior after being exposed to a violent game as has been alleged in Scenario 1?

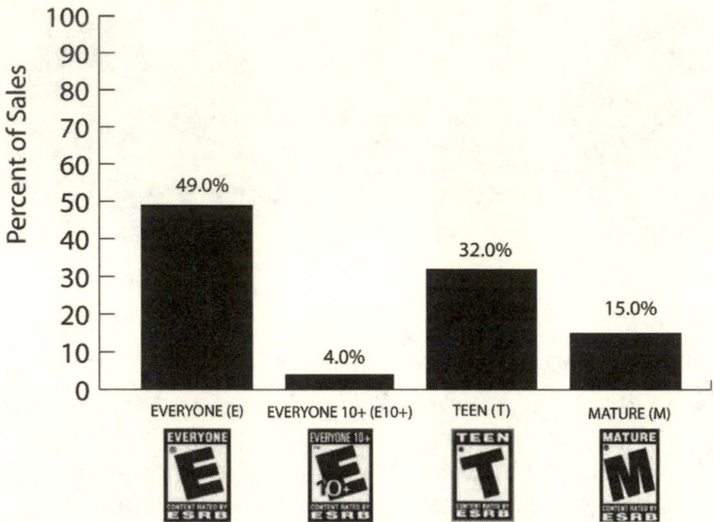

Figure 15.4. Proportion of sales of four ratings of video games and their Entertainment Software Rating Board (http://www.esrb.org/) symbols.

The gaming industry is certainly aware of the concern. The Entertainment Software Rating Board (ESRB; http://www.esrb.org/) provides the following six rating symbols for rating video games: "eC" for early childhood, "E" for everyone, "10+E" for everyone older than 10, "T" for teen, "M" for mature 17+, and "AO" for adults only. In addition to these ratings, the ESRB includes a list of content descriptors to detail specific elements that might be considered offensive, including violence, alcohol references, and nudity. Figure 15.4 shows the ESRB labels and the proportion of sales across four of these ratings.

The potential link between video game violence and aggressive behavior is based on theories of learning. Video games provide environments for participatory learning of aggressive solutions to conflict situations. The immediate consequences may be due to a priming of aggressive thoughts and behaviors. Long-term effects of violence are expected due to the acquisition of aggression-related scripts that become more and more available for application in real-life situations. Video games, as opposed to violence on television and in movies, are more insidious for three reasons. First, the player inherently identifies with the aggressor by playing and controlling his or her aggressive actions in the game. This is particularly true in "first-person shooter" games. Second, the player is active in making aggressive choices and being rewarded for the consequences. Active learning is more effective than passive learning. Finally, as noted previously, video games can be addictive. The reinforcement characteristics of violent video games that make them addictive also reinforce the learning of aggressive scripts that can drive violent behavior.

Anderson and Dill (2000) provided a two-stage model for the causal relationship between exposure to video games and aggressive behavior, as shown

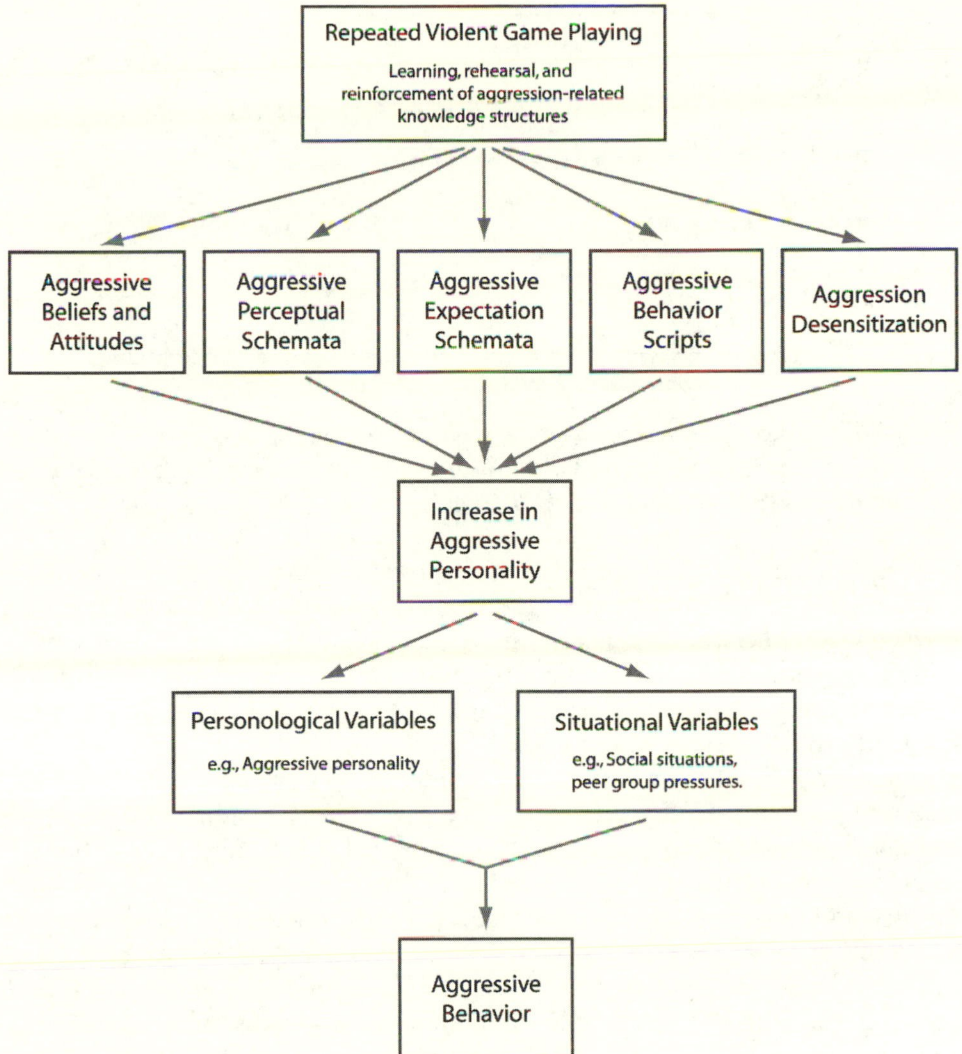

Figure 15.5. The causal network between violent video games and aggressive behavior. (Adapted from Anderson & Dill, 2000.)

in Figure 15.5. In the first stage, the repeated exposure to violent games alters a number of aspects of the individual and serves to generate an aggressive personality. In the second stage, personality (internal) variables and situational (external) variables combine to produce overt aggressive behavior.

A number of empirical studies have been conducted in which children and college students are randomly assigned to be exposed to a violent video game or a neutral video game. Following the game, they were observed for a period of time as they interacted with others. Most of these studies have shown statistically significant elevations in aggressive behavior (e.g., pushing, shoving, hitting) by the children exposed to the violent game and increased tendencies to aggressive. However, it is not a simple effect. Anderson and Dill (2000) showed that there are at least two very important

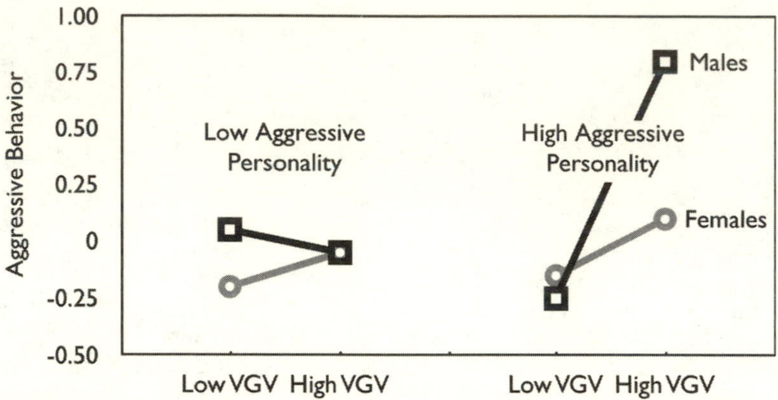

Figure 15.6. Aggressive behavior as a function of exposure to low versus high video game violence for individuals with low versus high aggressive personality. (From Anderson & Dill, 2000.)

factors: gender and predisposition to aggressive behavior. In one of their experiments, they divided males and females and those with a high versus low aggressive personality. The results are shown in Figure 15.6. Males with a high aggressive personality were most affected by the exposure to video game violence. Females and males that are not prone to aggression are not substantially affected by the violence.

Overall, the results are clear. Violent video games are significantly associated with 1) increased aggressive behavior, aggressive thoughts, and affect; 2) increased physiological arousal; and 3) decreased prosocial (helping) behavior. However, one may question whether violent games lead to violent behavior or whether it is merely correlational, and aggressiveness in the individual leads him or her to play violent video games. Nevertheless, because the average effect sizes for experimental studies (which help establish causality) and correlational studies (which allow examination of serious violent behavior) appear comparable (Anderson & Bushman, 2001), it seems that there is a causal effect in place.

It has been argued that even though there are statistically significant effects, they are small and trivial. However, meta-analyses reveal that the effect sizes for violent video games are larger than the effect of second-hand tobacco smoke on lung cancer, the effect of lead exposure to IQ scores in children, and calcium intake on bone mass. Moreover, it should be emphasized that because so many youths are exposed to such high levels of video game violence, it further increases the societal costs of this risk factor (Rosenthal, 1986).

In the end, the results appear conclusive. As Anderson, Gentile, and Buckley (2006) have argued, video game violence does translate into overt acts of aggression. To make matters worse, things are not expected to get better with respect to the effects of violent video games and their impact on society. Fueled by industry desire for profits, the games are increasing in realism and complexity, and marketing campaigns are designed to increase their popularity.

Entertainment

Entertainment covers a wide range of human activity of individuals and groups that involves pleasure, relaxation, and recreation. Entertainment involves an event, a performance, or an activity directed at an audience of one or many people. The audience may passively enjoy the entertainment, as in the case of watching a television show, a rock concert, or a football game. Alternatively, the people may be more engaged with the activity as in playing games and sports. We distinguish between live and recorded performances and between attending an event in person or watching it remotely. In both cases, electronics and digitization come into play. Human interface issues quickly emerge, dealing with everything from remote controls and menus of functions to understanding storage formats, program scheduling, and communication.

In the short history of personal computers, we have witnessed a rapid transition of computers as number crunchers to computers as multimedia entertainment systems. The legal battles of Apple Computer provide a perfect example. Apple Computer was incorporated January 3, 1977. Surprisingly, in 1978, Apple Corps, Ltd., the parent company for Apple Records, The Beatles' record label, filed suit against Apple Computer for trademark infringement. What could be more different than computers and records? Nevertheless, in 1981, Apple Computer, Inc., agreed to pay Apple Corps $80,000 and to stay out of the music business. Not surprisingly, Apple Corps sued again in 1989, when Apple Computers introduced a machine that had the ability to play MIDI music. In 1991, Apple Computer settled and paid Apple Corps around $26.5 million. Finally, in 2003, Apple Corps sued Apple Computer for distributing music when they introduced the iTunes Music Store and the iPod. This time, on May 8, 2006, oddly enough, Apple Corps lost the case in the United Kingdom. Then, on January 9, 2007, in a keynote address during which several Beatles songs were teasingly featured in a new product demo, Apple Computer announced that it would change its name to Apple, Inc. On that day, computers and music had converged.

Digital convergence is the process by which different entertainment media are converted to formats that can be transmitted and stored digitally and converted back to their original format for human use and entertainment. Books, photographs, music, and film are digitized into text (ASCII), image (JPEG, TIFF, PICT), sound (WAV, MP3), and video files (AVI, MOV, MP4). Digital convergence is driven by many factors. The media are much less expensive, storage is much smaller, it does not deteriorate over time, and it can be quickly copied and transmitted over networks. Although devices such as the Apple iPod are at the center of digital convergence, digital convergence itself is ubiquitous.

Digital convergence also includes computer programs and computer networks. Consequently, it allows digital games and simulations to interact with other entertainment media across the Web. The epitome of digital convergence is to attend a virtual music festival in a cyberspace such as Second Life.

There are a host of psychological questions that surround entertainment in the media. For example, what makes something entertaining in the first place? Zillman and Vorderer (2000) listed a number of psychological reasons, such as suspense, humor, sex, violence, and one's personality, to explain why entertainment in the media is so appealing. Shrum (2003) suggested that entertainment is also highly influenced by other psychological factors such as subliminal persuasion, identification, ownership, branding, memory, and judgment. These factors and others spill over into cyberpsychology as digital convergence pulls the entertainment industry into the realm of HCI. Following are some of the issues that will affect us in the area of digital media entertainment:

- *Media packaging.* Although digital convergence is a technological asset for the computer industry, it is not necessarily compelling psychologically because it disassociates the contents from both the sensory modality and the physical packaging of the media. e-Books have no physical pages, binding, or covers. Recorded music has no vinyl discs, CDs, record covers, or jewel cases. Games have no cardboard storage boxes, boards, 3-min glass timers, or little pieces. By not requiring physical storage or shelf space in one's home, they lose a sense of territory and display of personal ownership. The disappearance of the physicality of the media means that it must be replaced with virtual markers or interface object models such as icons and cover art. Index listings of titles, although useful, have not been sufficient enough to grab consumer's attention. Consequently, marketers and designers of online stores have resorted to surrogate packaging, using images of items placed in one's virtual shopping cart. The challenge to interface designers is to effectively replace our previous models of analog media with new mental models of digital media.
- *Media management.* In the recent past, one managed one's personal media by organizing photo albums, record collections, and libraries of books. When you looked for something in your collection, you could literally lay your hands on it. Today, storing, searching, finding, and retrieving multimedia entertainment is extremely complex. When digital television and radio provide hundreds of channels, searching for the desired program is not easy. When online movie stores sell downloads of movies and movies on demand provide thousands of titles, it is a daunting task just to find what you want to watch. Because the media objects are essentially digital files and sources, search for entertainment media becomes a human–computer interface problem as discussed in Chapter 7. It suffers the problems of menu navigation and query formulation but can benefit from the computational power and database management capabilities of computers. Well-designed systems should be able to offer consumers endless possibilities with easy-to-use, intuitive search and indexing.

- *Media control.* In the past, one could turn on the television, set the volume with one knob, and tune the channel with a second knob. Anyone could do it with no instructions. With home entertainment systems today, we are faced with half a dozen remote controls and a number of boxes for digital television, DVD players, surround sound, digital recording and playback, and video game systems, as well as the HD television itself. Needless to say, many consumers are totally befuddled and frustrated just trying to watch a simple football game. In some cases, consumer frustration with the complexity and unintuitive design of these systems has boiled over and led to "HDTV rage," the costly sister of computer rage. The new design challenge for consumer electronics is to develop a system that provides the same functionality and options as current digital systems, with the simplicity of yesteryear products.
- *Media multitasking.* Multitasking is when a person attempts to do several things at the same time or, more often, by quickly shifting attention back and forth between multiple tasks (Pashler & Johnston, 1998). Because cognitive resources (e.g., attention, information processing capacity, memory) are limited, performance is generally degraded on one or both tasks. We often try to work and be entertained simultaneously by listening to music or watching television while doing homework or reading. We may even try to entertain ourselves by watching several television shows at the same time, using picture in picture, split screen viewing, or channel switching. Digital convergence not only facilitates media multitasking, but it also seems to encourage it. Computer multitasking with multiple windows running different media players, rapid switching, and bite-size segments may lure us into highly interactive, yet mind-numbing media experiences that have little or no redeeming effect.
- *Media diet.* Finally, with the availability of vast multimedia options, anytime, anywhere, we need to consider its overall effect on the psychological well-being of the individual. How might overexposure of certain types of media lead to mood changes, desensitization to violence, and antisocial behavior? Parents of young children have to ask how early exposure of television to children affects their learning and cognitive development (O'Flynn, 2005). Analogous to our intake of food, we all need to consider what is a balanced media diet in terms of media mix and moderation for ourselves to promote a healthy and productive lifestyle.

Edutainment

To many of us, particularly in education, entertainment for the sole purpose of being entertained is pointless without some positive, lasting outcome. Entertainment that leaves a message, a learning experience, and a positive change in one's life serves two purposes: entertainment and education. Although this is inherently the goal of many writers, artists, composers, and performers, *edutainment* is specifically a form of entertainment that is meant to educate the audience or participant in the process of being entertained. It takes a familiar medium of entertainment, such as television programs, movies, cartoons, or video games, and embeds educational content.

Edutainment seeks to use the principles of attention, motivation, learning, and memory by packaging educational content in the interesting and reinforcing context of entertainment.

It has been argued that video games can not only embed educational material in the course of play, as with the games Where in the World is Carmen Sandiego? and Age of Mythology, but also teach important motor and cognitive skills. Gee (2003) gave a number of examples where good games teach skills such as problem solving (e.g., Half-Life), memory and comprehension (e.g., System Shock 2), planning and design (e.g., Rise of Nations), and decision making (e.g., Star Wars: Knights of the Old Republic).

Edutainment is also used within educational software to make learning a more enjoyable experience. This may be accomplished by embedding multimedia entertainment in the learning modules. The student's interest in a subject may be piqued by an intriguing video at the onset, performance reinforced by funny animations, and completion of the exercise rewarded by the opportunity to listen to music. In the last section, we finally turn to education itself. We explore how computers are revolutionizing the learning process and will complete the migration to digital convergence in the electronic educational environment (EEE).

Training and Education

One of the most important applications of computers today is in training and education. The purpose is not to only learn about computers (i.e., computer literacy), but to use computers as learning devices, teaching tools, and facilitators in training and education. The goal is twofold: 1) to increase teaching effectiveness in terms of amount learned in time spent and 2) to decrease cost in terms of labor and materials. The human–computer interface is generally seen as the key to achieving both of these goals.

Origins

In 1958, B. F. Skinner first proposed a learning technique called "programmed learning," based on his research on operant conditioning. The idea was to manage learning under controlled conditions. In the original method, the student was presented with the "to be learned" information in small steps called "frames." Each frame contained a small chunk of information and a blank space that the student was to fill in (e.g., "The three primary colors are RED, YELLOW, and ____."). The student then uncovered the correct answer ("BLUE") by moving a card down the page before going to the next frame. Each frame contained new information or reviewed material covered previously. According to the theory of operant conditioning, the student was reinforced by seeing the correct answer.

The idea of programmed learning was later applied in a method of instruction called the "personalized system of instruction" (PSI). PSI was self-paced and self-administered. The student mastered each unit before moving to the next. Active student involvement, immediate feedback, and reinforcement have made it an effective method of instruction (Reiser, 1984).

The ideas of programming, control, and feedback made it immediately obvious to educators in the 1980s that programmed learning could be implemented on a computer. This resulted in a wide range of computer learning applications known as computer-assisted instruction, computer-aided personalized system of instruction, and, more generally, computer-based instruction (CBI). Again, empirical research has, for the most part, found these methods to be effective educational techniques in terms of material learned and in terms of reducing the cost of teaching (Fletcher-Flinn & Gravatt, 1995).

Educational Software

Today, educational software is a big business appealing to companies, schools, and parents. Marketing claims for training employees, improving student test scores, and helping parents with their children's education abound. One promoter at a trade show claimed that with their software, trainees would learn "twice as much in half the time." Unfortunately, these exaggerated claims have created unrealistic expectations and made it difficult to objectively assess the efficacy of the programs.

After years of conflicting claims and experiences, the U.S. Department of Education (Dynarski et al., 2007) released the results of a comprehensive study on the effect of educational software on standardized test scores in the public school system. In the No Child Left Behind Act of 2002 (P.L. 107–110, section 2421), the U.S. Congress called for a study of the effectiveness of educational technology on academic performance. Sixteen software products were selected by the Department of Education in the areas of first-grade reading, fourth-grade reading, sixth-grade math, and algebra. The average cost per student per year for reading products was about $100, and $15 to $18 for math products. The study included 132 schools and 439 teachers. Within each school, teachers were randomly assigned to use the software product (treatment group) or not (control group). Tests were administered to the students near the beginning and end of the school year. Nearly all teachers in the treatment group received training on the products and believed that they were prepared to use them. Technical problems using the products were fairly common but minor. Student–teacher interactions changed such that the students were more likely to engage in individual instruction and the teachers were more likely to facilitate student learning rather than lecture to the class. Students in the treatment group averaged about 30 hours per year using the reading products, amounting to about 11 percent of their reading instruction time, and 15 to 17 hours per year using the math products, or about 10 percent of their math instruction time.

The results were extremely disappointing. According to the report, "Test scores were not significantly higher in classrooms using selected reading and mathematics software products. Test scores in treatment classrooms that were randomly assigned to use products did not differ from test scores in control classrooms by statistically significant margins" (Dynarski et al., 2007, p. xiii). Overall, the results indicated that the use of educational software in the school did not significantly increase the scores, despite a cost of hundreds of millions of dollars in software and hardware. Although experts are exploring possible reasons for this failure (e.g., poor teacher training, inefficient implementation), the results seriously question the use of computers for individualized learning in the classroom and as surrogates for human teachers. Nevertheless, educational software may be effective outside or in addition to classroom instruction. When teachers are not available, CBI may be the next best thing.

Multimedia Materials

Digital technology makes it possible for teachers to present old material in new ways, often called "new media." New media include graphics, multimedia, video, and all elements of digital convergence. What is exciting about new media is its ability to grab one's attention, to communicate ideas in effective ways, to be interactive, and to do so in individualized ways. In education, new media is the ultimate in audiovisual services, but again the question is whether multimedia materials actually make a difference or whether they will result in yet another unfulfilled promise. In 1922, Thomas Edison proclaimed that "the motion picture is destined to revolutionize our educational system and that in a few years it will supplant . . . the use of textbooks" (cited in Cuban, 1986, p. 9). Following a review of the role of motion pictures in schools over the decades following Edison's grand predictions, Cuban (1986) concluded that "most teachers used films infrequently in classrooms" (p. 17). However, to Edison's credit, classroom education is highly dependent on the electric light bulb.

Ample evidence exists that when used correctly, multimedia in education can effectively increase communication, understanding, and learning (Mayer, 2001). However, the use of multimedia in education can entice teachers to subject their students to a barrage of pictures, sounds, and animations in an attempt to convey more and richer information. Unfortunately, when misused, it can create confusion, information overload, and sensory saturation. Mayer and Moreno (2003) suggested ways of offloading information from one channel to another, reducing redundant information, and synchronizing information.

Mayer and Moreno (1998) argued that unless the application of multimedia in education is based on cognitive principles, it will go the way of one more broken promise. They listed the following principles for appropriate use of multimedia:

- *Multiple representation principle.* It is better to present an explanation in words and pictures than solely in words or pictures without words. For example, animations are better with narration than without, and illustrations are better with captions than without.
- *Contiguity principle.* When giving a multimedia explanation, present corresponding words and pictures contiguously rather than separately. For example, narrations should occur simultaneously with animations rather than before or after, and captions are best if placed close to the illustration rather than on separate pages.
- *Split-attention principle.* When giving a multimedia explanation, present words as auditory narration rather than as visual on-screen text. If written text is presented with the animation, students have to split their attention between watching the animation and reading the text.
- *Individual differences principle.* The foregoing principles are more important for low-knowledge than high-knowledge learners and for high-spatial rather than low-spatial learners. Students with low prior knowledge are more susceptible to multimedia and contiguity effects than students who have a higher prior knowledge. Students with high spatial visualization ability (SVA) also show stronger multimedia and contiguity effects by generating their own mental images and by holding images in memory longer than students with low SVA.
- *Coherence principle.* When giving a multimedia explanation, use few rather than many extraneous words and pictures. A coherent summary highlighting the relevant words and pictures is better than a longer version with redundant information.

Multimedia in education is undoubtedly here to stay for better or worse. Teachers need to learn how to harness the new media to increase teaching effectiveness without overwhelming the students. Students need to learn how to manage their attention and maximize learning according to their cognitive abilities.

Virtual Reality Training

VR is not only a form of entertainment in games, but it also provides exciting educational opportunities. VR environments, whether immersive or nonimmersive, provide 3-D visual and psychomotor simulations that can be used to train students in motor movements, procedural steps, and appropriate responses to events in context. In theory, VR training can take advantage of context-dependent memory by simulating the environment associated with the task to be learned (e.g., street scenes, factory layout, outerspace). Environmental stimuli then become available to serve as retrieval cues for memory (Mania & Chalmers, 2001). VR training has been used in place of real-world training in aviation with flight simulators, in biology with simulated dissections, and in medicine with various medical procedures. Nonimmersive VR can be relatively inexpensive and safe compared to real-world learning situations, which can involve expensive equipment (e.g., tanks, airplanes) and dangerous situations (e.g., fire, rescue).

When real-world, VR, and other types (e.g., videos, procedural manuals) of training have been compared, the results have been mixed (Sebrechts, Lathan, Clawson, Miller, & Trepagnier, 2003). VR training can be effective in learning routes and navigation through complex environments. For highly technical tasks, VR training has been successful and cost effective. For example, Hamilton et al. (2002) compared video training and VR training for laparoscopic skill of second-year residents. They found that VR training resulted in superior psychomotor skills and operative performance over video training. However, Kozak, Hancock, Arthur, and Chrysler (1993) reported an experiment in which they compared real-world training, VR training, and no training. They found no evidence of transfer from VR training to the world task and no difference in performance between the VR group and the group that received no training.

VR training is not for everyone. Between 10 percent and 60 percent of the population experience adverse reactions to computer displays of motion (Potel, 1998). VR sickness can involve nausea, dizziness, headache, and sweating. It is due to a number of causes, including motion sickness, lags and mismatches between visual and proprioceptive senses, and low-resolution rendering of images (Howarth & Finch, 1999). Things may improve with higher-resolution displays and faster processors; however, there will always be some form or level of discrepancy between the senses that will affect some portion of the population. Consequently, VR training may always be limited to specialized learning situations.

Electronic Educational Environments

Today, we are fast approaching digital convergence in education with online textbooks, online tests, computer simulations, online lectures, multimedia materials, electronic classrooms, and virtual campuses. EEEs attempt to bring together the pieces of education into one integrated, extensive package. The application of digital technology across all aspects of education leads to new potentials, new challenges, and new problems for students, teachers, and administrators.

Digital technology may be used in distance education courses, electronic classrooms, video conferencing, and blended courses that intermix classroom instruction with online materials and interactions. Many colleges and universities are turning to distance education over the Web not only to extend the reach of their degree programs over time and space, but also to reduce the cost of the physical plant and teaching faculty (Dede, Brown-L'Bahy, Ketelhut, & Whitehouse, 2004; Hezel, 1992). On campus, colleges and universities are providing electronic classrooms with workstations or wireless networks for the students and instructors and video projections systems to act as smart blackboards (Norman, 1990; Shneiderman, Alavi, Norman, & Borkowski, 1995). Videoconferencing and collaborative software link classrooms around the world for shared lectures, presentations, and student projects (Sebrechts, Silverman, Boehm-Davis, & Norman, 1995). Even traditional classes are supplemented with course management systems to host materials, assignments, discussion boards, and grade sheets for on- and off-campus access.

EEEs support many, if not all, interactions in the traditional classroom environment and afford a number of new possibilities, such as online discussions, polling of student responses, and instructor feedback with or without anonymity (Norman, 1994b). Norman (1990) listed the goals of these new environments as follows: 1) to provide a more interactive learning experience than is generally possible in traditional lecture and seminar courses at the college level; 2) to provide interactive and hypermedia technologies during lectures and seminars; 3) to increase student-to-student and student-to-faculty collaboration and group problem solving; and 4) to provide students with an integrated learning environment with access to hypermedia databases, communications, and simulations.

Norman (1990) presented a conceptualization of the types of interactions in EEEs between the students, instructors, course materials, and course products. Figure 15.7 illustrates the complexity of the areas of interactions and interfaces that should be considered in these environments.

Digital technology offers a number of advantages for EEEs (Norman, 1997). Electronic media provide the functionalities of input-ability, display-ability, store-ability, search-ability, copy-ability, and access-ability. The hypermedia and interactivity provide the functions of link-ability, manipulate-ability, compute-ability, and simulate-ability. Electronic communication makes possible the functionalities of communicate-ability, view-ability, and conference-ability. Altogether these create a powerful new environment for education if properly designed and managed.

Although tremendous effort and resources have been poured into the development of EEEs, their actual benefit to learning has not been unambiguously demonstrated. Too often, the user interface is itself difficult to learn, complicated, and time consuming to use, and a distraction in the learning process. Consequently, it has been emphasized that educational interfaces should 1) be easy to learn and use operating in an obvious way; 2) be integrated and seamless, requiring a minimum number of steps to perform desired functions; 3) reduce the cognitive load of students and instructors rather than increase it; 4) reduce the difficulty of instructors generating materials for the

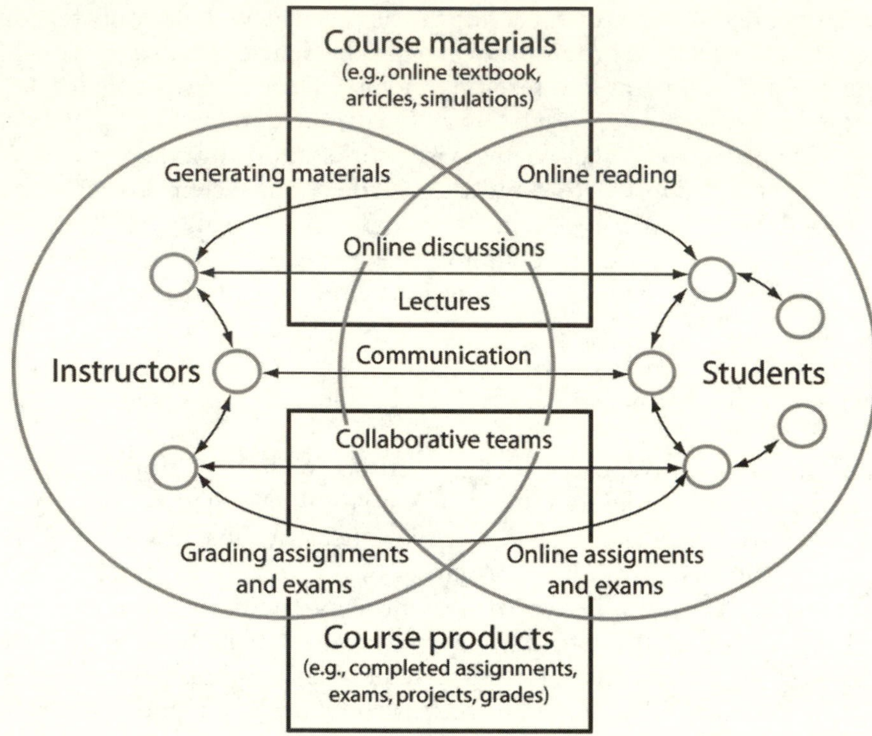

Figure 15.7. A schematic of agents, objects, and interactions in electronic educational environments. (From Norman, 1990.)

course and of students copying materials from the course; and 5) promote active interaction with course materials and collaboration among students and instructors.

Overall, the impact of EEEs has been positive, but not great, and sometimes negative. A meta-analysis of a number of studies of the effectiveness of distance education in K–12 by Cavanaugh (2001) showed a small positive effect, which was better for more interactive systems. But the situation is complex. Alonso and Norman (1996) conducted a study varying whether the instructor or the student was in control of the media and whether the interaction was simple (page turning) or complex (running simulations). They found that student-controlled interactivity was more beneficial for complex interactions, and instructor control was better for simple interactivity.

In the end, electronic education is an extremely complex system and an immense challenge to system and interface designers. For students, instructors, and administrators, it presents a new landscape for learning, teaching, record keeping, and management (Norman, 1994a). For students with low computer and navigation skills, education may become an even greater challenge when having to deal with hardware and software problems. For students that are highly facile with computer technology, education may be greatly facilitated. It has been speculated that the introduction of technology in education may not actually increase the overall performance of the class, but instead exacerbate the differences among the students with different technological skills (Norman, 1994c).

End Thoughts

The reason that three such different things – games, entertainment, and education – are in the same chapter is because of digital convergence. To the computer, they are all the same, files of 1s and 0s, but to the human they are categorically different. It may well be that psychologically we should keep them separate and even try to push the trend back to physical games with real objects and boards, to analog music and film, and to face-to-face education with real desks and blackboards. In each area, there are media Luddites who oppose digital technologies, audiophiles who claim that vinyl records are superior to MP3s, photographers who treasure old photographic film, and groups of board game and card players who treasure the time with friends around real tables. At present, however, digital convergence seems to be winning more and more territory in the attention and activities of humans.

In terms of impact and effect, however, there are two front runners and one lagging far behind. The video gaming industry has been a tremendous success, has pushed the development of new technologies, and has had a huge impact on psychology and society as a whole. The same is true in entertainment. Digital music, images, and video have had a significant impact on what we watch and listen to, how we store and find selections, and the devices we use to play this media. Unfortunately, in education, the results are marginal and mixed, at best. Although virtual courses, degrees, and universities abound, the cost and quality of education has seen little benefit, if any. Online courses and degrees are viewed with suspicion by prospective employers. Isolated success stories and testimonials exist, but by and large, digital technology in education has not produced anything near the claims of its protagonists. The challenge for psychologists and educators is to find out why.

Suggested Exercises

1. Select a set of five video games and classify them according to player versus opponent (Table 15.1), use of screen space (Table 15.2), and on the triangular coordinates of ludology, narratology, and simulation (Fig. 15.1).
2. Evaluate a "first-person shooter" computer/video game in terms of violence. How many kills occur on average per game session? How graphic are the animations of kills?
3. Conduct a controlled experiment on aggressive behavior after playing a violent video game. Randomly assign players to both violent and nonviolent games. Then observe the players' aggressive behaviors during the next 30 min. If possible, run this as a blind study so that observers do not know to which type of game the players were exposed.

4. Evaluate a piece of educational software. What educational and/or learning principles is the software using?

5. If you have or are taking classes using online materials, evaluate the system in terms of the interactions shown in Figure 15.5.

References

Alonso, D. L., & Norman, K. L. (1996). Forms of control and interaction as determinants of lecture effectiveness in the electronic classroom. *Computers in Education, 27*, 205–214.

Anderson, C. A., & Bushman, B. J. (2001). Effects of violent video games on aggressive behavior, aggressive cognition, aggressive affect, physiological arousal, and prosocial behavior: A meta-analytic review of the scientific literature. *Psychological Science, 12*, 353–359.

Anderson, C. A., & Dill, K. E. (2000). Video games and aggressive thoughts, feelings, and behavior in the laboratory and in life. *Journal of Personality and Social Psychology, 78*, 772–790.

Anderson, C.A., Gentile, D. A., & Buckley, K. E. (2006). *Violent video game effects on children and adolescents: Theory, research, and public policy*. Oxford: Oxford University Press.

Braun, C., & Giroux, J. (1989). Arcade video games: Proxemic, cognitive and content analyses. *Journal of Leisure Research, 21*, 92–105.

Cavanaugh, C. S. (2001). The effectiveness of interactive distance education technologies in K–12 learning: A meta-analysis. *International Journal of Educational Telecommunications, 7*(1), 73–88.

Crandall, R. W., & Sidak, J. G. (2006). *Video games: Serious business for America's economy*. Washington, DC: Entertainment Software Association.

Cuban, L. (1986). *Teachers and machines: The classroom use of technology since 1920*. New York: Teachers College Press.

Dede, C., Brown-L'Bahy, T., Ketelhut, D., & Whitehouse, P. (2004). Distance education (virtual learning). In H. Bidgoli (Ed.), *The Internet encyclopedia* (3 vols.; pp. 549–560). New York: John Wiley & Sons.

Dynarski, M., Agodini, R., Heaviside, S., Novak, T., Carey, N., Campuzano, L., et al. (2007, March). *Effectiveness of reading and mathematics software products: Findings from the first student cohort*. Washington, DC: U.S. Department of Education, Institute of Education.

Entertainment Software Association. (2006). *Essential facts about the computer and video game industry: 2006 sales, demographic and usage data*. Washington, DC: Author.

Fletcher-Flinn, C. M., & Gravatt, B. (1995). The efficacy of computer assisted instruction (CAI): A meta-analysis. *Journal of Educational Computing Research, 12*(3), 219–242.

Gee, P. J. (2003). *What video games have to teach us about learning and literacy*. New York: Palgrave/Macmillan.

Goldsmith, T. T., Grove, C., & Mann, E. R. (1948). *U.S. Patent No. 2,455,992*. Washington, DC: U.S. Patent and Trademark Office.

Hamilton, E. C., Scott, D. J., Fleming, J. B., Rege, R. V., Laycock, R., Bergen, P. C., et al. (2002). Comparison of video trainer and virtual reality training systems on acquisition of laparoscopic skills. *Surgical Endoscopy, 16*(3), 406–411.

Hezel, R. T. (1992). Cost-effectiveness for interactive distance education and telecommunicated learning. In University of Wisconsin–Madison, *From vision to reality: Providing cost-effective, quality distance education*. Papers from the eighth annual conference on distance teaching and learning, Madison, August 5–7, pp. 75–78.

Howarth, P. A., & Finch, M. (1999). The nauseogenicity of two methods of navigation within a virtual environment. *Applied Ergonomics, 30*, 39–45.

Klabbers, J. H. G. (2003). The gaming landscape: A taxonomy for classifying games and simulations. In M. Copier & J. Raessens (Eds.), *LEVEL UP: Digital games research conference* (pp. 54–68). Utrecht, The Netherlands: University of Utrecht.

Kozak, J. J., Hancock, P. A., Arthur, E. J., & Chrysler, S. T. (1993) Transfer of training from virtual reality. *Ergonomics, 36*(7), 777–784.

Lindley, C. A. (2003). Game taxonomies: A high level framework for game analysis and design. *Gamasutra*, October 3. Retrieved March 20, 2008, from www.gamasutra.com/features/20031003/lindley_01.shtml.

Mania, K., & Chalmers, A. (2001). The effects of levels of immersion on memory and presence in virtual environments: A reality centered approach. *CyberPsychology & Behavior*, 4(2), 247–264.

Mayer, R. E. (2001). *Multimedia learning*. Cambridge: Cambridge University Press.

Mayer, R. E., & Moreno, R. (1998). *A cognitive theory of multimedia learning: Implications for design principles*. Paper presented at the annual meeting of the ACM SIGCHI conference on human factors in computing systems, Los Angeles, CA, April.

Mayer, R. E., & Moreno, R. (2003). Nine ways to reduce cognitive load in multimedia learning. *Educational Psychologist, 38*(1), 43–52.

Norman, K. L. (1990). The electronic teaching theater: Interactive hypermedia and mental models of the classroom. *Current Psychology: Research & Reviews, 9*(2), 141–161.

Norman, K. L. (1994a). HyperCourseware for interactive instruction in the electronic classroom. *Behavior Research Methods, Instruments & Computers, 26*, 255–259.

Norman, K. L. (1994b). Navigating the educational space with HyperCourseware. *Hypermedia, 6*, 35–60.

Norman, K. L. (1994c). Spatial visualization: A gateway to computer-based technology. *Journal of Special Education Technology, 12*, 195–205.

Norman, K. L. (1997). *Teaching in the switched on classroom: An introduction to electronic education and HyperCourseware*. College Park, MD: Laboratory for Automation Psychology. Retrieved March 20, 2008, from http://lap.umd.edu/soc

O'Flynn, L. (2005). *Media diet for kids*. Hay House.

Pashler, H., & Johnston, J. C. (1998). Attentional limitations in dual-task performance. In H. Pashler (Ed.), *Attention* (pp. 155–189). East Sussex, UK: Psychology Press.

Piaget, J. (1962). *Play, dreams, and imitation in childhood*. New York: Norton.

Potel, M. (1998). Motion sick in cyberspace. *IEEE Computer Graphics and Applications, 18*(1), 16–21.

Reiser, R. A. (1984). Reducing student procrastination in a personalized system of instruction course. *Educational Communication and Technology Journal, 32*, 41–49.

Rosenthal, R. (1986). Media violence, antisocial behavior, and the social consequences of small effects. *Journal of Social Issues, 42*, 141–154.

Sebrechts, M. M., Lathan, C., Clawson, D. M., Miller, M. S., & Trepagnier, C. (2003). Transfer of training in virtual environments: Issues for human performance. In L. J. Hettinger & M. Haas (Eds.), *Virtual and adaptive environments: Applications, implications, and human performance issues* (pp. 67–90). Mahwah, NJ: Erlbaum.

Sebrechts, M. M., Silverman, B. G., Boehm-Davis, D. A., & Norman, K. L. (1995). Establishing an electronic collaborative learning environment in a university consortium: The CIRCLE project. *Computers in Education, 25*, 215–225.

Shneiderman, B., Alavi, M., Norman, K., & Borkowski, E. (1995). Windows of opportunities in electronic classrooms. *Communications of the ACM, 38*, 19–24.

Shrum, L. J. (Ed.). (2003). *The psychology of entertainment media: Blurring the lines between entertainment and persuasion*. Mahwah, NJ: Erlbaum.

U.S. Government. (2002). Public Law 107–110, 107th Congress. Last retrieved 4/12/2008 http://www.ed.gov/policy/elsec/leg/esea02/107-110.pdf.

Wolf, M. J. P. (1997). Inventing space: Toward a taxonomy of on- and off-screen space in video games. *Film Quarterly, 51*(1), 11–23.

Zillman, D., & Vorderer, P. (Eds.). (2000). *Media entertainment: The psychology of its appeal*. Mahwah, NJ: Erlbaum.

Sixteen

The Future

The Ultimate Human–Computer Interface

Scenario 1

The Cylons were built to serve humankind as robotic workers and soldiers. With time, they gained sentience. They rebelled and fought the human race in a major conflict that devastated both sides. An armistice was agreed on, but the Cylons then disappeared for 40 years. They evolved, and they had a plan. They created humanoid models. They returned, infiltrated security, and launched a nuclear attack that eliminated most of the twelve colonies. The humanoid models sought to interbreed with the human survivors. Some of the humans had developed romantic feelings for the humanoid Cylons. Were they "toasters," or were they human? Could they kill them without remorse? (Adapted from "Battlestar Galactica," the 2003 TV miniseries.)

Scenario 2

Kristina and Keith entered the name of their firstborn child into the genealogical database on the family HomeStation just as their ancestors had done for twenty generations. The screen had been replaced by their grandparents 50 years earlier, and the processor by their great-great grandparents 100 years earlier after a fire had damaged it. But Keith had to replace the data entry board every 10 years due to wear and tear. Virtually the same software had been running for all these generations. The OS and the applications for word processors, communications, record keeping, home control, etc., were all Version O, "O" for optimal. They had no need to change or upgrade. Any change would result in a problem or in lower performance. No one in their time thought to entertain the idea of technological change. What for?

Overview

What does the future hold for psychology, the human–computer interface, and cyberpsychology? Needless to say, predictions are all over the map, from moderate to extreme, positive to negative, and hopeful to dreadful. Some look forward to a world of "new computing," meeting our needs for creativity and self-actualization. Computer networks will host a new digital society with "social computing." Some look forward to an intelligent world where computers disappear into the background with "ubiquitous computing." Homes and appliances become "smart," and the walls of rooms become interfaces to controls and communication to the world. Some predict the blurring of the interface between human and machine, such that either we will become machines or our conscience processes will inhabit the machines. Or if AI leads to ultra-AI, as predicted by the coming "technological singularity," there may be no reason for humanity as we know it. Some predict a growing distance and disparity between humans and machines to the point of war, as in Scenario 1. Still others predict a leveling off of technological advances and even a stagnation of development into what might be called the "Digital Dark Ages," as suggested in Scenario 2.

Although these predictions have a life in science fiction from the world of the "Jetsons" to "Battlestar Galactica," each has an element of truth and a set of implications for cyberpsychology and future research, theory, and application in psychology. This chapter surveys a number of these ideas and discusses their implications.

The New Computing

A favorable initiative and projection into the future is the "new computing" in contrast to the "old computing." In his book, *Leonardo's Laptop: Human Needs and the New Computing Technologies,* Ben Shneiderman (2003) portrayed the future of HCI as a positive shift in focus from computers to people. He emphasized usable and universal interfaces rather than computers designed for a limited group of elite users. The challenge is to design the computer and its systems for all people. The *new computing* is about meeting human needs over computer requirements and human creativity over AI.

Shneiderman anticipated two transformations from the old computing to the new computing. First, there is a shift from numbers and technical specifications of computers to what users value. He focused on the values of communication, relationships, and communities. Second, there is a shift from machine-centered automation to user-centered services and tools. Shneiderman joins others such as Don Norman (1986) in calling for user-centered design, as we discuss in previous chapters.

The new computing is partially motivated by Maslow's hierarchy of human needs and the desire for self-actualization and by the development of

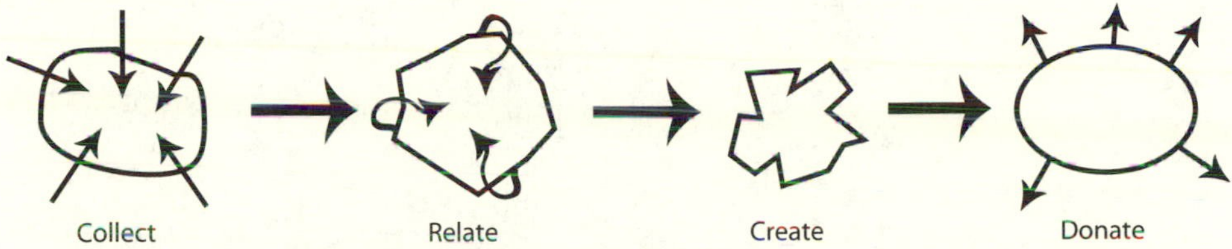

Figure 16.1. The "creative process" in the new computing. (Adapted from Shneiderman, 2003).

creativity support tools. Shneiderman (2003) advocated a process of human creativity supported by the new computing, as shown in Figure 16.1. The process is to collect information, relate the information, create a product, and, finally, donate the product to the common good of society. Shneiderman explored a number of the areas where the new computing meets human needs in e-education, e-health care, e-commerce, and e-government.

The new computing is extremely good news for psychology and those seeking employment in HCI-related fields. It invigorates the human side of the interface. It turns the focus of research and development from building a better machine to fostering a better understanding of the human user and designing a more usable interface to meet human needs. It requires an investment in psychological research to understand and model the user and an investment in user-centered design of computer interfaces. The new computing requires a careful assessment of human needs and abilities in the context of everyday life and new ways of integrating them into the design of user interfaces.

However, the bright side of new computing has its skeptics. The nature of humankind is not always so positive in promoting collaboration, philanthropy, honesty, open-mindedness, and love. Competition, greed, dishonesty, prejudice, and hatred can infect and derail the new computing. Nevertheless, the new computing suggests that we refocus on the psychology of the user rather than on the mechanics of the system. As such, we should ask the following questions:

- What are the human needs and aspirations that can be supported by the new computing? How do we assess these needs and aspirations, and make sure that they are correctly mapped onto the new computing?
- What negative aspects of the human character work against the new computing? What designs and interventions can be used to mitigate negative effects?

Social Computing

A related trend focuses on interpersonal relationships, communities, and societies, as discussed in Chapter 11. In its basic form, "social computing" refers to computer network activities that are of a social nature. It is not really new because e-mail itself is a form of social computing, but the sheer

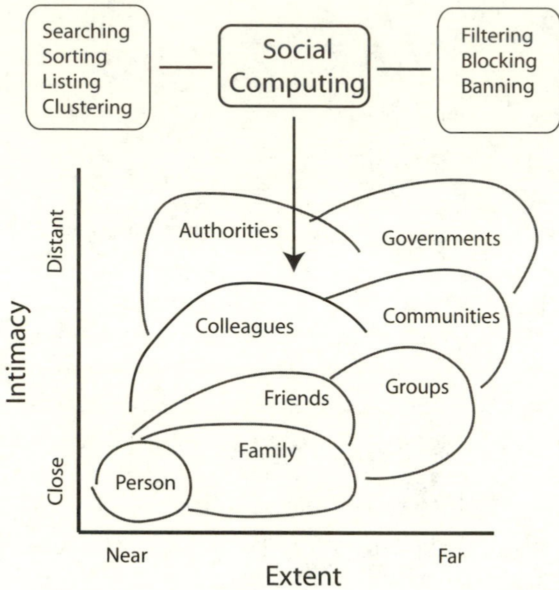

Figure 16.2. Schematic of the social computing network varying by extent and intimacy.

predominance and impact of social computing is what is new. Many predict that we will live and conduct our social lives primarily on the Internet. It will be where we turn when we are lonely, where we will find our mates, where we will share our intimate moments, and where we will guide and teach and play. Figure 16.2 shows the expanding circles of social computing from the person to social networks in families, work, communities, and beyond.

Any software running on LANs or WANs that supports communication or sharing of information between individuals and groups is part of social computing. It starts from peer-to-peer communication and reaches to network meeting places and enormous databases of shared personal information on social networking services, such as www.facebook.com, www.myspace.com, and www.blogger.com, to name a few. Rather than heading down to the pub, the commons room, or the mall, people are logging in to these sites.

Social computing provides a vast and fertile ground for human interaction; however, it also carries with it the computational aspects of computers, history files, searchability, data mining, and AI agents. In social computing, incredible amounts and types of information are stored. They can be related, associated, or inferred from stored profiles, networks of friends, preferences, etc. This information is easily searched, and new algorithms are constantly being generated to sift and sort through this information for various noble and ignoble purposes, from maintaining the security of the community to target marketing for advertising, and from providing freedom from constraints to totalitarian control of society. There are great concerns about privacy, surveillance, and data mining. Networking data are extremely detailed and

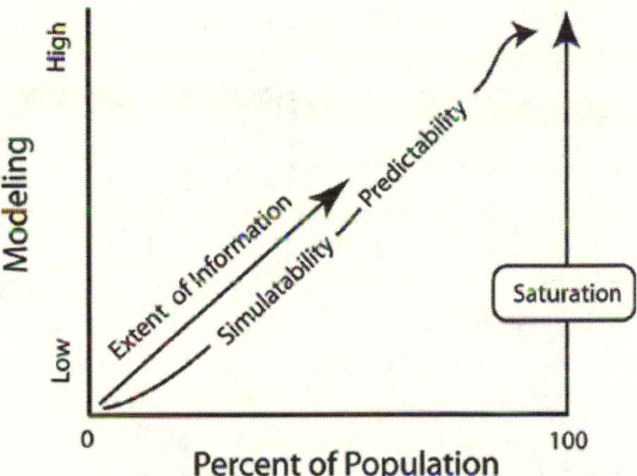

Figure 16.3. Projected increase in the extent of social knowledge and predictability as a function of the percent of the population online and its implications for modeling and predicting social behavior.

powerful for searching for people and for connecting the dots to reveal patterns of a person's or a group's activities. Government agencies and other organizations only need to run "social networking bots" to find suspected drug rings, terrorist cells, and prostitution networks.

It is expected that social computing will continue and become increasingly linked between different servers, shared among servers, and even internationalized. Identity theft, erasing one's identify, and simulating major parts of the social network will create interesting problems. One can imagine having imaginary friends, idealized situations, imaginary followers, and even profiles maintained after death by afterlife simulation agents.

One's social presence is reflected by the amount and frequency of social activity such as e-mails, message board postings, and updating preferences. But there are also implicit or automatic records that are related to one's social presence, such as court and police records, health records, census records, genealogies, and credit card purchases. When these services link records, incredible detail will be known about individuals, groups, markets, and economies.

As with the new computing, the field is wide open for psychologists. Data mining of these extensive databases can be used to study social networks and many of the phenomena discussed in Chapter 11, as long as anonymity of the individuals and groups is preserved. Over time, social computing will become more pervasive in terms of both the proportion of the online population involved and the extent of the interaction and information shared. As these increase, the degree and precision of modeling social behavior will also increase dramatically, as shown in Figure 16.3. Eventually, social scientists and social planners may be able to simulate and predict social behavior with great precision. If this is true, social computing societies may be controlled by authorities that are able to inject planned interventions to change the course of group behavior.

However, a recent Internet experiment suggests that random events in the social network may result in unpredictable outcomes. Salganik, Dodds, and Watts (2006) set up a Web site for listening to, rating, and downloading music. Some participants saw only the names of the songs and bands, whereas others saw the number of times the songs had been downloaded by other listeners. These last participants were subdivided into eight parallel "worlds." They could see the number of prior downloads only in their own world. The researchers hypothesized that if personal preferences and overall popularity alone determine which songs will be hits, the results should have been similar in all eight worlds. However, this is not at all what they found. The songs that became hits were not the same in the different worlds, apparently due to the effect of cumulative advantage building on small initial differences. Social influence did not just make the hits bigger, it made them unpredictable.

In networks, the attractiveness of something is influenced by the number of other people wanting, buying, or using it. The problem is that social networks not only reveal our preferences for something, but they also modify them. Because of the circularity of influence and the cumulative advantage that the popular get more popular, the relation between what we want now, what we wanted before, and what we will want in the future can become indeterminant.

Nevertheless, social experiments can be embedded in the social computing environments. Researchers could introduce fictitious events, groups, and individuals as friends in the network. However, enormous ethical issues emerge from such experiments because they involve deception. What happens when one falls in love with a person who is really just a confederate in an experiment on romantic ties or when a person is caught stalking a female undergraduate in a social sting operation. Consequently, we need to ask the following questions:

- How can social computing help us do research in social psychology?
- In addition to the current findings in social psychology, are there new, emergent phenomena in social computing?
- To what extent should social networking sites be allowed to or required to share information about participants with other sites and organizations? Should government authorities monitor and police social activities in cyberspace?

The Disappearing Computer

Computers started with toggle switches and keyboard interfaces. The mouse has been a useful addition, but it can often be an annoying way of pointing, clicking, and dragging objects on a screen. The early output devices were lights and alphanumeric output on paper or a monitor. Today, computer screens are small portals into the interaction with computers. They are workstations, play stations, kiosks, and terminals. But there is no reason why the interface cannot be spread across walls and desktops and into every sensory modality.

In the future, many predict that computers will in one sense be everywhere and in another sense disappear. At present, networks allow one to log into systems from anywhere, and wireless networks allow them to be mobile. Moreover, computers are becoming a pervasive part of our environment. Ultimately, according to Mark Weiser (1991), in "ubiquitous computing" machines will no longer be distinct objects but will be integrated into the environment. Computation will be embedded in the environment and into everyday objects around us. *Pervasive computing* will allow people to move around and interact with information more casually and naturally than we do today (Norman, 1998). The HCI will be wrapped into our entire environment.

In addition to being surrounded by visual displays, the computer interface will include an "all seeing eye" or video input of the user's every motion. Gesture recognition software will interpret our commands and even read our body language. Whatever we write on, whatever we move, wherever we go, and whatever we do will interact with networks and computation.

A number of projects are exploring these possibilities. "Smart Rooms" was a project at the MIT Media lab to provide a user interface to a virtual environment (Wren et al., 1997). The Smart Room acts like an invisible butler. Equipped with cameras, microphones, and other sensors, it tries to interpret what people are doing and looks for ways to help them (http://vismod.media.mit.edu/vismod/demos/smartroom/ive.html).

"Everyday Computing" is a series of projects to bring computation and information into the everyday lives of humans to assist in memory, in performing everyday tasks, and in monitoring the environment. Everyday computing involves the use of computers in informal and unstructured activities that have no clear beginning or end and that comprise much of our everyday lives (Abowd & Mynatt, 2000) (www.cc.gatech.edu/fce/ecl/projects/index.html).

Finally, "The Disappearing Computer" is a European Union project to investigate how information technology can be diffused into everyday objects to enhance personal experience, assist in collaboration, and create more engaging interactions with information artifacts (Streitz & Nixon, 2005) (www.disappearing-computer.net/).

Aside from the technology necessary to empower these ideas, there are a number of psychological questions that need to be addressed as these environments take shape:

- How will people know what to expect and how to interact with these new "smart" environments? How will people contend with these environments as more objects become interactive, programmable, and intelligent? Can they handle the complexity?
- Given that there are already inconsistencies, bugs, and glitches in the current screen-based human–computer interface, what will happen when these

problems are spread throughout the environment? Can people trust an environment whose parts can crash, freeze up, and not interact with each other?
- How will people form mental models of the environments involving the attribution of causes and effects? Will environments seem like an enchanted fairyland with elves and sprites and talking trees?

The Blurred Interface

The human–computer interface defined in Chapter 1 is pictured as an overlapping area of human and machine activity. However, there is a clear demarcation between human and machine. The human organism is an independent and intact unit separated by skin from the rest of the world. Even the BCI discussed in Chapter 14 was noninvasive and preserved the integrity of the human. However, science and technology are beginning to blur this line, exploring both AI implementations and invasive BCI.

Human in the Machine

Some have envisioned life in the machine. If a computer simulation of the human were so complete as to include a simulation of every cell in the body from neurons to fat cells and all tissues and organs, one could imagine that the simulation could also include a "self" and associated consciousness. Even relaxing the completeness of the simulation, it may be that whatever we mean by "person" or part of the person could reside in the machine. This is the idea behind science fiction movies such as "Lawnmower Man" (1992), "The Matrix" (1999), and "The Thirteenth Floor" (1999).

Such a possibility is beyond the computational power of current machines and well beyond our ability to simulate human cognitive and neurological processes. However, we already take for granted some of the components that will make machine habitation possible. We routinely transfer much of our memory and knowledge to the computer as we add to databases, calendars, preference files, blogs, etc., and as we program the machines and environments around us. As we discuss in Chapter 9, we already think of some part of our personalities as residing in the computer, especially in social networking and virtual reality sites. This transference will only continue in amount and quality over time, and we need to ask the following questions:

- How much of our personal information, characteristics, and programming will ultimately be transferred to the machine?
- At what point will the balance tip so that more of our personal knowledge resides in the machine than in our own brains?
- How will our attitudes about who we are and where we reside change as a function of this transference?

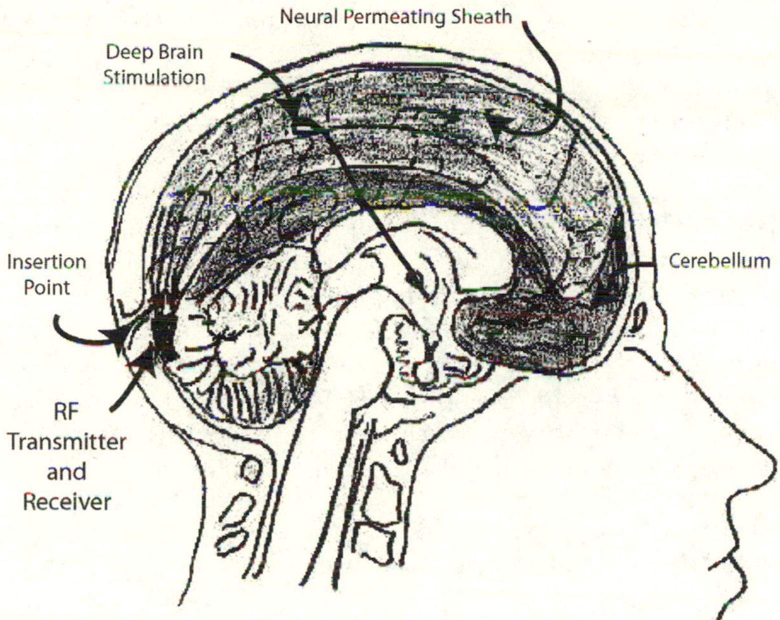

Figure 16.4. Diagram of surface and deep brain direct neural interfaces with RF (radio frequency) transmitter and receiver.

Machine in the Human

Alternatively, we may become more bionic with an invasive BCI. Implants of various types are common today and will increase dramatically in the future. Skeletal implants of knees and hips are mechanical and do not interact with the nervous system. Artificial pacemakers stimulate the heart muscles but do not directly interact with the central nervous system. Microchip implants can be used to store personal identification, medical information, and contact information. They can be used for GPS tracking, identity verification, and credit card information. Although these implants store and transmit data, they do not interact with the body, only with external wireless receivers.

However, a number of advances have been made with direct neural interfaces to the brain. Brain pacemakers are being used to send electric impulses to areas of the brain and nervous system to relieve symptoms of Parkinson's disease, epilepsy, and depression (Donovan, 2004; Mayberg et al., 2005). These devices are a one-way interface to the brain. True BCIs will involve a direct two-way, high-bandwidth channel between neurons and arrays of sensors and neural stimulators, as illustrated in Figure 16.4. After these are developed and implanted, an accommodation and learning period will have to occur during which a "handshaking" communication protocol is established. Communication may involve sensory channels so that one "hears" a phantom sound or "sees" a ghost image. Communication may involve direct conscious thought to send a signal to the computer and the interpretation of a feeling as a signal from the computer. Alternatively, communication may not involve consciousness intervention. The computer sensors may be used to pick up many brain functions and intervene to optimize the processing. Neuroprosthetics may be used to replace damaged or missing parts of the brain or nervous system. The cochlear implant currently used to restore hearing to the deaf is such a neuroprosthetic device. Work is being conducted for a visual neuroprosthetic device to restore vision to the blind.

Other possibilities for neuroprosthetics would be to bridge neural centers that may be malfunctioning, limiting short-term memory, or impairing transfer of information from short-term memory to long-term memory. If these were possible, it would also be feasible to augment brain functions, as discussed in Chapter 14. We could extend short-term memory, add math and logic processors to working memory, and link into extended databases, language translators, and AI systems. The research programs and psychological issues are extensive, and involve the following questions:

- What is involved in rewiring the nervous system, how will the system accommodate the changes, and how disruptive is it to the rest of system functioning?
- When do we cease being ourselves and become the machine?
- What about privacy, ethical, and legal issues? If something goes wrong and a person with a BCI commits a crime, who is at fault – the person or the prosthetic device?

Technological Singularity

Futurists predict that with the exponential increase in technological change, there will be a "spike" on the event horizon, at which point current models of the future cease to give reliable answers (Broderick, 2002). This point will occur following the creation of Strong AI or the amplification of human intelligence. Even as early as the mid-1960s, computer scientists speculated about the impact of super-AI (Good, 1965). The term "singularity" was introduced by the mathematician Vernor Vinge (1993) and recently popularized by Ray Kurzweil (2005) to represent that point in time where the models become indeterminant. After the singularity, humans, as we are today, will be obsolete. Super or ultra-super intelligence will rule the day. In 1993, Vinge wrote, "Within thirty years, we will have the technological means to create superhuman intelligence. Shortly after, the human era will be ended" (p. 1).

Bostrom (2003) noted that "Superintelligence may be the last invention humans ever need to make" (p. 12). Advances in all fields will be accelerated by superintelligence. At this point, scientific and technological advances will no longer be in the hands of mere humans. The study and development of psychology and certainly cyberpsychology will be conducted by superhuman intelligence. Our role as scientists will cease to exist. We will be the subject of study by superscientists. The results and theories of new ultraintelligent science may very well be beyond human comprehension, just as our psychology is beyond comprehension by the mind of a lab rat.

Even today, computer modeling and simulations, while programmed by humans, are incomprehensible to the human mind because they involve vast numbers of computations, equations, and variables. Vinge (1993) believed that when, not if, the singularity occurs, mind and self will be very different. In Kurzweil's (1999) view, the mind and consciousness will be liberated from the confines of human biology and will be able to transcend the information processing limits of the human nervous system and interact directly with computer networks. At the same time, the distinction of individuals as selves may merge into one global consciousness. Vinge noted that Freeman Dyson (1988) was correct when he said, "God is what mind becomes when it has passed beyond the scale of our comprehension" (p. 119).

Needless to say, the singularity has its proponents and opponents. Some futurists, mostly in computer science and science fiction, believe that we should hasten the day by investing billions in super-AI. They view it as inevitable and as representing the next step in the evolution of life, regardless of the consequences. Some note that such intelligence will not have human-like motives, but may be happy to act as a benevolent servant (Bostrom, 2003). Others fear that super-AI would be the demise of humanity as we know it and that we should put the breaks on AI research and development. Their view is that in the uncertainty of the future and from past experience with computers, things will not only go wrong, they will go very wrong. Interestingly, it seems that the majority of science fiction movies and novels on the subject (e.g., "Demon Seed" [1978], "Battlestar Galactica" [2003]) share this negative view.

In this text, there is little utility in following the apocalyptic path, so we assume a benevolent super-AI. As we discuss in Chapter 13, there are two basic issues in HCI with AI and super-AI. The first is the issue of the model of the mind. Is it modeled from the human mind or something else? If it is the human mind, then we may be able to understand it, relate to it, and avoid the "incomprehensibility" problem. This is a good reason for continuing research on the model of the human mind. If not, we must rely on the second issue of its interface. How do we interact with it? This will be a two-way street and will require greater investments in the theory of the interface than in super-AI itself. But in the spirit of the singularity, all bets are off. Nevertheless, a few issues that deserve consideration are 1) how should AI be developed to be commensurate with human intelligence?, and 2) how should we develop the interface between human and AI?

The War with Machines

There has and always will be a disconnect between humans and machines. Regardless of whether the singularity occurs, if there is any residual distinction between the human, machine, cyborg, or whatever, there is potential for conflict. The psychological issues of racial and ethnic prejudice, conflict, and discrimination are potential threats to trust and harmony in society. Power struggles in terms of who is right, who is more logical, who needs scarce resources, and who makes decisions can result in violence and war (Brown, Cote, Lynn-Jones, & Miller, 1998). It has even been theorized that war is a purely human and a predominately male phenomenon (Goldstein, 2001).

We are not at a point where computers have united as a nation state and declared war on humans. We do not need to redirect our military to fight an army of robots. However, there are numerous cases in which we have had to shoot down missiles whose computer guidance systems have gone astray or pull the plug on computers that are spreading viruses across the network. In recent human conflict, we have recruited the aid of computers and robots as allies against enemy forces who have also armed themselves with the same. It is unlikely that there will ever be a true war with computers, unless they somehow assume human characteristics as in Scenario 2.

The term "cyberwar" refers primarily to large-scale attacks using spam, viruses, jamming to disrupt services, corrupting databases, and infiltrating networks. As we become more reliant on technology, we become more vulnerable to cyberwar attack. In response, greater effort has been made to harden and secure networks and systems. Although much study has been devoted to the psychological effects of conflict and loss due to war, the uncertainty of cyberwar and its effects are not well understood at this point.

To a great extent, the military forces of developed countries have built and trained machines for war. When machines fight machines, it is a bloodless conflict. However, when humans are physically involved, loss of human life is the cost. It has been suggested that we should not take our conflict to the human battlefield but rather to the negotiation table for a peaceful settlement. Alternatively, we may fight our battles with machines or even on a game board to avoid the loss of life. There is a great psychological difference in the mind of a human soldier between blowing up a robot combatant versus killing another human. However, there is no difference in the logical circuitry of a computer between one or the other. Consequently, war with machines depersonalizes the effects of combat. Nevertheless, having your son or daughter killed by a human soldier, a robot controlled by a human, or even an autonomous robot changes nothing about the loss.

Indeed, there are many psychological issues that come to play with war, the threat of war, and machines. The two basic ones are as follows: 1) what are the psychological effects of the threat of war and warfare itself against machines?, and 2) what are the psychological effects of the threat of war and warfare itself among humans using machines?

Digital Dark Ages

We know the Dark Ages as a period in history from about 476 to 1000 AD, also known as the Middle Ages. It was first called the Dark Age by Petrarch in the 1330s. The Italian humanists retained the term, along with the Middle Ages, to distinguish it from the Renaissance Period. The Dark

Ages were characterized as a period of cultural stagnation following the Roman Empire and prior to technological change in the medieval period and cultural enlightenment in the Renaissance. However, according to the historian G. K. Chesterton (1909), the Dark Ages were not really so dark. Instead, he characterized them as a period of stability which served as a bridge to the Modern Age.

The Digital Age in which we live is an age of transition. We look to massive and rapid changes in technology. We point to Moore's law (Moore, 1965), the doubling of the speeds and capacities of our computers and networks. The "digital divide" between the young and the old, between the rich and the poor, and among the nations of the world marks the challenges of our age.

The digitalization of media, information, communications, and economy has its merits, but it imposes vast problems in change, customization, and standardization. The transition from analog to digital is transparent in many ways. Few consumers take note of the three-letter code on compact audio discs and the transition from AAD (*a*nalog recording, *a*nalog mixing, *d*igital storage) to DDD (*d*igital recording, *d*igital mixing, *d*igital storage). We appreciate the DVDs, the MP3s, the MP4s, and the JPGs from our digital cameras. But we are frustrated by having to change and upgrade the media (e.g., miniDV, Compac Flash, WAV) and OSs that are obsolete within days of their release.

Today, technology, information, and change itself is accelerating at such a rate that it may well be beyond the human capability to adapt. As humans, we may realize the need for usability, standardization, and stability. For these needs to be met, we need a period of little or no change in technology. Fortunately, even as technology develops, there will eventually come a leveling off due not so much to the limits of technology, but rather to the limits of the human mind, perceptual abilities, and motivation. Why should the speed and resolution of the media exceed the abilities of the human perceptual system to appreciate it? Why should the features of the software go beyond the abilities of users to use them? Why should hardware and software become obsolete every few years and new versions, formats, and upgrades be required? Why should the complexity of OSs and applications exceed the limits of one's cognitive abilities?

The Digital Age has witnessed tremendous advances in speed, quality, and creativity. But we may be coming to a point of wondering if "enough is too much." We have maxed out on the number of software functions that a typical human can fathom or would ever want to use in word processors, media players, etc. The new interface design slogan has become "less is more!" Instead of developing the faster and bigger, the effort will be fine-tuning the system and the human interface. At this point, the major questions will be whether it is easy to use, easy to learn, easy to transfer from one generation to the next, and easy to maintain. We are quickly coming to this point.

The turning point will also be marked by industry returning to older solutions that worked rather than to new developments to solve problems. One of the most remarkable of these in recent years has been the reactionary change in the OS of Apple Computer's Mac OS X. Rather than moving in the same trajectory of purely GUI systems, they made an about face and returned to an architecture with an underlying UNIX-based kernel with the Macintosh look and feel running on top.

The Digital Dark Ages refers to a period at which the human–computer interface will have achieved stability at a level to match human needs and limitations. The Digital Dark Ages may be the eventual outcome of the new or everyday computing, illustrated in Scenario 2. The focus will be on day-to-day human life supported by stable technology rather than on exponential increases in science and technology. Although some futurists hoping for the singularity may be disappointed, the Digital Dark Ages may be a protracted period of peace, enjoyment, and stability for humankind. The lack of change need not be construed as stagnation or failure. The positive side is that systems will have reached levels of perfection, completion, and finality. Although change can be a good thing, no change can be a better thing.

To round things out, it should be remembered that feudal kingdoms also marked the old Dark Ages. In stark contrast today, we see a unification of the world with the Web, globalization, and a vast pooling of human knowledge. However, some futurists see a deterioration of this trend. Networks will become more internal to protect themselves from viruses and spam. Blackouts, firewalls, and proxy servers will set up boundaries around the world. Languages, regional standards, digital rights management, and even accessibility requirements may work against the unification of knowledge and communication.

For psychologists and cyberpsychologists, the Digital Dark Ages may actually be a period of enlightenment during which the theories and techniques of psychology will be able to catch up with the technological revolution that has so far left us in the dust. Ultimately, in the distant future, there may be a new renaissance of technology. In the meantime, as psychologists, we can begin with the following questions:

- What is the best balance between change and stability and accommodation and adaptation to technology?
- What psychological forces are at work for and against opening and closing gateways in communication and knowledge sharing?
- What psychological theories and techniques need to be developed and refined during a period of stability?

Implications for Cyberpsychology

In the previous sections, a number of research questions and issues have been raised. I believe that psychologists have a lot of work to do now and into the future. We must be prepared for this work with multiple specialties,

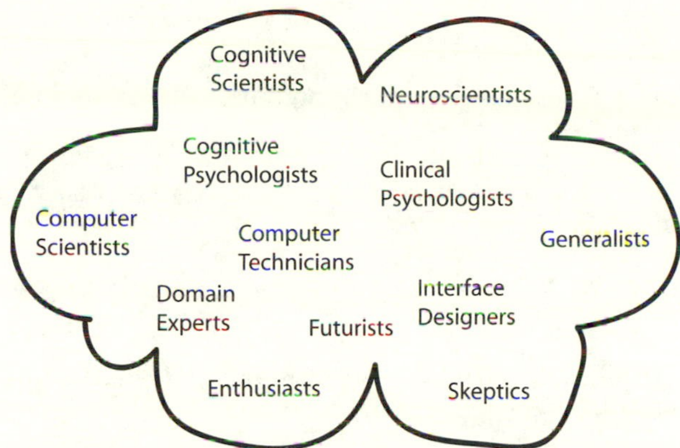

Figure 16.5. Network of collaborators required for research in cyberpsychology.

skills, and disciplines. Psychologists must be both generalists able to see the whole forest of theories, models, and approaches outlined in Chapter 3 and specialists in particular areas of application.

Some might worry that it is hard enough to keep up with the literature in one's own field, without trying to keep up with new technologies as well. We must keep abreast of new and changing technologies, but we do not necessarily need to understand how they work. Research and development in cyberpsychology will of necessity involve interdisciplinary teams, composed of project leaders, psychologists of various types, technicians, computer scientists, and often domain experts (e.g., business, medicine). Figure 16.5 shows the collaborative network that will be required for research in cyberpsychology.

End Thoughts

This brings us full circle back to the reason for this book. The overlap of human activity and computer technology is fast approaching a total of nearly 100 percent. To be a psychologist is to study HCI. To study HCI is to be a psychologist. This being the case, we must span the gap between psychology and technology. We cannot study human behavior in isolation from the environment. Rather, we study behavior in context. Today, the context is technology. Consequently, as psychologists, we must be fully aware of the impact and implications of technology. The direction of technology will, to a large extent, define the future of psychology in theory and practice.

However, this is not to say that technology totally dictates our future. Instead, as psychologists, we put the human, the person, and our values before technology. We hopefully shape technology to meet our needs and values, and not the other way around. The study of cyberpsychology is key to how this all fits together. As we build a new world based on new technologies, we must build it enlightened by the study of cyberpsychology.

Suggested Exercises

1. This chapter has a list of questions at the end of each section. Pick several and try to expand on them.
2. Watch a recent science fiction movie, and write down as many cyberpsychology issues as you can from the movie.
3. Visit the Web sites for futurism and futurists, and identify the issues in cyberpsychology.
4. Plan an interdisciplinary course of study to pursue a degree in cyberpsychology at your college or university.

References

Abowd, G. D., & Mynatt, E. D. (2000). Charting past, present, and future research in ubiquitous computing. *ACM Transactions of Computer–Human Interaction, 7*(1), 29–58.

"Battlestar Galactica," the 2003 TV miniseries. (2003). Universal Studios.

Bostrom, N. (2003). Ethical issues in advanced artificial intelligence. *Cognitive, Emotive and Ethical Aspects of Decision Making in Humans and in Artificial Intelligence, 2,* 12–17.

Broderick, D. (2002). *The spike: How our lives are being transformed by rapidly advancing technologies*. New York: Tor Books.

Brown, M., Cote, O. R., Lynn-Jones, S. M., & Miller, S. E. (Eds.). (1998). *Theories of war and peace.* Cambridge, MA: MIT Press.

Chesterton, G. K. (1909). *Orthodoxy*. New York: John Lane.

Donovan, C. E., III. (2004). *Out of the black hole: The patient's guide to vagus nerve stimulation and depression.* St. Louis, MO: Wellness Publishers, LLC.

Dyson, F. (1988). *Infinite in all directions*. New York: Harper & Row.

Goldstein, J. S. (2001). *War and gender: How gender shapes the war system and vice versa.* Cambridge: Cambridge University Press.

Good, I. J. (1965). Speculations concerning the first ultra-intelligent machine. *Advances in Computers, 6,* 31–88.

Kurzweil, R. (1999). *The age of spiritual machines: When computers exceed human intelligence*. New York: Viking.

Kurzweil, R. (2005). *The singularity is near: When humans transcend biology*. New York: Viking.

Mayberg, H. S., Lozano, A. M., Voon, V., McNeely, H. E., Seminowicz, D., Hamani, C., et al. (2005). Deep brain stimulation for treatment-resistant depression. *Neuron, 45,* 651–660.

Moore, G. E. (1965). Cramming more components onto integrated circuits. *Electronics, 38*(8), 114–117.

Norman, D. (1986). *User centered system design: New perspectives on human–computer interaction*. Hillsdale, NJ: Erlbaum.

Norman, D. (1998). *The invisible computer: Why good products can fail, the personal computer is so complex, and information appliances are the solution.* Cambridge, MA: MIT Press.

Salganik, M. J., Dodds, P. S., & Watts, D. J. (2006). Experimental study of inequality and unpredictability in an artificial cultural market. *Science, 311*, 854–856.

Shneiderman, B. (2003). *Leonardo's laptop: Human needs and the new computing technologies*. Cambridge, MA: MIT Press.

Streitz, N., & Nixon, P. (2005). The disappearing computer. *Communications of the ACM, 48*(3), 32–35.

Vinge, V. (1993). *The coming technological singularity*. VISION-21 symposium sponsored by NASA Lewis Research Center and the Ohio Aerospace Institute, March 30–31. Accessed March 24, 2008, from http://mindstalk.net/vinge/vinge-sing.html

Weiser, M. (1991). The computer for the twenty-first century, *Scientific American, September*, 94–10.

Wren, C. R., Sparacino, F., Azarbayejani, A. J., Darrell, T. J., Starner, T. E., Kotani, A., et al. (1997). Perceptive spaces for performance and entertainment: Untethered interaction using computer vision and audition. *Applied Artificial Intelligence, 11*, 267–284.

Index